THE OTHER TAIWAN

Political and Economic Development/Asia

Taiwan's dramatic postwar transformation from bomb-damaged former Japanese colony, pacified Chinese province, and Guomindang bastion to economic miracle and showplace of state-sponsored democratic transformation has been the subject of intense scholarly and popular scrutiny. Few studies, however, have confronted the other, darker side of the island's economic revolution. The contributors to this important new text address that imbalance by examining the effects of the socio-economic transformation of Taiwan's political system, environment, religious structures, the relationships between the sexes and the different ethnic populations. They also examine the way in which different segments of the economy have reacted to the government's attempts to maintain certain traditional sectors and to control basic interpersonal and intergroup relationships within the economic sphere.

What emerges from this important text is a decidedly revisionist portrait of a country that is far more complex than the one depicted in much of the existing "Taiwan miracle" literature.

In addition to his substantive introduction, Professor Rubinstein provides background and context for each of the major sections, making this new text user-friendly for a wide variety of courses.

TAIWAN IN THE MODERN WORLD

THE OTHER TAIWAN

1945 to the Present

Linda Gail Arrigo
Joseph Bosco
David W. Chen
Robert L. Cheng
Bi-ehr Chou
Hai-yuan Chu
Yun-han Chu

Catherine S. Farris
Shih-Chung Hsieh
Hsiu-Lien Annette Lu
Murray A. Rubinstein
Alan M. Wachman
Jack F. Williams
Jane Kaufman Winn

MURRAY A. RUBINSTEIN
Editor

An East Gate Book

M.E. Sharpe
Armonk, New York
London, England

An East Gate Book

Library of Congress Cataloging-in-Publication Data

The Other Taiwan : 1945 to the present /
Murray A. Rubinstein, editor.
p. cm.—(Taiwan in the modern world)
"An East gate book."
Includes index.
ISBN 1-56324-192-7.—ISBN 1-56324-193-5 (pbk.)
1. Taiwan—Politics and government—1945–
2. Taiwan—Economic conditions—1945–
3. Taiwan—Civilization.
I. Rubinstein, Murray A., 1942–
II. Series.
DS799.816.O74 1994
951.24′905—dc20
94-16058
CIP

Printed in the United States of America

The paper used in this publication meets the minimum requirements of
American National Standard for Information Sciences—
Permanence of Paper for Printed Library Materials,
ANSI Z 39.48-1984.

∞

BM (c) 10   9   8   7   6   5   4   3   2   1
BM (p) 10   9   8   7   6   5   4   3   2   1

Contents

Contributors

Linda Gail Arrigo is completing her doctorate in the department of sociology at the State University of New York at Binghamton. She also works with the Democratic Progressive Party on Taiwan.

Joseph Bosco is a member of the department of anthropology at the Chinese University of Hong Kong in Shateen, the New Territories, Hong Kong. He is also the editor of *Taiwan Studies: A Journal of Translations* published by M. E. Sharpe.

David W. Chen is a reporter for the Associated Press based in Hong Kong.

Robert L. Cheng is a member of the department of East Asian languages and literature at the University of Hawaii at Manoa.

Bi-ehr Chou is the chair of the recently established department of gender studies at the National Xinhua University in Xinju, Taiwan.

Hai-yuan Chu is a senior research associate at the Institute of Ethnology/Academia Sinica in Nanking, Taibei. He also conducts large-scale surveys for the agencies of the government of the Republic of China.

Yun-han Chu is a member of the department of political science, National Taiwan University. He is also associate director of the Institute for National Policy Research in Taibei.

Catherine S. Farris is a member of the department of anthropology/sociology at the University of Northern Iowa.

Shih-Chung Hsieh is a member of the department of anthropology at the National Taiwan University.

Hsiu-Lien Annette Lu is presently a member of the Legislative Yuan in Taibei, and has established an office in New York to lobby for Taiwan's readmission to the United Nations.

Murray A. Rubinstein is a member of the history department at Baruch College of the City University of New York. He is the current chairperson of the Taiwan Studies Group of the Association of Asian Studies.

Alan M. Wachman is the director of the Nanjing Program of the Paul H. Nietze School of Advanced International Studies of the Johns Hopkins University.

Jack F. Williams is the director of the Asian Studies Center at Michigan State University. He was one of the founders of the Taiwan Studies Group of the Association of Asian Studies and served as the editor of the *Taiwan Studies Newsletter* until the summer of 1994.

Jane Kaufman Winn is a member of the faculty of the School of Law at Southern Methodist University.

Note on Transliteration

The chapters in this book were originally written for different venues. Given the different time periods and socioeconomic circumstances they cover, the editor has decided to allow each author to retain his or her own system of Romanization.

THE
OTHER
TAIWAN

Introduction

"The Taiwan Miracle"

Murray A. Rubinstein

The Taiwan most written about—and thus the Taiwan that the West has come to know best—is a nation that is usually defined by such phrases as "economic miracle," "evolving democracy," or "anti-Communist bastion." Security has made Taiwan a safe haven for the Guomindang (GMD), the home of a dramatic export-oriented industrial revolution, the greenhouse for the evolution of an educated and Westernized middle class, and the laboratory for emergence of a presidential parliamentary system with an increasingly viable two-party system. Thus it is logical, and not at all ironic, that this island has also become a place where specific sets of organizations, interest groups, religious bodies, and representatives of specific ethnicities speak, with ever stronger voices, to the problems and the possibilities created by the very processes of economic, social, political, and spiritual/cultural transformation.

These different collectivities make up the "other Taiwans." Because those who represent such "other Taiwans" see Taiwanese realities differently from those in the establishment, they view the evolution of the island critically and present alternative visions of the island's future development. The essays in this volume focus on such critical voices—voices that often speak to the needs of the disenfranchised or the disaffected. They articulate problems too often neglected in mainstream accounts of the "Taiwan Miracle."

The "Taiwan Miracle" Defined

The central theme of this book is that the rationales and policies of the elites created disaffection, which in the fullness of time gave birth to political awareness, gender consciousness, ethnic self-realization, and spiritual rebirth. And a core reality of contemporary Taiwanese life is that such forms of consciousness, when articulated and then expressed in deed, as well as in word, by the actors themselves, threaten the status quo the power elites have so carefully constructed.

3

"The Taiwan Miracle"[1] began in 1949 when key GMD leaders and remnants of the Nationalist army conceded the mainland to the hated *gongfei* (Communist bandits).[2] As they did so they retreated to the island province they had reclaimed from the Japanese at the end of World War II.

Nationalist troops had come to Taiwan four years earlier, when they and a number of civilian officials had "liberated" and reoccupied the island. Whatever their faults as imperialists—and there were many—the Japanese had recognized the economic potential of the island and had developed it into a prosperous colony, one that also protected Japan's southern flank. Although GMD propagandists insisted that the return to Chinese rule was truly a restoration (*guangfu*), the populace soon felt that it was an occupation, one that proved to be much worse than that of the Japanese. As Suzanne Pepper has shown in *The Chinese Civil War*, the newly arrived troops and officials treated Taiwan as they treated other parts of Japanese-occupied China—not so much as areas liberated from an oppressive colonial rule and possessing brethren populations who had suffered the depredations of exploitation and war, but rather, the officers and their troops, and the bureaucrats, saw these areas as spoils of war, their populations tainted by the very experience of the occupation and thus looked on as traitors. They acted according to this perception, confiscating property and harassing the local populace.[3]

The Taiwanese populace first welcomed their fellow countrymen. However, as the nature of the new regime became clear, and as incidents of official theft, corruption, and sexual assault multiplied, the Taiwanese grew angry. A year and a half after the first troops had landed, a confrontation between a policeman and a woman selling cigarettes—an illegal act because the government controlled the sale of both tobacco and alcoholic beverages—escalated into a riot and resulted in the destruction of a Taibei police station.

This incident on a Taibei street on February 28, 1947—and the failure of authorities to deal with the violent response of the local populace—was a catalyst: Once word of the attack on the police station had circulated, the fighting spread throughout the island and the Nationalist authorities were soon forced to defend themselves. After gauging the resentment of the people, Taiwanese leaders organized themselves and attempted to negotiate with authorities, demanding reform and more local autonomy. As the Nationalist authorities negotiated with the Taiwanese leaders, seemingly in good faith, they brought troops from the Chinese mainland. These troops restored order and made numerous arrests; many of those arrested died in captivity and there was great bloodshed. The suppression of the rebellion provided the Nationalist authorities with the opportunity, first, to wipe out members of Taiwan's intellectual and managerial elites, individuals who were educated and trained during the years of Japanese control, who might threaten their hold on the island; and second, to cow the rest of the populace into submission. Most estimates place the dead at about 20,000. The suppression included the shutting down of local presses, and local Taiwanese institutions were targeted for further attention by the GMD authorities.[4] Taiwan was now pacified, and its elites and its general populace would remain docile—with certain notable exceptions[5]—until the early 1970s. However, the memory of the violence was kept alive in the minds of those who witnessed it and experienced its fury. The bitterness of that repression remains to this day. In Taiwan today, however, with its more open press, books and articles on the once-taboo 2–28 Incident are published and are widely read.[6] People have now begun to restore this episode to their collective past, and a new generation has come to learn of what took place. Furthermore, the leaders of such institutions as the Presbyterian Church in Taiwan and the Democratic Progressive Party have begun to use the 2–28 Incident as a powerful spiritual and political symbol as they articulate their positions on Taiwanese nationalism.

In the immediate aftermath of the 2–28 Incident, over the course of 1948 and 1949, the tattered Nationalist forces retreated to this pacified and secured Taiwan as control of the mainland slipped from their collective grasp. The GMD now ruled the island with an iron hand, readying itself for an invasion by the Chinese Communists that never came. North Korea's invasion of South Korea, the American intervention in that war, and China's subsequent decision to defend its communist brother in North Korea against U.S. imperialism were decisive in ensuring that an invasion would not take place: the United States shelved plans for recognition of the People's Republic of China, placed its Seventh Fleet in the Taiwan Strait, and promised to defend the Republic of China on its island bastion.

The United States did more than simply agree to defend Taiwan. It pledged massive amounts of aid and technical assistance in the hope that such aid might allow the ROC to defend itself and, at the same time, to become an economically viable and more democratic regime. The Republic of China/Taiwan became the paradigm of a successful program of assistance, bearing witness to the viability of a strong anti-Communist and capitalist United States.[7]

As defenders of the GMD often point out, however, the miracle was not only the product of American action. The GMD, they argue, learned from its painful experiences on the Chinese mainland and then worked to correct its flaws and to establish the institutional structures for further economic, political, and social development.

Internal housekeeping and a cleansing[8] of the Communist elements of the émigré community were a prelude to more systematic bureaucratic and systemic reforms, and ushered in the far-reaching socioeconomic changes that the GMD and its American advisors agreed needed to be put in place.

The "Miracle" that resulted, first fueled by direct American aid and expertise, and later supported by major American and Japanese corporations, earned that rubric by the standard of most available economic indicators. The statistical and anecdotal evidence amassed by such participant/observers as K.T. Li and Neil Jacoby and by Chinese and Western students of Taiwan such as Samuel Ho, Thomas Gold, and Ching-yuan Li[9] demonstrate that a massive transformation of the island's economy did take place.

There were, these scholars have pointed out, two major stages of the process of economic transformation that, when taken together, constitute the Miracle. In the first stage, a foundation for economic development was constructed. In the second stage, a strategy for economic growth through the creation of an export-oriented economy was designed and then implemented.

First, the government of the Republic of China, with the strong urging of American Agency for International Development (AID) advisors, and with the financial backing of the United States, introduced a widespread and effective land reform. By the terms agreed on, property was taken from the large landowners, in exchange for generous compensation payments, and redistributed among smaller landowners or former tenants.[10] Under the Japanese colonialists, the island's agrarian economy had been developed, at least in certain key sectors, but the allied bombing and the depredations of the newly arrived Nationalists had done much to destroy the gains that had been made. These land reforms gave agriculture—then the dominant sector of the economy—a needed impetus, and the island soon once again became a rice basket, a major producer of sugar and tropical fruits, a livestock exporter, and the center of a major tea industry.

But the effects of the land reform did not end there: A number of the major landowners invested the funds and the bonds they received as compensation for the lands they surrendered, and some of these funds were used as seed capital for the new industries that were either organized and run by the government or were, with government support, beginning to develop.

The economic revolution that took shape was neither directed nor fueled by free market factors, however. The Taiwan Miracle was, first and foremost, a directed and planned economic revolution, as K.T. Li, one of the key planners of that revolution, makes clear in his own account of this period.[11] By the mid-1950s, the government had set up organs to design and then implement a series of economic plans, plans that stressed large-scale development projects and the construction of new types of industrial facilities.

The objective of the planners was to reconstruct the existing nationwide infrastructure while constructing new elements of that infrastructure, thus providing the foundation for a modern industrialized economy. The transportation network—railroad lines, roads and highways, and harbor facilities—that had been developed by the Japanese had been damaged by the allied bombing of the island and was in need of repair and upgrading. Dams were needed to control the rivers that when swelled by monsoon rains ran over their banks and destroyed portions of the rich agricultural land of the island's western coastal plain. The waters from the reservoirs that formed upriver of the dams would be used for irrigation, thus helping agricultural development, while the force of the water as it flowed from the dams was to serve as a cheap source of much needed electric power in this oil-poor island nation (or *non-nation,* to use Thomas Gold's clever and ironic term).

A second objective of the planners was to establish factories that would provide the many construction projects with much needed materials. Various finished and processed goods were needed to construct the roads, the dams, the power stations, the irrigation systems, and the other types of systems and facilities the planners deemed necessary. In addition, other types of factories were planned that were intended to serve as models for new industries.

As Li has shown, many difficulties had to be overcome in introducing and then implementing such large-scale economic plans. The process of constructing a workable system of planning and implementation and assessment that began in the early 1950s continued in the 1960s and on into the 1970s, even after the economic growth desired had been achieved.[12]

Whatever the difficulties, and there were many, the strategy worked. The infrastructure was put in place and has been continually improved to meet the demands for better transportation and for more power, both commercial and private, that are made by a complex modern and prosperous society. The various factory complexes that pointed the island in the direction of new forms of industrial production were constructed with grants-in-aid received from the United States. Only when the factories neared completion, the government administrators discovered, did private mainland-born and Taiwan-born investors prove willing to invest their resources: In the early stages of this innovative development, what few investors there were simply were not willing to commit their capital resources. The student of East Asian development can see history repeating itself in all of this: The patterns of economic development that were implemented by the Meiji leaders in Japan some seventy years before were being replicated on Taiwan in the 1950s.

There was more to this first phase of the Miracle than raw economic development, however. The central planners and their American advisors realized that a modern society is one that possesses a well-educated managerial elite and a well-trained and highly skilled work-force. They also realized, as had the Japanese before them, that adequate sanitation and public health facilities were needed. During the occupation the Japanese had begun to develop both educational and public health systems,[13] and the administrators of the ROC were able to build on this foundation. This period saw the development of education at all levels—primary, secondary, and postsecondary. While much of this development was undertaken by the government, private groups such as the Presbyterian and the Catholic churches and various mission bodies also played their part in setting up primary and secondary schools and universities. These same groups also set up hospitals and developed local health care networks that complemented the institutions the government had established.

In the 1960s, the second stage of the island's economic miracle began to take shape. By the early sixties, Taiwan's planners and their American advisors saw that the foundations for a stable currency and for sustained economic growth had been laid—all the available economic indicators suggested this. Major decisions

now had to be made. Thus far the economy had faced inward, with self-sufficiency a fundamental goal of its import substitution strategy. But Taiwan could
never be as self-sustaining or as well rounded an economy as its leaders wanted
it to be. Because it was both energy poor and resource poor, a skilled and
ambitious population was perhaps the nation's major resource. The planning
strategists, aware of these realities, came to the conclusion, after lengthy
discussions with their American advisors, that Taiwan could no longer face
inward or rely on American grants-in-aid. One major impetus of the planned
realignment was a decision made in Washington in the early 1960s: American
officials were now told to wean Taiwan from its reliance on large amounts of
direct economic aid from the United States. Because there was a pressing need to
redirect the economy so that it could play a role in the larger world economy, the
government now had to change some of its basic economic policies. It had to
reduce its tight control of the economy, reduce tariffs, provide rebates if products
were exported, and liberalize controls on trade. In other words, Taiwan had to
open itself to risk. It had to face outward if it was to grow and prosper.[14]

K.T. Li, a protégé of K.Y. Yin who was the driving force behind the development of the 1950s, now came to the fore. Following in the footsteps of his
mentor, he pushed this transformation in basic economic policy. In doing this,
he opposed more cautious and conservative GMD leaders but acted, he later
said, with the support of Jiang Jieshi (Chiang Kai-shek) and other key leaders of
the regime.[15] The Americans played their part in this transformation. They had
threatened aid cutoffs if these steps were not taken; now they promised aid
amounting to 20 to 30 million dollars if the plans were implemented quickly.
The first two four-year plans (1953–56; 1957–60) had stressed development of
the infrastructure. The third (1961–64) implemented the Nineteen-Point Program of Economic and Financial Reform—the program that included those
reforms mentioned above. At the same time, the structure of the economic plan
was reformed and CUSA—the Council on U.S. Aid—was now integrated into
the newly established CIECD—the Council for International Economic Cooperation and Development—and this body became an organ of the Executive
Yuan, the ROC's executive branch. This demonstrated the Jiang regime's commitment to centralized planning.[16]

But how to implement such a plan? And how to draw the attention of
overseas companies that might take advantage of Taiwan as a possible site of
investment? As Thomas Gold has shown, AID contracted with the Stanford
Research Institute to "prepare reports on the feasibility of certain industries
of potential interest to foreign investors," industries that produced plastic
resins, synthetic fibers, electronic components, transistor radios, and watches.
AID then used these reports to publicize Taiwan. Other agencies of the
American government then made use of existing programs to help facilitate
and protect the flow of funds from the United States. The campaign was a
success. General Instruments committed its resources when it set up an elec-

tronics factory near Taibei in 1964. The factory proved successful, and seven other American firms took the plunge that same year. Seventeen more made the decision to set up facilities in 1965.[17] This was the beginning. Within the next few years, in an expanding and ever more integrated global economy, Taiwan began to be seen as an attractive site for major investment. Its government officials, following the lead of the Americans, stressed that they would provide the potential investor with a variety of incentives and that their nation possessed a large, educated, disciplined, and cheap labor force. The Americans were soon joined by their East Asian ally/rival, Japan, which now also saw the many advantages that its former colony offered.

In 1965 the government took another major step by establishing the first Export Processing Zones in Gaoxiong, on the southwest coast. Here an industrial park linked to a modern harbor was developed. The zone had its own administration, which facilitated decision making. Finally, the government offered tax incentives and eliminated duties on equipment imported to produce goods for export.[18] The basic rule was this: If the products produced by a foreign factory were intended only for export then that company could be held completely by a foreign corporation and could avoid various types of taxes and duties. If, however, the goods produced were intended for both the world market and the domestic Taiwan market, then ownership of that factory had to be 50 percent Taiwanese. Furthermore, at least half of the parts used in assembling the products produced by that factory had to be manufactured on Taiwan. To ensure that such products would find a captive market in Taiwan, tariffs on a wide variety of foreign goods were made so high as to make them virtually prohibitive to all but a select few. What made this system work, from the Taiwanese consumer's viewpoint, was that the quality of goods produced for the domestic market improved markedly.[19]

American firms that invested in Taiwan tended to be large in scale. While some Japanese giants entered the fray, most of the Japanese firms were small or medium sized. The larger Japanese firms took the next step and tried to gain entry to Taiwan's domestic market by means of joint ventures. The smaller firms followed suit by taking Chinese locals as partners.

This government-sponsored and foreign-financed redirection of the economy showed local Chinese entrepreneurs what was possible, and by the late 1960s, Taiwan-based investors began to commit both their resources and their skills to the new spheres of economic opportunity. These firms began to link themselves to the world network by entering into joint ventures, by serving as subcontractors for Western or Japanese firms, and by undertaking direct export. For many of those involved, these efforts proved successful. Lin Ting-sheng of Tatung, the island's major consumer electronics firm, is one example. Chen Mao-pang Hong of Sampo, another manufacturer of consumer electronics, is a second. C.C. Hong, of Matsushita Taiwan, is a third.[20]

Thus the gamble to establish an export-oriented economy paid off. By the early 1970s the economy was booming, and the trickle-down effect was felt by the majority of the island's citizens. New types of entrepreneurs appeared, and more and more people began to enter the ranks of the bourgeoisie. Business groups also began to appear as media for spreading risk and cementing relationships. Labor was still repressed, but many in the working class found a way out by accumulating capital and starting their own small enterprises, thus emulating those in the social strata above them. With more money available, consumerism became a way of life in this prosperous new socioeconomic environment. Economists who supported and who spoke for the GMD regime argued—and continue to argue—that growth-with-equity was a fundamental reality of the "Taiwan Miracle."[21]

The Miracle also produced a major shift in population as more and more people moved from countryside to city, transforming a landscape of small villages and plots of tilled land and rice paddies into a landscape of high-rises and sprawling suburbs linked by increasingly inadequate road networks and mass transportation systems, a landscape that was beclouded by ever increasing levels of pollutants thrown into the atmosphere. Thus the government-directed "Miracle" transformed both social and physical environments in ways the leaders of the island could not have imagined.[22]

But other acts of the Taiwan drama had to be played out. The economy, while strong, was vulnerable to vagaries in the world market and to crises that the larger world economy experienced. The 1967 Yom Kippur War between Egypt and Israel and the oil crisis it produced brought this fact home. The rapid rise in oil prices forced the government to take difficult and painful steps to deal with rising rates of inflation and to maintain some degree of price stability.[23] Beginning in 1973 the island's economy entered a sustained period of stagflation that lasted for about a decade. This, when combined with a series of diplomatic setbacks, gave rise to internal political protests.

This first wave of protests was spearheaded by students, intellectuals, and members of the Presbyterian Church. Challenged, the government responded with a combination of strength and flexibility that foreshadowed its handling of later crises. President Jiang Jingguo, Chiang Kai-shek's son, now asserted himself and assumed a position of dominance. He introduced important administrative changes and opened the government to more technocrats. However, he also showed the iron fist and suppressed dissent. One of his targets was the Presbyterian Church.[24] Further setbacks created new and more potent protests in the late 1970s. The canceling of elections in late 1978 led to the formation of the *dangwai*—the Outside-the-Party/Meilidao movement that challenged the GMD in a series of demonstrations that resulted in the Gaoxiong Incident of December 1979 and the clampdown on political dissent.[25] By the early 1980s the regime had weathered the worst of the political, diplomatic, and economic storms and the "Taiwan Miracle" was back on course.

The second half of the 1980s saw new stages in the "Taiwan Miracle" and in the nation's ongoing political development take place. The economy continued to develop, and with the approval of the government new initiatives were taken so that a viable economic relationship with the PRC could begin. A first step the regime took was to make room for political opposition by means of the de facto recognition of the *dangwai*. A second step was the opening to the PRC through a change in visa policy and through a change in monetary exchange policy. Chinese from Taiwan began pouring into the mainland via Hong Kong as tourists and as merchants seeking products for across-the-strait trade, and as possible business partners searching for joint enterprises to invest in.[26] Soon thereafter came the announcement that martial law would be ended. These measures were all part of Jiang Jingguo's legacy of creating a more politically open Taiwan. With Jiang's death, Li Denghui, a Taiwanese (and Presbyterian) without a power base in the security force, came to the fore as the successor to the now revered Jiang Jingguo. He, in turn, continued to open up the political process. He relaxed the government's control of the press, took a statesman-like position on the events at Tiananmen, and then, some nine months later, in March 1990, demonstrating his political astuteness and his flexibility as a leader and his responsiveness to the demands of the rising middle-class elites, agreed to convene the *Guoshihui*—the National Consultative Assembly. And, in June 1990, in yet another move that was meant to demonstrate that he was the president of a more open regime, he released a number of political dissidents imprisoned after the Meilidao incident and others put in jail for similar crimes against the state.[27]

This then was the miracle that transformed Taiwan. While I have tried to suggest what impact the Taiwan Miracle had on the people of the island and on their basic patterns of existence, I have not dealt with the complex effects this radical socioeconomic transformation has truly produced. Nor have I dealt with the ways in which different segments of the society have responded to these wide-ranging changes in the ways one earns a living, receives an education, engages in social interaction, involves oneself in the political system, or prays to one's deity or deities. It is to this task that the chapters in this book are dedicated.

The authors are diverse in background and in discipline, in life experience, in political orientation. Some are political activists, some journalists, some academics. They are from either Taiwan or the United States. All have learned about Taiwan firsthand. Some are nationals who play roles in the island's interrelated academic, political, and bureaucratic communities. Others are foreigners who have been either longtime residents or frequent visitors who have come to know the island and feel at home there. Each knows the island well, and while each is an objective observer, each also writes from the depth of his or her personal experience of a Taiwan in flux.

The Other Taiwan is divided into seven parts. The first is intended to give the reader a word picture of the island and some of the basic issues that confront its populace. Each of the other parts is made up of two or more chapters that focus on specific problems or themes or issues.

We hope that these topics will provide the student of Taiwan and the student of the Pacific Basin new insights into the way the people of one society were affected by its leaders' decision to transform their homeland and to make it a part of the global community.

Notes

1. There is a growing body of literature on this subject. I have examined books written from various perspectives and ideological viewpoints. Among the works consulted in developing this portrait are: Ralph N. Clough, *Island China* (Cambridge, MA: Harvard University Press, 1978); Marc J. Cohen, *Taiwan at the Crossroads* (Washington, DC: Asia Resource Center, 1988); John F. Copper, *Taiwan: Nation State or Province* (Boulder, CO: Westview Press, 1990); Thomas B. Gold, *State and Society in the Taiwan Miracle* (Armonk, NY: M.E. Sharpe, 1987); James C. Hsiung, ed., *Contemporary Republic of China: The Taiwan Experience, 1950-1980* (New York: Praeger, 1981); Kuo-ting Li, *Taiwan jingji kuqishi chengchang de jingyan* (The Taiwan experience in dynamic economic growth) (Taibei: Cheng-Chung Press, 1978) (this volume was also published in the United States under the title *The Taiwan Experience of Dynamic Economic Growth* [New York: Meiya Press, 1976]); Ching-yuan Lin, *Latin America versus East Asia* (Armonk, NY: M.E. Sharpe, 1989); Hung-mao Tien, *The Great Transition: Political and Social Change in the Republic of China* (Stanford, CA: Hoover Institution Press, 1989); Edwin A. Winkler and Susan Greenhalgh, eds., *Contending Approaches to the Political Economy of Taiwan* (Armonk, NY: M.E. Sharpe, 1988).

2. The Taiwan Miracle, in a formal sense, began only after 1951, when the United States made the decision to patrol the Taiwan Strait and defend the GMD regime in the wake of the Chinese involvement in the Korean War. However, since the essays in this volume focus on the political as well as the economic and social impacts of the island's transformation, one must begin in 1949 or, as I will argue, in 1945.

3. On the first stages of GMD takeover of these areas on the mainland and on Taiwan see Suzanne Pepper, *The Chinese Civil War* (Berkeley: University of California Press, 1980). On Taiwan see George H. Kerr, *Formosa Betrayed* (Boston: Houghton, Mifflin, 1965); and Min-ming Peng, *A Taste of Freedom* (New York: Holt, Rhinehart, and Winston, 1972).

4. The best Western account of the incident remains by Kerr, *Formosa Betrayed*. An important and controversial new study, based on recently opened ROC archival materials, is Lai Tse-han, Ramon H. Meyers, and Wei Wou, *A Tragic Beginning: The Taiwan Uprising of February 28, 1947* (Stanford, CA: Stanford University Press, 1991).

5. Among the exceptions were Peter Huang, who bore witness to the repression and who provided American authorities with detailed accounts of what had taken place. Another was Shi Mingde, who as a young military cadet plotted against the GMD regime and who, like Peter Huang, spent much of his adult life in prison for "treason."

6. Within the past three years, and coinciding with the political liberalization, there has been a plethora of books dealing with 2-28 that have been published on Taiwan. They range from collections of documents, to eyewitness accounts, to historical analyses that discuss the events and their significance. The Lai book mentioned in note 4 is the most recent English-language work on the subject, but, given the new material now available, more will undoubtedly follow.

7. Students of the Vietnam War often refer to the American experience in both Taiwan and the Philippines as setting the stage for the United States' involvement in South Vietnam after 1954. For example, see Neil Sheehan, *A Bright Shining Lie* (New York:

Random House, 1988). On the term "miracle" see the discussion in Gold, *State and Society in the Taiwan Miracle.*

8. One can gain a feel for life in Taiwan at this time and a description of this process of *cleansing* by the GMD in an account by a British reporter then on the island. See M. Mclear Bate, *Report from Formosa* (London: London, Eyre, and Spotswoode, 1952).

9. K.T. Li, *The Experience of Dynamic Economic Growth on Taiwan* (Taibei and New York: Meiya Publications, 1976); Neil Jacoby, *U.S. Aid to Taiwan* (New York: Praeger, 1966); Samuel Ho, *Economic Development of Taiwan* (New Haven: Yale University Press, 1978); Gold, *State and Society in the Taiwan Miracle;* Ching-yuan Lin, *Latin America versus East Asia .*

10. Gold, *State and Society in the Taiwan Miracle,* pp. 65–66.

11. Li, *The Experience of Dynamic Economic Growth on Taiwan.* See also a more objective and less favorable picture of the planned economic development during the 1950s that is drawn in Gold, *State and Society in the Taiwan Miracle,* pp. 67–73.

12. Li, *The Experience of Dynamic Economic Growth on Taiwan,* pp. 87–101.

13. E. Patricia Tsurumi, *Japanese Colonial Education* (Cambridge, MA: Harvard University Press, 1977).

14. Gold, *State and Society in the Taiwan Miracle,* p. 77.

15. Li, *The Experience of Dynamic Economic Growth on Taiwan,* pp. 87–101; Gold, *State and Society in the Taiwan Miracle,* p. 77.

16. Gold, *State and Society in the Taiwan Miracle,* p. 78.

17. Ibid., p. 78; Li, *The Experience of Dynamic Economic Growth on Taiwan,* pp. 138–41.

18. Li, *The Experience of Dynamic Economic Growth on Taiwan,* pp. 352–58.

19. The system was not foolproof, however. In the late 1970s, seconds from some of the Western clothing factories, with their name brands attached, could be purchased in discount clothing stores, and by the 1980s, factory-direct discount stores—discount-outlet malls of the sort often found in Manchester, Vermont, or Glenns Falls, New York—were established in the newer and pricier shopping areas of Taibei.

20. Li, *The Experience of Dynamic Economic Growth on Taiwan,* pp. 131–35, 359–70; Gold, *State and Society in the Taiwan Miracle,* pp. 79–87.

21. On the results of the miracle see Hsiung, ed., *Contemporary Republic of China: The Taiwan Experience, 1950–1980,* pp. 119–217. This book was reviewed quite critically by some scholars who felt that it was produced by scholars who were strong supporters of the GMD-led regime; in addition its publication was subsidized by the Pacific Cultural Foundation, a body closely connected with the regime. While I recognize the source of support and agree that its editor stands openly and unashamedly as a strong and articulate defender of the ROC, I find the book to be a useful compendium that contains papers that both praise and attack the politics and programs of the regime.

22. Hsiung, ed., *Contemporary Republic of China,* pp. 219–81.

23. Li, *The Experience of Dynamic Economic Growth on Taiwan,* pp. 134–35, 171–77.

24. On the Presbyterian Church's actions at this time see Murray A. Rubinstein, "Mission of Faith, Burden of Witness," *American Asian Review,* vol. 9, no. 2 (Summer 1991): 70–108.

25. See Gold, *State and Society in the Taiwan Miracle,* pp. 97–121, for a summary of the events of this period. As is true of the 2–28 Incident, there is much interest in this period, and as a result, a rich literature is evolving on Taiwan that deals with these events, with the Meilidao movement, and with the major actors in it. Western scholars now have a rich body of material to work with.

26. I was able to see firsthand that people on Taiwan were taking advantage of this opening to the PRC in the summer of 1990 when I visited cities in Fujian, the ancestral home province of those Chinese who had gone to Taiwan in the centuries since the final decade of Ming rule. I met Taiwan entrepreneurs involved in import-export trade and those looking for investment opportunities. These individuals saw Fujian as a new frontier for Taiwanese economic enterprise.

27. Many of these political issues are examined in Harvey Feldman, ed., *Constitutional Reform and the Future of the Republic of China* (Armonk, NY: M.E. Sharpe, 1991).

Part I

CONTEXTS

The two chapters in this section provide background and context for the more detailed studies to follow.

Alan Wachman's chapter attempts to come to grips with two central issues that the people of Taiwan are now facing. One is political liberalization. The second is the way in which one defines Taiwan in terms of what Wachman has called the "competing claims" of national and ethnic identity. By using a host of very diverse and often antagonistic voices, Wachman conveys the sense of crisis now pervading Taiwan and provides some explanations for this many layered crisis.

Hai-yuan Chu's chapter provides an understanding of how Taiwanese see their lives today. Comparing survey data over a five-year period, he begins by asking his informants how satisfied they are with the lives they lead in modern Taiwan. He focuses on questions of personal relationships such as those between husband and wife, parent and child, and friend and friend. Here he finds high levels of satisfaction. However, when people are asked about how they feel about their own level of academic success, their own financial condition, and their own sense of the time they have for leisure activities, their responses were far less positive.

Next, Chu explores how his respondents view the public realm. He asks how people feel about the political changes taking place on the island and then inquires about their connection to the society—the degree of alienation they feel. Attitudes toward the work ethic and toward instruments of social control are next. This, in turn, leads to a series of questions about the way people see Taiwan's social problems. These problems include juvenile delinquency, public security, pollution of the environment, the rising cost of living, and political corruption.

He concludes by examining how people see and respond to the increasing secularization of life. He finds that people are aware of and disturbed by such secularization and that they are responding to this "assault of the modern" by returning to folk religion and by involving themselves in such sectarian religions as Yiguan Dao (the Connected Path).

Chapter 1

Competing Identities in Taiwan

Alan M. Wachman

The two political problems most evident in Taiwan since the mid-1980s have been: (1) the demands for greater participation, fairness, and equity in the political system, and (2) the absence of consensus regarding national identity. These problems are related. In the past, those who believed that Taiwan should be governed as a sovereign state by officials elected exclusively from among the residents of Taiwan demanded greater opportunities for political participation from those in power who restricted political participation by authoritarian means. The aim of those in power was to ensure that they could maintain the claim that they were not simply the rulers of Taiwan, but the sole legitimate government of all China, of which Taiwan was one part.

Until the middle of the 1980s, those people demanding greater opportunities to participate in the political process that governed their lives were repressed—sometimes quite brutally. At issue in the competition between the government and the opposition were fundamental questions of political power. Whether one associated oneself with the government or the opposition, however, was a matter of identity. Although the conflict between competing views of national identity has been a central characteristic of political life in Taiwan and, to a great degree, defined the struggle between the opposition and the government, as a subject of investigation it has been largely ignored by those who study Taiwan.

Analysts of Taiwan tended to examine the island from an economic or international perspective. The dynamism of Taiwan's economic growth from a poor agricultural-based economy at the end of the Second World War to a thriving,

This chapter was adapted from my dissertation, which concerns the relationship among identity, nationalism, and the process of democratization in Taiwan. Funding for research was generously provided by the Center for International Affairs at Harvard University in the form of a K.T. Li Dissertation Research Fellowship and was supplemented by a research grant from the Pacific Cultural Foundation.

industrialized, export economy with one of the world's greatest reserves of foreign exchange in the current era was, naturally, an attractive subject of examination. People were more curious about the "Taiwan miracle" or about Taiwan as one of East Asia's "four little dragons" than about the internal politics of the island.

Taiwan's conflictual relations with the People's Republic of China (PRC), the quandary concerning reunification, and decisions made by many states to abandon formal ties with Taiwan as a way to grease relations with Peking all contributed to a view of Taiwan as a piece of the international affairs puzzle. Yet, works about Taiwan's role in the diplomatic or strategic realms paid scant attention to the restive domestic politics of the island or to the controversies festering there.

Indeed, the struggle for political reform in Taiwan was not studied much by scholars outside the island until liberalizations initiated in 1987 were well under way. From the onset of reforms, scholars began to show interest in the political life within Taiwan, rather than simply viewing Taiwan as a factor affecting politics elsewhere, and as those reforms have proceeded, political liberalization in Taiwan has attracted attention from scholars scrambling to offer explanations of the changes that are taking place. Even so, far less attention has been paid to Taiwan's progress toward democracy than, for example, to the PRC's resistance to reform. Perhaps because Taiwan is not the PRC, it is overlooked, save by a small community of subspecialists in the "China field" and, of course, by the island's own social scientists.[1] So far, no work has focused on national identity as a matter of contention that both drives the process of reform and threatens the consolidation of democracy in Taiwan.

China's Tribulations

Problems in Taiwan pertaining to national identity reflect a dilemma that has burdened Chinese political and intellectual elites for most of the twentieth century. In the past, there was little question that China—*Chung-Kuo*—was a term that represented a nation, a culture, and a polity. In common parlance the term "Chinese" has been used as an ethnic category referring to those who are considered Han.[2] Chinese were assumed to come from a common racial type, a common linguistic stock, and a common cultural heritage. To be Chinese implied not only a particular ethnicity, but that one lived in the Chinese polity, or considered China as home if one resided abroad. These assumptions are no longer unquestioned on Taiwan.[3]

The conflict with Western powers that flared up in the mid-nineteenth century was a watershed. It marked the start of a long, gradual unraveling of the Chinese illusion of cultural supremacy and political cohesion. The process that began with the Opium Wars was advanced by China's losses to Japan and Russia around the turn of the century, and went into full spin through the 1920s and 1930s. The consciousness of China as a unity and as a bastion of civilization was shattered by the trauma of repeated ruination.

The incursion of Western forces—brash, demanding, and different—led to a vain attempt by the empire to repel its assailants. These efforts only highlighted China's weakness and vulnerability and made a mockery of the accepted notion of greatness. Proposals for reform at the end of the last century and early in the twentieth century led to failure. By the second decade of this century, the empire had disintegrated and then vanished. The hope for recovery grew more and more remote as, again, China tumbled into the churning uncertainties of anarchy. The successive acts played out by pompous and ineffectual figures in Peking made manifest the irrelevance of the drama itself. There was no leadership, there was no capital, there was no state. Again, China was ground into defeat.

The Treaty of Versailles, which followed World War I, brought fresh evidence of China's powerlessness and marginality in the minds of the strong and wealthy states of the West. Shan-tung Province, recovered from the German colonial grasp, was turned over to Japan, another reminder of China's decrepitude. Unable to rise beyond internecine struggles, corruption, and dissolution, Chinese intellectuals lashed out with frustration, anger, and despair at their own civilization. They felt betrayed by the values and institutions they had been primed to preserve.

During the May Fourth Movement (1919), intellectuals flaunted China's helplessness by seeking cures from beyond China. Throughout the 1920s and 1930s, young minds viewed the hapless state into which China had deteriorated as a mirror of its cultural and political hubris. They sought to cure China's ills with medicines from abroad. They looked to the powerful and prosperous states of Europe for tonics and relief. But the palliatives from the West were not easily injected into the body China.

During this century, China's intellectuals have sought in vain for ideological systems that would make China strong again. Despite the conscious efforts to sustain some aspects of China's past, without the unity provided by a moral order under which political, social, and personal norms cohered for long stretches of Chinese history, elements that survived the collapse of the empire now lay in an unstructured store of memories and sensibilities. Chinese intelligentsia have picked at this heap of unintegrated cultural ingredients like scavengers in the hope that a strand here or a shred there could be woven into a new cultural fabric. Now, as in the past, whatever they create will be influenced by the world outside China and is very likely to incorporate values and institutions that were once alien to the Chinese.

Taiwan's Travails

Taiwan's most intractable problems are political and stem from differing views of the island's national identity. The roots of these matters lie deep in Taiwan's past. For one thing, Taiwan's political status has never been unassailable. China (understood as the mainland) has been governed in several ways: by Chinese exercising dominion over the entire empire, by Chinese exercising power in regions that competed for control of the whole empire, and by foreigners who wrested control of China from Chinese, but who were ultimately routed and replaced by Chinese rulers. This has not been the case in Taiwan. Taiwan has not always been considered part of China, has often been governed by non-Chinese, and has never been ruled exclusively by people who consider Taiwan as home.

Taiwan was first inhabited by Chinese immigrants in the seventeenth century, but was then under the control of the Dutch until 1662, when the island was taken by a colorful figure known as Koxinga (Cheng Ch'eng-kung), the son of a Chinese pirate and a Japanese woman. The island was ruled as a separate kingdom until 1683 when it was conquered by forces of the Ch'ing, the Manchu dynasty that had taken control of China in 1644. Taiwan was then "under the careless and weak" control of the Manchus who were, themselves, alien rulers of China. Although the Manchus adopted Chinese manners, values, and administrative systems, they were foreigners.[4]

When the Ch'ing dynasty was defeated in war by Japan in 1895, Taiwan was severed from the rest of China and taken by the Japanese as part of the settlement extracted under the Treaty of Shimonoseki, and from 1895 until Japan was defeated at the end of the Second World War fifty years later, Taiwan was a Japanese colony. The legacy of Japanese rule runs deeply among those residents of Taiwan old enough to remember and has shaped mannerisms and customs on the island. Japan's presence is visible even to those who have no personal memory of Taiwan's days as a colony because Japan directed the construction of an industrial base and transportation infrastructure that is often cited as a contributing factor in Taiwan's subsequent "miraculous" economic development.[5]

It was decided at the Cairo Conference of December 1943, and reaffirmed at the Potsdam Conference of July 1945, that following the defeat of Japan, Taiwan would be turned over to China. As Chiang Kai-shek and the Nationalist Party (*Kuo Min Tang,* or KMT) were viewed as governing the Republic of China (ROC), it was to KMT forces that the Japanese formally surrendered control of Taiwan on October 25, 1945. The KMT military administration that took control of the island initiated "a period of rapid underdevelopment," as Taiwan was plundered for booty that could be used to support the KMT's battle with the Communists on the mainland. "Economically, politically, and culturally [Taiwan] was suddenly yanked out of the Japanese orbit and appended to China in another colonial relationship."[6]

The relationship between the residents of Taiwan—newly freed from Japan's colonial rule—and the representatives of the KMT was sour from the start. Those who first arrived from the mainland to take control of the island were viewed as carpetbaggers, bunglers, or thieves. By 1947, the animosity had built to such a degree that the unintentional shooting by a government agent of a bystander present at the arrest of a street vendor triggered a demonstration that led to a violent island-wide uprising.[7] Residents of Taiwan lashed out against the KMT and other immigrants from the mainland. This outbreak of hostilities was brought under control and Taiwan was thereafter subjected to a brutal period of repression, retribution, and mass executions.

In 1949, when the KMT lost control of the mainland to the Communists, between one and two million civilian and military refugees retreated to Taiwan—which then had a population of about six million—where the Nationalist government set up shop. Although the KMT intention was to use the island as a temporary haven from which to launch an assault to recover the mainland, in more than forty years, it has been unable to realize its goal of national recovery. During that time, it thoroughly subjugated the island to its own purposes. An authoritarian oligopoly dominated by the political elite who had escaped from the mainland established itself without regard for the wishes, sentiments, or consent of the island's preexisting population. The constitution of the ROC was suspended, and the island was ruled under emergency provisions that institutionalized a prolonged period of martial law. Dissent of any form was suppressed and opposition severely punished.

Chiang Kai-shek ruled with the impunity of a charismatic autocrat. After his death in 1975, his son Chiang Ching-kuo—first as premier and eventually as president—succeeded his father as paramount leader. Chiang Ching-kuo was a more moderate, less doctrinaire soul than his father. Under his leadership, a range of programs were undertaken with the aim of invigorating the economy and the viability of the island itself. Taiwan was no longer viewed simply as a temporary base that would be abandoned and disregarded once the mainland was recovered. Although one may dispute the precise relationship between economic prosperity and political liberalization, what is clear is that as the island's economy began to flourish, demands for political change increased in vigor and frequency.[8] Beyond dispute, though, is that as Chiang Ching-kuo neared the end of his life, he oversaw the initiation of dramatic political reforms that gave rise to a process of democratization that is still very much under way.

The Turmoil of Change

Prominent among changes that have been brought on by political liberalization in Taiwan is the liberty to address divisive questions concerning national identity that might have been considered taboo only a few years ago. Discussions of identity prompt some people to express intense, roiling emotions and vast litanies of frustration. Others disclaim a personal concern for such matters but do, invariably, disclose strong views.

Uncertainty about the national identity of the island is tied to deep anxieties about the future of Taiwan. This results from a clash of nationalist visions: the Chinese nationalism manifested by the KMT and its supporters, and the Taiwanese nationalism manifested by those who advocate that Taiwan be an independent state.[9] This conflict reveals ingrained hostilities and mistrust between segments of the population that threaten to destabilize Taiwan.

Despite the steady progress of democratization, which has been trumpeted by the KMT as evidence that it can lead all China from authoritarianism to democracy, the volatile uncertainties about national identity are not likely to be dampened unless the populace is able to exercise the right of self-determination. As repression gives way to liberty, problems that reflect conflicting notions of identity may become more nettlesome, and the demands to rectify long-standing inequities may intensify.[10] While Taiwan faces many problems that appear more immediate, underlying tensions related to national identity affect nearly every sphere of island-wide political and social interaction and guide the attitudes, decisions, and behavior of the political elite. At the national level, even apparently mundane decisions may be couched in terms of the conflict between Chinese and Taiwanese nationalists.

Tearing down the citadels of authoritarianism entails challenging formerly unassailable truths. In Taiwan, liberties newly wrested from the authorities have led people to depart from past orthodoxies. Free to express their genuine sentiments, people assert political identities that threaten the cohesion of the state in which they live and complicate efforts to reform the system by which they have been ruled. The absence of consensus about political identity in Taiwan may be seen as both a contribution to rapid change and an outgrowth of change.

One fundamental change has to do with attitudes people hold toward China and Taiwan. Residents of Taiwan have been impelled by changes in the political and social realms to reexamine their cultural and political identities, and as they do, many find that the simple truths to which they clung in the past are certainly not simple and may not even be true. The nub of debate is whether Taiwan itself is a country or whether it is, as the ruling parties in both Taipei and Peking have claimed, only part of a larger country: China.

Perplexities about Identity; Decisions about Democracy

This controversy encompasses subsidiary questions that also affect Chinese living beyond Taiwan, including:

1. What constitutes China? Is the PRC China? Is Taiwan?
2. Does China only exist when both the mainland and the island comprise a single polity with one government?
3. Is it possible to differentiate "Taiwanese" from "Chinese"?
4. Is it possible to be culturally Chinese and politically Taiwanese?
5. Which Chinese—those on Taiwan alone, or all Chinese—should decide these matters and by what means should they decide?

Viewed narrowly, this debate concerns a competition for power among the twenty million residents of Taiwan. Taken broadly, the debate pertains to the nature of China as a polity and the existence of the Chinese nation. These are matters that affect Chinese everywhere and reflect long-standing anxieties triggered by the dissolution of the empire at the end of the last century. In essence, what does it mean, now, to be Chinese?[11]

As scholars play with the intellectual consequences of these questions, people in Taiwan confront divisive choices linked to demands for reform. The authoritarianism of the past has been discredited and a new political system is evolving fitfully. The national goals and political rules of the game articulated by the KMT, which have prevailed since the late 1940s, are being scrutinized and adapted to accommodate demands for reform. Disputes about the development and future of Taiwan hinge on two overriding uncertainties: (1) how to democratize Taiwan's political system and (2) what relationship Taiwan should have with the mainland. These are not simple matters of policy preferences. They pertain to people's deeply felt sentiments of identity, fear that the values of others threaten that identity, and fear that the conflict about identity may jeopardize the security of the island.

The Players

In Taiwan, people are commonly categorized according to their place of origin: Taiwan or the mainland. "Mainlanders" were born on the Chinese continent and came to Taiwan in the late 1940s or early 1950s to escape from communism.[12] "Second generation Mainlanders" were born on Taiwan to parents who are Mainlanders. Although one hears about the "second generation" of Mainlanders, the fact is that many of them are now middle aged and are producing a third generation.[13]

"Taiwanese" does not simply refer to everybody living in Taiwan. It is a term used to denote only those Han Chinese who already lived on Taiwan prior to the wave of migration that occurred at the end of the 1940s and their offspring.[14] Despite an earlier taboo against "mixed" marriages, there are many people who were born to one Mainlander parent (generally the father) and one Taiwanese. This group defies classification and complicates any effort to calculate the number of Taiwanese and Mainlanders in Taiwan.[15]

Taiwan's population is generally described as slightly less than 85 percent Taiwanese, about 14 percent Mainlanders, and a bit more than 1 percent aborigines.[16] In fact, the 1990 census states that the total population is 20,366,325, of which 87.11 percent are Taiwanese and 12.74 percent are Mainlanders.[17] While the proportions are about right, the labels are not as meaningful as they might first seem.[18] A survey conducted by the government-sponsored research institution, Academia Sinica, found that when asked "where are you from?"[19] 76.1 percent of respondents identified themselves as Taiwanese, 12.4 percent said they were Hakka from Taiwan,[20] 10.1 percent said they were from the mainland, and 1 percent identified themselves as aborigines. Asked "where is your native place?"[21] 78.4 percent listed a county or city on Taiwan, another 11 percent said only that they were from Taiwan, just 7.5 percent identified themselves as from the mainland, and about 2.5 percent identified themselves in other ways.[22]

In the same way that classifying people by place of origin offers only ambiguous labels, so, too, does the effort to classify people by party affiliation. The KMT has long been seen as the party of Mainlanders and predominantly concerned with the reunification of China. Until the onset of reforms in the mid-1980s, the KMT ruled with such impunity that Taiwan was essentially a one-party state and the government of the Republic of China was virtually indistinguishable from the KMT.

This has changed. For one thing, approximately 70 percent of the KMT membership of 2.4 million is now Taiwanese. This includes key figures in the highest echelon of the party including the president, Lee Teng-hui.[23] In addition, the party is seriously divided about the pace and direction of reforms. "Hard liners" seem not to have noticed that authoritarianism has gone out of fashion.[24] Their passion for order and control, their willingness to manipulate the organs of government to execute their will, and their visceral mistrust of anyone who seems to disagree with them reflect values that run deeply in Chinese political history. They cling to old ideas and old ways, continue to enjoy spheres of power—although more circumscribed than in the past—and impede the pace, if not the direction, of political liberalization. This group, many of whom are now quite elderly, take exceptional pride in what they see as the KMT-led development of Taiwan. They genuinely fear that the loss of central control and the greater pluralism of contemporary Taiwan politics will lead to calamity.

The Democratic Progressive Party (DPP), the strongest opposition party, is the only party that has offered any credible counterbalance to the KMT.[25] It was formed in 1986 out of a loose coalition of opposition activists who sought to assert the interests of the Taiwanese who had for many years been restricted from effective participation in Taiwan's politics. The absence of experience and the turmoil that result from establishing a new political party have limited the DPP's effectiveness. The party remains divided between those in the *Hsin Ch'iao-liu* (New Tide) faction, who are eager to promote Taiwan independence, and those in the *Mei Li Tao* (Formosa) faction, for whom democratization is a more urgent objective. There are also independent satrapies that operate under the umbrella of the DPP because they are comprised largely of Taiwanese opposed to the KMT, but their nominal association with the DPP does not imply ideological conformity.

The DPP has the reputation for sponsoring visible public demonstrations, initiating melees in the parliament to embarrass the KMT, and standing up to unfair practices of the KMT at every turn. While these forceful and theatrical ploys attracted attention and support from disaffected Taiwanese in the early years of the party's life, the DPP is now seen by many as lacking the capacity to take over the reins of government. Taiwan's residents are most in agreement when talking about the need for improved social order and continued economic development. KMT officials gleefully suggest that the DPP has undermined its own credibility by failing to address the concerns of the growing commercial middle class, which associates disorder with the opposition. The DPP must "decide whether it will develop into a responsible opposition party of democracy or continue to serve merely as a political instrument for Taiwan independence and other protest movements."[26]

The Stakes

The catechism of Chinese Nationalists, as embodied in Article II of the KMT charter, is that

> the Kuomintang shall be a revolutionary and democratic political party charged with the mission of completing the National Revolution, carrying out the Three Principles of the People, *recovering the Chinese mainland, promoting Chinese culture*, aligning with other democratic nations, and building the Republic of China into a unified, free, peace-loving, and harmonious democracy based on the Three Principles of the People. [emphasis added][27]

The recovery of China and the promotion of Chinese culture have been the focus of KMT policy on Taiwan since 1949, and the bane of many Taiwanese. These goals have manifested themselves in grand campaigns, symbolic gestures, as well as countless restrictions and requirements meant to embed these aims in the minds of Taiwan's population. Those who identify with China and the nationalism of the KMT view their efforts as a sacred trust.[28] They express their interest in providing greater stability and opportunity to the next generation by ameliorating the tension between the PRC and the ROC, in playing a key role in the modernization of the mainland after the passing of communism, and in realizing an historic imperative to reunify China.

If Chinese nationalists accept the protestations of the Taiwanese as genuine, and many do not, they are incredulous that their promotion of Chinese culture and the recovery of the mainland are not universally accepted.[29] For them, the concepts of a distinct Taiwanese culture and nation and an independent state are nonsensical and heretical. They fear that crafty local politicians have manipulated the notion of Taiwanese identity to veil a menacing quest for personal power which might accrue from an independent Taiwan.

Those who believe that Taiwan itself is a country challenge the long-standing belief in the unity of a Chinese culture, nation, and state. They identify themselves as Chinese—which they see as a cultural or ethnic designation—while identifying themselves as citizens of Taiwan.[30] They reject the idea that all Chinese must live under the same government within the same polity. They reject the idea of a Chinese nation-state. Some even reject the idea of a Chinese nation. Chinese, for them, is a cultural or ethnic category, not a political category.[31] A commentator in the pro-opposition newspaper *Tzu-li Wan-pao* (Independence Evening Post) wrote, "The Taiwanese nation is not the same as the Chinese nation; Taiwanese are not Chinese, just as Americans are not Englishmen."[32]

Challenging the view of a single Chinese culture, nation, and state has led some to assert that Taiwan has been autonomous and deserves an independent political status.[33] Politically active Taiwanese press for greater and more sweeping liberties in Taiwan and have pressured the KMT to loosen its control of the political and ideological restraints that had limited discussion and political participation. Taiwanese who hope to establish an independent Taiwanese state, as well as those who simply want to preserve the ambiguous status quo vis-à-vis the mainland, are united in their demand that they be given more opportunities to compete for political power. This is commonly expressed in terms of a desire for democracy.

Those who hope to preserve a unified Chinese culture and promote the reunification of Taiwan and the mainland have struggled to moderate their inclinations to dominate Taiwan's political sphere so as to offer a controlled release for the hostility and frustration of their opponents. Still, for ideological and temperamental reasons, some conservatives are disinclined to liberalize. Many in the KMT fear that democracy will enable Taiwanese activists to push for Taiwan independence, and that, in turn, would invite a military response from the mainland.[34] Questions of identity, therefore, are not idle matters. They spill over into nearly every political debate and are especially prominent in discussions of democratization and the political status of Taiwan.

Identity and Power

Taiwan's most fundamental problem is who should govern the island. This is a question of power. In earlier phases of the island's past, there was competition for control among the Dutch, the Spanish, pirates, and the court in Peking. Finally, with the Treaty of Shimonoseki in 1895, Japan took Taiwan and the question of which power would rule there was suspended. Those who lived in Taiwan had no say in the matter. That was a decision made between powers based elsewhere. There was no thought that the island's residents had sufficient political standing to question such decisions; they were expected, simply, to acquiesce.

From the moment the first Nationalist forces of Chiang Kai-shek arrived in Taiwan in 1945, the issue of power was paramount. Not only was there a conflict about power among the people living on the island, but the status of Taiwan came to dominate relations between the Communists in Peking and the Nationalists in Taipei. For the Taiwanese, both the internal and external competition to control the island is indicative of a history of subjugation by forces that came from elsewhere. Repeated efforts to assert control over Taiwan by people from afar have made the people who lived in Taiwan prior to 1945 feel increasingly victimized and frustrated.

The conflict between the Nationalists and the Communists concerning the control of Taiwan expresses itself in terms of the issue of reunification. Leaders in Taipei and Peking are committed to the idea that, ultimately, Taiwan and the mainland should be reunified under a single authority. They disagree about which authority that should be and under what conditions the reunification should be effected, but they share a belief that Taiwan is a part of China.

The Nationalists' perpetual concern with reunification and their restrictive and manipulative control of the population of Taiwan led to demands on the part of the preexisting population of Taiwan to establish an independent state. Those who advocate that Taiwan be independent regard the effort by the KMT to reunify with the mainland as just another example of an exogenous force imposing its will over the people of the island. Advocates of independence decry the absence of democracy because if Taiwan were governed by the consent of the majority, the population would be at liberty to determine its own national identity. Until 1992, the island's residents were not able to participate in decisions that affected the determination of Taiwan's political status. That privilege was reserved for a tiny group of politically powerful rulers in the KMT. Most of them were men who emigrated to Taiwan in the late 1940s from the mainland, or their offspring. In 1992, the newly elected National Assembly and the Legislative Yuan elections scheduled for the end of the year helped to introduce popularly elected representatives into the process and laid the foundation for self-determination.

The denial of self-determination has contributed to a Taiwanese identity, a consciousness born of isolation and frustration. Part of Taiwanese identity is tied to the island itself, rather than China, as a motherland. The hundred miles or so that separate Taiwan from the mainland also separate its people from the people on the mainland. Those on Taiwan have developed a sense of belonging to a group defined by residency on the island. History has reinforced this distinction. The Taiwanese have been treated differently by foreign powers and by governments on the mainland than the people living elsewhere in China. The island was repeatedly amputated from the body China and its people regarded as distinct.

When the KMT arrived, it too treated the population it found on the island as a group that differed from other Chinese. Part of the KMT concern was that after fifty years of Japanese colonization those on the island were not sufficiently loyal to China and needed to be indoctrinated to become fully Chinese. The failure of the KMT to institute democracy earlier in its tenure led to frustrations among the Taiwanese that reinforced the differences they felt between themselves and those who had come from the mainland. The deeper the frustration and the greater the sense that they were being ruled by outsiders, the more intense was the demand for self-determination.

Considering that Taiwanese constitute more than four-fifths of the population of the island, self-determination may be equated with democracy. The assumption is that if the political system were completely open, the Taiwanese would be able to exercise self-determination through the ballot box, because as a cohort they far outnumber those from the mainland who have manipulated the political system on the island to sustain themselves in power. Repression by the ruling minority of the demands for self-determination of the ruled majority served to intensify the identity Taiwanese felt as they differentiated themselves from the rulers who came from outside Taiwan. The competition between Taiwanese and the ruling minority now threatens the possibility of establishing a democratic system that will endure.

Identity and Views of the "Other"

We and They

To consider matters of identity, one must depart the world of facts and enter a realm of sentiment and beliefs. It is important to understand how artificial the notion of identity is and, yet, how exceptionally potent it can be when entangled with political objectives. The identity one has with a group—regardless of how that group is defined—may be more apparent than real.[35] After all, identity is a sentiment of attachment based on one's belief that a community exists and that one "belongs" in that community.

One is usually not compelled to sense the attachment; one chooses to do so (although there are circumstances in which an individual is pressured by the group to behave as though the person feels an attachment when in fact there is none). There is generally no proof that a community exists. As Benedict Anderson writes, communities are "imagined." The sense of belonging one feels is frequently a nebulous form of alliance—a consciously constructed view of oneself in relation to others with whom one perceives a commonality.

As one begins to probe, it soon becomes evident that the convictions people have about their own identity are not necessarily consistent with reason. Identities are driven by emotion, are dynamic, and are seldom exclusive. Individuals have multiple, overlapping, or competing identities, and the bases for a person's disparate sentiments of identification may differ.[36]

People also have different notions about what it means to identify with a particular social category. For instance, one person may believe that being Chinese encompasses cultural, national, and political factors. Another person may distinguish between being culturally Chinese and politically associated with a country that is not China. There is no list of criteria by which one may determine who is *really* Chinese when people from Vancouver to Penang, Tsing-Tao to Lukang, all claim the same label.[37]

The inability to define who is Chinese may make for interesting academic discourse, but it also leads to considerable political discord. Such pluralism may be acceptable in other contexts, but conformity and unity have long been prized in Chinese society. Collective consciousness rather than idiosyncratic expression is valued highly. In contemporary Taiwan, the expectation of uniformity—rather than of pluralism or polarity—persists. Yet, no individual or group has sufficient moral suasion to ensure, as the KMT did for so long, a single view of the national identity, Taiwan's relations to the mainland, or the cultural and political identities of Taiwan's residents.[38]

Examining how residents of Taiwan view themselves, one finds that some seem clear that they are part of the Chinese nation—where nationality is defined in terms of "shared identity and feelings of affinity."[39] This sense of belonging cuts across the divide between Taiwanese and Mainlanders and across class boundaries, too. Others acknowledge their Chinese origin but identify themselves as Taiwanese. This group, in turn, is divided between those who consider Taiwan as their nation and those for whom Taiwanese is an ethnic category within the Chinese nation. In short, there is an absence of consensus.

The disparity of views has made people on Taiwan highly sensitive to the origins of others with whom they interact. Hill Gates observed some years ago that in social settings

> new acquaintances were usually "placed" for me . . . as Taiwanese or Main-landers. The common social chat among strangers attending dinner parties begins by establishing the origins of all persons present with jocular references to foods, speech peculiarities, or personality traits supposedly characteristic of each ethnic group.[40]

Beyond the prejudicial views that people who identify with one group have of people they identify with another group, the state employed administrative procedures that encouraged people to identify themselves on the basis of their ethnic identity.[41]

> Ethnic group membership . . . is based on one's father's place of origin, and this information is a necessary item on the identity cards carried by all persons aged fifteen and over. Children are socialized by the state to accept ethnicity as a primary identity; in many elementary and high schools, children are asked publicly to state their province of origin at the beginning of the term, and the census of students by province is posted.[42]

The inclination to pigeonhole someone as either a Mainlander or a Taiwanese was easier in the years soon after the KMT retreated to Taiwan. At that time, the distinctions were fairly obvious, and the criteria for labeling a person rather simple. With time, intermarriage, and the birth of a second and third generation, these distinctions have become more difficult to draw and the criteria rather tenuous.

Among the elite, it is apparently now considered parochial to draw social distinctions on the basis of one's province of origin. People demur at the suggestion that stereotypes of Taiwanese and Mainlanders persist.[43] Indeed, in 1990, "social surveys found public consciousness of ethnic differences to be disappearing. Nevertheless, cultural liberalization allowed overdue exploration of localist issues."[44]

One influential journalist, a second generation Mainlander, recalled:

> When I was young, when I talked to people, I used to ask, "where are you from?" But now that question never jumps into my mind. I just look at [the person to see] whether he is very well educated, is he boring, is he articulate, is he interesting? It is not the first question which jumps into my mind, "is this stranger Taiwanese or Mainlander?"[45]

Despite what people would like to believe about the nature of contemporary society in Taiwan, and even if distinctions on the basis of identification are not as blatant as in the past, one cannot escape the impression that people in Taiwan are aware of a "we" and "they" dichotomy. The propensity to classify people in "we" and "they" categories is a reflection of the division between Taiwanese and Mainlanders. The distinction between these groups is sometimes cultural, sometimes national, and nearly always political. Even if it is no longer fashionable, mannerly, or official policy to divide people in this way, the legacy of four decades during which these distinctions were sharply drawn abides. A television series on one of the three national television networks accentuates the stereotypes that many claim no longer matter. A television critic writes that the series is imbued with Han chauvinism:

> It emphasizes the superiority of Mainlanders and, as the plot unfolds, blurs a number of factual situations regarding the Taiwanese and even makes them feel inadequate. Throughout the plot, every law-abiding and just person, every reasonable person, and every cultivated person seems to be played by a Mainlander and the hoodlums, petty thieves, snobs, money-grubbers, and vacillators, seem to be Taiwanese.[46]

For some people these distinctions may be more consequential than for others. In some contexts the distinctions may be more apparent than in others. In the political context—especially among the political elite—the distinction between "we" and "they" is both consequential and apparent.

Who Are They?

When prodded to describe how one distinguished between Mainlanders and Taiwanese, people have no difficulty calling up the characterizations of the "other." The assumption that underlies these prejudices is that one's place of birth determines one's identity and world view. Crude distinctions between Mainlanders and Taiwanese do not always make a great deal of sense, logically, and one must remember that the identity a person feels—or that one attributes to others—is an emotional attachment, not a carefully reasoned position.

For example, Taiwanese tend to view Mainlanders as a monolithic group. Among the Mainlanders, however, are immigrants from the very same provinces—and perhaps the same villages—from which the Taiwanese trace their own origins.[47] Not only is the effort to distinguish between Taiwanese and Mainlander on the basis of original locale questionable, but these categories are too broad to have much meaning. A Taiwanese whose family came from Fukien in the seventeenth century will have much more in common (dialect, diet, and deities) with a Mainlander who arrived from Fukien in 1949 than that Mainlander might have with someone from Szechwan or Shantung who arrived on Taiwan at the same time and on the same boat. There is also a tendency to blur the distinction between the Mainlander elite who came from the mainland as the cream of China's intellectual, commercial, and political crop, and the Mainlanders who came as soldiers in the ragtag army of the KMT. The former are privileged and powerful. The veterans and their families have led much simpler lives.

The real line of demarcation is not province of origin, although that is relevant, but time of arrival on Taiwan and attitude about Taiwan's political status. Among those who were adults in 1945, the issue is where they lived at that time. If they were already on Taiwan, their political identity was probably shaped by their experience under Japanese rule and as the object of KMT control in the years that followed. They are unlikely to have much interest in reunification, may or may not actively support the Taiwan Independence Movement, but almost assuredly hope to preserve and expand Taiwan's autonomy under any guise that will work.

If they were on the mainland in 1945 and then made their way to Taiwan, it is likely that they associate themselves with the policies of the KMT—particularly the promotion of reunification, as many left parents, siblings, spouses, children, and friends on the mainland. More importantly, Mainlanders understand that their fate hinges on the KMT remaining as the ruling party. If the Taiwanese opposition gains control, Mainlanders fear they will rapidly begin to feel the minority status the KMT has been able to shield them from for the past four decades.[48]

Taiwanese tend to view Mainlanders as different from themselves. Taiwan has been separated from China for so long that there evolved a set of social mores peculiar to Taiwanese. This sense of difference causes Taiwanese to see themselves as belonging to a group of which the Mainlanders are not a part, even if they cannot agree on the principal differences.

Comparing Taiwanese with Mainlanders, Antonio Chiang said, "we are easy-going, much [more] easy-going, more aggressive, [and we have] more individual spirit."[49] A Taiwanese executive ruminated about a distinction in the way Taiwanese and Mainlanders think. In his eyes, Taiwanese are practical people because they are all basically farmers. Mainlanders, on the other hand, excel at "reasoning by talking" but cannot *do* very much because they do not reason in a rigorous, mathematical fashion.[50]

By contrast, elite Mainlanders spoke of Taiwanese as unsophisticated farmers and of Taiwan itself as a frontier. Cosmopolitan Mainlanders were apprehensive about coming to what they viewed as the remote and undeveloped island of Taiwan in 1949 and, once they arrived, saw their Taiwanese compatriots as unpolished.[51] For some Mainlanders, the difference between themselves and the Taiwanese was a matter of economic class distinction. One second generation Mainlander explained that as a schoolgirl she carefully chose her friends from among other second generation Mainlanders because she could communicate with them and because she saw them as more polite than the Taiwanese children. She said that their family backgrounds were similar.

> We [have] very similar lifestyle[s], we can share the same life experience.... [U]sually the Mainlanders will teach their kids very politely. Filial piety is very important in a Mainland[er] family. You say, "good morning," [and] "good night." When guest[s] come, you have to come out to say, "hello," bring tea, [and] bring slippers. You have to do all kinds of those things. But, I don't know if the Taiwanese kids are trained that way. I never lived with them. Maybe they do in a big, rich family. But usually in the rural area[s], I don't think they really teach kids to do that.[52]

Who Are We?

For those born on Taiwan after 1945 (those who constitute the "second generation" Mainlanders and their offspring, the Taiwanese, and all those who were born to mixed parentage), identity revolves largely around the issue of Chinese unity. Many Taiwan-born Mainlanders feel that they are just as Taiwanese as the Taiwanese. They complain that they are excluded from Taiwanese society because one or both of their parents was born on the mainland. Some even fear that because they are considered by Taiwanese as second generation Mainlanders, not Taiwanese, they may be persecuted and deprived of their present social standing if Taiwanese extremists come to power.[53]

One influential professional born on Taiwan to Mainlander parents said he "belongs" on the island of Taiwan and regards it as his home. He shares a sense of Taiwan consciousness with Taiwanese and resents being excluded from the Taiwanese category because of his reliance on Mandarin and his parents' province of origin. He found it difficult to accept that in the eyes of Taiwanese he represents a class of repressors and expressed frustration that Taiwanese did not consider him to be a compatriot.[54]

C.V. Chen (Charng-ven), an exceptionally visible attorney who wears many hats in the public and private sector, said that he was born in 1944 in the city of Kunming in Yunnan Province on the mainland, but moved to Taiwan when he was five years old. Technically, he is not a member of the second generation but asks, after forty-two years on Taiwan, "Am I not a local Taiwanese?" He believes he is. He sees no contradiction between his identification with Taiwan as his home and his identity as a Chinese that impels him to push for reunification. For many Taiwanese, however, C.V. Chen is the archetypal, privileged power-holder from the mainland whose interest in Taiwan is overshadowed by his greater concern for unification.[55]

Taiwanese vehemently distrust Mainlanders committed to promoting reunification. Conversely, Mainlanders deeply resent and distrust Taiwanese devoted to working toward independence. Each group sees the other as foolishly irresponsible, tempting fate, and spoiling a good thing. The visceral repugnance people who identify with one group—whether Mainlanders or Taiwanese—hold for the activists and extremists of the other group contributes to a general characterization of "we" versus "they."

It is clear from conversations and observations that these distinctions have meaning when politics are at stake. The inclination to classify people as either Taiwanese or Mainlander—even though the categories do not make as much sense today as they may have in 1949—still expresses itself in the ordinary affairs of politics. The prominence of the "we" and "they" distinction in politics has to do with the role the KMT claimed for itself on Taiwan, the conflict between the KMT and the CCP for the right to rule the mainland, and the unresolved matter of Taiwan's national identity. It is not surprising, then, that people claim the distinction between Mainlanders and Taiwanese is no longer as conspicuous a factor in their daily lives, but it remains an essential ingredient in the political sphere.

Where Do We Live?

While people may have clear convictions about their identity as either Chinese or Taiwanese, there is considerable uncertainty about the identity of the polity in which they live.[56] It is unclear whether Taiwan is a country itself or only part of a larger country. If it is part of a larger country—China—that leaves open a question about how to classify Taiwan under the circumstances that have prevailed since 1949 in which China is divided and governed by more than one regime. Some of the Mainlander political elite speak of the current situation as an anomaly that will be normalized only after Taiwan and the mainland are united. If China only exists when the mainland and Taiwan are united, it suggests that in the absence of that unity, there is no place that may properly be considered China.[57]

As they try to define their identity, people blur the distinctions among different forms of identity. They mingle references to their identity as Chinese or Taiwanese (cultural, ethnic, or national identity), about the political entity to which they feel a sense of attachment (political identity), and the identity of the polity in which they live. This confusion hints at the problem contemporary Chinese have reconciling their emotional attachments with political realities.

For the Chinese elite, it is difficult to define either China or Taiwan as a political unit without tripping into ambiguity. One might suspect that those who were born and raised on Taiwan would identify with Taiwan and those born and raised on the mainland would identify with the mainland. Actually, loyalties are complicated by other attachments and emotions. To define their political identity, people conjure rationales comprised of two key ingredients: history and pragmatism.

Those who appeal to the past cite historical data or theories to justify their views. For example, some endeavor to show that Taiwan was always a part of China and, therefore, should not be considered an independent state today. Alternatively, others argue that for the past 300 years Taiwan was rarely under the effective control of the Chinese court and, therefore, should not relinquish its *de facto* independence now. They assume that if they accrete sufficient evidence that the way things were accords with their view of how things should be, then the weight of history itself will be persuasive.

Those who appeal to pragmatism seem less concerned with how well the present and future mimic the past, and more concerned with what can really be accomplished given the international context and domestic conditions that inhere. For instance, it is common for advocates of reunification to criticize those who demand independence, saying that the latter are impractical and irresponsible because they neglect the adamant views of the communist authorities in Peking who oppose an independent Taiwan. They claim to fear that the PRC will use military force against Taiwan if it even seems that the ROC government has relaxed its opposition to independence.

Those who advocate independence, on the other hand, claim that the notion of reunification is unworkable because of the tremendous gap in the standard of living, political liberties, and opportunity that exists when the mainland and Taiwan are juxtaposed. They view official attempts to improve relations with the mainland as opening the door to a Hong Kong–type settlement in which Taiwan may be absorbed by the Communists and its prosperity threatened. They wonder what Taiwan has to gain by sacrificing its autonomy to be a junior partner in an enterprise it will not easily influence. In the end, they are skeptical that KMT claims of fearing PRC reprisals is a ruse to keep Taiwan from becoming democratic. Chang Chun-hung, secretary-general of the DPP, said the KMT does not, fundamentally, want to reunify with the mainland, but hoists the banner of reunification to justify its claim to rule Taiwan as part of China.[58]

The difficulty is that both those who appeal to history and those who claim to be more pragmatic are selective in their reading of the past or present. How one presents historical evidence or assesses contemporary political realities depends as much on the view one espouses as on the evidence. Evidence used to underscore one position can be countered easily by other evidence or an alternative interpretation that undermines that position.

Perhaps there is no correct view of the past or the present. There may be no truth to which one can appeal or any way to determine who is right and who is wrong. Indeed, in some ways each claimant is partially right and partially wrong. Yet, each side dismisses the arguments of the other as a distortion of the past, a misreading of the present, a cunning effort to deceive, or a foolishly idealistic crusade. There has been very little effort to empathize with the other, to understand why others make the claims they do, or to reconcile one's own perceptions with the views of one's opponents.

Different Views of China

Taiwan's historical association with the mainland is an exceptionally thorny issue. Those who favor reunification look to the past to emphasize how long Taiwan has been (*de jure*) under the control of the Chinese court. Those who favor independence for Taiwan emphasize how the island has, in the past, maintained (*de facto*) autonomy. Since 1949, one of the few things about which officials in both Peking and Taipei have concurred is that Taiwan was and is a part of China.

One's identity as either Chinese or Taiwanese is tied to how one views China and Taiwan. For some people, China exists as a place; for others it is a concept. Often, though, the line between China as a concept and China as a territory is blurred. Tsiang Yien-si, secretary-general of the Office of the President, writes that "[m]ore and more people would now accept the view that China is a trinity of culture, nation, and state."[59] Shaw Yü-ming believes:

> "China" names a country and symbolizes a cultural system of which Confucianism has long been a fundamental ingredient. . . . Since ancient times, the notion of one unified China has been deeply embedded in the minds of all Chinese. Perhaps alone among the major world civilizations, China is marked by a single, unbroken line of cultural identity.[60]

For many Mainlanders, particularly the older ones who were adults when they took refuge on Taiwan, China consists of the mainland and Taiwan together. This has been the official view of the KMT. Tsiang Yien-si writes:

> For more than forty years, we consider ourselves—the Republic of China—the legitimate representative for the entire Chinese nation, including both the mainland and Taiwan. In other words, we have never given up our sovereignty over mainland China.
>
> You may not understand why we maintain our claim of sovereignty over the mainland. But why should we give up that claim? What good would it bring us? In fact the claim is a reflection of our sense of responsibility, as long as we maintain our sovereignty, we would never forsake our duty in bringing freedom, democracy and prosperity to our compatriots on the mainland.[61]

People who hold this view object to the idea that Taiwan should be a separate political entity. To them, Taiwan used to be part of the empire and, therefore, *is* part of China.[62] Many Taiwanese, by contrast, oppose this view and claim that for most of the time Han Chinese inhabited the island, they were not under the jurisdiction of the central authorities on the continent.

Taiwanese feel it is ludicrous that the KMT, a party that traces its roots to a revolutionary ideology aimed at overthrowing the alien Ch'ing emperor, claims Taiwan as part of China because it was taken more than 300 years ago by forces who were themselves foreign rulers of China. When confronted with the argument that Taiwan has only been under the effective control of the Chinese government on the mainland for four years this century (1945–1949), Chinese Nationalists discount the period of Japanese rule because China was forced to cede Taiwan in 1895. The Nationalists also consider the separation that has lasted since 1949 as invalid because the communist authorities are an illegitimate power.[63]

From the perspective of those who lived on Taiwan during the Ch'ing dynasty, it is not clear whether they felt any sense of identity as Taiwanese.

> If people thought about it at all, most would probably have identified themselves as Chinese. They would also identify with their family or local village, with their ethnic group (Fukienese or Hakka) and, among the Fukienese, with place of origin in Fukien.[64]

One is left to wonder what it may have meant to people to identify themselves as "Chinese." It is not clear whether that was viewed as a political denomination, a national one, or a cultural one. In addition, if people identified themselves as from Fukien or as Hakka, it is not clear how they viewed the relative importance of this designation vis-à-vis their identity as Chinese.

Contemporary residents of Taiwan differ in how they view China. Ma Ying-cheou said that for government officials China is synonymous with the ROC. However, the ROC government has acknowledged that

> there is a[nother] political entity in actual control of the mainland area to which we cannot extend our jurisdiction. That we understand. And we have gone so far as to acknowledge that. But the other side [the CCP] has not done that. They still refuse to recognize, or at least acknowledge, the political entity here. And they said, "if you *are* a political entity, then you are a subentity."[65]

C.V. Chen objected to the common misconstruction of China taken to mean the PRC. He said that the Communists have long claimed that because the PRC is larger than Taiwan, it is, indisputably, China. Chen discounts the idea that merely because the territory and population of the PRC is larger, it necessarily represents China.[66]

A senior official in the Foreign Ministry explained that traditionally China was seen as a politically unitary state and a single economic unit. With the circulation of goods and the exposure of China to markets beyond its borders, Chinese have become more enlightened and there has been a diffusion of economic and political interests. Development has engendered several different forms of China: a Hong Kong–China, a Taiwan–China, an eastern seaboard China, a southern China, and a middle China. He believes that no Chinese really want to see their country divided into a "China A, China B, and China C" and, in spite of these different notions of China, the ideal of a unity persists. This forms the core of China's nationalism: the view of a single, grand, unified China dominated by a central government.

The same official said that "in people's hearts, honestly (we) feel we are still one China." Then he admitted that it may no longer be practical to think in terms of one China. He discussed the idea of a Chinese federation and suggested that during much of China's history there actually was some sort of federation of feudal states loosely allied under an emperor to whom they all paid tribute.[67]

Li I-yuan said that, while the notion of China as a unified political and cultural entity has been destroyed by the current political division, "culturally, every Chinese is in search of a kind of equilibrium, a total system of equilibrium." This view is expressed by many Taiwanese and second generation Mainlanders who view China as a concept. It is the homeland of their ancestors and the source of their cultural heritage, but it does not currently exist in a political sense. Ming Chu-cheng said China represents, in order of significance, a (1) culture, (2) people, and (3) nation.[68] He explained that Chinese cultural and political identity are not fully integrated anymore, but that they are also not fully opposed, either. Mournfully, he concluded, "[w]e don't know who we are. Taiwanese are losing our own identity, yet we have not erected a new one."[69]

For those who promote reunification, the concept of unity is the highest ideal and a prominent theme in Chinese political thought.[70] Knowledgeable Mainlanders distinguish between unity as an ideal and as a historical reality. They reject the view of China as a predominantly unified realm and describe how frequently China was divided as regional power-holders contended for control. Division, however, was ultimately viewed as intolerable; unity remained the objective.[71]

For people who hold this view, it is difficult to define what and where China is at present. They are reluctant to identify China as the mainland alone, because that would exclude Taiwan and play into the hands of those who promote Taiwan independence. At the same time, they would never say that China is only Taiwan. Their view of China is of a unity—the mainland and Taiwan subsumed in a single political entity. They vehemently oppose becoming citizens of the PRC and are viscerally disinclined to communism. Yet, they cannot envision a China that does not encompass the mainland.

To extend the logic of their argument that China is comprised of both the mainland and Taiwan, one would have to say that China only exists when the mainland and Taiwan are governed as part of the same polity. That, however, would put them in the untenable position of admitting that China does not now exist. Ordinarily, advocates of reunification faced with this awkward realization point out that China is now divided as Korea is and as Germany was.[72]

In Taiwan, the conflict between these two visions of China is not limited to abstract, scholarly ruminations. It is the stuff of daily political struggle. While this debate may not be prominent in the minds of the majority of Taiwan's residents who concern themselves primarily with earning a livelihood, among politicians, officials, intellectuals, and any people who travel beyond Taiwan— particularly for business—this matter is of pressing importance. It affects people's views of a wide range of choices that must be made about Taiwan's ongoing political and social development.

From the perspective of the observer, the stalemate between advocates of unification and advocates of independence seems a burlesque of exceptional complexity. Those who claim to favor reunification readily confess that they do not expect to resolve the matter any time soon, not as long as the Communists continue to rule in Peking. For them, the status quo—a tacit acceptance of Taiwan as an autonomous, sovereign state—is a necessary evil that they will not admit is preferable to reunification (as long as the mainland is governed by Communists). The status quo enables them to perpetuate themselves in political power by invoking their role to keep the extremists in the opposition at bay. They cannot tolerate an outright declaration of independence, even though, for all practical purposes, Taiwan is already independent, because either they fear that the PRC would use force to drag Taiwan back into the Chinese fold, or because they wish to create a sense of impending calamity that will cause the populace to resist the entreaties of the opposition and enable the KMT to maintain some degree of legitimacy to rule the island.

Those who demand independence insist that there be a formal acknowledgment of Taiwan's independent status so that the Mainlander-dominated KMT can be dislodged from power and a government elected from among Taiwan's populace with Taiwan alone as its purview. Simply accepting the status quo—though Taiwan is essentially independent even without a formal declaration—is inadequate because that leaves the KMT in charge. This means a perpetuation of the myths that have enabled the ruling party to subjugate Taiwan's populace and its interests to the ambitions of the Mainlander elite for the past forty years.

The advocates of independence believe a formal declaration that Taiwan is independent—while unlikely to alter Taiwan's actual autonomy—would discredit and displace the KMT and allow a Taiwan-elected government to prevail. The U.S.-led U.N. response to Iraq's invasion of Kuwait in 1991 and the general acceptance into the community of states of the former republics of the Soviet Union offer succor to those who assume that if the PRC threatened to use force in response to a declaration of independence in Taiwan, other states—notably the United States—could be counted on to deliver assistance.

Identity and the "Rectification of Names"

Beyond the self-conscious responses people offer about the nature of their own identity, one can learn something from the words people choose to describe themselves and their polity. In Chinese, there are several terms that refer to the nation, each of which carries political import. The term *Chung-kuo,* literally "central kingdom," is generally used to identify the entity that, in English, is China. The term *jen* means man, or, in the generic sense, person, and when appended to *Chung-kuo* creates the term *Chung-kuo jen,* which, in English, is translated as Chinese—referring to the people, not the language.

The Chinese language is replete with terms that describe like phenomena or objects that are not identical. In this vein, there is another term, *hua,* comparable to the term "Cathay," a poetic, archaic reference to China. This term is more conceptual. While *Chung-kuo* implies a centralization of power in a single state and reflects the way the Chinese empire actually emerged out of a morass of smaller, sovereign states, the term *hua* evokes an indistinct image of splendor that might be more appropriately applied to the Chinese nation and its culture than to the Chinese polity. For this reason, Chinese people who do not want to associate themselves with the Chinese state may identify themselves as *Hua jen,* not *Chung-kuo jen.*

One official noted that an overseas Chinese in the United States is likely to identify himself as an American, indicating his country of citizenship, and also as a *Hua jen,* indicating his identification with the Chinese nation. It is unlikely he will call himself a *Chung-kuo jen,* as that would imply that he is a citizen of China, not the United States.[73]

Yao Chia-wen said that as a Taiwanese he does not identify himself as a *Chung-kuo jen.* "I prefer to say, 'I am a *Hua jen.*' A Chinese, yes ... but a *Chung-kuo jen,* no."[74] His concern for linguistic propriety and symbolism is common among Chinese and manifests itself in conversations with others about identity.

Ma Ying-cheou, whose official duties are concerned with Taiwan's relationship to the mainland, raised another issue of terminology. He said that the KMT and the DPP make subtle political statements in the words they choose to describe the other side of the Taiwan Strait. Ma said that the KMT refers to the other side as "the mainland" whereas the DPP makes a conscious effort to call it "the Chinese mainland." By adding the term "Chinese," the DPP hopes to distinguish "Chinese" from Taiwanese. The KMT, on the other hand, regards both the mainland and Taiwan as Chinese.

Ma observed that Chinese from the PRC residing abroad use the term *kuo-nei* (meaning internal or domestic) to refer to the PRC. People from Taiwan—even those who oppose Taiwan independence—use the same term "internal" to refer to events in Taiwan. In this way, those from Taiwan who consciously oppose designating Taiwan as a separate state inadvertently imply that it is so by using the term *kuo-nei.* Ma said:

Since mainland China is also part of the idea of *kuo*, . . . we have to be very careful and we try to avoid terms like "third country" because that would imply that the Chinese mainland is the second country. Actually, we don't consider that [the mainland is] a second country.[75]

Identity, Socialization, and Culture

Another factor that has affected the tension pertaining to people's identity as either Chinese or Taiwanese is the KMT effort to socialize the population of Taiwan. When the advance guard of the KMT arrived on the island in 1945, it considered that many of the residents had been overly influenced by Japan. In response, and out of suspicion about the loyalties of the island's population, the KMT established policies that were intended to re-sinicize the Taiwanese. The KMT promoted a form of orthodox, Chinese gentry culture and represented it as national culture—the culture of all Chinese. China's monuments and geography, the high culture of its elite, the Mandarin dialect adopted as the national language, and the history of its heroes, achievements, and development dominated the school curriculum and were validated by public, official expressions in word and deed. Taiwan, and all that is distinctive about it, was largely ignored.[76]

Taiwanese have been alienated by the incessant, pervasive focus on China as a whole at the expense of Taiwan. Antonio Chiang said:

> My daughter now is in high school. She has to memorize all the cities, all the agricultural products, and industrial products of every province [of China], the weather, the rivers, and the natural resources. Everything. We had to memorize all this before, thirty years ago. I forget everything. Now, my daughter . . . has to memorize what I had memorized and we know so little about Taiwan. . . . We are forbidden to learn. We have no access. No resources. Some get into trouble when they began to know about Taiwan. When you begin to identify with Taiwan . . . people feel you are associated with independence or the opposition.[77]

Chiu I-jen, of the DPP New Tide faction, said that when he was in junior high school, there were six semesters over the course of three years. During each semester students were issued a history text and a geography text, but in those twelve volumes, there were only two chapters that mentioned anything about Taiwan's history and only two that mentioned anything about Taiwan's geography.

Curricula are standard in Taiwan, and most schools assign texts used island-wide for each course in each grade. It was reported that in the twelve volumes used to educate elementary school students about social studies, about 30 of approximately 1,200 pages mention Taiwan. These passages emphasize the importance of Taiwan as a base from which to recover the mainland, but depict the island simply as a temporary refuge. The standardized college entrance exam, required of any student hoping to get a college education, also deals sparingly with Taiwan. In 1987, of the forty-two items pertaining to geography, four were related to Taiwan, and of the thirty-two items dealing with history, only one dealt with Taiwan.[78]

In January 1991, the Ministry of Education announced that it would revise geography textbooks to bring them into line with "factuality." One report stated: "[C]urrently, Taiwan students . . . are taught the old names of mainland China places, railways, and administrative divisions. They learn names that were used before the ROC government relocated to Taiwan forty-two years ago." These names will be revised to reflect current PRC usage, but the changes will appear only in the appendices of the texts, where the differences will be explained.[79]

These illustrations are suggestive of the imbalance between the attention given the mainland and that given to Taiwan in public school curricula of which Chiu spoke. This sort of indoctrination is effective when people are young, but after they graduate and take up roles in society, people are confronted with a reality that does not match the lessons they were taught in school. This leads to a feeling of betrayal that has resulted in a degree of animosity directed toward the KMT.[80]

People resent that they are caught between an abstract notion of a remote China, about which they know many facts, and a concrete reality in Taiwan, about which they know too little to make sense of their experiences. This emphasis on Chinese culture, Chiu suggested, results from the KMT's efforts to strengthen a Chinese identity and assimilate the Taiwanese. By purveying a false sense that there is a single Chinese culture and by denying the possibility that Chinese culture is comprised of many local variants, the KMT inadvertently fostered the development of Taiwanese identity.[81]

When questioned about the effort of the government to create a unified sense of Chinese culture on Taiwan, the influential Tsiang Yien-si writes:

> No effort as [far as] I know of was ever made to "unify" Chinese and "Taiwanese" culture. . . . However . . . we would not deny that we Chinese are always very proud of our culture and treasure our tradition and heritage. . . . The ROC Government on Taiwan . . . made urgent efforts to promote what is known as the "Chinese Cultural Renaissance Movement" to counter any possible devastation of the [Communists' Cultural] "Revolution." . . . The purpose of our renaissance movement has always been to affirm and restore those traditional value[s] in the Chinese culture which would help to enrich our spiritual life in a rapidly developing society that can become also increasingly materialistic.[82]

Tsiang's disclaimer notwithstanding, it seems evident that the KMT has fostered a particular view of China, history, and culture associated with a value system that validates the adoption of the appropriate—Chinese—identity and denies the legitimacy of any rival, subordinate, or alternative construction of cultural identity. At first this resulted in an effort to reorient the Taiwanese "from Japanese to mainland influence by installing a Nationalist curriculum and culture." After decades of failing to eradicate the Taiwanese cultural element, "Nationalists gradually began to accommodate cultural localism, but still defined Taiwaneseness as just one local variant of a national Chinese culture."[83]

It is easy to understand that the KMT hoped to promote a set of attitudes, attachments, and beliefs that would perpetuate Chinese culture as the political elite knew it and advance the cause of reunification—an aim dependent on popular identification with the mainland. What the KMT did not anticipate is that by promoting Chinese identity as exclusive and trivializing or denying the validity of sentiments Taiwanese had for their own subcultural forms, the KMT ended up emphasizing, rather than muting, the differences between its view of culture and that of the Taiwanese. The very effort that the KMT made to foster a sense of identity—because it insisted on the exclusivity of that identity—impelled Taiwanese to cling to and cultivate their own sense of self. This ensured that "cultural policy is likely to remain a political issue, as Taiwanese dialect, history, and culture struggle for a larger place in education, media and public life."[84]

Origins of Taiwanese Identity

Competing claims of identity in Taiwan reflect the consternation that is nearly universal among Chinese intellectuals this century about what it means to *be* Chinese. This communal existential predicament manifests itself in Taiwan as a conflict between two strains of national identity. While a good deal has been written about Chinese nationalism and the titanic battle with communism, Taiwanese national identity, by contrast, has been much less studied, and comparatively little has been written about it, especially in English.[85]

Ernest Gellner argues that it is not nationalism that imposes a sense of group identity, but that a "homogeneity imposed by objective, inescapable imperative eventually appears on the surface in the form of nationalism."[86] At issue, then, is what caused the emergence of Taiwanese nationalism; what "objective, inescapable imperative" led Taiwanese to sense that they have an identity as a group apart from other Chinese? Gellner cautions against assuming that any "category of persons (say, occupants of a given territory, or speakers of a given language, for example) becomes a nation" by virtue of their distinctiveness. More is needed. In his view "it is their recognition of each other as fellows . . . which turns them into a nation, and not the other shared attributes, whatever they may be, which separates that category from non-members."[87]

If Gellner is correct, it is the collective consciousness that "we" are a group that is the basis of a national spirit. To locate the source of Taiwanese national identity, then, would be to identify reasons why Taiwanese think of themselves as a group distinct from other Chinese. There are many. Among those factors Taiwanese themselves commonly see as shaping their identity are:

(1) the separation from the rest of China and the collective memory of succeeding periods during which forces came from elsewhere to impose control on the island's people,

(2) the friction between the KMT and the Taiwanese stemming from persistent memories of initial misperceptions and early conflicts,

(3) the sense that a distinct Taiwanese culture and consciousness differs from Han culture and Chinese consciousness, and

(4) a legacy of frustration resulting from the authoritarian nature of KMT rule which seemed to favor Mainlanders and their interests over the Taiwanese and which, in an effort to resocialize Taiwanese as Chinese, inadvertently reinforced mutual perceptions of difference.

How one assesses the origin and development of Taiwanese identity, how one regards Taiwanese nationalism, the weight one accords to the various contributing factors, and how one sees their mutual influence depends largely on one's identity and consequent world view.

Separation and Alien Domination

As an island, apart from the continent, Taiwan has been subjected to political, military, and commercial forces that did not affect Chinese living across the Taiwan Strait. It may be that people who are separated from others by natural boundaries—like those who live on an island—sense a kinship with those who share the same territory and an alienation from others who do not. The people of an island cannot help but view themselves as distinct from all others who might claim them as compatriots because they are divided by more than a town line or provincial boundary. Even though there are visual and social similarities between Taiwan and, say, Fukien Province, there is no way to get from the mainland to Taiwan without feeling that one has left one place, traveled across an expanse of neutrality, and arrived in another. It is likely that the residents of Taiwan have been conditioned to view themselves vis-à-vis the mainland in a manner that reflects this spatial dimension.

Chang Chun-hung portrays the initial migration from the mainland to Taiwan in the seventeenth century as a process of fleeing from adversity. Those who came to Taiwan, he claims, had fled as far as they could and had nowhere else to flee. He muses that the common sense of having taken refuge on the island contributes to an identity that distinguishes the people of Taiwan from those across the strait.

> The reason why Taiwan consciousness succeeded is, on the one hand, because they had fled to a place from which they could no longer flee, because they had to have an identity for the sake of survival, and because they were dominated by outsiders which prompted a rather strong emotional reaction.[88]

However, the development of a distinct Taiwanese identity was not simply a product of being isolated on the island. From the earliest times, succeeding waves of invaders have tried to sever the island from what were seen as tenuous bonds to the authorities who governed Chinese on the mainland. Taiwanese have inherited a legacy of subjugation by aliens: Spanish, Dutch, pirates, Manchurians, Japanese, and, in the minds of some, the KMT and refugees from the mainland.[89]

The most enduring foreign influence for Taiwanese with memories that reach back before 1945 is the Japanese, stemming from the period of occupation. In 1895, at the conclusion of the Sino-Japanese War, Taiwan and the Pescadores were ceded to Japan in perpetuity, a period that lasted only until Japan's defeat at the end of World War II.[90] The fifty years of Japanese occupation affected Taiwanese in a significant and complex manner. Detached from China, residents of Taiwan were effectively exiles in their own homeland. Among other things, the Taiwanese were educated in Japanese in the schools[91] and were restricted politically and economically on the basis of their identity as Chinese.[92] Occupation reinforced people's identity as Chinese and, to some degree, as Taiwanese.[93] Even though their boys were drafted into the Imperial Japanese Army during World War II, Taiwanese claim their loyalty to China remained unshaken.[94]

Japan brought order and development to Taiwan but may also have affected the growth of a nationalist sentiment among Taiwanese.[95] Japanese occupiers discriminated against the Taiwanese and monopolized high-ranking posts in the government, the military, the state-run industrial enterprises, and the schools. Managers, teachers, and policy-makers were predominantly Japanese, even though the population was overwhelmingly Taiwanese. Bartoleme Martinez, a Spanish priest who lived on Taiwan through much of the Japanese occupation, observed that "the more stupid Japanese always gets any available government position first, can rise higher, and is paid from fifty to eighty percent more for the same work than a Formosan (Taiwanese)."[96] The half-century of Japanese rule

> prepared the ground for a genuine sense of national unity. It had provided the first effective island-wide administration, substituted comparatively modern education for old superstitions, cut off most ties with mainland China, raised living standards far above those on the turbulent Asian continent, and encouraged a cash crop economy with per capita foreign trade 39 times greater than China's and higher than that in Japan itself. The growth of urbanization, along with the rise of an articulate middle class, helped to weld the Formosan population together at the same time that the irritant of the Japanese presence further united it.[97]

One may conclude, then, that the mentality of isolation coupled with the experiences of being ruled by outsiders contributed to a sense, among Taiwan's residents, of group consciousness. This identity evolved more fully and was politicized after the KMT arrived on the island.

Friction with the KMT

The first encounters with the Mainlanders who arrived to replace the Japanese after the Second World War caused some Taiwanese to acknowledge, with chagrin, that in many ways, the Japanese were superior to the Chinese. It also caused them to see themselves as different from the Mainlanders. Those old enough to recall the transition of power once the Japanese had left Taiwan recounted how an air of jubilation prevailed in anticipation of being rejoined with their homeland and governed again as Chinese by Chinese. These high spirits quickly sagged on seeing the Nationalist troops. One eyewitness writes that after the soldiers arrived in Taiwan they were expected to fend for themselves:

> No camps had been set up to receive them. Clusters of dank hovels—improvised with coconut palms, flattened rusted tins and flimsy bamboo strips—sprouted in back alleys all over town. Cowering soldiers, ashen and skeletal, some only 14 or 15, others decrepit with age, limped around unshod, in tattered uniforms stiff with filth and dried sweat. Local residents shunned them, and if they ventured to better areas of town the police shooed them away brutally as they did unsightly beggars.... What depraved inhumanity had press-ganged those who had no means of bribing their way out, used them ... to stop the deluge of enemy onslaught, and failing, shipped them to a remote island to keep them from joining the enemy?[98]

Chang Chun-hung commented:

> We all took up flags and went to welcome them [the KMT]. ... President Chiang has come to take over Taiwan! That was really how we felt—entering the embrace of our fatherland. But although we genuinely accepted the mainland takeover, we immediately began to sense the conflict of culture. Moreover, that conflict of culture was extremely intense. It was discovered that the Japanese culture which we had originally loathed was, as compared to the culture of our fatherland, a strong culture, a superior culture. And the culture of the rulers [the KMT] is a worthless, inferior—an inferior kind of barbaric culture. ... That kind of conflict was extremely intense and transformed us from the heights of identification to the heights of hostility.[99]

One Taiwanese, now a highly placed senior official in a government ministry, observed that the Japanese had promoted a set of social values that had been derived long ago from China but that had been corrupted on the mainland. When the KMT arrived and began to set up institutions to govern the island, the Taiwanese elite who had assimilated the standards and values with which the Japanese had imbued them were disheartened to see that their Chinese brethren were corrupt, decadent, and backward as compared with the Japanese. One commentator writes:

> Although we bitterly detested the brutal colonial rule of the Japanese, we cannot deny that, under Japan's perfected system of civil service, obedience to

the law and administrative efficiency made the Japanese incomparable to the KMT's corrupt feudal regime. Even though it was the rule of a different race, Taiwanese of the older generation believed in the fairness of the Japanese courts. How many today believe in the judicial system manipulated by the KMT?[100]

Initially, Taiwanese hoped that the Japanese surrender would signal the start of a happier phase of life in Taiwan. Mutual misperceptions, corrupt and inept leadership, misconduct on the part of the KMT soldiers, and a host of other irritants soon soured the views of the residents of Taiwan toward their mainland cousins and reinforced whatever notions of Taiwanese identity already existed.[101]

One hears different tales about the first encounters with the Mainlanders. Nationalist soldiers were perceived by Taiwanese as unsophisticated country bumpkins. Some Taiwanese claim that Taiwan had been more highly developed by the Japanese than almost anywhere else on the mainland and that urban residents in Taiwan were far more "modern" than the Chinese who came from across the strait.[102] Several people explained with great mirth how a Mainlander soldier—having never seen running water before he arrived in Taiwan—purchased a spigot, took it home, forced it into the wall, turned the knob, and was angered that no water flowed from it. Furious, and feeling that he had been cheated by the Taiwanese merchant who sold him the fixture, he returned to the store where he bought it and threatened the proprietor with violence for having deceived him. This story is emblematic of the sentiments some of the urban Taiwanese had with regard to the Mainlanders.[103]

The tension that emerged between the Taiwanese and Mainlanders had less to do with inherent characteristics and initial impressions and much more to do with the quality of early interactions.[104] While the residents of Taiwan recall welcoming the Nationalist troops as liberators, the leaders of the KMT apparently suspected that the Taiwanese had collaborated with Japan while the KMT had been battling Japanese savagery on the mainland. The KMT also feared that Taiwan had been infiltrated by communist provocateurs. Given the KMT's stunning loss to the Communists on the mainland, it is easy to see how reasonable this insecurity seemed to them at the time.[105]

Lai, Myers, and Wei chronicle the various causes of friction between the two groups of Chinese which, ultimately, led to a violent uprising and a brutal KMT response. They assert that after Japan's surrender, the KMT took control of many territories that had been under Japanese rule, but only Taiwanese revolted.

> KMT misrule in Taiwan … in contrast with KMT misrule in the coastal provinces recovered from the Japanese, aroused the anger of an especially coherent, ethnically bounded "we-group" animated by a deeply shared sense of being victimized and insulted by outsiders inferior to it.[106]

On February 27, 1947, there was a confrontation between investigators of the Monopoly Bureau (a government agency that monopolized the sale of alcohol and tobacco) and a woman who was illegally selling matches and cigarettes on a Taipei street. Unexpectedly, the incident turned ugly and a government officer unintentionally shot a Taiwanese bystander. That night, and all the following day, mobs of Taiwanese in Taipei and other cities across the island went on a rampage, assaulting Mainlanders and destroying their property.

The violence continued for two weeks as Taiwanese vented the anger, frustration, and hostility toward the Mainlanders that had mounted in the year and a half since the KMT came to Taiwan. This was followed by several months of terror imposed by the KMT who had troop reinforcements sent from the mainland to Taiwan. What actually happened may never be fully known. The perception among Taiwanese is that the KMT authorities systematically wiped out the political and intellectual elite of Taiwan.[107] When it was over, thousands had been executed.[108] The KMT claims that it was quelling a rebellion and that the lives of many Nationalist troops and those of innocent mainland refugees were lost as well.

With this bloody preface, the story of Taiwanese and Mainlander animosity unfolded as the two groups were riveted to opposing camps. The whole episode is referred to in Taiwan as the 2–28 Incident (for February 28, the day the killing started in earnest) and impeded subsequent efforts at integration because of residual hostility and mistrust. Until the end of the 1980s, it was not even permissible to discuss this matter openly in Taiwan. Now, as many other things have changed, this taboo, also, has been shunted aside.[109]

Searching for a cause of 2–28 in the Taiwanese identity, Chang Chun-hung explains:

> Originally [Taiwanese] thought that the culture of their fatherland was noble. This sort of esteem is just like that of a son who has for a long time been cut off from his parents and . . . in his thoughts his father is exalted, noble, and abounding [in fine qualities]; so, when the son enters back into the embrace of his father he is full of excitement and illusions; to be let down from such a high point of illusion is really dreadful; to discover suddenly that the parent for whom you yearned, whom you held up with such illusions is actually quite low class and lacking in fine qualities—the impact of that was a factor in the eruption of the 2–28 Incident and a reason why the heights of acceptability were transformed into the heights of animosity; it produced an extremely serious fissure.[110]

One gathers from conversations with Taiwanese—even those too young to have any memory of the 2–28 Incident—a severe sense of victimization. To this day, the failure of the KMT to address adequately the anger Taiwanese feel about the random, pervasive terror associated with the crackdown by Nationalist troops has caused this sense to fester. Memories of the 2–28 Incident also provided a rallying point for the opposition movement, an effective tool to mobilize support for Taiwanese nationalism. The indignation Taiwanese repressed since the KMT crackdown in 1947, a gnawing sense of hatred, was fed at each turn by any perceived impropriety or inequity in which Taiwanese were victimized by Mainlanders. Regrettably, the KMT has fanned the flames of resentment and animosity in the forty years since it came to Taiwan both by actions that wronged Taiwanese and by inaction.

Some academics point out that the friction the Taiwanese had with the KMT was not so much a clash between the native population and Mainlanders as it was an example of the way the KMT behaved wherever it took power. There are those who say that before the KMT came to Taiwan, its relations with the local people of Nanking and Chungking were also soured by brutality and high-handedness. Speaking of those who now advocate independence on Taiwan, James Chu said, in an astoundingly candid remark:

> During World War II when the central government was seated in Szechwan ... Szechwanese had such [an] element, such sentiment. . . . It was fortunate that [the] Japanese occupation ... only last[ed] eight years. Had it lasted for forty years, probably [there] would be some kind of Szechwan Independence Movement.[111]

The indignations the Taiwanese feel they have suffered at the hands of the KMT have probably been the most potent source of group consciousness. In this sense, the notion of Taiwan consciousness—as opposed to a Taiwanese culture—may be viewed primarily as a political, not a cultural, phenomenon.

Taiwanese Culture, Taiwanese Consciousness

Some Taiwanese have justified their demands for independence by claiming Taiwanese culture and Chinese—or Han—culture are different. For example, Hsieh Chang-t'ing writes:

> Taiwan's traditional culture originated from the Han culture of mainland China. But because it was separated from the mainland for long periods of time, and also due to its oceanic location, it was able to absorb foreign cultures easily and it gradually developed a lifestyle and values that were suited to its own survival. Thus, in many ways there was a significant difference between it and the original Chinese culture.[112]

Chiu I-jen acknowledged that Taiwanese culture is similar to the culture of Fukien Province. However, the KMT has worked hard to foster a sense of unity, to eradicate any source of Taiwanese opposition, and has systematically repressed any expression of Taiwanese history, dialect, folk-operatic forms, songs, and so forth. In reaction, Taiwanese who felt that their sense of identity was being smothered arose to assert their differences. The implication is that had the KMT been more inclusive, less suspicious of Taiwanese cultural forms, and tolerant rather than repressive, there would have been little impetus for Taiwanese political action and, therefore, a weaker sense of Taiwanese identity.[113]

Chang Chun-hung agreed that "[b]asically we cannot deny that Taiwanese culture is an extension of Chinese culture." He accounts for the emergence of Taiwanese identity not in cultural differences, but in persecution and repression.[114] It would be wrong to attribute the animosity and distrust between Taiwanese and Mainlanders today to cultural differences, as some have tried to do. Essentially, Taiwanese culture is a regional variation of Chinese culture. It is not wholly unique and shares a good deal with the culture of southeastern China, particularly of Fukien Province, across the Taiwan Strait. Yet, the identity Taiwanese feel and the reason why some have tried to promote the idea that Taiwan has a separate culture has to do with Taiwanese reactions to political repression. The frustration Taiwanese have endured has caused them to challenge the legitimacy of the KMT and all it represents. That has created an atmosphere in which regional distinctions that might otherwise have been ignored have become potent symbols of a group consciousness, or identity, that empowers Taiwanese to see themselves as different.

It is evident that Taiwanese differ from most Mainlanders in that they speak a different dialect, worship different deities, have cultivated a self-referential literature, perform distinct forms of folk-opera and puppetry, and practice different funeral and burial customs. What some Taiwanese refer to as Taiwanese culture is most easily characterized as the transported culture of Fukien Province (from which most Taiwanese families trace their roots), leavened with bits of other southern Chinese cultural ingredients and flavored with the peculiar historical experiences of Taiwanese interactions with Japan and the West.

Every civilization that extends over a wide territory and a vast population is bound to have regional variations and discernible differences in practice, customs, and beliefs. These differences do not necessarily constitute a different culture.[115] That Taiwanese distinguish between their own expressions of culture and the ways of other Mainlanders may have to do with the gap between the folk culture of Taiwan and the elite, gentry culture that the KMT has portrayed as Chinese national culture. This gap, naturally, has led Taiwanese to see themselves as different, but may not necessarily be attributed to the existence of a distinct Taiwanese culture.

Ch'en Li-li writes about the cultural elite's perception of the mainland during the period that the KMT first came to Taiwan. She offers insight about the gap between the Han culture purveyed by the KMT as national culture and Taiwan's indigenous culture. The elite believed Chinese civilization

> resembled a tree, and China at any given generation was a cross-section of the trunk with concentric rings. Occupying the core was the cultured elite—erudite gentry and well-born scholar officials.... Less cultured groups occupied successive outer rings with the outermost ring occupied by the untutored masses. Generation after generation of descendants kept their places in their appropriate rings....

> Horizontally, in good times, the core sent its sap outward to nourish the other rings, but when the times were bad, outreaching altruism could be retrenched and the core need only protect its own survival. . . . Vertically, each generation's core must pass on its values and cultural heritage to the next generation's while constantly harkening back for sustenance to its predecessors. As long as the continuity was maintained, Chinese civilization would be safe.[116]

From the perspective of those about whom Ch'en writes, imbuing Taiwanese with the sap of Chinese civilization was something they were obliged to do for their own survival. Of course, there are some Taiwanese who view the KMT effort to assimilate the Taiwanese into "Chinese" culture as an effort to smother any indigenous Taiwanese culture with the form of nourishment that Ch'en describes.

As liberalization proceeded in Taiwan, a flood of publications gave voice to the Taiwanese need to redefine their culture and to rectify the problems with contemporary Taiwanese society that stem from the abiding uncertainty people feel about their identity.[117] Taiwanese seem willing to acknowledge that Taiwan's culture evolved from the Han culture of the mainland, but claim the peculiar circumstances of Taiwan's history have resulted in the emergence of a new cultural form which must be accepted for what it is, rather than that be molded to suit an idealistic notion of what Chinese culture must be. Many intellectuals object to the idea that Taiwanese must be remade in the KMT's image of what Chinese used to or should be. Taiwanese social critics view contemporary society in Taiwan as profoundly unhealthy because for forty years people have strained to maintain a false sense of attachment to China when they are mired in a society on Taiwan that they have been cued by socialization and propaganda to disregard or disdain.

Taiwanese intellectuals make the plea that all residents of Taiwan—Mainlanders and Taiwanese alike—must accept the culture they live with as a new form of Chinese culture. The culture of Taiwan, a departure from the Chinese culture of the past, is depicted as arising from the struggle of Taiwan's people to cope with the pressures of adapting traditions to suit modernity. This is an embracing ideology that looks from the present forward to what Taiwan must be, rather than from the present backward to cling to an ideal that was not realized. It is a declaration of cultural independence that is intended to offer the residents of Taiwan a more realistic image of themselves and their future. It is a new identity that has vital political import.

> Taiwanese have been a prisoner of the yoke of Han culture for almost 400 years, especially after 1949. Large scale traditional culture was forced onto the Taiwanese by a fascist regime and today . . . finally there is a turning point for a complete reform in Taiwanese society. Taiwanese have had all kinds of new consciousness and they are alive and bravely pursuing freedom, emancipation, egalitarianism and self-respect.[118]

The author of this passage, Lin Yang-min, dismisses the focus on national recovery that has served as the essence of KMT ideology and the plinth on which its legitimacy rests. He emphasizes the importance of accepting Taiwan, not the mainland, as one's fatherland. Taiwanese have been on the island at least as long as Americans have been in America, and Lin suggests that there is no reason for them to look to a land across the ocean as their home. He implores his compatriots to reject the idea that their fatherland is elsewhere and accept the island as home. He upbraids the Mainlanders and exhorts them, too, to accept Taiwan as a homeland instead of longing to be elsewhere.[119]

> The so-called "Mainlanders in Taiwan" who came after 1949 have lived here for forty years and have set down roots here and have given birth to offspring here. They don't plan to leave. Why don't they take Taiwan as their own country? Even when they have a chance to visit the so-called fatherland across the Taiwan Straits, they still come back to Taiwan to live. Therefore, they have to take Taiwan as their fatherland. We are not from the mainland anymore, we are Taiwanese. Taiwan is our native place, our country, and our fatherland.[120]

This is a common theme. Hsieh Chang-t'ing writes that because of the "stalemate between the KMT and the CCP" the people on Taiwan have developed a sense of sharing a common fate. "This new Taiwanese consciousness accommodates all the Mainlanders, Taiwanese, Hakka, and aborigines. It is a new consciousness that will allow all of us to harmonize and become one."[121]

This rich literature is a grave threat to the KMT. It denies Taiwan's ties to the mainland, undermines the basis of KMT rule, inspires people to view Taiwan as a distinct polity, contributes to the drumbeat of the Taiwan independence movement, and amplifies the call for democratic reform as a step toward self-determination. The most potent theme in this literature is the appeal to Taiwanese to take pride in who they are and where they live, rather than to continue viewing themselves as orphans who must be returned, someday, to their fatherland.

Legacies of Frustration and Authoritarianism

Taiwanese and Mainlanders have been wracked by frustrations that have reinforced their own senses of cultural and national identity. For Mainlanders, the gradual realization that they will not be able to recover and return to the mainland—as Chiang Kai-shek led them to expect they would—came as a shattering disappointment. They have become more sensitive to their plight as alien figures in a society in which they do not, nor generally wish to, belong. Taiwan is a cramped, truncated semblance of the China with which many of the older Mainlanders identify.

For Taiwanese, the authoritarian system imposed by the KMT robbed them of dignity in a way that has proven hard to accept. Intense socialization in the schools emphasized Chinese mainland history, heroes, geography, language, literature, and values at the expense of any attention to Taiwan. The KMT exercised complete control over the island and the affairs of its residents according to a set of "Temporary Provisions Effective During the Period of Communist Rebellion," which essentially suspended constitutional law.[122] KMT officials scrupulously point out that this period was a state of emergency and temporary; they rankle at the suggestion that what they imposed was a form of martial law.

Still, an elaborate domestic security apparatus—ostensibly to safeguard against communist infiltration—put every citizen within earshot of government agents, informants, or undercover police and effectively strangled all but the boldest critics. Reports of the intimidation, blacklisting, apprehension, torture, imprisonment, and murder of political dissidents and critics of the KMT have punctuated the history of Nationalist rule on Taiwan.[123]

As Taiwanese bore the brunt of this political repression, it is understandable that they came to see themselves as the victims and the KMT, represented by the Mainlanders, as the victimizers, underscoring another apparent difference. In truth, the situation was far more complex, and there have been plenty of Mainlander victims as well as Taiwanese beneficiaries of KMT domination. While it appears that the "new" KMT is eager to distance itself from the abuses and excesses of the past, it has been hard to slip out from under the shadow of suspicion that even now, former leaders cast from their graves.

Rigid KMT policies directly and indirectly reinforced distinctions between Mainlanders and Taiwanese in a way that undermined the party's goal of social integration. These institutionalized manners of distinction have contributed to the emergence and sustenance of Taiwanese identity.[124] Among those policies that highlighted the distinctions directly was the KMT attitude toward the use of Mandarin versus Taiwanese—probably the irritant that Taiwanese most often speak of when explaining their sense of frustration and their flagging sense of self. Another way in which the KMT plan to create a sense of unity backfired was the official attitude toward Taiwan.

Attitudes toward Language

Contemporary life in Taiwan bustles without many visible clues of the divisions that seethe beneath the surface or the memories of harsher times, not long in the past. One source of daily frustration that results from KMT cultural policies and continually reinforces the Taiwanese sense of group identity is the issue of dialect.

Mainlanders came to Taiwan from various provinces of China speaking different regional dialects.[125] Few spoke the dialect of Taiwan, which is a variant of the dialect spoken in southern Fukien Province, from which most Taiwanese forebears had come.[126] To communicate, the Mainlanders used Mandarin, the dialect of the north, which had been selected as the "national language." Few Taiwanese spoke this dialect.

As part of its effort to reintegrate Taiwan into the Chinese fold, the KMT enforced a strict policy that entailed using only Mandarin for official affairs, in schools, on radio, and on television.

> Television was first aired [in Taiwan] in 1962 and Taiwanese shows were most popular, which caused some jealousy. So in 1972 the government ordered that all television stations could not air more than one hour per day of Taiwanese-language programs and that hour had to be broken up into two segments at lunch and at night. During the 6:30 P.M. prime time hour, only one of the three stations could air a Taiwanese-language program. In 1976, another rule was passed which said that all television shows had to be in Mandarin and the shows in Taiwanese would be gradually phased out over the year.[127]

This contributed to the immense sense of frustration that Taiwanese felt—having been forced by Japanese to speak Japanese and by Mainlanders to speak Mandarin, the Taiwanese resented the imposition that restricted the use of their own mother tongue.[128]

In time, Taiwanese came to feel that their dialect, literature, poetry, songs, and drama were all inferior to Mandarin and the cultural works of the mainland.[129] One consequence of this sense of inferiority was the illogical assumption that Mainlanders' pronunciation of Mandarin was "standard" and the accented Mandarin that Taiwanese spoke was inferior. In a culture that emphasizes heavily the importance of conformity with ideals and in which mastery of language is, by tradition, accorded a very high degree of respect, Taiwanese were often made to feel inferior.

In schools, speech contests intended to promote fluency in Mandarin caused many Taiwanese to feel inadequate. Taiwanese, which was still the dialect of the home and marketplace, was forbidden in class. It seems that every adult Taiwanese who was educated since the KMT arrived recalls the fines, slaps, and humiliations that were meted out as punishment to students heard speaking Taiwanese at school.[130] Taiwanese were made to feel their dialect was somehow less dignified, dirtier, than Mandarin. Taiwanese who spoke Mandarin encumbered with a Taiwanese accent felt vulnerable each time they opened their mouths and ashamed that culturally—and, perhaps, inherently—they were inferior to Mainlanders.

The fallacy of this assumption is that not all those who came from the mainland spoke with the much-coveted "standard" pronunciation.[131] In each region of China, Mandarin is tinged with the accent of the dialect that is spoken there as a primary tongue. The Mandarin taken as "standard" is that which is spoken in the north, particularly in the area surrounding Peking, where the court was located.[132] However, the Mandarin spoken in Peking is not at all like that spoken in Chungking, and that not a bit like the Mandarin spoken in Shanghai. Indeed, even Chiang Kai-shek spoke Mandarin with a thick accent of his native Chekiang Province. From the vantage of pronunciation alone, a laborer or rickshaw puller in Peking may have spoken more standard Mandarin than the president, who spoke it with an accent no less heavy than many Mandarin-speaking Taiwanese.

Restrictions on the use of Taiwanese have loosened in recent years, and it has become more acceptable—even fashionable—to speak Taiwanese in certain settings. Taiwanese is now the language of commerce outside of Taipei, has slowly reentered the realm of officialdom—even, for symbolic purposes, in the Legislative Yuan—and is apparently a *sine qua non* in campaigning for elected office. Kang Ning-hsiang illustrated this change in attitudes by recounting a dinner conversation he had had with a U.S. government official who had returned to Taiwan after a long absence.

> I asked him "is there any difference between the time you were in Taiwan [before] and now?" He said, "When I was in Taiwan before . . . you knew [if someone] was Taiwanese, [even though he tried to] speak Mandarin. Although the Taiwanese spoke Mandarin . . . their Mandarin was very poor. But things are different this time . . . [because] there are also Mainlanders speaking Taiwanese . . . everybody speaks Taiwanese. Even the Mainlanders . . . try their best . . . the louder they speak [Taiwanese], the more proud they are."[133]

The latitude to speak Taiwanese is, itself, emblematic of the rise of Taiwanese nationalism. The Taiwanese dialect is reclaiming social respectability because Taiwanese have asserted their identity.[134] It is still the case that most Mainlanders do not speak Taiwanese, even those who were born on Taiwan. This is a source of great uneasiness in settings where Mainlanders, second generation Mainlanders, and Taiwanese are expected to mix.

Shaw Yü-ming, in a candid statement about the KMT's language policy, remarked that people should be grateful that the government insisted on teaching Mandarin. He said that fostering a universal dialect is an essential part of nation-building and enables Taiwanese entrepreneurs to communicate when conducting business on the mainland. However, he does rue one thing. He said that "if something can be criticized, maybe the Mainlanders should [have been] taught Taiwanese on the side. Then you [would] have [had] a true integration."[135]

Attitude toward Taiwan

When Mainlanders arrived in Taiwan, the Taiwanese saw them as interlopers with little concern for the island and no respect for the Taiwanese. For decades, all Mainlanders spoke of was their desire—and intent—to return *home* to the mainland. This attitude was bolstered by official government pronouncements and, therefore, provided a measure of legitimacy that affected notions of identification.

Mainlanders sensed that they were not welcome, felt uneasy about being uprooted and deposited on the distant island, hoped only that they would soon return home, and felt alienated from the Taiwanese. One second generation Mainlander spoke of her father's attitude toward Taiwan saying that for the first decade after their arrival

> he still thought we were going back there [to the mainland], so we didn't buy anything. We didn't buy a house, we didn't buy anything. We were poor . . . but we still could have managed to have some real estate, but he didn't do that [buy any]. And that made us . . . relatively poor compared with other Main-landers, [not to mention] with indigenous people because they owned land, they owned houses, they [had] been here many, many generations. So, my dad was . . . very disillusioned when he knew that he was going to settle down here and organize his family here probably all his life. . . . [He said,] "I planned not to stay here very long, but now I'm doomed to stay here the rest of my life, even my children will probably stay here the rest of their lives."[136]

For Taiwanese, who had only recently been freed from a half century of colonial administration, Taiwan was home. They expected to be integrated into the Chinese community. Instead, they were viewed with hostility, suspicion, or indifference. Many claim they felt like second-class citizens in their own home. Antonio Chiang recalled with some bitterness the sense he got from his KMT-regimented education, which ignored Taiwanese culture.

> Under KMT indoctrination . . . we not only don't know much about Taiwan . . . we learn[ed] to despise Taiwaneseness, Taiwanese language. They said Taiwan has no language, no culture. Taiwanese history started from the day the KMT arrived in Taiwan. Taiwan has no purpose in itself. The purpose of Taiwan is to be a stepping stone to go back to China. It is a transition. It is like a hotel. So, the only hope for Taiwanese is the mainland. The ultimate goal is in the mainland. Everything here is so small. Mountains are small, rivers are so short. [There are] volcanoes, earthquakes. "So, how can we stay here [Main-landers asked]?" The KMT brought that kind of philosophy, that kind of view to Taiwan and imposed that . . . view on Taiwanese. So, we feel humiliated . . . downgraded. . . . We have no hope because we are too small. We have no culture.[137]

City streets in Taiwan were renamed by the KMT for cities on the mainland, for Nationalist ideals, and for Confucian virtues. The vast plaza on which a grandiose monument to Chiang Kai-shek was built is surrounded by four major roads: Chung-shan South Road on the west—named for Sun Yat-sen, Hang-chow South Road on the east—named for the Southern Sung dynasty capital of China, Hsin-i Road on the north—a reference to the Confucian virtue of living up to one's word to manifest significance, and Ai-kuo East Road on the south—literally, "love the country," or Patriotism Road.

Antonio Chiang said, "[t]he map of Taipei is a map of China; it is easy for [Mainlanders] to go back to visit the mainland, from Chungking to Heilungkiang, in just twenty minutes. From Nanking to Hsinkiang, from Canton

to Shanghai is two blocks."[138] Another source points out that the entire environment created by the KMT and the Mainlanders reinforced the idea that everything of importance was on the mainland and nothing on Taiwan was of
importance.

> You live in Taiwan yet you do not see any reference to Taiwan, only to China,
> Chung-kuo, Chung-hwa. Even restaurants and company names very seldom
> used local names. All the famous restaurant names from mainland China were
> used. Even the laundries or the provincial assemblies were all intended to
> remind citizens of China. "You do not belong here, you are only passing
> through. Do not ever forget your motherland. And Taiwan is not your country.
> . . . Taiwan is not a country, it is only a place."[139]

There's No Place Like Home

Attitudes toward the mainland—and Taiwan—have changed since the government lifted the ban on travel from Taiwan to the mainland in 1987. Since that
time, Mainlanders have had an opportunity to return to see relatives and homes
left behind forty years ago, their children have had a chance to get a glimpse of
the place that their parents had primed them to reunify with, and Taiwanese have
had the chance to see the land and people with whom they have been told they
shall unite. Reactions of people who have made the trip across the Taiwan strait,
predictably, differ according to their identity and have affected people's views of
Taiwan and themselves.[140]

Many Mainlanders have found the return visit a disheartening ordeal. They
are deeply affected by the sense of deprivation in the PRC, often give voice to a
form of "survivor's guilt," and seem thoroughly disabused of any residual
illusions of ever moving home again. Beyond the shock of revisiting loved ones
and sights not seen for four decades is the realization of how terribly far apart
Taiwan and the PRC have grown in that time. While Mainlanders spent much of
the past forty years on Taiwan yearning to return home, upholding the dream of a
unified Chinese state and belittling the value of Taiwan, they have discovered
that homes they left have vanished and that, after forty years of communism,
more of the China and Chinese culture they value has been preserved in Taiwan
than on the mainland.

As compared with the PRC, Taiwan has a highly developed infrastructure,
economic vitality, elevated standard of living, and relatively free social milieu.
People on Taiwan perceive the PRC as backward, still heavily repressed, and
depressingly hopeless. Relatives who have lived through the vicissitudes of communist rule also bear scars from past campaigns—some the result of denuncia-
tions that were based on family ties to Taiwan and the KMT. The most prevalent
comments heard from embittered Mainlanders who return to Taiwan after a visit
to the PRC is that family members still living in the PRC ply guilt to drain their
Taiwan relatives of money and gifts of consumer products.

For the most part, Taiwanese who traveled to the mainland for the first time were taken by the similarity between themselves and their brethren across the strait. While people are highly sensitive to the economic disparity that separates Taiwan from the PRC, they seem impressed that—despite KMT propaganda to the contrary—their "communist" cousins are just as "Chinese" as they are.

Ma Ying-cheou summed up the different reactions to the mainland, saying that Taiwanese returning from the PRC are

> . . . quite fascinated by the mainland; the vast land, the rich resources, everything is fascinating. Cheap labor. Everything. But Mainlanders, particularly those who have lived in the mainland [before], are very frustrated. Very disappointed. Many of them say, "I don't want to go back again."[141]

Shaw Yü-ming pointed out that most of those from Taiwan who have invested in the mainland in recent years are not Mainlanders, but Taiwanese.

> It's the Taiwanese businessmen who are most directly involved in the indirect trade [with the PRC]. Its not the Mainlanders. If we [Mainlanders] go back to the mainland, [we] mostly just look at the Great Wall . . . look at the relatives. Not much else to do. And most of the old soldiers, after a few trips, they don't want to go back to their roots . . . spend all their money. They're not that welcome. They pretty much satisfy their homesickness and they want to stay here [in Taiwan]. Mainland, to them, is more sentimental, or cultural. . . . But mainland to many Taiwanese businessmen is a market. They are the ones who . . . crashed down the door of the mainland. They are the ones who are active [there], not the Mainlanders.[142]

Indeed, there is a lot of anecdotal evidence about Taiwanese rediscovering their roots in the mainland. In addition to building up the economy of coastal, southeastern China, there are stories of temples, hospitals, and schools being built with money donated by wealthy Taiwanese. Religious pilgrimages from Taiwan to the mainland add to the sense that many Taiwanese, secure in their political identity as Taiwanese, find fulfillment in the reestablishment of cultural contact with their origins.[143]

This suggests that the policies of the KMT that tried to associate cultural and political identity with a unified China have not fully succeeded. Mainlanders who, one assumed, would naturally identify with the place from which they came, now find themselves repulsed by poverty, backwardness, and greed on the mainland or are just indifferent. Taiwanese, who have not had a political affinity for the mainland, are comfortable looking to Fukien as the touchstone that reinforces their cultural identity, as long as they can look at it from Taiwan. Taiwanese and Mainlanders are equally comfortable pointing to economic disparities and experiential differences that divide the PRC from Taiwan and, in the eyes of most, this justifies keeping Taiwan politically separate from the mainland as long as the Communists remain in charge.

The ravages of the past four decades in the PRC have done more to accentuate economic and social differences than to cultivate a commonality between the mainland and Taiwan. Although the KMT endeavored to foster the sense that unifying China was critical to the glory of Chinese civilization and the betterment of all Chinese, the strategy it adopted for this task ended up alienating the Taiwanese from this vision. The KMT tried to persuade those it forced to listen that there is only one China and China means unity. Over the years, the KMT has worked hard to promote itself as a more credible source of leadership than the CCP. It has done this, in part, by extolling the glories of Taiwan's economic development, cultural renaissance, and the political liberalization that has evolved under its guidance on Taiwan. At the same time, to discredit the CCP, the KMT ranted about the depravity, oppression, and hopelessness of life under communist rule in the PRC.

While this dual appeal was intended to bolster the party's image as better suited to being the "sole legitimate government" of all China, the KMT succeeded only in persuading residents of the island that they are better off living in Taiwan than on the mainland and that self-rule would be infinitely preferable to rule from Peking. The KMT expected people to take from this the message that it would lead China and all Chinese to flourish, but the CCP could only cause China to perish. What people heard, however, was not what the KMT had hoped.

The incessant comparison of Taiwan to the mainland caused many to identify success and modernity with autonomy, and deprivation with reunification. For both Mainlanders and Taiwanese, there is a palpable sense that Taiwan is successful, prosperous, and increasingly open politically. People gripe about the cost of living, the stench of pollution, the unrelenting traffic congestion, and other social ills on the island, but they have no interest in trading any of that for life on the mainland. Disgruntled residents of Taiwan might gladly jump at an opportunity to relocate to Vancouver or Los Angeles, but few would see any advantage at all in moving to the mainland or forming a union with the mainland that would be likely to dilute the riches Taiwan has earned for itself.

Taiwanese have been particularly attentive to the woes of what used to be West Germany. Reflecting on the way the new Germany must absorb the impoverished, undisciplined, disorderly, and demanding population of the former East Germany, Taiwanese opposed to reunification see the German case as a strong incentive to maintain Taiwan's autonomy. If Taiwan and the mainland are reunified anytime soon under KMT control, the frustrations and cost to the former West Germans will be dwarfed by the costs Taiwanese will incur. What Taiwanese fear even more is that in the hubristic desire for historical significance, leading figures in the KMT will work to reunify Taiwan with the mainland, but will end up "selling out" Taiwan for their personal aggrandizement. The greatest fear is that the Communists will end up taking control of Taiwan.[144]

The fear that Taiwan will be sold out is an anxiety that comes from a historical consciousness of being treated like chattel by self-serving political regimes over several centuries. Taiwanese elites have cultivated a sense that in the past, Taiwan and its people have been treated as objects of exchange—political booty—in machinations effected by alien governments too powerful for the island's residents to resist. Taiwanese have been sold out before and, therefore, have severe misgivings about any deals that would lead to a political arrangement in which Taiwan is governed from Peking.

Uneasiness about reunification affects Mainlanders, too. While the party continues to promulgate reunification as a national goal, it is getting increasingly difficult to believe that many people on Taiwan genuinely expect reunification to benefit them as long as the CCP remains in Peking. Surely, people are happy to fantasize about a time in the future when the CCP falls and there is an opportunity for reunification with a new form of Chinese government. Until the Communists are eliminated from the political stage, however, even Mainlanders on Taiwan are wary of moving too quickly to reunify.

There are different perspectives about these matters, but they seem to lead to the same conclusions. It is difficult to imagine the aging Mainlander elite having a pressing desire to live in the mainland as it is today. They have become too accustomed to the comforts of air-conditioning, Mercedes Benzes with car phones, Italian suits, French brandy, gaudy and sensually indulgent nightlife, freedom to travel at will, and other dimensions of the high-life that is available to them in Taiwan.[145]

For the elderly KMT soldiers who were pressed into military service as young men, brought to Taiwan in the aftermath of the KMT defeat, and consigned to depressing retirement villages, there is nothing for them any longer in the PRC. Family they left behind may resent the old soldiers for having "had it so good" in Taiwan while their kin in the PRC suffered the fate that the CCP visited on its citizenry. Those who were married before they left the mainland may have married and sired again in Taiwan. Even those who would like to return to be with their family fear they may be regarded as politically undesirable or worse by the Communists against whom they once fought.

As to the "second generation" that was born and raised on Taiwan, the only home they have known is the island, and if they cannot identify with that home, they are unlikely to find the mainland more hospitable. The generations that have been raised in Taiwan since the KMT arrived have been influenced by American and Japanese popular culture in a way that their cousins in the PRC have not. The material advantages and political liberties to which they have become increasingly accustomed would not be as readily available in their "home province." To their misfortune, the growth of Taiwanese identity on the island is decreasing the psychic "space" for Mainlanders. Politically, the KMT has been far more welcoming to Taiwanese than has the opposition to Mainlanders. For many, this disturbing turn of events is cause to reevaluate their relationship to Taiwan and their cultural and national identity.

Conclusion

The cultural identity of Taiwanese appears to have been "invented" in reaction to the efforts of the mainland elite to make residents of Taiwan cleave to the Chinese motherland, its culture, and its people.[146] The KMT endeavored to reinforce—or establish—a sense of nationality by intense socialization in the schools, in public places, and through the media in Taiwan as it did elsewhere on the mainland prior to 1949. When the state acts in this way to assimilate a segment of the population under its jurisdiction, the process is often "forcible, involving the repression of [the] language and culture of subordinate groups."[147] Surely, by viewing the Taiwanese as a group that needed to be assimilated forcibly, the KMT inadvertently nourished the Taiwanese sense of distinctiveness that was the seed of the Taiwan independence movement.

Two contextual factors affected the emergence of this Taiwanese sense of national identity. The defeat of Japan in 1945 ended fifty years during which the residents of Taiwan were subjected to the Japanese system of rule. The arrival of the KMT from the mainland shortly thereafter made for a highly disruptive transitional period. This period may be characterized as one in which there was a sudden:

(1) disruption in the preexisting sense of security people had in their insular community, and

(2) recognition of sharp contrasts between the indigenous community and the rulers, who are seen as alien to that community.[148]

Disruptions may come about because of economic forces, as with industrialization, or because of political forces, as with decolonization and conquest. In the case of Taiwan, the disruptions were caused by decolonization and effects analogous to conquest.

Even though there had been a sharp contrast between the Taiwanese and their Japanese rulers, these were to be expected as the Japanese were aliens. Residents of Taiwan were surprised by the sharp contrast they detected between themselves and the Chinese from the mainland who had come to restore China's sovereignty over the island. The most tangible divisions between the rulers and the ruled were political and cultural. The KMT constrained Taiwanese from meaningful political participation and caused them to feel that the manifestations of their own vernacular, regional, and cultural forms were less valued than the state-sponsored manifestations of high Chinese culture.

Mainlanders tend to dismiss the sincerity of those who promote Taiwanese cultural distinctiveness. For Mainlanders of this school, those who promote the notion of a Taiwan culture are either seriously misguided or merely seeking personal aggrandizement.[149] Some Taiwanese opponents of the government dismiss the determination of the Mainlander elite to promote Chinese culture as an effort calculated to smother Taiwanese and stymie would-be challengers to KMT supremacy. They question the sincerity of Mainlanders and denounce the focus on Chinese unity as a shield for political expedience. To denigrate the Mainlanders' view of China as solely instrumental is as cynical as denouncing Taiwanese nationality as a fabrication concocted for the personal gain of the Taiwanese elite.

One must take quite seriously the sense of threat the Mainlander elite must have felt in 1949 and the devotion they felt both to their notions of cultural norms and to political unity. The deep commitment of the Mainlander elite to their vision of China and Chinese culture—coupled with a habitual and unexamined reliance on authoritarian mechanisms of governance—is the most likely source of the cultural repression that the KMT visited on the Taiwanese.

By favoring the culture of China's elite, the KMT intended to promote what it took to be the genuine culture of the Chinese nation, but ended up imposing a "high culture" on a society "where previously low cultures had taken up the lives of the majority, and in some cases the totality, of the population."[150] Party leaders do not believe that they have imposed a foreign culture on Taiwan. However, the regime made clear to the Taiwanese how different they were from the standard that the authorities endorsed. By reinforcing Taiwanese notions of distinctiveness, the KMT inadvertently boosted people's identity as Taiwanese rather than fostering a deeper identity as Chinese.

Taiwanese recognize the Chinese origin of their own culture, but also sense that beyond sharing in the national culture manifested by the Mainlander elite, they have ties to a more compelling, more immediate set of cultural impulses. These they share with other Taiwanese in a manner that differentiates them from the Mainlanders.[151] The peculiar experience of people living on Taiwan during the past four decades of economic and political development—quite apart from whatever historical ties people have with Taiwan of the past and with China— has imparted to a new generation a sense of being distinct. To those who see themselves in this way, it is from the recent past, not the distant past, that they take cues about their identity.

To summarize:

(1) Mainlanders who associate themselves with the KMT tend to embrace all Han Chinese as part of the "Chinese" nation.

(2) Many Taiwanese see themselves as constituting a nation distinct from the Chinese—even as they acknowledge that they are *culturally* Chinese. Some of these Taiwanese claim to be culturally Taiwanese and reject "mainland" culture.

(3) Other Taiwanese recognize that they are part of the Chinese nation, but demur at being subsumed by the Chinese state—where the Chinese state means the PRC.[152]

(4) Taiwan-born Mainlanders cannot comfortably identify themselves as either Taiwanese or Chinese. They recognize there is a Taiwanese nation of which they are not a part and yet they do not share their parents' sense of identity with the Chinese nation. This sense of rootlessness is doubly confusing for those whose parentage is "mixed."

(5) Taiwanese born, educated, and socialized by the KMT may, like the Taiwan-born Mainlanders with whom they have grown up and gone to school, suffer from divided loyalties and confusion about their identity. Having known nothing other than KMT rule and the values proffered by the state, many are not as exclusive about their ties to Taiwan as their parents are. They may, or may not, speak Taiwanese and may, or may not, promote independence. They do speak Mandarin, however, and have been vigorously prompted to see themselves as part of the Chinese nation.

In short, the generation that was adult at the time the KMT came to Taiwan have views of identity that are more easily characterized than the generations raised and socialized since the KMT arrival. The older generation is, generally, polarized as either Taiwanese or Chinese depending on where they were born. The generations born since the KMT came to Taiwan are more deeply troubled about their identity.

While Taiwanese are a majority on Taiwan, they comprise a small fraction of all Chinese. That they identify themselves as a group, apart from other Chinese, is curious, considering that they are not racially, ethnically, religiously, or even linguistically distinct from Chinese elsewhere. Many factors have contributed to the emergence of their sense of group identity including:

(1) the historic mentality of geographic isolation, coupled with the experiences of being ruled by outsiders;

(2) tension resulting from the KMT effort to impose an elite, gentry culture represented as the national culture of China, at the expense of the native, folk culture of Taiwan;

(3) tension that emerged from early confrontations between Taiwanese and Mainlanders—culminating in the 2–28 Incident—that may have been fueled, but not caused by, inherent characteristics and initial impressions of differences;

(4) residual indignation, mistrust, and hostility Taiwanese have toward the KMT stemming from 2–28, which was reinforced by perceptions of official impropriety or inequities that victimized Taiwanese—especially those inequities resulting from repression of political demands; and

(5) a wide range of policies that institutionalized differences between Mainlanders and Taiwanese—especially those concerning language, culture, and attitudes toward Taiwan.

Other than the first, these characteristics are not based on discernible, objective distinctions between the two groups of people. Taiwanese identity has arisen largely in response to the frustration and anger people feel about being belittled, repressed, and victimized by the KMT. The Taiwanese independence movement, which has promoted the notion that there is a distinct Taiwanese identity, has fed off of these political irritants as a way to mobilize support from among Taiwanese. The result has been a combustible admixture of passions manifested in the KMT's determination to perpetuate its power and in Taiwanese demands for self-determination.

APPENDIX: BIOGRAPHICAL LIST OF INTERVIEW SUBJECTS

The following is a list of individuals interviewed. Names in brackets are those by which the person is commonly known in the English press:

Chang An-p'ing [Nelson], President, Chia-Hsin Cement Corporation

Chang Chun-hung, Secretary-General, Democratic Progressive Party (DPP)

Chang Yan-hsien, Sun Yat-Sen Institute for Social Sciences and Philosophy, Academia Sinica

Chang Yu-sheng, President, Pacific Cultural Foundation

Chen Charng-ven [C.V. Chen], Attorney-at-Law; Vice Chairman and Secretary-General, Straits Exchange Foundation

Chen Yi-ren, Entrepreneur, philanthropist

Chiang Chun-nan [Antonio], Publisher, *Hsin Hsin-wen* [The Journalist]

Chien Hsin-chu [Edward], Professor, Hong Kong University of Science and Technology; formerly, Professor, Department of History, National Taiwan University

Chin Hsiao-yi, Director, National Palace Museum; Director-General, Party History Committee, Central Committee, KMT

Chiu I-jen, Publisher and Editor-in-Chief, *Hsin Chiao-liu* [The New Tide]; Member, DPP Central Executive Committee

Chu Chi-ying [James], Director, Department of Cultural Affairs, Central Committee, Kuomintang; KMT Spokesman

Chu Kao-cheng [Ju Gau-jeng], Representative, Legislative Yuan; Chairman, Chinese Socialist Democratic Party

Ho Chen-Hsiung [Earle], Chairman, Taiwan Steel and Iron Industries; President, Tung Ho Steel Enterprise, Corporation

Hsiao Hsin-huang [Michael], Institute of Ethnology, Academia Sinica; Professor, National Taiwan University

Hsu Chi-ming [Steve], Deputy Chairman, Research and Planning Board, Ministry of Foreign Affairs

Hsu Hsin-liang, Chairman of the DPP

Hsu Lu, Correspondent, *Tzu-li Wan-pao* [Independence Evening Post]

Hsu Shao-p'o [Paul], Senior Partner, Lee and Li, Attorneys-at-Law; Professor, National Taiwan University

Hsueh Kwang-zu, Educator

Hu Fo, Professor, Department of Political Science, National Taiwan University

Huang Chu-wen, Member, Convenor, Legislative Yuan; head of Wisdom Club

Jen Chi-p'ing, Professor, Department of Political Science, Tunghai University

Kao Hui-yü [Alice], Correspondent-at-large, *Lien-ho Pao* [United Daily News]; Member, Central Committee of the KMT; Deputy, National Assembly

Kang Ning-hsiang, Adviser, DPP

Lee Yi-yuan, Member, Academia Sinica; Dean, College of Humanities and Social Sciences, National Tsing-hua University; President, Chiang Ching-Kuo Foundation for International Scholarly Exchange

Li Hsin Chu [Nigel], Attorney, Lee and Li, Attorneys-at-Law; Professor, National Taiwan University; Member, Central Committee, Kuomintang

Li Kuo-ting [K. T. Li], Senior Adviser to the President; Member, National Science Council; Member, Central Standing Committee, Kuomintang

Lin Cheng-chie, Representative, Legislative Yuan

Liu Chin-tien, Director, People's Service Division, Kaohsiung County, Kang-shan Township, Kuomintang Headquarters

Lü Hsiu-lian, Feminist, political activist, lawyer, author; Founding Director, Coalition for Democracy

Lü Ya-li, Professor, Department of Political Science, National Taiwan University

Ma Han-pao, Grand Justice, Judicial Yuan; Professor of Law, National Taiwan University

Ma Ying-cheou, Deputy-Director, Mainland Affairs Council

Ming Chu-cheng, Professor, Department of Political Science, National Taiwan University

Po Yang [Kuo Ying-ting], Author, social critic

Shaw Yü-ming, Director-General, Government Information Office, Government Spokesman

Shieh Sen-chung [Samuel], Governor, Central Bank of China

Soong Chu-yü [James], Secretary-General, Central Committee, Kuomintang

Ting Shou-chung, Representative, Legislative Yuan

Tsai Jen-chien, Director of Propaganda, Democratic Progressive Party

Tsiang Yien-Si, Secretary-General, Office of the President

Wang Hsing-ching, Editor-in-Chief, *Hsin Hsin-wen* [The Journalist]

Wang Yi-hsiung, Attorney

Wu Tsu-ping, Honorary Consul-General to Malta, Swaziland

Yang Hsien-hung, Environmental activist, author

Yang Kuo-hsu, Institute of Ethnography, Academia Sinica; Professor, Department of Psychology, National Taiwan University

Yao Chia-wen, Member, Central Standing Committee, DPP

Yü Tsung-hsien, President, Chung Hwa Institute for Economic Research

Yü-Chen Yueh-ying, Magistrate, Kaohsiung County

The following individuals were consulted—some repeatedly—in informal discussions:

Chung Kuo-hsien, Reporter, China Television System

Coliver, Edith, Representative, Asia Foundation

Hou Teh-chien, Political activist, popular songwriter

Hung Wang-sheng, Professor of Mathematics, National Taiwan Normal University

Kornbluth, David, General Affairs Section, American Institute in Taiwan

Luo Ching-chung, Political cartoonist, *Liberty Times*

Pascoe, **Richard,** Chief Representative, Reuters

Shih Chih-yu, Visiting Associate Professor, Department of Political Science, National Taiwan University

Sun Yang-ming, Correspondent, *United Daily News*

Vuylsteke, **Richard,** Senior Editor, *Free China Review*

Wang Lin-lin, Chairman, Association of Chinese Congressional Assistants; Confidential Secretary, Office of Representative Huang Chu-wen, Legislative Yuan

Wang, **Rex,** Asia Foundation

Wen Chen-hwa, Professor of History, National Taiwan Normal University

Notes

Interviews cited in this study were conducted in 1991 when I met with more than fifty prominent figures in the KMT, DPP, academic, journalistic, and commercial sectors (see Appendix). No standard questionnaire was used, nor was my intention to analyze responses statistically. I am indebted to all those who graciously consented to be interviewed. Interviews were conducted in Mandarin and/or English. Translations from Mandarin are my own (with occasional assistance), and quotations from interviews conducted in English have been edited slightly for the sake of clarity.

1. In the past several years, a number of worthy publications about Taiwan's domestic politics have been written. The most useful include: Simon Long, *Taiwan: China's Last Frontier* (New York: St. Martin's Press, 1991); Peter Moody, *Political Change on Taiwan: A Study of Ruling Party Adaptability* (New York: Praeger, 1992); Tien Hung-mao, *The Great Transition: Political and Social Change in the Republic of China* (Stanford, CA: Hoover Institution Press, 1988); and Tun-jen Cheng and Stephan Haggard, eds., *Political Change in Taiwan* (Boulder, CO: Lynne Rienner, 1992).

2. There is a common belief among Chinese that they are both culturally as well as racially distinct from other Asians and that the purest Chinese are descendants of a people called the Han who originated in the central plains of China. China has not always been governed by Han people. During the Yuan dynasty (1279–1368) it was

governed by Mongols, and during the last dynasty, the Ch'ing (1644–1911), it was governed by Manchus. At other times, other people were incorporated into China, and even today the PRC boasts of fifty-five minority groups in addition to the vast Han majority. One can read about the use of the term Han to represent the Chinese people in Denis Twitchett and Michael Loewe, eds., *The Cambridge History of China*, vol. I: *Ch'in and Han Empires, 221 B.C. –A.D. 220* (Cambridge: Cambridge University Press, 1986), pp. 369–373.

3. One can regard this debate as a challenge to accepted notions of what it means to be Chinese. Indeed, there are those who question whether the notion of Han Chinese as a homogeneous ethnic group is anything more than a product of Chinese nationalism. While China's borders expanded and receded around a central core, the populations on the fringes of China's territory were absorbed and sinicized as, indeed, were foreign rulers who came from beyond to conquer China. Chinese culture, too, is an amalgam of indigenous ideas, beliefs, inventions, and practices, as well as those synthesized from communities outside China. The idea that the Chinese are a pure race or that their culture is unadulterated by foreign elements satisfies a certain chauvinistic desire but cannot be substantiated.

4. Even if one accepts that Ch'ing emperors had inherited the right to rule China, official representatives of the court stationed in Taiwan exercised very little influence outside the cities in which they lived, and the government in Peking "repudiated all responsibility for the central mountains or the narrow east coast" of Taiwan. See Douglas Mendel, *Politics of Formosan Nationalism* (Berkeley: University of California Press, 1970), pp. 13–14.

5. For a more detailed discussion of these developments, see Thomas B. Gold, *State and Society in the Taiwan Miracle* (Armonk, NY: M.E. Sharpe, 1986), especially chapters two and three.

6. Ibid., pp. 49–50.

7. This incident in Taiwan's history is known as the February 28 (2–28) Incident. See Lai Tse-han, Ramon H. Myers, and Wei Wou, *A Tragic Beginning: The Taiwan Uprising of February 28, 1947* (Stanford: Stanford University Press, 1991).

8. It is entirely possible that as Taiwan began to thrive economically, the cost to the regime of suppressing opposition rose, too.

9. To date, there are no reliable statistics about the proportion of Taiwan's population that supports each of these positions.

10. The idea that democracy will not resolve Taiwan's troubles but may cause more problems to emerge has been suggested by Po Yang, the noted author, social critic, and former political prisoner. Interview with Po Yang, Hsintien, November 28, 1990.

11. The broad question about Chinese identity is taken up in a compendium of probing essays published as "The Living Tree: The Changing Meaning of Being Chinese Today," *Dædalus*, vol. 120, no. 2 (Spring 1991).

12. The term "Mainlander" refers to Chinese in Taiwan who either (1) came from the mainland in the late 1940s or early 1950s, or (2) bore their offspring in Taiwan. It does not refer to Chinese currently living in the PRC. These distinctions are easier to denote in Chinese than in English. Tien Hung-mao reports that in 1989 just over 2.8 million (14.3 percent) of Taiwan's total population were Mainlanders, but of those, 1.5 million (55 percent of all Mainlanders) were born on Taiwan. That means that about 93 percent of Taiwan's population was born on the island. See Tien, "Transformation of an Authoritarian Party State," in *Political Change in Taiwan,* Cheng and Haggard, eds., p. 36.

13. It is also worth noting that the "first generation" should actually be viewed as two generations. There was the generation of people who were adult in 1949 when they came to Taiwan, and the generation of their mainland-born children. Obviously, it is not possi-

ble to encompass everyone in these general terms, but with regard to the governing elite of the KMT, the first generation of leaders—Chiang Kai-shek and his contemporaries—are now dead or quite elderly. Their sons are now mature adults and, in many cases, have followed in their fathers' footsteps to take a prominent role in public affairs.

14. Approximately 1 percent of the island's population of 20.1 million are non-Han residents of several distinct ethnic groups who are referred to collectively as aborigines, *yuan-chu min,* literally "original dwellers."

15. For a discussion of intermarriage between Taiwanese and Mainlanders, see Hill Gates, "Ethnicity and Social Class," in *The Anthropology of Taiwanese Society,* Emily Martin Ahern and Hill Gates, eds. (Stanford: Stanford University Press, 1981), pp. 265–66.

16. In Chinese, Taiwanese are also referred to as native people, *pen-ti jen,* literally "people from this land"—not to be confused with the aborigines. Mainlanders are known as outsiders, *wai-sheng jen,* "people from outside the province."

17. *China Post,* April 3, 1991, p. 1.

18. Tien Hung-mao writes, "It is difficult to get an accurate count of mainlanders in Taiwan. Available figures range from 12 to 14.3 percent of the total population. The discrepancy may stem from differences in counting intermarried couples and their children." He points out that the proportion of Taiwan's population born on the mainland has decreased significantly since 1950 when it was about 15 percent and even since 1985 when it was 5.7 percent. To be sure, "The majority of those classified as mainlanders are now Taiwan-born. . . . Native Taiwanese who speak the Fukien dialect constitute almost three quarters of Taiwan's population." See Tien, *The Great Transition,* p. 36.

19. In Mandarin, *"ni shi na-li jen?"* is literally a question that asks "where are you from?" but can be taken to mean "are you a Taiwanese or a Mainlander?" It can also mean "where did you grow up?" to which one might respond with the name of a specific place, say Taipei, or Tainan.

20. Among the first Chinese to settle on Taiwan were the Hakka from Kwang-tung Province. The Hakka (literally meaning "guests") were a persecuted minority that spoke their own dialect and had been "driven from their homes in Henan Province in northern China fifteen hundred years ago. They took up residence in southern China, engaging in fishing and trading in coastal areas, and from there migrated to the Pescadores, then on to southern Taiwan" where they have been since about A.D. 1000. See John F. Copper, *Taiwan: Nation-State or Province?* (Boulder, CO: Westview Press, 1990), p. 8. Although individual Hakka have risen to prominence in the political system of Taiwan, as a group the Hakka have not significantly influenced the politics of the island by expressing communal political demands.

21. This question pertains more to the place from which one's father comes—the place one considers the province of family origin—rather than the actual spot where one was born or raised.

22. See Hsiao Hsin-Huang (Michael Hsiao), *Sheng-chi jen-ting yü sheng-chi wen-t'i* (Provincial Identification and the Problem of Provincial Origin), in Chung-yang yen-chiu yuan, *T'ai-wan ti-chu she-hui i-hsiang tiao-ch'a,* Academia Sinica, January 1991, pp. 42–43.

23. See Tien, *The Great Transition,* p. 85. For a comprehensive discussion of political parties in Taiwan, one may wish to read Tien's fourth chapter. It should also be noted that in 1991 Taiwanese continued to speak of the KMT, and therefore the government, as dominated by Mainlanders who have made token, but not thoroughgoing, reforms. While it is true that a majority of the ruling party is Taiwanese, of the most powerful 120 positions in the government apparatus, 77 of the posts are held by Mainlanders. See Chen Jou-chin, "Premier's Version of Taiwanization Challenged," *Hsin Hsin-wen* [The Journalist], no. 224, June 30, 1991, in JPRS-CAR–91–057, October 18, 1991, pp. 40–42.

24. Cheng and Haggard offer very useful definitions of these terms. They write:

> With the KMT, it is useful to distinguish between "hard-liners" and "soft-liners." The hard-liners included party cadres in the internal security apparatus who were concerned with the potential social disorder accompanying political change and the old guard, who defined the KMT's mission in conservative terms: staunch anti-communism abroad, continued commitment to recapturing the mainland, and KMT dominance and "tutelage" at home. The soft-liners included younger cadres in the Department of Organization, a division responsible for conducting elections and intraparty affairs, and newer, Taiwanese recruits throughout the party. See Cheng and Haggard, "Regime Transformation in Taiwan," in *Political Change in Taiwan*, Cheng and Haggard, eds., p. 12.

25. Before the initiation of liberalization, there were three political parties: the KMT, the Young China Party (YCP), and the Democratic Socialist Party (DSP). All three were formed on the mainland before 1949, but the YCP and the DSP on Taiwan have remained small parties of Mainlanders with little political clout. Since 1987, there has been a proliferation of political parties. During 1991, there were sixty-eight different parties, but, other than the KMT, the only party with any real political influence was the DPP, which, at the end of 1990, had slightly more than 20,000 members. See Tien, "Transformation of an Authoritarian Party State," p. 45, n. 35.

26. Tien, *The Great Transition*, p. 101.

27. "The Charter of the *Kuo Min Tang* of China," Article II, in Department of Cultural Affairs of the Central Committee of the *Kuo Min Tang*, ed., *Getting to Know the KMT: The Nationalist Party of China* (Taipei: China Cultural Services Co., Ltd., 1989), vol. 2, p. B–4.

28. Chen Charng-ven (C.V. Chen) expressed this view passionately by saying:

> I'm for reunification of China. I know unification is extremely difficult if not im-possible. Yet, on the other hand, I do know I am Chinese—by history, by blood, and also by [my] ideal[s]. . . . I know that if China could be united under a system comparable to what we have now [on Taiwan] . . . with freedom for the people . . . be it economic, political, or social . . . all Chinese, be it on Taiwan or on [the] mainland, [would] have a great future. . . . But, I am not blind to the fact that if China is . . . ruled by the same leaders [they have now], we have a problem. But, I'm hopeful that if we all work hard, we may achieve something, not only for us [in] this generation, but also for the generations to come. That is the belief I have, that is the hope I have. Whether or not I will succeed, God knows, but I think that at least it is worth trying. What do we stand to lose? . . . We stand to lose very little, but [have] something to gain. Yet, on the other hand, if we now say we should go independent . . . that is really too provincial . . . if not irresponsible.

Interview with Chen Charng-ven, Taipei, June 24, 1991.

29. Typical of the sort of skepticism one hears about the idea of a Taiwanese culture distinct from a Chinese mainland culture is a comment by James Chu, director of the Cultural Affairs Department of the KMT and the party's spokesman. Chu said:

> I have a theory. This hypothesis would have to be verified. . . . I believe a small group of people, when they talk about the difference between the Taiwan culture and mainland culture . . . [that is, in] distinguishing between Taiwan culture and main-land culture there is a political motivation behind it. Okay. In their mind and heart they believe there is no such great difference between Taiwan culture and mainland culture. I believe they know Taiwan culture is rooted in mainland culture.

Interview with James Chu, Taipei, July 4, 1991.

30. Taiwanese speak of their Chinese lineage (*hsueh-t'ung*), acknowledging their ac-ceptance of a "blood-relationship" to Chinese from the mainland.

31. Of course, "overseas Chinese" have for centuries lived in countries other than

China while clinging to their essential Chineseness. The sense that they are "overseas" implies that their real home is China. They may identify politically with Malaysia, Thailand, or Indonesia, but they still view themselves as part of the Chinese nation. Their nationality as Chinese inheres even though they are citizens of non-Chinese states. Not even Singapore, where the majority of the population is Chinese, is really a Chinese state if to be a Chinese state means to occupy territory that, historically, was associated with the Chinese empire.

32. *Tzu-li Wan-pao*, [Independence Evening Post], May 17, 1991, p. 4. See JPRS-CAR–91–039, July 5, 1991, p. 94.

33. Professor Hu Fo suggested two political concepts common to Mainlanders. *I-t'ung* is an ideal that the state, China, encompasses all regions and all ethnic groups under a single, unified moral system. It is a cultural perspective of oneness in which individuality and distinctiveness are surrendered to unity so that virtue may spread to the four seas. *T'ung-i* is the action needed to bring this about after China has been divided.

Hu observed that one legacy of Japanese influence on Taiwan is that Taiwanese no longer abide by the notion of *i-t'ung* and already see themselves as having separate cultural and political identities. Many Taiwanese feel that Taiwan is already independent and that the Mainlanders and government should simply acknowledge that reality. Hu said this practical assessment is unacceptable to Mainlanders whose sense of *i-t'ung* is an emotional attachment not subject to reason. Interview with Hu Fo, Taipei, June 13, 1991.

34. Whether the KMT now sincerely believes in the possibility of an attack by the PRC or whether this is the residue of an earlier ideological creed remains to be investigated more thoroughly. Certainly KMT officials are eager to explain the equation: Democracy + Taiwan Identity = Taiwan Independence + Chinese Communist Policy = PRC Attack on Taiwan. Opposition leaders dismiss these alleged fears of a PRC attack as a ploy to restrain the pace of political liberalization; simply, a way for the KMT to retain power. For a sense of how the KMT regards the threat of attack, see Government Information Office, *A Study of a Possible Communist Attack on Taiwan* (Sanchung: Good Earth Printing Company, 1991).

35. To understand how this imagined identity functions in the case of cultural and political communities, see Benedict Anderson, *Imagined Communities: Reflections on the Origin and Spread of Nationalism* (London: Verso, 1991), chapter one, and Ernest Gellner, *Nations and Nationalism* (Ithaca, NY: Cornell University Press, 1983), chapters one, four, and five. My objective here is to analyze the way in which people in Taiwan view themselves and their relationship to others on the island and across the Taiwan Strait. Readers should know that there is a vast literature concerning the concepts of identity and nationalism that this chapter only hints at, but cannot encompass fully.

36. This thought was suggested by Professor Benjamin Schwartz in conversation, September 13, 1991.

37. If one considers a Chinese-American Methodist from Taiwan and a Chinese Buddhist from Bangkok it is difficult to determine which of the two—if either—is *really* Chinese and in what way they are Chinese when they have other identities, too.

38. I am grateful to my colleague, Lin An-chi, for helping me to understand this point more fully.

39 Rod Hague and Martin Harrop, *Comparative Government and Politics: An Introduction* (Atlantic Highlands, NJ: Humanities Press International, Inc., 1989), p. 32.

40. Hill Gates, "Ethnicity and Social Class," p. 254.

41. According to the *American Heritage Dictionary*, ethnicity pertains to "a social group within a cultural and social system that claims or is accorded special status on the basis of complex, often variable traits including religious, linguistic, ancestral, or physical

characteristics." On this basis, the division between Taiwanese and Mainlanders is really not an ethnic one, but I retain the term here as a shorthand and for consistency with Gates's comments.

42. Hill Gates, "Ethnicity and Social Class," p. 255. As of 1991, these practices were being revised to downplay provincial origin as an official mode of classification.

43. Hsu Hsin-liang, chairman of the DPP, explained what one often hears: that the difference between Mainlanders and Taiwanese used to be quite sharp but in recent years has diminished. Interview with Hsu Hsin-liang, Taipei, June 3, 1991.

44. Edwin Winckler, "Taiwan: Changing Dynamics," in William A. Joseph, ed., *China Briefing, 1991* (Boulder, CO: Westview Press in cooperation with the Asia Society, 1992), p. 165.

45. Interview with Alice Kao (Hui-yü), Taipei, May 24, 1991.

46. Liu Fang, "As People of Integrity, Taiwanese Should Refuse to Watch the Excesses of the TV Series 'Love'," *Tzu-li Wan-pao* [Independence Evening Post], March 11, 1991, JPRS-CAR–91–028, May 22, 1991, p. 109.

47. Many of the old, red-brick family compounds that were constructed by rural families in Taiwan centuries ago are still standing and inhabited. These multigenerational homes are built around a courtyard and oriented so that a pavilion in which the family's ancestral tablets are preserved is the centermost chamber of a generally symmetrical array of buildings. Over the main door to the central pavilion, a place of architectural focus and symbolic import, one commonly finds a plaque on which is inscribed the name of the village on the mainland from which the family originated. Family crypts may also bear an inscription of the location on the mainland from which Taiwanese families came. I am indebted to Wang Ch'ing-yi, a journalist and scholar from Kang Shan Township in Kaohsiung County, for pointing out to me the significance of these architectural features.

48. These generalizations mask a host of more complex attachments as suggested in the short story by Ch'en Li-li, "When Jackals Rule," *Mother Jones*, July 1983, pp. 12–19.

49. Interview with Antonio Chiang, Taipei, May 20, 1991.

50 Interview with Earle Ho, Taipei, June 24, 1991.

51. One second generation Mainlander said that it is possible to tell a Taiwanese even before he opens his mouth. The subject said that body language is different and offered an illustration by comparing the hand gesture used when a Taiwanese indicates the size of an object versus the gesture used more commonly by a Mainlander. This individual seemed to feel it is possible to distinguish Taiwanese from Mainlanders on the basis of demeanor. This sense of the other was expressed by several Taiwanese who claimed to be able to tell who in a room is Taiwanese and who a Mainlander. When I asked for specific details— the things one notices to distinguish the two—the subject demured and said, essentially, "you can just tell." People also indicated that the ability to distinguish between Taiwanese and Mainlanders was easier in the past than it is now.

52. Interview with Alice Kao (Hui-yü), Taipei, May 24, 1991. She pointed out that this attitude toward Taiwanese began to change when she reached junior high school and encountered better educated and more refined Taiwanese. Still, she recalled enjoying the occasional opportunity to accompany a Taiwanese friend to a religious ritual at which there was a lot of praying and eating. Her description suggested that she viewed Taiwanese folk customs as quaint or exotic.

This, of course, is the view of a Mainlander who is one of the political elite. The distinction between the KMT soldiers who followed Chiang Kai-shek to Taiwan and their Taiwanese compatriots is not so clearly a reflection of class differences or social polish. The veterans and their families who live in military villages and retirement homes and the vast cohort of aging single men, who either left wives on the mainland or never married in Taiwan, came from the lowest rungs of China's society before 1949. If one is to measure by reference to social polish, there is probably less of a difference between them and the Taiwanese than between them and the Mainlander elite. All of this is to say that the distinctions between Mainlanders and Taiwanese are simplifications that mask a wide range of actualities.

53. Some second generation Mainlanders who support reunification exaggerate their interest in being considered Taiwanese as a way to undermine the credibility of those who assert that the distinctions between Taiwanese and Mainlanders are a justification for Taiwan independence.

54. He said that after a recent trip from Taiwan to the mainland, he felt more intensely than ever his association with Taiwan and said he would happily fight alongside Taiwanese to defend the island against any assault from the Communists. He fully identified with Taiwan as his home. Still, he hopes that ultimately Taiwan may be reunified with the mainland. Understandably, he asked that he not be cited by name.

55. Interview with Chen Charng-ven, Taipei, June 24, 1991. At that time, Chen was the vice chairman and secretary-general of the Straits Exchange Foundation, a private agency with semiofficial status and a mandate to serve as the ROC's designated liaison to the mainland. Chen was also the director of the Red Cross of the ROC, another private agency that had been used for humanitarian interactions with the mainland, as well as a lawyer in a well-respected international firm and a professor of law at National Taiwan University. In these posts, Dr. Chen has, indisputably, contributed to Taiwan's development, even though he and his critics differ about long-range political objectives.

56. The term used in Chinese to connote the problem is *kuo-chia jen-t'ung*, which one might translate as "national identity" except that it does not really pertain to the nation as "the people" as much as to the nation as "the country."

57. Actually, something rather like this view was espoused by C.V. Chen when he visited Peking under the auspices of the Straits Exchange Foundation. Chen is quoted as saying: "If Taiwan is a part of China, then the mainland is also a part of China; if Taiwan is part of the mainland, then the mainland is also a part of Taiwan. Only when the Chinese in Taiwan and the mainland are added together will China be complete." "Taiwan Feelings, Chinese Heart," *Yuan Chien* [Global Views Monthly] 62, July 15, 1991, p. 123.

58. Interview with Chang Chun-hung, Taipei, May 28, 1991.

59. Letter from Tsiang Yien-si, July 8, 1991.

60. Shaw Yü-ming, *Beyond the Economic Miracle: Reflections on the Republic of China on Taiwan, Mainland China, and Sino-American Relations* (Taipei: Kwang Hwa Publishing Company, 1989), pp. 6–7.

61. Letter from Tsiang Yien-si, July 8, 1991.

62. In their eyes, Taiwan was ruled by China prior to 1895 when it was ceded to Japan. In October 1945, the Japanese on Taiwan surrendered to the forces of the ROC and the island was returned to China. See Ralph Clough, *Island China* (Cambridge: Harvard University Press, 1978), p. 6.

63. This is a moralistic argument based on a selective interpretation of international legal and historical data. Proponents of this view expect that the indignity of China's loss to Japan in 1895 invalidates the Treaty of Shimonoseki, which ceded Taiwan to the Japanese. Despite their willingness to invalidate that treaty, they uphold the Cairo Declaration and the Japanese surrender in 1945. Put simply, this position is: When Japan wins and China loses, the outcome is invalid. When Japan loses and China wins, the outcome is valid.

I am grateful to Professor Alfred Rubin of the Fletcher School of Law and Diplomacy for his instruction about international law in which this style of reasoning seems to arise with regularity.

64. Peter R. Moody, *Political Change on Taiwan: A Study of Ruling Party Adaptability* (New York: Praeger, 1992), p. 39.

65. Interview with Ma Ying-cheou, Taipei, July 3, 1991.

66. Interview with Chen Charng-ven, Taipei, June 24, 1991.

67. Regrettably, the individual who made these observations asked that he not be cited by name.

68. By using the word nation, Professor Ming was somewhat ambiguous about whether he was thinking of the nation as a people or as a country. From his other comments, however, it seems that he meant nation as a political entity.

69. Interview with Ming Chu-cheng, Taipei, March 11, 1991.

70. One high-ranking KMT official summed up this line of thinking by paraphrasing the opening passage of the epic novel *Romance of the Three Kingdoms:* "A world long divided must unite and when long united must divide." Lo Kuan-chung wrote *Romance of the Three Kingdoms (San-Kuo Yen-i)* in the fourteenth century about the period of chaos following the collapse of the Han dynasty in the third century.

71. Interview with Ma Han-pao, Taipei, March 9, 1991.

72. This line of reasoning has spawned its own debates and has frequently been featured as the subject of commentaries and editorials in the press. Some, like Hsu Hsin-liang, say that the reunification of Germany occurred only because both West and East Germany were internationally recognized political entities with equal status and, therefore, it is important to have *de jure* independence for Taiwan as a precondition to any negotiations with the authorities on the mainland. Others, like KMT central committee member Alice Kao (Hui-yü), point out that even though Korea is now divided, the residents of both North and South Korea see themselves as Koreans and are eager for the reunification of their state. Interviews with Hsu Hsin-liang, Taipei, June 3, 1991; Alice Kao (Hui-yü), Taipei, May 24, 1991; as well as James Chu, Taipei, July 4, 1991.

73. Interview with James Soong, Taipei, June 28, 1991.

74. Interview with Yao Chia-wen, Taipei, June 7, 1991.

75. It was revealing that in his explanation about the use of the term *kuo* and third country, Ma used the terms "mainland China" and "Chinese mainland." He reflexively used terms that he had just explained were tainted with political implications he hoped to avoid. This suggested that he has not fully integrated these terminological distinctions into his own vocabulary. Interview with Ma Ying-cheou, Taipei, July 3, 1991.

In this regard, the English-language *China Post* reported that ROC Minister of Transportation Eugene Y.H. Chien commented, "Flights between Taiwan and mainland China will not be called domestic routes or international routes, but will be 'mainland routes' once direct aviation links across the Taiwan Straits are established." See *China Post,* November 27, 1991, p. 1.

76. Richard W. Wilson, *Learning to Be Chinese: The Political Socialization of Children in Taiwan* (Cambridge: M.I.T. Press, 1970); Lin Yu-t'i, *T'ai-wan chiao-yü mien-mu 40 nien* [Faces of Taiwan's Education Over Forty Years] (Taipei: Cultural Division of *Tzu-li Wan-pao* [Independence Evening Post], 1987).

77. Interview with Antonio Chiang (Chun-nan), Taipei, May 20, 1991.

78. Lin, *T'ai-wan chiao-yü mien-mu 40 nien* [Faces of Taiwan Education Over Forty Years], pp. 117–19.

79. *Free China Journal,* January 7, 1991, p. 3.

80. This sentiment was verified by Professor Hu Fo, who said that according to popular opinion surveys he has conducted, people begin to break away from the orthodoxies fed to them by the KMT during a critical period between the second and third years of high school and the second and third years of college. Before that time, children display no signs of challenging the attitudes they are expected to adopt about China. By the time

many complete college, however, they attest to feeling as though they were deceived by the KMT about political and cultural realities. This, Hu says, is the cause of intense anxiety. Interview with Hu Fo, Taipei, June 13, 1991.

81. Interview with Chiu I-jen, Taipei, March 21, 1991.

82. Letter from Tsiang Yien-si, July 8, 1991.

83. Winckler, "Taiwan: Changing Dynamics," p. 165.

84. Ibid.

85. See George Kerr, *Formosa: Licensed Revolution and the Home Rule Movement: 1895–1945* (Honolulu: University Press of Hawaii, 1974); Lai Tse-han, Ramon H. Myers, and Wei Wou, *A Tragic Beginning: The Taiwan Uprising of February 28, 1947* (Stanford: Stanford University Press, 1991); Douglas Mendel, *The Politics of Formosan Nationalism* (Berkeley: University of California Press, 1970).

86. Gellner, *Nations and Nationalism*, p. 39.

87. Ibid., p. 6.

88. Interview with Chang Chun-hung, Taipei, May 28, 1991.

89. For a thorough study of Taiwan's pre-twentieth-century history, see the reprint of the 1903 tome by James W. Davidson, *The Island of Formosa: Past and Present* (Taipei: Southern Materials Center, Inc., and Oxford University Press, 1988).

90. Hungdah Chiu, *China and the Taiwan Issue* (New York: Praeger, 1979), pp. 16 ff., p. 214.

91. W.G. Goddard, *Formosa: A Study in Chinese History* (London: Macmillan, 1966), pp. 262–63.

92. I was frequently told that the Japanese forbade Chinese from studying law or politics. A promising student would be directed to medicine or commerce, and higher education for the best was often available only in Japan. See John F. Copper, *Taiwan: Nation-State or Province* (Boulder, CO: Westview Press, 1990), p. 24. Taiwanese who commented to me about this restriction generally were trying to explain the frustration they felt that for so long they had little voice in their own governance. Mainlanders cited the restriction against Taiwanese learning law or politics as a justification for dominating political and legal affairs in Taiwan for the first decades of KMT rule. They stated that once the Japanese were expelled from the island, the dearth of trained Taiwanese lawyers or public officials necessitated that Mainlanders who had had experience governing in other provinces assume positions of responsibility for the welfare of the island province, especially because it was a time of crisis when there was a perception of imminent attack from the communist-controlled mainland. One source explained that during the Japanese occupation, no Chinese were permitted to hold management positions. Even those who oversaw the crews of laborers who gathered the nightsoil were Japanese. When the Japanese left, Taiwanese were not even capable of managing the collection of human excrement by themselves and were dependent on Mainlanders to re-regulate society.

93. Goddard, *Formosa: A Study in Chinese History*, pp. 164–66. Goddard writes about repeated efforts to oppose Japanese occupation and the wistful poetry and songs composed during the occuption that express a longing for China.

94. According to a front-page story in the English-language *China News,* July 6, 1991, "The government had listed 31,000 Taiwanese drafted into the Japanese Imperial Army before 1945."

95. See, for example, Goddard, *Formosa: A Study in Chinese History,* chapter 9; Gold, *State and Society in the Taiwan Miracle,* chapter 3; Kerr, *Formosa: Licensed Revolution and the Home Rule Movement 1895–1945*; Lai, Myers, and Wei, *A Tragic Beginning: The Taiwan Uprising of February 28, 1947,* chapter 2; and Mendel, *The Politics of Formosan Nationalism,* pp. 16–25.

96. Goddard, *Formosa: A Study in Chinese History*, p. 163.

97. Mendel, *The Politics of Formosan Nationalism*, p. 25.

98. Li-li Ch'en, "When Jackals Rule: A Defiant Year Under Chiang Kai-shek," *Mother Jones*, July 1983, p. 12. Having looked forward to a restoration to the Chinese realm, Taiwanese were disappointed to see the gap between Japanese values and those manifested by the Chinese. Peng Ming-min, a Taiwanese activist, recalls watching the first Nationalist troops disembark at a welcoming ceremony staged by the vanquished Japanese colonial forces:

> The ship docked, the gangways were lowered, and off came the troops of China, the victors. The first man to appear was a bedraggled fellow who looked and behaved more like a coolie than a soldier, walking off with a carrying pole across his shoulder, from which was suspended his umbrella, sleeping mat, cooking pot, and cup. Others like him followed, some with shoes, some without. Few had guns. With no attempt to maintain order or discipline, they pushed off the ship, glad to be on firm land, but hesitant to face the Japanese lined up and saluting smartly on both sides. My father wondered what the Japanese could possibly think. He had never felt so ashamed in his life. Using a Japanese expression, he said, "If there had been a hole nearby, I would have crawled in!"

Peng Ming-min, *A Taste of Freedom: Memoirs of a Formosan Independence Leader* (New York: Holt, Rinehart and Winston, 1972), pp. 51–52.

99. Interview with Chang Chun-hung, Taipei, May 28, 1991.

100. Liu, "As People of Integrity, Taiwanese Should Refuse to Watch the Excesses of the TV Series 'Love'," p. 109. The passage is taken from a commentary about a contemporary television series broadcast on a national television network with ties to the military.

101. See George Kerr, *Formosa Betrayed* (Boston: Houghton Mifflin Company, 1965); Lai, Myers, and Wei, *A Tragic Beginning*, and Mendel, *The Politics of Formosan Nationalism*.

102. Chang Chun-hung, in an assertion that mirrors what Mendel writes, said that in the 1920s and 1930s, per capita income in Taiwan exceeded that of Japan. He argued that the standard of living in Taiwan was much higher than that on the mainland and says that if Japan had continued to rule Taiwan, the current standard of living on the island would be even higher than it is. He labels assertions to the contrary that Taiwan was less developed than the mainland as lies. Interview with Chang Chun-hung, Taipei, May 28, 1991. See also Mendel, *The Politics of Formosan Nationalism*, p. 25.

103. This story was told to me several times in interviews with Taiwanese. I challenged one subject, a responsible figure in the DPP, asking him whether this had really happened. He stated that it had; that people of his "era" witnessed the encounter with their own eyes. The story is also recounted in the autobiography of P'eng Ming-min, a dissident well known in the United States. P'eng, *A Taste of Freedom*, p. 53.

While interviewing two Taiwanese women, one told the same story, which she attributed to her father. The second woman objected, saying that her family did not have running water for many years after the Mainlanders came in the late 1940s. After a discussion, they concluded that there was running water in most cities in 1947, but not in most rural homes. When I expressed to another Taiwanese friend my amusement at the frequency with which I heard this running water story, my friend advised me with some gravity that this story was just one of several illustrations of how much more advanced the Taiwanese were compared with the Mainlanders—implying that this friend, too, abided by the tale.

104. Certainly the mythology of superiority and inferiority is affected by economic status. That is, the Mainlanders who arrived in the late 1940s and early 1950s were

comprised of two distinct groups: the educated, polished, cosmopolitan elite and the simple, uneducated, unwashed soldiers. Taiwanese, too, may be divided into simple rural types and more sophisticated urban elites. Characterizations of Mainlanders and Taiwanese must be calibrated by reference to the status of the one doing the characterization and the one being characterized.

105. Once the KMT officially reassumed control beginning on October 25, 1945,

> Taiwan was treated as though it were Fukien, i.e., a potentially wealthgenerating but relatively peripheral frontier province dangerously exposed to Japanese influence and dangerously populated by what was perceived as a dissident intelligentsia.

See Edwin Winckler, "National, Regional, and Local Politics," in Ahern and Gates, eds., *The Anthropology of Taiwanese Society*, p. 15.

106. Lai, Myers, and Wei, *A Tragic Beginning*, p. 173.

107. Ibid., p. 160. The authors attempt to deal with the wildly divergent claims of casualties in a dispassionate manner. They dispute the claim that the KMT wiped out all of Taiwan's elite and write:

> We can assume that around 325,000 people, or 5 percent of Taiwan's population of 6.5 million or more in 1947, were members of the elite. Even an overly cautious estimate of 1 percent of the population yields 65,000. If we conclude that 8,000 persons at most were killed and that half of that number were members of the elite . . . we can surmise that 0.012 percent of the elite were killed.

Their effort to hold irresponsibly exaggerated claims of annihilation up to the light of reason may be commended. Yet, troubling matters persist. First, although they seem to have arrived at casualty figures in a considered fashion, estimates are inconclusive. To draw conclusions about casualties from an equation in which each factor is merely an estimate leads only to a suggestion of the scale of death involved and is not conclusive. Second, to be drawn into the morbid debate of death tolls, in the way many scholars were in the aftermath of the June 4, 1989, crackdown in Peking, distracts attention from more telling analyses of the mentality of repression in which killing one's own citizens—no matter how many—may be justified as expendable casualties of overriding concerns for ideology and security. Finally, that an event such as the 2–28 Incident is inflated to mythological dimensions is, itself, as significant a clue to the nature of the conflict as is the conclusive resolution to the question: how many died?

108. The precise number of executions, if it was ever known by the authorities, has not been released. Estimates run from a conservative 1,000 dead to an extreme of more than 100,000. An official account says 6,300 and there is a popular conception that approximately 10,000 were executed. See Lai, Myers, and Wei, *A Tragic Beginning*, pp. 155–64.

109. In 1990, a film, *City of Sadness*, won popular acclaim for its startlingly frank depiction of the period of "white terror." The government has gone a long way in recent years to deal with the animosity generated by the 2–28 Incident. While President Lee Teng-hui and Premier Hau Pei-tsun have each addressed the matter in public—a momentous step—and even though an official report about the incident has been issued and plans for a monument to the victims have been announced, Taiwanese activists championing the cause are now pressing for a formal apology acknowledging the KMT's role and for reparations by the government to the families of the victims.

110. Interview with Chang Chun-hung, Taipei, May 28, 1991.

111. Interview with James Chu, Taipei, July 4, 1991.

112. Hsieh Chang-t'ing, "*T'ai-wan ming-yün kong-tong-t'i ti chung-chi kuan-huai*" [The Ultimate Concerns of Taiwan's "Body of Common Destiny"], *Hsin Wen-hua* [New Culture], February 1989, p. 5. I am obliged to Louisa Chiang (Hue-na) for her translation of this and other passages.

113. Interview with Chiu I-jen, Taipei, March 21, 1991.

114. Interview with Chang Chun-hung, Taipei, May 28, 1991.

115. Cultural-anthropologist Li I-yuan suggests that culture encompasses a basic framework for ordering one's relationship to one's self and the universe, which, in many ways, operates unreflexively. At a basic level, Taiwanese are like Chinese from elsewhere in that they abide by notions of fortune-telling (*suan-ming*) because they have the same views of the temporal and supernatural dimensions. They abide by geomancy (*feng-shui*) because they have the same sense of spatial and cosmological dimensions. Their attitudes toward interpersonal relations—in the family, community, and the state—are the same as Chinese elsewhere, as are their attitudes toward food and health. Li suggests that these similarities affirm that the culture of Taiwan is Chinese. Interview with Li I-yuan, Taipei, July 2, 1991.

116. Ch'en Li-li, unpublished manuscript, "When Jackals Ruled," p. 18–19. This passage was among those edited out of the version of this story that appeared in *Mother Jones* in July 1983. Ch'en Li-li is a professor of Chinese language and literature at Tufts University and chairman of the Chinese Language Division.

It is worth noting that the issue of *Dædalus* devoted to the question of contemporary Chinese identity is entitled "The Living Tree: The Changing Meaning of Being Chinese Today." See *Dædalus*, Spring 1991.

117. Ch'en Yung-hsing, *Cheng-chiu T'ai-wan-jen ti hsin-ling* [Saving the Heart of Taiwan] (Taipei: Vanguard Press, 1988); Li Ch'iao, *T'ai-wan-jen ti chou-lou mien* [The Ugly Side of the Taiwanese] (Taipei: Vanguard Press, 1988); Lin Yang-min, *T'ai-wan-jen ti lien-hua tsai-sheng* [The Lotus Rebirth of the Taiwanese] (Taipei: Vanguard Press, 1988); and Sung Tz'o-lai, *T'ai-wan-jen ti tzu-wo chui-hsun* [The Taiwanese Pursuit of the Self] (Taipei: Vanguard Press, 1988).

118. Lin Yang-min, *T'ai-wan-jen ti lien-hua tsai-sheng*, [The Lotus Rebirth of the Taiwanese] p. 5. I am indebted to Piper Tseng for her assistance in translating this and other passages.

119. Lin writes that "Taiwanese should take Taiwan as their one and only country and should also take Taiwan as the fatherland of the Taiwanese ... [t]he Fukienese or Hakka—those Taiwanese who descended from the Han line ... haven't they lived in Taiwan for generations?" Ibid., p. 6.

120. Ibid.

121. Hsieh Chang-t'ing, *"T'ai-wan ming-yün kong-tong-t'i ti chung-chi kuan-huai"* [The Ultimate Concerns of Taiwan's "Body of Common Destiny"], p. 4.

122. These provisions were enacted on May 10, 1948, and lifted on July 15, 1987. They were replaced in 1987 by a National Security Act which critics claimed offered the same sweeping, unregulated powers to the government, but finally, in 1991, the state of emergency was ended with a declaration that the period of mobilization to resist communist aggression had passed.

123. For a sense of this sordid side, see Marc J. Cohen, *Taiwan at the Crossroads: Human Rights, Political Development and Social Change on the Beautiful Island* (Washington, DC: Asia Resource Center, 1988). Cohen's research is presented in a more polemical style than is customary in academic works, but nonetheless provides much valuable information.

124. Arend Lijphart describes in a general sense the approach the KMT employed in its attempt to foster national unity as resulting in the "gravest practical consequences." He writes that:

> Although the replacement of segmental loyalties by a common national allegiance appears to be a logical answer to the problems posed by a plural society, it is extremely dangerous to attempt it. Because of the tenacity of primordial loyalties, any

effort to eradicate them not only is quite unlikely to succeed ... but may well stimulate segmental cohesion and intersegmental violence rather than national cohesion.

Arend Lijphart, *Democracy in Plural Societies: A Comparative Exploration* (New Haven: Yale University Press, 1977), p. 24. Lijphart's theory of consociationalism is taken up in chapter four of this volume.

125. In Chinese, some dialects differ as little as English does between New York and Mississippi. Other dialects are mutually incomprehensible—sounding as different as English and Dutch or German. The dialects of Taiwan—"Taiwanese"—and Mandarin are mutually unintelligible.

126. The region of southern Fukien from which many Taiwanese families originated is south of the Min River. Taiwanese call themselves *Min-nan jen* (people from south of the Min), and the dialect they speak is called *Min-nan hua* (south of the Min speech). Contemporary Taiwanese language evolved from this dialect and other southern linguistic influences. See Copper, *Taiwan: Nation-State or Province?* p. 39.

127. Lin, *T'ai-wan chiao-yü mien-mu 40 nien* [Faces of Taiwan's Education Over 40 Years], p. 114.

128. In September 1991 it was announced that there would be television news broadcasts in the dialect of the Hakka. The three television networks are now required to air daily newscasts that run at least fifteen minutes and must precede or follow those broadcasts in Taiwanese. *China Post,* September 2, 1991, p. 4.

129. Interview with Chiu I-jen, Taipei, March 21, 1991.

130. In the very earliest years after the KMT arrived, teachers still used both Mandarin and Taiwanese to explain material in class. In 1953, the government mandated that neither Taiwanese nor Japanese be used as a language of instruction, and in 1964 a law was passed to forbid the use of Taiwanese in schools or official settings. This was accompanied by a campaign that emphasized the grace of Mandarin and the comparative vulgarity of Taiwanese. See Lin, *T'ai-wan chiao-yü mien-mu 40 nien* [Faces of Taiwan's Education Over 40 Years], p. 114.

131. Americans are often seduced into attributing intelligence, wit, and erudition to speakers of Oxbridge English and falsely assume that all Englishmen speak that way. On arriving in England, one instantly learns that the myriad variations of the "English accent" are not all as pleasing to the ear or even comprehensible.

132. Indeed, the very term Mandarin refers to the court officials with whom foreigners dealt first in the early years of contact with China. Europeans may have mistaken the Chinese of court officers for the standard language of the entire country and, in any event, labeled the dialect with the same name as the office that the court representative held: Mandarin.

133. Interview with Kang Ning-hsiang, Taipei, July 1, 1991.

134. It is now fashionable for Mainlanders to study Taiwanese. Indeed, it has become a badge of honor for high-ranking KMT officials from the mainland to flout their newly found interest in studying Taiwanese. One report in a government-sponsored popular journal wrote that Taiwanese-language courses are even being offered in certain public schools out of concern that "the dialect could someday vanish, since the number of young people who cannot speak Taiwanese has been increasing." The report continues, a bit disingenuously, "In fact, in the 1950s and early 1960s, when the government was working hard to promote Mandarin, use of the dialect in classrooms was strongly discouraged. . . . Even with increased promoting, Taiwanese still faces a long climb to overall acceptance."

As an aside, in the same issue, there was a commentary about the importance of learning how to read critically. The author was concerned that with the relaxation of regulations concerning the press, people would be exposed to a vast array of new ideas in uncensored form. The author advises that one must develop "the ability to tell truth from falsehoods, facts from sheer fabrications and outright deception. One must acquire the ability to either know when something is truly informative or when to suspect that it might be in error—deliberate or otherwise." It is amusing that such advice appears several pages after a statement about Taiwanese that is so fundamentally skewed. See Julian Baum, "Vernacular Vogue," *Far Eastern Economic Review,* August 30, 1990, p. 32; Yu Shiao-min, "Acceptance of Taiwanese Gaining Impetus," and Huang Jen-yu, "Readers Have to Learn to Read Between the Lines," *Free China Journal,* January 28, 1991, pp. 1, 3.

135. Interview with Shaw Yü-ming, Taipei, June 15, 1991.

136. Interview with Alice Kao (Hui-yü), Taipei, May 24, 1991.

137. Interview with Antonio Chiang, Taipei, May 20, 1991.

138. Ibid.

139. Lin, *T'ai-wan chiao-yü mien-mu 40 nien* [Faces of Taiwan's Education Over 40 Years], p. 117.

140. See Hu Chang, "Impressions of Mainland China Carried Back by Taiwan Visitors," in *Two Societies in Opposition: The Republic of China and the People's Republic of China After Forty Years,* Ramon H. Myers, ed. (Stanford: Hoover Institution Press, 1991), pp. 141–58.

141. Interview with Ma Ying-cheou, Taipei, July 3, 1991.

142. Interview with Shaw Yü-ming, Taipei, June 15, 1991.

143. Ma Ying-cheou told of a place in northeastern Taiwan where there was a rivalry between two temple communities whose primary deity of worship is Matsu, a benevolent, female protector of seafarers. Worshipers at one temple went on a pilgrimage back to Mei-chou island off the coast of Fukien, where the cult of Matsu originated, and brought back with them to Taiwan a statue of Matsu. When the statue was installed, the temple became a popular center of worship because people attributed to it a heightened degree of spiritual authenticity. Not to be outdone, worshipers from the rival temple that also revered Matsu went on a pilgrimage to the same island off the Fukien coast and returned to Taiwan with religious icons. Ma recounted how he visited the temple and, on seeing the newly installed icons, asked:

> "Who are they?" "Those are Matsu's parents." I said, "How come Matsu's parents and not Matsu herself?" They say, "Look, Matsu is a very filial person. [She] always obey[s] what the parents say. So, to worship the parents may be even more effective than if you worship Matsu."

Interview with Ma Ying-cheou, Taipei, July 3, 1991.

144. KMT officials vehemently deny any intention to reunify with the mainland as long as the CCP is in control. The whole point of the newly articulated National Unification Guidelines is to map out a policy that appears to be moving toward reunification, but one that is dependent on political reforms and economic development in the PRC that is unlikely to occur under CCP rule. In effect, it is a plan that allows the KMT to say that it is still determined to reunify, but a plan that cannot be effected as long as the current system in the PRC prevails.

145. Indubitably, some high-ranking cadres in the PRC have access to these goodies, too, but the access to privilege in Taiwan probably extends farther down into society than on the mainland.

146. In Benedict Anderson's view, however, even the idea of the Chinese nation must be challenged. Indeed, that which the Mainlander elite refer to as Chinese culture and their view of the Chinese nation itself may be as imagined a community as the Taiwanese nation they so vigorously oppose. Anderson's proposition leads one to question whether

there is in fact a Chinese nation, a Chinese culture, or a Chinese state. If all communities are simply imagined, it is possible that the political and cultural elite have established intellectual constructs to promote a vision of a unified nation, one they alone have the bureaucratic and political power to enforce on others.

Anderson speculates that the vision the Chinese elite wanted to promote was not the "Chineseness" of their civilization. "The Middle Kingdom . . . though we think of it today as Chinese, imagined itself not as Chinese, but as central." It is the visceral conviction that this centrality is real and that there is a cultural elite whose responsibility it is to perpetuate it and keep it vital that informs the cultural policies of the KMT. Anderson, *Imagined Communities*, pp. 12–13.

147. Hague and Harrop, *Comparative Government and Politics*, p. 32.

148. Gellner discusses the transformation of a community by reference to a hypothetical nation called Ruritania. He offers a detailed explanation of the characteristic way in which such transformations take place. Gellner, *Nations and Nationalism*, pp. 58–62.

149. Gellner defends the birth of nationalist sentiments such as those of the Taiwanese, although he ascribes economic causes to their origins. He writes:

> It would be genuinely wrong to . . . reduce these sentiments to calculations of material advantage or of social mobility. . . . [T]his is a misrepresentation. In the old days it made no sense to ask whether the peasants loved their own culture: they took it for granted . . . [but] they soon learned the difference between dealing with a co-national, one understanding and sympathizing with their culture, and someone hostile to it. (Ibid., p. 61.)

150. Ibid., p. 57.

151. Gellner writes that "if the rulers of the political unit belong to a nation other than that of the majority of the ruled, this, for nationalists, constitutes a quite outstandingly intolerable breech of political propriety. This can occur . . . by the local domination of an alien group." Ibid., p. 1.

152. Hakka Chinese, who comprise about 15 percent of the Taiwanese, may see themselves as tied to three nations: their own, the Taiwanese, and the Chinese.

Chapter 2

Taiwanese Society in Transition: Reconciling Confucianism and Pluralism

Hai-yuan Chu

In the near future, Taiwan is going to be an open, pluralistic, and democratic society if the ongoing reforms are not seriously set back. The main features of Taiwanese society today might be summarized as unusual economic growth, reform that is conservative and passive, scattered social movements under political and social control, increasing numbers of autonomous associations or groups, changing values and attitudes with persistent traditionality, increasing anomie or alienation, secularization and religious revival, and identity crisis. In the original plan for writing this chapter, I hoped that I could elaborate on all these features. Unfortunately, given limitations of time, I can only discuss some of the issues.

Satisfaction with Personal Life

According to the Social Attitude-Opinion Survey (September 1990), 79 percent of Taiwan's adults express satisfaction with their personal life in general, while 15 percent show dissatisfaction. Taiwan's adults are very satisfied with the parent-child relationship (94 percent), friendship (93 percent), and marriage (92 percent). On the other hand, they are much less satisfied with their own educational achievement (38 percent), leisure (51 percent), and financial condition (58 percent). Thus, people in Taiwan are satisfied with their social life but much less satisfied, even dissatisfied, with their living standard. The average level of satisfaction for all items relevant to social life is 89 percent, which is

This chapter appeared in *The Chinese and Their Future: Beijing, Taipei, and Hong Kong*, ed. Zhiling Lin and Thomas W. Robinson. Washington, D.C.: The American Enterprise Institute for Public Policy. Reprinted with the permission of The American Enterprise Institute for Public Policy Research.

much higher than that for personal life in general. On the other hand, the average for all items regarding living standard is only 61 percent.

Compared with results from a 1985 survey that had the same set of items, the overall change is slight.[1] Personal satisfaction with leisure activity decreased between 1986 and 1990 by 16 percent, but only a 3–6 percent decrease occurred for the rest of the items, including the financial conditions, and neighborhood and friendship status of the respondents. Thus, the decreasing satisfaction with leisure activity is a significant and substantial change.

Although the residents of Taiwan spend more and more money for leisure and entertainment, the quality of leisure has tended to decline seriously. Official statistics show that 2.2 percent of the total amount spent per capita went for leisure and entertainment in 1974, increasing to 4.5 percent, 5.3 percent, and 7.0 percent in 1980, 1985, and 1988, respectively.[2] Government records also show that an increasing number of people traveled around the world: twelve persons per thousand went abroad in 1980, seventeen in 1985, and thirty-four persons in 1988. However, the domestic resources for leisure activities are limited and are getting worse. The playground area per 10,000 population has decreased from 27.35 hectares in 1981 to 23.65 hectares in 1988. Although four national parks were set up in the mid-1980s, people still do not have enough outdoor space for leisure activities. People's need for improved leisure time has thus become stronger but their resources have become more limited, leaving people dissatisfied with the situation. In the future, leisure will be an increasingly important part of life, with the potential to change life-styles and develop cultural activities.

Although other aspects of the quality of life have changed less significantly, the tendency is clear and meaningful. From table 2.1 it is clear that people in 1990 tended to be slightly more satisfied with the parent-child relationship and with their marriages than in 1985. People are less satisfied with their relationships with relatives and neighbors, however. This trend is meaningful in terms of alienation.

There is a clear and consistent tendency of decline for other items listed in the table regarding standard of living. All the differences between 1985 and 1990 are negative and significant. In other words, people in 1990 were less satisfied with their education, work, housing, health, and financial situations than they were in 1985. The largest difference occurs for the satisfaction with financial conditions (6.6 percent), and the smallest for health conditions (2.5 percent). It is reasonable to predict that people will still be dissatisfied with their education, financial situation, and other aspects of living in the future. Leisure conditions show no signs of improving, and people's need for high-quality leisure activities will be heightened. Thus, the satisfaction with this aspect of living is going to decrease.

Changing Social Attitudes

In the past five years, structural transformation has taken place in Taiwan. People's social attitudes are likely to be affected by this great transformation. In

Table 2.1

Satisfaction with Quality of Life (1985 and1990)

	Satisfied 1990	More satisfied than 1985	Less satisfied than 1985	Other	G^2	df	p-value
Parent-child relation	94.9	+2.5	−1.5	−2.2	.6	2	.729
Marriage	92.6	+1.9	−1.6	−.4	3.8	2	.149
Relation with relatives	86.4	−7.9	+2.1	+5.8	158.4	2	.000
Neighborhood	82.5	−8.0	+.5	+7.4	188.8	2	.000
Health	77.0	−2.5	−1.0	+3.5	147.2	2	.000
Housing	71.8	−2.8	−1.4	+4.1	109.2	2	.000
Working	68.0	−4.3	−4.2	+8.5	170.0	2	.000
Financial	58.4	−6.6	−.7	+5.9	103.9	2	.000
Leisure	52.1	−16.7	+7.6	+9.1	195.7	2	.000
Education	37.6	−4.4	−2.8	+7.2	161.4	2	.000

Sources: Data are from the General Survey on Social Change (1985) and Social Opinion Survey (1990).

Note: G^2 shows the maximum likelihood estimates of partial association by controlling sex, age, education, and marital status.

turn, the changing social attitudes also influence the path and the magnitude of the structural change. For instance, the ongoing process of liberalization and democratization has had a significant impact on individuals' attitudes and values. People have become more open-minded and more tolerant toward different political opinions, and more emphasis has been placed on the need for political reform.

These changing attitudes are the foundation of further democratization. The situation is similar for other social attitudes. Two different surveys reveal the changing social attitudes (see table 2.2, pages 84–85).

Liberalization and Changing Attitudes

The ongoing reform and political change are the very focus of the changing phenomena of Taiwan. The respondents of the two surveys show the changing political attitudes. Generally speaking, liberalization becomes the main theme in the process of political reform. This process affects individuals' attitudes significantly. For instance, fewer people agree with such items as "political decisions

Table 2.2

Changing Social Attitudes, 1985 and 1990

	Agree 1990	More agree than 1985	More disagree than 1985	Other	G²	df	p-value
Bearing hardship leads to success	78.3	−12.5	+6.9	+5.6	324.9	2	.000
For the rich to earn more is good for all	21.4	−10.1	+9.5	+.6	63.5	2	.000
The rich should always be respected	21.9	+5.3	−6.1	+1.3	30.0	2	.000
Political decisions should be made by older men	15.8	−23.1	+27.7	−4.7	488.2	2	.000
National affairs should be decided by the government head	32.9	−9.2	+10.6	−1.4	43.2	2	.000
Violent criminals should be immediately punished	62.4	−.1	0.0	0.0	4.6	2	.099
Different thoughts result in social chaos	62.7	−7.7	+10.1	−2.4	56.0	2	.000
Government should decide circulation of an opinion	32.8	−13.1	+14.7	−1.6	122.0	2	.000
The more interest groups, the less stability	57.9	−8.8	+10.4	−1.7	59.1	2	.000
Parliament's interference leads to poor administration	28.9	+3.3	+2.0	−5.4	12.0	2	.003
It's wrong to ask congressmen to vote for or against an act	42.3	+.6	−.9	+.4	12.9	2	.002
Officials should obey orders rather than serve the people enthusiastically	16.1	+3.3	−.6	−2.7	22.8	2	.000
People change their minds at all times	49.7	+6.5	−1.1	+5.3	13.0	2	.000
Too many decisions have been made to do anything	56.9	−3.8	+3.0	+.8	15.1	2	.000

No trust among people	24.8	+2.8	−4.6	+1.8	33.2	2	.000
Common people can influence public policy	51.4	−6.2	+4.6	+1.6	44.0	2	.000
It is meaningless to be a man	10.7	−1.3	+2.8	−1.6	5.8	2	.055
Do not care about public affairs	39.4	+11.8	−14.0	+2.2	192.3	2	.000
Less contact with neighbors avoids trouble	10.3	−.3	+.2	+.3	.7	2	.691
Social development can be influenced by presenting opinions frequently	55.3	−4.0	+2.4	+1.7	18.3	2	.000
Spirit exists after death	55.3	−5.5	−5.0	+10.4	83.4	2	.000
More people believing in God leads to more stable society	47.0	−9.1	+.1	+8.0	76.6	2	.000
Work hard rather than depend on God	83.1	−3.4	−.5	+3.9	36.7	2	.000
Madness is due to offending God or ghosts	12.9	−1.3	−5.7	+7.0	112.3	2	.000
No criminal charges should be levied against a mentally ill person	32.3	−13.1	+.2	+6.9	135.1	2	.000
Stricter discipline leads to more achievement	18.1	−17.5	+4.1	+13.4	658.1	2	.000
Sufficient freedom is good for development of children	25.5	−15.0	+2.5	+12.4	543.3	2	.000
Like to increase knowledge	80.3	−6.8	+1.7	+5.1	151.4	2	.000
Feel the importance of family when it is left	83.2	−7.7	+2.7	+4.9	133.4	2	.000
Like quiet life with less change	86.4	+.9	−.5	−.4	1.6	2	.442
Like to socialize with relatives	81.4	−7.4	+2.8	+4.6	109.0	2	.000
Like to be self-actualized	70.4	−10.4	+.9	+9.5	224.3	2	.000
Protection is more important than promotion	70.7	−12.8	+2.8	+10.0	235.5	2	.000
Like to experience varieties of living	79.8	−13.5	+4.1	+9.4	344.9	2	.000

should be made by older men" (23 percent less), "government should decide circulation of an opinion" (13 percent less), "national affairs should be decided by the government head" (9 percent less), and "so many different thoughts result in social chaos" (8 percent less).

All these attitude changes demonstrate that the people of Taiwan have become more liberal in the process of structural liberalization. Although a few citizens were liberal before the political reform, more people became liberal after the structural changes occurred. The acceleration of structural transformation is slowed down, however, by the politically "oversocialized" persons who insist on their conservative ideology. The majority of Taiwanese people seem not to be pluralistic, even now. They are afraid of having many different thoughts; they like stability. For similar reasons, the majority of people still believe that the existence of more social groups might hurt social stability. Fifty-eight percent of respondents in 1990 agreed with the conservative argument. Thus, freedom of speech is not firmly established in Taiwanese society. When an authoritarian government limits this freedom, many people accept the argument that it is necessary for reasons of stability.

Some of the people's representatives, elected almost forty years ago, still control three organs of the parliament. They are so old and so loyal to the ruling party that they cannot take responsibility as people's representatives. Some 39 percent of respondents in 1985 agreed with the statement that political decisions should be made by the old representatives, but almost the same number (38 percent) disagreed with the statement. More and more people have become convinced that the old representatives must retire. Thus, only 16 percent of respondents in 1990 agreed with the statement above, while 66 percent disagreed. However, the old representatives have yet to retire. The changing attitude of the people should play a significant role in bringing about a change in this situation.

While significant changes in political attitudes can be empirically detected and statistically tested, therefore, freedom of speech and freedom of association cannot be taken for granted. The majority of people do not support the liberal position under the shadow of possible instability and chaos. Surprisingly enough, 15 percent disagree with the government's right to decide whether an opinion can be circulated; 33 percent, however, feel that the role of the government involves inspection of its citizens.

Alienation

Data on eight items are exactly the same for the two surveys. In terms of statistical inferences, by controlling the effects of age, sex, education, and marital status, changes from 1985 to 1990 can be asserted on six items involving alienation.

More people are feeling powerless and normless. Compared with the response in 1985, fewer people in 1991 thought ordinary citizens could influence public policy (6 percent less) or could affect social development by presenting opinions frequently (4 percent less). More important, 12 percent more people say they do not care about public affairs. In 1985, 28 percent of the people thought that way, but 39 percent felt that way in 1991. Thus it is clear that there is an increasing tendency to feel powerless. This tendency should be carefully examined in light of political liberalization and democratization.

Such results seem to contradict the need for political reform. In other words, while the main purpose of political reform is to add to people's power by liberalizing and democratizing, more and more people feel they are powerless. This contradiction indicates the difficulty involved in carrying out reform or any other expected change. It is possible that when rising expectations cannot be satisfied for long and the establishment holds on to power tightly, people tend to be disappointed but inactive. In fact, in spite of the rapid and tremendous change, the progress of reform has not been able to meet the expectations of the people. Furthermore, the government and its public policies in recent years have become more ineffective under the pressure of released social and political forces.

In a rapidly changing society with a weakening authoritarian regime, the norms in the different areas are being transformed. In the political sphere, the fundamental law and the basis of the institution are in the process of stagnant reform. Newly emerged party politics and social movements forcefully challenge the old norms and values, and there is a dilemma between maintaining power and creating a compromised set of norms. Liberalization and internationalization of the economy are the main policy of the government. The economic strength of the private sector is so energetic that the related regulations cannot be effectively constrained. Many businessmen and industrialists violate regulations and public policies. Thus, the underground economy booms domestically and Taiwan people's investment in mainland China grows. Finally, the social order and norms are in a confusing condition. The crime rate increased around 1986, and various gambling activities have become popular in recent years. In general, people emphasize deregulation in various domains. On the contrary, the government and the conservatives try to emphasize and restore the social order. In sum, social norms and values are changing and are seriously affected by the structural transformation. More important, people are confused by the ongoing change.

Work Ethic and Social Control

Some sociologists and economists suggest that the work ethic of people in East Asia is a main factor facilitating the economic growth in this area, and the majority of Taiwanese people emphasize the necessity of hard work. According to the surveys, in 1985, 91 percent of the respondents agreed with the statement that bearing hardship leads to success. The emphasis on hard work is obviously overwhelming. Nevertheless, only 78 percent of the respondents in 1991 confirmed this statement. The 13 percent discrepancy shows the critical change in the work ethic.

Since 1989, the president and premiers have claimed the seriousness of the problem of public security. The majority of people have been willing to support the suppressive policy of the authoritarian regime. Based on the surveys, it can be stated that people still want to see violent criminals punished immediately. In 1985, the percentage who agreed with this statement was 62.5 percent; in 1990, it was 62.4 percent. This consistent attitude shows the conservative orientation toward the strategy of social control. In another survey conducted in 1990, two-thirds of the respondents stated that criminals should be executed in public. Traditional ideas about legal justice thus seem to persist.

Social Problems

According to a survey conducted in 1990, the following ten social problems are rated as most serious:

Problem	Respondents rating problem serious
Juvenile delinquency	83%
Transportation	82
Public security	79
Environmental pollution	77
Vice and prostitution	73
Getting elected by bribery	72
Speculating	70
Poor–rich discrepancy	69
Rising prices	69
Gambling	66

At least two-thirds of the respondents rated these problems as serious. In addition, seven other problems were rated as serious by over half of the respondents. These were moral degeneracy (63 percent), corruption (60 percent), politicians colluding with the rich (58 percent), economic crime (58 percent), providing for the aged (56 percent), social welfare (55 percent), and consumer protection (54 percent). These problems obviously cannot be ignored. In addition, there are five more problems that can be considered serious: getting higher education (49 percent feel this is serious versus 33 percent who feel it is not), population problems (45 percent versus 38 percent), worker's rights (43 percent versus 34 percent), divorce (43 percent versus 33 percent), and judiciary injustice (38 percent versus 22 percent).

Almost all of the problems listed in the questionnaire are thus rated serious. However, the seriousness of each problem is different. Three major categories can be identified. The social meaning and impact of these problems have different effects on the changing social and political situation of Taiwan. For example, the problem of public security is presumed to be serious by almost 80 percent of the adult population, and government efforts to adopt forceful measures to improve the situation are supported by the majority of people. On the other hand, although 43 percent of people rate the lack of protection of workers' rights as serious, 34 percent rate the problem as not serious. Thus, when workers' movements have been repressed by the government, workers do not get support from the masses. The majority of people tend to accept the argument that frequent social movements hurt public security, and thus hurt the economy.

The Five Most Serious Social Problems

Juvenile delinquency is the most visible and serious social problem. People's subjective feelings can be matched with the objective situation shown by the official statistics. Although the fluctuation of juvenile criminal cases since 1985 has not shown a consistent trend in terms of the proportion of juvenile crime in comparison to criminal cases, juvenile crime has increased in proportion to the population under eighteen. For instance, eighteen children in ten thousand young men under 18 were charged in 1985, but twenty-eight per ten thousand were charged in 1988.

Since 1985 the number of registered motor vehicles has skyrocketed. There were 698 cars per ten thousand people in 1985, but 1,057 in 1988. Traffic jams have become a popular topic among the residents of metropolitan Taipei. Before the transit system is fully constructed, the transportation situation will become even more serious and chaotic. People in Taiwan rate transportation as the second most serious problem (i.e., 82 percent of respondents rate it this way). Again, the subjective rating corresponds to the objective situation.

Since August 1989 President Lee and Premier Lee have repeatedly emphasized the worsening situation in public security. President Lee even unexpectedly nominated a military general to be premier in an attempt to restore public security. Mass media frequently report information relevant to public security, giving it enormous publicity. Such reports have led the people of Taiwan to become even more nervous about the public security situation. However, formal statistics on crime show that public security has not become worse since 1989. In fact, the situation was worse in 1986 but improved in mid-1989 before the president proclaimed the seriousness of the problem. The crime rate in 1985 was thirty-two cases per ten thousand persons, increasing rapidly to forty-nine cases in 1986. Since then the crime rate has declined slightly but continuously. In 1988 the rate was forty-five per ten thousand, and it has improved ever since.

In 1989, 63 death sentences were executed. The total number of death sentences carried out from 1979 to 1988 was less than the total number in 1989. From 1979 to 1990, 156 men were executed, but the total number for 1989 and 1990 was 137. It is clear that the judiciary system cooperated with the administration in trying to reduce the crime rate by imposing severe punishments.

The bubble economy, including speculating on the stock exchange, skyrocketing real estate prices, and collective gambling, came to an end in mid-1990. The whole economy seemed to be in a state of depression. Public security had become a serious excuse for economic troubles for both government officials and capitalists. In addition, after the government was forced to lift martial law, high-ranking officials identified public protests as one of the most important causes of public security problems. For instance, among the ten most important causes cited by the National Police Administration for public security problems, social protest was the second most important. Therefore, restoration of public order has become most important in reinforcing capitalists' confidence. To achieve this political goal, the government has suppressed the people and businesses that have been assumed to be harmful of public security, in addition to suppressing social protest and other social movements. A new authoritarian regime seems to be emerging.

In recent years, the environmental movement has grown fast. Protests and other kinds of collective action occur frequently. Environmental pollution has not decreased, and the new cabinet, which is headed by an army officer, is quite friendly with the industrialists and hostile to the environmental movement. Nonetheless, the people do feel that environmental pollution is a serious problem: 77 percent of survey respondents show their dissatisfaction.

The Bureau of Environment Protection was established in 1987, but the environment is still seriously polluted. The number of days on which the PSI value was larger than 100 was 13.75 in 1986, 17.33 in 1987, and 15.09 in 1988. Water pollution has become an even bigger problem. The proportion of rivers that are not polluted has decreased from 73.7 percent in 1986 to 71.6 percent in 1987 and to 67.3 percent in 1988. Under this unfavorable condition, the government is not willing to adjust the economic policy to reduce the size of industries with high pollution levels. By emphasizing economic growth in a condition of depression, the government tends to repress the environmental movement.

Public security is yet another problem in Taiwan. Some 79 percent of survey respondents indicate that public security is a concern for them. The problem of prostitution has been troublesome both to the government and to ordinary people. Since the mid-1970s the national government has executed several policies to try to solve the problem, but prostitution and its related social problems are still quite serious. At the end of the 1970s the famous Peitou area of prostitution was closed, and the government raised fees levied on several businesses in order to weaken prostitution-related activities, but the size and profits of the business are still increasing. The majority of the business is now conducted less openly, so the problem has become much more serious and complicated.

According to official statistics about sex offenses, especially pornography and prostitution, the situation has been worsening since 1970. In 1971, 298 persons were charged for crimes related to pornography and prostitution; the number increased to 682 in 1979 and 2,088 in 1987. The figures reflect only a small part of the problem. People have begun to feel that pornography and prostitution are invading their private lives, leading various neighborhood organizations and women's groups to protest and try to organize to protect themselves. Seventy-three percent of the survey respondents rate the problem as serious, and only 14 percent suggest that it is not serious.

The Five Worst Social Problems

In the past five years, Taiwanese society has experienced tremendous, dramatic changes that might have meaningful effects on social problems in terms of both the objective situation and subjective experience. Table 2.3 lists data from a 1985 and 1990 social survey on sixteen social problems. Compared with this 1985 survey, seven problems are rated more serious in the 1990 survey (table 2.2). The problem that has become most serious is rising prices. Only 30.5 percent of respondents rated this problem as serious in the 1985 survey, but 69.2 percent of respondents in 1990 rated it as serious, an increase of 39 percent. Other problems with worsening situations are the poor–rich discrepancy (27 percent increase); environmental pollution (25 percent); getting elected by bribery (18 percent); public security (15 percent); transportation (14 percent); and caring for older people (13 percent).

The changes in the respondents' ratings between the two surveys are meaningful because they can be correlated with the corresponding changes occurring in the objective situation. Rising inflation has meant that people feel that commodity prices are rising. Similarly, actual income inequality has increased in recent years, and therefore people feel the widening discrepancy between rich and poor. The Gini concentration coefficient for 1980 was .277 but it increased continuously, to .283, .287, .296, and .303 for 1982, 1984, 1986, and 1988, respectively. Furthermore, increased amounts of currency in circulation have allowed more people to become involved in various money games, such as illegal private lotteries, speculative stock exchanges, and illegal investment companies. It is likely that the discrepancy between rich and poor is actually much bigger than the official Gini coefficients show. When the actual distribution of wealth becomes more unequal and people feel the inequality subjectively, social stability and other social problems might be influenced. In other words, inflation and inequality might contribute to the dissatisfaction of people.

Environmental pollution and public security have been discussed above. Another increasingly serious problem, however, is getting elected by bribery. In 1985, 54 percent of respondents felt it was a serious problem, but in 1990, 72 percent of the people surveyed rated it as serious, an 18 percent increase. Although getting elected by bribery has been a serious problem for a long time, the Kuomintang, the ruling party, usually has more financial resources for winning an election. Facing strong challenges from the opposition in recent decades, the Kuomintang has tried very hard to stay in power and has spent large amounts of

Table 2.3

Respondents' Judgments on Seriousness of Social Problems, 1985 and 1990

	Serious 1990	More serious than 1985	Less serious than 1985	Other	G^2	df	p-value
Juvenile delinquency	83.4	+2.1	−3.5	+1.3	19.7	2	.000
Transportation	81.7	+12.9	−13.2	+.3	102.2	2	.000
Public security	79.1	+15.0	−15.4	+.5	151.0	2	.000
Environment	77.0	+25.1	−24.3	−.8	297.2	2	.000
Vice and prostitution	73.2	+5.3	−4.5	−.8	14.5	2	.001
Getting elected by bribery	72.3	+17.8	−11.2	−6.6	125.6	2	.000
Rich-poor discrepancy	69.3	+26.9	−26.6	−.3	412.8	2	.000
Prices	69.2	+38.7	−38.2	−.5	809.9	2	.000
Moral degeneration	62.8	+6.7	−7.9	+.7	36.3	2	.000
Corruption	59.9	+1.5	−4.4	+2.9	28.5	2	.000
Economic crime	58.1	−10.1	0.0	+10.0	127.6	2	.000
The old are not taken care of	55.9	+12.5	−17.9	+5.5	188.8	2	.000
Entering a higher school	49.3	−9.7	+2.6	+7.0	105.4	2	.000
Population problem	44.4	−26.3	+18.0	+8.4	392.2	2	.000
Divorce	43.2	+3.1	−9.4	+6.1	65.3	2	.000
Unemployment	35.0	−33.4	+22.4	+9.0	536.5	2	.000

money to get its candidates elected. Numerous rumors about bribery were spread during the election in 1989. Since the Kuomintang will experience a continuous decline as democratic reform goes on, the situation will not improve. The Kuomintang will be under ever stronger pressure to give up its unjust, even illegal, strategy.

Secularization and Religious Revival

The majority of people in Taiwan believe in folk religion. Although negatively affected by modern education and other social institutions, folk religion still persists. In the past five years, some secularization has taken place. Few people still believe that the spirit exists after death, for example. In 1985, 53 percent of the adult population felt that the spirit existed, but in 1990 only 48 percent thought so. The decline is similar in the percentage of people who feel that believing in God leads to a more stable society. In spite of such significant changes, however, the majority of people still maintain their religious beliefs. For instance, 48 percent believe that the spirit exists after death while only 20 percent do not. Forty-seven percent insist that the society tends to be stable if more people believe in God, and only 31 percent do not think so. Thus, on the basis of the persistent religious beliefs of the people, government control over folk religion, huge and increasing contributions to religious groups and temples, and large-scale religious activities should be expected to continue.

The strong utilitarian orientation of folk religion motivates people to accumulate as much wealth as they can. When structural conditions are favorable to the development of a capitalistic economy, this utilitarian orientation is enforced and leads to actual accumulation of wealth. Furthermore, the continuing economic prosperity resulting from high economic growth enriches the temples, and in turn, the enriched temples with their new or renovated buildings and great festivals reinforce people's commitment to folk religion with a utilitarian orientation.

The persistent solidarity of local religious organizations is still a major force maintaining local group identity and motivating group action. Furthermore, sophisticated state policy toward folk religion has led to a stable and desirable political situation that facilitates the capitalistic development of Taiwan. Temples and other religious organizations are often integrated into the dominant local political power of the Kuomintang. In addition, the contributions of entrepreneurs and local leaders to local religious organizations, especially to major temples, not only obtains the respect and approval of local residents, but also obscures the boundary and conflict between classes. Religious activities, especially festivals, distract people from becoming involved in political and social protests and help them overlook the repressive political and economic measures of the government.

Despite the strong impact of popular secular humanism represented by modern education, folk religion is still the most popular religion in Taiwan. While the number of believers has decreased, the number of temples, the property holdings of temples, and the extent of large-scale religious activities have increased. Although folk religion in Taiwan will never be as strong as it once was, it will continue to influence Taiwan society.

Buddhism is also an influential religion in Taiwan, but the number of orthodox Buddhists is not large. According to the surveys, 10–15 percent of the adult population can be identified as Buddhists. Nonetheless, Chinese Buddhism has significant influence over those in Taiwan who believe in folk religion. Support for Buddhism grew steadily over the period from 1950 to 1980, and in recent years it seems to have revived.[3] Activities promoted or arranged by Buddhist devotees are becoming increasingly visible. Taiwanese Buddhist groups have successfully played active roles in helping people cope with the worsening social situation. Recently, for example, a huge Buddhist organization initiated by the nun Cheng-yen has emerged, with over one million members committed to charitable and pious deeds. This organization, the Tsu-Chi Charity Enterprise Foundation, set up a huge hospital and a nurse's school in Hualien to serve the people of that remote eastern area, and the fame of the nun and her organization has spread. There are also other Buddhist organizations that have contributed substantially to the development of Buddhism and the society. Many well-educated Buddhists have joined these programs and activities. Taiwanese Buddhism can be expected to be a vital force in Taiwan's changing society and culture in the future.

After a decade of stagnant development, Christianity seems to be in a crisis in Taiwan, with limited hopes.[4] An interdenominational committee has been established to promote Christianity in Taiwan, with a target to double the size of the island's Christian population.[5] According to the plan, an annual growth rate of 23 percent is expected. Realistically, however, such a goal is exaggerated and almost impossible to reach. Although the growth rates of some Protestant denominations have been larger than that of the total population of Taiwan, these growth rates are unstable. In addition, other denominations have smaller or even negative growth rates. From 1950 to the mid-1960s, the Christian churches experienced a wave of strong growth, but since the mid-1960s many churches have shown a tendency to decline.

Despite such decline, however, Christian churches are still influential in the society, culture, and politics of Taiwan. Among high-ranking government officials, the proportion of Christians is much higher than that for the general population. President Lee, who frankly admits that he prays every night, claims that he has had revelations about how to solve his political problems. The Christian organizations of Taiwan are very active in terms of education, medical service, social welfare, and other charitable and sociocultural activities. The impact of the Christian church can thus be expected to continue.

In the 1980s the people of Taiwan faced a rapidly changing polity and society. These changes, including political liberalization, economic growth, and social pluralization, will continue. On the other hand, the essential conservatism of the society and the complexity of the problems being faced will hinder progress. With rising expectations, people tend to feel more powerlessness and normlessness when the reforms are obstructed. Religiosity correlates with powerlessness and normlessness, so religion could help those people who feel powerless or normless cope with the stresses of rapid change. Religion will continue to be an influential force in the changing society.

Notes

1. Yang, Kuo-shu, and Hei-yuan Chiu, eds., *Taiwanese Society in Transition* (in Chinese) (Taipei: Institute of Ethnology, Academia Sinica, 1988).

2. Directorate-General of Budget, Accounting, and Statistics, *Social Indicators in Taiwan Area of the Republic of China* (1989).

3. Yau, Li-shiang, "An Exploratory Study on the Changes of Buddhism in Taiwan since 1950" (in Chinese), ms., 1988.

4. Chiu, Hei-yuan, and Lis-hiang Yau, "On Religious Changes in Taiwanese Society," in *Social and Cultural Change in Taiwan,* ed. Hei-yuan Chiu and Ying-hwa Chang (Taipei: Institute of Ethnology, Academia Sinica, 1986), pp. 655–86.

5. Strickler, Rahn, and Chung-chien Hsia, *The Church in Taiwan: Present Situations and Projections* (in Chinese) (Taipei: Gospel Movement for Year 2000, 1990).

Part II

POLITICAL CHANGE

One of the major results of the socioeconomic change that has altered the nature of Taiwan's reality is political ferment. The truism that a newly educated and prosperous middle class will demand political change has been demonstrated in the Republic of China over the course of the past three decades, since the Daoyutai crisis of 1972. The authors in this section are students of this political change, and each demonstrates his or her insight into the reasons for and the nature and potentials of the process of political transformation that they have witnessed, both close at hand and from afar.

The first chapter in this part is by Yun-han Chu, a political scientist and one of a group of scholars who are redefining the discipline on Taiwan. Chu explores the interaction between the bursts of street protests on Taiwan in the late 1980s and early 1990s and the process of political democratization ushered in by the ruling elites of the KMT even as it was pushed forward by the leadership of the *dangwai* opposition.

Chu begins by placing the island's multidimensional political change within the context of Taiwan's economic modernization. He then places the explosion of protest within the context of Taiwan's recent political development. He shows how the KMT was able to maintain an entrenched political dominance to control politics down to the local level by creating a combination of administrative and representative organs. An elaborate and eclectic ideology and highly penetrating political apparatus serve to keep the KMT in control. Since the regime did recognize the need for the people to play some role, however minor, in the political process, it also provided for an electoral system that was used to coopt the local elite.

As the economic revolution took hold and the populace gained both higher income and higher levels of education, the new middle class began to demand greater control of the political realm and to see how electoral politics could be used to obtain this end. As a result, politics became more complex and more useful as a means of expanding the power of the middle class. The key moment in this transformation came in the late 1970s when an informal political opposition, the dangwai, took shape. The dangwai challenge came at a time when the regime was especially vulnerable. Although the government held the opposition in check in late 1979 by making use of the military force that lay at the base of its real power, it eventually lost its resolve to use its weapons of repression, and by the late 1980s a transition to a more open, multiparty system began.

Chu narrates this process of political development and then shifts to a more theoretical mode to analyze how the new political climate allowed popular demonstrations to become a major political tool. He concludes by demonstrating that seemingly abstract political theory can be used to help understand the nature of the Republic of China's political realities.

Joseph Bosco also deals with Taiwanese politics, but he sees things from the perspective of a political anthropologist. In his chapter on factions, he provides a micropolitical analysis of Taiwanese politics. Bosco's chapter focuses on political life in the township of Wandan as a means of exploring the origins, nature, and significance of factions in Taiwan. He first discusses the literature on the subject of factions, showing where his concept of factions fits in. His basic thesis is that factions are a product of a particular state-society articulation at a particular point in history. He combines an overview of factions and factional politics with a specific discussion of the place of factions within the framework of Taiwan's postwar political history. He analyzes faction membership and leadership, and the relationship between *guanxi* (connections) and the ability of factions to mobilize for elections. The chapter concludes with a discussion of the complex relationship between local factions and the Guomindang.

The third chapter in this section is by Linda Gail Arrigo, who begins by questioning how democratic Taiwan is today and wondering whether the opposition party has been bought off and corrupted by the ruling party. Her chapter is an attempt to answer this deliberately provocative and disturbing question. Her chapter discusses the political culture that now exists on the island, explores the history of the Minjindang and the background of the various factions that make up the Democratic Progressive party, and provides a step-by-step account of party development over the course of 1991.

The three chapters in this section suggest that political life in Taiwan is a complex and multidimensional entity. As seen in the chapters that follow, the vision of a neat and linear progress toward democracy is not reflective of Taiwan's real situation.

Chapter 3

Social Protests and Political Democratization in Taiwan

Yun-han Chu

For a long time Taiwan has been known among students of comparative politics for its economic dynamism and political stasis. But since the early 1980s the political landscape of the island has changed almost beyond recognition. One of the most salient aspects of the political change taking place in the last few years has been the sudden upsurge of organized contentious collective actions in the form of citizen petitions, demonstrations, wildcat strikes, civil disobedience, and riots—almost two reported incidents a day in 1987.[1]

Only a few years ago, incidences of organized protest that pressed demands on the authorities were few and far between. In the past, few segments within Taiwanese civil society escaped the immediate control of the authoritarian regime. But recent years have witnessed an explosion of autonomous social mobilization throughout the society. In its most ostensible form, it manifested itself in the outburst of reported incidents of social protest, which increased from 143 in 1983, the year the data series begins, to 676 in 1987 (see table 3.1).[2] Contentious collective actions as a means of pressing collective demands have proliferated into all kinds of issue areas and spread across the island within a very short time span. Most notably, four major types of social protest have emerged in recent years—political, environmental, economic, and labor (see table 3.2).[3] Except for political protests, which were typically organized by the political opposition, most types of social protest were initiated by ordinary citizens making claims over issues of livelihood.

This chapter explores the interplay between the assertion of autonomous social forces in the form of social protests and the process of political democratization, a process that has been pushed forward by the political opposition as well as

An earlier version of this essay first appeared in *The National Taiwan University Political Science Quarterly Review* vol. 1, no. 1 (March 1990): 65–88.

Table 3.1

Reported Frequencies of Social Protest Incidence in Taiwan, 1983–1987

Year	1983	1984	1985	1986	1987	Total
Frequency	143	183	243	271	676	1,516
Growth rate	—	28.0%	32.8%	11.5%	149.4%	

Table 3.2

Reported Frequencies of Social Protest Incidence in Taiwan by Type of Issue, 1983–1987

Issue	1983	1984	1985	1986	1987	Total	Col. Percent
Political							
Frequency	5	4	20	35	106	170	11.2%
Growth rate	—	–20.0%	400.0%	75.0%	202.9%		
Environmental							
Frequency	43	61	34	78	167	383	25.3%
Growth rate	—	41.9%	–44.3%	129.4%	114.1%		
Economic							
Frequency	57	72	89	101	257	576	38.0%
Growth rate	—	26.3%	23.6%	13.5%	154.5%		
Labor							
Frequency	20	37	85	38	63	243	16.0%
Growth rate	—	85.0%	129.7%	–55.3%	65.8%		
Other							
Frequency	18	9	15	19	83	144	9.5%
Growth rate	—	–50.0%	66.7%	26.7%	336.8%		

ushered in by the ruling elite.[4] This chapter examines the impact of political democratization on the recent upsurge of contentious collective actions and evaluates the implications of this development for the political transition process.

The Political Setting of the Explosion of Social Protest

In comparative perspective, Kuomintang (KMT) one-party rule in Taiwan is distinctive among third world authoritarian systems in two important aspects: First, the KMT regime on Taiwan is one of the few entrenched authoritarian regimes that have effectively combined political stability with successful economic development in the postwar era. The KMT regime has enjoyed undisrupted rule for almost four decades in a context of a dynamic industrialization and social transformation. Second, in the contemporary era, few authoritarian regimes in developing countries have been able to do without some form of democratic facade,[5] but since its initial consolidation on Taiwan, the KMT regime has relied very little on democratic legitimacy for its rule.

The KMT regime in Taiwan entered the 1970s with a proven formula for maintaining the entrenched political dominance of the mainlander elite at the national level and for controlling a limited popular electoral process at the local level. Formally the KMT state maintained a complicated five-branch (*yuan*) national government, with a functioning legislature claiming to represent all the provinces of China with its life-term members elected in 1948 on the mainland. It also intentionally retained a cumbersome four-tier administrative system designed for all of China, from the national down to provincial, county/city, and town/borough levels. Limited home rule was implemented in 1950. Native Taiwanese were allowed to elect their own representatives up to the provincial level, and executive officials up to the county/city level.

But under the surface, the KMT maintained a stable political order through an elaborate ideology akin to socialism, a cohesive and highly penetrating party apparatus organized along Leninist democratic centralist lines, and a powerful, pervasive, but less visible security apparatus reinforced by martial law. The official ideology, Sun Yat-sen's eclectic "Three Principles of the People"—nationalism, democracy, and people's livelihood—advocated the commensurability of the interests of the capitalist class and working class, the need for regulating private capital, and the advancement of state capital. Through their exclusive control over such socialization agents as schools and mass media, the mainlander elite constructed an ideologically indoctrinated popular coalition where all members of society believed that the KMT state embodied the interest of all classes and that they had a stake in preserving the political status quo.[6]

The party apparatus consisted of cross-cutting functional units organized along both regional and corporatist (sectorial) lines. At the grass-roots level, the KMT utilized the existing social structure to establish complex local political machines built on patron–client networks within the party structure throughout the island. Within each administrative district below the provincial level, the KMT nurtured and kept at least two competing local factions striving for electoral offices and other public offices in such quasi-state organizations as Farmer Associations, Fisherman Associations, Irrigation Associations, Produce Cooperatives, and, more important, for a share of region-based economic rents in the nontradable goods sector to be distributed by the party-directed local spoils system.[7] Above the local level, the KMT controlled and demobilized all modern social sectors through preemptive incorporation of business and professional associations, labor unions, state employees, journalists, intellectuals, students, and other targeted groups. Few autonomous social forces escaped the immediate control of the authoritarian order. The party apparatus filled up all the political space in the society, and party membership reached almost 15 percent of the entire adult population. Also, the KMT captured the rents created by natural monopoly and governmental procurement at the national level and used them to cushion the economic security of their loyalist mainlander followers. Finally, wherever indoctrination or cooptation failed, the security apparatus picked up. Under the rule of martial law, the security authority was prepared to suppress even a hint of political stirring. For almost three decades of its rule, the KMT faced a very unorganized and weak political opposition consisting primarily of defiant local factions that had no national political aims and posed little threat to the KMT's dominant position. Thus for an extended period of time, the ruling elite saw no pressing need for even a limited electoral opening at the national level.

Initially, the electoral system was installed by the emigrant regime at the local level to coopt the native elite and incorporate existing local patron–client networks into a superimposed party apparatus. A series of developments, however, have gradually transformed both the nature and the significance of the electoral process.

First, as it evolved, the election has become the major institution to assimilate emerging economic and social forces into the political system. Facing recurring electoral challenges, the party-sanctioned local factional networks are more adaptive than the formal party apparatus to socioeconomic changes. When traditional clientelist networks could no longer deliver votes as effectively as they once did, faction-centered or candidate-centered clientelism was expanded to incorporate more secondary associations and regional business concerns, especially in rapidly urbanizing areas. Also, more and more new contenders were drawn into the electoral process to seek political access and economic privilege, since electoral success could be readily translated into instant social prestige and handsome economic gain. With an ever-expanding economy, both the cost and the stakes of elections became ever greater for the established factions. Thus as more social resources were mobilized into the electoral process, elections became more institutionalized. Elections became the institution in which the local political elite found their self-identity and on which the entire local power structure rested. Increasingly, the national ruling elite found out not only that they could not do without elections, but that they had to deal with the rising pressure from both inside and outside the party for electoral openings at a higher level.

Another unavoidable political consequence of rapid socioeconomic changes has been the rise of a new breed of political opposition in the elections. With rapid urbanization, diffusion of education, and a general rise in material well-being, the opposition, who dared to initiate a challenge to the legitimacy of the KMT regime, have found more and more open ears among an increasingly articulate, self-assured, and economically secure electorate. This development culminated in the local election of 1977, in which a loosely coordinated opposition group, bearing the label of *dangwai* (outside the party), made considerable gains in contesting local and provincial electoral offices. Since 1977, more and more activists have dared to test the permissible limits of public defiance of political taboos. The opposition has turned the campaign process into an effective medium of "resocialization" for fostering the growth in popular demands for democratic legitimacy. On the other hand, it has become increasingly costly for the ruling elite to use repressive measures against popularly elected opposition leaders. To do this, the KMT regime had to pay a considerable price at the cost of its own legitimacy, as the ruling elite soon found out in the aftermath of the Formosa incident, in which a number of prominent dissident leaders were prosecuted and jailed for treason. The incident also precipitated great political strain on the political system. After a temporary period of disarray, *dangwai* members soon regrouped and regained their electoral momentum. Building on increased electoral backing, the opposition became even bolder in their political demands.

Drastic changes in the external environment also compelled the ruling elite to become more responsive to the rising popular demand for political opening. During the 1970s a series of diplomatic setbacks, including the loss of Taiwan's United Nations seat to the People's Republic and derecognition by major allies, severely undermined the KMT's claim to be the sole legitimate government of China. A series of peace overtures initiated by the PRC in the late 1970s and the emerging détente atmosphere in the Taiwan Strait also began to melt down the "besieged mentality" among the public. Thus the KMT elite felt the need to turn inward and to rely more on the legitimating function of electoral institutions. Thus limited electoral opening of national representative bodies was first instituted in 1972 and expanded in 1980. But the overall institutional arrangements retained the necessary design to ensure that the opposition that emerged in the election and the competition it brought about would in no way pose a real challenge to the regime.

The limited opening of national representative bodies to electoral contests provided a fertile ground for the formation of an islandwide coalition among independent candidates with national political aims. Also, increased electoral support has emboldened the opposition to break the legal limitations on their organizational growth. Since 1979 the opposition has moved cautiously toward forming a quasi-party despite stern warnings from the government of its resolve to enforce the legal ban. After a temporary setback in the aftermath of the Formosa incident, the opposition regrouped and united under various forms of quasi-party organization.[8] Also, beginning in 1984 the *dangwai* gradually stepped up their push for democratic changes in ways never before tolerated. They organized mass rallies, staged street demonstrations, and engaged in other kinds of confrontational strategies to undermine the political support for the KMT regime on three fronts: at the levels of political community, political regime, and policy performance.[9] They confronted the regime on the sensitive issues of constitutional reform, Taiwanese identity, and self-determination. Facing the opposition's intensified challenge, the KMT regime evidently lost its resolve to use repressive measures against the opposition, especially during the last two years of Chiang Ching-kuo's tenure (1985–86). Thus the opposition effectively expanded the public space the ruling elite decided to tolerate at the beginning of the transition. On the eve of the 1986 election, a formal party, the Democratic Progressive party (DPP), was declared in defiance of the legal ban.[10]

In retrospect, the limited political opening that started in the early 1980s clearly has had an effect on loosening the regime's authoritarian grip on society. It ignited a broadly based popular demand for political decompression and started a reciprocal cycle between political liberalization and democratization in the early 1980s. Suddenly the KMT regime found itself reigning over a resurrected civil society that expressed itself in the mushrooming of autonomous social groups breaking out of the corporatist straightjacket and in the upsurge of social protests and all kinds of contentious collective actions. The following section examines the impact of political democratization on social movements in the light of recent literature on social mobilization.

Some Theoretical Considerations

As I explore the interplay between the recent democratic opening and the upsurge of social protest, two questions are particularly relevant: "How" and "Why." The domains of these two questions, and therefore the kinds of answer, are different. "How" questions are concerned with the domain of the possible, whereas "why" questions are concerned with the domain of the actual.[11] The former is dealt with in terms of structural analysis, which tries to answer "How is A possible?" Structural analysis uncovers "tendencies" for structures to be actualized in certain ways but does not directly account for the production of particular events.[12] The latter is dealt with in terms of causal analysis, which tries to answer "Why did A happen rather than B?" and thus takes as unproblematic the possibility that those events *can* happen in the first place.

In searching for answers in these two explanatory domains, two theoretical perspectives are particularly relevant in the analysis of the structural and conjunctual causes for the explosion of social protest in Taiwan: Charles Tilly's comprehensive analytical framework for social mobilization and contentious collective action, and recent literature on transition from authoritarianism.[13]

The conclusion that Tilly has drawn from his analysis of how collective action in Europe evolved under the influence of long-term structural transformation brought about by industrialization can be summarized as follows: Rapid urbanization and industrialization did exert stress on existing social fabrics and stimulate social conflict over the long run, but the changes labeled as modernization had no uniform effects on the level, form, or timing of major bursts of contentious collective actions. Instead, shifts in the struggle for political power explain the timing and intensity of contentious collective actions better than hypotheses based on social breakdown or economic hardship. Major bursts of violent social protest usually accompany large-scale realignments of the political system. Finally, the main determinants of a group's mobilization and possible forms of collective action are its organization and the current opportunities and threats confronting its interest, in particular the possibility of its subjection to the repression of the state. In sum, Tilly's mobilization model directs one's attention not just to the long-term disrupting effect of industrialization but more to the larger political process and the microscopic social settings of protesters.

The emphasis on state power and political process is also brought up by O'Donnell and Schmitter in their analysis of the democratic opening in Latin America and southern Europe. They contend that the opening of authoritarian rule usually produces a sharp and rapid increase in general politicization and popular activation. This explosion has to be set against the background of the success of most authoritarian regimes in depoliticizing as well as atomizing their respective societies. Once the government signals that it is permitting contestation on issues previously declared off limits and is lowering its willingness to use coercive forces, these regimes quickly discover that the so-called peace and consensus were, at best, "part of an imposed armistice."[14] This limited concession is usually forced on the ruling elite by the effective mobilization and confrontational political strategies of the political opposition. Other groups from a rather different segment of the society also take rapid advantage of political liberalization. Once most social actors learn that they can engage in collective actions at lower cost to themselves and their followers, an enormous backlog of grievance, anger, and conflict long repressed or ignored by the authoritarian rule is unleashed and results in an explosion of grass-roots organizations and contentious collective actions.

Against this theoretical backdrop, one can consider the social and political sources of the recent burst of social protest on the island in two domains. In the domain of structural analysis, the recent upsurge of contentious collective actions in Taiwan should be understood as a result of a number of structural factors—the social conflict and social mobilization brought about by the island's rapid industrialization in the last three decades, the structural characteristics of the authoritarian state itself, and the facilitating effect of the existing social fabric at the communal level.

In Taiwan, as in many other developing societies, industrialization and urbanization as a long-term force stimulated social conflicts. New forms of production relations generated a structural situation of potential conflicts between modern economic actors, in particular between the capitalists and the workers. Also, popular grievances held by the victims of many forms of negative externality of production and consumption accumulated rapidly in the process of growth-first industrialization. This was further aggravated by increased social density of exchange, interaction, communication, and interdependence in a highly compact ecological environment.[15] A general rise in education level also increased the level of awareness among the masses of the complex causal mechanism that bears one's own interest or the interest of other contenders. All of the aforementioned conflict-prone changes have taken root in Taiwan's rapid industrialization.

Next, some inherent features of the state structure are also possible structural sources of the outbreak of popular discontent. One of the weaknesses of one-party authoritarian rule is the underorganization of secondary associations, most of which are not functional under the KMT's strict control. Thus the inability of functional intermediaries to translate popular discontent into effective policy responses has been an enduring feature as well as a weakness of the political system. With the arrival of an articulate and partially mobilized civil society, the ruling elite is constrained by a lack of an effective organizational instrument to assimilate these emerging social forces into the institutionalized political process. In many cases, the existing local factions can hardly make up the void. Next, the organizational characteristics of the state apparatus also constrain the capacity of the state to respond effectively and in a timely fashion to emerging popular demands and thus prevent a backlog of popular discontent from accumulating. The cumbersome multilayer state administrative apparatus that the KMT elite insisted on tends to reduce the state's capability to group the acuteness and urgency of popular discontent at the grass-roots level. At the same time, over-centralization of power and resources at the national level leads to severe undercapacity of local governmental agencies. As the society becomes more industrialized and urbanized, increasingly it shows signs that the state apparatus as a whole just cannot keep up with the magnitude and complexity of social problems at hand in terms of institutional design, personnel competence, and disposition. Furthermore, the proliferation of local rent-seeking factions in local politics has skewed the quality of public policies intimately affecting the livelihood of common people. Local authority becomes highly susceptible to particularistic demands, which usually involve extra-legal or illegal economic privileges. This erodes the popular faith in the impartiality of public authority. These structural tendencies for contentious collective actions, however, have seldom been actualized in the past under the highly restrictive political environment.

Effective collective actions always require organization. Thus it is necessary to identify certain features of the micro-socioeconomic setting in Taiwan society that are conducive to the organization of collective actions at the local level. Most small-scale collective actions, which were typical in the early phase of the recent upsurge, benefited from the existing organizational endowment commonly found at the communal level in both rural and urban areas. Specifically, the long-standing hierarchy and social networks in the local community, in the form of lineage ties, brotherhood gangs, workshop circles, and local factions, are crucial. These existing organizational endowments minimize the free-rider problem in organizing effective collective action and provide instant leadership. For all reported incidents of social protest during the 1983–87 period, in at least 45 percent the participants shared lineage, communal, religious, or factional ties.[16]

While it is part of a complete explanation of actual events, the structural explanation has its limits. It explicates the *possibilistic* relationship between structural factors, on the one hand, and the explosion of social protest, on the other. However, it hardly explains the timing and intensity of social protest. Most of these conditions that are conducive to the outbreak of contentious collective actions existed long before the actualization of social protest in the 1980s. What is missing in the complete explanation is the more immediate antecedent of the upsurge of social protest. In the domain of historical analysis, the timing and intensity of the recent burst of social protests, I argue, can be better explained by the perceived erosion by the social actors of the willingness of the state elite to use coercive forces against open defiance of public authority. Specifically, the *dangwai* agitation spearheaded the whole process as it continued testing the will and resolve of the state elite and the limits of its toleration. Moreover, with the political opposition in the forefront of challenging the authoritarian order, other social actors might have perceived a strategic opening for exerting their claims, as the government concentrated its coercive resources on meeting the more obvious threat to its authority.

Statistical Evidence for the Contagious Effect of
Political Protest on Other Types of Social Protest

The preceding argument about the direct impact of political protest on other types of social protest can be recast in terms of the vector autoregression (VAR) framework.[17] A four-variable VAR model can be constructed as follows:

$$
\begin{Bmatrix} \text{Political}_t \\ \text{Environment}_i \\ \text{Economic}_t \\ \text{Labor}_t \end{Bmatrix} = \begin{Bmatrix} A_{11}(B)\ A_{12}(B)\ A_{13}(B)\ A_{14}(B) \\ A_{21}(B)\ A_{22}(B)\ A_{23}(B)\ A_{24}(B) \\ A_{31}(B)\ A_{32}(B)\ A_{33}(B)\ A_{34}(B) \\ A_{41}(B)\ A_{42}(B)\ A_{43}(B)\ A_{44}(B) \end{Bmatrix} + \begin{Bmatrix} \text{Political}_{t^{-1}} + e_{1t} \\ \text{Environment}_{t^{-1}} + e_{27} \\ \text{Economic}_{t^{-1}} + e_{3t} \\ \text{Labor}_{t^{-1}} + e_{4t} \end{Bmatrix}
$$

Note: A_{ii} is a vector of coefficient parameters where
$A_{ii}(B) = A_{ii1} + A_{ii2}B + A_{ii3}B^2 + \ldots$
B is the backward shift operator
e_{1t} is the residual white noise series

One of the functions of the VAR system is to assess the causal interdependence, in the sense of Granger causality,[18] among the variables. My arguments about the relation between political protest and other types of social protest revolve around all four equations in the system. The first equation assesses the impact of the past history of environmental, economic, and labor protests and of political protest itself on the current level of political protest. One can verify whether changes in the reported frequencies of environmental protest, economic protest, and labor protest have a lagged impact on the ebb and flow of political protests by assessing the joint statistical significance of A_{12}, A_{13}, and A_{14}, respectively. F tests or specially constructed likelihood ratio tests can be used for this purpose.[19] Similarly, the joint statistical significance of A_{21}, A_{31}, and A_{41} can be used to assess the causal dependence of environmental protest, economic protest, and labor protest on the past history of political protest. The discussion can be extended to other A_{ii} in the matrix of VAR coefficients in a straightforward fashion.

Based on the above characterization of the interplay between political liberalization and social protests in Taiwan, it can be expected that the F statistic for A_{21}, A_{31}, and A_{41} is significant, and all statistically significant regression coefficient estimates in vector A_{21}, A_{31}, and A_{41} carry positive signs, or substantively, the faster the rise in the level of political protest, the more frequent the social protests centered around environmental, economic, and labor issues. This also means that political protest is causally prior to other types of social protest. In addition, I expect that the F statistic for A_{12}, A_{13}, and A_{10} will be insignificant. This means I expect that the overall impact of past history of other types of social protest on the current level of political protest should be negligible. In other words, political protests tend to precipitate more types of social protest at a later time, but not vice versa. There is no prediction for A_{23}, A_{24}, and A_{34} or A_{32}, A_{42}, and A_{43}, or causal interdependence among environmental, economic, and labor protests. Finally, since we have no prior knowledge about what lag structure best characterizes the relation, we will have to determine the appropriate lag length empirically.

I fit this four-factor VAR model in the monthly time series data for the period from January 1982 to December 1987.[20] All series were checked for stationarity as required by the VAR model. First differenced values of each series, instead of original scores, were used in the estimation. Since the same right-side variables appear in all four equations, one ordinary least square method is used to fit the model.[21] Preliminary investigation reveals that two lags of each variable should be included in the model.[22] The results of the Granger causality assessment are summarized in table 3.3.

According to the F statistic, among the four monthly indices of different types of social protest, the past changes in the reported frequency of political protest help predict the current level of environmental protest, economic protest, and political protest itself. The significance level of the F statistic for A_{41} is close to .05,[23] which suggests that the level of political protest also has some lagged impact on the level of labor protest. The overall effect is on the border line of being statistically significant.[24] The two lagged regression coefficient estimates in vector A_{21} both carry positive signs. The same applies to A_{31}. The F statistic

Table 3.3

Assessment of Causal Independence Between Different Types of Social Protest: Monthly Time Series, January 1982 to December 1987 Vector Autoregression Version of the Direct Granger Method

		Past History of			
		Protest for political issue	Protest for environ-mental issue	Protest for economic issue	Protest for labor issue	
	R^2	$F_{2,45}$	$F_{2,45}$	$F_{2,45}$	$F_{2,45}$	Q_{21} (P)
Current Level of:						
Political protest	.69	35.34**	.43	1.63	.05	22.0 (.40)
Environmental protest	.43	6.71**	6.82**	2.59	2.41	16.9 (.71)
Economic protest	.38	4.94**	.55	3.89*	.31	14.1 (.86)
Labor protest	.41	3.01	.67	.37	11.02**	19.3 (.56)

$*P < .05$
$**P < .01$

for coefficient estimates in vectors A_{22}, A_{33}, and A_{44} are all significant. This means the current level of environmental, economic, and labor protest, respectively, is influenced by its own past history. On the other hand, the F statistics for A_{12}, A_{13}, A_{14} are all insignificant. This suggests that as long as its own past history is taken into account, neither the immediate history of environmental protest nor of economic protest nor that of labor protest helps predict reported frequencies of political protest. Overall, the VAR analysis provides strong statistical evidence to support the argument that a rise in the reported frequencies of political protest tends to bring about a higher level of other types of social protest, but not vice versa.

Lastly, the detected nonstationarity in each of the four time series begets substantive explanations. Nonstationarity can be understood as the result of certain endogenous dynamics within each type of social protest. These endogenous dynamics might involve the spillover effect of some established grass-roots organizations that continue to agitate other, like-minded people with their existing mobilization resources. Also, through diffusion or other mechanisms, the positive responses or concessions that the protesting groups usually got from the authorities simply invited more similar collective actions or more contentious forms of social protest.

Conclusion

The data clearly suggest that the recent bursts of social protest were encouraged by the intensified confrontation staged by the political opposition against the KMT regime. This answers only part of the larger question. The political consequences of the burst of social protest are also of interest here. They can be evaluated along two lines of analysis. First, it can be convincingly argued that the outburst of social protest widens the cracks of the existing authoritarian order, creates potential resources for the political opposition to exploit, and thus tends to hasten the process of political liberalization. Direct evidence for this line of analysis is not difficult to come by. Evidently the KMT regime was compelled to respond to these developments in recent years with an accelerated "Taiwanization" within the party's power structure and a general political decompression culminating in the lifting of the martial law and other longtime political bans at the end of 1986.

On the other hand, one might also ponder whether the recent upsurge really weakened the authoritarian order and if the state power has been substantially pushed back. Is the strong state in retreat or just in the process of repositioning itself? The responsive and adaptive strategies of the state elite in other areas seem to suggest that the incumbent elite is trying to protect the authoritarian core from popular control while liberalizing and democratizing the system at the margins. To this end, it has reorganized the state administrative apparatus and revitalized the existing corporatist structure. New state agencies, such as Labor, Social Welfare, and Environmental Protection, are being created to take over the emerging issues and coopt new social groups. Also, the ruling party has indicated its intention of retaining the Temporary Articles,[25] which protect the apex of state power structure, the presidency, from direct popular accountability. Thus it is still too early to give a definite answer at this point. We have to wait for the transition process to run its full course.

Lastly, one might wonder if democratization in Taiwan will ameliorate social protest. It depends on the development of political parties and the kind of interest intermediation and representative institutions in the making. Alfred Stepan reminds us that a critical question for democratization is how the gap between the new movements based in the civil arena and the organized opposition in the political arena can be bridged.[26] There are no sure signs that the gap will be bridged in Taiwan.

Notes

1. The data set used in this chapter was constructed by a research team led by Professor Ya-li Lu. The data set is essentially a collection of archival event-based time series data covering the period from the beginning of 1982 to the end of 1987. The data are constructed from a content analysis of newspaper reports about social protests in Taiwan.

In recording these events, our research assistants searched through all editions of China Times, one of the two leading newspapers with a circulation over 1 million, to locate news stories about events that fit a standard definition of social protests. We then coded relevant information about the event on a uniform coding sheet. The basic unit of the data set is a record of a dated event described by its qualitative and quantitative characteristics. At the next level, a series of events that involve the same group of participants and the same issue constitutes a social movement. Thus the characteristics of a movement are constructed, by rules of aggregation or composition, from the characteristics of its constitutive events.

2. In this chapter, I define an incidence of social protest as an occasion on which a number of people gather in a publicly accessible place and make claims that are directed toward public authority or any party believed to bear on the interests of the participants. This broad definition includes all kinds of contentious collective actions, from citizen petitions, demonstrations, civil disobedience, and strikes to riots. This rather broad definition of social protest is justified considering the island's highly restrictive political atmosphere during the past four decades. Before July 1, 1987, the day the martial law statute was formally lifted, any public gathering without the government's approval in advance was prohibited under the martial law.

3. For analytical purposes I classify events of social protest by nature of the issue. Environmental protests refer to events precipitated by pollution or the perceived possibility of pollution. Political protests refer to contentious collective actions precipitated by the dissatisfaction with certain features of the existing political structure, institutions, and power configuration or with certain concrete official measures believed to be the consequences of these features. Any protests involving disputes over wages, working conditions, and labor practice regulations belong to the category of labor disputes. Economic protest is a residual category for social protests caused by disputes over the distribution of economic resources other than labor and environmental protests.

4. I share the view of Share and Mainwaring that democracy implies the possibility of an alternation in power. In this sense, a transition to democracy involves more than a liberalization of an authoritarian regime. Democratization refers to the establishment of institutional arrangements—free competitive elections, universal adult suffrage, freedom of speech, of press, and of political association—that make possible such an alternation. Transitions to democracy involve what O'Donnell and Schmitter call "democratization" and "liberalization." See Donald Share and Scott Mainwaring, "Transitions Through Transaction: Democratization . in Brazil and Spain," in *Political Liberalization in Brazil: Dynamics, Dilemmas, and Future Prospects,* ed. Wayne A. Selcher (Boulder, CO: Westview Press, 1986); Guillermo O'Donnell, "Introduction to Latin American Cases," in *Transitions from Authoritarian Rule: Latin America,* ed. Guillermo O'Donnell, Philippe C. Schmitter, and Laurence Whitehead (Baltimore: Johns Hopkins University Press, 1986).

5. Edward Epstein, "Legitimacy, Institutionalization, and Opposition in Exclusionary Bureaucratic-Authoritarian Regimes," *Comparative Politics* (October 1984): 37–54.

6. Thomas Gold, *State and Society in the Taiwan Miracle* (Armonk, NY: M.E. Sharpe, 1986).

7. Edwin Winckler, "National, Regional and Local Politics," in *The Anthropology of Taiwanese Society,* ed. Emily Ahern and Hill Gates (Stanford, CA: Stanford University Press, 1981).

8. Hsiao-fong Lee, *The Forty-Year Democratic Movement in Taiwan* (in Chinese) (Taipei: Independent Evening News, 1987).

9. David Easton, "A Re-assessment of the Concept of Political Support," *British Journal of Political Science* 5 (1975): 435–57.

10. Fu Hu and Yun-han Chu, "Electoral Competition and Political Democratization in

Taiwan," paper presented at the Joint Conference of the Center for International Affairs of Harvard University and the Institute for International Relations of National Cheng-chi University on Democratization in the Republic of China, Taipei, January 1989.

11. Alan Garfinkel, *Forms of Explanations* (New Haven: Yale University Press, 1981): 21–48.

12. Andrew Sayer, *Method in Social Science: A Realist Approach* (London: Hutchinson, 1984): 216–17.

13. Charles Tilly, *The Rebellious Century, 1883–1930* (Cambridge, MA: Harvard University Press, 1975); *From Mobilization to Revolution* (Reading, MA: Addison-Wesley, 1978); Guillermo O'Donnell, "Introduction to Latin American Cases," in *Transitions from Authoritarian Rule: Latin America*, ed. Guillermo O'Donnell, Philippe C. Schmitter, and Laurence Whitehead (Baltimore: Johns Hopkins University Press, 1986); James Malloy and Mitchell Seligson, eds., *Authoritarian and Democratic Regime Transition in Latin America* (Pittsburgh: University of Pittsburgh Press, 1987).

14. Guillermo O'Donnell, "Introduction to Latin American Cases," in *Transitions from Authoritarian Rule: Latin America*, ed. Guillermo O'Donnell, Philippe C. Schmitter, and Laurence Whitehead (Baltimore: Johns Hopkins University Press, 1986): 40.

15. Taiwan is one of the most densely populated countries in the world.

16. Yun-han Chu, "The Social Structural Causes of the Recent Upsurge of Social Protest in Taiwan," in *Public Authority and Social Protest* (in Chinese), ed. Ya-li Lu (Taipei: Ming-teh Foundation, forthcoming).

17. Christopher A. Sims, "Macroeconomics and Reality," *Econometrica* 48 (1980): 1–49; John Freeman, "Granger Causality and Time Series Analysis of Political Relationships," *American Journal of Political Science* 27 (May 1983): 327–58.

18. A variable X is said to Granger cause another variable Y, if Y can be better predicted for the past of X and Y together than the past of Y alone, other relevant information being used in the prediction (Pierce and Haugh, 1976 [source as given]). A thorough review of the concept and its application in political analysis can be found in John Freeman, "Granger Causality and Time Series Analysis of Political Relationships," *American Journal of Political Science* 27 (May 1983): 327–58.

19. John Freeman and John Williams, "Modeling Macro Political Processes," presented at the Third Annual Political Methodology Conference, Harvard University, August 1986, 44–45.

20. I aggregate the event-based time series into monthly time series because incidents of social protest are discrete, rare events and thus might be best analyzed as Poisson outcomes.

21. A check of the Q statistic of the four residual series verified that they are all serially uncorrelated. The correlation matrix of the residuals, however, does indicate that the three economic series are weakly correlated. This should not be of any concern. As long as the same right-side variables appear in all four equations, GLS reduces to OLS. OLS estimator is still unbiased and consistent regardless of the possibility of contemporaneously correlated disturbances (Johnston, 1984: 338 [source as given]).

22. Models with different lag length—two, three, and four—have been investigated. The selection of lag length of two is based on the likelihood ratio statistics, following the method introduced by Litterman (1984 [source as given]). The likelihood ratio statistic, chi-square, has the values of 11.36 with 16 degrees of freedom (P = .79) for the test of two versus three lags; for the test of three versus four lags it has the values of 24.06 with 16 degrees of freedom (P = .09), and for the test of two versus four lags it has the values of 34.13 with 32 degrees of freedom (P = .35). The likelihood ratio statistic was corrected by the number of variables in each unrestricted equation as suggested by Christopher A.Sims, "Macroeconomics and Reality," *Econometrica* 48 (1980): 17.

23. The probability level is .059.

24. There are a number of possible reasons why labor protest is least affected by the level of political protest. First, the level of labor protest, in contrast to other types of social protest, is more likely to be affected by some short-term ups and downs in the economy. Second, in the time series of reported frequencies of labor protest, there is a strong seasonal component. Most labor protests took place around the Chinese New Year, the time when the issue of the year-end bonus strains the labor–employer relationship.

25. The articles, having been in effect since 1948, supersede the constitution.

26. Alfred Stepan, *Rethinking Military Politics: Brazil and the Southern Cone* (Princeton, NJ: Princeton University Press, 1988).

Chapter 4

Taiwan Factions: *Guanxi,* Patronage, and the State in Local Politics

Joseph Bosco

There are two discourses on factions in Taiwan. One attributes the rise and persistence of factions to Taiwanese reliance on connections to relatives and friends. The other sees factions as the result of meddling by the ruling Kuomintang (KMT or Nationalist party) using state patronage and party favors. These discourses capture only part of the nature of factions. This chapter argues that Taiwan's factions are neither the "natural" expression of Taiwanese culture nor the nefarious creation of the ruling party-state, but rather the product of a particular state-society articulation at a particular point in history.

Factions mediate between the state and local society. Understanding the organization, mobilization, and operation of Taiwan's local factions (*difang paixi*) sheds light on the island's society and political economy. In addition, the ethnic separation between state and local factions highlights the state's role in local factions. The state in Taiwan has been dominated by mainland Chinese ("mainlanders") who came to the island with Chiang Kai-shek and the KMT upon losing the civil war with the Chinese Communist party in 1949. Local factions are the preserve of native Taiwanese but have been key to KMT rule by coopting native elites. KMT control over local factions has created an institution different from factions elsewhere that adds to our understanding of factions and state-society interaction.

Factions have typically been defined as political conflict groups that are not corporate and whose members are recruited by a leader on diverse principles (Nicholas 1977: 57–58). Most definitions have focused on the relationship formed between individuals, stressing the dyadic bonds between leaders and

---

This chapter was previously published in *Ethnology*, April 1992, vol. 31, no. 2, pp. 157–183. Reprinted with permission.

followers, and the transactional (Bailey 1969: 52) and shifting nature of these bonds. Other characteristics of factions include "uncertain duration, personalistic leadership, a lack of formal organization, and a greater concern with power and spoils than with ideology or policy" (Landé 1977: xxxii).

Taiwan's local factions fit these definitions except that they are more grouplike, permanent, and sharply defined than factions elsewhere. They have permanent names, a strong sense of identity, and a stable leadership. Lasswell (1938: 49) notes that the term "faction" "drops out of usage when certain lines of cleavage have become rather permanent features of the political life of the group; these divisions are accepted as parties." Bailey (1969: 53–54) argues that if a faction becomes a group, develops into a moral community, or develops the functional specialization and structure of a bureaucracy, then it ceases to be a faction and is a party. Taiwan's factions are grouplike and do, to some extent, develop into a moral community because they are political machines, but they have no functional specialization. Taiwan local factions are not parties, however, because faction leaders have nearly all been members of the KMT, the ruling party. Factions by definition do not reflect major ideological differences (Lasswell 1938: 49; Bailey 1969: 52); in Taiwan as elsewhere, local factions do not differ in their political program. They cannot be considered parties, but are more grouplike than most factions.

This chapter combines the insights of seeing the factions as a group and the insights of seeing the factions as alliances. Taiwan's factions are held together not by common ideology or class but by social ties (kin, patron–client, friend, etc.) forming a chain of dyadic relationships linking leaders to voters. Yet the factions are more than the sum of the leaders' dyadic ties, because factions persist and continue after leaders' deaths. Using an analogy from physics, just as light needs to be considered both a particle and a wave in order to fully describe its properties, so too must Taiwan factions be described both as a group and as a chain of dyadic relationships.[1]

Previous work on Taiwan's local factions has focused on factions as cultural institutions. Gallin (1968) described the emergence of the faction as institution, but he does not examine the source of factionalism except as a requirement for coalescing an electoral majority. A broader view that includes patronage and the year-round operation of the faction helps to better understand local factions. Jacobs (1980) studied local factions in an attempt to extract the cultural principles that guide Chinese politics generally. He focused on the culturally Chinese aspects of local politics, hoping analyses of *guanxi* (connections), solidarity, "face," and factional organization and operation would shed light on Chinese politics in historical periods and in the People's Republic. Though he found much of interest, his approach tended to reify Chinese culture and missed many of the specific features of Taiwanese factions that stem from their mediating role between society and the state. This chapter shows how factions are manipulated by social actors and tied to the larger political-economic system.

This chapter examines Pingdong County and Pingdong County's Wandan Township.[2] Although no single country or township or village is typical of all Taiwan, political races in Pingdong and Wandan bring the relevant processes to the fore and help shed light on faction-based political mobilization on the island.[3]

Pingdong County is the southernmost of Taiwan's twenty-one counties and agriculturally one of the most fertile. But since farming has not been profitable since the late 1960s, many residents have gone to work in industry and construction or moved to the city. Wandan Township, with a population of 50,000, is about one hour from the large industrial city of Gaoxiong. Wandan families combine agricultural work—now mostly mechanized and thus requiring little labor—with industrial work. Many Wandan residents commute to factory or construction jobs on the outskirts of Gaoxiong, and a number of small factories and assembly plants have moved to Wandan to hire the cheaper rural labor.

An Example

On Sunday, February 17, 1985, Farmers' Association elections were held throughout Taiwan. The Farmers' Association is a semigovernmental organization that controls much patronage, so its political offices are sharply contested by local factions. Its elections follow the same rules as elections for government office and thus illustrate the operation of factions. The most interesting and revealing election was the one I observed in a village in Zhutian Township, the township adjacent to Wandan. Its factions are known as the Wu and Lai factions, instead of North and South factions as in Wandan, but the operation of factions is the same.

At 8:00 A.M. the ballot box was displayed to show that it was empty, and then the lid was sealed to prevent tampering. Four officials ran the election: the village clerk (*cunganshi*), the policeman assigned to this village, and two Farmers' Association employees. Two persons came to watch the poll-opening ritual: the village head and one of the candidates, Mr. Lim. Villagers came throughout the day to vote and chat with a small group of persons who congregated outside the village office where voting took place. There was no obvious campaigning that day, nor, for that matter, is there open campaigning in the weeks leading up to the election for the Farmers' Association. At 3:00 vote counting began. A crowd of about 100 persons crowded by the windows to watch the poll personnel hold up each ballot so everyone could see it and read out *Lîm Thiam chit-phiu!*—the candidate's name followed by "one vote" (*yi piao* in Mandarin). The votes were then marked on tally sheets hanging on the wall for all to see using the traditional five-stroke character *zheng*, each stroke representing one vote. Shortly after the people left, firecrackers could be heard in the village celebrating the victors' election.

Although electioneering was not public, there was intense jockeying behind the scenes. In fact, the margin of the Lai faction victory over the Wu faction was two votes. The main contest was for Farmers' Association member representatives (*nonghuiyuan daibiao*), of which this village elected four (one for every fifty member families). The other electoral contest, for agricultural small group head (*nongshi xiaozuzhang*), was not contested since only one candidate ran for this powerless honorific position. The purpose of Farmers' Association elections is to select representatives, who elect the Farmers' Association board of directors, who in turn elect a general manager (*zongganshi*). The general manager controls Farmers' Association patronage, so each faction seeks to win at least half the representative positions to be able to elect this valuable post.

Since four candidates were going to be elected from the village, under the single nontransferable vote system (which means voters can only cast one vote for one candidate) and two "parties"—here factions—five candidates could be expected (one more than the number of positions).[4] Six candidates registered for the election, but by election day there in fact were only five active candidates. A sixth candidate, the weakest of the Wu faction candidates, withdrew after ballots were printed when it became clear that at most two Wu faction candidates could win. Three candidates (numbers 1, 2, and 4) were correctly predicted by informants as being winners; in the afternoon, well before ballots were counted, I was told the real contest was between the final two (numbers 3 and 6), one each from the two factions (see table 4.1). Even though faction affiliation is not listed on the ballot, the election boiled down to a test of whether the Lai faction could win three of the four positions. In the end, the Lai faction won the voting 117 to 79 (60 to 40 percent), and was able to win three of four seats because it better distributed its votes. Candidate 6 lost to candidate 3 by two votes; if just 3 of the 51 votes candidate 2 received had gone to candidate 6, the Lai and Wu factions would both have won two representatives' seats. But the strength of faction discipline can be seen in that no one, not even the candidate himself, voted for candidate number 5. The 93 percent turnout also shows how closely fought the elections were: four votes were disqualified (most for being marked twice), and 16 voters did not vote out of the total of 216 eligible voters.

Later that evening, I learned that the Lai faction had bought votes for NT $1,000 (U.S. $25) each, while the Wu faction could only muster NT $300 (U.S. $7.50) per vote. Candidate 1, Mr. Lim, happened to be the Lai faction choice for chairman of the board of directors; as the local Lai faction leader, he got the extra votes for candidate 3, which contributed to his election as chairman.

Taiwan's Factions

Scholars have long noted that "the less competitive the party system (i.e., a one-party system), the greater will be the tendency toward factionalism in the main party" (Beller and Belloni 1978: 12; see also Lasswell 1938: 51). The Japanese Liberal Democratic party and the Chinese Communist party display this type of factionalism. Taiwan also has such factions. At the central party

Table 4.1

**Farmers' Association Election, Jiadongjiao
Village, Zhutian Township, February 1985**

Candidate number	Faction	Votes	Comments
1	Lai	47	Lai leader
2	Wu	51	
3	Lai	30	
4	Lai	40	
5	Wu	0	Withdrew
6	Wu	28	The only loser

level, both the KMT and opposition Democratic Progressive party (DPP) are divided into two high-level party factions. The DPP (founded in 1986 when the ban on opposition parties was relaxed; martial law, which justified the ban, was ended in 1987) is divided more ideologically between the Formosa faction, which advocates moderation and electoral contestation, and the New Tide faction, which promotes mass party politics and supports Taiwan independence. The KMT has a Mainstream faction of reformers who support President Li Denghui and an Antimainstream faction opposed to President Li, which tends to be more conservative and of mainlander origin. These factions affect only the highest levels of the parties and do not have branches at the local level. In addition to factions at the central party level, however, a second type of political faction, the local faction, has developed at the county and township levels as a separate institution that plays an important role in mobilizing votes, distributing patronage, and assisting the KMT to control the island. This chapter concentrates on local factions.[5]

Taiwan's local factions are not only factions of the KMT but also political machines. A political machine "is a special case of a regime that bases its authority largely on its distributive activity (service, effectiveness)" (Scott 1972: 109). Taiwan's politicians often say that "service" is most important in getting elected and reelected. Political machines are most durable when they are local rather than national and when there is an external guarantor of the electoral process (Scott 1972: 156). In Taiwan, local elections were guaranteed by the KMT due to its need to present itself to the world as democratic "Free China" despite its single-party rule. With the national parliament dominated by mainlanders frozen in office since 1948, only elections for local government offices were held in Taiwan. Factional machines developed to compete in these local elections.

Taiwan voters do not vote according to faction because they are ignorant or irrational. Taiwan's electorate is generally well educated and sophisticated, as befits a society in a newly industrialized economy having a per capita GNP of

$8,000. Nevertheless, not all voters vote on issues or the ideological positions of candidates. Indeed, until the rise of the anti-KMT opposition in the 1980s and the founding of the DPP in 1986, no alternative ideology was offered to voters even though elections have been held in Taiwan since 1946. Candidates claimed to be more competent than their competitors, not to have an alternate vision. More important, many voters, especially in rural areas where social networks are more stable and long-standing, vote according to faction because it benefits them. Factions tap social networks and trade particularistic political favors for votes. The family that loyally supports a faction's candidates can count on his faction's representative for help. Factions dispense patronage in the form of jobs, local improvements (e.g., roads, lights, community centers), and assistance in the bureaucratic problems of businesses (e.g., licenses, tax audits, pollution standards, land-use regulations, electric power) and of ordinary citizens (e.g., population and land registration, dispute mediation, government and Farmers' Association benefits). Village faction leaders gain power, prestige, and authority by delivering votes, thereby helping candidates win, and by gaining favors from office-holders, thereby serving their constituents.

It is difficult to estimate what proportion of votes are cast according to faction. Most Taiwanese take a dim view of factions (especially when speaking with foreigners), believing them to be symptoms of strife, social division, and instability. Unity in society, politics, and nature is a major theme of Confucianism and makes many persons reluctant to admit to participating in factions. KMT officials especially seem to downplay factions' importance, though to many Western observers, factional electoral competition in the years before the legalization of opposition parties was the only basis on which Taiwan could claim to have even a modicum of democracy. Because many voters downplay the role of factions, public opinion surveys and voter behavior studies tend to overlook the importance of local factions in analyzing voting patterns (see Hu and Yu 1983 [cited by Tien 1989: 190–91]; Niou and Ordeshook 1989; Hu and Chu 1992; Sheng 1986). Other studies focus on party competition and campaign issues and interpret voting results as voter preference rather than voter mobilization through personal connection and faction (see Ts'ai and Myers 1990; Li 1989; Ting 1989; Copper 1984; Lasater 1990; He 1989). Yet factions are sometimes acknowledged: newspapers now regularly report on faction support for candidates[6] (albeit often circumspectly), and when faction members speak among intimates, they speak as self-conscious faction members who stress faction loyalty.

In all elections, factions provide the core of support. Informants estimate that on average two-thirds of the voters are divided between the two factions and the remaining one-third are the free voters not tied to either faction that each faction and candidate tries to reach with personal and popular appeals. But the proportion of votes cast according to faction depends on the level of the election. For township executive, a middle-level election, faction mobilization in each village is the key to victory, since most voters will decide strictly according to their faction representative's recommendation. In high-level elections (e.g., county executive), image or popularity are also important in mobilizing voters. At this countywide level, voters have fewer qualms about voting against the faction, since the candidate is socially more distant. The DPP recruits its supporters not with factions (which it does not control) and political favors (which it is in a weak position to offer), but by attracting ideologically committed protest votes with calls for more democracy and the advocacy of Taiwan independence.[7] A few charismatic candidates can win with such appeals when they run for high-level offices such as county executive or Provincial Assembly representative, but most candidates for these offices win with faction support. For township-level elections, however, factions are essential, because the social network between the candidate and voter is stronger. Thus, although the DPP made important gains on the KMT by winning 29 percent of county executive seats in December 1989, the DPP won a dismal 2 percent of township executive seats just six weeks later. In local elections, the factions were able to squeeze out the opposition candidates who did not have a factional base and tried to run on an ideological appeal (see Bosco in press). Even in elections where factions may control only about half the votes, it is clear that factions can deliver a sizable block of votes so that no politician can ignore them.

For the lowest-level elections in the village (e.g., village head and Farmers' Association representatives), the candidate's personal ties to other village members are important, although the candidate's reputation and wealth—known to all voters—have a direct influence in addition to faction.[8] These personal ties are the same ties that make up factions, and they usually but not necessarily lead to straight faction voting: a voter may support his North faction neighbor for village head, but vote South faction in most elections because his brother-in-law is in the South faction core. In village elections, personalistic faction voting—as opposed to issue voting—dominates.

Faction Origins and History

The local faction typical of Taiwan arose from loose personal networks already present in pre-1945 colonial Taiwan. Political competition and personal animosities between the major local political figures of the early post–World War II period led, with the establishment of local elections, to named and loosely organized factions. The loss of face in losing elections led to sharpened divisions (Jacobs 1980: 114–15). Wandan Township, for example, has North and South factions, which arose in the first postwar local election. According to informants, Li Ruiwen and Huang Hongji were both elected County Assembly representatives from Wandan, but Huang refused to vote for Li in Li's bid to become speaker of the County Assembly. This led to a serious and permanent rupture in relations between the two. Huang's refusal to support Li probably reflects already bad relations, but the public nature of elections, in which Huang had to be either for or against Li, sharpened their previous tensions. Huang was supported by leading political figures from the township's northwest and together with them formed the core of the North faction. Li was supported by Zhang Shanzhong and what became the South faction based in Xinzhuang in the township's south. Today faction strength and leaders are more evenly distributed, but the North and South faction names persist.

Similar binary factions arose at the same time in townships throughout Taiwan, and they also arose at the county level. In a few counties, personal antagonisms and local social cleavages led to the creation of three factions (e.g., in Gaoxiong County) or even more (e.g., Taoyuan County), but in most counties two county-level factions developed that corresponded with two township-level factions. Pingdong County was divided into the Zhang and Lin factions. The Zhang faction was named after the first county executive, Zhang Shanzhong, elected in 1951. After his three-year term as county executive, he was not nominated by the KMT and withdrew his bid for reelection. According to many informants, Zhang felt it beneath his dignity as a local elite (Ph.D. in medicine and one of the area's largest landlords) to pay the courtesy visits necessary to secure the KMT nomination. Others point out that the KMT was afraid to let any one person develop a strong popular following and independent political base. The person the KMT nominated, Lin Shicheng, became the key leader and namesake of the Pingdong County Lin faction. Taiwan's factions arose because though power and authority were concentrated in the hands of the KMT, the central authorities had to deal with local politicians like Zhang and Lin whose wealth and vote-getting abilities gave them some leverage over the KMT.

County-level factions are a nearly permanent alliance of township-level factions. In Wandan Township, the North faction has always supported the countywide Lin faction, and the South faction has supported the Zhang faction. These alliances are stable since faction loyalty is a key value for all politicians and because top township faction leaders concurrently constitute the county faction core. Less stable and predictable are the motivation of faction members and the effectiveness of faction activists in getting votes. Individual candidates have switched faction, and township factions have at times refused to support the county faction candidate, but these disputes over particular candidates have not disrupted long-term county–township faction alliances. Villages are also divided in two, but the factions are only branches of the township faction and do not have a separate name or identity. The named factions are thus organized at the two key administrative levels, the township and the county, where patronage from elective office is available.

Factions mobilize voters at the village level. In Wandan Township, each village (average population about 1,600 persons) is a voting precinct. Full township faction meetings involve at least one faction leader from each village. The village faction head is known as *thiāu-á-kha* in Hokkien (*zhujiao* in Mandarin, but the Mandarin term is never used in ordinary speech), meaning "stake" (as for a tent), a term that is also used for the neighborhood faction heads under his control.

For example, one village of 350 families and 15 administrative neighborhoods (*lin*) has 40 *thiāu-á-kha* in all. Village *thiāu-á-kha* are sometimes the village head or Farmers' Association representative. Often, however, the village *thiāu-á-kha* is a government employee, legally barred from seeking elective office and yet politically powerful because of his education and political connections.[9] In another village, for example, the village head belonged to the South faction in 1990, but he was young and inexperienced. The real South faction head was the vegetable market manager, who was very well connected because he was the younger brother of a former township executive. The North faction was led by the previous village head who had run for office to validate his family's financial success. He chose not to seek reelection because the position of village head was too much trouble, but he continued to be a primary North faction leader.

It might be expected that county-level factions would seek to organize island-wide factions, or that elected provincial and national representatives would seek to form voting blocs. In Japan, where the voting system is the same as in Taiwan, local factions are in fact connected to national factions. Units that went beyond the county, however, would have impinged on KMT power and were thus ruthlessly suppressed when they first appeared in the early 1950s (see Chen 1989: 13). Chiang Kai-shek blamed the KMT failure on the mainland on excessive factionalism and thus enforced unity and central control. Furthermore, since high-level government positions were either appointed (e.g., provincial governor) or elected by the mainlander-dominated National Assembly (e.g., president), there was little need for an organization that went above the county level, this being the largest district and highest level at which elections were held to fill offices (Tien 1989: 165). Only in the late 1980s did a few legislative "clubs" reappear, and even then attempts were made to force them to disband. Factions were therefore constrained by state power to be merely county and township electoral machines.

Political patronage can be defined as politicians' turning of public institutions and public resources to their own ends, exchanging favors of various kinds for votes (Weingrod 1977: 324–25). Government and state-company jobs, construction contracts, government benefits, public works, and nonmonetary favors all are part of a politician's store of patronage. The power to decide, for example, which road will be paved and who will do the paving offers faction leaders the opportunity to reward supporters. In fact, public construction is notoriously afflicted with bid rigging, inside information, and favoritism.

Patronage jobs are important in holding a faction together.[10] Many informants in Wandan claim Farmers' Association elections have been the most hotly contested elections in the township and that conflict over the Farmers' Association is what sharpened factional alignments. Farmers' Associations are officially semigovernmental, but in fact closely regulated and controlled by the state (Stavis 1974; Lasson 1989). The Farmers' Association's ability to dispense patronage is limited by a competitive examination system and higher-level administrative control. But there are still ways for officials to help fellow faction members get jobs or transfer to a more desirable office. In addition, licenses for export crops, subsidies and loans for new machinery, and information on new seeds and techniques all provide additional patronage to bolster factional control.

In Wandan, the South faction is known as the Farmers' Association faction (*nonghui pai*). After 1950 when the Farmers' Associations were first reorganized and elections were held to select representatives, the North faction at first took control. In the second half of the 1950s, when South faction (and countywide Zhang faction) leader Zhang Shanzhong no longer held public office and there was dissension among its leaders, the South faction appeared to be headed for extinction. In the late 1950s, however, a new group of leaders emerged able to unite the South faction and, in a surprise result, defeated the North faction for control of the Farmers' Association. The South faction has continued to control the Farmers' Association since that time and to use it as its patronage base; hence the appellation of "Farmers' Association Faction."

In the 1970s, the South faction also controlled the Township Office. The North faction was a weak opposition. Although able to elect its share of County Assembly representatives,[11] the North faction could not muster a majority to elect a township executive. Since 1982, however, the North faction has controlled the Township Office. Though it seemed less powerful than the South faction in the 1986 elections, and only able to win reelection for township executive because of the candidate's personal appeal, eight years of rule have made it the equal of its opponents, and in 1990 informants began to call the North faction the "Township Office Faction" (*xianggongsuo pai*).

Faction Membership and Leadership

A person is in a faction if he or she exchanges favors with other faction members; no ceremony or formal act indicates a person has joined a faction. Exchanging favors is not merely a transaction but implies a relationship, the tie that is at the heart of factions. Informants estimate that on average about one-third of voters are not closely tied to either faction; they are a shifting constituency both factions try to attract and keep.

Factions are inherently vague and ambiguous. A faction's ambiguity is in part responsible for the recurrent difficulties in defining and describing factions that are noted in the literature (Firth 1957: 292; Boissevain 1977). This ambiguity is due not to the observer's lack of knowledge but to the contingency of the support given by faction members. The dyadic relationships underlying factions are, to some extent, constantly being reinforced, manipulated, and renegotiated. Defections, both temporary and permanent, do occur, and new political support needs to be recruited for each election. Many persons avoid being too closely associated with one faction; businessmen, for example, are said to fear alienating clients. These persons are often known to lean toward one faction (because their friends or relatives are members of that faction) but avoid antagonizing the other faction. Thus Mr. Li, a teacher who with his wife owns a children's clothing shop on Wandan's main street, does not campaign for the South faction even though his mother's brother is an old South faction leader and his friend teacher Wang is also a South faction activist. Mr. Li says he does not want to lose North faction families as clients. If a businessman begins exchanging favors with and openly campaigning for one faction, he begins to be associated with that faction.

Although factions exist in a social sense, they do not have an office or paid cadres. Administrative offices controlled by the faction and faction leaders' homes act as informal offices. Powerful leaders and village *thiāu-á-kha* serve as the personnel. Temples and other social organizations often become the foci for faction organization. Seaman (1978) has described a village temple whose cult also served as a force for dominating village politics. Mazu is a goddess of the sea widely worshiped in Taiwan, and in Wandan Township the Mazu temple is the principle townshipwide temple. It is run by a board of directors made up of the township elite. When the board of directors became dominated by South faction members in the early 1970s, the North faction members from six villages in the township's northwest resigned in protest, pulled their villages out of the townshipwide procession, and organized their own Mazu procession. Projecting the factional dispute to the religious realm, they no longer accept the primacy of the Mazu temple in Wandan's town over their villages and have elevated a Mazu temple in their own area to what they consider to be equal status. Other organizations have also been divided by faction: the Wandan Rotary Club (founded by the chairman of the Wandan Mazu temple), rather than be a bridge between North and South factions, became a club for wealthy businessmen who leaned toward the South faction.

Factions are strongest in rural areas, where people have the strongest webs of connections. Even in villages of 200 to 300 families, adults know other villagers' friendship and kin networks and can guess for whom many of their neighbors are likely to vote. Women have ties with groups of women who tend to socialize more often in their neighborhood; they typically also have relatives and female friends from their natal village living in other parts of the village (see Wolf 1972: 42–52). Men have similar but broader village networks because, following Chinese patrilocal residence patterns, they live in the same village in which they were raised. They have age-mates throughout the village with whom they went to school, and their childhood playing throughout the village and their longer residence make their web of village connections wider and knowledge of villagers deeper than for most women. In the neighborhood for which a *thiāu-á-kha* is responsible, each family's web of kinship and personal friendships is intimately known. In many cases, this web indicates—to those who are interested in politics— for which faction or which candidate a voter is likely to vote.

Taiwan factions have a collective leadership and are not simply the network of one leader or family, as they have been in many parts of Latin America and the Philippines. Death or departure of a leader does not lead to the collapse or dissolution of the faction (cf. Nathan 1977: 385). The Lin faction is no longer led by a Lin, but the name persists because of organizational continuity. One of the Zhang faction leaders is in fact Zhang Fengxu, the son of faction founder Zhang Shanzhong, but he is only one of several high-level leaders of the Zhang faction. His family connections doubtlessly helped his career, but he has earned his factional leadership position through his own career in county and national politics (served as county executive, mayor of Taibei, and Minister of the Interior, and at present is president of the Chinese-Taipei Olympic Committee).[12] His faction-based power was greatest when he served as county executive, but it has waned now that he lives in Taibei and is out of touch with the day-to-day politics of Pingdong. Nevertheless, his prestige and national connections give him status and power in the Zhang faction. Faction leaders can claim a seat among the fluid and informal leadership based on their ability to deliver votes, which in turn depends on their personal wealth, prestige, and ability to dispense patronage.

Faction leadership is often poorly defined and ambiguous since it is based on prestige. Faction leadership is informal and unstructured, with no posts or formal hierarchies. By virtue of its informality, the faction could not be penetrated by the KMT and could include and exclude whoever the core leaders wished. Taiwan's rapid economic mobility and the lack of a landed elite in large part explains this collective and fluid leadership. Office holders and prominent faction supporters who can mobilize votes participate in strategy meetings. Since the faction has no structure or office, the faction is held together by political favor-trading. Support for one leader's candidate can be had in exchange for supporting another leader's candidate or for supporting a local development project. Prestige and influence of the leaders—largely determined by their ability to mobilize votes—helps decide who gets what. The overriding goal of defeating the opposing faction helps faction leaders focus on what is best for the faction.

The collective and diffuse leadership of Taiwanese factions is in part due to local elites' lacking total local control, or what Silverman (1977a: 294) calls "near-exclusivity" in performing economic and political functions. Before 1945, when Taiwan was a colony of Japan, landlords and peasants were tied in a landlord patronage system that "had its basis in the peasants' dependence upon the landlords, who historically were the peasants' sole recourse to physical protection and economic aid" (Silverman 1977a: 298, referring to a similar situation in central Italy). Landlords were mediators between the Japanese colonial government and the general population. The colonial government consciously worked through landlords in promoting agricultural development, and landlords had privileged access to the Japanese state. In addition, landlords used their personal resources to maintain patron-client ties. With the arrival of the KMT, the Japanese-educated landlord elite lost its tie to the state, and then with land reform it lost much of its economic base. Older informants, for example, recall that tenants had to give special gifts to their landlord to maintain their *guanxi* or affective relations in the hope that they could continue renting land. Since land reform, they note, such deference has been unnecessary (see Gallin 1963). Some landlord families have continued to be prominent, but farmers have many more channels to the state than they did under the colonial government. More persons now are part of the elite, and the economic and status differential has diminished. New elites are recruited to factions; wealthy entrepreneurs have been allowed (and often courted) to use their newfound wealth and prestige in politics. The prewar landlord patronage has given way to faction machine patronage (see Silverman 1977a; Weingrod 1977: 325). In contrast to the landlord patrons, faction leaders offer a channel to state resources and do not generally offer goods and services of their own. Not only were the old mediators largely eliminated, but the relationship between state and society was changed, offering individuals more avenues to the state. Factions, and the local elite who lead them, are not gatekeepers; though factions specialize in offering individual favors and patronage so as to build up political support, other connections (kin, friend, classmate, etc.) and/or the use of money can make up for weak links to a faction.

Guanxi and Faction Mobilization

Factional mobilization and leadership is based on *guanxi,* a term for particularistic ties connoting connections, network, and patron-client relations (see Fried 1974; Gallin 1966; Jacobs 1980; King 1991; for the PRC, see Gold 1985; Yang 1989). Taiwanese think of themselves as tied to other persons in a web of social relations rather than as free individuals. These webs or networks are made up of many types of connections. Kin connections are the most obvious type of *guanxi,* and they range from the important parental and sibling ties to the weaker distant agnatic and affinal ties. Other types of bonds include neighbor, classmate, co-worker, and sometimes coreligionist. In each case, friendship and affect will influence the degree of cooperation. Some *guanxi* ties are among equals; others are vertical. In all cases, they are cultivated from the much wider range of possible ties; though certain social bonds (such as patrilinial, affinal, and class-mate bonds—see Jacobs 1980) are important sources of *guanxi,* these bonds do not have a predetermined strength but must be built up and maintained. A good politician or businessman must be able to keep a great number of these strands active and strong. The expression *"wode pengyou hen duo"* (I have many friends) is frequently used by faction leaders and by prominent businessmen; though in English it appears odd and immodest, it expresses the importance of *guanxi.*

Factions can thus be viewed as two mostly exclusive *guanxi* networks. The overlap between the two networks is greater as one gets further away from the faction leaders. Although factions operate at all times by dispensing political favors, they are most clearly visible during elections, when the normal network of social relations crystallizes into separate groups (us versus them). Outside of election periods, most villagers maintain social relations without consideration for faction. Core members only socialize with fellow faction members, but even *thiāu-á-kha* faction heads maintain cordial relations with neighbors who are supporters of opposing factions. A village head, though elected as a faction representative to a largely ceremonial post without pay, must offer to assist fellow villagers of both factions if he is to avoid alienating the key shifting middle vote. Even so, families closely associated with the opposing faction are not likely to seek him out for help but use their own faction *guanxi* connections. In general, what is good for the person with whom I have *guanxi* is good for me; the idea of voting according to *guanxi* is accepted and indeed expected.

At the faction leadership level, the *guanxi* network has many cross-cutting strands that tie leaders to one another in a stable web, making the faction grouplike (similar to parties). At lower levels, dyadic ties between activists and voters are more important. Neighborhood *thiāu-á-kha* use their personal ties to mobilize as many votes as possible. A *thiāu-á-kha* will have some persons with whom he has close ties on whom he can count, and will also try to influence persons with whom his *guanxi* is weaker. One voter may have ties with several persons involved in politics, in which case he may find it difficult to choose without damaging some relationships.

Faction leaders, including the lowest *thiāu-á-kha,* stress loyalty to the faction; one *thiāu-á-kha* went so far as to say that anyone who betrayed his faction was just as likely to betray his country. Faction supporters believe their faction to be good (*shan*) and their opponents' evil (*e*), and they frequently suggest that their faction opponents are immoral and have underworld connections, often attributing other candidates' wealth to ownership of brothels or gambling dens. Since both sides cite similar stories, the tales appear to be a form of ritualized political posturing. The tales make faction members feel virtuous in contrast to their immoral opponents and make changing factions difficult, since it is "going to the dark side." Faction members thus have a moral rather than a transactional relationship since they cannot change faction without losing credibility. Leaders may "bracket" a race and temporarily support a nonfaction candidate for a particular race if kin or other personal reasons intervene, but they cannot always take their supporters with them. Followers (i.e., voters) can change sides, although they do so quietly and without publicity (cf. Bailey 1969: 46–47).

The *thiāu-á-kha* must estimate faction strength and then deliver the vote on election day. The village *thiāu-á-kha* tells faction leaders how many votes he can deliver, a process one referred to as *bao piao,* or "contracting for votes." The faction delivers money to the village *thiāu-á-kha*, who distributes it to neighborhood *thiāu-á-kha,* who distribute it to supporters to firm up the vote. Often extra money is made available to pay a small premium to swing votes, depending on the availability of funds and the electoral strategy. To estimate a faction's strength, the village *thiāu-á-kha* reads down a list of voters[13] with his neighborhood *thiāu-á-kha,* determining one by one whether the voters are likely to vote for their candidate. This determination is easier than it may seem, because although most people do not openly discuss or advertise how they intend to vote, the *thiāu-á-kha* knows who they are related to, who their best friends are, who they visit, who they invite for feast day banquets, and thus how their *guanxi* connections are likely to lead them to vote. This connection between *thiāu-á-kha* and voter is not necessarily clientelistic; as Lasswell (1938: 49) put it, "This primitive alignment rests on no deep calculation of personal interests. Emotional relations of varying degrees of intimacy are already established, and the crisis of personnel selection provides but a special occasion for their expression."[14]

A *thiāu-á-kha*'s value to the faction is not only in winning votes through his social ties but also in accurately measuring voter support before the election. Indeed, the faction values accuracy above high numbers because it needs to know at the last minute if additional vote-buying will make a difference. The *thiāu-á-kha* is evaluated depending on how many votes he delivered, how accurate his estimates were, and how he did compared to the previous election. The key to the KMT's success in most recent elections has been not fraud but organization (Wu 1987: 103–4); the party has worked through factions, and the *thiāu-á-kha* is the basic link of the faction's—and thus the party's—organization.

Although it is often said that *thiāu-á-kha* keep some of the money themselves, it seems more common that they actually contribute out of their own pocket to the faction's funds. One village *thiāu-á-kha* who held a patronage job gave one month's salary or about NT $20,000 to his faction, and another who was an older farmer gave NT $10,000. *Thiāu-á-kha* who keep part of the money they receive are not able to deliver the vote and are not likely to be entrusted with money and responsibility in the future.

Vote Buying

There are two types of vote buying. In the vast majority of cases, money is merely a gift; indeed, many candidates give soap, towels, or china in addition to money, and the KMT gives gifts such as pens, paperweights, and watches. When money is a gift, it represents less than the value of a day's work: in January 1990 voters in Wandan received from NT $200 (U.S. $7.70) to NT $300 (U.S. $11.50) for the township executive and NT $200 for County Assembly representative. Nearly every rural voter receives money; only oppositionists hostile to factions are skipped by *thiāu-á-kha*. Money is given in loose bills along with a flyer or small advertisement for the candidate. The money is sometimes referred to as a *hongbao* (or "red envelope" used for gifts—the term also used as a euphemism for corrupt payoffs), but the money is not placed in envelopes. Though money is often viewed as a crass gift in the United States, in Taiwan money is the standard gift at weddings and is the customary religious offering to gods and ancestors (Gates 1987). In this form, money does not buy votes but firms up the loyalty of supporters. As Jacobs (1980: 148) puts it, "the vast majority of votes in rural Taiwan elections are bought, sold, and cast on the basis of *guanxi*."

Most rural voters do not see the transfer of money as "buying" so much as an expression of, or a forced attempt to create, a relationship between the voter and the candidate. Similarly, the campaign style in Taiwan is for the candidate to stand in a vehicle (previously on the back of a pickup or flat-bed truck, now often in a convertible all-terrain vehicle or a sedan with a sun-roof) and drive around the district, waving to villagers like a beauty-pageant contestant: this behavior, like the money-gift, creates a connection (albeit a weak one) between the candidate and voters. Elections in the past were usually contests between largely identical candidates who had little effect on policy but could dispense patronage. Receiving money made it clear to whose patronage network one belonged. Money is not given to voters who vote on ideological issues or who have made a decision to vote for another candidate; many of the recipients of money would have voted the same way even without the gift. Because money is viewed as a gift and not a purchase, many informants note that they feel obligated to accept the money because they know the person giving it to them.[15]

Since money is channeled through an existing social network, it is impossible to bring charges of vote buying against candidates; almost no one is willing to testify against the relative, neighbor, or friend who delivers the money, regardless of how much one may disagree on politics. Furthermore, as one *thiāu-á-kha* noted on the eve of the January 1986 election with a wad of NT $100 bills in his hands, "Reporting vote-buying does no good here because the courts are not independent of the party. The courts will always support the power of the [KMT] party."

The second type of vote buying is true vote buying, when a candidate spends much more per vote and solicits in areas where he or she would otherwise receive no support. In the January 1990 Pingdong County Assembly election, several representatives were elected in this way, viewed by local observers as a surprising success for this tactic. The fourth district (including Wandan Township, Xinyuan Township, and Donggang City) elects seven representatives. Xinyuan Township, with only about one-fifth of the district's population, normally elects only one or two representatives. It was a surprise, then, when in January 1990 Xinyuan managed not only to have three native sons elected as representatives, but to have one of them win as the district's high vote getter. Informants and even newspaper accounts attributed this success to vote buying, with votes selling for NT $500–600 (U.S. $19–23) each, compared to the NT $200 or so most other candidates were paying.[16] In 1986 a political novice from Wandan was elected by paying NT $300 per vote instead of the NT $100 other candidates paid. The candidate's organization seeks opportunistic or disgruntled *thiāu-á-kha* or other influential persons and gives them the money in return for their support. These votes are bought in areas far from a candidate's base. Since the candidate did not expect to win any support in that area, it is simple to measure the effectiveness of the *thiāu-á-kha*; if money was delivered for thirty votes and only ten votes are delivered, the *thiāu-á-kha* loses face. Although the *thiāu-á-kha* has social ties to the voters, the candidate's social and physical remoteness to the voter make this expensive vote buying a more contractual and short-term deal.[17]

The difference between money as a gift and money as a purchase should not obscure the fact that both are illegal and viewed as at best necessary evils. Money is delivered discreetly and often at night, not publicly with a written record as is the custom for wedding gifts. The distinction between money as gift and money as purchase also fades in close elections, where last-minute vote-buying at higher prices is common late on election day. Reliable informants said that the winner in the Wandan Township executive election bought last-minute votes for as much as NT $1,000 each (compared to the NT $200 he had paid the night before). His opponent spent NT $3,800,000 (U.S. $150,000) of his personal money in the last day when the election appeared close.

The total amounts spent in campaigns are staggering: well-connected informants agreed that both factions spent about NT $10,000,000 (U.S. $370,000) on the 1990 Wandan Township executive race, or an average of about NT $400 for every vote cast. Candidates for County Assembly representative spent NT $4–5,000,000 (U.S. $148–185,000) according to a village *thiāu-á-kha*. These representatives in turn sold their own vote, receiving NT $500,000 (U.S. $18,500) for their vote for County Assembly speaker.

The faction's money comes from three sources. Core faction members donate money to their faction, but the amounts are relatively small. A second source of money is the KMT, but it only spends money on politically significant elections, such as county executive, Legislative Yuan, and National Assembly, and when the election is close. Then it can spend a great deal of money. Third, businessmen give the bulk of the money. As Wurfel (1963: 766) notes for the Philippines, " 'Expediting' a businessman's request to a government agency is a valuable service which congressmen can provide; its value is usually well-recognized, and rewarded." Included among these businessmen are factory owners and pig farmers seeking waivers on environmental standards, and *liuhecai* numbers games organizers who seek political protection for their illegal businesses. For example, the Wandan campaign manager (i.e., the largest township contributor) for the 1985 KMT candidate for county executive was a major contractor who built many government projects. In the township executive race two months later, a major pork-processing factory gave NT $2,000,000 (U.S. $50,000) to the South faction candidate trying to unseat the North faction incumbent. The election contribution came just a few months after the factory was levied fines for pollution. Much of the money is donated by faction members and businessmen not as a direct quid pro quo but to earn status, prestige, and influence within the faction. As one informant put it, the *thiāu-á-kha* who donates NT $10,000 to the faction coffers is not going to earn the money back, but he will get faster service at the Township Office. Yet, in the long run, political influence yields financial advantages.

Many Taiwanese argue that politicians lose money in running for and holding public office because they are seeking fame or face to go with the money they already have. Jacobs (1980: 64–67) also argues that candidates cannot get this money back and would not jeopardize their careers by accepting bribes. My best informants note, however, that politicians have numerous opportunities to earn back the money they invest in elections. In Pingdong, where most land is restricted for agricultural use, advance knowledge of government projects—and the power to decide where these projects will be built—presents politicians with the possibility for extraordinary profits. Furthermore, Yun-han Chu (1989: 151–52) has identified four kinds of economic privilege the KMT grants faction leaders to keep local factions beholden to it. First, the KMT protects the monopoly status of a number of enterprises that earn great profit and/or provide disposable patronage to local politicians (such as credit cooperatives, local vegetable and fruit markets, Farmers' Associations, and local bus companies). Second, Provincial Assembly representatives and their factions have preferential access to loans from the provincial government-owned Cooperative Bank. Third, politicians can take advantage of procurement budgets and construction contracts by directing contracts to faction members' enterprises or earning a broker's commission. Fourth, politicians can profit personally in the course of carrying out official duties, for example, by speculating in land involved in urban planning or public construction projects or by protecting or operating underground dance halls and betting parlors (on economic privileges and local factions, see also Chen 1989). Money is not merely buying face but is an investment in power and prestige that offers many money-earning opportunities.

The impoverishment of some politicians is not proof that a politician cannot earn back money invested in elections (cf. Jacobs 1980: 66) but merely shows that some politicians are unskilled at redistributing patronage and acting as a political entrepreneur. Elected officials and faction leaders must act like "big men" in distributing their resources so as to maintain support. Politicians have to be able to dip into their pockets, but they must do so judiciously. One politician in Wandan was criticized for charging money for providing favors to faction supporters, and there were rumors that he had pocketed KMT money. There was even suspicion that he was against "arranged elections" (in which the two factions agree not to contest each other's position) because, although such arrangements save factions a great deal of money, they do not allow faction leaders to skim faction funds. These charges may be scurrilous rumors, but they illustrate the pressure on politicians to distribute patronage widely and wisely.

Vote buying is only part of a larger pattern of selling influence and exchanging favors, ranging from the exchange of minor gifts among businessmen to the purchase of government favors (import licenses, exclusive contracts, etc.). Many voters see the money they are paid as the trickling down of the large sums exchanged between businessmen and candidates—several considered it their fair share. Influence selling is a widespread phenomenon (see, for example, Amick

1976), and vote buying as a part of this phenomenon is also common (see Scott 1972; Wurfel 1963; Curtis 1983: 67–68). Many informants feel that once vote buying began in the early 1950s it became a "cultural" trait and hard to stop. But only the style of pulling strings (*la guanxi*) is culturally Chinese, as shown by the success of Taiwan's businessmen in getting things done in the People's Republic (knowing who to pay, how much, and how); the pattern is widespread. The use of cash gifts to express reciprocity and the distribution of the gifts through traditional social ties are cultural aspects of a broader phenomenon common to electoral politics, influence buying or "money politics" (*jinquan zhengzhi*) (Scott 1972).

The KMT has used vote buying to affect electoral outcomes, but it has also restrained vote buying in several ways. In many areas the KMT divides a district among its candidates, designating an exclusive territory where a candidate can canvass for votes. This KMT-imposed order prevents a bidding war among candidates and prevents multiple selling of votes, which would lower the bene-fits of vote buying. In rural areas this KMT-imposed order has been supple-mented (if not rendered unnecessary) by factions' localism—the preference to vote for candidates in one's own village or township (see Jacobs 1980: 41–42). Candidates use gifts to solidify the support of voters in their township; only candidates who need to purchase votes will go out of their natal area.

When money is used as a gift, vote buying does not appear to affect the outcome of elections because the money is simply used to firm up support. Without money, voters question the seriousness of the campaign. In the January 1990 Wandan Township executive race, the DPP candidate charged after the election that his support should have been about 5,000 votes—not nearly enough to win, but respectable—except for the fact that the other candidates spread rumors that he had withdrawn from the race. They claimed Li continued to campaign to save face, a claim that, without vote buying, made it difficult for Li to prove he was still an active candidate. This caused his support to plummet to under 2,000 votes. If vote buying is viewed as firming up support, it will be viewed as not making a difference in overall electoral outcome. Its main effect will be in distributing votes among KMT candidates.

Opposition candidates argue that money is the meat on the faction skeleton; without vote buying, factions are worthless bones. This view exaggerates the role of vote buying by ignoring the social networks that underlie factions, that is, the connections of kinship, friendship, and business that connect faction leaders to voters through *thiāu-á-kha*. Opposition candidates consider all vote buying to be "purchase." Elections cannot usually be "bought." Though money can swing the outcome of a close election, the number of votes it can affect is limited. DPP County Executive Su Zhenchang at first argued in an interview that "Money is to factions what gas is to a car," but he later admitted that money only helps if the abilities of the two candidates are similar. If one candidate is far superior, he said, money will not make up the difference. In another example, an informant commented on a wealthy and highly esteemed businessman who did not run for township executive despite rumors that he would: "Even though he has a lot of prestige and money, elections are funny some times. He does not have the same contacts with everyday people, so he would have to spend more money. But you are never sure to win."[18]

By focusing on the dyads (or patron–client ties) that are the building blocks of factions (see Landé 1977), one can argue either of two opposing views: that factions do not exist because they are merely personal networks (an argument a number of KMT cadres made to me in the mid-1980s) or that factions depend entirely on money and vote buying for their survival (the DPP position). Both views exaggerate one aspect of the clientelist nature of factions: the KMT view focuses exclusively on the personal ties, and the DPP view focuses exclusively on resources. Personal networks and resources together can mobilize factions. Vote buying is not the only mobilizing force, but given the history of vote buying, money is clearly an essential campaign resource for all but the most charismatic of candidates.

The KMT and Factions

The KMT maintains a party organization of paid cadres that is parallel to but separate from the faction hierarchy. At the township level, the party office, known as the People's Service Station (*minzhong fuwuzhan*), has a local party secretary appointed by the county KMT office. He is assisted by three full-time cadres and several part-time and volunteer personnel, many of whom grew up and live in the township, and nowadays all of whom are college graduates. The cadres, although generally considered government employees, are paid about 30 percent more than comparable civil servants to elevate their status and facilitate their leadership work. The party secretary leads the township's party members who are organized in village and neighborhood cells. The party is supposed to hold regular meetings of all members, but the cells in Wandan have become dormant since the mid-1970s. Members feel that the meetings are pointless; one party member, a businessman who would like to see the party run more like the Lions or Rotary Club rather than the current centralism, said "it is like a dog barking at a train" (*káo-á pūi hóe-chhia*). Although no one attends the meetings, the party office, like all party offices in Taiwan, regularly sends reports of meetings to higher levels.

At the provincial and national levels of government, the party cadres and the elected politicians form a dual elite structure (Wu 1987; see also Winckler's [1981] "managers" and "contenders"), but at the township level, politicians are able to mobilize votes, whereas the party secretary is an outsider standing above and controlling the politicians. The party secretary's duty to select which faction nominee will receive the KMT nomination gives him power over factions since, at least until the late 1980s, nomination virtually assured a candidates' election.

Candidates were willing to make sizable donations to the KMT in return for the nomination (Gallin 1968: 387). Today nomination still means important campaign support (polling data, tactical advice, and mobilization through the party) and often convinces other KMT members not to run. The local cadres help extend the KMT candidate's network and use their intimate knowledge of the township to promote the KMT nominees' campaigns. They even help win some votes in return for having helped township residents with legal and administrative problems, from applying for a driver's license to mediating disputes.

Informants often note two KMT strategies in dealing with factions: (1) The KMT supports the likely winner, to earn prestige from the success of the local candidate; (2) the KMT supports the underdog to make the factions more equal so it can pit the two factions against each other and better control local politics. Although seemingly contradictory, both strategies exist but are applied depending on the local situation. When one faction is clearly dominant, the KMT tries to prop up the weak faction. Where strength is reasonably even, the KMT is free to support the better candidate or likely winner, and thereby coopt the victor and strengthen the party's image. The township party secretary is supposed to be a neutral arbiter between the factions, managing the factional conflict to the benefit of the party. In deciding on nominations, he or she considers (1) a candidate's wealth (necessary for the expensive campaign), (2) the candidate's loyalty to the KMT, and (3) the factional balance of the district.[19]

Factions tend to be limited to two per county or township because they are struggling for access to elected office and the patronage that comes with it. Internal cleavages within the faction are suppressed for the sake of victory. Factions that are rent by dissension have difficulty winning elections, and electoral defeats reduce the power and prestige of the leaders and leave an opening for new leaders and candidates that can unite the faction. Many scholars argue that bifactionalism is the creation of the KMT (see, for example, Wu 1987: 307–17). The KMT has indeed promoted factionalism through divide-and-rule tactics: by keeping the two factions roughly even in strength, the KMT could maintain control over the rural areas in which mainlanders had no social or political ties. Although factions are based on networks that predate the arrival of the KMT, factions have only become an institution under the KMT. The KMT used factions to help it control the countryside by inserting itself in the fissure between the factions. Since party nomination virtually assured a candidate's election, the KMT acted as a kingmaker and used this power to prevent any faction from gaining too much power. The mainlander KMT elite allowed Taiwanese to compete for elective office at the local levels while not allowing elections to determine the composition of the national government (with the argument that national elections had to wait for the defeat of the Communists). But bifactionalism itself is not a KMT creation: the literature on factions is full of examples of binary factions. The KMT has been to able manage factions to advance its own interests, but it did not have to create factions or work very hard to promote them.

The KMT's official pronouncements have been hostile to local factions, despite (or perhaps because of) the party's reliance on them. Chiang Kai-shek suppressed central party factions when he retreated to Taiwan in 1949; factional competition was widely blamed for weakening the party and leading to the Communist takeover. Most Taiwanese also hold a negative view of factions. The widespread claim of informants (before strong rapport is established) that they do not belong to either faction is due in part to the traditional and KMT ideals of unity, but also because they are trying, as businessmen, politicians, or civil servants, to maintain a network as large as possible to further their career. Businessmen in particular deny favoring any faction, much as they claim to have no interest in politics, when in fact they nearly always have ties to persons in politics, ties that are essential for conducting business.

The Confucian ideal of unity and harmony was kept alive by the corporatist ideology of the KMT, which tried to represent all groups and classes and to promote an image of the government united with the people in one harmonious whole (see Tien 1989: 44–45). The party divided society into functionally specialized groups, labor unions, or trade associations (e.g., Farmers' Associations, Irrigation Associations, and furniture manufacturers), each of which, until the liberalization of the late 1980s, had only one government-recognized union or association. Because these associations were official and closely controlled by the KMT, they had little or no autonomy and functioned more to control the membership and to preempt any autonomous organizations than to represent members' interests. Corporatism was the centralizing force used by the KMT to maintain control over the island.

But because of the KMT elite's lack of roots in Taiwan, the KMT had to use patronage to reach out and coopt the local elite. Because elections were instituted shortly after the KMT's takeover of the island (elections had been held under the Japanese and were thus not new to Taiwan), elite recruitment was structured by the elections (Chen 1990). After a few free elections up through 1951, the KMT began to use its power as the only legal party to influence local election results. Patronage and party nominations gave the KMT considerable influence over the selection of candidates. In addition, locally elected officials had "extremely limited budget-approving power and negligible regulatory power" (Cheng 1989: 478). Thus, whereas in Mexico a national elite that changed with presidential elections every six years (because of a ban on presidential reelection) dealt with local elites who were stable (Purcell 1981), in Taiwan a stable central elite dealt with a local elite that had limited governmental authority and was forced to change frequently through elections and election rules that limited executives to two terms (to prevent person-based machines). Locally based clientelism is a decentralizing force (Purcell 1981: 200), but local factional power in Taiwan was countered by the KMT's control of national politics. Corporatism and clientelism became concurrent principles of KMT rule (Chen 1989: 6–7). Local candidates organized into factions to compete for elections by distributing patronage and favors to hold their coalitions together. The local factions that developed represented local interests but were not a decentralizing force because they were subordinate to the KMT. Despite the leadership's opposition to factionalism, local factions became an essential institution in KMT rule.

The Taiwan case seems paradoxical: factions elsewhere arose when a weak or new state did not reach down to the local level, allowing brokers to fill the space between the village and the state (classic examples come from Latin America, Mediterranean Europe, and the Philippines; see Chalmers 1977; Campbell 1964; Landé 1964). In late-nineteenth-century Italy, for example, the new nation-state had not penetrated local semifeudal society (Silverman 1977a). But Taiwan has been characterized as having a "strong" state (Amsden 1985; Gold 1986) led by a vanguard party. The solution to the paradox is that though the KMT state was indeed a strong state that had great freedom to set economic policy free of interest group interference, the KMT elite were an immigrant elite socially and ethnically different from, and previously unconnected to, the Taiwanese local elite. To govern, the KMT needed a compliant local elite. Elections selected these local elite. Factions formed to compete for elective office. Factions developed into political machines to win elections by distributing patronage, but they were prevented from becoming political parties by the KMT. Factions became the bridge between Hokkien politicians and mainlander party cadres; faction candidates attracted the popular following, but the central KMT authorities could remain in control.

Factions also help the KMT win local elections. I describe elsewhere how the KMT uses factions to win under Taiwan's election rules. Briefly summarized, the single-vote multiple-member district system requires that the party allocate an equal number of votes (*pei piao*) to each candidate for representative office. Candidates try to win as many votes as possible to assure their election, but winning too many votes hurts the party because all votes beyond the minimum needed to get elected could have gone to help elect another candidate and thus could have increased the party's representation. Spreading votes requires organization; factions provide it by mobilizing and distributing votes. The KMT has consistently been able to win about 10 percent more seats than votes (Winckler 1989; for the 1989 election, see Bosco in press).

An additional benefit to the KMT of reliance on local factions is that intraparty competition caused by the multiple-member districts is reduced because each candidate has a factional base. Pingdong's fourth district elects seven County Assembly representatives. Each of the district's three townships' factions is virtually guaranteed a representative, leaving only the seventh seat open for competition. Most factions will back only one candidate in the race to prevent diluting their strength and electing no one. Many elections result in no competition because the two factions agree informally on how to divide the seats. In the 1985 Wandan Farmers' Association election, thirteen of thirty villages had no competition, saving the candidates and factions money. In villages where the results are less predictable (e.g., two evenly divided factions that must divide three seats), competition is intense but still structured by factions, avoiding uncontrolled bidding and allowing the use of vote buying to firm up support. Viewed another way, under a one-party authoritarian system, "the party's main problem is preventing those party politicians denied nominations from sabotaging the nominee or running as mavericks" (Winckler 1984: 496); the KMT reduces this problem by counting on factions to discipline their members.

The KMT cannot completely control factions, however. Factions will at times campaign against the party nominee. They can spend great sums of money to build up their power and prestige and to tear down the other faction even if it subverts party designs. It might seem that the factions have an "overwhelming rational incentive" to unite against the DPP, but they have a countervailing incentive to keep their organization alive by fielding a candidate no matter what the odds. Factions must remain well oiled for the next battle and thus have a contrarian tendency (Winckler 1990). This is characteristic of factions; "the same set of people fight at one another's side through a series of engagements, while displaying a cavalier disregard for the ideological consistency of the causes they support" (Bailey 1969: 52). If the South faction supports the KMT nominee, that is reason enough for the North faction to support the DPP.

Conclusions

Taiwan's factions combined elements of political machines and party factions because they could not develop into formal political parties. With the liberalization since 1987, the ban on new parties has ended. But local factions still serve the KMT well in most elections, and it is likely that the ruling party will try to preserve this base of strength. Factions may make alliances with legislative coalitions once the representative bodies have true law-making powers, or some factions may become associated with the opposition party. With constitutional changes still uncertain, it is too early to predict the future of local factions.

The factions literature suggests that mobility, transportation, literacy, and education will speed the breakdown of factions (Silverman 1977a: 301–3). Affluence decreases the dependency of villagers, making them less beholden to patrons. New and more persons become intermediaries, so that in the end the junctures between the national and local systems "can no longer be 'guarded' by any group" (Silverman 1977a: 303). Public-interest groups of all kinds have arisen in Taiwan representing farmers, women, consumers, aspiring homeowners, and others, ending the KMT's corporatist monopoly. Based on experiences elsewhere, faction and machine politics may give way to interest group politics and mass parties (for Italy see Caciagli and Belloni 1981: 36–37). So far, however, even opposition DPP candidates have used personal networks and patronage to hold electoral coalitions together. As one *thiāu-á-kha* noted, DPP candidates "buy" votes with public projects. Corporatism is dissolving, but clientelism is as strong as ever.

A faction-based strategy may soon begin suffering from diminishing sources of patronage. In the more complex and internationalized industrial economy, state-owned enterprises (the traditional source of sinecures) represent a smaller share of employment and are in many cases being privatized. Perhaps most important, to defend itself against charges of corruption and excessive use of influence, the KMT is beginning to turn patronage positions into meritocratic (or bureaucratic) positions.

The growing power of elected officials over the central government is also changing the role of factions. Both the KMT and the government were run by mainlanders who last faced election in 1947. The replacement in 1991–92 of all representative bodies with persons elected in Taiwan promised to end their role as rubber-stamp bodies and give them greater power. As the party becomes more representative of Taiwan, the old pattern of managing factional rivalries to maximize central party power is giving way to a variety of central party factions and personalities attempting to use local factions. Factions developed in Taiwan as local machines, with local elections guaranteed by the state but national politics closed to debate. Now that national policy is open for debate, factions may link up with national-level politicians and become part of islandwide factions as in Japan, or they may become local party branches as in Italy. But in the short term, factions still serve the interests of many of Taiwan's politicians; election rules such as the single-vote, multimember district help preserve the faction since factions can better distribute votes and can continue electing their representative. Reports from the press and from informants that true vote buying is becoming more common suggest the unraveling of the KMT order that made most vote buying a form a gift-giving and prevented a free market in votes. The inability of the KMT to control vote-buying may lead to higher prices for votes and to an escalation of factions' money politics and a devolution of power from the KMT to elected politicians.

The irony in all this is that factions were molded and used by the KMT to allow the mainland elites to rule the native population; by keeping local political leaders divided in two nonideological camps and maintaining the role of kingmaker in the nomination process, the KMT inserted itself into a social environment where it not only had no previous support, but after the rebellion of 1947, actually was the target of resentment. To promote the notion of "Free China," the authoritarian national government was forced to preserve and guarantee local elections that spawned and preserved factions. For decades, factional elections were presented to the outside (i.e., the United States) as evidence of democracy while factions were decried internally as a dangerous lack of unity in the face of the Communist threat. Factions gave a democratic appearance without threatening KMT power. Over time, however, the factions have taken on a life of their own, draining power from the party. The KMT has lost control over the local factions, so that putatively KMT faction leaders now think nothing of openly supporting non-KMT candidates if this strengthens the faction. The factions' local power is a reemergence of a force nearly wiped out when land reform eliminated local landlords. With the recent democratization of the central government, local factions have gained some autonomy. Elections, originally of the "elections without choice" (Hermet, Rose, and Rouquié 1978) variety that helped the state control local elites, have now become an arena for wider political competition. Despite the eroding base for factions as Taiwan moves to mass politics, factions and not parties will continue to structure local politics for the near future.

Although the cultural pattern of tapping *guanxi* connections made factions possible, it would be a mistake to view factions as merely the product of traditional culture, an immature electorate, or irrational clannishness. As Silverman notes, " 'the' political culture tends to be treated as a substratum of values and predispositions that defies (or at least does not demand) explanation, yet has causal significance" (Silverman 1977b: 18). Factions are part of the structure of society, the channels through which political favors and resources flow. Voters align themselves with one faction or the other (or remain neutral) based on their social networks, and they develop their networks and factional contacts to advance their interests.

Neither Taiwanese culture nor the KMT government was solely responsible for the development of factionalism; factions arose to mediate between the mainlander state and local society, earning power and prestige by their ability to help individuals unable to appeal directly to the KMT-controlled government and courts. Culture and structure develop together and cannot exist without each other. The *guanxi* basis of social relations has not determined faction structure, and has in fact permitted several different forms of patronage. The dyadic *guanxi* ties and the political structure have developed together from landlord clientelism to machine factions and now, possibly, to mass party clientelism. In turn, the factions have had an important—albeit unintentional—effect on Taiwan political culture: muting class consciousness. "The effect of machine rule under universal suffrage is to submerge growing collective policy demands with immediate payoffs, thereby retarding the development of class-based political interests among the lower strata. The machine's lower-class voters are disaggregated and dealt with particularistically while its upper class financial backers and bureaucratic capitalists find their collective interests well cared for" (Scott 1972: 151). Local factions thus have structured local politics and been an important influence in national politics, and have been key to KMT rule in Taiwan by connecting Taiwanese to mainlanders and by promoting a nonideological political culture.

Notes

1. My intent in using an analogy from physics is merely pedagogic. Whereas the concept of the photon is often presented as a temporary theoretical compromise or as a

riddle of science, ambiguity is inherent in social phenomena and not to be resolved or removed.

2. Fieldwork for this chapter was carried out from June 1984 to August 1986 and supported by a Columbia University Traveling Fellowship, an American Council of Learned Societies Pre-doctoral Dissertation Research Fellowship, and a Fulbright-Hays Doctoral Dissertation Research Abroad Fellowship for research in Taiwan. Additional research in Taiwan in November–December 1989 and January–February 1990 was supported by the Taiwan Area Studies Program of the East Asian Institute, Columbia University, a program that is supported by a grant from the Institute of International Relations of National Chengchi University. Many of the ideas in this chapter were learned or sharpened during discussions with members of the Columbia election trip study group (Andrew J. Nathan, Thomas Bernstein, James Seymour, Douglas Chalmers, Hung-mao Tien, and Mingtong Chen), and long conversations with Ed Winckler and Yun-han Chu. Richard Lufrano, Chen-Chia Cheng, Andrew Nathan, Murray Rubinstein, Sara Bosco, and anonymous reviewers offered comments on an earlier version of this essay. Remaining errors are my own.

3. Taiwan's administrative levels can be confusing, in part because there is no consensus on the English translation of the Mandarin terms. The following chart shows the administrative levels used in Taiwan. The three types of unit below the county are administratively identical and vary only in relative urbanization. This level will all be glossed as "township." County and township "head" (*xianzhang* and *xiangzhang*) will be glossed as "executive."

4. If voters could cast four votes or vote for a party list, one would expect eight candidates to run, four from each faction.

Republic of China on Taiwan				
Province *sheng* (i.e., Taiwan) (Governor appointed by central government)				Municipality (city) *shi* (i.e., Taibei, Gaoxiong) (Mayor appointed)
County *xian*			City *shi* (e.g., Taizhong City)	District *gu*
Township (rural) *xiang*	Township (urban) *zhen*	City *shi*		
Village *cun*	Neighborhood *li*	Neighborhood *li*	Neighborhood *li*	Neighborhood *li*

5. For a discussion of factions' relationships with the opposition party and of factions' future in a more democratic Taiwan, see Bosco (in press).

6. After the January 20 election, the *China Times* (January 22, 1990, pp. 6–7) had a two-page, county-by-county report on the changes in factions.

7. Native Taiwanese who oppose the KMT government have questioned the legitimacy of a legislature representing all of China by calling for the independence of Taiwan, which would require a government elected by residents of the island. Under recent reforms, mainlanders retired in 1991, and Taiwan-elected representatives were elected in 1991 and 1992.

8. Because village head is largely an honorary position, few seek the post, and many villages do not have two qualified candidates running, in which case faction looms as less important.

9. Civil servants and teachers often claim that they must be scrupulously above factional politics and show no favoritism (*bufen dangpai*). In fact, however, many of these

persons are local faction leaders because of the prestige their education and work commands and because of the connections and resources they can mobilize.

10. The system is not mired in corruption because the state sets and enforces high employment standards and, with the KMT, supervises hiring closely to prevent extreme abuse. As will be seen, the party allows some patronage but seeks to prevent any one faction machine from becoming too strong. In addition, most people have a broad range of *guanxi* connections that they can tap to find out about jobs and other important information. Furthermore, although the security of government jobs is sought after, many private-sector jobs and businesses are more lucrative. Nevertheless, the personalism that is possible is an important source of patronage for factions.

11. Because of Taiwan's single-vote, multiple-member district system (described more fully below), a faction or party that does not have a majority to elect an executive can still elect at least one representative.

12. Some factions are indeed largely led by one family (for example, the Black faction in Gaoxiong County, known as the Yu Family faction), but these are the exception. Generalizations from these few cases suggesting Taiwan factions are family- or lineage-based are attempts to make the factions and their networks appear to be concrete when they are inherently vague and informal.

13. This list of voters can technically only be copied from the Household Registration Office three days before the election, which is not sufficient time to plan the campaign strategy. Factions therefore use personal contacts inside the office to get copies ahead of time. Maps that officially are state secrets also end up in candidates' hands. Even DPP candidates, although often viewed by civil servants as agitators, have little difficulty getting these materials, showing the strength and importance of personal connections.

14. I am not trying to claim the ties are not based on self-interest, but only to stress the primacy of personal ties, which already have an element of mutual self-interest.

15. The use of money to create a sense of obligation in the recipient is not unusual or exclusively Asian. The Simmons market research firm mailed a questionaire to U.S. attorneys along with a crisp new one-dollar bill "as a token of [their] appreciation." Simmons research shows that making personal contact with respondents and giving them a token gift raises response rates for surveys, but that as the burden of the survey increases, respondents expect to receive not just token but fair compensation (Donato 1991). Voting is not an onerous burden in Taiwan, especially since election day is a national holiday, so token monetary gifts coupled with a visit from the *thiu-á-kha* are effective in mobilizing voters.

16. A rumor said that the high vote winner's brother-in-law, a wealthy Taibei industrialist, told him to spend as much as was necessary to get elected.

17. Votes are not being sold to the highest bidder; candidates pay more to help assure a more reliable return. The local candidate with a smaller gift may be able to lay claim to the vote unless the outsider offers a sufficiently large gift to make the voter feel indebted.

18. Another revealing factor in the businessman's decision not to run was that as a businessman, he was not openly a South faction supporter but only leaned toward it, trying to be on good terms with all political leaders. His power within the faction was thus less strong than that of the openly factional politicians; he would have been welcome to run only if no core faction members wished to run.

19. KMT tactics on factions have not been unchanging. Winckler (1984; 1988: 169) describes how in the 1973 and 1977 elections Chiang Ching-kuo, advised by Lee Huan, switched from a divide-and-rule strategy of balancing local factions to parachuting outsiders skilled in administration. The tactic failed because some of the young candidates defected to the opposition, and the KMT returned to traditional tactics. This new tactic was primarily applied to county executives, however, and not to township executives.

References

Amick, G. 1976. *The American Way of Graft*. Princeton: Princeton University Press.
Amsden, A.H. 1985. "The State and Taiwan's Economic Development." In *Bringing the State Back In*, ed. P.B. Evans, D. Rueschemeyer, and T. Skocpol. New York.
Bailey, F.G. 1969. *Stratagems and Spoils: A Social Anthropology of Politics*. New York.
Beller, D.C., and F.P. Belloni. 1978. "The Study of Factions." In *Faction Politics: Political Parties and Factionalism in Comparative Perspective*, ed. F.P. Belloni and D.C. Beller, pp. 3–17. Santa Barbara.
Boissevain, J. 1977 (1964). "Factions, Parties, and Politics in a Maltese Village." In *Friends, Followers, and Factions*, ed. S. Schmidt, J. Scott, C. Landé, and L. Guasti, pp. 279–87. Berkeley: University of California Press.
Bosco, J. In press. "Faction Versus Ideology: Mobilization Strategies in Taiwan's Elections." *China Quarterly*.
Caciagli, M., and F.P. Belloni. 1981. "The 'New' Clientelism in Southern Italy: The Christian Democratic Party in Catania." In *Political Clientelism, Patronage and Development*, ed. S.N. Eisenstadt and R. Lemarchand, pp. 35–55. Beverly Hills.
Campbell, J.K. 1964. *Honour, Family, and Patronage: A Study of Institutions and Moral Values in a Greek Mountain Community*. Oxford.
Chalmers, D.A. 1977 (1972). "Parties and Society in Latin America." In *Friends, Followers, and Factions*, ed. S. Schmidt et al., pp. 401–21. Berkeley: University of California Press.
Chen, Ming-tong. 1989. "Quyuxing lianhe duzhan jingji, difang paixi yu shengyiyuan xuanju: Yi xiang shengyiyuan houxuan ren beijing ziliao de fenxi" (Regional oligopoly, local factions, and provincial assembly elections: An analysis of the background of candidates), ms.
————. 1990. "The Mobility of the Local Political Elite Under an Authoritarian Regime (1945–1986): An Analysis on the Taiwan Provincial Assemblymen." Ph.D. dissertation, National Taiwan University (in Chinese).
Cheng, T.J. 1989. "Democratizing the Quasi-Leninist Regime in Taiwan." *World Politics* 41, 4: 471–99.
Chu, Yun-han. 1989. "Guazhan jingji yu weiquan zhengzhi tizhi" (Economic oligarchy and the authoritarian system). In *Longduan yu boxue: weiquanzhuyi de zhengzhi jingji fenxi* (Monopoly and exploitation: Political economic analyses of authoritarianism), ed. Hsin-huang Hsiao et al., pp. 139–60. Taibei.
Copper, John F. 1984. *Taiwan's Elections: Political Development and Democratization in the Republic of China*. With George P. Chen. Occasional papers/Reprint Series in Contemporary Asian Studies. Baltimore.
Curtis, G.L. 1983 (1971). *Election Campaigning Japanese Style*. Tokyo.
Donato, P. 1991. "Mechanisms for Improving Response Rates in Complex Surveys." Simmons Market Research Bureau, New York, ms.
Firth, R. 1957. "Factions in Indian and Overseas Indian Societies. Introduction." *British Sociology* 8:291–95.
Fried, M.H. 1974 (1953). *Fabric of Chinese Society: A Study of the Social Life of a Chinese County Seat*. New York.
Gallin, B. 1963. "Land Reform in Taiwan: Its Effect on Rural Social Organization and Leadership." *Human Organization* 22:109–12.
————. 1966. *Hsin Hsing, Taiwan: A Chinese Village in Change*. Berkeley: University of California Press.
————. 1968. "Political Factionalism and Its Impact on Chinese Village Social Organization in Taiwan." In *Local-level Politics*, ed. Marc J. Swartz, pp. 377–400. Chicago.

Gates, H. 1987. "Money for the Gods." *Modern China* 13, 3: 259–77.

Gold, T.B. 1985. "After Comradeship: Personal Relations in China since the Cultural Revolution." *China Quarterly* 104:657–75.

———. 1986. *State and Society in the Taiwan Miracle.* Armonk, NY: M.E. Sharpe.

He, Ying'ai. 1989. *Taiwansheng xianshizhang ji xianshiyiyuan xuanju zhidu zhi yanjiu* (Research on the Taiwan province's county/city executive and county/city representative election system). Taibei.

Hermet, G., R. Rose, and A. Rouquié, eds. 1978. *Elections Without Choice.* New York.

Hu, Fu, and Yun-han Chu. 1992. "Electoral Competition and Political Democratization in Taiwan." In *Political Change in Taiwan,* ed. Tun-jen Cheng and Stephan Haggard, pp. 177–203. Boulder, CO: Westview Press.

Hu, Fu, and Ying-lung Yu. 1983. "Xuanminde dangpai xuanze: Taidu chuxiang ji geren beijing de fenxi" (Partisan choice of the voter: An analysis of their attitudes and background). *Zhengchi xuebao* (Journal of politics) 21 (December 16): 31–53.

Jacobs, J.B. 1980. *Local Politics in a Rural Chinese Cultural Setting: A Field Study of Mazu Township, Taiwan.* Canberra.

King, Ambrose Yeo-chi. 1991. "Kuan-hsi and Network Building: A Sociological Interpretation." *Daedalus* 120:63–84.

Landé, C.H. 1964. *Leaders, Factions, and Parties: The Structure of Philippine Politics.* Monograph no. 6, Yale University Southeast Asian Studies. New Haven.

———. 1977. "The Dyadic Basis of Clientelism." In *Friends, Followers, and Factions,* ed. S. Schmidt et al., pp. xiii–xxxvii. Berkeley.

Lasater, M.L. 1990. *A Step toward Democracy: The December 1989 Elections in Taiwan, Republic of China.* American Enterprise Institute Special Analysis. Washington, DC.

Lasson, A. de. 1989. *A Restudy of the Taiwan Farmers' Associations.* Socioeconomic Studies on Rural Development, vol. 82. Aachen.

Lasswell, H.D. 1938 (1931). "Faction." In *Encyclopaedia of the Social Sciences,* vol. 5, pp. 49–51. New York.

Li, Wen-lang. 1989. "Structural Correlates of Emerging Political Pluralism in Taiwan." In *Taiwan: A Newly Industrialized State,* ed. H.H.M. Hsiao, W.Y. Cheng, and H.S. Chan, pp. 265–84. Taibei.

Nathan, A.J. 1977 (1973). "A Factionalism Model for CCP Politics." In *Friends, Followers, and Factions.* ed. S. Schmidt et al., pp. 381–401. Berkeley.

Nicholas, R.W. 1977 (1965). "Factions: A Comparative Analysis." In *Friends, Followers, and Factions,* ed. S. Schmidt et al., pp. 55–73. Berkeley.

Niou, Emerson M.S., and P.C. Ordeshook. 1989. *The Republic of China's Emerging Electoral Pluralism: A Spacial, Game-theoretic Interpretation.* Working Papers in Asian/Pacific Studies, Asian/Pacific Institute, Duke University.

Purcell, S.K. 1981. "Mexico: Clientelism, Corporatism and Political Stability." In *Political Clientelism, Patronage and Development,* ed. S.N. Eisenstadt and R. Lemarchand, pp. 191–216. Beverly Hills.

Scott, J.C. 1972. *Comparative Political Corruption.* Englewood Cliffs, NJ.

Seaman, G. 1978. *Temple Organization in a Chinese Village.* Taibei.

Sheng, Hsing-yuan. 1986. *Guomindang yu dangwai zhongyanghouyuanhui xuanju jingzheng zhi yanjiu: Minguo qishier nian Taiwan diqu zenge quyu lifaweiyuan xuanju zhi fenxi yu tantao* (Research on KMT and dangwai campaign assistance committee electoral competition: Analysis and discussion of the 1983 Taiwan area supplementary legislative Yuan elections). Taibei.

Silverman, S.F. 1977a (1965). "Patronage and Community-Nation Relationships in Central Italy." In *Friends, Followers, and Factions,* ed. S. Schmidt et al., pp. 293–304. Berkeley.

———. 1977b. "Patronage as Myth." In *Patrons and Clients in Mediterranean Societies,* ed. E. Gellner and J. Waterbury, pp. 7–19. London.

Stavis, B. 1974. *Rural Local Governance and Agricultural Development in Taiwan.* Ithaca.

Tien, H.M. 1989. *The Great Transition: Political and Social Change in the Republic of China.* Stanford: Stanford University Press.

Ting, Tin-yu. 1989. "Who Votes for the Opposition in Taiwan: A Case Study of Chia-yi City." In *Taiwan: A Newly Industrialized State,* ed. Hsin-Huang Michael Hsiao, Wei-Yuan Cheng, and Hou-Sheng Chan, pp. 285–312. Taibei.

Ts'ai, Ling, and R.H. Myers. 1990. "Winds of Democracy: The 1989 Taiwan Elections." *Asian Survey* 30, 4: 360–79.

Weingrod, A. 1977 (1968). "Patrons, Patronage, and Political Parties." In *Friends, Followers, and Factions,* ed. S. Schmidt et al., pp. 323–37. Berkeley.

Winckler, E.A. 1981. "Roles Linking State and Society." In *The Anthropology of Taiwanese Society,* ed. E.M. Ahern and H. Gates, pp. 50–86. Stanford: Stanford University Press.

———. 1984. "Institutionalization and Participation on Taiwan: From Hard to Soft Authoritarianism?" *China Quarterly* 99:481–99.

———. 1988. "Elite Political Struggle, 1945–1985." In *Contending Approaches to the Political Economy of Taiwan,* ed. E. Winckler and S. Greenhalgh, pp. 151–71. Armonk, NY: M.E. Sharpe.

———. 1989. "The 1989 Taiwan Elections: What They Mean and How They Work." New York.

———. 1990. "The 1989 Taiwan Elections: A Preliminary Post-election Assessment." Paper presented at the Association for Asian Studies meetings, Chicago.

Wolf, M. 1972. *Women and the Family in Rural Taiwan.* Stanford: Stanford University Press.

Wu, N.T. 1987. "The Politics of a Regime Patronage System: Mobilization and Control Within an Authoritarian Regime." Ph.D. dissertation, University of Chicago.

Wurfel, D. 1963. "The Philippines." *The Journal of Politics* 25:757–73.

Yang, M.M.H. 1989. "The Gift Economy and State Power in China." *Comparative Studies in Society and History* 31, 1: 25–54.

Chapter 5

From Democratic Movement to Bourgeois Democracy: The Internal Politics of the Taiwan Democratic Progressive Party in 1991

Linda Gail Arrigo

Taiwan is awash with money. It has the highest foreign currency reserves in the world per capita. Its GNP per capita is soaring and may soon surpass U.S. $10,000; it is the Taiwan miracle, proof of the export industrialization strategy.[1] It is also a bustling, internationalized economy laid haphazardly upon the remnants of an agricultural society of personalistic loyalties.

It has a Chinese-born regime, long frozen in anxious confrontation with its distant nemesis, the People's Republic, that has finally put down roots and begun to go native. In the words of the *New York Times Magazine* of February 16, 1992, it is "a dictatorship that grew up.... In Taiwan despotism passes post haste into democracy."

Yet what kind of democracy is that? The question can only now be answered with greater verisimilitude following the December 1991 elections for the Republic of China National Assembly, only the second time in the forty-five-year history of that body that it has been fully subject to election by the populace. This was to be a seminal election, with the shape of a new constitution and presidential elections at stake. Other functions of democracy have also been revived. Martial law was repealed in 1987. Activists espousing a formal declaration of Taiwan independence are still being jailed, about a dozen a year, and

---

This chapter is based largely on interviews and discussions conducted during six weeks in Taiwan, from late December 1991 to early February 1992, plus newspaper and documentary sources.

statements of opposition candidates that "contravene national policy" are still censored from their printed platforms; but they are hardly deterred, and thus freedom of speech advances with a slightly hobbled gait. The 72 percent popular vote victory of the ruling party, the Kuomintang, cannot be attributed to intimidation, ballot-box stuffing, or simple electronic falsification, as before—although vote buying, now on a colossal scale, continues.

But is this democracy, a measured and well-informed judgment of the populace on the choices that best safeguard their interests and future? The democratic process calls for an articulation and organization of contending opinions and personnel, such that the electorate is accorded substantial options. This function would seem to be provided by the Taiwan Democratic Progressive Party, at present the only major opposition party, founded on September 28, 1986—in personnel and continuous history the carrier of the legacy of the democratic movement of 1977–79, which culminated in the 1979 establishment of *Formosa Magazine (Meilidao)*, the Kaohsiung Incident of December 10, 1979, and the public trials the following March.

Many of the leaders of the democratic movement have spent six to ten years in incarceration. Some have suffered the murder or maiming of family members, in periods (as late as 1984–85) when security agency arrogance surpassed governmental concern for embarrassment in foreign affairs. In 1991 they were substantially the same as the leadership of the Democratic Progressive party, both in social composition and in specific personnel. It would seem that this past assures an adamant and unyielding stance of opposition. Certainly the ruling party, for one, is happy to legitimize its democratic credentials and let foreign visitors know it faces an obstreperous if small opposition; but despite past fist fights in the legislature, the DPP could perhaps now be appropriately portrayed, as the ruling party would like, as a loyal opposition. Its social composition is still the same. But given the substitution of incorporation and cooptation for repression in the core of the regime's policy, the social dynamics are different now. To be abrupt, if one has a lot of money, it is easier and less damaging to business as usual to try to buy off one's opponents rather than to jail or kill them.

Has the DPP been bought off? It would be premature to answer this in the affirmative. Even in a measured affirmative, it would have to be qualified that it is no more bought off than the generally accepted social custom, and certainly much less than the politicos of the ruling party. But all the same its bite has been blunted, its critical stance as the champion of the masses subtly compromised.

The particulars of how this has happened will be the main content of this chapter. This involves a sketch of the composition of the party and its supporters: its factions and their related social bases and the interactions among these in the shifting currents of the popular clamor for liberalization. This is shown in the struggle among the factions in 1991, leading up to bitterly contested intraparty elections for chairman and Central Committee in mid-October 1991, and thence to a poorly coordinated bid for representation in the National Assembly two months later. Finally, the complementary processes of democratization and cooptation must be understood in the context of Taiwan's expanding economy, and this in turn can be seen as part of the dynamics of a global shift in economic and political relations.

The Kuomintang, the Opposition, and Taiwanization

While ostensibly the opposition party is the amalgamation of all that is different from the ruling party, it is truer to portray it as a microcosm whose internal dynamics and factional disputes are analogous to those of the whole society, albeit played out more intensely under the prying eyes of the press. The conflicting needs for money and for popular mobilization are felt sharply, particularly at the commanding heights of the DPP central party headquarters: money from capitalist supporters, to sustain the functions of the party apparatus; mobilization, to cajole the government into concessions and to win elected posts. Here mobilization means acceding to the issues of the left faction of the party, or at least mouthing the aspirations of the disadvantaged.

The ruling party is secure in its power and privilege; yet it too is swept along with internal and societywide demand for rationalization and restructuring of the polity. The tasks are reorientation to the de facto national identity—Taiwan—and balancing of the forces of an industrialized, internationalized society—political accommodation and legitimation, a.k.a. democratization. (Social balancing, of course, does not mean that all sectors are accorded equality, only that the clamor of workers and peasants can at least be quieted with some welfare palliatives from the full coffers of the state.)

And so while the opposition party appears to be at a standstill in terms of voter response and finds its issues repeatedly coopted by the ruling party, the overall dynamic rolls both ahead to new territory. This is especially the case on the issue of national identity, "Taiwan Independence." What government bureaucrats proclaim now as policy would have been tantamount to sedition a decade ago.

A further sketch of the social history of the two parties may be useful to set the stage, although it may be familiar to the reader. The central government of the Republic of China, along with its military and security organs, fled to Taiwan in 1949; having subjugated a native Taiwanese uprising in 1947, they proceeded to rule by white terror for several decades, from the Japanese-built governor's palace. They fed their hordes of bureaucrats and soldiers with requisitioned Taiwanese rice; handed over the Japanese monopolies to the management of Shanghai capitalists and Nanking functionaries; and set up party-owned monopolies to provide employment for retired soldiers and other minions. To many Taiwanese nationalists, the government is still the "foreign regime," an ethnic minority of less than 15 percent that rules the majority.

But at least by 1975, when Chiang Ching-kuo took over from his father, a new direction had been set: incorporation of the newly expanding native Taiwanese entrepreneur and professional classes. It sought the sons of Taiwanese corporate heads to be its candidates for public office, to the extent that the second generation of mainlanders complained of lack of opportunities for advancement. It may be speculated that the Kuomintang then proceeded to sink roots and increasingly incorporate leaders of the native population into its networks of patronage and payoff. It paid substantial bonuses to its provincial assemblymen on the occasions of important votes. It manufactured consent among trade union representatives, aborigine leaders, youth groups, and others by means of small subsidies, feasts, and free trips.

On the side of opposition to the Kuomintang, since the early days of show elections local leaders had voiced the plaints of farmers, victims of the squeeze of the agricultural sector, and found themselves jailed for sedition or, if they were lucky, merely framed on corruption charges. But such local leaders usually represented local clan or faction interests that could be played off against one another, or bought off. In a recurrent pattern, local notables arose and garnered a popular following through vociferous oratory damning governmental exploitation and cultural suppression of the Taiwanese, but then traded that popular support for government-appointed office, or mitigated their vituperation in the face of monetary inducement and police threat.

It was not until the mid-1970s that a new generation of Taiwanese intellectuals/ politicians in the capital city, many having already been frustrated in their efforts at reform within the Kuomintang, linked with the local opposition politicians to form the challenge of the democratic movement of 1977–79. They could be said to reflect the discontent of small Taiwanese manufacturers chaffing under monopolistic governmental regulation, and of middle-class professionals, lawyers and teachers, insulted by government censorship and propaganda; these were a large part of urban supporters.[2] That movement utilized as well the populist appeal of leftist academics and students inspired by the Chinese Cultural Revolution and American radicalism of the 1960s, and of young Presbyterian ministers rooted in the long native history of the church and contemporary liberation theology. It moved forward on a groundswell of mass rallies, scenes populated with market hawkers, shopkeepers, farmers, artisans, laborers—rough hands, grimy baseball caps, broken teeth stained red-brown with betel nut.

To a large degree this is still the basic equation for the composition of the opposition party; but the contradictions within this amalgamation have been played out. I believe that my essay, "The Social Origins of the Taiwan Democratic Movement," written in 1980–81 for an overseas Taiwanese audience, shows a certain prescience in this.

But now Taiwan is an advanced industrialized nation virtually sinking under its own material wealth. It is a sophisticated, largely middle-class society with an extravagant nouveau riche segment. In the new East District of Taipei, massive art deco towers and department stores line broad boulevards choked with traffic. Japanese cuisine, ritzy disco, and karaoke with private rooms are the rage. Older areas of the city are stained cement blocks of buildings, refurbished piecemeal, but are abustle with commerce. When the streetside night food vendors close at 3:00 A.M., they leave five-foot-high piles of used styrofoam dishes. Or to stave off midnight hunger you can buy microwaveable *baoze, jiaoze,* or *chongze*—spongy and flavored by cellophane wrapping, but still better than American fast food—at the twenty-four-hour OK or 7–11 store. The lanes behind the boulevards are packed solid with parked cars and nearly impassable. Given the ubiquitous automobile—generally foreign-made, often with real leather upholstery—it is not surprising that the dense population of the city is seeking fresh air and expanding the urban sprawl. The five-hour freeway stretches down the west coast, never out of sight of buildings, past factories belching noxious fumes. Luxury apartment buildings are going up in what were originally semirural towns or farmers' rice fields. Originally lush terraces lie abandoned for want of labor; flat paddy land is dug into to make fish ponds. There are even pockets of foreign laborers and housekeepers kept like indentured servants, from Thailand, Philippines, Bangladesh, and smuggled from China in boats, to fill out the worker shortage.

The problems of Taiwan are now the problems of a modern urban industrial society, one with a legacy of particularly haphazard and cannibalistic development: disastrous environmental degradation, lack of city services and planning, capital flight and worker discontent, family instability, crime, youth alienation and drug use. The opposition party cannot address these with merely the cry of "Taiwan Independence!" or by railing against government inaction.[3] It must propose programs and solutions, and in fact it is already faced with the tasks of administration in the six counties where the DPP has won the post of county executive, out of thirteen total. But the obstacles to dealing systematically with environmental and social problems lie largely in patronage and payoff, and the party demurs to take these on.

It would not be fair to criticize without taking cognizance of the environment from which the DPP has grown and in which it operates. I will take a certain poetic license in the description.

Patronage, Payoff, Political Office

Even decades ago Taiwanese were known to revel in culinary delights, in time-honored tradition, as far as their budgets permitted. Now, to say that Taiwan is awash in money is to say that it is awash in food, very expensive food. The pools of oil dripping from the delectables lubricate not only gullets, but the business deals that thrive in the idiom of personal relations. The American visitor to Taipei, finding prices in the range of New York City, cannot but choke in amazement at the sums splashed in restaurants even by people of ordinary means. But the standard of consumption is really set by the business of business entertainment, with exotic seafood in elegant place settings, imported XO brandy gulped for "bottoms-up," and hostess companions. In Taiwanese dialect, *kha yiu,* literally "skim oil," is to skim a profit.

Such Dionysian indulgences are not merely recreation, but the process of development of a discrete understanding of political/economic arrangements. Construction companies are particularly known for lavish entertainment, because they are involved not merely with customers, but with a myriad of subcontractors, banks, and government offices, for zoning, licensing, and inspections.

According to an informed observer, the overall price of construction undertaken under government contract can be estimated at 20 percent drinking, eating, and entertainment, 30 percent kickback and payoff, and 50 percent cost of construction. Thus positions on the city planning commissions of large city councils are particularly remunerative. A single city council vote in favor of a particular zoning or construction—or even abstention from objection—may commonly be rewarded by NT $20 *wan* (U.S. $8,000).[4] More directly, city council members can set up their own real estate and construction companies. A person with real clout can stage a coup by wrapping up exclusive deals with all the available subcontractors and monopolizing the construction market; it is not necessary actually to own equipment or to be involved in construction. In the process of multiple subcontracting the actual builders are squeezed to a low margin and are likely to *tou gong jian liao,* steal labor and decrease materials, resulting in the generally expected low quality of government construction.[5]

The process works similarly for zoning. It is said that all of the land adjacent to the cleaned-up and renovated Love River and promenade was bought up by Kaohsiung City councilmen. In a small, simple case in January 1992 it was revealed in television reports that all the saplings of a particular kind of tree specified for a large river beautification project in Taipei had been bought out ahead of time from nurseries throughout the island. Such revelations are always followed by indignant statements by officials that they will get to the bottom of the matter and punish the culprits. But investigations are frequently stymied, and pundits quip that exposure and punishment are related to infighting of political factions or retribution by those cut out of the deal, not the frequency of malpractice.

A conspicuous case of corruption in 1991 was that of Hua Lung Investment Company. An assistant to the DPP legislator Hsu Kuo-tai obtained copies of receipts that showed that the minister of communications was profiting from insider trading. (As in real estate and construction, astounding profits in the Taiwan stock market are generally suspected to be due to insider sources, even where no evidence is exposed.) The prosecutor, a young Taiwanese woman, refused to let go of the investigation and circumvented some of the usual judicial conventions to indict him. The minister was forced to resign, the prosecutor became a folk hero, and a conflict of judicial authority is still under way.[6] But another sly interpretation common to those who read the newspapers carefully is that the Hua Lung group, which supports the military-man-in-business-suit Premier Hao Bo-tsun, was given a blow by "KMT mainstream" President Lee

Teng-hui, who is supported by Taiwanese capitalists such as the Evergreen group, which incidentally sponsors the Institute for International Policy Studies, a very liberal think tank espousing government adjustment to a sovereign state of Taiwan. To add to the Byzantine twists of this scene, in December 1991 the recent chairman of the DPP, Huang Hsin-chieh, brought with him to a campaign appearance the manager of Hua Lung (who perhaps had tried to redeem public relations by making a contribution to the party), leaving the observers in confusion.

This account is not an effort to make sense of this case, but only serves to illustrate the flows and eddies of a social process in which the sides are not clearly white or black. It further shows the role of the opposition as a watchdog and possibly a conciliator, and this relates to the dynamics described by an opposition legislator who will remain unnamed here, as follows.

Like officials of the ruling party, independent or opposition politicians can parlay popular election into bank account balances. In fact, their structural role as opposition may command even higher inducements. After this decade of overheated economic growth, both local big men and Taipei political science professionals wear three-piece suits; both may be supported by those who resent losing contracts to KMT favorites and want to compete. But in this role they act individualistically.

The mechanisms are numerous and range from an active search for deals, to a passive, tacit acceptance of misdoing, to a mild voicing of concerns that have no appearance of impropriety. The official may own an office machine company, and the city may place a large order for copiers. Or the legislator may act as mediator for a company that has been subject to tax audits and is under threat of being fined five times the delinquent amount. If the penalty is NT $2,000 *wan* (U.S. $800,000), the matter may be resolved with NT $200 *wan* (U.S. $80,000) to the tax auditor and NT $300 *wan* (U.S. $120,000) to the legislator, dispersed through discrete channels where trust has been built up through repeated mutual enmeshment. Even a telephone call or a courtesy visit to "show concern" that a party in litigation is not mistreated may influence the outcome with no transfer of cash—but alliances are built up and expressed in campaign contributions. In such fashion the government agencies can neutralize the supposed watchdogs one by one by entangling them in questionable exchanges.

It is not surprising, then, that businessmen cluster around certain political figures, and that the supporters' political ideals cannot be clearly differentiated from their pecuniary purposes. For example, perhaps thirty businessmen can sustain one legislator, and they would provide about 90 percent of that legislator's income. According to the source, the danger of this, even without overt corruption, is that the legislator comes to see the financiers as a constituency and a sounding board for political direction, and these may also be beholden to Kuomintang-influenced interests, and/or fearful of tax audit or other retribution. In fact, the Kuomintang can act on an opposition legislator through the intermediary of these financial sources.

It is only with this background that it is possible to understand the election of members of the National Assembly on December 21, 1991. The results overall had little to do with nationalism, either Taiwanese or Chinese, or with the role of the National Assembly as framer of the constitution. Of the 470 who ran for the assembly in city and county races, 225 were victorious; between 20,000 and 30,000 votes were required to win by plurality in each district. Some 78 percent of the victors were KMT-nominated. But as investigated and analyzed in detail by the *Independence Post*,[7] the election was really a victory for "gold cows," moneyed interests. The amount of money necessary for a candidate to "spread around" in handouts was NT $3–5,000 *wan* (U.S. $1.2–2 million), distributed by elected neighborhood heads (overwhelmingly KMT) and by specialized intermediaries (*thiau kha*). A control center for handing out money in Taichung operated with a computerized database listing four thousand intermediaries. Most of over one hundred reports of vote buying detailed by the newspaper were in the range of NT $300–500 (U.S. $12–20). One can only surmise that it is worth spending all this money because the rake-off of a public official, even in realms apparently unrelated to the office, is so great.

The cartoon accompanying the newspaper report shows a character resembling President Lee Teng-hui muttering in the streets under a shower of NT $1,000 (U.S. $40) bills fluttering down from high buildings: "Has Taiwan been declared independent? Why are the candidates throwing out currency like trash?"

Only a few DPP candidates are rumored to have engaged in vote buying. The DPP candidates generally do not have that kind of money. They must rely instead on appeals to the issues, particularly Taiwanese nationalism. Some voters take money from candidates but still vote their consciences. All the same, a major campaign for a DPP candidate easily costs NT $500 *wan* (U.S. $200,000), requiring considerable commitment by financial backers. One of three Labor party candidates, Wang Yao-nan, by his own account spent only NT $50 *wan* (U.S. $20,000) and directed his speeches to the specifics of constitutional reform; he received precisely 1,026 votes in the Kaohsiung City second district race.

Another 100 seats in the National Assembly were apportioned to candidates nominated by the Central Committee of each party according to the percent of popular votes received overall: 80 seats as if to represent some unseen Chinese population (a nod to the old National Assembly, 90 percent of which represented a long-gone Chinese constituency), and 20 to represent overseas Chinese. Of these the DPP was apportioned 20 and 5 seats; no third party rated representation. This arrangement resulted from a deal drawn between the KMT and the DPP following the National Affairs Conference of July 1990. The DPP assigned at least seven of its seats to the party chairman, general secretary, and other functionaries in or allied with the central party headquarters, allowing them to circumvent the time and expenditure of local campaigns. This move brings us back to examine the internal politics of the party.

Inside the Democratic Progressive Party

The political scene of the opposition politicians in Taipei runs at a feverish pace, a cyclone in which it seems a race merely to catch up with the actors. The reporters, now only young men and women with considerable physical stamina and command of Taiwanese dialect as well as Mandarin, chase the press conferences and news leaks daily, pounce on the juiciest bits like flocks of birds of prey, and rush back to home offices to write and file. They must know both the history and the latest moves to interpret what is happening. It can be seen that each notable continually seeks to rally alliances and hatch crusades that will put him or her at the center of the limelight. They carry their portable telephones and must turn them off to grab a moment of rest. Their itinerary books might read as follows: Attend weekly party committee meetings. Meet with prospective contributors. Appear at press conferences. Seek talented young assistants who will work for low wages for an unspecified length of time. Appear at benefits for auspicious social causes. Drink to feigned drunkenness with allies and supporters. Parry with the ruling party; ferret out its maneuvers from the information mongers. Organize demonstrations. Attend appreciation banquets. Banquet lunch at Hoover Hotel. Meeting at coffee shop, NT $150 (U.S. $6) a cup. Banquet dinner at Ambassador. Appear at 9:00 P.M. at wedding in cheap hall in Panchiao, hour's drive through gridlock traffic, toast with rice wine and shake hands with a hundred people: i.e., extend influence by lending prestige to event. 11:00 P.M. snack, rice porridge at fancy Taiwanese restaurant, together with confidantes and senior editorial writers. 1:00 A.M., midnight vigil outside prison for Taiwanese émigrés arrested upon return, for membership in seditious Taiwan Independence organization;[8] give impromptu speech. In brief, this is an intense, grueling way of life that expands the waistline and raises the blood pressure.

There is hardly time to reflect in this whirlwind, and yet somehow an observer must seek analysis that is beyond the event of the week, a significance that is in social forces and not in personalities. Any history is to some extent an abstraction, and social analysis is even more an interpretation based in repetitious experience and perception of pattern, shaped and limited by the environment of the observer. In exposition the concrete events must be laid out with considerable simplification. Here the cast of characters is real, and representative of many more. With this caveat, I will proceed to tell the tale.

A Decade in Review

Looking back over the years since the Kaohsiung Incident of December 10, 1979, which is generally seen as the watershed in Taiwan's recent political history, I see two basic changes in the wider environment that have shaped the evolution of the opposition forces.

The first is a complex of changes, the upward shift of Taiwan's position in the world economy and a change in the ruling forces that seems to have been derived ultimately from the relative decline in U.S. power. Let me recreate the atmosphere of 1979. U.S.-supported military regimes presided in much of Latin America and East and Southeast Asia, many having taken power with bloody suppression of democratic functions. Just as the democratic movement was suppressed in Taiwan with extensive arrests and heavy sentences, December 1979–April 1980, so in Korea the Kwangju uprising of May 1980 was crushed with much greater loss of life and U.S. complicity. Even Taiwanese activists without an anti-imperialist understanding (by far the majority) at that time saw the political question as one of armed revolution, like Iran or Nicaragua, although they were at a loss for any military capacity. For example, in response to the Kaohsiung Incident arrests on December 15, 1979, a coalition of overseas Taiwanese independence organizations headed by Hsu Hsin-liang (one of the leadership core of the democratic movement, but studying abroad since September 1979) vowed to "wipe the Kuomintang off the face of the Earth."

Yet despite the despair of those dire moments, the Taiwan democratic movement did begin to revive in late 1980 with the highest-vote election success of the wives of the arrested leaders, and broad social reaction against the suppression began to be felt. Finally, in the larger perspective a series of international events seemed to signal a new U.S. posture and the end of easy living for dictatorships. The frozen face of Latin American military regimes began to thaw; their dead victims were exhumed by human rights groups that indicted even those in power. Closer to Taiwan, Cory replaced Marcos on a wave of people power on the occasion of U.S.-forced elections. For Taiwan, the bungled assassination of Henry Liu in Daly City, California, in October 1984 exposed the vicious ambitions of the heirs to the security apparatus and irritated Washington. In retrospect, the turning point probably came as early as 1983 when General Wang Sheng was removed from his position as apparent successor to President Chiang Ching-kuo and shuffled off to Paraguay as ambassador. Now it can be seen that military-muscle strongmen from Korea to Singapore—in the "little dragons" of export-led growth—voluntarily gave way to softer, more technocratic versions of control in the years 1988–90, following the earlier trend. In this perspective there is no reason to credit especially either Chiang Ching-kuo's belated conversion to liberalism in the last year of his life, or even heroic struggles of a democratic movement with being the ultimate force behind Taiwan's relatively bloodless transition to democratic forms.[9]

Given that with the establishment of a functioning opposition party and also relative prosperity and full employment a revolutionary scenario could no longer be projected, overseas revolutionary organizations began in 1985 to change their rhetoric and their strategy to civil disobedience; and in 1991 even the diehard World United Formosans for Independence dropped its call for violent overthrow of the government. The opposition party and related organizations within the island have become the focus of activity.

The second factor is more internal to Taiwan, and that is the issue of nationalism. Whereas in 1980 there could be said still to survive a genuine Chinese chauvinism within Taiwan, to thence fuel elite government ideology and suppression of Taiwanese identity as a heterodox form, by 1990 the internal issue had devolved to one of who controls the spoils of government. Since the 1987 opening of legal travel to China, the poverty of China has been seen in stark contrast to Taiwan's wealth, and the Tiananmen massacre of June 1989 wilted any desire for political reunification. The most conservative, Chinese-nationalist rhetoric (that of the "nonmainstream" KMT) depicts China as a threat against the formal declaration of independence, not a beacon for cultural or other emulation. The president's policy ("mainstream," heavily Taiwanese KMT), labeled *du tai*, "Taiwan alone," by its right-wing critics, can hardly be distinguished from the seditious *tai du*, "Taiwan independence," and is thus the butt of many jokes. As for opposition forces, the pro-China and socialist-sounding Workers' Party (*Lao Dong Dang*) with its party emblem of a red star rising over a green patch received less than a thousand votes for its candidate in 1989.[10] There were fifty-one candidates announced from ten small parties with "China" in their names running in 1991, but not one was elected.[11] In sum, the DPP's poor showing in the elections—just after its October 1991 embracing of a Republic of Taiwan platform—indicated rather that the ruling party has successfully taken over much of the territory of Taiwanese nationalism with its Taiwanese-born president.[12]

There is a new cultural vibrancy in Taiwan, one that moves freely among Mandarin and native dialects, both Hokkien (usually generalized as "Taiwanese") and Hakka. This is widely reflected in television programming, notably in advertisements, and in the new prevalence of native cuisine and nostalgically decorated tea shops.[13] The relics of the agricultural society now seem quaintly endearing—they are far enough away in time that they no longer reek of poverty and hard labor. But this cultural renaissance is also not the exclusive province of the opposition party, although most vanguard intellectuals are loosely affiliated.

Now for the course of recent chronological events that are the waves above these tidal changes, here in brief are the events that are most significant to the opposition:

May 1986, New York. Drive by overseas Taiwanese groups for opposition party formation, by supporting return of Hsu Hsin-liang to Taiwan following pattern set by Benigno Acquino and Kim Dae-jung.

September 28, 1986, Taipei. Establishment of Democratic Progressive party, largely by elected wives and lawyers of those incarcerated following the Kaohsiung Incident.

July 1987. Government declaration of end of martial law, replaced by enactment of national security laws.

1986–88. Upsurge of social movements and street demonstrations: labor strikes, farmers' organizations, antinuclear and antipollution community organizations, women's protests against police-protected prostitution, aborigines' land struggles.

May 1988. Bloody confrontation of riot police with farmers' demonstration against unlimited imports of U.S. agricultural goods—sobering blow to social movements.

April 1989. Tseng Nan-jung, outspoken advocate of Taiwan Independence (TI), immolates himself rather than accept arrest: most stirring sacrifice among unceasing activities of TI networks and recurrent government crackdowns.

March 1990. Massive student movement against "old thieves" (national assemblymen elected in 1947 in mainland China) and their control of presidential selection, with sit-in of 60,000 at Chiang Kai-shek Memorial. Constitutional convention demanded.

May 1990. Release of remaining *Formosa Magazine* political prisoners, notably Shih Ming-deh and Hsu Hsin-liang, on accession of new president, Lee Teng-hui.

May 1990. Demonstrations against President Lee Teng-hui's appointment of military strongman Hao Bo-tsun as premier.

July 1990. National Affairs Conference, convened by President Lee, calls together liberal KMT party front, DPP moderates, academics, and overseas dissidents; ostensibly a constitutional convention for national reconciliation. In following months KMT reneges on most agreements.

April 1991. March against KMT convening lame-duck session of old National Assembly to extend national security laws. Show of DPP party unity. Prestigious professors form "100 Action Association" to oppose security laws, carry on struggle independent of opposition party.

October 1991. Annual party delegate convention passes resolution advocating establishment of Republic of Taiwan, replacing previous self-determination platform; new element this year is support of academics. Hsu Hsin-liang elected chairman over Shih Ming-deh.

December 1991. "Old thieves" retired. In elections for new National Assembly KMT gets 72 percent of votes, 78 percent of seats, and claims populace rejects Taiwan independence.

The Meilidao Faction and the Heritage of *Formosa Magazine*

In 1991 we see the old core of the democratic movement continuing as the present leadership of the opposition, but bitterly divided. The five central figures, plus the grand old man figurehead, have been embattled in internecine struggle.

The more traditional faction, which occupies the central party headquarters and has appropriated the name of the 1979 magazine organization, Meilidao, is headed by Huang Hsin-chieh, recent chairman; Chang Chun-hong, secretary general; and Hsu Hsin-liang, chairman since October 1991. In 1979 they were opposition champions as national legislator, provincial assemblyman, and executive of Taoyuan County, respectively. This faction continues the form of the *Formosa (Meilidao) Magazine* in that it is a coalition of Taipei intellectuals with local politicians. It is only weakly ideological in seeking democracy and national realization and is mostly oriented toward election results. The intellectuals have a genuine legacy of sacrifice in the democratic movement, Chang and Huang having each served eight years. But the faction overall has been unflatteringly described as *ji de li di jie he,* "a confederation of interests." The direction of the Meilidao faction has been to seek a solid base in the middle class through moderate and rational challenge to the contradictory laws and self-defeating international policy of the ruling party.

Chang Chun-hong, its most articulate spokesman, has emphasized the party's sense of social responsibility: that it does not sow divisiveness to disturb the economy, nor will it recklessly provoke the People's Republic of China. In this respect Meilidao is much rankled by the street fighting set off in some New Tide–sponsored actions. For Chang Chun-hong, however, a compromisist attitude toward the ruling party (such as his much-criticized decision for the party, represented by Kang Ning-Hsiang, to participate in the president's National Reunification Committee, established under his cabinet as a sop to the KMT hard-liners following the July 1990 National Affairs Conference) is based in a sense of impotence of the popular forces, that the populace is weary of endless street marches, and such shows of reaction do not remedy the disparity of power.[14]

Hsu Hsin-liang, never a good public speaker and better known for his unchangingly optimistic countenance in evasion of knotty questions, has, however, articulated a direction that gives maximum leeway to Taiwan's commercial interests. In a July 1990 public speech at the Tien Educational Center in Taipei he espoused a laissez-faire attitude to investment by Taiwanese capitalists in China and abroad, dismissing the suggestion that unrestrained capital flows could damage the development of the national economy or Taiwan nationalism. In May 1991 in an internal speech to the Taiwan Democratic Movement Overseas annual meeting in Los Angeles, an organization of which he still held the chairmanship, he cautioned that labor and environmental activism could drive Taiwanese capitalists into closer alliance with Premier Hao Bo-tsun, who was attacking social movements under the guise of cleaning up gangsterism.

With both Chang Chun-hong and Hsu Hsin-liang in the DPP central party headquarters—the two members of the Formosa core who emerged from among early 1970s liberal reformers within the KMT central party headquarters, grouped around the magazine *The Intellectual (Da Xue Ca Jer)*—the earlier tendency of the Meilidao faction has been made manifest. In preparation for the National Affairs Conference, Hsu Hsin-liang forced through a DPP position paper proposing a mongrel governmental structure combining contradictory features of presidential and parliamentary-cabinet authority, supposedly the "French model." The unstated logic for this seemed to be that it proffered a face-saving formula to President Lee Teng-hui's continuing standoff with the premier. Consistent with this, the DPP strategy at the National Affairs Conference, directed largely by Hsu, was to pry the "mainstream" Taiwanese-rooted KMT away from its conservative wing and into agreements for liberalization under the pressure of the public scrutiny of the event. This strategy seemed to be largely successful at the time. Chang Chun-hong, consistent with his previous statements but astonishing in timing, only a week after the embarrassing December 1991 showing stated publicly and unilaterally that if the DPP won 40 percent of the vote for the new Legislative Yuan in December 1992, it would be willing to enter into a coalition government with the ruling party. Hsu Hsin-liang, pressed in private conversation, denied that this would result in a Korea-style split of the opposition party and insisted that the KMT would split instead. Chang Chun-hong reportedly has spent considerable effort seeking the weak link in the KMT, a few tactical allies who could at least allow the DPP to sway 25 percent of the next National Assembly sessions in March 1992 and block the KMT from steamrolling through a one-sided constitution, but without success yet. Hsu has persistently asserted that the party must reach power soon—his famous "three years to government rule" statement of mid-1990. This can hardly be imagined attainable except by the DPP being accepted into a coalition with the "mainstream" KMT. There is great disagreement among political commentators as to whether this is probable.

All the same, Hsu Hsin-liang is well known for clever strategies and startling changes of direction. While overseas, he successively joined in various united fronts: first with the politically conservative World United Formosans for Independence (WUFI), attempting to seize leadership and move the organization to more open action in Taiwan's political scene; ejected, he set up *Formosa Weekly* in Los Angeles in mid-1980, and then the next year allied with an old-time Marxist based in Japan, Shih Ming of the Taiwan Independence Army (which much alarmed U.S. congressional members lobbied by Taiwanese-Americans); then in 1984 he joined the Taiwan Revolutionary party, a splinter from WUFI with a revised social democratic line. This last organization, later Taiwan Democratic Movement Overseas, renounced armed struggle and propelled Hsu in redeveloping links with the Taiwan democratic movement and attempting to reenter Taiwan.[15] Hsu was on the wanted list for sedition, but the government, embarrassingly enough, was afraid to arrest him; he finally managed to land by boat and be arrested in 1989. His political philosophy has been disclosed in several statements quoted in the press: "Politics is like business. If you win, you have done it right," and "Any politician who is serious has the ambition to be president." Hsu has been called a chameleon, but his unpredictability may in itself be a potent weapon.

As for the other three core leaders of the *Formosa Magazine* period—Lin Yi-hsiung (formerly provincial assemblyman), Yao Chia-wen (candidate in 1978), and Shih Ming-deh (fifteen years imprisonment before the Kaohsiung Incident, behind-the-scenes organizer)—they are alienated from the Meilidao faction and by default have served as standard-bearers of the New Tide faction, because New Tide has stood behind whoever challenged the monopoly of the Meilidao faction. Lin Yi-hsiung has become a distant voice of moral authority and indignation, only rarely on the scene since the murder of his mother and twin daughters on February 28, 1980. Yao Chia-wen served as DPP chairman with a strong TI stance from October 1987 to October 1988, following his January 1987 release, but then was defeated in bitter competition by Huang Hsin-chieh and Chang Chun-hong, released the following year. Yao's wife, Chou Ching-yu, is now executive head of Changhua County, a powerful position.

Huang Hsin-chieh was reelected chairman and the term lengthened to two years. Then in late 1990 the newly released Shih Ming-deh appeared to be the heroic heir apparent and was much heralded by the media. But he persisted in advocating a policy of evenhanded balancing of the factions and of diversifying the sources of party funds, rather than relying on large contributors. Thence it seems that the Meilidao faction, unwilling to release its monopoly on the central apparatus, decided to jettison him. This is the story of 1991, to be recounted below.

Aside from the core figures of the *Formosa Magazine* period, there is on the scene the next chronological echelon of leadership, the lawyers who defended them against the charges of sedition and, together with the wives of the defendants, carried forward the torch of the democratic movement in the difficult period 1980–87. Chiang Peng-chien served as first chairman of the DPP. You Ching, educated in Germany, was the first opposition leader to be elected to the Control Yuan, and since 1989 he has been executive head of Taipei County, in which position he is challenged with the practical tasks of traffic and trash in a huge industrialized area and frazzled in frays with the Kuomintang-fed civil servant bureaucracy. Hsieh Chang-ting and Chen Shui-bien (whose wife has been paralyzed from the shoulders down following a traffic "accident" in 1985) serve as a rambunctious challenge to the KMT in the national legislature. They are not members of the Meilidao faction but independent figures with their own contributors and offices. It was prematurely announced in January 1992 that these independent figures, loosely allied in the so-called Independence coalition (*Du Pai*) with the New Tide faction and the re-turned-émigré World United Formosans for Independence, would formalize a third faction to assume their own autonomous power. But it seems that the opposing Meilidao and New Tide factions are the ends of a pole on which no third power can exist as an unpolarized force.

As a social artifact, it may be noted that in recent years doctors, another well-respected profession in Taiwan's society, have increasingly joined in open political activity. These are, notably, Chen Yung-hsing and Tsai Sze-yuan, national assemblymen who serve in important positions in the central party headquarters, and though functionaries for the Meilidao faction, are often seen as less partisan; and the legislators Wei Yao-chien and Hong Chi-chang, both associated with New Tide.

The New Tide Faction

Finally we may explore the origins and composition of the New Tide (*Xin Chao Liu*) faction, named for the founding magazine.

My essay "The Social Origins of the Taiwan Democratic Movement" described some incidents of tension and differing perspective between the elected officials of the democratic movement coalition in 1979 and the young intellectuals who worked for them in campaigns and on editorial staffs. At that time there was a general alignment of liberal ideology (democratic procedures, constitutionality) with Taiwanese nationalism, on one hand, and radical ideology (egalitarian ideals, social movements) with Chinese nationalism, on the other hand. The latter encompassed a small but intellectually important minority of personnel. All the same, the different groups were forced into an uneasy coalition by the overwhelming threat of the Kuomintang and its security agencies, as well as by the expediency of arousing the populace to resistance with populist slogans.

The exception to this congruence was a small segment of young liberation theology ministers in the Presbyterian church, which had called for Taiwan independence since 1971. The Presbyterian church had not only a solid place in native Taiwanese society going back to the conversion of modernizing elites by British missionaries in the 1890s but also many decades of missions among the exploited aboriginal people, and thus a social conscience.

Despite the pattern of nationalism at that time, in 1980 I thought the logic of the situation boded the emergence of a Taiwanese nationalism with an ideology of mass mobilization. A decade later that is the new constellation, though I cannot say I precisely foresaw the sources of this development. Now it is the liberals, allied with opportunistic local politicians, who are reluctant to risk confrontation with the Kuomintang on the issue of Taiwanese nationalism; whereas the organizations with a philosophy of grass-roots mobilization use "Taiwan Independence!" as a rallying cry that means uprooting the whole structure of special privileges for the ruling elite and along with it local patronage politics.

Chinese nationalism now has no significant presence in mass politics: a few of the diehard professors and writers of the *China Tide* group, such as Chen Ying-chen, Wang Ching-ping, and Wang Shao-po, formed the Labor party (*Gong Dang*) in 1987 and then split off into an exclusively pro-China party, the Workers Party (*Lao Dong Dang*) a year later. Su Ching-li served in both as secretary general.[16] Both parties have met with pathetic voter response but are said to have had some impact in practical work with labor. However, the Chinese nationalists of the Taiwan democratic movement can be proud that they have also played a pioneering role in China's democratization in recent years.[17]

A small number of left- and/or once-upon-a-time China-leaning intellectuals are of common Hakka background with Hsu Hsin-liang and more personalisticly tied to his past populist programs—for example, Chang Fu-chung and Chen Chung-hsin. With Hsu's accession to the chairmanship they have new and more central roles. Others, such as Wang Tuo (*China Tide* background, jailed following the Kaohsiung Incident, elected national assemblyman December 1991) and Chen Chao-nan (émigré with Austrian citizenship but strong Taiwanese nationalism, worked with Hsu in Los Angeles, jailed briefly on return in June 1990) are in similar positions, professing a Marxist social vision but tied to Hsu for their present work at the central party headquarters. It remains to be seen whether Hsu Hsin-liang will choose to play populist ploys. A few other intellectuals educated abroad and with strong social convictions have taken up practical programs under DPP county executives.

The New Tide group, however, unambiguously weds a strong Taiwanese nationalism to the force of social movements. The group emerged from among idealistic assistants to the elected opposition figures in a gradual development in the mid-1980s. They reacted against the hierarchical and particularistic structure of relations within the opposition itself, in which elected officials gained fame and fortune riding on the issues researched by their assistants. A central figure, Chiu Yi-jen, studied political science at the University of Chicago in 1978–82 and at that time seemed to discount class analysis. Wu Nai-jen did not leave Taiwan for studies but now discourses in mature Marxist terms. As editors for Hsu Jung-su (wife of the then imprisoned Chang Chun-hong, Hsu was then an important legislator; in the mid-1980s she became independently wealthy from stock market investments) on her magazine *Plow Deep (Shen Geng)*, 1982–84, they found contradictions between their efforts to report on labor issues and the preferences of her financial backers, as well as resistance to their critique of opportunism within the opposition. They encountered similar problems managing Hsu Jung-su's constituent service center in Nantou, where they set up a democratically governed oversight committee to promote community self-rule and grass-roots organization. They left and in May 1984 started a separate journal with a social democratic philosophy, a drawing point for the younger generation of activists. Ho Duan-fan, Lin Chuo-shui, Liu Shou-cheng, and Hong Chi-chang were among the founders.

As developed to the present, the New Tide faction is virtually a party within a party, reportedly holding a membership of about one hundred persons (not publicly identified) who are subjected to training and discipline of their ideology, activities, and financial dealings. The group has a Central Committee, procedures of internal democracy, and requirements for participation in interminable reports and meetings. On occasion notable public office holders have sought to join the group together with their underlings, in which case they might form a block and overshadow others; but such requests have been rebuffed. The tight egalitarian organization of New Tide seems to have developed gradually in reaction to the Meilidao, as a tactic to outflank it.

In recent years, however, New Tide has assigned its own members to run as candidates in elections: legislator Hong Chi-chang; the writer Lin Chuo-shui, author of the DPP's Republic of Taiwan resolution; the wife of Tsai You-chuan (liberation theology Presbyterian minister, served second sentence for TI), Chou Hui-ying; and the pioneer in the student movement, Lee Wen-chung. It also strategically allies with or puts forward candidates that it deems will promote a strident Taiwanese independence demand or the interests of a social group that warrants protection: Yeh Chu-lan, widow of Tseng Nan-jung, now legislator; Chen Hsiu-hui, founder of the Homemakers' Union for environmental protection, now in the National Assembly. New Tide seems to have hit upon a pattern for candidates: young, educated, idealistic, personable, physically attractive, energetic, and ready to get their hands dirty in local organizing.

New Tide is a formidable challenge to the Meilidao faction, which has absolutely no systemic discipline. It has a network of offices in the names of regional constituent service offices for particular office holders—for example, for legislator Lu Hsiu-yi in Panchiao, Taipei County—entirely separate from those of the formal party command. It must have at least a dozen such offices, with a constant programming of activities, hung solid with colorful banners and slogans: "New Nation Movement," "Build a New and Just Society," and so forth. The DPP apparatus has its regional offices, and independent office holders also have theirs, but most are said to rev up only before elections. There has been recurrent struggle between the factions over control of various regional branch offices, but at present most seem to be Meilidao-controlled.

The element of financial discipline is extremely significant and unusual in the Taiwan political scene. New Tide members, if elected, are required to turn over all of their government salaries and allowances to the organization and live on salaries as service center activists. In recent elections even donations are reported and recorded for central management. Those members elected are required to keep squeaky clean in an environment where money flows easily for slight favors, and constituents expect that service means special intercession at the price of a gratuity. According to one service center manager, the New Tide public office holders he knew were so pressed for financial survival, especially with the heavy expenses incurred, that they had to start a business on the side to make ends meet, but tried to pick one that would not lead to errant suspicions. Reciprocal to this discipline, the organization must deal with the debts left over from campaigns, especially failed campaigns, and make sure its activists sustain a minimum standard of family income. Funds go to support a joint think tank to assist its legislators, as well as assistance for other organs, such as the affiliated Taiwan Association for Labor Movement, in operation seven years.

According to some descriptions of the New Tide faction, its actions may be more indirect but broader in influence than apparent. For example, it claims to have initiated organization of farmers' groups and community campaigns against polluting manufacturers, but these organizations take on a life of their own and are not directly controlled. The Urban-Rural Mission, linked with Canadian religious social activists through WUFI and also in communication with the Korean Urban Rural Mission (URM), has provided training for home-grown agitators; it has been a target of the KMT security agencies. The situation is similar in fields of cultural development and historical studies. Quiet ties with social groups, even the newly emerging "liberation theology" schools of Buddhism that have made yellow robes a colorful presence at demonstrations against political arrest,[18] have given the faction a secret potential in election campaigns. New Tide may have the possibility of maturing into a powerful election machine, but some members do not wish to be distracted from what they see as the basic goal of grass-roots organizing.

At any rate, there has been a realization among members that organization must also be addressed to the middle and professional classes on issues such as environment and education, given the structure of Taiwan's modern society. The leadership of New Tide has reached the difficult admission that, despite several years of efforts, the industrial working class is not particularly responsive except to palpable economic gains, and it frequently trusts to continuing standard of living improvements under the ruling party. Nonpolitical social activists, such as those with the Catholic church, have commented that the Taiwan workers do have serious grievances, but that they do not trust any of the political parties. A common comment among social activists is that there is a wide gap between the opposition party and the social movements, and the politicians rarely show evidence of any long-term concern. For example, in 1991 the government moved to turn back several of the provisions of the labor law that are favorable to workers, but the DPP remained silent. Most of the public does not clearly understand the existence of different groups and social directions within the DPP.

Membership and Operations

In contrast to the financial pooling of New Tide, prospective candidates in the Democratic Progressive party at large are self-selecting and must supply their own financing. Therefore the process is individualistic and depends to a large degree on previous public exposure, social connections, and even whether one has a large circle of clan relatives that can be mobilized to assist. Given the effect of personal ties to office holders, as described above, it is not surprising that financiers want to give their money discretely, and without public accounting, directly to the candidate they are cultivating. (Small contributors usually want their contribution recognized on slips posted on boards at their affiliated DPP offices, but those with enterprises are wary of KMT reprisal; e.g., a tax auditor was stationed to stand right next to the cashier of the large Pirate King Restaurant, a DPP supporter). This process works overall to build up a number of "mountain tops" (*shan tou*) in the party who dispense money according to their own political interests and programs, while the common coffers of the party are nearly bare and long-term programs and policy development are starved. Moreover, it generally is not appropriate to inquire as to what money a party leader has, and to which purposes it should be applied; that is considered a matter of individual discretion, and, especially if powerful, the person should not be questioned.

The dearth of ideological unity and discipline has led over a period of time to a hidden crisis for the party: registered party members often have no political commitment, and those with political commitment, even some persons who work for the party virtually full-time as volunteers, refuse to enter membership. There are something under twenty thousand registered members in the party. That is less than 1 percent of the minimum number of DPP voters (about two million in the last poor showing). The membership does not represent the voters, and it also does not represent a trained or disciplined vanguard, though the majority are enthusiastic supporters. A party delegate can be selected by each thirty party members. To address the problem of the gap between membership and voting constituency, however, DPP elected officials are automatically accorded delegate votes. Over the long run this works to maintain the status quo of the party.

The source of the problem of party membership is, first, that in the initial rush of expansion of the party, control over access to membership was lost; and second, every time an election nears, those hopeful of nomination in the internal party primaries stuff the rolls with friends, relatives, and anyone they can induce to sign a party membership form. The sponsor also pays the annual dues, about U.S. $50 for each member, part of which is sent to the central party headquarters. Such nominal members are called "head count party members" (*ren tou dang yuan*), and a cautious conjecture is that they account for 20 percent of the rolls overall. A more extreme artifice has now been rumored, "pocket party members," in which a great number are all registered at one address (in Kaohsiung reportedly two hundred at one address), and their signature chops kept on hand for easy voting. By now there have been cases of party dues paid to Taipei in one chunk but not remitted to the regional office, of the losing faction in a regional branch struggle withdrawing en masse, and of the central party headquarters derecognizing a local membership in total.[19] Both Meilidao and New Tide factions have been accused of padding the rolls, but it is generally thought that New Tide cannot make the match in money. Nominal party members affect the outcome of nominations. One long-term party member without direct affiliation to any candidate commented acerbicly on recent nominations, "The DPP came to Kaohsiung and picked up trash."

A similar problem of the internal composition of party membership involves the class character of the supporters of the party, who, compared to those of the ruling party, are frequently the less advantaged, more marginal, some even lumpen proletariat, with simultaneously politically valid and socially invalid reasons for resenting authority. Especially given the lack of enforced standards within the party, operations depend on goodwill and intentions. There has been some effort at regulating the quality and image of membership; in Panchiao in January 1992 the membership was reviewed, and those operating disreputable enterprises such as massage parlors and gambling halls were asked to withdraw. About 10 percent of the membership was challenged for various reasons.

It may be obvious in this account that the factions do not seem to be treated equivalently, that there has been no extended description of the social policy of the Meilidao faction. This unevenness quite accurately reflects the different concerns of the factions. Although Meilidao has had a public policy section, headed by the scholarly Huang Huang-hsiung, and also an organization section, it is difficult to find anyone at the central party headquarters who cares to make an extended social analysis. Actions vis-à-vis the Kuomintang, election results, financing, and personnel assignments are the major concerns. Critics of New Tide say that it allies with questionable local politicians as much as does Meilidao, and in regional branch struggles it really just comes down to a senseless competition over territory. Candidates within the party tend to try to dig into each others' constituency (most races are a plurality, some with as many as eight seats to be assigned, so there may be candidates from both factions as well as the KMT and other local factions all running together), especially in the heat of the last days when it is easier to appeal to DPP supporters than to convert KMT loyalists.

Although serious, the factional disputes are not as severe or as publicly aired as two years ago, many say. There is now a basic agreement on two matters: the Meilidao faction has accepted the explicit call for a Republic of Taiwan, and New Tide has entered the parliamentary arena. While not forsaking either grass-roots organizing or demonstrations, New Tide has recognized the public backlash against street brawling with the riot police (the example of Korean students throwing Molotov cocktails was briefly emulated in May 29, 1990, demonstrations, which the government turned to its propaganda advantage) and has sought to distance itself from the rabid bands abetted by the World United Formosans for Independence, despite previous alliance. There is still no general agreement in the party on how best to deal with the issues in practice or promote them in propaganda. There are naturally differences in local conditions—for example, rabidly Hokkien-chauvinist areas like Chiayi versus Hakka areas like Hsinchu County—that make it unwise to apply uniform literature islandwide.[20] But the "mountaintop" structure of personal relations and the factional cleavage impede the development of a coordinated strategy. The central party headquarters is weakened by lack of capacity to direct, and the regional offices are left to fend for themselves.

This disunion is highlighted in the matter of financing. The central party headquarters of course runs a large literature and propaganda department, which puts out a party newspaper and special election reports. The headquarters also organizes a cast of party notables who speak at local campaign rallies. Candidates are supposed to contribute to the cost. The government reimburses campaign funds to successful candidates after the election in the amount of NT $30

(U.S. $1.20) per vote received. Unsuccessful candidates get three-quarters of that as long as they receive a minimum of about a thousand votes. The DPP party headquarters in the past requisitioned 10 percent of the refund, but in 1991 demanded 50 percent. New Tide is discussing whether, as policy, its candidates should hand over that amount, which could well be NT $35 *wan* (U.S. $14,000) each. It is unlikely that either New Tide or other candidates will submit the full amount.

Most scuttlebutt on the specific incidents within the party cannot be readily verified. Or the sources may be deemed knowledgeable, but different versions of the reasons and rationale, who did what to whom first, may be floated. It is not practical to try to pin down every item as a point of fact, and yet recurrent themes may be taken as indication of the actions and interactions within the party, and of the kind of information to which people are reacting. In recent interviews there has been concern voiced about the quality of some DPP members who have reached high rank within the party, and such concern, expressed among those in all parts of the party, involves a few named individuals who may be representative of a more general problem.

The Course of 1991

Huang Hsin-chieh, the DPP's stubby, bristle-haired chairman with a country-Taiwanese accent, has been overshadowed by the KMT's polished technocrat Lee Teng-hui for the last three years. Still, he has a kind of old-time-politician quality that is endearing, a straightforward wheeling and dealing in traditional *guanxi* that is more appealing than the machinations of clever political scientists. He has never been the brains of the democratic movement, but he has stood with it generously and loyally, like a father to a profligate son, through eight years of prison and a few million in contributions—even when the party treasury sank to rock bottom after the spending spree engendered by vying with the KMT at the National Affairs Conference.

At the end of 1990 Huang Hsin-chieh seemed outpaced by the rapid changes in political forces and discomfited by the prospect of his reign coming to a close in 1991. The party charter, recently amended, limits the chairman to two two-year terms. Huang ventured to argue that since his first term had been only one year, before the amendment, he should be eligible for another term. No one in the central party headquarters dared to gainsay him openly. As months passed and the news media played on the image of Shih Ming-deh as the heir apparent, Huang seemed alternately to acquiesce and then to cast about the names of many candidates, as if he were magnanimous to bestow the seat on others—while still not disavowing his own intentions of continuing. For perhaps six months the headquarters seemed paralyzed on the issue of succession; the credentials committee seemed likewise to lack the nerve to make a ruling based on the charter. A columnist queried sarcastically whether Huang Hsin-chieh wanted to emulate the five-term record of Chiang Kai-shek.

In the meanwhile, Shih Ming-deh continued with plans to prepare for the year-end election by gathering together academics and social activists to write policy papers; and Hsu Hsin-liang set up a large office to work for islandwide organization. Both swore they would work together and with the party. Shih declined to question publicly the propriety of Huang, whom he respectfully addressed as *ojisan*, "old gentleman," from the days of *Formosa Magazine*, in claiming another term; and Hsu claimed his target was the future election for governor of Taiwan. There was speculation that the outcome would be Shih as chairman, Hsu as secretary general.

In 1989 and 1990, while still in prison, Shih Ming-deh had written bitter diatribes against the New Tide faction, accusing them of crassly using social mobilization issues for the purpose of a power grab. It was anticipated that he would align with the Meilidao tradition, due to historical and personal attachments. Soon after his release, however, he renewed contacts with his former disciple Chiu Yi-jen and gave an exclusive interview to *New Tide* magazine on his first imprisonment as a military cadet.[21] He tried to maintain good relations on all sides on the basis of his personal authority and charismatic sway as a popular hero, "Taiwan's Nelson Mandela." On a triumphant trip to the United States, he sought to press the two contentious émigré factions, World United Formosans for Independence and Taiwan Democratic Movement Overseas, into joint cooperation in November 1990, but this resulted in offense to the TDMO, allied with Meilidao on Taiwan. Moving into 1991, Shih confronted some DPP office holders in Kaohsiung whom he accused of profiteering and dishonorable relations with the KMT.

When the KMT announced a convening of the "old thieves" National Assembly in April 1991 and suddenly introduced a draft for continuing the functions of the security agencies spawned during martial law, the DPP was stung by the about-face on what had been thought to be the achievements of the National Affairs Convention. The New Tide faction pushed for resolute action, a mass demonstration. The Meilidao faction was reluctant and initially let New Tide figures take the front-line roles. Suddenly, New Tide felt hung out to dry. Shih Ming-deh stepped in to mediate and draw all the party leadership into an impressive display of unity in the march of April 17, 1991. At that point his accession to the chairmanship seemed unchallenged; the cover of the party charter booklet printed in sharp color soon after shows the front rank of the march with Huang Hsin-chieh, Shih Ming-deh, and Chang Chun-hong lined up in center focus.

In reminiscing, Shih feels that the turning point also came in April when he repeatedly refused to make an explicit agreement that if he were chairman Chang Chun-hong could continue as secretary general. Shih had from the start insisted that he would act as chairman for the whole party and give all factions and figures a stake in participation. He did not so much object to Chang continuing as secretary general, he says, as to appearing to "cut a deal" with one faction. At that point the Meilidao faction began to set in motion other plans for the succession, and enlisted Hsu Hsin-liang.

According to a reliable leak, Hsu made secret plans to wrap up the party delegate vote before he left for a United States trip, and he confirmed these islandwide plans on his return in mid-May. The DPP headquarters in June approved the establishment of an overseas party branch, and in short order the TDMO transformed itself into that role with a cutoff date of July 6 to apply for DPP membership and vote for delegates. The Meilidao faction likewise stuffed the regional party branch rolls just before the cutoff. However, the crucial element in commanding the majority of delegate votes against the formidable personal aura of Shih Ming-deh was a tit-for-tat exchange with a number of local DPP politicians, the delegate votes they controlled in exchange for positions in the central party committee and the national assembly. This is not denied by insiders of the Meilidao faction, and many also decry the deleterious effects. This is detailed below.

A subsequent incident heralded the coming confrontation. Two members of *Min Chung Daily News* (a strong supporter of the DPP, a large newspaper based in Kaohsiung) known to have spent a great deal of time drinking late into the night with Shih Ming-deh, Deputy Managing Editor Mou Shang-sang and writer Tseng Chia-lun, and others wrote a series of articles printed July 20–22. These articles sharply criticized the DPP center and Chang Chun-hong for lack of resolution and private dealings in relations with the KMT. Whereas in a famous satire of twelve years ago, a democratic movement cartoonist called the vestige parties brought from the mainland the KMT's "flower vase in the toilet," a token opposition, the *Min Chung* articles suggested the DPP might become the KMT's "flower vase in the parlor." They also revealed that Hsu would make a bid for the chairmanship. Both Chang and Hsu denied these allegations and reacted vigorously with a threat to picket the newspaper and push a campaign to drop subscriptions. After a tense week-long standoff, the publisher printed an apology and demoted the offending staff.[22]

A week after this furor broke, Hsu Hsin-liang publicly announced his candidacy. However, the toll in media relations continued. In an article commenting on the upcoming party chairmanship elections, The *Journalist (Xin Xin Wen)* weekly magazine ran two pictures, a broadly smiling Shih Ming-deh with his trademark Errol Flynn mustache, and the shiny back of Hsu Hsin-liang's Franciscan-fringe pate. Even now Shih Ming-deh is featured in newspaper articles for his role as president of the Taiwan Association for Human Rights as often as is the DPP chairman.

The Democratic Progressive party is a poorly coordinated, fractious organization that lacks the resources of even some of the new religious sects in Taiwan. And yet it is a large presence in the media and in the intellectual life of the country because it signifies and moves much more than just its own mass. It seems to some extent to set the agenda to which the ruling party and government must react. It is not surprising, then, that Hsu Hsin-liang and Shih Ming-deh met for a public, partly televised debate in the Sun Yat-Sen Memorial Auditorium, almost as if submitting the chairmanship race to the entire population. Hsu glowed with his perpetual confidence, proclaiming that with proper organization and good candidates the party would sweep the year-end elections and move toward governing. Shih, his eyes cast upward, pronounced in an apocryphal tone that if he had learned anything in his twenty-five years of dark imprisonment, it was that "it is more difficult to resist temptation than to endure suffering"; and that the party faced the temptations of power. Hsu ended with a soft statement that he never thought it necessary to flaunt the difficulties of his ten years of exile.[23]

On the first day of the DPP delegates convention, October 12–13, the vote for the central committee of eleven produced the following: Meilidao, four—Hsu Hsin-liang, Yu Chen Yueh-ying (executive of Kaohsiung County, old Yu clan local faction), Lin Wen-lang (originally Taipei city councilman), Chu Hsing-yu (city councilman from Kaohsiung); independent figures, four—Hsieh Chang-ting, Shih Ming-deh, Yao Chia-wen, Yen Chin-fu (Taipei city councilman), the last two closely allied with New Tide; New Tide members, three—Chiu Yi-jen, Hong Chi-chang (legislator), Liu Shou-cheng (provincial assemblyman from Ilan). For the moment it seemed that Meilidao would lose the chairmanship and the crucial control of the party apparatus. The next morning a resolution for making the establishment of the Republic of Taiwan a goal of the party passed with a two-thirds show of hands; it had only been slightly softened, under KMT threat, with the condition that independence would be subject to a plebiscite. The Meilidao faction was not enthusiastic about taking on this platform explicitly, but feared it would lose the chairmanship if it abjured.[24] The difference from previous times when it had been voted down was the support of prestigious intellectuals outside the party. In the following vote for the chairmanship Hsu narrowly prevailed over Shih, 180 to 163. The two shook hands like gentlemen.

The central party headquarters had been unprepared for the aftermath of the Republic of Taiwan platform. Hsu Hsin-liang left for Japan on October 15 and Chang Chun-hong shortly after, no doubt on prearranged business, but some of the populace felt that the leadership deserted just as the gauntlet fell. There was sparse headquarters reaction to the arrests of nine Taiwan independence activists over the next few days.[25] The response to the government's threat to ban the party was nonchalant.

It has been alleged that Meilidao supporters applied monetary inducements to a few swing delegate votes in the final showdown, in amounts of up to NT $30 *wan* (U.S. $12,000), which sounds rather fantastic. This seems to have been inferred because a few delegates bargained with both sides in the chairmanship race. The counterevidence against the possibility of vote buying is said to be that the Meilidao faction controlled 180 or so delegate votes anyway, as shown in the central committee voting, but did not have them well enough apportioned to take more central committee seats. Whether or not delegate buying occurred in the chairmanship vote, there is a reliable report that one "mountaintop" attempted to get a seat on the central committee by distributing checks for NT $10 *wan* (U.S. $4,000), but was unsuccessful. For a party only recently emerged from the golden age of the democratic movement, when one risked death and destruction for the sake of freedom of speech, vote buying seems to fall short of idealism. No one in the party has wanted to make charges openly, for fear of "scratching your own face"; but this reluctance also allows rumors to fly unrepudiated.

As far as trading delegate votes for central party headquarters–supported positions, there seems to be little ambiguity. Although not unique examples,[26] Chu Hsing-yu's seat on the central committee and Du Wen-ching's assignment to a party-apportioned seat in the new National Assembly are the two most bandied about.

Du Wen-ching is a young protégé of central committee member Lin Wen-lang, a financial source for the democratic movement going back to the heroic days of *Formosa Magazine*. Lin was originally a Taipei city councilman who was respected for refusing to join the KMT, but then he made his fortune in construction contracts, allegedly with the aid of KMT connections. Lin Wen-lang has shown considerable largess to many in the democratic movement, and also provided an apartment gratis to Shih Ming-deh soon after he was released from prison. It is said that Lin obtained a staff position for Du at the central party headquarters; then Lin got Du appointed to be head of the party branch at Miaoli, where he stuffed the party rolls using Lin's funds. Controlling a number of delegate votes, Du was then able to assure Lin a seat on the central committee. Now Du is a DPP national assemblyman. No other critique of him personally has been heard, except that his past contribution does not warrant the position.

Chu Hsing-yu, a small man, fairly young, with a pug nose and round-cropped, short hair somewhat incongruous with his usual formal black three-piece suit, is given credit for having his own popular base as a Kaohsiung city councilman. However, he is also seen as a gangsterish figure who has built up his constituent base by weeping crocodile tears at every local funeral and taking oaths while chopping off roosters' heads, a traditional swearing-in ritual that does not seem to bind him for long. He is rumored to have made his money through construction company deals of the usual suspicious sort. How much of this description, oft-repeated in party circles and now in the press,[27] is accurate cannot be verified here. Chu Hsing-yu has reportedly bragged that he donated NT $200 *wan* (U.S. $80,000) to Hsu Hsin-liang, and reportedly a single night's party for Hsu and his entourage in Kaohsiung cost him another NT $20 *wan* (U.S. $8,000) as well.

The issue of the chairmanship vote recently emerged over into the media eye in a way that party members must have winced to read. At the end of January 1992 the DPP held a Lunar New Year's party at Meilihua Hotel to show its appreciation to the media and display a front of unity. Under the influence of alcohol Chu Hsing-yu began to badger Shih Ming-deh and boast of wealth, including the U.S. $90,000 Swiss watch on his wrist; Shih promptly held up Chu's wrist to photographers, to be compared with Shih's electronic giveaway watch. The issue for tension was that both Shih and Chu had thought they were to be contestants for legislator in the same Kaohsiung district in December 1992. Chu was reported in newspapers the next day to have then said, to the effect, "Don't think you're such a hero that you can get anything you want. You didn't get the chairmanship because I didn't support you. . . . If you run in my district, NT $5,000 (U.S. $200) a vote says that you'll lose to me." Shih Ming-deh's rejoinder was likewise intemperate. "If you win, I'll cut my gut and die. If you lose, you can commit suicide and Chang Chun-hong and Hsu Hsin-liang can be buried with you." The incident was papered over later with an apology from Chu, who claimed he meant the KMT, not himself, would defeat Shih by buying votes.

This makes for colorful reporting; but let us return to the moment of the DPP delegate convention, October 1991. The Meilidao faction had kept its place in the central party headquarters, but was only a minority on the central committee. The accession of the new chairman was later feted with a gala reception at the cost of nearly NT $100 *wan* (U.S. $40,000). Hsu nominated Chang to continue as secretary general, but the central committee refused to ratify the appointment; after bitter wrangling it was agreed that Chang would continue until February 1992. A physical attack on Yen Chin-fu at the entrance to the building, dutifully reported by the press, further tarnished the party image. Little time remained for adjustment of staff at the central party headquarters and preparation for the December elections.

Given this and the organizational constraints, from the vantage of Taipei the party headquarters waged an uphill propaganda battle with the KMT, which had grown very slick, low-key, and sophisticated, in contrast with the heavy-handed and laughable pronouncements it had produced a decade before. The television stations were directed to broadcast the taped messages of four political parties who were allotted time proportional to their number of candidates, after they were passed by censors. The film of the KMT, forty-five minutes at a cost of over NT $1,000 *wan* (U.S. $400,000), took as its theme prosperity and security for future generations; proclaiming Taiwan independence would provoke the wrath of the PRC. Its emblem was a healthy baby boy frolicking on a blue cloth with white sun, the KMT party emblem. The DPP film, twenty-one minutes at a cost of NT $550 *wan* (U.S. $220,000) sarcastically parodied this image with a long sequence of plastic baby kewpie dolls coming off an assembly line—and those not meeting the standards of uniformity thrown back into the furnace to melt down.[28] For this, campaign literature, and expenses of the central party campaign speakers group, the total cost was about NT $2,000 *wan* (U.S. $800,000), which led some to gasp in astonishment. Meanwhile, Shih Ming-deh announced the New Constitution Campaign Speakers Group, a few dozen professors, editorial writers, and other well-known figures who agreed to speak in favor of the party and its issues; he raised NT $200 *wan* (U.S. $80,000) to cover its operations. The effectiveness of the group was generally acknowledged, but Shih was criticized for going his own way after losing the chairmanship election.

The ruling party relied almost exclusively on television broadcasting, in which it has a virtual monopoly,[29] to set the agenda for the election (Chang Chun-hong's efforts at setting up a broadcasting station have met with interdiction and confiscation). It held very few rallies or campaign speeches. While DPP candidates identified themselves clearly with the green and white party flag, KMT candidates did not fly the white sun on blue. At most they printed the slogan "reform, prosperity, stability" on their posters. It is not known whether this lack of stated affiliation was party policy, to blur the line between independent and party candidacies, or to avoid identifying the ruling party with rampant vote buying, while allowing local interests to pursue their natural cupidity. There are laws against vote buying, but they seemed to be in abeyance for this election. DPP members of the government's election supervisory commission found the commission completely ineffectual.[30]

In Taiwan the hegemonic political culture is composed of several strands that are familiar in Korea as well and in other Confucian authoritarian environments: The rulers are stern but benevolent, and keep social order for the sake of all. Democracy is advancing with the development of parliamentary procedure, and all must play by the "rules of the game," even if they may be rigged. The opposition is dangerous radicals who stir social discontent. Politics is dangerous and dirty; all politicians are more or less corrupt. Society accepts collusion, so it should not be resisted. This myopic blend of smug idealism and cynicism is being challenged by some news commentators and academics in Taiwan, as well as by some of the younger generation of social activists. However, it is the stuff of ordinary discourse, and much of the behavior of the opposition falls into the mold.

Following the relative failure of the election, there was a flurry of self-examination in all sectors of the party and some finger-pointing.[31] Substantial unity did not emerge from this. This was shown at the caucus of the DPP national assemblymen, seventy-five including a few remaining from previous supplemental elections, in preparation for the March 1992 session. The caucus was held January 10–11 in a chilly mountain lodge near Hsitou, Nantou County. The task was the election of a head convener of the group and his staff, who would lead strategy in confrontation and negotiation with the ruling party. The Meilidao faction insisted on monopolizing the positions, and New Tide called for a showdown after negotiations advanced by Shih Ming-deh broke down the previous day. There were no nominations (all were eligible) and hardly any discussion in the hall, where assemblymen, reporters, and a few observers sat bundled against the cold. The politicking had already been done within the factions, each pulling the unaffiliated votes aside. Assembly members (among them about ten women) mounted the stage and dropped their ballot when their name was called. Chen Bo-wen, a New Tide candidate, Presbyterian minister, and representative of social rights for the handicapped, was lifted up in his wheelchair and then down. Finally, as the vote was counted the hall fell silent: Huang Hsin-chieh, the old chairman, 32, to Lin Chun-yi (Edgar), the antinuclear activist professor promoted by New Tide without public nomination, 30.[32] At the end of the meeting large traditional carved wooden plaques were presented to each national assembly member in the name of Huang Hsin-chieh and Hsu Hsin-liang. According to the person delivering them, these cost NT $6,000 (U.S. $240) each, at least NT $45 *wan* (U.S. $18,000) in all.

This is a standoff that the leadership of New Tide expects will continue for some time, and that, surprisingly, they do not seem overly concerned about. It is recognized in all sectors that the populace does not want to see the opposition party split, and whoever splits off bears the onus of blame. It may be projected that their strategy is to organize slowly from the bottom up, including also liberal and middle-class new social movements such as environment, women, and cultural renaissance, and thus engulf the party. The Meilidao faction, with its loose organization and lack of social activism, hardly impedes this. But the central party of course gets credit in the public eye for the social concern activities of New Tide. The ruling party is sharper in preventing New Tide from monopolizing these social issues by putting forth high-profile gestures such as the appointment of Chao Shao-kang to head Taiwan's Environmental Protection Agency.

One issue on which New Tide may be able to capitalize is regional branch resentment of profligate spending at the headquarters. The annual budget of the party headquarters is said to be about NT $4,000 *wan* (U.S. $1.6 million), but under Hsu the previously lavish socializing has been brought to new heights, "as if there were no tomorrow" in the words of one high-ranking Meilidao figure. Hsu is increasing the central party staff from about twenty-three to about thirty-five, which may indicate more ambitious programs. On the other hand, program funding is very constrained, and efforts to placate the disparate interests of personal power within the faction result in inappropriate personnel assignments. The unrestrained expenditure scares some potential contributors, and it has even been reported that some capitalists with deeper political intentions are shifting their sponsorship toward New Tide figures. Such effects will probably only be apparent in a year or so.

For the larger picture, if the Meilidao faction moves into a closer relationship with the KMT, it may be anticipated that the party will split, and the factions go their separate ways, as happened in Korea.[33] On the other hand, the government has made a feeble threat to disband the DPP for advocating the establishment of the Republic of Taiwan, and some members even relish the prospect of such a government move, saying it would reunify and revitalize the party. Such moves would originate in the dynamics of the factions of the ruling party, which is outside of the purview of this chapter, but which can still be envisaged from tangential observations, and thence placed in a wider context.

Cooptation and Inclusion

This chapter has detailed the mechanisms by which a democratic movement in strong opposition to an authoritarian state has been partly compromised and reintegrated into a role of cooperation with the state. This is a process in which vertical ties of patronage are continually respun across what would be potential rifts along the horizontal cleavage of class—alliances of workers demanding new industrial relations, or communities demanding environmental protection against the incursion of industry. Such a controlled opening to bourgeois democracy occurs in the realm of daily political relations, in the opposition party as described, and in ideology and information as well.[34]

This is a democracy in which different fractions of capital jockey for position, but can reach at least a strained consensus on the direction of evolution. The direction would only be apparent after the accession of a new legislature in December 1992. However, in Control Yuan and Legislative Yuan internal votes of early 1992, after the forced retirement of the old rubber-stamp representatives, it can be seen that the Kuomintang party structure is fast losing its ability to discipline its own Taiwanese representatives of moneyed interests.[35]

It may be speculated that this opening to bourgeois democracy can occur because the regime still has sufficient repressive capacity to control it in slow fall, but also sufficient economic resources to coopt it. It must occur, however, because of the internationalization of capital under export industry development, and the inability of the regime to limit capital mobility.[36] At the same time that segments of Taiwanese capital are brought into political deliberations, the original social base of the mainlander elite,[37] the government-owned corporations, are privatized, and thus the fractions compete more equally while retaining control over their respective domains.

The process of democratization in Taiwan can be understood within the pattern proposed by Nigel Harris on the basis of studies of South Korea, South Africa, Mexico, and Indonesia: a prolonged process of "bourgeois revolution" against the state which was in fact the midwife of the bourgeoisie as a class.

> However, when the State establishes a system for forced accumulation, this is not simply a set of arrangements that can be changed at will. It constitutes a social order, with a weight of inertia constituted by vested interests, the immediate beneficiaries, that inhibits the creation of any other order. What was set up to speed development becomes an inhibition of growth as capital develops, as output diversifies, as businessmen are increasingly drawn to participate in the world economy, and as the need for the psychological participation of a skilled labour force supersedes the dependence upon masses of unskilled labour: capitalism "matures." The old State must be reformed or overthrown, to establish the common conditions for all capital: a rule of law, accountability of public officials and expenditure, a competitive labour market and, above all, measures to ensure the common interests of capital can shape the important policies of the State.[38]

This quotation seems to contain hints of tendencies seen in Taiwan, even aside from the incorporation of the opposition party into a bourgeois democracy as has been described in detail in this chapter: first, a rationalization of the bureaucratic role, gradually stripping it of its extraordinary and particularistic economic powers, as seen in pressures for prosecuting official corruption and discussions of possible disclosure of officials' holdings and income;[39] second, a momentous political change since 1990, a realignment of academics and intellectuals to favor Taiwan independence and substantial governmental restructuring.

The interests of the mass base of the populace are not equally represented in the process of bourgeois democratization, but the benefits of patronage are indeed more widespread than before due to competition between the ruling and opposition parties, and each internally between their factions, and in this one can acknowledge some small measure of effective economic democracy. This inclusion also affects the populist base of Taiwanese nationalism, rendering it more complacent and patient with gradualistic change.

To acknowledge this cooptation is not to say, however, that social issue activism is not at the same time intensifying; to the contrary, Taiwan's society is bubbling with new voluntarist associations that at present have little apparent role in the formal political process, including religions with social and political agendas, groups of students and intellectuals more leftist than the New Tide group, and performers and teachers reaffirming minority cultures. The past progress in inclusion, however corrupted, feeds the hopes of those who are still relatively excluded. These forces and the dynamic they exert on the ruling and the opposition parties will not go away.

Notes

1. A lively account of Taiwan's recent economic development, and one closer to the ground than most "economic miracle" analyses, is to be found in Simon Long, *Taiwan: China's Last Frontier* (New York: St. Martin's Press, 1991), pp. 75–109. On several points it is relevant to the discussion in this chapter:

> The structural problem in the credit industry is the predominance of state ownership combined with the lax enforcement of legal requirements. . . . This creates an environment where the "kerb" market of illegal financing companies can flourish. . . . The commitment to privatisation (since 1989) was both a victory for the "liberal" strain in the Taiwan policy debate, and an effort to add more stock to the very limited number of companies listed on the Taipei Stock Exchange (TSE). In the late 1980s, the TSE enjoyed a boom of phenomenal proportions, which saw market capitalisation reach double the size of Taiwan's GDP, and daily trading volumes regularly surpass those on all the world's exchanges other than Tokyo and New York. The scale of investment in the TSE owed far more to extraneous considerations than to the underlying health of the listed stocks. (p. 107)
>
> The most important reason for the balloon-like expansion of stock-market capitalisation is the extraordinary degree of liquidity slopping around the financial system in 1986–88. This is a result of two of the most striking characteristics of the

Taiwan economy: one is the level of current account surplus (exports over imports) achieved from 1986 on; the other is the remarkable propensity of Taiwanese residents to save. (p. 108)

2. The comparison with Korea is very instructive for understanding the rise and form of the democratic movement in Taiwan. Almost all of Hagen Koo's article, "Middle Classes, Democratization, and Class Formation," *Theory and Society* 20 (1991): 485–509, can be said to apply to Taiwan. To quote from his conclusions,

In late industrialization, as occurred in South Korea and other East Asian countries, the new middle class has emerged as a significant social class, before the capitalist class established its ideological hegemony and before industrial workers developed into an organized class.... The Korean experience also highlights the significant role of the state in class formation. The predominant role of the state in economic and social development puts it at the center of major social conflicts.... The role of the middle class in the South Korean democatization process has been complex and variable, in part because of its internal heterogeneity and in part because of shifting political conjunctures in the transition to democracy.... This analysis suggests that political behaviors of different segments of the middle class can be explained in terms of their locations within the broad spectrum of middle-class positions between capital and labor and by the changing balance of power between the two major classes. (pp. 505–6)

Hagan Koo, "From Farm to Factory: Proletarianization in Korea," *American Sociological Review* 55 (1990): 669–81, is also useful.

3. The same point is made in Harvey J. Feldman, "Taiwan: The Great Step Forward," *The National Interest,* no. 9 (1987): 88, regarding the 1986 elections.

4. The exchange rate is very close to U.S. $1 = NT $25, rising rapidly in value since late 1985, from the U.S. $1 = about NT $40 maintained from 1960 to 1983 (Long, *Taiwan,* p. 105). In this article NT $ will be quoted in *wan,* ten thousands, as is common in Asian usage, because of the large sums involved. NT $1 *wan* = U.S. $400.

5. The kickback economy in Taiwan is worthy of study by itself, especially given the scale on which it operates. Unfortunately, a common response to the revelations as given in this article is to brush them off with the comment "It happens in every society," or "That's Asian culture." But such would be a very careless approach to social science. The kickback economy is a system, both social and economic, and should be examined as such. What its effect is on various social classes should also be examined, and a political or moral judgment may be argued from that knowledge.

As ubiquitous as the kickback economy is, economic anthropologists should be able to do an interesting study of at least a few industries. Many observers in Taiwan can describe its patterns and pieces, e.g., it depends on whether the item is in a buyers' market or a sellers' market, as to whether the seller's rep or the purchasing agent gets a kickback. On items subject to competition, such as automobiles, the kickback may be low, only U.S. $100 on a U.S. $15,000 car. Kickbacks can extend a long way; for example, an electronics engineer who designs a product using a particular U.S. $3.00 circuit that has only one manufacturer may receive 20 cents from the sales representative.

6. *Independence Weekly Post,* no. 128 (November 22, 1991): 2–3. "A wind to support Hsu A-Kuei and oppose her impeachment sweeps all Taiwan," "Hua Lung's black ploys are too many."

7. *Independence Weekly Post,* no. 134 (December 27, 1991): 1–5, on election results. "The greatest winner of the National Assembly election is the 'Gold Cow' party," p. 4.

8. *Independence Weekly Post,* no. 132 (December 13, 1991): 2. Return of Chang Tsan-Hong (George), twenty-five-year leader of World United Formosans for Indepen-

dence, and his arrest at airport, December 7. Two other émigré officers at large for several months arrested in following days.

9. The reader may note from Long, *Taiwan,* that there are several elements of U.S. economic coercion on Taiwan that are common to other Asian NICs: liberalization of foreign investment in export industries in the 1960s (p. 83); and then in the mid-1980s several measures to help remedy American balance-of-payments problems: i.e., upward valuation of currency, enactment of Taiwan labor standards laws in 1987 under pressure of the AFL-CIO (p. 103), opening of markets in 1986–87 to U.S. agricultural products despite protests of local farmers (p. 99). These plus the common heritage of Japanese colonization and current economic links go far in explaining the parallels between Korea and Taiwan; see Bruce Cummings, "The Origins and Development of the Northeast Asian Political Economy: Industrial Sectors, Product Cycles, and Political Consequences," *International Organization* 38, 1 (1984): 1–40.

Long also sees an economic reason for political liberalization: "There is a convincing school of thought that what persuaded Chiang Ching-kuo to open the floodgates of political and economic reform was not so much any broad perception of historical necessity as a rather murky financial scandal (the Tenth Credit Co-operative and the Cathay Investment and Trust) that erupted in 1985, with dire consequences for the whole economy" (p. 106).

10. The Workers' party candidate in 1989 was Wang Ching-ping, formerly a professor at Tamchiang University and a leading figure in the *China Tide* group since the late 1970s. In December 1991 the Workers' party came close to getting a candidate elected; Luo Mei-wen, one of the few party founders with real credentials as a worker and a union activist, received 18,000 votes in Hsinchu County.

11. See table on party affiliation, *Independence Weekly Post,* no. 130 (November 29, 1991): 1. According to hearsay, about 14 of the 179 KMT district seats achieved were candidates who appealed to mainlander constituencies, and perhaps as many as 60 are affiliated with the "nonmainstream" conservative KMT faction.

12. Whereas the *New York Times* accepted the KMT's claim that the people of Taiwan had rejected independence ("A Strong Vote for One China," December 24 editorial, rebutted by election observer Timothy Gelatt on January 6), the Asian edition of *Newsweek* (January 13, 1992) more accurately reported it as "a mandate to do nothing."

13. *Far Eastern Economic Review,* February 27, 1992, pp. 48–49, "Nostalgia for Paradise."

14. Chang Chun-hong, presentation at Columbia University on October 17, 1990, on the National Affairs Conference. Proceedings in *Constitutional Reform and the Future of the Republic of China,* ed. Harvey Feldman (Armonk, NY: M.E. Sharpe, 1991). The New Tide faction accused Chang and the Meilidao faction of merely serving as an accessory for KMT renovation and legitimation at the NAC. See *New Tide,* no. 14 (July 1990): 10–17.

15. Linda Gail Arrigo, "The Logic of Taiwanese Nationalism and the Recent Development of the Taiwan Independence Movement Abroad, 1980–85," ms., October 1985. Marc Cohen's *Taiwan at the Crossroads* (Washington, DC: Asia Resource Center, 1988) devotes a whole chapter to overseas Taiwanese, and pp. 291–92 mention Hsu's role.

16. The development and activities of labor parties and unions are most thoroughly written up in English in Ho Shuet Ying, *Taiwan—After a Long Silence: The Emerging New Unions of Taiwan* (Hong Kong: Asia Monitor Research Center, 1990).

17. Professor Chen Ku-ying (purged from National Taiwan University philosophy department in 1971 Diaoyutai movement, opposition candidate in 1978), Huang Hsun-hsin (long-time veteran of local political struggles in Taitung and Changhua; National Legislator), and Chang Chun-nan (candidate in 1978 and 1980, insist that Taiwanese nationalists must know more about China) all made their way to Beijing in the 1980s. The former was given a post at Beijing University, the latter two token Taiwan seats in government bodies. In 1986

Chen lectured on democratization in Taiwan on many college campuses, implying the same for China. According to news reports, Huang and the Hong Kong representative were the only members of the People's Congress publicly to oppose the Tiananmen crackdown. After 1989 all three sought to leave the mainland and return to Taiwan. The author met with Chen and Chang in Beijing in December 1986 and also in the United States since.

18. Interview on February 4, 1992, with Buddha-Intelligence-Mysterious-Gold-Spear Master (*Fo Hui Jin Gang Cang Shang Shi*), head of the Ten Thousand Buddhas sect, Dragon Spring Mountain Temple (*Wan Fo Hui, Long Quan Shan Si*). The temple has large calligraphy on one of its walls saying "We love Taiwan," implying its Taiwanese nationalism. It provided its halls for meetings of a professors' and students' mobilization against national security laws. The master has written a tract justifying Buddhist social activism and participation in demonstrations on the basis of Sukyamuni's mendicant travels.

19. In July and August 1990 the author accompanied Shih Ming-deh on three trips to Chiayi to negotiate between DPP headquarters and the party branch on the nomination of a candidate for legislator. Local party members, strong advocates of Taiwan independence, resented Huang Hsin-chieh's endorsement of a non-DPP local candidate in an earlier race, and his further attempt to assign a candidate from the central headquarters. Several procedural clashes ensued.

20. The Hakka minority areas commonly are not enthusiastic about Taiwan independence, because if the Hokkien majority took over fully from the mainlander Kuomintang their angle on linguistic and political alliance with the ruling minority would be lost. This can be seen in the low number of DPP votes in areas dominated by Hakka: Taoyuan, Hsinchu, and Miaoli counties, outside of the cities where Hokkiens are usually the majority.

21. *New Tide (Xin Cao Liu, The Movement* in English on cover), no. 14 (July 1990): 4–9.

22. Interview with Wang Yao-nan, January 1992.

23. *Democratic Progressive News,* no. 76 (October 1, 1991): 4, statement by the two candidates for chairman on the fifth anniversary of the party, September 28, substantially the same as televised debate of October 5. Full debate available on VHS video, two cassettes.

24. *The Journalist,* no. 241 (October 21, 1991): 40–41. "For the throne of chairman, they all vie to be the 'black face': The background behind the DPP's Taiwan independence resolution."

25. Ibid., pp. 12–13, "The Bureau of Investigation starts the arrests!" "Attacking First the Periphery of the Opposition." On October 17, six members of the Organization for Taiwan Nation Building were arrested, and the next day the office in Taichung was forcibly dismantled. On October 18, agents arrested three leaders of an activity planned for October 20 in which a hundred people would reveal membership in the "seditious" World United Formosans for Independence and vote for Taiwan chapter officers.

26. Of forty-four DPP nominees for party-apportioned National Assembly seats, five were current and at least one a past regional branch head officer; the head officers are in a position to control new party enrollments. *Democratic Progressive News,* no. 80 (November 16, 1991): 4.

27. Chu Hsing-yu was featured in the *Independence Weekly Post,* nos. 140 and 141 combined (February 7, 1992): 5. "Firebrand, much gold, where does Chu Hsing-Yu's money come from?" This article notes, among others, that Chu was the only DPP public official to participate in the Control Yuan vote five years ago, and he bought a BMW soon after.

28. *Independence Weekly Post,* no. 132 (December 13, 1991): 1. "Taiwan finally enters the television election campaign era." Article describes the process of censorship and adjustment of content.

29. Tien Hung-mao, *The Great Transition: Political and Social Change in the Republic of China* (Stanford, CA: Hoover Institution Press, 1989), pp. 195–206.

30. January 30, 1991, report by Yang Tse-chuan, professor of business administration at Cheng Kung University and member of election supervisory commission group.

31. The author was present at several election analysis sessions: Christian Social Research Office, December 30, 1991, attended by prominent academics and Presbyterian ministers; DPP Taipei City Branch Head Office, January 16, 1992; same evening, DPP Taipei County, Panchiao Office, issues include arrest of campaign assistant.

32. *The Journalist,* January 19–25, 1992, pp. 42–49. "The old generation and the young upstarts bare their swords in the three factions' verbal sparring at San Lin Hsi."

33. *China Times Weekly,* August (date unknown) 1991, "The Future of Coalition Government," by Huang Chun-Cheng (Jacob).

34. Analysis courtesy of DPP legislator Wei Yao-chien. Major newspapers supporting the DPP are *Min Chung Daily* in Kaohsiung, *Independent News* group in Taipei, *Liberty Times* in Taipei, and *Taiwan Times* in Kaohsiung. Supporting means they report fully, objectively, and generally favorably on the opposition. They criticize the KMT, but the KMT is long since inured to it. However, according to Wei they occasionally make back-handed critiques that considerably negate the support, and they are all subtly limited by majority investment from directorates that interlock with KMT interests, even security agencies. See also Tien, *Great Transition.*

35. *Independence Weekly Post,* no. 138 (January 24, 1992): 3, on election of Shen Shih-hsiung as vice-chairman of the Legislative Yuan. Editorial, "Who Is Paving the Road for the Power of Money?"

36. The analysis of capital mobility and political opening for Taiwan is courtesy of Su Ching-li, private communication, 1987. Also see Long, *Taiwan:* "Even the [1987] removal of restrictions on the holding of foreign currency by individuals and banks had a very limited effect in reining in money supply growth. Much of the potential of this measure had been exploited by the evasion of exchange controls for many years by traders and exporters. . . . Indeed, having devoted much energy over the years to salting away their foreign currency profits overseas, Taiwan's business community now seems to have become adept at bringing it back" (p. 108). Also see *Far Eastern Economic Review,* December 12, 1991, p. 62–64, on internationalization of financial markets.

37. On the cleavage between mainlander and native Taiwanese capitalists, see Ichiro Namazaki, "Networks of Taiwanese Big Business: A Preliminary Analysis," *Modern China* 12, 4 (1986): 487–534.

38. Nigel Harris, "New Bourgeoisies?" *J. Development Studies* 24, 2 (1988): 237–49, quote from page 247.

39. An extraordinary current example of this is a February 29, 1992, move by more than thirty members of the Provincial Assembly to impeach twelve members of the Control Yuan, with a statement that "recently, following on criticism of money entering into every aspect of Control Yuan election activities, although presently within the country every election of officials has rumors of corruption," this should be corrected, beginning with the Control Yuan, which is supposed to be an oversight organ. *Independence Weekly Post,* no. 144 (March 6, 1992), p. 4. As of March 1992 the factions of the Kuomintang were publicly warring against each other and creating a kind of democratic opening in their solicitation of public support.

Bibliography

Democratic Progressive Party Officers and Elected Officials

Shih Ming-deh, president of Taiwan Association for Human Rights, DPP central committee

Huang Hsin-chieh, chairman, Democratic Progressive party 1988–91

Wei Yao-chien, national legislator

Chen Chu (Ms.), National Assembly, formerly director of Taiwan Association for Human Rights

Chen Hsiu-hui (Mrs. Ho Wen-chen, Mary), National Assembly, director of Homemakers Union & Foundation

Chen Chao-nan, vice-director of Organization Section, DPP Central Party Headquarters (émigré returned from Austria)

Wu Nai-jen, New Currents founder, formerly DPP central committee

Lin Yi-cheng (Daniel), director, DPP Taipei City Branch

Yuan Yen-yen (Theresa), administrative director, Lu Hsiu-yi and Chou Hui-ying Joint Service Center in Panchiao

Tseng Wan-hsin, former director, DPP Hsinchu City Branch

Huang Chun-cheng (Jacob), formerly director of Hong Chi-chang's service center in Tainan, now of DPP New York

Chou Bo-ya, Taipei city council, and wife Yeh Ch'i-lin (Inca), student activist

Chou Bo-lun, Taipei city council

Party branch organizers and members in Hualien and Penghu Islands

Other

Chien Hsi-chieh, Taiwanese Association for Labor Movement

Tseng Dze-tsai (husband of Wu Ch'ing-kuei, National Assembly), implicated in 1971 attempted assassination of Chiang Ching-Kuo in New York, returned to Taiwan 1991

Wang Su-ying (Ms.), Director of Kaohsiung County Women, Youth and Child Welfare Service Center, Fengshan City

Lin Mei-jung (Yvonne), Grassroot Women Workers' Center

Wang Yao-nan, secretary general of Labor party, also deputy editor of *Min Chung Daily* in Kaohsiung

Willi Boehi, correspondent for *Tages Anzeiger* of Zurich and associated with Catholic workers' organizations in Taiwan

Chan Hsi-kuei (pen name Lao Pao), editorial writer for *Liberty Times*

Periodicals

Independence Weekly Post (Ze Li Zhou Bao), Overseas Edition, in Chinese.

The Journalist (Xin Xin Wen), weekly, in Chinese.

China Times Weekly (Shi Bao Zhou Kan), Overseas Edition, in Chinese.

Taiwan Communiqué, monthly, in English.

City Paper, English weekly, free in Taipei.

Part III

THE OTHER ECONOMY

Each chapter in this section deals with a different facet of the related Taiwanese economy. The "economic miracle" that Taiwan experienced has been closely studied as a unique phenomenon, as has been suggested in the introduction to this volume. The effects of this miracle, however, as well as the facets of the economy that did not experience the explosive growth found in the industrial sectors, have been neglected by students of the island's economic development. The two chapters that make up this section examine such hitherto neglected facets of the "Taiwan miracle."

Jane Kaufman Winn's chapter demonstrates the insights she has gained into the complex socioeconomic environment of the Republic of China. In this detailed and multifaceted study, she deals with the informal sector of Taiwan's economic life. Winn explores a world where the government operates at arm's length.

Jack F. Williams explores a very different world, that of the agrarian economy. Here the government plays a major role in what has become more a symbol than a viable economic sphere. What emerges from Williams's essay is a fleshed-out picture of Taiwanese agriculture that is different from the rather rose-tinted and romantic one usually presented in accounts of the farmer's world on Taiwan.

The common thread tying these two essays together is that Taiwan's economic system is not as miraculous as one might think.

Chapter 6

Not by Rule of Law: Mediating State–Society Relations in Taiwan through the Underground Economy

Jane Kaufman Winn

Following the repeal of martial law in Taiwan, the tempo of progress toward economic liberalization and political reform has increased as the government of the ROC and the people of Taiwan search for new forms of cooperation and interaction. Any new system that evolves will still have to cope with a large informal sector,[1] a legacy of the former social and political order.

Chai Sung-lin, chairman of the Environment Foundation, has estimated that the underground economy of Taiwan may be as large as 50 percent of the reported ROC GNP.[2] Dr. Chai's definition of the underground economy includes not only criminal activities such as smuggling and prostitution but also merely illicit activities such as the underreporting of income by otherwise legitimate businesses. While some aspects of the informal economy such as *biao-hui* (rotating credit clubs) may raise few concerns, other aspects raise serious social policy issues. For example, the spectacular rise and subsequent collapse of the underground investment companies in the late 1980s demonstrated clearly that such operations could threaten the stability of Taiwan's regulated financial system. Another example is Taiwan's serious pollution problem, which will be even more difficult to solve to the extent that the sources of the pollution are informal enterprises outside effective government surveillance and control.

The informal sector has served as an important safety valve in the often strained relations between the people of Taiwan and the KMT regime. In the past, while political self-determination was severely constrained, economic free-

A version of this chapter titled "Relational Practices and the Marginalization of Law: The Study of Informal Practices of Small Business in Taiwan" will be published in *Law and Society Review*, vol. 28, no. 2, 1994.

dom was tolerated and even encouraged as part of the unwritten compromise between the KMT and the people it governed. Small and medium-sized enterprises were permitted to flourish without interference from the central government. Where government-controlled resources, such as bank credit, were in short supply, informal alternatives were allowed to grow up to meet demand. Now the informal sector constitutes a significant proportion of all economic activity in Taiwan, and the social structures of the informal sector will have a major impact on current moves to reform political and economic institutions. Attempts at liberalization undertaken without regard to the magnitude of informal economic activities in Taiwan are not likely to succeed.

The first part of this chapter will analyze the relationship among the legal system, the formal economy, and the informal economy in Taiwan. The second part will describe in greater detail one prominent feature of the informal economy in Taiwan, the informal financial sector. My central thesis is that Taiwan's political and legal processes cannot be understood apart from the role played by institutions in the informal sector. The informal sector in Taiwan plays a role not unlike that ascribed by Frank Upham to informal bureaucratic procedures in Japan:[3] it diffuses and obscures the exercise of power in Taiwanese society while simultaneously providing a forum within which that power can be exercised. To incorporate the informal sector explicitly into any general interpretation of economic, political, and social change in Taiwan, however, it is necessary to address cultural biases implicit in existing theories as well as to develop several new categories of analysis.

Law, the Formal Economy, and the Informal Economy in Taiwan

What separates the informal sector from the rest of society is, by definition, the legal system. According to conventional liberal theories of the role of law in a modern state, the legal system is the ultimate arbiter of conflicting values because legal judgments are backed by the full force of public authority.[4] A modern legal system should embrace and order the law-abiding elements of society, while excluding and punishing any criminal elements. From this modern liberal perspective, an informal sector floats in a kind of limbo between crime and conventional social practices that are technically illegal.

The assumption that state-sponsored values are primary, universal, and apparently costlessly transmitted throughout society by the legal system has been labeled "legal centralism" and criticized by scholars who advocate a more complex and pluralistic vision of social organization.[5] From a more pluralistic perspective, the informal sector, like the regulated economy or any other part of society, is composed of various "fields" of social interaction.[6] This alternative perspective has been labeled "legal pluralism." Law is seen as only one of many competing value systems, albeit a value system with a stronger ideological claim to primacy and deploying harsher sanctions than the alternatives can muster.

At least at a superficial level, the legal centralist ideas of modern liberal political and economic theories would seem to be a good description of the actual social organization of a Western nation like the United States, while legal pluralism would seem to be a good description of Taiwan's social organization. To assume such a simple, symmetrical relationship between theory and practice may be misleading, however. While the U.S. legal system seems to be fairly well integrated into the fabric of society—the common-sense perceptions and intuitions of the average person seem to harmonize fairly often with the results dictated by statutes and regulations, and the administration of justice seems generally to be thought of as fair—this does not necessarily support the conclusion that legal centralism accurately describes American society. Empirical studies have demonstrated a wide divergence between the ideas actually held by many apparently law-abiding people in the United States and the ideas that social scientists and jurists too readily assume are universally held. Similarly, empirical studies have demonstrated the widely disparate impact of legal institutions at different levels of American society.[7] So even in an apparently legalistic society, legal institutions may not be mediating between the people and their elected government in quite the manner commonly assumed, and it would be a mistake to assume that informal social, political, and economic institutions are only significant in non-Western or developing countries.

The difference between the roles of law in Taiwan and those in the United States lies as much in the contrasting official ideologies concerning law as in the different social practices of each country. The pretensions of the legal system in the United States to articulate fundamental social values are certainly a part of the ideology regarding law, whether or not they are true in fact. In Taiwan, the official ideology with regard to law has been influenced by traditional Confucian values such as a preference for personal relationships at the expense of the legal system, as well as by a regime of martial law, which until 1987 undermined the effectiveness and autonomy of the ROC legal system. Given the ambivalence toward the rule of law at the ideological level, it should not be surprising to find that Taiwan's legal system plays an even more attenuated role in mediating between the people and their government than does that of the United States.

Even the most superficial observation of the ROC legal system reveals that it cannot possibly be providing a universal, fundamental value system for Taiwanese society. The formal, technical requirements of ROC law often seem deliberately to have been set at variance with conventional social practices or legitimate business interests. Rigorous enforcement of the law is the exception rather than the rule. The divergence between what the law requires and what people commonly do, combined with lax enforcement, encourages people to find a basis for interaction outside the letter of the law.

The ROC authorities would face serious resistance if the rather formal, unrealistic standards embodied in ROC law were actually enforced. This is where Confucian-influenced popular attitudes about law seem to mesh with contemporary practices of patronage and corruption. One Confucian-inspired attitude to law is that if the social order is functioning well, then the law need not be invoked and the informal, particularistic social order of human relationships, face, and personal connections can govern.[8] The stilted and narrow perspective implicit in much ROC legislation does not disrupt the social order in Taiwan when it is ignored, as it is much of the time. If law plays only such a marginal role in Taiwanese society, however, it becomes difficult to say where the regulated economy ends and the informal economy begins.

A plausible interpretation of the role of law in Taiwanese society is that it is held in reserve, to be used only when the normal social order is under unusual stress, or that it is a bargaining chip that can be introduced to tip the balance in relationships or negotiations. The stilted, unduly restrictive laws and regulations of the ROC, combined with the (de facto) option to waive them at any time, clearly expand the scope of discretion government officials can exercise in their dealings with the public.

A simple example can illustrate the difference between the United States and ROC approaches to law and business activity. The general rule in the United States is that a corporation can be formed for the purpose of engaging in any lawful business. Once the business is incorporated, it may then be necessary to apply for a license to engage in a line of business subject to regulation. In the ROC, by contrast, incorporation is granted only for narrowly defined purposes, and anything for which permission is not granted is not allowed. The applicant must specify the particular activities the corporation will undertake, and some government official has discretion to grant or withhold permission to engage in those activities. In Taiwan, problems arise because the authorities refuse to grant permission for many lines of business, but once a business is incorporated, there is little monitoring of what the business is actually doing. This gives rise to the common practice of seeking permission for something that is routinely granted (such as selling refreshments or operating a trading company) and then doing whatever one wants but for which the authorities are unlikely to grant permission (such as opening a KTV parlor[9] or underground bank). As a result, a large proportion of apparently legitimate businesses in Taiwan are engaged in at least some underground activities.

Disregard of formal law and preference for personal relationships influence not only state-society relations, but also relations between private parties where no government interest is directly involved. Prior to the repeal of martial law and the current political and economic reforms, the KMT regime was notable not only for its repressive, Leninist political organization but also for its relative isolation from much of local society and business enterprise. To a considerable extent, the small and medium-sized businesses, which still constitute the greater part of Taiwan's economy, have operated free from central government interference. Lax enforcement of tax, labor, environmental protection, and zoning laws meant that small businesses operated with considerable autonomy but little support from the central government.

While personal relationships are often a good substitute for enforcement of legal standards, in extreme cases too much reliance on personal connections and informal procedures can undermine fundamental modern values such as respect for human rights. It is common for family members and friends in Taiwan to guarantee each others' debts, or even without a formal obligation, to underwrite each others' business ventures. The Confucian ideals of family solidarity and a sense of honor are not enough, however, to contain all the conflicts that arise in a modern economy. In Taiwanese society today, it is not uncommon to supplement traditional values with the threat of violence to settle what would otherwise be legal disputes.

Where government institutions fail to regulate the local economy, private parties will have to assume the costs of organizing and policing business relationships. In some sense, the costs borne directly by participants of maintaining the institutions of the informal sector are the functional equivalent of taxes paid by participants in the regulated economy for the maintenance of formal institutions by a central authority. A major component of those costs is the time and effort invested in maintaining networks of human relationships.[10] Those costs may vary from choosing not to seek any redress for a wrong suffered to the expense and danger of hiring gangsters to resolve a dispute.[11] In a highly competitive economic environment where the security of traditional relationships is being eroded but where government intervention is still limited, private parties may turn to alternatives like organized crime for services not provided by official sources, such as dispute resolution services.

Allegations are widespread in Taiwan that people in business often resort to gangsters to resolve serious disputes. A common sign that organized crime has become involved in an argument is the appearance of unidentified strangers, perhaps seated in the office lobby of one party to the dispute. The strangers need not even identify themselves because their silent presence telegraphs the fact that gangsters are now involved. Most people rush to settle the problem at this point, but the threat of violence can escalate to threats of bodily harm or kidnapping family members if the dispute is not resolved promptly.

One local lawyer described in detail a client's harrowing experience with gangsters hired to collect a debt. The client acted as agent for a foreign entity in soliciting funds in Taiwan for investment overseas and received a commission on all funds invested. The investors later learned they had lost all their money when the foreign entity went bankrupt. They insisted that the lawyer's client repay their investments in full, an amount equivalent to U.S. $200,000. The lawyer advised the client not to pay because the client, as mere agent, was not liable for the money lost by the overseas organization. The investors hired gangsters who appeared at the client's new place of employment, according to the conventional scenario. When this had no effect, they began telephoning the client's wife to threaten the client's children. These threats had to be taken seriously because in the late 1980s Taiwan was plagued with a rash of kidnappings and extortion rackets, but the client continued to follow the lawyer's advice and still refused to pay. The gangsters then waited for the client to leave work one day, forced him at gunpoint into the back of a car, and drove off with him. A coworker who witnessed the abduction telephoned the client's wife, urging her to notify the police. The wife called the police, who declined to take any action because they said they were too busy with the then upcoming elections. The client was taken to an undisclosed location and, at gunpoint, instructed to write out checks to the investors for the full amount of their investments. The client did so and presumably was able later to raise the money from friends and relatives to cover the checks when they were presented for payment. The lawyer recounting his client's misadventure ruefully added that the client then refused to pay the bill for the lawyer's services on the ground that the lawyer had not been of any assistance to the client.

The KMT has generally tolerated the existence of, or in any event been unable effectively to suppress, organized crime in Taiwan. The involvement of gangsters in local factional politics is well documented,[12] but this may stem as much from the inability of the central government fully to penetrate local society as from tacit complicity between organized crime and the ruling party. Although there have been periodic crackdowns, the magnitude of the problem seemed to increase following the repeal of martial law and erosion of KMT hegemony. According to several sources in 1989, individuals with known underworld connections have been elected to local government office in recent years.

Organized crime can openly compete with the legal system in providing coercive debt collection and dispute resolution services in part because the legal system is not always seen as a practical alternative. One reason effective access to the legal system in Taiwan is limited is the small number of trained legal practitioners.[13] Not only is the total number of lawyers small, but lawyers with training relevant to business and commerce are in the minority among all licensed lawyers. Until very recently, the legal profession was dominated by retired military personnel. The majority of licensed lawyers in Taiwan today received their training in the military. There are several methods to gain admission to the bar in Taiwan, and until very recently, passing the bar exam has been by far the most difficult. Until 1989 the pass rate hovered around 1 percent of the approximately 3,000 students who sat for the exam each year.[14] Other methods of becoming a lawyer include service as a military officer with legal responsibilities after having received training from the law faculty of a military college, or getting a Ph.D. degree in law and teaching in law school for a designated period of time.[15] While lawyers with legal training during military service will be well equipped to handle a law practice based on litigation and lobbying the government, such lawyers will not generally be well equipped to cope with a commercial law practice. Recent moves to permit more of the brightest graduates of Taiwan's regular law faculties to pass the bar exam may begin to alleviate the shortage of trained personnel.

Effective access to courts may be restricted by popular attitudes toward litigation as well. According to one ROC judge, most parties to civil litigation do not hire lawyers because they do not believe the benefits would justify the costs. The lack of representation by the parties increases the burden on the judge to formulate the legal issues and guide the litigation, slowing the proceedings and clogging the dockets. The perception of the parties that the standard of proof required is too high and the formalities of litigation are oppressive is likely to be accentuated if the parties are not represented by legal counsel. In criminal proceedings, by contrast, the perception is that it is worthwhile to pay for a lawyer so that the lawyer can try to bribe the prosecutor or judge. The allegation that bribes are routine in criminal proceedings is often made but difficult to verify.

Even if resort to gangsters to collect debts or settle disputes is relatively infrequent, it still parallels the marginal role played by the legal system in Taiwan. When the legal system and any alternatives are reduced to mere bargaining chips held by some but not all members of society, then the legal system cannot act as a countervailing force to the power exercised by elites in local society. Without effective access to a low-cost forum such as courts to seek redress, individuals have a strong incentive to maintain networks of personal relationships to protect them in the event that serious conflicts arise.

Doing Business Informally

While networks of personal connections are common to both the formal and informal economy in Taiwan, they are essential to business practices in the informal sector. In the informal economy there are fewer alternatives to such networks than in the formal economy, and state-sponsored initiatives have less impact than in the formal economy, but the difference is one of degree, not of kind.

Pressure to develop and maintain networks of relationships in Taiwan comes not only from inadequate protection of legal rights, but also from inadequate alternative sources of information about business opportunities and risks. Financial information about business operations that would be public or at least standardized in the United States either is not available or, when available, is generally so unreliable that its value is severely discounted. In Taiwan, information about reputation, profitable investment opportunities, and other economic variables are the currency used to exchange favors and build networks. The continued viability of networks of human relationships thus undermines attempts to bring the exchange of economically relevant information out into the public sphere.

One of the most obvious obstacles in Taiwan to the free flow of economic information outside networks of personal contacts is the low standard of accounting practices. Taiwanese businesses historically have not implemented sophisticated bookkeeping systems for a variety of reasons, including tax evasion. It is proverbial that local businesses maintain several sets of books: inside accounts (*nei zhang*) for the owner and outside accounts (*wai zhang*) for others, or even one set of books for the bank (overstating profits), one set for the tax authorities (understating profits), and one for the owner. The Income Tax Law indirectly sanctions the practice of not maintaining adequate accounting records by providing that the tax collecting authority may use industry standards for profitability to estimate the income of a business that cannot produce evidence to prove its actual income.[16] In practice, permitting the tax authorities to estimate the profitability of a firm will often lower the effective tax rate compared with paying taxes based on actual revenues. The reluctance of local businesses to establish and maintain reliable financial records shows some signs of diminishing, however, especially as the benefits of being a publicly listed company became apparent during the stock market boom of 1987–89.

As with the legal profession, Taiwan suffers from a severe shortage of properly qualified accounting professionals. In the past, as many as 80 percent of local CPAs were retired military or government personnel with training and experience in accounting for governmental entities, not private businesses.[17] The problem of a large number of CPAs with qualifications not directly relevant to the expansion of private-sector finance was compounded by an artificially low pass rate on the CPA examination for students graduating from the universities in Taiwan with no connection to the military. The professional standards of the accounting profession have not been very high in part because no legal liability is likely to result from certification by a CPA of false or misleading financial statements.[18] Endemic tax evasion within the private sector could only be maintained through cooperation between accountants and managers, and a profession of underground accountant has even emerged to meet the demand for keeping duplicate books.[19]

The poor reputation of the accounting profession in Taiwan is due not only to a shortage of qualified personnel, but also to the inadequate accounting standards professionals are called upon to apply. Even reputable accountants have only vague and incomplete standards with which to work, as evidenced by the fact that the accounting and auditing standards issued by the National Federation of CPA Associations of the ROC totaled only thirty-four pages, compared with thousands of pages for the U.S. equivalent.[20]

Rampant speculation on the Taiwan Stock Exchange is a good example of how the shortage of reliable, publicly available information and the local preference for information obtained through personal contacts can undermine the efficiency of an organized market. ROC authorities are aware that the overwhelming majority of the investing public in Taiwan are unconcerned with the economic fundamentals that should be reflected in stock prices, but trade instead on rumors and speculation. In the past, financial information filed with the ROC Securities and Exchange Commission was not always reliable. In recent years the SEC has attempted to raise the standards of such information by requiring that it be audited by one of only a handful of major, reputable accounting firms. The SEC is also gradually opening the local market to foreign institutional investment because institutional investors are more concerned with fundamental analysis than are individual investors, and thus can exert a stabilizing influence over market values. But institutional investors remain a minor force in the Taiwan Stock Exchange while individual speculators still dominate trading.

Is Informality Efficient?

The tremendous economic growth achieved by Taiwan in the last thirty years would hardly be possible if business done on the basis of informal networks of relationships was substantially less efficient than business done in regulated open markets. Although conventional economic analysis is based largely on assumptions (e.g., perfect information, no transaction costs, uniform enforcement of legal entitlements) that are of limited use in analyzing many business transactions conducted in Taiwan, some economists in recent years have attempted to develop analytical models that would take account of the type of institutional arrangements that prevail in an informal sector.

The noted economist Ronald Coase pointed out in 1937 that although economic analysis treats all economic actors as individuals, the assumption that large, complex economic organizations such as corporations can be analogized to individual persons may be seriously misleading even from the rather abstract perspective of economic theory. Coase argued that whenever business activity is not conducted by individuals but instead is organized into firms, the individual participants in the firm have made a collective decision to withdraw from the rigors of the free market into an alternative—presumably less costly—form of business organization.[21] Coase suggested that the decision to organize firms be taken as evidence that it may be more efficient to organize production bureaucratically in some instances rather than conforming to the radical individualism assumed by the concept of the free market. The new institutional economics, associated principally with Oliver Williamson, takes Coase's insight further and attempts to specify the efficiency conditions that would justify use of institutions other than markets to coordinate economic activity.[22]

Williamson argues that when "idiosyncratic" investments are made, the risk of opportunistic behavior and the limits of bounded rationality will lead the parties to adopt flexible governance structures to build mutual trust so that the transaction can go forward. He defines idiosyncratic investments as those with great value within the context of a particular transaction or relationship but with few alternative uses. Opportunistic behavior is defined as unprincipled selfishness such as lying or cheating. Bounded rationality refers to the inability of the parties to foresee all future contingencies relating to a particular transaction.[23] While the firm is an example of a governance structure designed to minimize the costs associated with opportunism and bounded rationality, Williamson argues that relational contracts are also examples of such structures.

Relational contract is a term coined by Ian Macneil to describe long-term commitments to cooperate in order to realize a particular venture in which many of the key elements of the agreement to cooperate are left ambiguous at the time agreement is entered into.[24] In a relational contract, the parties commit to a long-term relationship in which problems will be dealt with in a cooperative manner as they arise. Relational contract is contrasted with the conventional image of contracts as discrete, short-term transactions in which all possible future contingencies can be identified and risks allocated between the parties at the time the contract is entered into.

The concept of relational contract is clearly rich in potential for analyzing the informal sector. According to Williamson, under certain circumstances parties will realize their objectives more efficiently by forming relational contracts rather than entering into a series of discrete, short-term contracts on the one hand, or establishing a hierarchical organization such as a corporation, on the other. If the networks of relationships in the informal sector in Taiwan can be described as a form of relational contract, not only is it possible that these networks may be as economically efficient as free-market transaction, they may even be more efficient. Such a quantitative comparison cannot accurately be made, however, until the institutions of both a relational contract system and a free-market system are specified in an equivalent level of detail and valued according to some more general standard than market prices.

Williamson, like other economists, implicitly assumes the existence of a free market operating in the background of his analysis of relational contracting or firm governance because he argues that parties opt out of market governance and choose an alternative only under certain limited circumstances.[25] Because Williamson is postulating a free market as a sort of institutional foundation or baseline from which the parties are free to depart, and because the operation of a free market requires, among other things, the enforcement of property and contract rights, he is still tacitly accepting the idea of legal centralism. Economic analysis of relational contracts thus postulates a priori the existence of universal legal structures that the parties are free to reject or accept on an individual basis. It is fundamentally incompatible with the idea of legal pluralism, which assumes that social values are fragmented into competing fields.

The fact that specific institutions are required to support the operation of the price mechanism, and that there must be some social cost attributed to the maintenance of those background institutions, such as the legal system, is an inference that can be drawn from Coase's 1937 article. That subsequent debate over Coase's theory of the firm has focused on the nature of, and costs attributable to, alternatives to the firm,[26] only reflects the general reluctance of economists to tie the operation of the price mechanism to empirically testable foundations. Coase criticized this tendency of conventional economic analysis, complaining that too much economic analysis exists only on blackboards or "floats in the air."[27] The consequence of this tendency consistently to understate the costs of maintaining actual market structures is that economic analysis cannot provide a neutral standard to evaluate the relative effectiveness of both competitive markets and relational alternatives as actual institutions in a real world context. The bias toward understating the actual costs of markets is shared even by transaction cost economics because it assumes a background of state-centered legality that may be lacking or less developed in a relational system. A less biased standard of comparison between markets and flexible or relational economic organizations might be a theory that explicitly treats all economic institutions as embedded in a larger system of social relations.[28] By focusing on the degree to which even competitive markets cannot function without connections to and reinforcement from other institutions in society, a theory of markets as embedded within other social relations could counteract the proclivity of economists to elide the costless price mechanism of "blackboard" economics with the actual operation of markets in society.

The operation of relational economic institutions may be facilitated in Taiwan because such economic relations harmonize with other social relations and draw on social values unlike those usually postulated in economic theory. The work of the social psychologist K.K. Hwang suggests that the system of relational norms supporting social interaction in Taiwan manifests a form of rationality very different to the individualistic, formal rationality commonly invoked in economic analysis but that is still highly calculating and also quite effective in allocating resources.[29] In Hwang's model of decision making in a relational system, he argues that family-based or familylike relationships are the preferred basis for social exchanges in Taiwan while discrete, individualistic exchanges are the exception. The relational system Hwang describes is dynamic and interactive, with participants constantly reappraising the quality of their relationships and critically assessing the ability of prospective or existing partners to deliver access to social or economic resources.

Hwang's research captures the common perception in Chinese society that conduct undertaken on an individual basis is fraught with peril whereas initiative undertaken from within relationships or groups is less daunting.[30] The tacit assumption of legal centralism, that is, that there is a state creating a universal normative order, is lacking in Hwang's model. This contrasts with the basic image of the model of perfectly competitive markets, in which individuals are free to produce as much or as little as they like because an unlimited number of potential consumers await in the anonymous forum of the market. In Hwang's model, the possibility of anonymous, discrete transactions still exists, but it is no longer the standard for comparison. This model is more useful than conventional economic models for understanding relationships in the informal economy in Taiwan because it explicitly accounts for the activities of choosing to create a relationship, choosing to maintain relationships, and choosing to deny the existence of relationships, which then permits an anonymous transaction to take place. Free-market-type transactions are thus available to participants as a sort of default option, to be exercised only when relational alternatives are not available.

Existing legal and economic analyses of relational institutions in the United States that treat them as exceptional or marginal are merely mirroring the general bias in favor of universalizing interpretations of the role of law in modern society. These interpretations are a poor model to apply to Taiwan because both the state and society are so obviously embedded in the system of networks of personal relations. In Taiwan, relational contracts are the norm, not the exception, at all levels of state-society relations. The universal norms of liberal political theory and individualistic competitive market forces are more properly treated as marginal or exceptional institutions in Taiwan.

The possibility of economic regulation systematically organized along informal, relational lines to the exclusion of formal legal regulation has been suggested by Upham in his analysis of legal institutions in Japan and their displacement by what he calls bureaucratic informalism.[31] Upham views Japanese economic regulation as a form of institutionalized informality. If he is correct, then it is further evidence that it is not necessary to assume that parties opt out of regulated free markets on a selective basis, but rather that an entire economy might be organized along predominantly relational lines and still be economically efficient.

To make a cross-cultural comparison of the efficiency of markets in a legalistic society like the United States and the efficiency of relational economic systems within relational social and political systems such as arguably exist in Taiwan and Japan, it is necessary to avoid the cultural bias in favor of Western institutions implicit in prevailing economic theories. Coase pointed out that even so basic a concept as time is treated as only a transaction cost and not generally accounted for in economics.[32] Williamson added language as a transaction cost,[33] but there is no reason not to include as well the cost of institutions charged with socialization of economic actors such as schools, the media, and religion. Such institutions are essential to ensure that the expectations of individuals engaged in productive activities are consistently fulfilled by others operating within the same system. Only when the concept of transaction costs has been expanded to this point would it be possible to overcome bias in favor of Western-style institutions implicit in the concept of the price mechanism and the free market. With such a broad concept of transaction costs it would be possible not only fully to price the networks of informal relationships that support business transactions in Taiwan, but also to price the maintenance of institutions that legitimate and facilitate the operation of markets in the United States. Such a theory of transaction costs would necessarily be interdisciplinary, drawing not only on economics but also on sociology and anthropology.

In a theory capable of evaluating both conventional market economies and informal economies, an analogy could be drawn to concepts like human capital[34] and symbolic capital[35] to develop a concept of relational capital.[36] The economist Gary Becker coined the term "human capital" to account for the relationship between education, on-the-job training, and variations in earnings over time and with age. The social theorist Pierre Bourdieu developed the concept of symbolic capital to designate productive capacity accumulated in the form of authority, knowledge, reputation, or relationships but which may be converted to capital assets recognized by economists.[37] In Taiwan, relational business practices can constitute a loosely institutionalized framework for economic activity because there has been a large investment of social resources to focus individuals on the importance of human relations. This investment of social resources should be recognized as relational capital.

Relational capital serves an economic purpose because, once established, it lowers transaction costs. Transaction costs that are reduced include evaluating the integrity of a potential colleague to minimize the cost of opportunistic behavior, comparison shopping for better quality or price terms, full specification of all terms of an agreement in advance, or design and implementation of monitoring systems. Although the decision of the parties to do business through relationships constitutes a withdrawal from free-market competition, it need not result in the kind of inefficient allocation of resources associated with monopoly or oligopoly. If the terms of the ongoing relationship are fair to all the parties, the resulting distribution of resources through relationships may approximate the competitive free-market result.[38]

To account for relational capital in Taiwan but not to account for the investment of social resources that make markets work in a country like the United States would overstate the costs of maintaining a relational system and understate the costs of a market system. The tendency of economic analysis to assume that the price mechanism operates costlessly and that externalities and transaction costs not reflected in market prices are not significant, represents precisely this type of understatement of the social investment in maintaining market institutions. The accounting for the equivalent to relational capital in a market system would require accounting for the socialization functions performed by institutions of education, religion, the mass media, and popular culture, which facilitate market transactions while marginalizing relational networks. It might then be possible to demonstrate that while markets appear to operate with fewer social costs in societies whose members are socialized to believe in universals and understand themselves as individuals, and relational systems appear to operate at lower social cost in societies whose members are socialized to believe in the importance of human relationships and to understand themselves through membership in groups, there are significant hidden costs in either form of organization, the magnitude of which is disguised by culture and ideology.

Since the functions of formal political, economic, and legal institutions are merged in the activities of various participants in the informal sector, a concept such as "relational entrepreneur" could be developed to describe the activity of individuals who, like impresarios, orchestrate the networks of relationships that constitute the informal sector. The activities and the rationality of relational entrepreneurs could be compared to the rationality of managers, workers, politicians, voters, judges, and others as analyzed in conventional social sciences. Hwang's analysis of the dynamics of maintaining networks of relationships is a first step toward such a theory of relational entrepreneurship. If the flexibility and ambiguity of relations in the informal sector translates into the ability of any capable individual to act as a relational entrepreneur, and thus the ability to shape consciously the development of social institutions, this has significant implications for political theories of expanded participatory democracy.[39]

A social theory that would permit unbiased comparisons between formal and informal economic institutions would not treat informal institutions such as relational contracts, relational capital, and relational entrepreneurship as options available only as elective alternatives to more fundamental institutions. Such a theory could recognize relational institutions as genuine alternatives to and at least potentially equivalent to institutions such as representative government and competitive markets. When relational institutions are no longer presumed to be derivative or defective, then an unbiased appraisal of their fairness or efficiency is possible. Until such a theory of social and productive relations emerges, however, comparisons between the efficiency of competitive free markets and relational contract systems in the informal sector remain fraught with unexamined cultural biases.

Democracy and the Informal Sector

The current conditions of rapid social and political change in Taiwan have brought calls from the political opposition for the rule of law and the reform of the legal system. Bolstering the authority and integrity of the ROC legal system would reduce the possibility of patronage, corruption, and official abuse of discretion, and it would reduce the individual need to rely on personal relationships for economic security. It is not clear, however, that Taiwan is moving in that direction. The current attempts at liberalization of the social and political order in Taiwan will necessarily require a more vital legal system, but that is not the only path reform may take. If political innovation in Taiwan moves in the direction of Japan rather than the United States, the ROC legal system may remain marginalized indefinitely.

With regard to the Japanese legal system, Upham has concluded that Japan's leaders have managed to coopt political dissent and to minimize the public expression of criticism in part through the practice of "bureaucratic informality."[40] Bureaucratic informality involves a preference for informally mediated solutions over formal adjudication of disputes in court, and a preference for enforcing bureaucratic priorities through informal techniques such as "administrative guidance" rather than through formal legal processes such as promulgation of regulations. A bias in favor of informal bureaucratic procedures minimizes the role of the legal system in mediating conflicts between the state and society and substitutes less public channels of communication and influence that are more easily subject to elite manipulation.

The role of the informal sector of Taiwan in mediating conflict is similar to informal bureaucratic procedures in Japan because it may facilitate elite domination of society by obscuring the exercise of power. On the other hand, the operation of the informal sector in Taiwan is unlike Japanese bureaucratic informality because it is not actually administered by the government but is beyond direct government control. The informal sector in Taiwan is therefore even further removed from public perception or critical review. While the language of laws and regulations in Japan is sufficiently open-ended and aspirational to sanction official recourse to bureaucratic informality in enforcement, ROC laws do not sanction informal economic activity, but specifically proscribe it. Thus the blending of formal and informal institutions in Taiwan must take place entirely outside the public view and direct official control. The use of gangsters in Taiwan to settle disputes arising in the informal sector may seem a far cry from the use of government-sponsored mediation procedures in Japan, yet both structures involve no public awareness or independent review of the results achieved. Both can be contrasted with the generally public, open nature of litigation and the possibility of judicial review.

While the example of Japan suggests that economic development can be achieved within a predominantly informal or relational institutional framework, this does not answer the question of whether a society organized along such lines is more or less just than a society where legal institutions are emphasized. The ideal of universal respect for fundamental human rights is a quintessentially liberal concept, and the realization of that ideal is generally assumed to take place within a legal framework. Whether the ideal of fundamental human rights is actually given concrete recognition in any modern liberal society is another question, however. In the United States, for example, where human rights are generally discussed under the rubric "constitutional rights," they are understood to pertain primarily to civil liberties and not to include any claim to economic subsistence or material well-being. Given that the ideal of human rights is only imperfectly realized in liberal societies, it is possible that the concept of human rights might find an equivalent degree of practical recognition in a society dominated by networks of human relationships if individuals are understood to have rights against not only the state with regard to civil liberties, but also intermediate institutions based on relational networks.

The Informal Financial Sector in Taiwan

Although informal economic relations are pervasive in Taiwan and an empirical study could be based on any number of industries or sectors of the economy, this chapter will focus on the informal financial sector. Although financial relations differ in some significant respects from business relations based on the production or marketing of goods, the informal financial sector is representative of informal economic activity generally in that its influence is pervasive in

Taiwan's economy. The empirical component of this chapter will therefore not attempt an encyclopedic, superficial description of the informal sector, but instead focus in depth on informal financial relationships.

Until recent years, most enterprises in Taiwan faced an acute shortage of bank credit. From the 1950s to the late 1980s, entrepreneurs were forced to find alternative sources of finance for their businesses. Some alternatives included traditional forms of finance such as rotating credit clubs (*hui*), while others were of more recent derivation, such as discounting postdated checks. The development of an informal financial system was tolerated by ROC authorities as an apparently unavoidable consequence of trying to encourage rapid, decentralized economic growth while retaining tight central control over the banking system.

Although precise estimates of the magnitude of the informal financial sector are not available, the consensus is that it constitutes a major component of Taiwan's financial system. An economist in Taiwan has estimated that from 1964 to 1988, 34 percent of the financial resources of private enterprises in Taiwan came from the curb or informal market.[41] A former minister of finance estimated that 30 to 40 percent of all financial transactions took place in the informal sector.[42] Another estimate of the total size of the informal financial system in Taiwan is 30 percent of all loans processed through the financial system.[43] Wade notes that interest rates in curb markets ranged from 300 percent higher than bank loan rates in the 1950s to 50–100 percent higher during the 1970s. Wade also observes that while public enterprises receive almost all their credit from banks, small businesses rely most heavily on the informal financial system.

One of the most obvious factors contributing to the growth of the informal financial system in Taiwan was the conservative, bureaucratic orientation of regulated financial institutions. The unresponsive attitudes of bankers are in turn a function of excessive government interference in all aspects of bank management. Until very recently, ROC authorities have pursued a apparently paradoxical policy of stifling regulated financial institutions such as banks through overregulation while virtually disregarding the activities of informal financial institutions.

Retaining direct government control over most of the ROC banking system was a fundamental KMT policy until it was finally officially renounced in 1989. Until the decision was made in 1989 to grant licenses to new, privately owned commercial banks, virtually every major commercial bank in Taiwan was owned by either the central, provincial, or local governments or the KMT. The actual historical origins of this policy are not clear, although several justifications of it have been offered. The policy might be attributable to memories of the hyperinflation experienced in the late 1940s, which reflected the failure of the KMT to retain control over the financial resources necessary to finance its operations and also contributed to the KMT defeat at the hands of the Communists.[44] The policy might also be attributable to the Three Principles of the People, the official KMT ideology. The principle of People's Livelihood calls for an economic order that combines private property with government control over important public resources, of which finance may arguably be one. Although the justifications for the policy may be open to debate, there is no question that for forty years, the official KMT policy was to maintain oligopolistic control over banking in Taiwan.

Central control is exercised over these banks in part through periodic audits based on standard accounting and financial principles and performed by Central Bank of China or Ministry of Finance personnel. External audits performed by government regulators are a form of bank regulation practiced in any country with a modern banking system, however, and not only government-owned banks but also foreign banks and the small number of privately owned financial institutions are subject to the same type of audits. The problem of excessive governmental interference experienced by government-owned banks does not arise because of periodic audits, but arises because the banks are subject to other, more intrusive and oppressive forms of governmental interference with internal operations and management.

Government-owned banks suffer from substantial interference in personnel and management matters because whenever various divisions of government or government agencies are majority shareholders in a bank, the employees of that bank are considered civil servants under ROC law. Through these various forms of regulation, ROC authorities have been able to use the government-owned banks as conduits for expressing government priorities in economic planning as well as for distribution of patronage, although at a cost of making the management of the banks very conservative and unresponsive to the needs of bank customers.

The authority of the Control Yuan to investigate the conduct of bank employees is another major factor stifling initiative in government-owned banks in Taiwan. Employees are hired and promoted according to civil service standards, which interfere with the power of bank management to set personnel policies. Government employees or employees of government-owned enterprises are held to be fiduciaries with regard to the government property they control. If any government property is lost under their stewardship, these individual civil servants may be held personally liable for the loss. Whenever a government-owned bank wishes to write off a bad loan, the Control Yuan has the authority to investigate the facts of the loss to determine if any of the bank employees involved should be held liable for civil or criminal penalties. The fear of personal liability for the amount of the credit extended by the bank would tend to stifle any initiative by lending officers.

During the decades when demand for credit exceeded supply, official policies on credit allocation could be translated directly into concrete results, given that most bank credit was under government control. ROC credit allocation policy has been to give access to bank credit at below market interest rates[45] for projects or enterprises supported by the government (which were often KMT-controlled or government-owned enterprises) while also permitting access to bank credit for a limited number of privately owned enterprises that were not directly affiliated with the government or KMT but were able to qualify under conventional lending standards. While small and medium-sized enterprises did not receive any subsidies in the form of access to cheap credit, they were not prevented from devising alternative sources of finance.

Institutions that received bank financing enjoyed not only an interest-rate subsidy but also access to what was known as "evergreen" financing. The decision to grant a loan was based on either the existence of real property as collateral or two guarantors known to the bank, not based on the anticipated profits of the enterprise. The lender and borrower knew that although the loan was nominally made for a fixed term of several years, in fact the term was indefinite. This was because upon maturity, the loan would be rolled over as a matter of course if the collateral was still intact or the sureties were still available. A business that could secure "evergreen" financing from a bank enjoyed what was in effect an equity investment but with no obligation to pay dividends. The borrower's only obligation was to make low fixed payments in the form of below-market interest.

The focus on secure forms of collateral, combined with a disregard for the profitability of the borrowing enterprise, gave rise to the charge that government-owned banks suffered from a pawn-shop mentality. By requiring that the collateral be in place before the credit was extended, not only was there little reason to reconsider a credit once it was extended, but there was little a small or growing enterprise could do to qualify for credit. Bank lending officers were unwilling to lend based on cash-flow or projections of profitability based on accounting information because of endemic fraud in accounting practices in Taiwan. Given the generally poor state of financial records at all levels of business enterprise in Taiwan, this pawn-shop mentality was a reasonable response on the part of bankers trying to minimize losses. However, the focus on real property or the reputation of the guarantors has prevented bankers from adopting modern financial standards for credit based on the profitability of the ongoing business operations.

In the fluid and dynamic world of small and medium-sized enterprises in Taiwan, the rapid pace of economic development did not stop because most did not qualify for subsidized bank credits. Small entrepreneurs had a variety of alternative sources of credit, although at higher interest rates and for shorter terms than bank credit. The simplest source might be working capital provided as credit from suppliers or purchasers, documented in the form of a postdated check.

Working capital supplied by customers or suppliers in Taiwan is generally supplied with a postdated check as evidence of the obligation. At different times, the same enterprise might be either a lender or borrower of this type of working capital. A promissory note or a draft is normally thought of as a credit instrument, while a check is considered a cash equivalent, but in Taiwan, post-dated checks are more popular credit instruments than promissory notes. The ROC practice of using checks as credit instruments dates back to the 1960s, when criminal penalties were established for dishonoring checks but not for dishonoring promissory notes. The policy behind this seems to have been the desire to enhance popular confidence in checks as an equivalent to cash payment, but it missed the mark for several reasons. Banks restricted the number of checking accounts they granted because of the seriousness of the consequences for bouncing checks. Private parties were comforted by the thought of potential criminal liability of the issuer of the check and began to rely on the threat of criminal prosecution as a guarantee of creditworthiness. Thus, postdated checks became a common credit instrument instead of a common cash equivalent.

The ROC authorities were indirectly subsidizing the development of the informal financial system by providing government-subsidized debt collection services (in the form of the public prosecutor and threat of imprisonment) to creditors that demanded checks as evidence of debt. As the tempo of economic development quickened throughout the 1960s and 1970s, and as the cohesiveness of traditional social ties based on family or place was eroded by increasing social and economic mobility, the ROC authorities provided a convenient, effective alternative for reinforcing the security of business transactions. The threat of criminal penalties for bouncing a check acted as a surrogate for reputation or face, but also inhibited the development of financial and accounting standards of creditworthiness.

In a typical trade transaction financed with a postdated check, the party supplying the goods accepts a postdated check in exchange for delivery of the goods. The check may be payable, for example, three months after the date of the transaction. The seller can either hold the check until it is payable or sell it at a discount. Banks will discount postdated checks for their customers provided a copy of the invoice for goods sold accompanies the check. The practice of requiring supporting documents to establish that the check was given in the context of an actual sale of goods or services was adopted by banks in the early 1980s to prevent the practice of exchanging postdated checks for the sole purpose of getting bank credit (*huan piao*). By exchanging postdated checks, two businesses that did not otherwise qualify for bank credit could borrow based on each other's credit. The banks thought they were extending a self-liquidating trade credit secured by an underlying transaction in goods, but in fact they were extending unsecured credit for working capital to small businesses.

In 1987, in spite of vocal opposition from local business interests, the criminal penalties for bouncing checks were repealed. Although many observers anticipated a severe credit contraction as a result, the reform apparently had very little impact on the system of using postdated checks to raise working capital. There are several reasons that might account for the easy transition away from criminal penalties: first, by 1987, the previously chronic credit shortage had been replaced by a surplus of funds for investment; second, although criminal penalties inspired confidence in the parties accepting postdated checks, they actually had little other impact on business behavior; and finally, even without criminal penalties, a party that bounces checks may have their account closed (losing access to postdated checks as a form of finance) and be unable to open another one because the banks share information on dishonored checks. Parties entering into transactions in bad faith were smart enough to evade prosecution under the law, and the parties actually prosecuted were often the victim of circumstances beyond their control who would have made good on their obligations had they been able to. The large number of hapless wives (who had permitted their husbands to do business under their names) languishing in ROC prisons after the failure of their husband's business was noted as a significant human rights abuse by the U.S. State Department in 1985 and 1986.[46]

The withdrawal of criminal penalties was not accompanied by a significant reform of the credit policies of government-owned banks. Most small and medium-sized businesses apparently continue to rely on the informal financial sector for much of their credit needs. This contrasts with the normal business practice in the United States, for example, where small businesses might raise working capital by offering security other than real estate, such as equipment, inventory, or accounts receivable, to a professional financer such as a bank or finance company. Such a professional financer would apply recognized financial standards to audited accounting information as well as personal knowledge of the borrower and the borrower's business to determine creditworthiness. Credit extended between small businesses in Taiwan would more likely be based on reputation and a preexisting relationship, which can only indirectly take account of the profitability and soundness of the underlying business.

The assumption behind credit obtained through rotating credit clubs (*biao hui* or *he hui*), like credit obtained with postdated checks, is that personal relationships or reputation are an adequate guide to creditworthiness. The structure of a *hui* is as follows: the *hui-tou* or leader of the *hui* brings together the members of the *hui*. The amount of the regular contribution is set, and the *hui-tou* takes the first collected amount. The *hui* meets at regular intervals, and members who have not yet received the collected amount can bid competitively for the right to receive it. A member can take the collected amount once, but at all other meetings must contribute the designated amount. The *hui-tou* assumes responsibility for the performance of each member in the event of default, so the reputation of the *hui-tou* is crucial to the success of the *hui*. Even though the members of the *hui* have no legal obligation to each other (their obligations run only to the *hui-tou*), their reputations are indirectly factors in the success of the *hui*.

Hui generally offer savers a higher return than financial institutions like banks, although this is offset in part by the higher risk of default and the higher monitoring costs assumed by the participants. *Hui* may be organized on a friendly basis as a form of savings club, as between coworkers or neighbors, or to raise capital for a business venture. While in a friendly *hui* most participants are already known to each other, in business *hui* only the organizer of the *hui* may know all the members.

Hui can be used to acquire capital assets such as real estate for which purchase money financing is not available from regulated financial institutions. Once an asset has been acquired, it can be offered as collateral for bank finance at lower interest. Unlike their equivalents in the United States, banks are not very involved in financing purchases of major assets. For example, in Taiwan there is no equivalent of the residential real property mortgage payable over up to thirty years such as has been used in the United States to facilitate home ownership. If a *hui* is used to acquire a major asset, the term of the credit will be determined by the total number of participants, but would generally not exceed several years at most.

Business enterprises in Taiwan were once permitted by ROC authorities to receive savings deposits from their employees, although this practice is now officially proscribed and continues only in the informal sector. Employee deposit taking was originally encouraged by the authorities during the 1960s and 1970s when credit was in short supply. The MOF gave companies incentives to borrow from employees by granting favorable tax treatment to the interest expense incurred on such borrowing.

Although the tax incentive no longer exists, the practice of business enterprises taking savings from the public has proven difficult to stamp out. From the point of view of the employer, encouraging employees to save through investing in the company gives them an incentive to support the company and also relieves the pressure to seek finance from outside sources.[47] Higher interest rates have usually been the incentive offered to lure employees away from the regulated financial system. Although the 1989 revision of the ROC Banking Law attempts flatly to prohibit deposit taking by nonbanks, the Central Bank of China Economic Research Department still publishes a figure for the average interest rates on "deposits with firms." For example, for April 1990, the average interest rate for deposits with firms in Taipei City was 1.51 percent a month, with a high of 2.30 percent and a low of 0.90 percent. This compares with a 9.25 percent annual interest rate on a one-year time deposit with the Bank of Taiwan.[48]

Transfers of title of real property in Taiwan are handled by notaries (*daishu*), who also participate in the informal financial system by providing introductions to individuals willing to finance real estate transactions in exchange for a mortgage. Such individuals can earn a higher rate of interest than available through banks combined with the security of a real property mortgage as security. The notary can profit in two ways from providing such introductions: directly, from charging for the introduction itself, and indirectly, by facilitating deals that might otherwise fail to take place for lack of credit. Although the borrower is able to obtain purchase money financing not available from regulated sources, private lenders of this type are usually only willing to lend money for a year or two. This transaction thus differs from land contracts in the United States, in which a seller may take the buyer's obligation to pay for twenty years or more in exchange for the real property.

While a *daishu* may be able to introduce borrowers to prospective lenders interested in investing in real estate, this should not be confused with another category of professional private moneylenders, *dixia qianzhuang* or underground banks. These moneylenders often charge high interest rates for relatively short periods of time (from a few days to a few weeks, or at most months), often with security such as automobiles or stock certificates but not usually real estate. This type of moneylender cannot operate without some connection to organized crime, and some gangs in Taipei even specialize in this type of moneylending operation. Many customers of this type of moneylender are persons borrowing to cope with a personal emergency or to cover gambling debts. Businesses may be forced to deal with moneylenders if the principal of the business has withdrawn too much money from the business, leaving it undercapitalized and at risk from minor fluctuations in the volume of business. These moneylenders, however, do not extend long-term credit, and failure promptly to repay amounts borrowed is understood to entail the threat of dire reprisals. Although such a moneylender may take a postdated check as evidence of the debt, the lender would rely on faster, more effective underground sanctions to ensure repayment rather than the threat of criminal prosecution.

Relational Capital and Financial Pluralism

Whether credit is extended by government-owned banks or by participants in the informal sector, several common features of financing transactions in Taiwan emerge. These common features contrast with what are understood to be the basic elements of a financing transaction in a country like the United States that has a more developed regulated financial system. The features common to financial transactions in Taiwan but absent from similar transactions in the United States reflect the fact that parties in Taiwan can count on the existence of highly developed networks of relationships to order economic activity, while parties in the United States can count on the existence of complex, well-recognized accounting and legal standards to govern their activities.

Sophisticated creditors in the United States monitor the performance and creditworthiness of debtors based in large part on financial information derived from accounting data. When summarized, accounting data should give a reasonably accurate picture of the health of the business enterprise whose profits ultimately guarantee repayment of the loan. Collateral is taken to limit the magnitude of problems that might arise after default, not as a substitute for understanding the business of the borrower. In Taiwan by contrast, both informal and regulated lenders seem to alternate between two major forms of debtor-creditor relationship. In one, the creditor is not concerned with the personal integrity of the borrower but only with the availability of reliable mechanisms for recovery upon default. In the other, the creditor is concerned with the degree to which the borrower is integrated into the networks of connections and personal relationships and the status of the borrower within those networks. In neither form of debtor-creditor relationship is the profitability of the enterprise expressly addressed.

Creditors concerned only with reliable mechanisms for recovery upon default may be either regulated lenders or participants in the informal financial sector. When banks, for example, insist on collateral, the preferred form of collateral is real estate. The value of real property collateral is less subject to variation based on the vagaries of the debtor's conduct than personal property collateral such as inventory or equipment. Thus the relationship between lender and borrower is attenuated, with the borrower focusing on the value of the real estate to guarantee repayment of the loan without much regard for the borrower's conduct. When professional moneylenders lend, they rely on fear of the steps they are willing to take to recover their money to frighten borrowers into repaying. Professional moneylenders, like mortgage holders, are not really concerned with how the borrower will repay, only that the borrower understand that default entails high costs.

Similarly, creditors concerned primarily with the standing of the borrower within the dense fabric of personal relationships in Taiwanese society may be either regulated lenders or participants in the informal financial sector. If the loan is not secured by real estate or the threat of bodily harm, then the focus of the lender shifts to an evaluation of the personal integrity of the borrower. The practice of requiring guarantors reflects the continuing importance of relational standards to the operations of regulated lenders, even in large-scale commercial transactions.[49]

When commercial banks ask for two guarantors as a substitute for real property collateral, the focus is on the reputation of the guarantors. The caliber of the guarantors is based in part on their apparent wealth but part of the analysis focuses on softer variables such as general reputation. The standing of the guarantors is an indication of the reputation of the borrower. By adding two guarantors, the bank has three parties it can turn to in the event of default, but defaulting debtors can fairly easily evade legal process instituted by creditors, so a bare legal right to repayment is of little comfort to a creditor after default. Ultimately, the willingness of the borrower and the guarantors to repay amounts they are legally liable for is a function of their concern for their reputations in the community. Capitalizing on this concern for reputation is also found in informal financing techniques such as *hui* and employee deposit taking.

Knowledge of how to move in the system of relationships, face, and favors is therefore an essential element in unsecured lending and borrowing in both the formal and informal financial systems in Taiwan. This knowledge and ability to function would be the "relational capital" referred to above. The individuals able to amass and deploy this type of relational capital would be "relational entrepreneurs." Although these labels are not used by participants in the informal financial sector in Taiwan, the underlying concepts are recognized and coexist with other forms of financial and economic analysis to create the equivalent of legal pluralism. The resulting patchwork of perspectives might be labeled "financial pluralism."

The ability to evaluate critically another person's personal integrity, future prospects, and connections is in some sense the Taiwanese equivalent of financial analysis performed by financing companies in the United States. Concern with the personal integrity of borrowers is also a concern of lenders in the United States, but the availability of financial information through national credit reporting services and reasonably reliable audited financial statements means that lenders in a country like the United States can supplement or even replace their personal judgment with mathematical formulas applied to financial data. In Taiwan, the lack of reliable credit reports and accounting information may be both a cause of the failure to apply financial standards in credit transactions and a symptom of the fact that there is a reasonably effective parallel system in operation. To the extent that the relational entrepreneurs are able to evaluate the borrower's reputation and connections accurately enough to predict ability to repay a loan, then there is no real pressure to transform the Taiwanese system into a credit system based on principles of modern financial analysis. Only when the somewhat subjective evaluations of relational entrepreneurs do not adequately predict the probability of repayment will there be pressure from lenders for change in the terms of lending in Taiwan.

A financial system based in substantial part on relational capital and relational entrepreneurship will have certain structural differences compared with a conventional system of financial markets organized around universalized accounting and legal standards. Some of the most important differences will be fewer long-term financing vehicles and generally higher interest rates to cover higher costs of monitoring that have been transferred from the state to private parties. Borrowers in Taiwan have many options for credit outside banks, but all are relatively short term and expensive compared with bank credit. The variables taken into account in evaluating reputation and connections cannot be projected very far into the future. This system also entails high monitoring costs for the lender, which are in some sense the obverse of lower public investment in legal institutions financed through taxes. In a regulated financial system, the monitoring costs assumed by legal institutions like courts and police become externalities not reflected in the prices charged by financial institutions to the extent that the costs of these institutions are borne by the taxpaying public in general. The higher monitoring costs of financial informality can be passed on as higher interest rates, effectively shifting the cost directly onto the end user.

The short-term, high-interest-rate, informal system of finance in Taiwan may have served the economy well in the early years of industrialization where development was concentrated in labor-intensive, light industries. As Taiwan now tries to shift its economy into high-technology, high-capitalization industries in the 1990s, entrepreneurs will face a more acute need for long-term credit at moderate interest rates or for greater access to equity capital. The decision by the ROC authorities to grant fifteen new commercial bank licenses in July 1991 may facilitate the development of a more competitive, less bureaucratically regulated financial system that may be better able than the present system to meet the needs of borrowers for stable, low-cost sources of capital.

Liberalizing the regulation of commercial banks and modernizing their management are not necessarily the only options ROC authorities could consider in their efforts to make the financial system more responsive to local needs, however. Expanding the formal banking system will expand the legalistic, market-oriented component of Taiwan's financial system at the expense of the relational, informal financial system. An alternative to emphasizing conventional modern banking institutions at the expense of informal relational institutions might be a regulatory regime that explicitly recognizes the pluralistic structure of Taiwan's financial system. Such an alternative would be difficult to fashion but is not without precedent.

There exists in Taiwan today a small subcategory of commercial banks known as small and medium enterprise banks (*zhongxiao qiye yinhang*). Although one small and medium enterprise bank is effectively owned by the government (because its shareholders are government-owned banks), the remaining eight of these banks are privately owned. The scale of each of the privately owned small and medium enterprise banks is limited by the fact that their authorization to do business is restricted to a small geographical area. Before their reorganization in the late 1970s as modern banks, these institutions once functioned as state-sponsored umbrella organizations coordinating large numbers of *hui* operating between private parties. Although this hybrid form of regulated banking institution and traditional financing vehicle was officially abolished with the 1975 reform of the ROC Banking Law, it remains an interesting example of a successful, if not enduring, combination of modern and relational financing practices.

The evolution of the small and medium enterprise banks, known before their reorganization as mutual savings societies (*hehui gongsi*), took place in three stages. At first, the representatives of the mutual savings societies were sent out by their employers to set up *hui* among their friends and relatives. In the second stage, the mutual savings societies encouraged depositors and borrowers to enter into relationships directly with the financial institution, not with fellow members of a *hui*, but on terms that approximated participation in a *hui*. In the third stage, the *hui* model was completely abandoned, and depositors and borrowers dealt with the reorganized institutions just like any other bank. In part, this evolution took place independent of changes in official regulatory policy as management began to focus on lowering transaction costs and interest rates. Government incentives, however, accelerated the demise of *hui*-type activities after the mutual savings societies reorganized as banks.

In the first stage of development, the representatives of the *hehui gongsi* went out (often on bicycles) into communities and organized *hui*. These representatives earned commissions from the *hui* they helped establish, and the earnings of these representatives could be much higher than the salaries of the employees of conventional banks. The *hehui gongsi* assumed the role of the *hui-tou*, or organizer of the *hui*.[50] Because the contributions of each *hui* member were relatively small and the *hui* members were often known personally to the *hehui gongsi* representative, no collateral or personal guarantee was required of *hui* members in order for them to participate. Although this was a labor-intensive form of credit (because the *hehui gongsi* representative was required to call on the *hui* members personally to collect their contributions), the high interest rates and commission charges covered the high operational costs. Participants using the *hui* to borrow money were willing to pay the high interest rates because the credit was unsecured, and unsecured credit was not available from conventional banks. Participants using *hui* as a form of savings were able to earn higher interest rates than were available from other regulated institutions, while being exposed to less risk than they would be participating in *hui* organized by private individuals with no institutional intervention. At this stage of development, one bank officer estimated that 80 percent of all *hehui gongsi* credit was in the form of *hui* and unsecured, while only 20 percent was in the form of a bank loan secured either by collateral such as real property or by personal guarantees.

In the second stage of development, the various *hehui gongsi* wanted to expand their conventional lending, but were frustrated by a shortage of deposits. The *hehui gongsi* wanted to expand their conventional lending because it can be done on a larger scale and is less labor intensive than establishing and monitoring *hui*. They expanded their access to deposits from the public by offering a new service—special accounts that resembled *hui*. The *hehui gongsi* created special deposit accounts and special loan programs that copied the pattern of payments associated with *hui* membership. The *hehui gongsi* made up schedules of deposits or loan repayments for different time periods and different total amounts, for example, for ten, twelve, eighteen, or twenty-four months in duration, and for NT $10,000, NT $50,000, or NT $100,000. *Hehui gongsi* customers were allowed to choose the total amount of the loan or savings plan and the duration of the loan or savings plan. The *hehui gongsi* would then set a schedule of payments of varying amounts that its customer would bring in each week or month. There were two sets of tables: one for savings plans and one for loans. A customer who began a savings plan could convert to a loan in the middle of the plan and then would begin making payments according to the corresponding loan repayment chart. These payments varied over the life of the program because *hui* participants were used to periodic *hui* contributions varying because of the bidding process involved. The *hehui gongsi* also wanted to confuse their customers and prevent them from being able to calculate the actual interest rate. By offering this new service, the *hehui gongsi* were able to make a small change in customer relations (asking customers to come to the *hehui gongsi* to make their periodic payments instead of waiting for the *hehui gongsi* representative to visit them and collect the payments), and also expand the amount of deposits they received.

In the third stage of development, the various *hehui gongsi* were converted to small and medium enterprise banks by the ROC government. A ceiling was set on the amount of *hui*-style financial services the newly organized banks could offer and incentives were given to the banks to eliminate this form of financial service altogether. According to Ministry of Finance regulations, small and medium enterprise banks may engage in foreign exchange services only when they have eliminated *hui*-type financial services. In 1991, for example, the Medium Business Bank of Taiwan, which is government owned, had already taken this step, while the Taipei Business Bank, which is privately owned, had not yet done so but anticipated doing so in the future. Because these banks have already eliminated activities related to administering *hui* and only offer special accounts that resemble *hui,* the elimination of *hui*-style financial services is now only a small step. One bank officer estimated that 80 percent of the bank's credit is in the form of conventional bank loans requiring security such as real property collateral or two guarantees, and only 5 percent of the bank's business still had any resemblance to *hui.*

The transformation of the *hehui gongsi* into banks may have increased the size and profitability of each institution, but at a cost of reducing the volume of unsecured credit available to small borrowers. Small and medium enterprise banks have merely adopted the same standards as larger commercial banks in Taiwan (i.e., requiring either a real property mortgage or two guarantors), and thus no longer maintain interactive relationships with small borrowers and lenders. By intervening in the informal financial sector to stabilize *hui* transactions, bank regulatory authorities facilitated the accumulation of relational capital and recognized the fact of financial pluralism in Taiwan. By "modernizing" the *hehui gongsi* into banks, the authorities have forced financial transactions in the form of *hui* out of the regulated economy and into the informal sector. By removing the stabilizing influence of institutional sponsorship of the *hui* while permitting the small and medium enterprise banks to adopt the conservative standards of larger banks, the authorities undermined the value of individual investments in relational capital without achieving any progress toward modern financial practices.

Conclusion

The informal sector is not only a substantial element of Taiwanese society when judged by its sheer magnitude; it is also an important forum for mediating disputes and exercising economic, social, and political power. Drawing a sharp line between the informal sector and law-abiding society is difficult in Taiwan because law is not generally perceived as the expression of the fundamental social order. Law is marginalized while networks of human relationships take center stage in many social arenas, so in some respects, the informal sector tends to become indistinguishable from the rest of society.

The legal system is not irrelevant in Taiwan, however. The legal system, like organized crime, is a potentially powerful tool in the hands of some people that can be used to adjust the terms of relationships. Prior to the lifting of martial law, the rigidity and formality of the legal system both complimented the isolation of the KMT regime from much of Taiwanese society and also helped obscure the informal compromises and patronage systems that connected the ROC state to its citizens. If the current pressures for democratization of political processes in Taiwan are to achieve lasting reforms, it will be necessary to reform the legal system and bring the letter of the law closer to the lives of the people of Taiwan. The informal sector could diminish in relevance as a mechanism for mediating state-society relations as the formal institutions of government become more directly responsive to public demands.

Liberalization of the ROC legal and political systems is not the only option open to the people of Taiwan and their leaders, however. Japan offers an example of a modern nation that has institutionalized informal, relational channels of communication between the government and the people, and has also achieved a high level of economic development. The displacement of informal ties between groups in society and between the state and the people of Taiwan would require a profound reorganization of the fabric of society. Taiwan could instead follow the example of Japan with a far smaller degree of social dislocation. Implementation of the rule of law in Taiwan would constitute a radical challenge to accepted business and social practices, and it is not clear if the public commitment to democratization is deep enough to support such profound reforms at all levels of state and society.

Are human rights protected within a system of relational institutions? Are relational institutions a distinct and viable alternative to competitive markets? These important questions cannot yet be addressed because of the cultural biases implicit in most modern political, legal, and economic theories. Only when the culturally and historically determined assumptions of conventional economics and jurisprudence are examined and replaced with more general or pluralistic theories can the important process of critically evaluating the informal sector begin in earnest.

Critical evaluation of relational institutions is important not only for Asian societies like Taiwan's, where the official ideology and popular social practices openly acknowledge the importance of networks of relationships. If all societies are composed of a complex patchwork of legalistic institutions and relational institutions, a theoretical perspective that ferrets out and explicitly incorporates the roles played by relational institutions would provide challenging new insights into the dynamics of even liberal democratic societies. Contemporary social theories, with their implicit bias in favor of ideas like legal centralism and competitive markets, even when applied to social institutions in a country like the United States, tend to obscure the roles played by relational institutions.

Introducing new concepts such as "relational capital" and "relational entrepreneurship" to describe institutions in the informal sector in Taiwan is just a first step toward reappraising common assumptions about the workings of "modern" or "developed" nations. Within the models often used in conventional social theories, the true social costs of maintaining the core institutions of liberal democratic societies are not accounted for on a systematic basis because many of the costs of maintaining those institutions are understated or ignored. While modern institutions are often treated as though they operated virtually costlessly, the social costs imputed to maintaining relational institutions are often distorted and overstated because of implicit cultural biases. To overcome such biases, it will be necessary to assign concrete values to the contributions of popular culture, educational and religious institutions, and the mass media in maintaining liberal institutions in Western as well as non-Western societies. Only when the true social costs of modern institutions like competitive markets or representative democracy have been estimated can they be compared to the social costs of relational institutions in non-Western societies. When such an unbiased comparison is possible, questions of justice and equitable economic development can be addressed critically and impartially not only with regard to Taiwan but with regard to the United States as well.

Notes

1. The informal or underground economy is also known as "black, cash, clandestine, irregular, parallel, subterranean, secret, shadow, submerged." Linda Weiss, "Explaining the Underground Economy: State and Social Structure," *Brit. J. of Soc.* 18, 216 (1989). In this essay, the terms "informal sector" and "informal economy" will be used to describe the same group of institutions, although the term "informal sector" better conveys the sense that distinctions conventionally drawn among political, economic, legal, and social institutions may not always be valid if extended to informal institutions.

2. Chai Sung-lin, "Tai wan de di xia jing ji—xing cheng yuan ying, chung lei fen bu, gu ce gui mo, ying xiang he dui ce," undated memo.

3. Frank Upham, *Law and Social Change in Postwar Japan.* Cambridge, MA: Harvard University Press, 1987.

4. See, e.g., Oliver Wendell Holmes, "The Path of the Law," *Harv. Law Rev.* 10, 8 (March 1897); or Hans Kelson, *Positive Law.* Mexico: Unam, 1986.

5. Marc Galanter, "Justice in Many Rooms: Courts, Private Ordering and Indigenous Law," *J. Leg. Pluralism* 19, 1 (1981); John Griffiths, "What Is Legal Pluralism?" *J. Leg. Pluralism* 24, 1 (1986).

6. Pierre Bourdieu, "The Force of Law: Toward a Sociology of the Juridical Field," *Hast. L.J.* 38, 805 (1987); Sally Falk Moore, *Law as Process.* Boston: Routledge and Keegan Paul, 1978.

7. See, e.g., Macauley, "An Empirical View of Contract," *Wisc. L. Rev.* 465 (1985), and sources cited therein.

8. Chu T'ung Tsu, *Law and Society in Traditional China*. Paris: Mouton, 1961.

9. KTV parlors provide patrons with rooms equipped with large-screen televisions and a karaoke music system. A karaoke system includes a microphone and background music so that a patron can provide the vocals to recordings of well-known songs. KTV parlor patrons can select various music videos to be shown in their room and are aided in singing along by the words that appear on the TV screen, complete with a bouncing ball.

10. For a description of the rational calculations necessary to maintain an effective network of relationships, see K.K. Hwang, "Face and Favor: The Chinese Game of Power," *Amer. J. Soc.* 92, 944 (1987).

11. Felstiner divides possible responses to disputes into litigation, mediation, and "lumping it" or not trying to shift the loss onto the other party. Felstiner, "Influences of Social Organization on Dispute Processing," *Law & Society Rev.* 9, 63 (1974).

12. Arthur J. Lerman, *Taiwan's Politics: The Provincial Assemblyman's World*. Washington, DC: University Press of America, 1978, p. 170.

13. Although I have no precise statistics, several local observers have estimated the number of licensed lawyers at several thousand in a population of twenty million. This would be supplemented by an equivalent number of lawyers in government positions such as judge or prosecutor.

14. The pass rate for the annual bar examinations administered in 1989 and 1990 increased from approximately 1 percent to approximately 10 percent.

15. In recent years, the procedure for converting an academic law qualification into a local law qualification by teaching in a law school for several years has been tightened up, while the pass rate of the bar exam has gone up.

16. Article 83, paragraph 1, of the Income Tax Law, as amended through December 30, 1987, provides: "A taxpayer shall, during the conduct of an investigation or reinvestigation by the collection authority, produce account books and related documents of evidence that will prove the amount of his income. Where such account books and documents of evidence are not produced, the collection authority may determine the amount of his income on the basis of available taxation data or the profit standard of the trade concerned" [translation by Lee & Li, Attorneys at Law].

In 1986, the Ministry of Finance published average profitability figures for 9 major categories and approximately 750 subcategories of trade and industry.

17. M. Shao, "Taiwan: CPAs under Fire," *Asian Wall St. J.,* June 27, 1983.

18. According to one foreign accountant doing business in Taiwan in 1986, a local bank sued a local accounting firm for having certified a false financial statement. The court held that the bank had not relied exclusively on the financial statement and so the accountant could not be held liable even though the statement included false information. While under ROC law, judicial decisions do not generally have precedential value and are not usually published, this accountant recalled that the defendant accounting firm took the unusual step of mailing copies of the judgment to various parties to inform them of the decision.

19. Wou Young-Ie, "The Informal Sector in the Construction Industry in Taiwan: A Case Study of an Informal Contractor," M.Arch. thesis, University of California at Berkeley, 1982.

20. Robert Wade, *Governing the Market: Economic Theory and the Role of Government in East Asian Industrialization*. Princeton: Princeton University Press, 1990, p. 269.

21. Ronald Coase, *The Theory of the Firm*, Economica 4 (November 1937).

22. Oliver Williamson, *The Economic Institutions of Capitalism: Firms, Markets, Relational Contracting*. New York: Free Press, 1985.

23. Herbert A. Simon, *Models of Bounded Rationality*. Cambridge, MA.: MIT Press, 1982.

24. Ian Macneil, "Contracts: Adjustment of Long-Term Economic Relations under Classical, Neoclassical and Relational Contract Law," *Northwestern L. Rev.* 72, 854 (1978).

25. Oliver Williamson, "Transaction Cost Economics: The Governance of Contractual Relations," *J. Law & Econ.* 22, 233 (1979); Michael H. Best, *The New Competition.* Cambridge, MA: Harvard Unversity Press, 1990.

26. For a summary of the response to Coase's article, see William W. Bratton, Jr., "The New Economic Theory of the Firm: Critical Perspectives from History," *Stan. L. Rev.* 41, 1471 (1989).

27. Ronald Coase, *The Firm, the Market and the Law.* Chicago: University of Chicago Press, 1988, pp. 19 and 28 (1988).

28. Mark Granovetter, "Economic Action and Social Structure: The Problem of Embeddedness," *Am. J. Soc.* 91, 481 (1985).

29. Hwang, *supra* note 10.

30. For similar conclusions, see Ambrose Yeo-chi King, "Kuan-hsi and Network Building: A Sociological Interpretation," *Daedelus* 63 (June 1991); and J. Bruce Jacobs, "A Preliminary Model of Particularistic Ties in Chinese Political Alliances: Kanch'ing and Kuan-hsi in a Rural Taiwanese Township," *China Q.,* no. 78, (1979), p. 237.

31. Upham, *supra* note 3.

32. Ronald Coase, *The Firm, The Market and the Law,* 1988.

33. Williamson, *supra* note 25.

34. Gary Becker, *Human Capital.* New York: National Bureau of Economic Research, 1964.

35. Pierre Bourdieu, *Outline of a Theory of Practice.* Cambridge: Cambridge University Press, 1977.

36. My thanks to Mike Davis for suggesting this label.

37. Richard Terdman, translator's introduction to Bourdieu, *supra* note 6.

38. Roy W. Kenney and Benjamin Klein, "The Economics of Block Booking," *J. Law & Econ.* 26, 497 (1983).

39. Roberto Mangabeira Unger, *False Necessity.* Cambridge: Cambridge University Press, 1987; and Benjamin Barber, *Strong Democracy.* Berkeley: University of California Press, 1984.

40. Upham, *supra* note 3.

41. Shea Jia-dong, "Financial Development in Taiwan: A Macro Analysis," in H. Patrick and Y.C. Park, eds., *Financial Development of Japan, Korea, and Taiwan: Growth, Repression, and Liberalization.* New York: Oxford University Press, forthcoming.

42. Hsu Li-teh, *Financial Reform in the ROC—Employing a Financial System Designed to Spur the Development of Science and Technology,* speech delivered at USA-ROC/ROC-USA Economic Councils meeting, November 27, 1983.

43. Wade, *supra* note 20, at 161.

44. The fear of inflation almost amounted to a superstition, as evidenced by the long-standing refusal of the Bank of Taiwan to issue currency in denominations greater than NT $100. Lundberg, "Fiscal and Monetary Policies," in W. Galenson, ed., *Economic Growth and Structural Change in Taiwan.* Ithaca, NY: Cornell University Press, 1979.

45. Wade, *supra* note 20, at 59.

46. U.S. Department of State, *Country Reports on Human Rights Practices,* 1985, 1986.

47. Although the structures of the arrangements are very different, in this regard employee deposit taking in Taiwan serves a similar purpose to employee stock ownership plans or granting stock options to management in the United States.

48. CBC Economic Research Department, *Financial Statistics Monthly Taiwan District The Republic of China,* May 1990, at 110 and 119.

49. According to one bank lending officer I spoke with in 1990, a government-owned bank initially denied the application of the Ford Motor Company joint venture in Taiwan on the grounds that its general manager was unwilling to personally guarantee the loan and that there was no other form security offered, such as a real estate mortgage. It was only after the intervention of high-level bank personnel in the review of the loan application that the requirement of a guarantor was waived. Similarly, Y.C. Wang, head of the largest industrial conglomerate in Taiwan, has assumed personal liability for the debts of many of the enterprises he controls. Although a wealthy man, even the assets of Y.C. Wang are inadequate to cover a default by a major corporation. Richard Y.C. Chuang, *Legal Aspects of Related Enterprises in Taiwan,* S.J.D. thesis, University of California at Berkeley, 1987.

50. This role includes the right to take the first collection of money without paying interest and guaranteeing the performance of all *hui* members.

Chapter 7

Vulnerability and Change in Taiwan's Agriculture

Jack F. Williams

Any country's agricultural policy should consist of three objectives. One is to ensure that farmers can earn a decent living from farming. A second is to produce as much food and raw materials for the domestic market as resources and economic circumstances permit, and possibly a surplus for export. A third objective is to protect the country's physical resources for agriculture from destruction; otherwise, the first two goals become more difficult to attain. Thus, agricultural resources management involves much more than protection of physical resources but includes also the farmers and their farming system.

A fundamental question is whether or not a strong agricultural sector is necessary if that country is highly industrialized and can afford to buy its food and raw materials from abroad at lower cost than if those goods were produced domestically. Some countries without many agricultural resources, such as Singapore, have little choice in the matter. But other countries that do have significant agricultural resources, such as Taiwan, are faced with this basic development question. In practice the principles of comparative advantage and regional specialization, insofar as agriculture is concerned, are allowed to function only partially especially in the densely populated nonsocialist states of East Asia (Japan, South Korea, Taiwan) (see Hayami et al. 1979).

One can see this situation operating in various stages of these three countries' development. Willingly or not, circumstances have pushed Japan, South Korea, and Taiwan toward subsidization of economically inefficient agriculture for the sake of maintaining farm income and producing some minimum threshold of domestic food production for national security considerations. Japan has moved the furthest in this direction, a legacy of postwar land reform and the desire of the government to protect the livelihood of the nation's small family farms. In return, the farmers, who are now a small minority within the nation's work force, have been a powerful lobby that has successfully beaten back efforts to change

This chapter originally appeared in *Pacific Viewpoint*, vol. 29, no. 1, 1988, pp. 25–44.

agricultural policy (Yuise 1987). Taiwan and South Korea have remarkably similar agricultural environments to Japan: static (or declining) arable land, growing populations, and small farms. For basically the same reasons as Japan they are also increasingly subsidizing their own agricultural systems.

Supporters of subsidization of agriculture in Japan argue that the system is essential, especially for rice farmers, for three main reasons: (1) Agriculture is more than just an economic activity; it is part of the nation's cultural heritage and must be protected as such. (2) The nation needs to protect its food security. Japan could not be assured of adequate supplies of rice (or other commodities) at reasonable prices if it switched to reliance on imports. (3) Paddy land once converted to other uses could not easily be changed back to rice cultivation if the need occurred. Critics of subsidization argue, in turn, that, first, Japan is predominantly urbanized and industrialized, that cultures and societies change, and that the farmers have to accept that inevitable fact. Second they argue that the food security issue is a false one. As long as Japan is an effective exporter, it will always have the money and ability to buy whatever foods it needs abroad. Third, the critics argue, subsidization is an admission that Japan has lost its comparative advantage in rice production as well as in cattle raising and dairying, leaving only fruit and vegetable production as economically efficient. The nation should not prop up an inefficient sector of the economy. Substitute the names of "Taiwan" or "South Korea" in the above argument and nothing else would need to be changed. To be fair, Taiwan and South Korea both have special security considerations that perhaps partially justify the move toward subsidization. South Korea faces a genuine threat from a militant North Korea. Taiwan sees itself threatened by the People's Republic of China, which refuses to renounce military force as a possible option for reuniting Taiwan with the mainland.

Agriculture in Taiwan

The government in Taiwan must make policy decisions in relation to the fact that agriculture plays a relatively minor role in the economy today, compared to the 1950s or even 1960s. Agriculture's share in gross national product fell from 35.1 percent in 1952 to just 26.4 percent by 1965, but plunged the sharpest after that, to a mere 6.5 percent by 1984 (table 7.1). Likewise, agriculture's share of total exports was a high 95.5 percent in 1952, a still significant 57.8 percent in 1965, but a tiny 6.8 percent in 1984. In fact, what had happened was that agriculture's growth curve tapered off, especially after the mid-1960s, at the same time that the industrial growth curve was accelerating rapidly. Using 1952 as a base of 100, total agricultural production (here including food production, fisheries, livestock, and forestry, as defined by the government) reached 190.2 by 1965, almost doubling, but then in the next nineteen years rose to only 300.3 by 1984. The trend for just food production is even more striking. By 1965 the index reached 172.1, but then rose very slowly to just 200.8 by 1984. The lesson is unmistakable. Taiwan's small family farm system was approaching the limits

Table 7.1

Taiwan's Changing Agriculture

	1952	1965	1984
Cultivated land (ha)	875,000	890,000	892,000
Total cropped area (ha)	1,521,000	1,680,000	1,285,000
Multiple cropping index (MCIO)	174	189	144
Irrigated land (% of cultivated land)	61	60	56
Paddy fields (ha)	533,600	536,800	496,900
Number of farm families	679,000	847,000	792,000
Average farm size (ha)	1.29	1.05	1.12
Farm population (millions)	4.25	5.74	4.25
Agricultural employment (millions)	1.64	1.75	1.29
Agriculture's share in GDP (%)	35.1	26.4	6.5
Agriculture's share in total exports (%)	95.5	57.8	6.8
Agricultural production (1962 = 100)	100.0	190.2	300.3
Food production only (1952 = 100)	100.0	172.1	200.8
Composition of agricultural production (%)	68.6	64.6	46.6
Crops	68.6	64.6	46.6
Livestock	15.8	21.2	29.3
Fisheries	9.1	8.7	22.9
Forestry	6.4	5.4	1.3

Sources: Taiwan PDAF (1985) and Taiwan CEPD (1985).

of its productive capacity by the 1970s and 1980s and required major structural changes if productivity was to rebound.

The statistically much diminished role of agriculture is belied, though, by the physical impression conveyed by the rural landscape. Traveling through the lush green countryside of Taiwan, one is impressed by the extraordinary degree of human occupancy. The entire area from seashore to the lower slopes of the mountains in the center of the island is minutely parceled out in tidy fields and irrigation ponds, punctuated by innumerable rural villages and larger cities and towns, all connected by an intricate web of roads, railways, and canals. Scarcely a speck of lowlands seems unused. It is an intensely green and vivid landscape that leaves a lasting impression, particularly for someone used to the spacious checkerboard pattern of the American Midwest. The observer tends to assume that the land must be intensively productive. Moreover, the generally prosperous appearance of the farmhouses and rural people seems to support the impression of a thriving, healthy agricultural system. The reality, however, is not so simple. Everything is relative, of course. Compared with probably a majority of Asian or Third World countries, farmers in Taiwan are well off, and the island is a bountiful producer of a rich variety of agricultural commodities, sufficient to maintain the people in a well-fed condition. Nonetheless, the agricultural system of Taiwan has a number of weaknesses that present a challenge to the government's efforts to meet the three basic objectives of agricultural policy outlined earlier. These weaknesses of the agricultural system can be seen by examining Taiwan's agricultural system today from the perspective first of the farmers and then of the government (or national interest).

Earning a Living: The Farmer's Perspective

The basic fact of life for the average farmer in Taiwan today is that his farm is too small to make a living from. In 1952 the average farm was just 1.29 ha. That figure fell to its lowest level of 1.02 ha in 1972 and then increased slightly by 1984 to 1.12 ha (Taiwan, Executive Yuan, CEPD 1985). The minor rebound in the 1980s has been due to the fact that the total number of farm families finally started to decline in 1979, after steadily increasing up to then, peaking in 1979 at 898,000. By 1984, the number of farm families had decreased to 797,000 or a decline of about 100,000 in five years. Correspondingly, agricultural employment rose from 1.64 million in 1952 to a peak of 1.81 million in 1964, and then fairly steadily declined to 1.29 million by 1984 (Taiwan, Executive Yuan, CEPD 1985). (The total agricultural population started declining somewhat earlier, around 1970, as family sizes began to shrink.)

Most farmers have less than the average size holding. In 1980, 43 percent of farm households cultivated less than 0.5 ha, 73 percent farmed less than 1 ha, and only 2.5 percent had 3 ha or more, which is generally regarded as the minimum farm size needed to make a living from full-time farming in Taiwan (Taiwan, Executive Yuan, COA 1985a). Obviously, the majority of farmers in Taiwan would have to be described as marginal, in that they simply do not have enough land to make a living as farmers, even if they wished to farm full-time. The fact is, of course, that the vast majority are now only part-time farmers. Of the average farm income in 1984 of NT $256,000 (U.S. $6,400), agriculture accounted for only 35 percent (Chen 1984); this is shown in table 7.2. Of some 670,000 part-time farm families (83 percent of total farm families) 470,000 (58 percent of all farm families) earned the majority of their income from sideline nonagricultural activities (Taiwan Provincial Government 1985, p. 293). Those activities are predominantly in the form of work in rural industries, which have transformed the rural economy and society of Taiwan since the 1960s and 1970s

Table 7.2

Farm Household Income and Expenditure

	1958	1965	1984
Income			
Total (NTS)	37,914	68,773	256,261
On-farm income (%)	86.2	87.2	36.6
Off-farm income (%)	13.8	12.8	63.4
Expenses			
Food	46.3	41.2	36.4
Housing	0.4	1.3	11.9
Clothing	8.7	7.4	4.5
Fuel and electricity	10.6	8.1	4.7
Other	34.0	42.0	42.5

Sources: Taiwan PDAF (1985) and Taiwan CEPD (1985).

Note: The average farm household (farm family) in 1984 consisted of 5.3 persons (compared with 4.5 persons in the average family island wide). There were 121,000 full-time farm families compared to 670,000 part-time farm families. 1952 data not available.

(Ho 1979; Thompson 1984). In other words, farming has become the real "sideline" for most farm families!

In spite of rural industrialization, which has helped boost farm incomes, the gap between rural and urban families remains significant. In 1966 the per capita income of farm families was 69.8 percent of that of nonfarm families. That fell to 60.2 percent in 1970 and rebounded to 68.3 by 1984 (Taiwan, Executive Yuan, COA 1985a, p. 38). In other words, farm families are still about where they were, relative to nonfarm families, nearly twenty years ago. Moreover, since most farm family workers are actually engaged in nonfarming activities most of the time, and large numbers of rural people have left the rural areas entirely, the result has been a shortage of labor in rural areas, especially at peak labor demand periods of planting and harvesting. The result is that rural labor costs have escalated rapidly, making mechanization an increasing necessity. However, most farmers find mechanization too costly with their small farms. This situation encourages the farmers either to further reduce their intensity of farming or to try to mechanize in a roundabout way. The government's implementation of price supports for rice in the early 1970s has, however, helped some farmers to at least partially mechanize their operations.

Thus, in looking at the first objective of a country's basic agricultural policy, namely, to ensure a decent living for farmers, one would have to conclude that farmers are not making an adequate living, if one is thinking of agriculture only. In terms of total income, however, farmers are not too badly off, although not faring as well as urban workers. From the government's perspective, though, there is concern that part-time farming represents an inefficient use of the country's agricultural resources and poses potential long-term threats to the security of the island's food supply.

Food Security: The Government's Perspective

The government of Taiwan, while dealing with the problem of trying to help farmers maintain an adequate standard of living, must also struggle with the other two objectives of agricultural policy, that is, seeing that domestic production of food and raw materials is maintained at reasonable levels, and that the resources for agriculture are protected from destruction. In regard to the first of these two other goals, Taiwan is in a seemingly paradoxical situation. On the one hand, the island has an abundant food supply with high caloric intake, yet at the same time it is faced with declining relative food self-sufficiency (Chen 1980; Liu 1983; Shei 1983; Wu 1980).

One of the root causes of this paradox has been a steady decline in the intensity of use of farmland since the 1960s (Wang 1983, 1984a). The intensity of use is measured by the multiple cropping index (MCI), which is the total annual cropped area divided by the total cultivated area multiplied by 100. The MCI peaked in the mid-1960s at around 188–189 and has been falling steadily ever since, reaching 144 in 1984, the lowest level since 1947 (table 7.1). The figure of 144 derives from a total cropped area in 1984 of 1,285,000 ha on a total cultivated area of 892,000 ha (Taiwan, Executive Yuan, CEPD 1985, p. 58). The island has a year-round growing season, and 48 percent of the farmland was irrigated in 1984, with double-cropped fields accounting for 21 percent of the cultivated area (Taiwan Provincial Government, 1985 p. 286). Thus, even though not every plot of farmland can support two irrigated crops a year, rain-fed crops can still be grown in the nonirrigated areas or season. Basically, what has been happening with the MCI is that the total cultivated area has been slowly decreasing (or at best stagnating) since the mid-1970s as loss of land to urban/industrial and other uses has exceeded the amount of marginal land reclaimed for agriculture. At the same time, the total cropped area has been decreasing much more rapidly since the mid-1960s under the compound pressure of too small farms and expanded employment opportunities in rural industry. Rather than sell their land, most farmers prefer to retain ownership, perhaps growing just one crop a year, or none at all. The land is insurance against downswings in the industrial economy, but it is also part of the farmer's cultural tradition (Gallin and Gallin 1982; Thompson 1984).

Closely related to the fall in the MCI is the problem of simultaneous surplus and shortage of food supply. As of the mid-1980s, the overall food self-sufficiency of Taiwan had fallen to around 70 percent, measured in calories, which is a more effective measure of self-sufficiency than monetary value or other indices (Chen 1980). While 70 percent self-sufficiency is a quite respectable level by world standards, considering that a number of countries with significant agricultural resources now import the major portion of their food supply, nonetheless, the current level for Taiwan represents a sharp drop from the virtually 100 percent self-sufficiency status of the early 1960s. Taiwan has a surplus of rice, sugar, fruits and vegetables, eggs, and fish, and a deficit of other grains and dairy products. In the case of nonfood agricultural products, Taiwan is highly deficient in cotton, hides, and forestry products (Taiwan, Executive Yuan, COA 1985a, p. 10).

This situation is the result of several factors. The rice surplus has been accumulating since the mid-1970s, as a result of reforms in the agricultural system begun around 1972. Those reforms were designed to stem the stagnation in agriculture, which was reaching serious proportions by then. From 1953 to 1956, total agricultural production value grew by an average of 4.9 percent a year, from 1957 to 1960 by 4.2 percent, from 1961 to 1964 by 5.8 percent, and from 1965 to 1968 by 5.7 percent. During the two decades of the 1950s and 1960s, the small farm system worked well enough to maintain agricultural productivity increases at quite respectable levels. However, from 1969–72, the growth rate fell to only 1.5 percent a year, and from 1973 to 1975 to just 1.1 percent a year. The rate recovered somewhat in the late 1970s, to 2.7 percent a year from 1976 to 1981, but then declined again, from 1982 to 1984, to 1.4 percent (Taiwan, Executive Yuan, COA 1985a, p. 10). The basic reason for the decline in productivity has been the small size of farms, in spite of improvements in fertilizer availability and usage, improved irrigation, mechanization, increased unit area yields, and other aspects of Taiwan's version of the Green Revolution.

Rice is the overwhelmingly dominant crop in the island's agricultural system, and also the basic foodstuff in the diet. Hence the government tried to help rice farmers boost their incomes and also meet what was then perceived as inadequate rice production. This was done by establishing a subsidization program in 1974 that guaranteed rice farmers unlimited purchase by the government of their rice production at a price 20 percent higher than production costs (which were computed by survey). That proved too costly, however, and in 1977 the system was modified to guarantee farmers purchase by the government of 970 kg, or about 25 percent, of each hectare of rice production (Taiwan, Executive Yuan, COA 1985a, p. 10).

The subsidization program did help. The rice-planted area rebounded from a postwar low of 724,000 ha in 1973 to 790,000 ha in 1975. Rice production peaked at 2.7 million metric tons (mmt) in 1976, the highest level in Taiwan's history (Taiwan, Executive Yuan, CEPD 1984). Unfortunately, this production increase occurred at the same time that rice demand in Taiwan was starting to experience a steady decline, because of declining income elasticity of demand for rice. Annual rice consumption has fallen to under 2 mmt, even as the total population continues to grow and is pushing 20 million now. Production of rice has remained in the range of 2.2–2.5 mmt each year (Taiwan Executive Yuan, CEPD 1985, p. 63). Thus, each year several hundred thousand tons of surplus rice have been accumulating, and by the 1980s the government had to begin a program to reduce rice production.

The dilemma of the rice surplus is widely illustrated by comparing the data for 1975 and 1984. In 1975 the rice-planted area was 790,000 ha (48 percent of the cropped area), the peak level of the postwar period. Rice production that year was 2.49 mmt and the rice yield was 3.16 metric tons/ha (mt/ha). In 1984 the rice-planted area had shrunk to 586,000 ha (46 percent of the cropped area), and rice production had declined to 2.24 mmt, still a surplus condition, partly because yields had risen to 3.83 mt/ha (Taiwan, Executive Yuan, CEPD 1985; Taiwan, Executive Yuan, COA, 1984a). In other words, a 21 percent increase in rice yields had partially negated the efforts of the government to reduce the rice planted area and hence rice production. The surplus can only be stored for two to three years before it begins to deteriorate. The government wants to maintain a surplus stock of around 0.6 mmt for emergency use, thus the current surplus of 1.5 mmt is far in excess. It also is not easy for Taiwan to export the surplus rice. Even if markets can be found, the rice has to be sold at a substantial loss, of U.S. $400–500 per ton, because of subsidized production in Taiwan. Moreover, Taiwan has run into difficulties with the United States over rice exports in recent years, with the United States putting pressure on Taiwan to cut back its rice exports, charging Taiwan with dumping of its surplus rice and thus undercutting U.S. rice exports (*China Post* 1983).

Meanwhile, Taiwan has been steadily increasing the volume of its imports of certain key agricultural commodities, mainly cereals, plus some agricultural raw materials. Because of declining rice consumption and increasing consumption of wheat flour products, plus feed-grain produced meat (mainly pork), imports of wheat, corn, sorghum, and soybeans have been very large since the mid-1970s. Westernization has played a key role in these increased imports, in that as per capita incomes have risen, food tastes have been changing, with people wanting to eat more Western-style foods. This is particularly true in Taipei, where the Westernization process is most advanced and fast food chains are a lucrative high-growth business. By 1984, total agricultural imports came to U.S. $2.55 billion, compared with agricultural exports of only U.S. $570 million, or a deficit of nearly U.S. $2 billion (Taiwan, Executive Yuan, CEPD 1985, p. 201). Agricultural imports, in decreasing order of value, were cereals (wheat, corn, sorghum), logs and lumber, raw cotton, soybeans, hides and leather, dairy products, and fish meal.

The focus of this chapter is on food production, but there is also growing dependence on imported agricultural raw materials for industry as well. To protect the soil cover in Taiwan's fragile ecosystem, the emphasis in forestry is now on conservation and hence importing of logs and lumber. Hides and leather are also in large demand for the footwear industry. Agricultural exports in decreasing value were fish products, vegetables and processed products (dominated by canned asparagus and mushrooms), fruit and processed products, timber and bamboo products, and pork (Taiwan, Executive Yuan, COA 1985a, pp. 22–23). Agricultural exports have increased much more slowly over the past decade than have agricultural imports. Fortunately, this deficit is not yet a serious problem for Taiwan, at least insofar as the balance of payments is concerned, because the island's total trade balance is heavily in Taiwan's favor due to the huge surplus of manufactured exports over imports.

Thus, in regard to the second objective of agricultural policy, feeding the population adequately (and producing raw materials for industry), Taiwan is doing a relatively good job. However, the trend clearly is one of increasing dependence on certain imported commodities.

Policy Options

In light of these trends and problems facing agriculture in Taiwan, the question arises as to what the government can do to correct the imbalances. On the assumption that the government wants to and ought to maintain a viable livelihood for farmers, from farming, then a logical goal should be to raise the level of farm incomes (Mao 1981). If this could be achieved, it might result in more farmers spending more time on farming, thus reversing the decline in the MCI. Unemployment in the secondary/tertiary sectors of the economy might also be eased, and the imbalance in agricultural trade might be improved. Migration pressure on urban areas could be reduced as well (although migration has, in fact, already slowed down significantly). Incomes can be raised by a combination of reduced production costs and stabilizing support prices for agricultural products at reasonable levels. The government began implementing a number of financial measures with the Accelerated Rural Development Program (ARDP) in 1972. In 1979 the Program to Enhance Farm Income and Strengthen Rural Development was launched. These programs were further refined in 1983 under the Integrated Program to Strengthen Basic Infrastructural Development and Enhance Farm Income ("Macro-economic Planning" 1980). While these measures over the past fifteen years have brought undoubted benefits to farmers, the still sluggish growth rates of agriculture suggest that the most basic problem of the agricultural system has not been solved. In other words, improvements such as abolition of the rice-fertilizer barter system, better agricultural taxation, subsidies to farmers incurring electricity bills for irrigation and grain drying, and improved agricultural credit, among others, have not been enough. The issue is not that the productivity of part-time farmers is so much lower than that of full-time farmers in terms of unit-area yields. Rather, the problem is that land is underutilized, not cultivated when it could be, and this contributes to the declining food self-sufficiency of the island.

The ultimate solution to Taiwan's farm problem is widely regarded as lying in enlargement of the operational size of farms. Various methods for attaining this goal are being promulgated under what is called "The Second Stage Land Reform," following the First Land Reform in the 1950s when tenancy problems were corrected and public lands distributed (Taiwan, Executive Yuan, COA 1984b). Under the Second Land Reform, enlarging the operational size of farms is being accomplished by promoting larger private farms, various cooperative farming approaches, further land consolidation, and mechanization.

The preferred solution is for a much smaller number of larger farms. As already noted, the number of farms families has fallen within the past five years to just under 800,000. Nonetheless, the average farm is still too small, mainly because too many marginal farmers are still reluctant to part with their land. Unfortunately, rural industrialization has probably contributed to this tendency. Nearby sources of off-farm employment make it easier for farmers to retain their land and work part-time in factories, even commuting between farm and factory each day. The long-range goal is to have only about 610,000 people employed in agriculture by the year 2000, compared with 1.3 million in 1984. The government also hopes to see some 80,000 large modern farms in existence by then, using the latest technology and machinery (Myers 1984). These farms would be in the forefront in stimulating agricultural advances. To get there, however, farmers have to be persuaded to sell their land, and those who want to buy land must have assistance.

Since the first land reform in the 1950s, there have been no legal limits on how much land an individual can own. The only restriction was on the amount of land that could be leased to other farmers (maximum of 3 ha of paddy land), to prevent the return of large-scale tenancy (Taiwan, Executive Yuan, COA, 1985b). Now the government is providing low-interest, long-term loans to farmers who wish to purchase additional land. To qualify, the farmer must own at least 1 ha, although this rule is waived if the purchase includes all the land of a farmer who is leaving agriculture entirely. Preference is also given to those purchasing land immediately adjoining their property, to help prevent further fragmentation of holdings. Purchases exceeding 3 ha will not receive government loan support, however.

Those getting out of farming entirely will be encouraged to go to secondary and tertiary cities to help promote more balanced regional development of the island, under the concept of Nonmetropolitan Living Perimeters, a regional planning approach that the government has developed since the late 1970s (Tsai 1984). The living perimeters are functional regions in which transportation, economic development, and services are emphasized with the goal of enhancing the quality of life to discourage outmigration and promote balanced regional development. In other words, the government wants the marginal farmers out of agriculture, and definitely off their land, but does not want those people migrating to the four major metropolitan regions of Taipei, Kaohsiung, Taichung, or Tainan, which have been the foci of rural-to-urban migration over the past thirty years.

The other approach to expanded farm sizes is to accept the propensity of farmers to retain their land, but to achieve larger farm sizes nonetheless by encouraging various types of cooperative farming. These can range from simple cooperatives involving sharing of machinery and other inputs all the way to full-fledged collectives in which the farmers agree to physically pool their land and share in the proceeds of an agribusiness. All types are being tried, with the encouragement and assistance of the government (Ch'en 1983). By 1983, approximately 150,000 farm households (about 19 percent of all farm families) were participating in some kind of cooperative venture (Chen 1984, p. 19). However, most are relatively simple in nature; few farmers are willing to go all the way and pool their land with neighbors. Fragmentation of farm lands, especially on dry uplands, tends to work against cooperative ventures. The individualism of Chinese farmers, centered on the deeply rooted family system, is another obstacle. Unlike on the mainland, the Taiwan government has neither the authority, nor the desire, to impose cooperative farming. The government can only set up experimental operations and try to persuade other farmers to participate.

Another part of the Second Land Reform is consolidation of an additional 60,000 ha of land. As of 1984, a total of about 329,000 ha of land had been consolidated, since the program began in the 1950s (Taiwan, Executive Yuan, PDAF 1985, p. 285). Consolidation is designed to help farmers overcome the limitations of fragmented holdings (Taiwan, Executive Yuan, COA 1984b). In theory, consolidated land is more efficient to use, because it lends itself better to mechanization and modern methods of production. On the other hand, fragmented holdings have the virtues of spreading risk as well as possibly enhancing opportunities for diversified production on different types of land. Regardless, the government clearly favors consolidation, wherever possible. Moreover, the government is strongly promoting specialized agriculture, rather than diversification, as the key to the long-range future of the island's agricultural system (Taiwan, Ministry of Economic Affairs 1980).

Thus, further consolidation, concentrated primarily in the better paddy lands, is being promoted. Unfortunately, consolidation is not easy to carry out in the upland areas, which constitute 44 percent of Taiwan's cultivated area. With the 60,000 ha addition, roughly three-quarters of the paddy land in Taiwan will have been consolidated, or approximately 37 percent of the total cultivated area.

Mechanization is the fourth component of the Second Land Reform. Farm mechanization actually has been under way since the 1950s, beginning with the use of power tillers to substitute for draft cattle. However, the rapid exodus of rural manpower and rising labor costs by the 1970s required the government to assist mechanization much more vigorously (Kuo and Peng 1983). A Farm Mechanization Funding Program began in 1978, which, combined with price supports for rice and other financial reforms, greatly stimulated the spread of mechanization, resulting in a dramatic transformation of agricultural practices on many farms in Taiwan. The numbers of power tillers, tractors, rice transplanters, sprayers, water pumps, rice combines, and rice threshers, plus other machinery, have all increased significantly. Nonetheless, the mechanization process is still far from complete and the government recognizes the importance of mechanization in helping overcome the labor constraints facing agriculture today. Mechanization will be much easier, however, with larger size farm operations. It simply is not cost effective, without high, firm price supports, for Taiwan's smaller farms to purchase and maintain large machinery, although this does not preclude them from hiring the services of machinery owners.

An alternative argument has been made that the Taiwan government really does not want to push too vigorously for drastically fewer farmers because the large number of marginal farms provide a useful safety valve to absorb unemployment in times of economic downturn. With far fewer farms, the island would need a much more elaborate and expensive social security net than it currently has and which the fiscally conservative government is probably reluctant to develop soon (Eberstadt 1983). While there may be an element of truth in this argument, the role of the farming system as a form of natural unemployment compensation system is being increasingly outweighed by the negative consequences of the current landholdings and land-use systems.

Of course, improving the size of landholdings is not a panacea for the agricultural woes of Taiwan. Improving the quality of rural life is also a prerequisite. Again, everything is relative. Compared to the 1950s, life in rural Taiwan is immeasurably better today, in virtually all respects. But there is still room for improvement. If rural life can be enhanced, farming might be seen as a more attractive way of life for enterprising young men and women, so that they do not go off to the cities to work. A healthy agricultural system, in the long run, requires that the ablest people for agriculture remain on the farms. They are more likely to do that if they can have access to services and conveniences similar to those enjoyed by urban dwellers. That means good housing, electricity at reasonable rates, good running water and sewage disposal systems, good transportation access, good schools and medical care, entertainment, and cultural opportunities. Even in the most advanced countries, of course, rural areas seldom can match urban centers in all aspects of services and facilities. Nonetheless, the gap in Taiwan, while narrowed over the past thirty years, still exists. This is especially true in education and health care, a fact corroborated by a number of studies (Li 1983). The Farmers Associations are one means of providing some of the needed services, but they are not the only answer (Liu 1985). Major government-funded public works projects aimed at improving the rural infrastructure, among other objectives, have been a key means of enhancing the rural environment since the early 1970s. These projects started with the Ten Major Development Projects in 1972, and continued with the Twelve New Development Projects in 1979 and the fourteen Key Projects beginning in 1984 ("Macro-economic Planning" 1980; Taiwan, Executive Yuan, CEPD 1984).

Food Supply and Demand: Reducing the Imbalance

Reducing the imbalance between supply and demand of foodstuffs is another area of major policy concern to the government. While it is probably impossible for Taiwan ever to return to the days of 100 percent food self-sufficiency, some corrections in the imbalance can be achieved. Reducing the rice surplus was a major objective of the 1980s. In 1983 the government began a Six-Year Rice Conversion Program, aimed at transferring 146,000 ha of rice fields to other uses, namely, 95,000 ha to switch to production of corn, sorghum, and soybeans, another 31,000 ha to horticultural crops and aquaculture (fish ponds), and the remaining 20,000 ha to nonagricultural uses (Taiwan, Ministry of Economic Affairs 1983). The prospects for this program are problematic, however. For one thing, the three crops of corn, sorghum, and soybeans do not yield well in Taiwan. Without high price supports, farmers are reluctant to grow them, even though they are much in demand and must be imported in huge quantities each year. Comparing the 1978 planted areas for these three with their 1984 planted areas, corn showed a fairly healthy increase, most of that occurring after 1983 when price subsidies started, sorghum also nearly doubled (although it remains a minor crop), whereas soybeans declined disastrously. The total planted area for the three in 1984 of 65,892 ha was only slightly more than their 64,905 ha in 1978 (Taiwan Provincial Government 1985). . . . In any event, the net impact on domestic demand has been slight, considering that in 1984 Taiwan produced only 190,000 tons of corn, compared with imports of 2.96 million tons (Taiwan Provincial Government 1985). The argument is also made by some economists that Taiwan should not try to subsidize inefficient production of these grains that can be bought more cheaply from abroad.

What about the chances of switching rice fields to horticulture crops? Fruit and vegetable production has increased significantly over the past thirty years, and especially since the mid-1970s. Nonetheless, the domestic market of twenty million, in spite of relatively high spending power, has definite limits that have been or soon will be reached for a number of fruits and vegetables. Moreover, the prospects for exporting surplus production of fruits and vegetables are limited, partly because of the perishability of the goods and the fact that most have to be shipped fresh, as opposed to processed. Exports are also limited by difficulties in finding markets. The major markets are the developed countries that are either too far away or have import restrictions to protect their own producers. Taiwan's processed foods also face increasingly stiff competition from lower-cost producers, such as the People's Republic of China (PRC).

Assuming the government succeeds in converting 146,000 ha of rice fields to other uses, that would mean a reduction in annual production of rice by about 560,000 metric tons (assuming yields remain around the current 3.8 mt/ha). Compared with 1984 production of 2.24 mmt, that would mean a production total of approximately 1.7 mmt, just about the amount consumed in 1984. But what about the 1990s? Even with continued population growth, per capita rice consumption appears likely to decline faster than the fall in population growth, so that further reductions in the rice planted area are likely to be needed in the 1990s. The hard fact is, as the preceding discussion of alternative crops was meant to indicate, that much of the rice land in Taiwan is best suited to production of rice, and that the options for alternative crops are limited. Moreover, a majority of farmers are used to growing rice and are reluctant to switch (Tai 1983).

One should be careful, of course, not to overemphasize the inelasticity of land input to be used for purposes other than rice. For one thing, there was an enormous change in composition of agricultural production between 1952 and 1984, in which crop production fell from about 69 percent to 47 percent share of total production, while fisheries rose from 9 percent to 21 percent, and livestock from 16 percent to nearly 30 percent (table 7.1). This compositional change was the result of rising living standards and improved diets, and greater income opportunities in raising of fish and livestock. However, livestock production (mostly hog raising, plus poultry) uses relatively little land, since it is mostly done by the feedlot system (and relying primarily on imported feeds, as already noted). Likewise, fisheries production occurs primarily outside the land area of Taiwan. In 1978 deep sea, inshore, and coastal fisheries collectively accounted for 81 percent of total fisheries production, while fish culture (in ponds, mainly converted agricultural land) accounted for the remaining 19 percent. By 1984 the corresponding proportions were 76 percent and 24 percent, indicating a substantial growth in fish culture. During the same six years, a total of 7,046 ha of paddy fields and 2,196 ha of upland fields were converted to use as fish ponds (Taiwan Provincial Government 1985). Thus, one can say that growth of fisheries and livestock has been a decidedly healthy thing for Taiwan's agriculture and for the diet of the people. However, the growth of these activities can have only a modest impact on and relationship to the problem of rice surplus and alternative uses of paddy land.

Even assuming success in the riceland conversion program, anyway, Taiwan's huge imports of agricultural commodities would be only marginally affected, and the chances for significantly increasing agricultural exports are small. Thus, the trade deficit in agriculture is likely to remain a persistent, and probably growing, problem facing Taiwan for the foreseeable future. The lesson of all this is that governments have only limited abilities, in the best of circumstances, to control cropping systems and land-use practices.

Protecting Agriculture's Physical Resources

In regard to the third objective of agricultural policy, protecting the physical or natural resources for agriculture (basically land, soil, and water), Taiwan's record over the past thirty-five years is also a mixed one. Although the government has made noble efforts in policy formulation to protect these irreplaceable resources, enforcement of these policies has often been less than adequate, partly because of the extreme population pressure.

First of all, it has been an ongoing struggle to maintain the total cultivated area. That area peaked in 1977 at 922,000 ha, which was some 50,000 ha greater than the amount for the early 1950s. Nonetheless, in just seven years that gain was eroded by 30,000 ha, to a cultivated area of 892,000 ha in 1984. Unfortunately, paddy land, which is the best land, has suffered the most. Between 1978 and 1984, paddy land had a net decrease of over 23,000 ha (Taiwan, Executive Yuan, CEPD 1985, p. 57). This land is lost mainly to urban/industrial expansion. Pressure on top-grade land is intense.

Nowhere is this better illustrated than in the Northern Planning Region, which includes the Taipei Metropolitan Region, the key urban and economic center of the island. In the Northern Region, the total cultivated area fell from 241,000 ha in 1948 to under 160,000 ha by the early 1980s, a loss of 78,000 ha. The total cropped area declined even more sharply, from 501,000 ha to 248,000 ha in the same period, a loss of 253,000 ha (Wang 1984a, 1984b). Within the Taipei basin itself, there is relatively little agricultural land still being used for food production, the main exception being floodplain areas along the Tanshui and Keelung rivers (Williams, Sutherland, and Chang 1988).

Theoretically countering the loss of paddy land is the acquisition of new farmland through the government's reclamation program. Most of the reclaimed land is found in the slopelands, especially that band under 500 meters elevation that encircles the central mountain spine of Taiwan. This slopeland (or "upland" as it is officially classified) already accounts for 44 percent of the island's total cultivated area. This proportion is likely to grow, although there are in fact strict limits as to how much of the slopeland can be brought into cultivation. Aside from the slopelands, the only other lands suitable for potential cultivation are some riverbeds and seashores. These amount to only a few thousand hectares at best, are extremely expensive to reclaim, and are low yielding (Williams 1981; Williams, Chang, and Wang 1983).

In other words, for all practical purposes Taiwan is faced with a static total cultivated area at best, and a steadily declining area at worst. And even if the total can be maintained, as it has been at roughly 890,000 ha since 1982, the composition of that total area, in terms of the ratio of paddy land to upland (marginal land), is slowly changing for the worse.

A further serious problem in preserving the land resources of Taiwan is soil erosion. This is not the place to go into a detailed analysis of this problem. Suffice it to say that Taiwan has always suffered a serious problem with natural soil erosion, caused by heavy annual precipitation, subtropical climate, steep and mountainous terrain over two-thirds of the island, and weak geomorphological structures prone to land slides and erosion. Added to that inherently bad mix is the intense population pressure, with 20 million people crowded into about 11,960 km^2 (the effectively inhabited part of the island), resulting in a real population density of around 10,660 per km^2, one of the highest densities in the world. With virtually no place to expand cultivation except up the hillsides into the lightly inhabited mountain regions, it is not surprising that soil erosion has increased in recent decades, compounded by other assaults on the mountain interior resulting from building of cross-island highways and feeder roads into the slopelands. The government, through its Mountain Agricultural Resources Development Bureau (MARDB), plus the Council of Agriculture (formerly the CAPD and earlier the JCRR), and other agencies, has developed programs for control and selective development of slopelands for agricultural use (Hsieh 1984; Williams 1981). Since farmers are going to move into the slopelands one way or another, the government wisely reasoned that it was best to channel the settlement and development process in as healthy a manner as possible. Thus, each year a few thousand hectares of slopeland are carefully prepared, in terms of proper terracing, ground cover planting, installation of drainage ditches, and so on, to minimize the potential soil erosion. Careful testing has shown that fruits are the most suitable crops for the slopelands, because they involve the least frequent disturbance of the topsoil. The problem is that overproduction of some fruits is occurring, with few if any suitable replacement crops (Ch'en 1984). Getting farmers to observe proper soil conservation techniques is also a persistent problem, especially since some farmers are using the slopelands illegally. While Taiwan's slopeland development program is probably one of the best in the world, enforcement of rules and regulations is often less than ideal.

Protection of the island's water resources is also a problem. Fortunately, Taiwan has abundant annual precipitation, which, combined with a year-round growing season, makes it possible for a small island to support such a large population. As already noted, currently about 420,000 ha of farmland are irrigated, about 48 percent of the total cultivated area. Significantly, though, the irrigated area has actually shrunk since the late 1970s, partly because of decreases in paddy land. In addition, however, there is the growing problem of pollution of the island's rivers and underground water supply by effluents from factories and urban areas. The news in Taiwan frequently contains reports of environmental damage of this kind, which not only ruins the water supply but in severe cases has led to poisoning of the soil. The whole realm of environmental degradation is becoming a major public concern in Taiwan. In many ways, Taiwan is about where Japan was in the late 1960s after two decades of unrestricted and careless promotion of economic growth at any cost. Japan was finally forced to begin cleaning up its environment, starting in the 1970s. Taiwan now has its own Environmental Protection Agency, but in terms of effectively dealing with the serious air and water pollution of both urban and rural areas, the government is barely at the start of a long road.

Conclusion

In relation to the three basic objectives of agricultural policy, therefore, Taiwan's record, while good on a worldwide comparison, is nonetheless not the model picture that is sometimes painted in the literature. As long as Taiwan's industrial economy continues to prosper and the major export markets, especially the United States, on which Taiwan is so dependent, remain accessible to the island's products, then the agricultural trade imbalance and declining food self-sufficiency are not yet critical issues. Likewise, farmers can maintain their living standards in their part-time farming system. But if current trends continue, Taiwan's agricultural system is destined to become more and more like that of Japan, with increasing subsidization and rising domestic food costs as the likely outcome. The vulnerability and inefficiencies of this agricultural system are readily apparent, and the government is well advised not to be complacent about the situation.

References

China Post (Taipei), December 9, 1983.

Ch'en, C.J. 1983. "T'ai-wan ho-tso nung-ch'ang ching-ying wen-t'i chih yen-t'ao" (Study of the problems of cooperative farm management in Taiwan), *T'ai-wan Yin-hang chi'k-an* (Bank of Taiwan quarterly) 33, 2: 231–53.

————. 1984. "T'ai-wan shan-p'o ti-ch'u yu-mi ch'an-hsiao chih ching-chi yen-chiu" (Economic analysis of corn yields in the mountain slopeland area of Taiwan), *T'ai-wan Yin-hang chi-k'an* (Bank of Taiwan quarterly) 35, 1: 162–99.

Ch'en, H.H. 1980. "Food Supply and Agricultural Development Policy: The Taiwan Experience," *Industry of Free China* 54, 2: 7–13.

Chen, H.Y. 1980. "Food Price and Marketing Practices in Taiwan," *Industry of Free China* 54, 4: 9–23.

————. 1984. "Family Farms, Integrated Rural Development, and Multi-purpose Cooperatives in Taiwan," *Economic Review* (Taipei) (November–December): 7–32.

Eberstadt, N. 1983. "Asian Farm Policies Impeding Growth," *Asian Wall Street Journal*, September 5.

Gallin, B., and R. Gallin. 1982. "Socioeconomic Life in Rural Taiwan: Twenty Years of Development and Change," *Modern China* 8, 2: 205–46.

Hayami, Y., V.W. Ruttan, and H.M. Southworth, eds. 1979. *Agricultural Growth in Japan, Taiwan, Korea, and the Philippines.* Honolulu: University Press of Hawaii.

Ho, P.S. 1979. "Decentralized Industrialization and Rural Development: Evidence from Taiwan," *Economic Development and Cultural Change* 28, 1: 77–96.

Hsieh, H.H. 1984. "T'ai-wan shan-ti ching-chi cheng-ts'e yu ching-chi fa-chan wen-t'i (Economic development problems and policies in the mountain area of Taiwan), *T'ai-wan Yin-hang chi-k'an* (Bank of Taiwan quarterly) 35, 1: 126–61.

Kuo, Y.C., and T.K. Peng. 1983. "Land Tenure Systems and Farm Mechanization in Taiwan," *Industry of Free China* 59, 6: 1–11.

Lee, C.T. 1980. "A Review and Outlook of Taiwan's Agribusiness and International Cooperation," *Industry of Free China* 53, 1: 2–16.

Li, K.T. 1983. "Population Distribution and the Quality of Life in the Taiwan Area," *Industry of Free China,* part 1, 60, 3: 1–24; part 2, 60, 4: 17–31.

Liu, F.S. 1983. "Agricultural Marketing Improvements in Taiwan," *Industry of Free China* 60, 1: 21–34.

———. 1985. "The Contributions of the Farmers' Associations to the Agricultural Extension and the Developments (*sic*) in Taiwan," *Economic Review* (Taipei) 225: 8–16.

"Macro-economic Planning for Taiwan, R.O.C." 1980. *Industry of Free China* 53, 6: 11–31.

Mao, Y.K. 1981. "Agricultural Problems and Policy Issues in Taiwan," *Industry of Free China* 55, 30: 15–21.

Myers, R.H. 1984. "The Economic Transformation of the Republic of China on Taiwan," *China Quarterly* 99: 500–28.

Shei, S.Y. 1983. "Food Trade and Food Security of Taiwan," *Industry of Free China,* part 1, 60, 4: 1–15; part 2, 60, 5: 5–31.

Tai, H.Y. 1983. "T'ai-wan shuang-ch'i shui-tao ch'u nung-chia ching-ying chih chen-tuan" (Diagnosis of farm management in the double-cropped rice area of Taiwan), *T'ai-wan Yin-hang chi-k'an* (Bank of Taiwan quarterly) 34, 2: 254–73.

Taiwan, Executive Yuan, Council for Agriculture (CoA). 1984a. *Taiwan Food Balance Sheet.* Taipei.

———. 1984b. *The Second Stage Farmland Reform Program.* Taipei

———. 1985a. *Agricultural Development in the Republic of China on Taiwan—A Graphic Presentation.* Taipei.

———. 1985b. *Farmland Reform in the Republic of China on Taiwan.* Taipei.

Taiwan, Executive Yuan, Council for Economic Planning and Development (CEPD). 1984. *Shih-ssu hsiang chung-yao chien-she chi-hua shuo-ming* (Introduction to the 14 key projects). Taipei.

———. 1985. *Taiwan Statistical Data Book.* Taipei.

Taiwan, Ministry of Economic Affairs, Council of Agricultural Planning and Development. 1980. *Preliminary Report on Regional Agricultural Development Planning in the Taiwan Area.* Taipei.

———. 1983. *Six-Year Rice Project—Rice Production and Rice Field Diversion.* Taipei.

Taiwan Provincial Government, Department of Agriculture and Forestry. (PDAF). 1985. *Taiwan Agricultural Yearbook.* Taipei.

Thompson, S. 1984. "Taiwan: Rural Society," *China Quarterly* 99: 553–68.

Tsai, H.H. 1984. "Urban Growth and the Change of Spatial Structure in Taiwan," in *Conference on Urban Growth & Economic Development in the Pacific Region.* Taipei: Academia Sinica, Institute of Economics.

Wang, C.C. 1983. "Ts'ung tso-wu fa-tso chih-shu yu k'eng-ti li-yung shuai kai-suan t'ai-wan keng-ti te li-yung" (Land use in Taiwan from the perspective of the multiple cropping index and percentage of land use), *T'ai-wan nung-yeh* (Taiwan agriculture) 19, 6: 26–30.

———. 1984a. "T'ai-wan k'eng-ti li-yung pien-huan yin-tse te fen-che chi ying-yu tui-ts'e" (Analysis of factors affecting land use change in Taiwan and policy recommendations), *T'ai-wan t'u-ti chin-jung chi-k'an* (Taiwan land economics quarterly) 2, 1: 99–134.

———. 1984b. "T'ai-wan nung-yeh fa-chan fang-hsiang chih yen-t'ao" (A study of trends in Taiwan's agricultural development), *T'ai-wan Yin-hang chi-k'an* (Bank of Taiwan quarterly) 35, 91: 200–38.

Williams, J.F. 1981. "Agricultural Use of Slopelands in Taiwan." In C. Pannell and C. Salter, eds., *The China Geographer,* no. 11 (Boulder, CO: Westview Press).

Williams, J.F., C.Y. Chang, and C.Y. Wang. 1983. "Land Settlement and Development: A Case Study from Taiwan," *The Journal of Developing Areas* 18, 1: 35–52.

Williams, J., C. Sutherland, and C.Y. Chang. 1988. "Land Use in the Taipei Basin," *Annals AAG* 78, 2: map supplement.

Wu, T.C. 1980. "The Role of Administrative Support for Agricultural Development in Taiwan," *Industry of Free China* 54, 2: 14–27.

Yuise, Y. 1987. "Japanese Agricultural Policy," *Journal of Japanese Trade & Industry* 5: 49–52.

Part IV

THE ENVIRONMENTAL MOVEMENT

The multifaceted modernization that has transformed Taiwan has not been without its heavy costs, and nowhere are these costs more evident than in the island's environment. In their headlong rush to develop, governmental authorities and leaders of industry neglected to implement any environmental safeguards. Thus, when one lands on Taiwan, one sees the smog band on making the final approach to Chiang Kai-shek International Airport, an hour's bus ride southwest of Taibei. And when one approaches such major cities as Taibei, Taizhong, and Gaoxiong, one sees smokestacks belching fumes and rivers with their gray color and oily coatings.

This environmental devastation has not gone unnoticed, however. The middle classes that evolved as a result of the miracle are now demanding that the issue of environmental damage be dealt with as part of a larger struggle to improve the quality of life on the island. Wealth—a high per capita income—is not enough, the leaders of the evolving environmental movement are now saying. The two essays in this section deal with the growing recognition of an environmental crisis and with the development of an environmental movement.

Jack F. Williams sees Taiwan in the midst of what W.W. Rostow termed the "drive to maturity phase." A nation at such a stage of development often does not worry about environmental degradation, especially when it is attempting to attract foreign investment to its shores. Williams argues that Taiwan is now at such a stage, a stage that Japan reached at the end of the 1960s. He first points out the striking parallels between Taiwan and its Japanese trading partner, and then asks this important question: Will Taiwan follow Japan on the road to environmental destruction? Williams's answer makes up the body of this path-breaking chapter.

David W. Chen's chapter provides a detailed description of both the island's industrialization and the impact this virtually unchecked development has had on the environment. As it does so, it traces the origins of the public's recognition of the deteriorating environmental conditions on Taiwan.

In the final section of the chapter, Chen discusses the obstacles that block the path to future progress in the environmental sphere. Taiwanese leaders have difficult choices that pit environmental concerns against the need for sustained economic growth. These are choices, Chen makes clear, that must be made in an unstable political environment.

Chapter 8

Paying the Price of Economic Development in Taiwan: Environmental Degradation

Jack F. Williams
In collaboration with Ch'ang-yi Chang

> *The environmental crisis is an outward manifestation of a crisis of mind and spirit. There could be no greater misconception of its meaning than to believe it to be concerned only with endangered wildlife, human-made ugliness, and pollution. These are part of it, but more importantly, the crisis is concerned with the kind of creatures we are and what we must become in order to survive.*
>
> —Lynton Caldwell

As population grows ever larger on a finite resource base, and as nations scramble to industrialize and develop (however ambiguously the term "development" is interpreted), nation after nation is encountering its own version of the environmental crisis. Forty years ago, in the era of unquestioned dominance of the United States and the Western model of urbanization and industrialization, there was little if any concern about what industrialization and related processes could do to the environment. "Quality of life" tended to be interpreted largely in terms of rising per capita income and consumption of material goods. Today, as the twentieth century approaches its close, attitudes have changed dramatically. This change has been summed up thus: "environmental protection has gone from

This article is reprinted with the permission of the Centre of Asian Studies, The University of Hong Kong. It first appeared in the *Journal of Oriental Studies* vol. 27, nos. 1 and 2 (Special Issue), 1989, pp. 57–78. Hong Kong: Centre of Asian Studies, The University of Hong Kong and in *Taiwan: Economy, Society, and History*, edited by Edward K.Y. Chen, Jack F. Williams, and Joseph Wong, pp. 121–40. Hong Kong: Centre of Asian Studies, The University of Hong Kong, 1991.

being a luxury of the rich to being a requirement for the poor. Leaders of even the poorest countries . . . understand full well that future development depends on the sustainability of the resource base. Today many, if not most would agree with Tanzania's Julius Nyerere that 'environmental concern and development have to be linked together, if the latter is to be real and permanent'" (Brown 1988).

Taiwan's attitude toward the environment also has changed. From virtual indifference in the 1950s and 1960s, the position of the government and public is growing toward a determination to rescue the environment from past damages and to protect against future harm. Anyone who has studied Taiwan for any length of time must regard Taiwan's development experience with a mixture of admiration and dismay. Taiwan has achieved so much; yet Taiwan could be so much better than it is. Indeed, the contrasts between reality and potential assault one's senses every day there. On the one hand, there is the abundant material prosperity brought about by rapid increases in the standard of living. People live an increasingly good life, measured at least in terms of material possessions and personal consumption. These accomplishments are not to be sneered at, either, since hundreds of millions of people around the world wish they had as easy access to such wealth as the people of Taiwan. Yet one wonders if people in Taiwan are truly happier or have greater peace of mind than they did thirty or forty years ago. Taiwan faces a deteriorating environment that threatens the hard-earned quality of life and potentially the economic base of the island's prosperity. Taiwan is now in the midst of Rostow's drive-. to-maturity phase of development, and by the turn of the century hopes to be a fully developed country, or in Rostow's high mass consumption stage. This may well be the hardest phase of the development process for Taiwan, because what is called for is not only achievement of sustained economic growth, but also significant improvement in the environmental, social, and political spheres to support a mature economic system with a high "quality of life."

The argument is sometimes that LDCs cannot afford to worry about environmental degradation while they are in the process of developing the foundations for a sound economy. Particularly if a country is trying to attract private investment, the argument goes that the international division of labor and growth of transnational corporations has increased the degree of competition among LDCs to the point where it is suicidal for a country to impose too many restraints on investors. Otherwise, foreign investors will simply choose those locations with the fewest restrictions. Likewise, domestic investors will be discouraged from opening plants. There is certainly some truth in this argument, and it is difficult not to be somewhat sympathetic to LDCs in their predicament.

Nonetheless, one might expect countries such as Taiwan to have learned lessons from already developed nations about the consequences of unrestrained growth solely for the sake of GNP. Taiwan had a perfect example to learn from, namely, Japan. Chien Yu-hsin, director of Taiwan's newly created Environmental Protection Agency, has himself stated that taking appropriate environmental protection measures beforehand adds only 3 percent to total construction costs of projects. Corrective measures, on the other hand, increase costs by more than 40 percent ("Multi-Billion Program" 1987).

In the environmental battle, Taiwan today is about where Japan found itself at the close of the 1960s. At that time, after two decades of unrestrained promotion of economic growth, Japan found itself paying a high price in terms of environmental problems in its headlong drive to be number one in the world. Taiwan, fortunately, has never had that excessive an ambition. Yet might not some of the blame in Taiwan's case be placed on the ROC government's drive to build up the economic and military might of Taiwan at any cost in its determination to maintain the island's independence from mainland control?

Consciously or not, Taiwan has followed much the same path already trod by Japan. The parallels between the two countries are numerous. Both are densely populated with limited lowlands for human settlement. Both are resource poor in terms of minerals, agricultural land, and energy resources. Both opted for a high growth rate, export-oriented strategy of development, except that Taiwan, because of its smaller population, was forced to become even more dependent on export growth than Japan. Both put few if any constraints on factories as to what those establishments could do with their waste products. Both worried little at all about dumping sewage and other wastes directly into rivers and the ocean or into the air. Both encouraged development of motorized transportation, especially private automobile or motorcycle ownership, without much concern about what leaded gasoline and diesel fumes do to the air that people have to breathe, and before developing the infrastructure (roads, parking facilities, traffic control, etc.) to deal with large numbers of motor vehicles. Both were rather laissez-faire about zoning and ordinances to control incompatible land uses in both rural and urban areas. *Island of Dreams,* published in the mid-1970s, was a vivid and grim account of the ravages inflicted on Japan's natural environment and ecology, and ultimately on the people of Japan, by their neglect of the environment (Huddle, Reich, and Stiskin 1975). One is reminded of that book every time one is in Taiwan, especially in Taipei.[1] Who is going to write Taiwan's *Island of Dreams?*

Recognizing the Problem

Growth of the environmental crisis in Taiwan has been rapid, but recognition of the crisis was slow to develop, both within Taiwan, especially in government circles, and outside of Taiwan, in the way foreign scholars looked at Taiwan's development process. Even today, the literature from Taiwan often fails to mention the environmental crisis at all, or at best makes only vague reference to it. C.C. Chao (1986), in his analysis of the role of planning in Taiwan, ignores the issue entirely. Tsiang (1986), in his study of the reasons for the success of Taiwan's economic takeoff, also ignores the environmental factor. Indeed, might one argue that one of the contributing factors to Taiwan's successful takeoff was *not* diverting capital resources to environmental protection? Is this one of the lessons of the development process to be learned from Japan and the Asian NICs? One would like to think not, but the issue merits consideration. In much the same vein as Tsiang, Hsieh (1987) studied Taiwan's development process to see what relevance, if any, it had for other developing countries, but again with no mention of environmental degradation. Even the government's long-range forecast for the Taiwan economy up to the year 2000, prepared by the CEPD, makes only brief reference in one small subsection to the need for improved standards and investment in environmental protection. In a somewhat earlier and much quoted study in the literature, Li (1983) assessed Taiwan's population distribution and quality of life, but measured "quality" in a fairly narrow sense of mainly access of education, health care, and other public services. There was no mention of environmental problems.

Some Chinese scholars, however, have not ignored the environmental crisis. Liu (1980), in an interesting analysis of economic growth and quality of life, comparing Taiwan with the United States and other developed countries, developed a Quality of Life Index, in which environmental factors were explicitly included. In his ranking, Taiwan came out twentieth-eighth out of thirty-three countries compared, just on the environmental quality issue. However, his measurement of environment was quite limited, with population density being a major determinant. H.H. Tsai (1987), in a study of Taiwan's efforts to achieve a rational distribution of population, makes reference to environmental problems as a key factor behind the government's promotion of more balanced regional development, under the island's Comprehensive Development Plan officially adopted in 1979 (also see Williams, 1988b). Tsay (1986), in a study of Taiwan's changing demographic profile and related health problems, notes the growing rate of morbidity due to chronic illnesses associated with urbanization, industrialization, and environmental pollution.[2] In a related study, Ting and Jou (1988) examined the relationships between industrial pollution and regional variations of life expectancy at birth in Taiwan. Y.T. Chao (1986), chairman of the CEPD, perhaps best summed up the growing government recognition of the environmental crisis and the recognition of what Caldwell was getting at in his statement about the need to interpret the environmental crisis in broadest terms, by stressing the importance of "social cost" in the development process. Chao argues strongly that behavior be changed, and that Taiwan stress long-term benefits over short-term gains in its development policies.

Foreign scholars, sad to say, have paid very little attention to Taiwan's environmental problems. In nearly all the many economic and other studies of Taiwan over the last three decades or more, there is almost no mention of the environmental issue. Praise is heaped upon praise about Taiwan's development "miracle," and more recently about Taiwan's dramatic political and social progress. Yet one looks in vain for mention of the environmental cost of that development. Nickum and Schak (1979), for example, in comparing living standards and economic development in Shanghai and Taiwan, made no reference whatever to the environment, or for that matter to other nontangible elements of the quality of life. Selya's (1975) rather technical analysis of water and air pollution in the early 1970s is almost alone in its specific focus on environmental issues. Williams, Chang, and Wang (1983) did a case study of environmental problems arising from the building of the East-West Cross-Island Highway and development of the Lishan area in the central mountains. In an earlier study, Williams (1981) looked at the broader environmental issues of slopeland farming, especially soil erosion.

Defining the Problem: What Is the Environmental Crisis?[3]

Popular perceptions of the environmental crisis tend to be narrow and to concentrate on immediately perceivable manifestations of the problem, that is, air and water pollution. Certainly, pollution of the air, water, and land is a major component of environmental degradation. Much of this pollution, however, is not immediately visible, and its harm is often not felt until after prolonged exposure to it. Pollution can be divided into at least five types.

1. *Biologically Active Wastes.* These include food wastes, paper, fertilizers, human and animal wastes, and carcasses. Although these will eventually biodegrade, they are nonetheless highly offensive to see and smell, and they can contribute to air and water pollution and in turn to health problems. In all of Taiwan, less than 1 percent of human excrement receives even primary sewage treatment; in Taipei City the figure is below 3 percent. Not surprisingly, Taiwan has among the highest incidence of hepatitis B in the world. Another effect is eutrophication of water bodies, leading to depletion of fish. The lower reaches of most of Taiwan's major rivers and many reservoirs suffer now from this problem. This kind of pollution is generally highly visible and one about which the public complains. Its magnitude and effects may be difficult to quantify, but nearly everyone recognizes the existence of the problem. The technical solution to proper disposal of biodegradable wastes is well known, and the technology easily available. The chief issue in Taiwan's case, as in most countries for that matter, is political. Who will pay for the cleanup and control?

2. *Inert and Semi-Inert Substances.* These include plastics, glass, and metal found in ordinary garbage. Essentially harmless of themselves, these substances create problems because they are typically mixed with other refuse, including organic and toxic substances, which makes it difficult to separate them out. It has been calculated that between 1975 and 1985 in Taiwan, average garbage generation per capita rose from 0.5 to 0.74 kg per day, which works out to about a 4 percent annual increase, roughly the same growth rate as per capita income. Most garbage is disposed of in landfills. When dumped along with other substances, inert or semi-inert materials provide ideal breeding grounds for rats, flies, and other disease vectors. Toxic wastes contained in the mess may also seep into and contaminate groundwater. The problem is of course especially severe in the major metropolitan centers, particularly Taipei. There, incineration

is being tried as a possible solution, but it is costly. Moreover, some plastic substances release hazardous chemicals when burned at low temperatures. Taipei City is also trying very sophisticated landfill techniques, such as that at Futeken, that promise minimal environmental damage (*Guide to DEP* 1985). The problem is that nobody wants a garbage landfill site next to them. In a densely crowded basin like that of Taipei, it has become nearly impossible to find suitable landfill sites for future garbage disposal. One long-range solution is to separate garbage into different categories of biodegradable, inert, and toxic, before it is picked up by the sanitation crews. This approach, however, presents special problems in terms of getting the public to cooperate, and it would be costly.

3. *Hazardous Wastes.* These include caustic chemicals, pesticides, radioactive wastes, heavy metals, and a wide variety of other chemically potent substances used or produced by industry, agriculture, and sometimes consumers. These are the most life threatening in the long run because they are often unseen, even unknown, for long periods before the damage they cause becomes visible. Taiwan is probably most vulnerable right now in terms of controlling pollution by hazardous wastes and has yet to develop the institutional mechanisms and physical plant to deal with this growing problem. One can only wonder how long it will be before Taiwan has its Minamata or similar tragedy. The conditions are building for just such a situation. The general consensus on the island is that problems from hazardous wastes will escalate rapidly within the next decade or two as storage containers disintegrate and the latency periods for human health problems are exceeded.

4. *Atmospheric Emissions.* These include carbon monoxide, hydrocarbons, oxides of nitrogen and sulphur, polyaromatic hydrocarbons, chloroflurocarbons, and aerosols. "Air pollution," as it is loosely described, is perhaps the most readily visible aspect of the environmental crisis, at least in big cities. The extent of this problem remains not fully understood. On the one hand, existing quantitative measurements suggest no trend toward increased air pollution. For example, dust fallout in Taipei in 1985 was estimated by the EPB at 4500 tons/km^2, or 15 tons/km^2/day ("Thousands" 1985). Yet two years later the EPB claimed that air pollution was diminishing, with dust fallout at only 5.4 tons/km^2/month ("Cleaning" 1987). In other words, scientific measurement of the problem is still far from adequate, and simple observation strongly suggests that air pollution is worsening, at least in Taipei. Certainly there is broad public perception that the problem is getting worse. Fortunately, this is also a form of pollution that is relatively easy to solve technically. Developed countries, such as the United States and Japan, have made significant progress, through use of unleaded gasoline, catalytic converters, and other measures, to bring air pollution under greater control, although it is hardly eliminated.

5. *Noise.* An intangible but readily apparent aspect of the environmental crisis is noise. While this form of pollution can be easily measured, in terms of decibels, its effects on health are less measurable. Yet few would question the

negative effect on overall quality of life that excessive noise has, although what constitutes "excessive" is a subjective matter. Regardless, big city life tends to be very noisy, and in Taipei especially the noise levels can reach alarming levels. This can be debilitating for some people and interfere with work and school activities. Noise is a problem that can be brought under control, although not necessarily without difficulty, since it primarily involves altering public behavior (e.g., restricting honking of horns in traffic) or installing special equipment.

Eye Pollution. The above five categories, while generally regarded as the chief components of the environmental crisis, actually are only part of the picture. One could add what is sometimes referred to as "eye pollution," that is, the uglification of the environment through lack of planning, overbuilding, ugly architecture, indiscriminate advertising, and so on. Unfortunately, eye pollution seems to go hand in hand with the development process. Taiwan certainly has plenty of this problem, especially in the cities. This is also a highly subjective issue, however. A major component of eye pollution is simply the nature of the culture and society. Solution of the problem is partly a matter of levels of wealth, as well as changing cultural and social values.

Part of the environmental crisis also has to do with depletion or destruction of natural resources: land, water wildlife, unspoiled wild lands, and so on. The various forms of pollution already mentioned of course impact on natural resources in both rural and urban areas, but I am here referring mainly to nonurban areas and to other impacts of human settlement and development as well. There are at least four aspects that can be mentioned.

1. *Land for Agriculture.* Expansion of Taiwan's population, to around 20 million today, combined with massive industrialization and urbanization, has resulted in a shrinking land base for agriculture, in both quantitative and qualitative terms. The total cultivated area for the island peaked in 1977 at 922,000 ha. It has since fallen to around 870,000 ha and is projected to continue declining, to around 860,000 ha by early in the next century ("Rice" 1987). Moreover, the decline is even more serious in that marginal land (mostly slopeland) now accounts for 44 percent of the cultivated area and is growing proportionately at the expense of decreasing top-grade paddy land. Furthermore, soil erosion is a growing and serious problem, particularly on slopeland (Williams 1988a). What agricultural land remains is being polluted in many places by industrial and agricultural practices. Tsai (1987), in his study of rural industrialization and its impact on the rural economy, notes the severity, albeit highly localized in various places on the island, of poisoning of the soil and irrigation water by industrial pollutants, with deleterious effects on crop production and fisheries. Wang You-tsao, chairman of the Council of Agriculture, said recently that the productivity of Taiwan's farmland had fallen sharply because of abuse through overuse of fertilizers and pesticides that cause the soil to acidify ("Too Much" 1987).

2. *Impending Shortage of Fresh Water.* Taiwan, with its humid subtropical climate, would seem to have unlimited supplies of fresh water. But that is not the

case. Currently, about 95 percent of groundwater resources are being used. Over-drawing of groundwater is leading to subsidence and salt-water intrusion in a number of places. Although barely one-quarter of runoff is utilized at present, potential for tapping this resource further is limited, because of large seasonal fluctuations in stream discharge, limited reservoir capacity, and shortages of sites for further reservoir construction. Moreover, siltation in many existing reservoirs is seriously shortening their projected lifetimes.

3. *Wildlife Destruction.* It may be too late to save what little wildlife remains on Taiwan. There are some species still remaining, mostly in the mountain interior, and there is growing pressure by conservationists to protect these, pri-marily within the context of the evolving national park and nature preserve system (see below).

4. *Preserving Wildlands.* A growing conservation movement has resulted in the establishment of conservation areas and a national park system. The move-ment aims to protect still relatively unspoiled places and to preserve existing fauna and flora. These needs must be balanced, however, against the demands of an increasingly affluent population for domestic recreation and tourism, espe-cially places to get away from the crowded lowlands and cities. The major protected areas now consist of four national parks (Yangmingshan, Taroko Gorge, Yushan, and Kenting), seven ecosystem reserves, three nature reserves, and five coastal conservation areas (Eu 1986).

Environmental Degradation

Although I have already suggested some of the factors contributing to the envi-ronmental crisis in Taiwan, the causes can be summarized as follows.

1. One factor certainly is the unfortunate fact that Taiwan is simply too crowded. With some 20 million people squeezed into about 4,600 mi^2 (12,000 km^2), which is the effectively inhabited part of a mountainous island, the result-ing real population density of over 4,000/mi^2 (1,580/km^2) is one of the highest in the world. Thus, it is inevitable that some problems would be more severe and more difficult to solve than in countries with more favorable person/land ratios, such as the United States. However, it would be misleading to put too much blame on geographical circumstances for the severity of Taiwan's environ-mental crisis today. For one thing, there are a number of other countries in the world with similar person/land ratios that have managed to maintain both high per capita income and high quality of environment, such as the Low Countries in Europe.

2. There is little disagreement in or out of Taiwan that much of the blame lies in the failure of the government to monitor and protect the environment as industrialization and urbanization took place. Unfortunately, growth rates have been especially high in industries that tend to produce large amounts of hazard-ous wastes, namely, plastics, petroleum refining, pesticides, leather tanning, and

various chemical manufactures. Both local and foreign investors found Taiwan attractive for establishing these kinds of enterprises, not only because of cheap labor, political stability, and good infrastructure, but also because the government had minimal regulations or controls about factory emissions. Hence, waste liquids, gases, and solids were indiscriminately released into the environment of Taiwan for twenty to thirty years. Taiwan became known as a haven for so-called dirty industries.

3. Rural industrialization also played a role, in that much industrial growth since the early 1970s has been centered in factories scattered throughout the rural areas of Taiwan. This was a conscious policy of the government, designed to decentralize the industrial pattern, to help resolve the problems of the major metropolitan centers, as well as to help boost farm family income by providing off-farm sources of employment. From those perspectives, rural industrialization has been a great success. However, a negative consequence has been to spread pollution even more widely into once pristine rural environments.

4. The size of industrial plants has also been a factor. The large number of small and medium-sized factories, in rural as well as urban areas, has been a contributor to environmental problems, because these establishments have limited capital and hence are even more reluctant to use environmental safeguards than large businesses. Moreover, there are many illegal factories operating throughout the island, estimated in one account to number as many as 5,000–6,000 ("Crackdown" 1986). The mass poisoning of shellfish off the Tainan coast in 1986, which received widespread publicity at the time, was believed to have been caused by unlicensed factories discharging toxic wastes into nearby streams ("Initial Operation" 1986).

5. Urbanization has of course been a major contributor to the environmental crisis. In spite of promotion of balanced regional growth on the island, the two major metropolitan centers of Taipei and Kaohsiung have still tended to dominate the urban hierarchy. Taipei has been the most favored goal of migrants. The environmental problems of the cities have thus become especially acute, because of the extremely high population densities and relative lack of urban planning until fairly recently (Williams 1988b). One can only speculate on how much worse Taipei's problems would be if the government had not been promoting rural industrialization and other balanced regional development policies.

6. Transportation improvements, including the building of freeways and rapid growth in private automobile and motorcycle ownership, as well as electrification and expansion of the rail system, have made virtually the entire lowland region of the island highly accessible. While this has unquestionably been stimulative to economic growth and prosperity, it has also assisted in spreading pollution more widely as well as increasing the pollution in certain areas, such as the major cities. In Taipei, for example, the vehicular density is ten times greater than that of Los Angeles. In Taiwan as whole, there were more than 8 million motor vehicles by 1987, of which 83 percent were motorcycles and 75 percent of

those had two-stroke engines, which emit more toxic gases than other types. Add to that the many diesel buses and trucks, often poorly maintained, that belch out noxious black exhaust. Motor vehicles collectively are believed to contribute around 90 percent of the air pollution in Taipei (Benedicto 1987, 1988). Mass rapid transit has thus become essential for Taipei, not only to reduce traffic congestion but also to attack air pollution. The introduction of unleaded gasoline in 1986 was expected to prove beneficial in the long run also. By 1994 all new vehicles will be designed to run on unleaded gas (Wang 1986a).

Transportation access to the mountainous interior of Taiwan, including the several cross-island highways that have been constructed over the years, has also had negative consequences. It is true that the physical isolation of the east coast as well as that of people living in the mountains has been reduced, and slopelands opened up for fruit cultivation and other activities. Unfortunately, these developments have also led to serious soil erosion problems, leading to silting of rivers and reservoirs, as well as water pollution from fertilizers and pesticides washed into the drainage systems (Williams 1981; Williams, Chang, and Wang 1983).

7. The social and environmental attitudes of the people of Taiwan must also be faulted for contributing to the crisis. One can see indiscriminate dumping of trash and all sorts of pollutants in both rural and urban areas by many people. Who is to blame for this situation? Is it merely a matter of public education to get people to change their public behavior and increase their environmental consciousness? Can one argue that in a developing country public behavior toward the environment will mirror that of the government? Or is the root of the problem to be found in traditional Chinese society, with its strong (some might say excessive) focus on the family, at the expense of public welfare? There is plenty of evidence in Taiwan to support all of these arguments.

Growth of the Environmental Movement in Taiwan

There is hope for change. Within the last decade primarily, there has been a gradual awakening about the environmental crisis. This has resulted largely from growing public concern that has prompted the government to respond and to get serious about the problems. The parallels with Japan are again striking, because it was public pressure there that also got the government going on the road to its environmental protection program in the early 1970s.

The size of the environmental movement in Taiwan is difficult to measure, however. Based on routinely observed public behavior of most people, one might be tempted to state cynically that the majority of the public is still indifferent to environmental degradation, at least if it means inconveniencing themselves in their public behavior, or costing them extra money from their own pockets. Yet a newspaper survey in 1987 indicated that 60 percent of respondents would be willing to pay more taxes if the government increased its pollution-control budget ("Cleaner Air" 1987). M. Chang (1988), in his study assessing the quality of life in Taiwan, noted that his data clearly showed a direct correlation between a person's social class and one's perceived quality of life. He found that the most discontented group is Taiwan's middle class, which has spearheaded a variety of social reform movements, including environmental conservation. Some indication of this growing middle-class discontent is provided by the growth of private organizations, such as the Environmental Quality Foundation, and the New Environment Foundation of the ROC Consumers Foundation, which have been active in the environmental movement, have published periodicals on environmental issues, and serve as public watchdogs and pressure groups for policy changes (Crichton 1988; Moore 1988; Wang 1986b).

Might it also be argued that the authoritarian political system that characterized the island until the mid-1980s contributed to a reluctance by people to express publicly their unhappiness about environmental problems, let alone participate in public demonstrations? It seems hardly coincidental that the dramatic political reforms of the last two years have been paralleled by a suddenly strong public outcry against environmental deterioration. One can see this in several recent highly publicized cases.

Lukang

The charming old historic port city of Lukang, in Changhua County on the west coast, was shaken in June 1986 by strong opposition from local residents to a proposed Du Pont titanium dioxide plant ("Du Pont Meeting" 1986; "Control Yuan" 1986; "Keeping Taiwan" 1986; Reardon-Anderson 1992). The Lukang area remains one of the least environmentally disturbed regions of Taiwan, and aquaculture is an important part of the rural economy. In spite of assurances by Du Pont executives that the plant would be environmentally safe, opposition was strong enough to force government officials to side with the residents. In the end, the government canceled its approval of the project.

Houchin

A more recent case occurred in Houchin, a small town in the Kaohsiung area, in 1987. Here the guilty party was the government-owned Chinese Petroleum Company, which planned to add a fifth naphtha cracker to its existing plant there. (Naphtha is a flammable liquid obtained from crude petroleum and used as a raw material for gasoline.) Villagers of Houchin complained vehemently about the pollution they had already lived with for forty years and did not want any more. Protesters went by bus to Taipei to demonstrate at the Ministry of Economic Affairs and other agencies. In this case, the government has not backed down in its decision to go ahead with the fifth naphtha cracker, but it has promised to install the latest pollution control equipment in the facility. Local residents are reportedly unimpressed with the promises (Moore 1988; "Cleaner Air" 1987).

Ilan

The fishing town of Ilan in northeastern Taiwan has been the scene of protests against yet another planned naphtha cracker, this one to be built by Formosa Plastics, a private firm. Formosa Plastics is a huge conglomerate built up over the years by one of Taiwan's leading industrialists, Wang Yung-ching (Wang 1986b). The largest private corporation on the island, Formosa Plastics consists of more than twenty companies, plus overseas branches, and is the largest PVC resin producer in the world. Formosa Plastics thus is illustrative of the huge, often polluting firms that dominate Taiwan's industrial economy. Protests against the proposed facility in Ilan forced Wang to debate publicly with the governor of Ilan County on television about the plant project. The outcome of this plan is still undecided, but merely the fact that Formosa Plastics has had to make a public accounting and justification for its plans would have been unthinkable just ten or twenty years ago, when factories and other industrial facilities went up all over the island without the slightest consultation with local residents.

There have been innumerable other cases, some unpublicized, in which residents, distrusting the government's ability and/or determination to control polluters, have taken things into their own hands. One case occurred in Hsinchu in 1986 when residents physically interrupted operations of the Chang Yung Chemical Company by blocking the entrance for chemical tank cars. The protesters claimed the factory had polluted the groundwater, contributing to cancer deaths in the area. In an industrial park there the same week, protesters were upset by a fire at a garbage dump site for used-metal recycling that was causing severe air pollution in the surrounding area. The crowd broke into the industrial park and demanded compensation for injuries and damages to crops. Again, this sort of action would have been unthinkable not long ago ("Keeping Taiwan" 1986).

Government Response to the Environmental Crisis

Formal government response to environmental degradation dates technically from about 1972, when the Department of Health, under the Executive Yuan, set up a Bureau of Environmental Sanitation (renamed the Bureau of Environmental Protection in 1982) (*Republic of China—A Reference Book* 1986, 337–42). A Water Pollution Control Act was one of the first measures promulgated, in 1974. Because the bureau had no real enforcement powers, little was accomplished in the next ten years in terms of environmental improvement. There were a few isolated success stories, however.

Love River Cleanup

The Love River is one of the more significant early success stories in the environmental saga. The Love River is a very short and not terribly important stream that flows into Kaohsiung harbor. The river was very popular with Kaohsiung residents, however, as a recreational and fishing site in the heart of the city. Unfortunately, Kaohsiung's emergence as the key heavy industrial center of Taiwan in the last thirty years resulted in severe pollution of the river to the point where offensive odors from the river made even walking along the banks unpleasant. The river had become an open sewer by the 1960s. The disastrous Dragon Boat race of 1966 marked the end of the river's use as recreational site.

Plans were begun to clean up the river, but nothing much happened until Premier Chiang Ching-kuo got personally involved, so the story goes, and pushed through financing for the cleanup in 1974. Actual work did not begin until 1979, however, and the first stage of cleanup was completed in 1986 (C.H. Chang 1987a). Kaohsiung's controversial mayor, Su Nan-cheng, then got into political hot water by proclaiming the river cleanup completed, when in fact only the first phase of a long-range commitment was finished. Regardless, Kaohsiung set a powerful model for other pollution cleanup programs around the island, showing especially the importance of local effort and grass-roots support from the public as essential parts of a successful environmental improvement program.

Environmental Impact Assessments

In the 1970s the government began to require Environmental Impact Assessments (EIAs) for development projects. EIA studies were by and large ineffective, though, because they were not carried out until a site had already been decided upon for a project and construction work was already under way or nearly completed. EIAs were too late, for example, to stop construction of a third nuclear power plant on a beach next to some of the best coral reefs in southern Taiwan (Dong 1985a). Fortunately, in the last couple of years EIAs have become obligatory before all development projects even get official approval, let alone begin construction.

Establishment of the EPA

In 1984 regulations were added to the 1974 Water Pollution Control Act that put teeth into the law and expanded its coverage to include other sources of pollution. However, it was formal establishment of the Environmental Protection Agency (EPA) on August 22, 1987, that really marked Taiwan's coming of age in the environmental protection arena ("ROC Budgeting" 1987). The EPA, under the Ministry of Economic Affairs in the Executive Yuan, has greatly expanded powers over the old Bureau of Environmental Protection, and it has the budget to start getting serious about tackling the environmental mess. The 1988 budget alone for the EPA was set at some NT $17 billion (about U.S. $630 million at an exchange rate of 27:1). In the next ten years, it is estimated that pollution control and environmental cleanup will cost approximately U.S. $10–67 billion, indicating considerable divergence of opinion and a lot of guessing on the part of various agencies and individuals concerned with the environment ("Pollution Control" 1986; "Billions to Be Spent" 1988; "Clean Air" 1988). The government's own state-run enterprises, including the Taiwan Sugar Corporation's mills, and factories of the Tobacco and Wine Monopoly Bureau, will need to spend U.S. $1.5 billion on air pollution facilities and U.S. $250 million on water pollution control devices during the next eight years ("U.S. $1.5 Billion" 1985). The basic message is clear, anyway: cleanup and control will cost a great deal of money, as both Japan and the United States have already learned.

Tamsui River Project

One of the largest and most serious projects facing the EPA is the Tamsui River. The Tamsui drainage basin in northern Taiwan covers 1,000 mi and consists of the two major tributaries, the Keelung and Hsintien rivers, which flow into the Tamsui in the northern part of Taipei City. Some 4–5 million people live within the drainage basin, which is the center of the Taipei Metropolitan Region and the larger Northern Industrial Region, the most important of the four economic planning regions in Taiwan.

Once a lovely river that provided navigation all the way upstream to Taipei, as well as important fishing and recreation grounds, the Tamsui became dreadfully fouled with human and industrial wastes after the 1950s. (The river's navigability was already diminished by silting early in this century, but the beauty of the river lingered much longer than that.) Some 10,000 shops and factories directly front on the river and its tributaries now, with at least 500 continuously discharging large amounts of effluent into the drainage system. There are also innumerable private homes and duck farms along the system, adding their contribution of filth. The river has also been used for decades as a dumping ground for raw garbage from the metropolitan region. Small wonder, thus, that the name "Tamsui" (Tan-shui), which means "fresh water," has become a cruel misnomer, analogous to the no longer "fragrant harbor" of Hong Kong.[4]

Yet, if plans mean anything, the Tamsui River will be resurrected by the turn of the century, according to the government. The EPA, working with the Department of Environmental Protection in the Taipei Municipal Government, has a fifteen-year program to clean up the Tamsui (Chen 1987; *Guide to DEP* 1985). The key part of the plan is construction of sewage treatment plants around the metropolitan region, so that by the year 2000 no raw sewage will be dumped directly into the system (currently barely 2 percent of Taipei's sewage is treated at all before release into the river). In addition, factories and other businesses along the river will be required to stop dumping untreated effluents into the river. Garbage disposal is being improved by modern sanitary landfills, such as that at Futeken in southern Taipei, as mentioned earlier. Opened in 1983, Futeken was designed completely to prevent contamination of the groundwater. It is a showpiece project, but unfortunately was anticipated to be filled around 1990! By then, solid wastes from Taipei were to total more than 4,000 metric tons per day. Because of the near impossibility of finding future landfill sites in the basin, the government is turning to incineration as the long-term answer to garbage disposal. A total of three incinerators were in operation by 1989 and were expected to handle 98 percent of the basin's waste (Kuo 1986).

Nuclear Power: Controlling Potential Danger

Some of the greatest controversy over environmental pollution has taken place in recent years over nuclear power generating plants. Here the concern is really over potential long-range threats, since no actual harm has yet occurred from the island's nuclear power plants.

Aside from hydroelectric power, Taiwan has no significant domestic sources of energy and hence must import huge amounts of petroleum and coal for its thermal electricity plants. The island is about 90 percent dependent on imported sources of energy. By the late 1960s, therefore, the decision was made to develop nuclear power for electricity generation, to make the island less vulnerable, especially to the volatile oil supplies from the Middle East. The oil crises of the 1970s reinforced the government's determination in this regard. The first two nuclear reactors went into operation at Chinshan, on the island's northern tip, in 1978 and 1979. Two more reactors started up at nearby Kousheng in late 1981 and early 1983. The fifth and sixth reactors were opened at Maanshan on the southern tip of the island, near Kenting National Park, in 1984 and 1985. By that time, about half of the island's electricity requirements were supplied by these three nuclear plants, ranking Taiwan third in the world in terms of the proportion of actual supply contributed by nuclear power (behind France and Belgium) (Goldstein 1985a).

Growing international concern about the safety of nuclear power accelerated greatly with the Three Mile Island incident in the United States in 1979. Public opposition to nuclear power in Taiwan began to mount, not only because of environmental worries, but also because of concerns about the cost-effectiveness of nuclear power versus other sources of energy (Lew 1985; Dong 1985b). Moreover, concern mounted over what to do with radioactive waste. Orchid Island was chosen as the site for a modern, theoretically safe storage facility ("Orchid Island" 1985). The government approved a plan in early 1985 for a fourth nuclear plant to be built at the fishing village of Yenliao in northeastern Taiwan, arguing that growing demand for electricity required such a facility. However, a serious fire in one of the generators of the plant in southern Taiwan in July 1985 sparked heated debate about the wisdom of yet another nuclear facility ("G.E. to Negotiate" 1986; "Nuclear Energy" 1986; Goldstein 1985b). These reservations intensified with the much more serious Chernobyl disaster of 1986. Intense public debate continued through 1987. Unfortunately, preliminary construction work on the fourth plant had already been started before an EIA was carried out. Hence, the best that environmentalists have been able to achieve so far is simply postponing the project. As of mid-1988, the fourth was on hold, with Taipower arguing strongly for its resumption and warning of dire energy shortages without it ("Taiwan Warned" 1987; "New Nuclear Plant" 1986; "Nuclear Power" 1988; "Taiwan Postpones" 1988). In spite of less than complete success, the environmentalists have shown their new found muscle in bringing to public accountability such previously impregnable giants as Taipower.

Conclusion

What can be learned from Taiwan's experience with the environmental crisis? Several truisms seem to emerge from this experience.

1. Environmental protection is much cheaper if carried out before the damage is done, rather than after the fact.

2. Few governments have the foresight or courage to enforce environmental protection early in the development process, because of the desire to push economic development as rapidly as possible, partly to assuage public demands and expectations for improved standard of living.

3. The catalyst for environmental protection usually comes from a minority of concerned citizens, who prod the government into action, not vice versa.

4. Once the government is involved, however, environmental protection cannot be successful without active cooperation between government and public, and that in turn means the government has to convince the rest of the public that environmental protection is important not only to the quality of life but also to basic economic growth. In Taiwan's case, for example, the need to import pollution-control technology offers a multibillion dollar opportunity to reduce the unfavorable Taiwan–U.S. trade balance, which in turn could improve relations with the United States and help maintain a healthy bilateral relationship.

5. If environmental quality is going to be held in high importance by government and public, then economic growth will have to accommodate the needs for environmental protection. This could mean, for example, the phasing out of certain types of manufacturing that are highly polluting. Consumers will also have to sacrifice and put up with increased costs, higher taxes, and some inconvenience. For instance, the era of the motorcycle may have to come to an end in the cities at least, if technology is unable to come up with ways to control emissions.

Chien Yu-hsin, director of the EPA, had this to say about the environmental crisis (Yu 1988):

> We face a two-sided problem: one is pollution itself, the other is the structural limitations of the governmental administrative system. For more than thirty years we have pursued economic development as best as we can, but at the

same time we neglected environmental protection. As a result, our surroundings have greatly deteriorated. In addition, an ambiguous environmental protection policy aggravated the situation. When challenged by economic interests, environmental protection concerns were automatically compromised without exception.

Chien's remarks convey a bleak review of the past. One can only hope for greater success in the future. The task is daunting. An EPA staff of 318 is taking on 70,000 factories, more than 8 million vehicles, and some 20 million often stubbornly individualistic citizens. The EPA's long-range strategy is basically twofold: one is to use education, through school textbooks and programs, mass media, and direct appeals to industry; the other is to escalate the enhanced enforcement powers of the EPA.

Notes

1. One of the best places to observe the environmental crisis in Taipei is to walk across the bridge on Chung Shan North Road, just before the Grand Hotel, where the bridge crosses the Keelung River. The water pollution in the river is appalling; the murky brown smog is readily visible and smellable; the traffic congestion and noise at that spot are among the worst in Taipei.
2. Interestingly, a recent news item indicated that children in North Taiwan are more likely to get cancer than those elsewhere on the island ("Children" 1988).
3. Parts of this section are adapted from the preliminary, unpublished report of the *Taiwan 2000* Project. This is a multidisciplinary effort by scholars and other environmental activists in Taiwan, with the assistance of foreign technical experts brought in as consultants. Funding was provided partly by the Asia Foundation in Taiwan. The project's objectives were to analyze Taiwan's economy and ecology and to make recommendations to the government on how to balance economic development and environmental protection. The multivolume official report is due to be published and released in late summer 1988 and will in some ways be a master blueprint for the resurrection of Taiwan's natural beauty and ecology and the long-range protection of the quality of life.
4. One of the best (worst?) places to see this sad state of affairs is to hike along the dike near the Kuantu plain, where the Hsintien and Keelung rivers meet, and see the strewn black rubbish and malodorous waters. It is a depressing testimony to economic "progress."

References

Benedicto, Cindy M. (1987) "High-Tech to Be Used to Fight Problems That High-Tech Caused," *Free China Journal,* September 14.
———. (1988) "The EPA Attacks Air Pollution," *Free China Review* (March): 32–37.
"Billions to Be Spent Importing Equipment to Control Pollution" (1988) *Free China Journal,* January 4.
Brown, Janet Welsh (1988) "Poverty and Environmental Degradation: Basic Concerns for U.S. Cooperation with Developing Countries," proposals from the World Resources Institute for National Conference on Cooperation for International Development: U.S. Policies and Programs for the 1990s, Michigan State University, May 17.

Chang, Chiao-hao (1987a) "New Life for Love River," *Free China Review* (July): 24–29.

———— (1987b) "Pollution Controversies," *Free China Review* (July): 30–35.

Chang, Michael Mau-kuei (1988) "Assessing the Quality of Life" *Free China Review* (March): 24–27. This also appears as "Perceived Life Quality and Social Class in Taiwan," in Yu-ming Shaw, ed., *Reform and Revolution in Twentieth Century China* (Institute of International Relations, Taiwan, 1987).

Chao, Chieh-chien (1986) "Planning in a Market Economy: The Experience of Taiwan, ROC," *Economic Review* (Taiwan), no. 234 (November–December): 1–7.

Chao, Y.T. (1986) "Fostering New Economic Concepts in a Changing Economic Environment," *Economic Review* (Taiwan), no. 234 (November–December): 1–7.

Chen, Wen-tsung (1987) "Reclaiming the Tamsui River," *Free China Review* (July): 10–22.

"Children in North Taiwan Are More Likely to Get Cancer" (1988) *Free China Journal,* May 2.

"Clean Air in Taiwan to Cost Companies Billions, Says EPA" (1988) *Free China Journal,* February 8.

"Cleaner Air Worth Tax Hike to People, New Survey Reveals" (1987) *Free China Journal,* November 9.

"Cleaning the Air" (1987) *Free China Journal,* October 26.

"Control Yuan Members Analyze Pollution Problem" (1986) *China Post,* June 26.

"Crackdown on Unlicensed Factories" (1986) *China Post,* June 9.

Crichton, Tom (1988) "Consumer Rebellion," *Free China Review* (May): 49–53.

Dong, Yu-ching (1985a) "Experts Debate Controversial Fourth Nuclear Power Plant," *Free China Journal,* April 21.

———— (1985b) "Environmental Protection: A Matter of Choice," *Free China Journal,* July 28.

"Du Pont Meeting Does Little to Allay Fears of Factory" (1986) *China Post,* June 26.

Eu, Hunter Han-ting (1986) "An Overview of Environmental Conservation and Engineering Projects in the Republic of China," *Economic Review* (Taiwan), no. 234 (November–December): 8–18.

"G.E. to Negotiate Nuclear Plant Damage" (1986) *Free China Journal,* December 29.

Goldstein, Carl (1985a) "Taiwan's Delayed Reaction," *Far Eastern Economic Review,* January 10: 74–75.

———— (1985b) "Complacency Overpowered," *Far Eastern Economic Review,* August 8: 46–47.

A Guide to the Department of Environmental Protection (1985) Taipei: Municipal Government.

Hsieh, Sam C. (1987) "A Sequential and Integrated Approach to Economic Development," *Economic Review* (Taiwan), no. 235 (January–February): 17–25.

Huddle, Norie, Michael Reich, and Nahum Stiskin (1975) *Island of Dreams: Environmental Crisis in Japan.* New York: Autumn Press.

"Initial Operation Against Illegal Factories Fizzles" (1986) *China Post,* June 9.

"Keeping Taiwan a Beautiful Place to Live Is Winning More Converts" (1986) *Free China Journal,* December 22.

Kuo, Tai-Gong (1986) "Students Help "Uncle Chief Fight Pollution," *Free China Journal,* April 7.

Lew, Williams. (1985) "Concern Grows Over Nuclear Plant Safety," *Free China Jounal,* March 31.

Li, K.T. (1983) "Population Distribution and Quality of Life in Taiwan," *Industry of Free China* (September): 1–24; (October): 17–31.

Liu, Ben-chieh (1980) "Economic Growth and Quality of Life: A Comparative Indicator Analysis Between China (Taiwan), U.S.A., and Other Developed Countries," *The American Journal of Economics and Sociology* 39, no. 1: 1–21.

Miller, G. Tyler (1986) *Environmental Science: An Introduction.* Belmont, CA: Wadsworth Publishing Company.

Moore, Jonathan (1988) "Protests in This Green And Poisoned Land," *Far Eastern Economic Review,* February 25: 44–45.

"Multi-Billion Buck Program to Protect Taiwan Environment" (1987) *Free China Journal,* December 14.

"New Nuclear Plant Planned in ROC to Solve Power Needs" (1987) *Free China Journal,* December 12.

Nickum, James E., and David C. Schak (1979) "Living Standards and Economic Development in Shanghai and Taiwan," *The China Quarterly* 77: 25–49.

"Ninth Medium-Term Economic Development Plan for Taiwan (1986–1989)" (1987) *Economic Review* (Taiwan), no. 235 (January–February): 1–16; no. 236 (March–April): 1–15.

"Nuclear Energy Accident Hinders OK on New Plants" (1986) *Free China Journal,* September 29.

"Nuclear Power Stalemate" (1988) *Free China Journal,* March 7.

"Orchid Island's Radioactive Waste Storage Facility Determined Safe" (1985) *Free China Journal,* September 8.

"Perspective of the Taiwan Economy Up to the Year of 2000" (1987) *Economic Review* (Taiwan), no. 238 (July–August): 4–20; no. 239 (September–October): 620; no. 240 (November–December): 1–11.

"Pollution Control Costs: US $10 Billion over 10 Years" (1986) *Free China Journal,* October 6.

Reardon-Anderson, James (1992) *Pollution, Politics, and Foreign Investment in Taiwan: The Lukang Rebellion.* Armonk, NY: M. E. Sharpe.

Republic of China—A Reference Book (1986) Taipei: Hilit Publishing Company.

"Rice Paddies Now Factories" (1987) *Free China Journal,* November 23.

"ROC Budgeting Millions to Fight Pollution Woes" (1987) *Free China Journal,* September 2.

Selya, Roger Mark (1975) "Water and Air Pollution in Taiwan," *Free Journal of Developing Areas* 9: 177–202.

"Taiwan Postpones Fourth Reactor after Protests" (1988) *Far Eastern Economic Review,* April 7:14.

"Taiwan Warned of Brownouts" (1987) *Free China Journal,* November 23.

"Thousands of Tons of Dust Descend on Taipei Annually" (1985) *China Post,* November 13.

Ting, T.Y., and S. Jou (1988) "Industrial Pollution and the Regional Variations of Life Expectancy at Birth in Taiwan," *Sociological Inquiry* 58, 1: 87–100.

"Too Much of a Good Thing Hurting ROC Food Output" (1987) *Free China Journal,* October 26.

Tsai Hong-chin (1981) "Rural Industrialization in Taiwan: Its Structure and Impact on the Rural Economy," *Industry of Free China* (December): 17–32.

Tsai Hsung-hsiung (1987) "To Achieve a Rational Distribution of Population: The Experience of Taiwan," *Economic Review* (Taiwan), no. 236 (March–April): 16–31.

Tsay, Ching-lung (1986) "Consequences of Population Change for Health Services in Taiwan," *Economic Review* (Taiwan), no. 229 (January–February): 13–28.

Tsiang, S.C. (1986) "Reasons for the Successful Economic Takeoff of Taiwan," *Economic Review* (Taiwan), no. 232 (July–August): 1–20.

"U.S. $1.5 Billion to Be Spent on Air Pollution Prevention" (1985) *Free China Journal,* July 14.

Wang, Scott (1986a) "Unleaded Gas Makes Debut to Tackle Air Pollution," *Free China Journal,* June 16.

———. (1986b) "Huge Plastics Empire Built on Bold Management and Hard Work," *Free China Journal,* November 3.

Williams, Jack F. (1981) "Agricultural Use of Slopelands in Taiwan," in *The China Geographer,* no. 11 (Agriculture), ed. Clifton Pannell and Christopher Salter, pp. 89–111. Boulder, CO: Westview Press.

———. (1988a) "Vulnerability and Change in Taiwan's Agriculture," *Pacific Viewpoint* (May).

———. (1988b) "Urban and Regional Planning in Taiwan," *Tijdschrif Voor Economische En Sociale Geografie,* Fall.

Williams, Jack F., C.Y. Chang, and C.Y. Wang (1983) "Land Settlement and Development: A Case Study from Taiwan," *The Journal of Developing Areas* 18, no. 1: 35–52.

Yu, Kuo-sheng (1988) "Interview: EPA's Chien Yu-hsin," *Free China Review* (March): 34–36.

Chapter 9

The Emergence of an Environmental Consciousness in Taiwan

David W. Chen

Neihu Mountain in northeastern Taipei is one of Taiwan's most famous peaks, not because of its beauty or soaring height, but because of its contents: garbage.

During the 1960s, Taipei's lack of an adequate sanitation system made it all too convenient for local officials to use the Neihu site—which was then a small valley off a major road—as a perfect location for burying household waste. Up and down the island, other communities also tried to find the closest available nook to get rid of their refuse. Yet no public outcries could be heard, for people were more concerned with making ends meet than with caring about how to dispose of their garbage properly.

A decade or so later, however, the Neihu valley had grown into a 200-foot-high heap of foul, unsightly waste. Nearby residents, no longer worried about providing for their families because of their increased wealth, began to pinch their noses and complain. A few opportunistic politicians sided with the locals and mugged for the media cameras. After relentless pressure, authorities finally closed the mountain in 1985 and announced cleanup plans.

Today the mountain still stands, half-covered with garbage, half-covered with grass and mango trees, juxtaposing Taiwan's past problems and future hopes.[1] Unfortunately, though, Taiwan's garbage situation represents only a fraction of the island's environmental woes. Officially Taiwan's air is considered "harmful" one out of every five or six days, but many visitors to Taipei or Kaohsiung, the island's two biggest cities, swear that the air quality is never "good." Vehicular density in Taipei, to take one measure of the problem, is ten times higher than it is in Los Angeles.[2] Yet escaping the city by car can also have dire environmental consequences: the expanding network of roads necessitates more land, which often

---

This chapter was previously circulated as an Institute Report of the East Asian Institute, Columbia University, April, 1991.

means more deforestation. Even the more remote areas are vulnerable. Almost all of Taiwan's rivers are polluted, leaving little for recreational swimmers and fishermen to cheer about. In addition, the muck and trash in rivers and lakes are depleting the oxygen in the water by a process called eutrophication, which suffocates the fish and affects the food chain.[3] That Taiwan is the world's second most densely populated nation, after Bangladesh, only compounds and exacerbates these dilemmas.

There is, however, one positive and rather ironic note coming out of this squeeze: more people have been forced, out of sheer proximity, to become aware of their deteriorating surroundings. Recent public opinion polls provide some telling statistics. In one 1983 poll, people listed the environment as the sixth most serious social problem; by 1986, it was first.[4] A separate 1988 survey found environmental pollution as the second most important issue facing the government, behind social order and ahead of political liberalization.[5]

Despite these figures, however, the emergence of an environmental consciousness has been a recent phenomenon. And while environmental issues have begun to be addressed, albeit belatedly, on the national level, they may become diluted by other social concerns on an already crammed national agenda. If Taiwan is to resolve its mounting environmental concerns, activists say, more cooperation and action are needed from government officials, businesspeople, and ordinary citizens.

The Costs of Rapid Industrialization

The island had hardly any of these problems when the Kuomintang arrived in 1949, after being crushed by Communist forces on mainland China. Actually, the island didn't have much of anything. Scant natural resources confronted a mostly poor and illiterate population. Desperate, and determined to make the best of less-than-ideal circumstances, the government advocated all-out economic development in the 1950s and 1960s and launched ambitious land reform programs.

The results have been well documented. Taiwan has experienced unparalleled economic growth in making the transition from an agricultural society to an industrial one. Diseases associated with poverty, including tuberculosis, malaria, and cholera, "have all but disappeared as major causes of death."[6] Per capita GNP is soon expected to surpass $8,000, a level achieved by Great Britain in the early 1980s. Taiwan's trade surplus exceeds $10 billion; its foreign exchange reserves amount to $75 billion, the world's largest. In 1989 the Taipei stock market ranked as the world's third busiest in volume, behind New York and Tokyo—despite being open only six half-days a week.[7]

Until recently, however, these achievements could not be matched by any substantive political gains. In 1949 President Chiang Kai-shek declared martial law, effectively stripping people of basic liberties. Some of those freedoms were nominally restored in time, but with no legal opposition, the island's one-party and mainlander-dominated regime turned into an "authoritarian" and "development-oriented" government with a "top-down policy-making process." Party politics, not public opinion, guided the nation's direction. Instead of encouraging political liberalization in step with economic development, Chiang and the KMT government worried primarily about a Communist invasion and sought to clamp down on native Taiwanese resentment.[8] The government's monopoly on the media further hindered any chance for healthy debate or dissent. Yet many citizens did not seem to mind—at least openly—since they were presumably too occupied with family and work. And so by the 1980s, more than thirty years of martial law had conditioned many Taiwan residents to accept government policy and ignore political rhetoric.[9] Politics, after all, could not interfere with economic drive.

The combination of unchecked economic development and political lethargy eventually took its toll on something everyone took for granted: Mother Nature. With bigger pocketbooks leading to bigger appetites for consumption, people have been producing more trash than ever, almost two pounds a day. At present, 17 percent of that rubbish is comprised of nonbiodegradable plastics; in the United States, the figure is 7 percent.[10] Even more alarming, 87 percent of household garbage (much of which is wet and inflammable) still ends up in Taiwan's one hundred or so open landfills, and less than 1 percent of human excrement receives primary sewage treatment. Small wonder, then, that Taiwan has the world's highest rate of hepatitis B.[11]

The environmental record of industries and businesses is equally abysmal. In the past, the absence of tough and enforceable pollution regulations or a strong-armed watchdog agency often led to incessant polluting. Factories, whose numbers grew by an annual rate of 7.5 percent in the 1980s, belched wastes into the water, the air, and the earth, almost at will and without any governmental reproach.[12] That the economy grew by 7.1 percent in 1988, for instance, was marred by a 20 percent rise in pollution.[13] In Keelung, a northern port city, scientists recently discovered an inordinate quantity of lead in the soil, because of years of accumulated waste spewed out by the Hsin-Yeh Metal Company.[14] Worst of all, these cases may be but a sneak preview of how much nature has been abused; recently, the government admitted that it did not even know how much industrial waste was still being churned out.[15] The price of progress has been steep, indeed.

Although there was little manifest concern for the environment before the 1980s, there was some attention being given to a related area: nuclear power. While the government was going full speed ahead in advocating nuclear power as an efficient means of providing more energy to a rapidly industrializing country, an increasing number of scientists and intellectuals began to lodge objections as early as the 1960s.

But no organized opposition movement jelled until after a series of accidents in the late 1970s and early 1980s. To begin with, the nuclear accident at Three Mile Island near Harrisburg, Pennsylvania, coincided with the completion of the Taiwan Power Company's (Taipower) first nuclear power plant in 1978, prompting some academics to question whether a TMI-like disaster could be repeated on Taiwan. The accidental death of a worker in 1982 at one of the nuclear power plants did nothing to mitigate these fears. Then, in 1985, an explosion and fire "triggered by a loose blade in the stream turbine, designed and supplied by the General Electric Co. of the United States," occurred in Taiwan's third plant and lasted for three hours.[16] Luckily, no leakage was recorded.

What generated more controversy than any of these mini-accidents was Taipower's 271 percent budget increase proposal in 1984. Even some government officials argued against such a large increase; the money could be better spent elsewhere, they said. Taipower's planned fourth nuclear power plant in Taipei County's Kungliao Village only hardened opponents, who argued that having three plants in one, heavily populated area (Taipei) was a dangerous idea. With the exception of the KMT-run *Central Daily News,* Taiwan's normally prodevelopment newspapers also articulated antinuclear positions. Even though antinuclear groups did not enjoy a widespread popular base, they managed to make some headlines.[17] At first, these opposition views seemed to reflect more of a concern for self-interests than any concern for the environment. Some people, for instance, objected to nuclear power because they feared it would render Taiwan even more dependent on American technology. Others sought an opportunity to criticize Taipower and the government; one person dismissed Taipower's bid to build the fourth plant as "an excuse to make more money."[18] People living near the plants were equally critical: they accused Taipower and the Ministry of Economic Affairs (MOEA) of making arbitrary decisions without consulting any local residents.[19]

Scientists also raised doubts about the feasibility of more nuclear power. Radiation experts and chemical engineers criticized the temporary solution of storing high-level wastes in coolant reactors on plant sites. In addition, seismologists and meteorologists warned that a severe earthquake or typhoon—two common events in Taiwan—could have devastating effects. "If there's an earthquake," said Professor Lin Wu-nan, "you can say, 'Kiss your baby goodbye.' "[20]

These claims were largely ignored by government officials and unknown to most lay people until April 1986, when one incident thousands of miles away frightened just about everyone in Taiwan: Chernobyl. Reports of death, disease, and contamination in the Soviet Union and Eastern Europe were especially hard to swallow in Taiwan, because of the extrapolated fear of a similar catastrophe happening on such a small island.[21]

Chernobyl offered an excellent opportunity for antinuclear activists to drive home their warnings. Not only did they take the advantage, they began to blend in environmental concerns to make their arguments more appealing to the general public. "We are not against nuclear power," said one opponent, "but against the dangers to humans, animals, and plants caused by nuclear power."[22] Some people also spread widely believed rumors that much of Taiwan's nuclear waste was being used to manufacture nuclear weapons.[23] Large antinuclear rallies in

Taipei and Yenliao in April 1987 marking the one-year anniversary of Chernobyl demonstrated just how effective these efforts had been. Eventually these protests were loud enough to force the Executive Yuan to announce the temporary shelving of projects to construct more plants.

Those who were involved with environmental issues—and there were not that many yet—took the hint as well and began to align themselves more with the antinuclear movement. Environmentally oriented magazines like the *New Environment* also started to report more stories on nuclear power. Public concern for environmental issues grew until, in 1986, an environmental protection plank was included in most party platforms during that year's elections.[24] In tag-teaming with the stronger antinuclear movement, the environmental movement itself gained considerable muscle.

Political Liberalization and Environmental Protest

Conservationists began to flex this new power in a rash of protests after 1986. In June 1986, in what is now generally acknowledged as the first major grass-roots environmental protest in Taiwan, hundreds of people in Lukang broke through a police cordon and marched through the town in opposition to Du Pont's proposed $168 million chemical factory. Even though street demonstrations were banned under martial law, Lukang residents were defiant. More rallies occurred two months later, during which police detained for six hours some 270 Lukang citizens, many of whom wore T-shirts with such slogans as "I Love Taiwan But Want No Part of Du Pont." In December 400 Lukang residents marched again, this time in Taipei.[25] For one thing, these protesters were determined to preserve the historic flavor of Lukang, Taiwan's second oldest town.[26] More important, the demonstrations signaled the fact that "people were no longer prepared to put up with pollution, which spewed freely into the rivers and the air during the island's rapid industrialization in the 1960s and 1970s."[27] As for Du Pont, despite efforts to convince local residents that the chemical factory would not be hazardous, the company eventually backed down and announced that it would look elsewhere in Taiwan for an appropriate site.

Subsequent protests in other areas of Taiwan manifested how volatile and emotional some residents had become over newly discovered environmental dangers. In October 1988 Linyuan denizens attributed livestock deaths to water pollution from the Linyuan Industrial Zone and its eighteen petrochemical plants and two naptha crackers. Weeks of vocal protests ensued. But some residents became so incensed with industry's apparent indifference that they stormed their way into the control rooms of several plants and started pressing buttons and hitting switches. Plant employees could do little but watch and hope that no damage would be done to the equipment. Fortunately, the protesters did not trip on any wires or flick any wrong switches. But to calm the situation, the Ministry of Economic Affairs later agreed to pay about $10 million to the affected families.[28] At the same time, the officials from the MOEA and other government agencies implied that the government would consider using military action in future crises, to preserve safety and order.[29]

This veiled threat did not deter others from clamoring for a cleaner environment or for compensation for past industrial excesses. In 1988 inhabitants of Hungmao, a port near Kaohsiung, demanded that Taipower stop a coal facility because of dust pollution. The facility was temporarily shut off, and Hungmao residents were awarded a tidy $250 million settlement. A few months later, people in nearby Nanwan, perhaps impressed by the precedents in Linyuan and Hungmao, complained about a nuclear power facility's dumping of hot water.[30]

The protests were not confined to onshore sites, either. On Lanyu (Orchid) Island off Taiwan's southern coast, the fusion of antinuclear and environmental interests was never more in evidence as a group of islanders, made up mostly of students, marched against Taipower's storage of low-level nuclear waste near their homes.[31] In July 1989 a group of fishermen blocked Kaohsiung harbor, accusing the Monomer Corporation of discarding acid waste closer to the coastline than regulations allowed, thereby poisoning fishing grounds.[32] Everywhere, it seemed, people were crying "Foul!" against polluters.

In 1990 the most vehement local antipollution movement targeted the state-run China Petroleum Company, which planned to place the island's fifth naptha cracker in the Houching district, near Kaohsiung. Whereas company officials promised that the fifth plant would be much cleaner than the island's first few crackers and called the plant "absolutely essential" to Taiwan's economic survival, local residents were not buying it. During one demonstration on January 13, 1990, hundreds surrounded the company's headquarters, waving banners that said, "We Pledge to Fight the Fifth Naptha Cracker to the Death!"[33]

Had these protests taken place a decade earlier, or even five years earlier, they most likely would have been stamped out or simply ignored. But several factors accompanying Taiwan's modernization have propelled these as well as other social protests.

Thanks in part to an increasingly free and active press, the Taiwanese have become more aware of national affairs. Although television stations remain under government control, most newspapers have begun to assert their independence, and therefore have started to expand their operations and publish bolder stories.[34] For instance, media coverage of the controversial cleanup plans for two of Taiwan's worst-stinking rivers, the Tamsui in Taipei and the Love in Kaohsiung, garnered more publicity than had been anticipated.[35] Despite skepticism about how concerned the people were about pollution and other social issues, several polls, including the above-mentioned two on environmental concerns, suggested that at least overall ignorance was disappearing. In a disturbing 1983 survey, 46.2 percent of those polled did not even know that Taiwan had nuclear power plants; three years later, that number had been sliced to 19.3 percent.[36] Slowly, people were coming to realize that the environment was "the necessary material foundation for health, wealth, and enjoyment of life."[37]

The late President Chiang Ching-kuo's lifting of martial law in July 1987 further stimulated Taiwan's social development. Even though some activists had already defied the ban on street demonstrations, many more probably held back for fear of arrest. With martial law now spoken of in the past tense, anyone had a legal chance to air out some of his or her pent-up feelings. Apparently, people were so ecstatic about feeling psychologically unburdened that within one year Taiwan joined the Philippines as two of the world's hottest spots for street demonstrations. In Taiwan, there was an average of three rallies a day, with at least one of them focusing on environmental issues.[38] No martial law did not mean that Taiwan residents automatically enjoyed unlimited freedoms, but it was an important step forward.

As Taiwan inched toward becoming a more open society, the KMT's stranglehold on power gradually loosened. The opposition Democratic Progressive party (DPP) picked up considerable strength in the mid-1980s, as its mostly native Taiwanese members sounded pro-Taiwan and anticorruption themes. The DPP also linked itself with the antinuclear and conservation movements by sporting a green flag and supporting proenvironmental publications and rallies. Environmental pollution, went one popular DPP slogan, was mainly the doing of the KMT.[39] In the landmark December 1989 elections, some of these messages probably contributed to the DPP's gains: the party gathered more than 30 percent of the popular vote and snatched the all-important Taipei county executive seat away from the KMT. Much to the satisfaction of green activists, the new county chief, You Ching, was on record as being against the construction of the fourth nuclear power plant and being an avid environmentalist.[40]

The tide of democratization opened the gate to people trying to articulate their passions. Some voted with their emotions; others took the streets. "Social movements are not completely new to Taiwan," said Hsiao Hsin-huang, a sociologist at the Academia Sinica, "but in the past they were either masked by or only operated through approved institutions."[41] Before long, a myriad of impromptu social movements had erupted, involving issues such as farmers' rights, labor inequality, aboriginal rights, women's rights, consumers, and affordable housing.[42] The only notable absentee was the Taiwan Independence Movement, which was—and still is—considered subversive by the KMT government.

The Government's Response

No longer could the government ignore or underestimate the pressure from many different factions "to improve the quality of life on the island."[43] Faced with scores of pressing problems, the government took a first step in August 1987, when it beefed up its own infrastructure by transforming and upgrading the Bureau of Environmental Protection, previously an underfunded and understaffed office buried in the Department of Health, into the cabinet-level Environmental Protection Administration (EPA).[44] The government even provided the

EPA with a new ten-story building in downtown Taipei. The following year, the Taiwan provincial government and twelve other local administrations established their own environmental protection offices.[45] In addition, several conservation groups with government ties were established, including the Society for Wildlife and Nature (SWAN), which publishes a newsletter and *Nature,* a colorful quarterly magazine.[46] Though late, the government nevertheless had made a start.

To get even more people involved with nature—and to generate some favorable publicity—the EPA promoted education as one of the keys to a better and cleaner society. Television stations began, in conjunction with the EPA, to produce short commercials on how to throw away garbage and how to scold those who did not care about their environment. Similar shorts were introduced in movie theaters, too, sharing the spotlight with the singing of the national anthem. The EPA helped sponsor a television series on environmental protection, "The Earth Changes," and it mapped out a ten-year program to educate children and teachers.[47] The government did not have much financial difficulty in launching the ten-year program or any of its other environmental campaigns. And while critics have accused the government of not spending enough money on environmental research, the statistics do show that the EPA's overall budget has increased markedly since its founding. The 1990 budget, for instance, was 20 times greater than that of 1987. All told, the EPA plans on spending about $35 billion by the year 2000.[48] Some developers have grumbled about this price tag, but as Chao Shao-kang, the popular legislator, rebutted: "The question of money cannot be compared with the importance of life. Can money buy health?"[49]

The well-funded EPA has begun to tackle, on paper, many of Taiwan's worst environmental nightmares. In terms of general preliminary measures, the EPA has conducted over a hundred Environmental Impact Assessment (EIA) studies and has promised to complete even more in the 1990s. One broad, sweeping program is Project Rambo, which combats midnight dumping, the discharge of waste water, air emissions, and other violations.[50]

To reduce the garbage problem, the EPA has invested heavily in sanitary landfill technology and incinerating equipment. Most of Taipei City's refuse, for instance, is stored at the Futekeng Sanitary Landfill in the Mucha District; by "sanitary," the Taiwan authorities refer to the use of layered plastic barriers between the trash and the earth reinforced by clay, and the use of sophisticated monitoring equipment.[51] Since Taiwan has little space, though, there is a limit to using landfills, hence the move toward incineration. Even though some scientists warn that incineration is not the panacea to garbage mountains and valleys, EPA officials point to Japan and Europe as examples, where more than 50 percent of the solid waste is buried. By 1995, the EPA hopes to build twelve waste-to-energy incinerators; by 2000, a dozen more.[52]

Several projects are also on the drawing board to purify Taiwan's murky waters. According to a United States Department of State telegram, Taiwan plans on spending a lot of money over the next twenty years to improve its sewage system.[53] As for Taiwan's rivers, government officials assert that the rehabilitative process is under way. To give three examples: the government has allocated $1 billion to the Tamsui River reclamation project in order to construct sewerage, interceptor, and ocean outfall systems; $40 million to drinking water quality improvement problems; and $25 million to the Chi-sui Creek-to-Ocean discharge project.[54]

Until those projects are implemented, though, the most obvious problem is Taiwan's air pollution. The stench from Taiwan's open landfills and polluted waters has certainly contributed to the unpleasant atmosphere, but EPA officials point out that the air is fouled by many different pollutants: What is needed, they say, is a more scientific and comprehensive survey of air pollution sources.[55] Upon finishing this inventory, the EPA plans to take more concrete action, including the imposition of tougher, new vehicle emissions standards. One policy already under way is the gradual phasing out of leaded gasoline. Industry resistance notwithstanding, EPA personnel hope that within a few years Taiwan's cars only run on unleaded premium.[56] If not, Taiwan's air may be declared hazardous to everyone's health.

The drawback to the high visibility of Taiwan's garbage, water, and air troubles is the likelihood that other urgent problems, like soil despoilation, toxic wastes, and noise pollution, may get shoved aside. EPA Administrator Chien You-hsin has admitted, for example, that no law yet exists to control the amount of pollutants sinking into the soil.[57] For toxic chemicals, the EPA has only scratched the surface, spending a paltry $1.5 million to establish a toxic chemical information system and investigate toxic chemical distribution. A larger sum ($9 million) has been set aside for a traffic noise-monitoring network project, but this seems small given the fact that noise pollution is the biggest source of citizen complaints.[58]

To convince citizens of its sincerity in implementing these projects, the government has been attempting to soften its probusiness image. "Our policy is 'polluters pay,'" said Joseph Yang, an EPA adviser. "Industries that generate waste will pay to protect the environment."[59] Although the government's enforcement capabilities are weak, there have been a few positive signs. In cases where offending companies constantly appeal legal decisions, the EPA has paid for newspaper advertisements censuring the polluters, thereby making the companies "lose face."[60] Even Chen Li-an, the conservative and almost always probusiness minister of defense (and former minister of economic affairs), has said that new factories must meet environmental protection standards.[61]

But to appease industry, some government officials have also offered incentives to businesses to meet these tougher requirements. For instance, low-interest loans have been made available for medium and small companies—which make up more than 90 percent of all Taiwan companies—to purchase pollution control equipment.[62] As a bonus, the EPA has marketed environmental protection in the language businesses know and love: profits. According to one EPA adviser, Taiwan invites "businesses and consultants to develop and design management and technical systems for environmental protection."[63]

There have been a fistful of encouraging responses so far. According to Ma Wen-shung, director of the Safety and Health Program at Union Chemical Laboratories in Hsinchu, some industries have earnestly begun to research environmental issues, "realizing that a clean country is everyone's business." "It's not that industry is so evil," claims Ma, "it's just that twenty years ago, we had little knowledge of environmental protection."[64] In the area of garbage, the recently founded Taiwan Recycling Corporation is building a plant to recycle plastic bottles. A new biodegradable plate made of wheat may further reduce the volume of nonbiodegradable trash. According to the inventor, Chen Liang-san, these plates may initially be more expensive than the styrofoam *bian dang* lunch boxes now used, but they are better for the environment—and edible, too.[65]

Despite Chen's initiative and industry's claims, reaction from most businesses has been tepid. Less than 3 percent of private-sector capital is spent on pollution control; in Japan, the figure is about 15 percent.[66] Perhaps in the most telling sign of industrial neglect, China Petroleum (applying for the fifth naptha cracker) and Taipower (applying for the fourth nuclear power plant) are the top two polluters among state-run companies, between them accounting for more than 80 percent of all environmental violations.[67] With statistics like this, it is not surprising that industrial promises to meet environmental standards are greeted with cynicism. To accomplish any real progress requires much more private-sector investment.

Beyond the lack of genuine commitment, the shortage of industrial input to environmental protection can also be explained by the fact that the technology is simply not yet available domestically. But Taiwan needs the technology, and needs it now. The short-term solution? The Taiwanese have looked overseas for assistance. "We do not have any local companies which are qualified to provide these materials," confirmed Yuan Shau-ying of the EPA's Solid Waste Control Bureau, "so we expect many foreign companies will come in to help us out."[68] To entice foreign aid, Taiwan has also packaged waste management as a profitable business. In a meeting outlining some of Taiwan's major projects to some prospective foreign businessmen, for example, the closing message was: "God Luck and Welcome to a Promising Industry—We Need Your Help."[69] So far, the Japanese and the Americans have taken the early lead in securing waste management contracts. For instance, Takuma, a leading Japanese manufacturer of incinerators and water-treatment plants, won a $35.6 million bid for Taiwan's first incinerator to be located, fittingly, in Neihu.[70]

A Comparative Evaluation

Taiwan's reliance on the expertise and experience of the world's two most powerful economies should come as no surprise. Many Taiwan students have enrolled in American graduate programs, for instance, in order to absorb environmental management techniques, scientific know-how, and public policy. Younger students, too, are being groomed to be channeled into the same pipeline. In some circles, the joke is that Taiwan sends some of its most promising students overseas for a crash course in how to avert environmental disaster. But in all seriousness, Taiwan's situation is not unprecedented; in fact, it frighteningly parallels Japan's environmental problems of two generations ago.

As Japan recovered from World War II, its people contributed to a frenzied economic boom that quickly taxed the nation's resources and damaged the environment. With few policing mechanisms in place, the transition from agriculture to industry left in its wake a land littered with trash, rivers clouded by industrial waste, and air clogged by smog. According to political scientist David Apter, "The lack of effective due process in Japan—the inadequacy of consultative mechanisms outside of elite circles and the failure of local government to represent local interests—cannot be separated from the visible effects of economic growth, which in the name of progress resulted in pollution [and] environmental disaster."[71]

By the late 1950s, local protests had sprung up in the worst affected areas. Fishermen spearheaded much of the opposition, claiming that Japan's rivers had become too polluted. These voices, though, were originally snubbed by government and business leaders. The fishermen and other affected people were not shocked with this reaction, for the powerful ruling party, the Liberal Democratic party (LDP), practiced "corrupt and manipulative politics" and was beholden to "big business and to the United States."[72]

As would happen in Taiwan twenty years later, a number of high-profile environmental cases catalyzed even stronger protests. In Japan, fishermen and conservationists associated pollution with a dramatic rise in the number of victims affected by industrial diseases. The best-known, Minamata disease, was discovered in Minamata City, Kyushu, in 1956. Among other symptoms, the disease caused tremors, sensory disturbance, and paralysis; death was not uncommon as well. Even though some industrialists tried to blame the fish for the disease, researchers at Kumamoto University disproved this ridiculous theory and stated that the cause was the "consumption of seafood contaminated by methyl mercury released in industrial effluent."[73] Local residents were incensed with the findings. On October 17, 1959, some 1,500 fishermen forced their way into the river-poisoning Chisso Corporation plant in Minamata to demand indemnification for damages to the local fishing industry. A few months later, the Minamata fishery association commenced a two-month sit-in demonstration at Chisso's front gate.[74] From all appearances, an environmental movement had been born.

Many high-ranking officials proved resistant to change, though. Underscoring the "close and mutually interlocking relations of cooperation between Japanese industry and government,"[75] many of Minamata's top officials—including the mayor and the speaker of the Municipal Assembly—appealed to Kosaku Teramoto, the Kumamoto Prefecture governor, to permit the Chisso Corporation to continue dumping effluent. According to the officials, closing down Chisso,

Minimata's largest company, would cripple the city's economy. Police mobilization was then requested to deter violence and to ensure regular day-to-day business.[76] Hoping to ease tensions, Governor Teramoto agreed in April 1960 to mediate the dispute, and convinced the fishermen to end their sit-in and meet with Chisso officials to hammer out a settlement.

But the Minimata demonstrations were only the beginning. Eugene Smith's widely circulated, gruesome photographs of Minimata disease victims coupled with the reports of more deadly industrial diseases, like the Itai-Itai (Ouch! Ouch!) and PCB poisoning maladies, swayed public opinion toward the conservationist camp. That the air over Tokyo and other metropolises was turning into a thick, black smog only convinced more people of the dire straits their nation had fallen into.[77] Toward the end of the 1960s, opinion polls consistently showed a "dramatic rise in public concern about pollution." At times, that concern took on a pessimistic, even Doomsday-sounding tone. The question of whether environmental pollution was "an irreversible trend" lingered on many people's minds. "It is no exaggeration," went a typical remark, "to say that the most critical issue facing the human race today is the increasing destruction of the environment."[78]

The first Earth Day in April 1970 proved to be a rallying point for global environmental concerns. Started by a group of college students in the United States, the demonstrations aimed to galvanize environmental awareness and railroad legislative action. In Japan, Earth Day activists eventually forced the government to establish an Environmental Agency in 1971. Their enthusiasm proved to be contagious. By 1973, more than 1,420 environmental groups had been founded, urging recycling, environmental education, and the efficient utilization of Japan's precious resources.[79]

Due in part to grass-roots pressures, the Japanese government grudgingly allocated large slices of the budget pie to clean up its own backyard. By 1986, Japan had accumulated expertise, improved its technology, and cooperated with other nations in stiffening pollution standards. To take one example, the 1984 level of carbon monoxide in the atmosphere had shrunk to half of the 1965 level. Nevertheless, serious problems still remain, including filthy beaches, rapid deforestation, and more smog. But at least Japan has achieved some success in staving off environmental disaster.

That Taiwan seems to be "following the same path as Japan, in terms of agriculture and pollution,"[80] does not bode well for conservationists. The only solace they can find is the fact that Japan's environmental problems in the 1950s and 1960s were "much more serious"[81] than Taiwan's current ones.

In comparison with other Asian countries, though, Taiwan's condition is not that bad. In most developing countries, after all, the first priority is to create more wealth, even at the expense of environmental quality.[82] Economic development is still "Job One." Across the Taiwan Strait, China has the dubious distinction of having three of the world's ten most polluted cities.[83] Some other countries in the Asia-Pacific region have better track records, but not by much. In Malaysia, "environmentalism does not rank high with the government although it is becoming more accepted," said Gurmit Singh, president of the Environmental Protection Society of Malaysia, an independent NGO.[84] Even Taiwan's fellow newly industrializing countries (NICs) are lagging behind. Hong Kong's probusiness government has for the most part ignored its polluted harbor, while in South Korea, local residents have been too distracted by years of political and social upheaval to devote enough energy to environmental causes.[85]

Obstacles to More Effective Action

Unlike some of the Southeast Asian countries, Taiwan can pretty much scribble out a blank check to cover its environmental costs. But promises, plans, and a big bank account do not necessarily translate into action. In a sense, Taiwan is experiencing the pains of environmental adolescence, for it faces numerous technical, political, social, legal, and economic obstacles in trying to clean up its surroundings.

Inexperience, for one, has occasionally hampered some of the EPA's best-intentioned plans. The average employee age at the EPA is under 35; most of those in charge of major projects are fresh Ph.D.s who have just returned from five or more years of studying abroad.[86] Expecting these men and women to evaluate Taiwan's environmental problems immediately—no doubt the Taiwan they left is not the same now—may be too much to ask. To make up for the deficiency in technical and professional experience, the government often imports foreign experts or near-experts for policy recommendations and planning. But as EPA Administrator Chien You-hsin explained: "Thirty years of economic progress are all coming down at us at once; all the leftover problems are for us. We are quite late, and we are tying to make up for lost time."[87]

In trying to make up that time, however, the EPA can be a bit impatient, according to some analysts. The EPA's problem-solving approaches to water pollution and garbage disposal, for instance, have been called shortsighted and scientifically unsound. Some people doubt the effectiveness of the plastic layering in sanitary landfills; one consultant compared the landfill technique to burying two huge Hefty bags.[88] The EPA's eagerness to incinerate has also been questioned, since burning plastics and batteries releases PCBs, dioxins, and other toxins.[89] According to one Taipei environmental engineering consultant, "the government here looks upon incinerators as a magic bullet that can help them avoid dealing with nasty political battles over landfill siting."[90]

Indeed, politics seems to be inextricable from the environment. Internationally, Taiwan is isolated because of the China-Taiwan political conflict, and is thus prevented from joining important organizations such as the Worldwide Fund for Nature and the United Nations. Domestically, the EPA has come under fire for thinking politics first, environment second. The EPA head, Chien You-hsin, is a former Legislative Yuan member with close connections with the KMT but very little formal environmental training. One of Chien's top advisers, Joseph Yang, has a Ph.D. degree in computer science. And during the December 1989 elections, EPA employees were encouraged to go out and campaign for KMT candidates.[91] So despite the EPA's public relations efforts, a number of people wonder about the sincerity of the government's green thumb. At a 1988 public policy conference, for instance, a citizen complained that the EPA would often notify companies before a pollution inspection, thereby giving the companies time to clean up.[92] Political arguments continue, but they have done nothing but hinder environmental progress.

The close relationship between politics and the environment goes beyond the EPA and leads to a disturbing question: How sincere is official support? All over the world, being green is now viewed as being politically correct; even President George Bush, who made millions as an oil man, had the political sense and chutzpah to label himself the "environmental president." In Taiwan, the message is no different. Public figures who emphasize the importance of the environment are in a no-lose situation. During the December 1989 elections, the environment became sort of a nonissue, because both KMT and DPP candidates claimed to be the original nature lovers. But after the votes were tabulated, some legislators suffered political amnesia and flip-flopped on controversial issues such as the fifth naptha cracker and the fourth nuclear power plants.[93] To cynics, many politicians are merely paying lip service to the environment.[94]

Those who are genuine about their concerns for the environment, however, must face another daunting obstacle—the bureaucracy. Whereas other agencies, like the Ministry of Economic Affairs and the Ministry of Defense, share a significant portion of "centrally allocated budgets for environmental protection," coordination on projects is often difficult.[95] The tendency to deflect responsibility onto others is manifested in the regulations and laws governing the management of chemicals, where "nowhere is it specified clearly which department is responsible for handling problems or complaints arising from the mismanagement of chemicals."[96]

Taiwan's muddled and ineffective legal system has only complicated this bureaucracy. In the past, "the few laws that existed were poorly written and not enforced."[97] With a judiciary often accused of corruption and known to base decisions more on *guanxi* (personal relationships) than on statutes, environmental activists have long cried for an overhaul of the entire system. Frank government officials acknowledge that there are "weak environmental regulations" and that the judiciary "should be strengthened."[98]

Although political and legal hassles are big headaches, the biggest obstacle in the drive toward environmental action may be the perception that environmental momentum retards economic development. The two terms are not necessarily mutually exclusive; some foreign firms that have set up shop in Taiwan are "sensitive to public opinion" and try to produce environmentally efficient goods.[99] But the impression of incompatibility remains—and many politicians and industrialists are not willing to tinker with economic advancement. Premier Hau Po-tsun, for one, hardly ever mentions environmental issues in his speeches. And Defense Minister Chen Li-an has long pushed for the construction of the fourth nuclear power plant, calling it vital for "economic development and energy needs."[100]

The litmus test for the political battle between the developers and the greens may be Wang Yung-ching, the billionaire head of the Formosa Plastics Corporation. For many years, Wang has been stymied in his attempts to build a naptha cracker plant in Taiwan; wherever he goes, he hears boos and protests. His short-term remedy has been to look overseas for plants. In the United States, Wang plans on constructing a $2.1 billion rayon factory in Baton Rouge, Louisiana, and a $1.7 billion ethylene dichloride plant in Texas.[101] To developers, Wang embodies hard work, good business sense, and progress; to environmentalists, he symbolizes the cold-hearted industrialist bent on polluting for profit.

What stirred the most controversy, though, was Wang's January 1990 visit to mainland China—without government permission. Wang did not formally invest in any factories or enunciate any specific plans, but his actions forced a political scramble to reevaluate national goals. Would direct mainland investment be tolerated? Would Wang's actions be interpreted as a sign of Taiwan's increasingly flexible foreign policy? Would Wang be admonished for his behavior? The last question was least likely to be answered in the affirmative, since the petrochemical industry accounts for 38 percent of Taiwan's industrial output, and Wang's Formosa Plastics Group dominates the petrochemical sector.[102] The others were trickier. Though Taiwan President Lee Teng-hui said that Wang's trip was "no big deal,"[103] some politicians and businessmen worried that other big industrialists would also pull out of Taiwan and send feelers to the mainland. Most officials rode the fence, taking a wait-and-see attitude.

One other major element emerged from the controversial visit: the question of whether economic development was worth sacrificing for a cleaner environment. Wang made it clear time and again that Taiwan's worsening investment climate, attributable to "the labor movement and environmental consciousness," compelled him to look elsewhere. He implied, too, that if the government failed to curb environmentalists and restore "traditional work ethics," he would gladly invest in mainland China.[104] Despite the political delicacy of such an action, the mainland attracted Wang because of the dirt-cheap labor and the nonexistence of tough environmental regulations. With other industrial conglomerates like Yuen Foong Yu Paper already planting themselves in Southeast Asia, Wang may be itching to regain the competitive edge. "Now that he's missed the boat in Southeast Asia," said Taipei petrochemical consultant Wang Wen-po, "the mainland represents his last chance to go on polluting and still retain his market share."[105]

As if Wang Yung-ching and economic development were not enough to block environmental action, there are many other important tasks facing government and society. Chiefly, the wild speculation governing Taiwan's frenetic stock and real estate markets is driving prices through the roof. Since 1986, real estate prices have jumped up by more than 163 percent; stocks have gone up even more. Over the last year, stock prices have tumbled and fluctuated, but people are still finding sources of wild speculation. Waves of people have no doubt become instant millionaires, but others have not been as lucky. Finding affordable housing is almost impossible, as thousands demonstrated by participating in August 1989's "Snails without Shells" all-night vigil on Chung Hsiao East Road, the most expensive stretch of real estate in Taiwan.[106] The side effects of speculation have affected the environment as well. In the cities, the real estate craze has baited builders to prop up aesthetically displeasing, architecturally unsound, and energy-inefficient buildings. Construction also produces dust exhaust pollution. Out in the suburbs, most local contractors have little professional knowledge about how to develop slopelands; the usual method is to strip an entire area of trees and ground cover before building a house.[107]

For its part, the government has hardly budged. According to Chiang Ching-sen, a doctoral candidate at National Taiwan University's Graduate Institute of Building and Planning. "The ROC government and parliamentarians have done almost nothing, allowing property speculation to go unchecked for the last three years. They use the excuse that the operation of a free market should not suffer any interference. So the situation deteriorates."[108]

The situation for public housing is no better, as it accounts for only 5 percent of the local housing supply—far behind the percentages in Hong Kong and Singapore.[109] Various interest groups have formed, however, to press for housing reforms.

Taiwan's crowded conditions have intensified some of the island's other needs and wants. Although not everyone has an affordable apartment, more and more people are demanding the convenient trappings of modern society. Leisure time, for instance, is becoming more prized. For the Taiwanese, one of the best ways to relax—and to show off—is playing golf at one of the island's thirty or so courses. With skyrocketing land prices, golf courses have become a good investment as well; forty-six more links are in the planning stages. But even on the greens and in the bunkers developers must tangle with conservationists. Environmentalists worry that courses are taking away too much of Taiwan's land. What's more, the chemicals used to clear weeds may threaten the local water supply and upset local ecosystems.[110] Thus far the anti–golf course movement has only offered nominal resistance, but hopes to make up the handicap in the next year or so.

Less enjoyable signs of change have also emerged. Taiwan continues to suck up energy at record rates. Traffic remains clogged in the major cities, despite government promises to fine more motorists. The Taipei subway system is far from completion, but already subway operation offices have been jammed with complaints over noisy construction and cost overruns. More serious, crime—

especially money-related crimes such as robbery and kidnapping—has escalated at an alarming clip. In 1989 kidnappers held the son of shipping magnate Chang Yung-fa hostage for a multimillion dollar ransom, until police cracked the case. In January 1990 politicians agreed to pass a new anticrime law, stiffening penalties against murder and rape.[111]

Most politicians have been caught off-balance by Taiwan's faster-than-expected modernization and democratization. The potent opposition of the DPP and public demands for reform have forced members within the KMT to jockey for political power. The election of President Lee Teng-hui and Vice-President Lee Yuan-tzu, for instance, was not without political masquerading and intrigue. At one point, the extremely right-wing Chiang Wei-kuo, the half-brother of the late President Chiang Ching-kuo, threatened to run as a vice-presidential candidate with Lin Yang-gang, a moderate Taiwanese. Arguments and accusations reviving old political wounds flew for weeks. Chiang withdrew the nomination, but other political rumblings could also be felt. Unscheduled wrestling bouts featuring angry, disgruntled politicians broke out at restaurants and in the legislature. On February 20, dozens of riots, some of them organized by the DPP, broke out all over Taiwan objecting to the renomination of elderly, senile national assemblymen.[112] After the election of the Lee and Lee ticket, the internecine political squabbling toned down a bit, but divisions and scars may remain.

Public anger directed at the octogenarian and incapacitated representatives continued unabated. In March 1990 thousands of students rallied in the Chiang Kai-shek Memorial, demanding the retirement of the aged officials. Taking a page out of 1989's Tiananmen Square protests, scores of Taiwan students went on hunger strike and sat peacefully in the memorial. Some reactionaries suggested using military force to "relocate" the students, but the last thing Taiwan's leaders wanted was a rerun, Taiwan-style, of the Tiananmen massacre. Eventually, cooler heads prevailed and President Lee conceded to meet with student leaders later. Their point made, the crowds dispersed quietly, leaving behind trampled lawns and spray-painted political slogans on the National Concert Hall and National Opera House.[113]

The government's uncertain political footing has prompted different factions to push for even more demands. Splinter groups within the KMT want to institute a parliamentary system. The students want to retire the old "representatives" and abolish the electoral college system. Entrepreneurs want looser trade policies. And the DPP wants to perform a little liposuction on defense spending— said to gobble up as much as 50 percent of Taiwan's budget—and force constitutional changes. Whispers of Taiwan independence can be heard, as can the calls for the Taiwan government's renunciation of sovereignty over mainland China.[114]

These political spasms may ensure a freer Taiwan, but they also take away from other concerns—like the environment. With everyone so focused on politics and social order, the environment could slide down the administration's top ten list of things to manage. What's more, the DPP may look to other issues in an effort to broaden its base of support to further challenge the KMT. Environmental concerns could get watered down. From an institutional perspective, there is no happy resolution for now, since the government must also be responsible for all of the country's problems. But academics warn: "If environmental protection is not given high priority in the national policy agenda—Taiwan will be in danger of becoming a sort of poisonous garbage dump."[115]

Activities of Nongovernmental Organizations

While politicians bicker and fritter their time away, more nonprofit groups have been founded to amplify environmental concerns. As of November 1989 there were twenty-five environmental organizations, with a new one sprouting every one or two months.[116] Listed below are some of the more prominent groups:

The Taiwan Environmental Protection Union (TEPU), formed in November 1987 by professors, teachers, housewives, and "people from all walks of life," is one of the most vocal groups. Even though TEPU is considered the environmental arm of the DPP, the group says in its monthly newsletters that "environmental protection is the responsibility of all people, [and] knows no national boundaries, race, religion or political beliefs." Among other activities, TEPU members participate in the antinuclear movement, the preservation of forest and land, the study of official environmental policy, and education and training seminars.[117]

In 1986 the Homemakers Union was established by women concerned about an entire menu of social issues. "We founded this group," said former President Hsu Shen-shu, "so that housewives, often trapped in the house, could express their opinions about environmental problems more positively."[118] Membership now is well over 300—including men. Dedicated members have made the organization a "main force behind informal environmental education, both to individuals and to groups." Introducing environmental education into Taiwan's rigid and exam-oriented curriculum is the next challenge—and a difficult one, given the conservatism of the Ministry of Education. But for now, members are more than glad to dole out environmental tips such as "Take extra bags with you and refuse excess plastic packaging" and "Put away garbage in the proper bins." Perhaps the group's greatest impact has been on primary school children; the union runs the "Little Magic Scouts' Camp" for environmental awareness and has just published a cartoon book, "The Amazing Encounter of Hsiao-Chian."[119]

A third group, the New Environmental Foundation, has a smaller membership (about fifty) but tries to be just as active. The foundation first started as the *New Environment* monthly bulletin in early 1986, then decided, the following year, to expand its efforts. Their concerns overlap those of the above-mentioned two groups, but some of the New Environment Foundation members, made up mostly of technical and academic specialists, have personal reasons for fighting. Said Andrea Chen, the group's secretary general: "Many of my colleagues and I suffer from chronic coughs. Doctors tell us that we will recover only when air pollution subsides."[120]

The Beautiful Taiwan Foundation represents one of many groups combating a specific problem; in its case, the problem is garbage. Disgusted with the minimountains of trash accumulating on city streets, a small group of citizens formed this group in 1987. For starters, Beautiful Taiwan donated hundreds of new sidewalk garbage cans with separate bins for inflammable and nonflammable trash; the old cans had small and inconveniently placed holes about the size of a piece of pita bread. To reach the masses, the organization helped sponsor a commercial with television and movie celebrities using the new cans.[121]

The efforts of these four organizations have been complemented by an increasing number of college environmental clubs. "Campus life has been more active since the lifting of martial law," said one Taiwan reporter.[122] Ten years ago there were maybe one or two groups on the island; today there are at least a few on each campus. The Taiwan University Environmental Protection Club, for one example, was started in December 1987 and sponsors lectures and book exhibitions; publishes a newsletter; and conducts surveys all over the island on environmental issues.[123] No study has yet been done on how environmentally active these college students are after graduation, but older activists believe that the clubs are serving as solid training ground for future environmental leaders.

The most recent group of note is the Taipei-based Taiwan Youth Environment Network (TYEN), a nonprofit organization founded in January 1990 by local citizens and foreigners, most of whom are under thirty years old. In brief, the TYEN aims "to facilitate communication and cooperation among the many youth and study ecology groups springing up across Taiwan." Published monthly (on recycled paper) in both Chinese and English, the group's *Simple Earth* magazine provides environmental tips and information about grass-roots organizing. The best feature of the publication, though, may be its "Environmental Spaghetti" event calendar.[124] How long the TYEN remains in operation is uncertain because of the likelihood that many of the foreign volunteers will at some point return to their home countries. But TYEN members are hopeful that concerned citizens can always be found in Taiwan.

To an extent, though, the TYEN and some of these other groups contain restricted elements. For one thing, environmentalists seem to be comprised mostly of intellectuals and "young, more affluent, better educated people."[125] According to most journalists and academics, the environmental movement is not a genuine social movement in the sense that it is not all-inclusive and does not cut across class, sex, and income lines. What's more, there is the criticism that some of these protesters are, in the words of a popular Taiwan saying, "protesting for the sake of protesting." Some of the demonstrators, then, may not be green at heart but merely out there to "look" politically correct.[126]

Whatever the ulterior motives of the protesters, though, the bottom line is that there is strength in numbers. But herein lies another problem: So far, the organizations and the environmental protests have been too localized. As with many social groups, many of the conservationists are headquartered in Taipei or Kaohsiung and have problems getting the word out to people in rural areas. With most protests originating as a local gut reaction to an unwanted new factory or some pollutant found in the next town, environmentalists realize the need for stronger national and "regional branches" to broaden their base of support.[127] Lobbying groups—like PACs or congressional lobbies in the United States— would also help in applying constant pressure on lawmakers.

Even without these lobbyists, blaming big companies like Du Pont or agencies like the EPA has been easy. One chemical executive lamented that all industry was "a moving target to the whims of public opinion."[128] The people, he implied, were in an advantageous position because they could criticize without being criticized. Agreed a former Taiwan graduate student: "How can people point the finger at themselves?"[129]

Indeed, not enough people realize that they, too, are partially responsible for Taiwan's sad environmental state. And although people feel strongly about cleaning up, too many are enslaved by their own materialistic interests and habits—habits that often hurt the land even more. As a modern people, Taiwan residents want convenience, with good reason. But insisting on using styrofoam and plastics—the number of polyethylene terephthlate (PET) soda bottles has shot up from virtually none in 1980 to 250 million in 1989—makes bad environmental sense.[130]

This shortage of self-conscious action is probably a function of the following two conditions: Most people either don't know how to help or just don't have the energy to do anything. Besides, the Chinese have never had a strong history of voluntarism; there is no Chinese Jerry Lewis who urges people to participate in an annual twenty-four-hour telethon. To be sure, "whenever there's a fire, people will get there,"[131] but there is no preparation or sprinkler system, so to speak. The plain fact is, most Taiwan residents have been passive about the environment on a national, not to mention international, scale. According to cynics, perhaps the greatest exertion the average citizen may make is responding to public opinion polls about the seriousness of Taiwan's environmental troubles. "We may have more environmental consciousness," summed up Ma Wen-shung of Union Chemical Laboratories, "but we do not have environmental responsibility."[132]

Some people have even resisted responsibility. For instance, a recent proposal to include a small garbage tax as part of the electricity bill sparked complaints, not cooperation.[133] People must recognize the truth that everybody must sacrifice something. We must pay some cost to solve our own problem," said EPA Administrator Chien You-hsin.[134] Yet Chien and other officials understand it is only natural for people to oppose plans to place, say, an incinerator or a sanitary landfill in their neighborhood. In Taiwan as elsewhere, the not-in-my-backyard (NIMBY) syndrome prevails. In an effort to help people overcome NIMBY, the

EPA and some companies have been trying to buy out the neighboring towns with promises of new roads, schools, and nice facilities. The China Petroleum Corporation, to take one prominent example, has offered to build a swimming pool and hospital near its planned naptha cracker in Houching.[135] But the neighbors are still skeptical and are not taking anyone's word except their own.

No one wants to bear the brunt of any new operation. But when it comes to picking up and separating garbage, or carpooling, or using less plastic, too many Taiwan residents are thinking for themselves and not for their neighbors. In a sense, for the average Taiwan resident, the 1980s has been the "we-generation": we meaning me, my family, and my best friends, but not my community.

Unfortunately, what may energize people into becoming more community-oriented is some kind of shock or disaster. Unlike in the Japan of the early 1960s, in Taiwan medical data related to environmental problems have yet to be released. While scientists and doctors are worried about lung cancer, toxic poisoning, or the possible seepage of carcinogenic material into the groundwater, it may be at least a decade or so before they know any definitive information. According to the "Taiwan 2000" Study, "Present statistics cannot yet fully reflect the consequences of the environmental degradation of the last few decades because the more serious illnesses associated with complex toxification of the environment often come from cumulative exposure over decades, and often have very long latency periods."[136] Environmentalists hope that the Taiwanese will act now to prevent serious disease instead of passively waiting for disaster to strike.

Conclusions

On April 22, 1990, Taiwan organizers of Earth Day attempted to synthesize and draw attention to some of the island's pressing environmental problems and possible solutions. All over the island, popular celebrities and singers echoed the dangers in songs and words at a number of charity concerts. In Taipei, over 2,000 people crowded a gymnasium at National Taiwan University to hear music and speeches. Although it rained for the better part of the day, numerous events were held as scheduled: an environmental bazaar at the Chiang Kai-shek Memorial, a bicycle ride, tree-planting activities, a "recycled" art contest for children, and the distribution of "Campus Environmental Study Handbooks."[137] In a nutshell, what organizers hoped would last, in addition to the memories of music and fun, was a lesson in environmental history and a realization that each person can—and must—make a difference.

Twenty years ago, most Taiwan residents probably did not even know Earth Day existed. The situation is much better now, but like other Asian countries, Taiwan has many bridges to cross before the environment can be declared fit and healthy. The good news is that Taiwan has the fortune of having money—a lot of money—available to reverse the ecological mistakes of the past. The bad news is that unlike Japan, which already had achieved relative political and social stability by the 1960s, Taiwan must confront an army of social, economic, legal, and political problems and changes all at once. The task is formidable.

But since the mid-1980s, with some of the Taiwanese people gradually facing up to the island's depressing environmental history, there has been a noticeable, though not always smooth, shift toward environmentalism. As a result of political liberalization and a more enlightened media, those with the strongest convictions have spoken up, though frequently at just the local level. Environmental protests also broke out in greater numbers, and spokespersons demanded attention. Taiwan's waters were disgusting; its air filthy; its garbage unchecked. Ever the monitors of the nation's political pulse, some politicians and officials jumped on the conservation bandwagon. Others learned how to spit out green rhetoric to give the appearance of being sensitive. An environmental consciousness had definitely emerged, and the Neihu Garbage Mountain soon became a part of the past.

The future remains uncertain, though. Even the most earnest reform-minded, proenvironmental politicians are now saddled with other concerns, other lobbyists. With officialdom sputtering at times, more grass-roots environmental groups have taken it on themselves to assemble programs for teachers and children and to foster awareness. But activists cannot accomplish change by themselves. It is now up to all Taiwanese to act, no matter how reluctant they may be. If nothing is done, then the "further pollution and deterioration of natural resources may render [Taiwan's] homes and workplaces so unpleasant and unhealthy that rising incomes no longer compensate for declining environmental quality."[138] As Taiwan races toward the twenty-first century, the urgency of that message cannot be stressed enough.

Notes

1. I visited the Neihu Garbage Mountain on August 30, 1988, and talked with on-site personnel from Taiwan's Environmental Protection Agency (EPA). Contrary to public perceptions, the mountain no longer smells. See David W. Chen, "Garbage Disposal Dilemma," *Free China Review* (December 1988): 66–69. See also Carl Goldstein, "Cash from Trash," *Far Eastern Review* (September 21, 1989): 81–82.

2. "Costs of Success," *The Economist: Taiwan Survey,* March 5, 1988, p. 10. See also Cindy Benedicto, "The EPA Attacks Air Pollution," *Free China Review* (March 1988): 32. Two bonus statistics on Taiwan's vehicles: from 1978 to 1988 the number of cars went from 458,000 to 2.12 million; the number of motorcycles, from 2.7 million to 6.8 million. See U.S. Department of State, "Taiwan's Environmental Protection Administration after Two Years," telegram from David Dean (November 1989).

3. *Taiwan 2000: Balancing Economic Growth and Environmental Protection* (Taipei: Institute of Ethnology, Academia Sinica, 1989), pp. iv and 19. Pigs, which produce five times the amount of waste humans do, are also a major source of pollution in Taiwan. In 1989, an official census on pigs estimated nearly 7 million of them in Taiwan. See U.S. Department of State, "Taiwan's Environmental Protection Administration."

4. *Taiwan 2000,* p. 17.

5. "Costs of Success," p. 10.

6. *Taiwan 2000,* p. 18.

7. *Industry of Free China,* Council of Economic Planning and Development, Taipei, June 1990. Information was also gathered from Professor N.T. Wang's lecture on "Taiwan's Economic Relations with Mainland China" at Columbia University's East Asian Institute, November 14, 1989. Finally, see "The Miracle-Workers' Reward," *The Economist,* April 21, 1990, p. 42.

8. Mau-Kuei Michael Chang, "The Social and Political Aspects of the Anti-Nuclear Power Movement in Taiwan," in King-yuh Chang, ed., *Political and Social Changes in Taiwan and Mainland China* (Taipei: Institute of International Relations, National Chengchi University, 1989), pp. 114–16.

9. Chuang Kuo-lung and Huang Chin-hsien, "Taiwan's Nuclear Policy and the Popular Anti-Nuclear Movement," in *Papers from the 1988 Taiwan Public Policy Conference* (Taipei: North American Taiwanese Professor's Association and Taiwan Association for Human Rights, 1989), pp. 206–7.

10. Goldstein, "Cash from Trash," p. 82.

11. *Simple Earth* (March 1990): 1; Goldstein, "Cash from Trash," p. 81; "Costs of Success," p. 10.

12. U.S. Department of State , "Taiwan's Environmental Protection Administration."

13. Leu Chien-ai, "Volunteer Groups Arise!" *Free China Review* (December 1989): 59.

14. A number of articles provided good background on the lead poisoning in Keelung: "One Kilometer Danger Zone around Hsin-Yeh Metal Company," *China Times,* February 26, 1990, p. 6; "Lead Poisoning of the Hands Comes Without Sound, Without Warning and Corrodes the Health of Our People," *China Times,* March 7, 1990, p. 6; "Who Will Save the People Who Eat Lead?" *China Times,* March 11, 1990, p. 6.

15. Goldstein, "Cash from Trash," p. 81.

16. Chang, "The Anti-Nuclear Power Movement," pp. 112, 118, 122–23. See also Chang and Huang, "Taiwan's Nuclear Policy," in *Papers,* pp. 205–6.

17. Chang, "The Anti-Nuclear Power Movement," pp. 109, 118, 130. Antinuclear activists have also blasted Taipower for the lack of adequate evacuation plans.

18. Phone conversation with Donald T. Chen, consultant to the Taiwan EPA, on April 4, 1990.

19. Chang, "The Anti-Nuclear Power Movement," p. 122.

20. *Papers,* p. 286. See also Pierre Sigwalt, "Environmental Policies and Problems in Taiwan," in Chang King-yuh, ed., *Political and Social Changes,* p. 141.

21. Chang, "The Anti-Nuclear Power Movement," pp. 122–23. Taiwan is about the size of West Virginia.

22. Lin Wu-nan, "Covering Up Buried Nuclear Waste," in *Papers,* p. 175.

23. Suga Akiko, "The Power of Opposition Blowing Through the Grassroots of Taiwan," *AMPO Japan-Asia Quarterly Review* (January/February 1988): 85.

24. Chang and Huang "Taiwan's Nuclear Policy," in *Papers,* p. 205. Also Chang, "The Anti-Nuclear Power Movement," pp. 123, 125.

25. Jean Hamilton, "A Grassroots Rebuff for Du Pont," *Sierra* (May/June 1987): 68–69. See also Suga, "The Power of Opposition"; and James Reardon-Anderson, *Pollution, Politics, and Foreign Investment in Taiwan: The Lukang Rebellion.* Armonk, NY: M. E. Sharpe.

26. Chang Chiao-hao, "Pollution Controversies," *Free China Review* (July 1987): 34.

27. Hamilton, "A Grassroots Rebuff," p. 69.

28. "Potential Polluters Face Tougher Environmental Laws, Enforcement in Taiwan," *Business Asia,* November 28, 1988, pp. 383–84.

29. Fang Yang-chung and Huang Hui-chuan, "Full Moon Shining Upon a Strong

Fire: The War Over the Fifth Naptha Cracker Starts Again," *The Journalist*, January 15–21, 1990, p. 71.

30. "Potential Polluters Face Tougher Environmental Laws, Enforcement in Taiwan," p. 385.

31. Chang and Huang, "Taiwan's Nuclear Policy," in *Papers*, p. 206. Also, "Central Mountain Peaks New National Park Site," *Free China Journal*, February 15, 1990, p. 3.

32. "EPA Sets Sea Dumping Study," *Free China Journal*, July 31, 1989, p. 3.

33. "More Disturbance Over the Fifth Naptha Cracker Plant," *The Quest* (February 1990): 7. See also "Proposed Naptha Plant Faces Residential Siege," *Free China Journal*, January 18, 1990, p. 3.

34. Bolder does not necessarily mean better. Although the media have been praised for better and faster news coverage, they have also been excoriated for carrying overly sensational stories. There has also been a tendency for some journalists to report rumors; during the student demonstrations in Beijing last spring, for example, the Taiwan press reported the "confirmed" death of Deng Xiaoping and the "confirmed" shooting of Li Peng.

35. Chang Chiao-hao, "New Life for Love River," *Free China Review* (July 1987): 25. The Love River was so foul that Kaohsiung residents often told this story: A young woman wanted to commit suicide and decided to jump into the Love River. After impact, though, she was so overwhelmed by the stench that her body reacted against the will of her mind; she cried for help and was soon rescued.

36. Chang and Huang, "Taiwan's Nuclear Policy," in *Papers*, p. 207.

37. *Taiwan 2000*, p. 7.

38. "Costs of Success," p. 10.

39. Chen Chin-chung, "A Painful Disease Has Landed in Taiwan," *Taiwanese New Society* (January 1988): 35–37.

40. Chi Pi-ling, "Have the Plans for the Fourth Nuclear Power Plant Been Kicked onto the Iron Plate?" *China Times Weekly*, January 27–February 9, 1990, p. 28. The breakdown in the vote was as follows: KMT, 59 percent; DPP, 30 percent; other opposition parties, 11 percent. See "The 'Miracle-Workers' Reward," *The Economist*, April 21, 1990, p. 42.

41. Irene Yeung, "Special Interest Activists," *Free China Review* (December 1989): 48.

42. Leu, "Volunteer Groups Arise!" p. 54.

43. Hamilton, "A Grassroots Rebuff," p. 69.

44. Chen, "Garbage Disposal Dilemma," p. 66.

45. Leu, "Volunteer Groups Arise!" p. 59.

46. David W. Chen, "Key Dilemma," *Free China Review* (June 1989): 12–13. I also received some information about these groups during a conversation with Hsu Lu, a reporter for the Taiwan paper *Independent Evening Post*, on March 8, 1990, in New York.

47. "Educating Chinese about the Environment," *China Post*, March 9, 1990, p. 4. See also *An Introduction to Environmental Protection in the Taiwan Area, ROC* (Taipei: Environmental Protection Administration, October 1989), pp. 12–13. The national anthem (accompanied by a promotional short about Taiwan) is sung by standing audiences before each movie.

48. Chen Wen-tsung, "New Directions in Foreign Policy," *Free China Review* (February 1990): 8. Refer also to "Taiwan and Korea: Pushing Polluters to Pay," *Business Asia* (May 15, 1989), p. 153.

49. Huang Hui-chuan, "Can the Check for Environmental Legislation Be Cashed?" *The Journalist*, January 15–21, 1990, p. 73.

50. *Sino-British Environmental Protection Seminar Proceedings* (Taipei, January 1990), pp. 10–16.

51. I visited the Futekeng Sanitary Landfill site on August 30, 1988. Technicians and scientists explained that after being filled to capacity (about five more years), the landfill would probably be covered with topsoil and planted with trees. For the time being, though, there was little they could do about the (very) strong smells emanating from the landfill. Some local residents have complained, but not enough to mount any sort of concerted protest.

52. Goldstein, "Cash from Trash," pp. 81–82.

53. U.S. Department of State, "Taiwan's Environmental Protection Administration."

54. *Outline of Major Projects* (Taipei: Taiwan Environmental Protection Agency, 1989), n.p.

55. Ibid.

56. U.S. Department of State "Taiwan's Environmental Protection Administration." See also *Sino-British Environmental Protection Seminar Proceeding* (Taipei, January 1990), p. 6–4.

57. *An Introduction*, p. 32.

58. *Outline of Major Projects.*

59. Brian Caplen, "Cashing in on the Pollution Boom," *Asian Business* (April 1989): 31.

60. U.S. Department of State, "Taiwan's Environmental Protection Adminitration."

61. Fang and Huang, "Full Moon Shining," p. 71.

62. *Sino-British Environmental Protection Seminar Proceedings.* See also "'Miracle-Workers' Reward," p. 42.

63. Joseph Chi-hong Yang, *Recent Developments for Environmental Protection Activities in Taiwan* (Taipei: Environmental Protection Agency, 1989), p. 8.

64. Chen, "Garbage Disposal Dilemma," pp. 67–68.

65. Chang Chin-ju, "Recycling Bottlenecks," *Sinorama* (January 1990): 100–106. For the scoop on the wheat plates, consult "Edible Plates May Be Answer to Trash Woes," *Free China Journal,* January 18, 1990, p. 3.

66. Leu, "Volunteer Groups Arise!" p. 59.

67. "CFC Tops Polluter List," *Free China Journal,* August 7, 1989, p. 3.

68. Goldstein, "Cash from Trash," p. 80.

69. *Outline of Major Projects.*

70. Goldstein, "Cash from Trash," p. 80. For more information about businesses hoping to capitalize on Taiwan's trash troubles, see Caplen, "Cashing in."

71. David E. Apter and Nagayo Sawa, *Against the State: Politics and Social Protest in Japan* (Cambridge: Harvard University Press, 1984), p. 4.

72. Ibid., p. 9. On the fishermen's early protests, see Nobuko Iijima, ed., *Pollution Japan: Historical Chronology* (Tokyo: Asahi Evening News, 1979), p. 122.

73. Iijima, ed., *Pollution Japan,* pp. iv, 156.

74. Ibid., p. 148.

75. Jun Ui, ed., *Polluted Japan: Reports by Members of the Jishu-Koza Citizens' Movement* (Tokyo: Jishu-Koza Citizens' Movement, 1972), p. 10.

76. Ibid., p. 149.

77. Iijima, ed., *Pollution Japan,* p. 156. In 1960 Tokyo experienced sixty days of heavy black smog.

78. *Quality of the Environment in Japan* (Tokyo: Environmental Agency, 1973), pp. 2, 28, 38, 39.

79. Ibid., pp. 2, 40. See also Philip Shabecoff, "Veteran of Earth Day 1970 Looks to a New World," *New York Times,* April 16, 1990, p. B8.

80. Suga, "The Power of Opposition," p. 79.

81. Huang Hui-chuan, "Can the Check for Environmental Legislation Be Cashed?" *The Journalist,* January 15–21, 1990, p. 72.

82. Nicholas D. Kristof, "Taiwan Starts to Clean Up Its Air and Water," *New York Times,* December 29, 1986, n.p.

83. "Taiwan and Korea: Pushing Polluters to Pay," *Business Asia,* May 15, 1989, p. 156. The top 10 were not listed in this article, but it is likely that Tokyo, Taipei, Kaohsiung, and Bangkok are either included in that list or not far behind.

84. Caplen, "Cashing in," p. 31.

85. For Hong Kong information, see Nicholas D. Kristof, "The New, Revealing Look of Taiwan Elections," *New York Times,* February 12, 1989, p. 24. For South Korea, see "Taiwan and Korea: Pushing Polluters to Pay," pp. 153, 159.

86. Benedicto, "The EPA," p. 36.

87. Chen, "Garbage Disposal Dilemma," p. 68.

88. Phone conversation with Donald T. Chen.

89. *Taiwan 2000,* p. 20.

90. Goldstein, "Cash from Trash," p. 82.

91. Phone conversation with Donald T. Chen on April 29, 1990. Chen said that many employees heeded Chien's words, and the EPA was very quiet during the weeks before and after the election.

92. *Papers,* p. 284.

93. Fang and Huang, "Full Moon Shining," p. 72. During the early part of the campaign the environment was the focus of attention when Hsu Hsiao-tan, a Labor party candidate known more for her nude modeling than her politics, threatened to protest pollution by parading around a garbage dump—naked. See Nicholas D. Kristof, "The New, Revealing Look of Taiwan Elections," p. 24.

94. Conversation with *Independent Evening Post* reporter Hsu Lu on March 8, 1990.

95. U.S. Department of State.

96. *Sino-British Environmental Protection Seminar Proceedings,* p. 8–2.

97. U.S. Department of State, "Taiwan's Environmental Protection Administration."

98. *Taiwan 2000,* p. 34, and *Environmental Protection Recommendations Put Forth by the 1989 Nation Development Seminar* (Taipei: National Science Council, August 1989), p. 2.

99. "Taiwan and Korea: Pushing Polluters to Pay," p. 154.

100. For the Chen Li-an quote, refer to Chi, "Have the Plans for the Fourth Nuclear Power Plant Been Kicked onto the Iron Plate?" p. 28.

101. Lee Chu-yuan, "Wang Yung-ching Wants to Build an International Kingdom!" *China Times Weekly,* March 3–9, 1990, p. 54.

102. Lincoln Kaye, "Investment Incursion," *Far Eastern Economic Review,* February 8, 1990, p. 17.

103. Chuan Yi-chieh, "Lee Teng-hui Considers Wang Yung-ching's Mainland Visit No Big Deal," *World Journal Weekly,* February 18, 1990, p. 1.

104. Ibid. See also Kaye, "Investment Incursion," p. 17.

105. Kaye, "Investment Incursion," p. 17. Refer also to Jonathan Moore, "The Upstart Taipans," *Far Eastern Economic Review,* April 19, 1990, p. 84.

106. Leu "Volunteer Groups Arise!" p. 54.

107. Yang, *Recent Developments,* p. 3. See also Betty Wang, "Small Islands—Big Problems," *Free China Review* (June 1989): 10.

108. Leu, "Volunteer Groups Arise!" p. 54.

109. Ibid.

110. "Golf Rush," *Asia Magazine* (Weekend, December 8–10, 1989), pp. 8–17. In

Japan, the anti-golf course movement is quite strong. Apparently it is cheaper for the Japanese to fly to Hawaii—or Taiwan—to play a round of golf than it is to play at home. For information on chemicals, see Wang, "Small Island," pp. 10–11.

111. Kaye, "Investment Incursion," p. 17. In the Chang Yung-fa case, the kidnappers were quickly sentenced to death; just one example of how severe capital punishment is in Taiwan.

112. Chi Pi-ling, "Conflict, Blood, and Burning Cars," *China Times Weekly,* March 3–9, 1990, pp. 18–21.

113. "Chiang Kai-shek Memorial Damage Billed to DPP," *Free China Journal,* March 29, 1990, p. 3. I gleaned much of the information from the *World Journal* during the end of March and beginning of April.

114. *Independent Evening Post* reporter Hsu Lu said that defense may account for 40–50 percent of Taiwan's spending, but that it is difficult to pin down an exact figure, since much of the money is buried in different ministries, local administrations, and state-run companies. For more on the political situation in Taiwan, see Sheryl WuDunn, "New Taiwan Chief: Signal of Change?" *New York Times,* April 13, 1990, p. A6.

115. *Taiwan 2000,* p. 11.

116. Leu, "Volunteer Groups Arise!" p. 58.

117. For information about grass-roots groups, see *Simple Earth* (March 1990): 4–5, and *Taiwan Environmental Protection Union Newsletter,* December 20, 1989, p. 2.

118. Suga, "The Power of Opposition," p. 78.

119. Most of the information about the Homemakers Union was obtained through a conversation with Donald T. Chen on April 4, 1990, and *Simple Earth* (March 1990): 4.

120. Leu, "Volunteer Groups Arise!" pp. 58–59.

121. Chen, "Garbage Disposal Dilemma," pp. 66, 68.

122. Conversation with Hsu Lu on March 8, 1990.

123. *Simple Earth* (March 1990): 5.

124. Phone conversations with Donald T. Chen on April 4 and 29, 1990. Chen has also contributed to *Simple Earth.* I also referred to the *Simple Earth* issues of January, March, and April.

125. *Taiwan 2000,* p. 17.

126. Conversation with Hsu Lu on March 8, 1990. The expression is *wei fandui er fandui.*

127. Conversation with Hsu Lu on March 8, 1990 yielded information about the nature of these social protests. For the "regional branches" concept, see Leu, "Volunteer Groups Arise!"

128. "Potential Polluters Face Tougher Environmental Laws, Enforcement in Taiwan," p. 285.

129. Conversation with Hsu Lu on March 8, 1990.

130. Carl Goldstein, "Choking on Plastic," *Far Eastern Economic Review,* September 21, 1989, p. 82. A television commercial in the early 1980s showing a plastic container falling down the stairs—without breaking—probably contributed to the surge in PET bottles. See Chang, "Recycling Bottlenecks."

131. Conversation with Hsu Lu on March 8, 1990.

132. Chen, "Garbage Disposal Dilemma," p. 67.

133. Conversation with Hsu Lu on March 8, 1990.

134. Chen, "Garbage Disposal Dilemma," p. 68.

135. "Costs of Success," p. 10.

136. *Taiwan 2000,* p. 18.

137. Conversation with Donald T. Chen on April 29, 1990. See also *Simple Earth* issues.

138. *Taiwan 2000,* p. 30.

Bibliography

English Sources

Apter, David E., and Nagayo Sawa. *Against the State: Politics and Social Protest in Japan.* Cambridge: Harvard University Press, 1984.
Benedicto, Cindy. "The EPA Attacks Air Pollution." *Free China Review* (March 1988): 32–37.
Caplen, Brian. "Cashing in on the Pollution Boom." *Asian Business* (April 1989): 28–32.
Chang Chiao-hao. "New Life for Love River." *Free China Review* (July 1987): 24–29.
———. "Pollution Controversies." *Free China Review* (July 1987): 30–35.
Chang Chin-ju. "Recycling Bottlenecks." *Sinorama* (January 1990): 100–106.
Chang King-yuh, ed. *Political and Social Changes in Taiwan and Mainland China.* Taipei: Institute of International Relations, National Chengchi University, 1989.
Chen, David W. "Garbage Disposal Dilemma." *Free China Review* (December 1988): 66–69.
———. "Key Dilemma." *Free China Review* (June 1989): 12–13.
Chen, Donald T. Telephone conversations, April 4 and 29, 1990.
Chen Wen-tsung. "New Directions in Foreign Policy." *Free China Review* (February 1990): 4–11.
Chien Jen-ter. "Pollution Clouds the Economic Image." *Free China Review* (December 1988): 70–72.
Chien You-hsin. *Progress, Harmony and Balance: Building a Quality Society.* Taipei: Environmental Protection Agency, December 1989.
China Post (March 1990).
"Costs of Success." *The Economist: Taiwan Survey,* March 5, 1988: 10–12.
"Environmental Issues at a Glance." *Business Asia,* May 15, 1989: 158–61.
Environmental Protection Recommendations Put Forth by the 1989 National Development Seminar. Taipei: National Science Council, August 1989.
Free China Journal (July 1989–May 1990).
"General Instrument Taiwan's Route to Overcoming Environmental, Labor Hurdles." *Business Asia,* September 12, 1988: 294–96.
Gold, Thomas. *State and Society in the Taiwan Miracle.* Armonk, NY: M.E. Sharpe, 1985.
Goldstein, Carl. "Cash from Trash." *Far Eastern Economic Review,* September 21, 1989: 80–82.
———. "Choking on Plastic." *Far Eastern Economic Review,* September 21, 1989: 82–83.
"Golf Rush." *Asia Magazine* (Weekend, December 8–10, 1989): 8–17.
Hamilton, Jean. "A Grassroots Rebuff for Du Pont." *Sierra* (May/June 1987): 68–69.
Iijima, Nobuko, ed. *Pollution Japan: Historical Chronology.* Tokyo: Asahi Evening News, 1979.
Industry of Free China. Taipei: Council of Economic Planning and Development, June 1990.
An Introduction to Environmental Protection in the Taiwan Area, ROC. Taipei: Environmental Protection Agency, October 1989.
Kaye, Lincoln. "Investment Incursion." *Far Eastern Economic Review,* February 8, 1990: 17.
Leu Chien-ai. "Volunteer Groups Arise!" *Free China Review* (December 1989): 53.
"The 'Miracle-Workers' Reward." *The Economist,* April 21, 1990: 41–42.

Moore, Jonathan. "The Upstart Taipans." *Far Eastern Economic Review,* April 19, 1990: 84–87.

New York Times (December 1986–May 1990).

Outline of Major Projects. Taipei: Environmental Protection Agency, 1989.

"Potential Polluters Face Tougher Environmental Laws, Enforcement in Taiwan." *Business Asia,* November 28, 1988: 383–85.

Quality of the Environment in Japan. Tokyo: Environmental Agency, 1973, 1974, 1986.

Reardon-Anderson, James. *Pollution, Politics, and Foreign Investment in Taiwan: The Lukang Rebellion.* Armonk, NY: M. E. Sharpe, 1992.

Simple Earth (January–April 1990).

Sino-British Environmental Protection Seminar Proceedings. Taipei, January 1990.

Suga Akiko. "The Power of Opposition Blowing Through the Grassroots of Taiwan." *AMPO Japan-Asia Quarterly Review* (January/February 1988).

"Taiwan and Korea: Pushing Polluters to Pay." *Business Asia,* May 15, 1989: 153–57.

Taiwan Environmental Protection Union Newsletter (January 1990).

Taiwan 2000: Balancing Economic Growth and Environmental Protection. Taipei: Institute of Ethnology, Academia Sinica, 1989.

Ui, Jun, ed. *Polluted Japan: Reports by Members of the Jishu-Koza Citizens' Movement.* Tokyo: Jishu-Koza Citizens' Movement, 1972.

U.S. Department of State. *Taiwan's Environmental Protection Administration after Two Years.* Telegram from David Dean, November 1989.

Wang, Betty. "Small Island—Big Problems." *Free China Review* (June 1989): 6–11.

Wang, N.T. "Taiwan's Economic Relations with Mainland China." Lecture given at Columbia University's East Asian Institute, New York, November 14, 1989.

Yang, Joseph Chi-hong. *Recent Developments for Environmental Protection Activities in Taiwan.* Taipei: Environmental Protection Agency, 1989.

Yeung, Irene. "Special Interest Activists." *Free China Review* (December 1989): 46–52.

Chinese Sources

Chen Chin-chung. "A Painful Disease Has Landed in Taiwan." *Taiwanese New Society* (January 1988): 35–37.

Chi Pi-ling. "Conflict, Blood, and Burning Cars." *China Times Weekly,* March 3–9, 1990: 18–22.

———. "Have the Plans for the Fourth Nuclear Power Plant Been Kicked onto the Iron Plate?" *China Times Weekly,* January 27–February 9, 1990: 28–29.

China Times (January–May 1990).

Chuan Yi-chieh. "Lee Teng-hui Considers Wang Yung-ching's Mainland Visit No Big Deal." *World Journal Weekly,* February 18, 1990: 1.

Environmental Protection Weekly Newsletter (March–April 1990).

Fang Yang-chung and Huang Hui-chuan. "Full Moon Shining Upon a Strong Fire: The War Over the Fifth Naptha Cracker Starts Again." *The Journalist,* January 15–21, 1990: 70–71.

Hsu Lu. Conversation, New York, March 8, 1990.

Huang Hui-chuan. "Can the Check for Environmental Legislation Be Cashed?" *The Journalist,* January 15–21, 1990: 72–73.

Lee Chu-yuan. "Wang Yung-ching Wants to Build an International Kingdom!" *China Times Weekly,* March 3–9, 1990: 54–55.

"Let the Setting Sun of Industry Rise from the Dead and Return to Life." *China Times Weekly,* February 10–16, 1990: 24.

Meng Fan, ed. *1988 Taiwan Year in Review.* Taipei: Yuan-Shen Publishers, 1989.

"More Disturbances over the Fifth Naptha Cracker Plant." *The Quest* (February 1990): 7.

Papers from the 1988 Taiwan Public Policy Conference. Taipei: North American Taiwanese Professor's Association and Taiwan Association for Human Rights, 1989.

United Daily News (January–May 1990).

World Journal (January–May 1990).

Part V

GENDER ISSUES

The rapid modernization of Taiwan has had effects that have challenged the very nature of assumptions about the role of the sexes in Chinese society. Higher levels of education and the autonomy created by the need for both members in a nuclear family to help support that family have created the need to rethink the role of women and the relationship between the sexes. That ongoing attempt to redefine gender relationships is complex, and many men as well as many women find the process of redefinition and the act of transformation of relationships very difficult. The difficult process of implementing these changes in consciousness and behavior may be discerned by studying the three chapters in this part.

The first author is Hsiu-Lien Annette Lu. Her chapter serves as a summation of its author's long, challenging career as leader and as role model and is both history and autobiography. Much of its power lies in its clear narrative line and in the fact that its author lived many of the events being described. The chapter describes the origins of the awakening of women's consciousness and the feminist movement, suggesting that the impetus for that movement lay in the economic change that export-centered development helped to foster.

While Hsiu-Lien Lu focuses on women's attempts to gain a degree of empowerment in recent decades, Catherine Farris examines the way in which the roles that women play are perceived in contemporary Taiwanese society. She presents a detailed examination of the Taiwan literature on women written over the course of recent decades. She also suggests that Hsiu-Lien Lu was put into prison not so much for her efforts as a political activist but because she was the organizer of the very visible and troublesome feminist movement.

In her conclusion, Farris assesses the significance of the scholarly and popular literature and suggests that it has helped to redefine the way women are seen in Taiwan. This change in perception in turn has presented a challenge to the KMT-dominated state, which supported the traditional male-dominated social structure with its laws and its organs of control. Lu's emotional and powerful vision of the new role of women in Taiwan is supported by Farris's more detailed and objective analysis.

Bi-ehr Chou presents a third approach to the issue of gender and the relationship between genders. Her tightly focused chapter is based on extensive study of the theories that relate to gender and employment patterns in developed and developing nations and on a close reading of various types of statistical data. Zhou demonstrates her skill both in explaining seemingly abstract theoretical formulations and in showing how they can be applied to produce important insights into the nature of the changes women in Taiwan have experienced in the last three decades.

Chapter 10

Women's Liberation: The Taiwanese Experience

Hsiu-Lien Annette Lu

Following the breakthrough of the first Taiwanese opposition party—the Democratic Progressive party, founded on September 28, 1986—demonstrations for political or nonpolitical causes have become the general practice in Taiwan. Amidst the demonstrators, women activists are as vociferous as men. On some occasions, women lead the march with flowers in their hands to give to the heavily equipped security police, using the contrast to make an ironic statement. Is the Taiwanese women's awakening purely a side effect of democratization, as is the increasing consciousness of other social issues, such as environmental protection? Or does women's liberation in Taiwan have its own origin?

Fourteen years prior to the establishment of the DPP, a feminist movement had already been spearheaded. Not until its founder participated in the democratic movement and later was jailed for more than five years, however, was women's liberation connected with general politics. Although inspired by the political reforms, struggles for women's rights are by no means on the male freedom fighters' agenda. Rather, women have trodden a long, tough path of their own.

This chapter will deal with experiences of contemporary women's liberation in Taiwan, starting from a background understanding of Taiwanese society under which the feminist movement was launched and ending in a objective review of its impacts. Due to the fact that I happen to be the founder of the movement, and that the first wave of the movement was almost a "one-woman crusade," an overtone of personal reflection is inevitable. However, discussion will be ex-

---

This chapter is reprinted with the permission of The Centre of Asian Studies, The University of Hong Kong. It first appeared as "Women's Liberation Under Marital Law," in *Taiwan: Economy, Society, and History*, edited by Edward K.Y. Chen, Jack F. Williams, and Joseph Wong, pp. 339–354. Hong Kong: Centre of Asian Studies, The University of Hong Kong, 1991.

tended to cover the second wave of the movement, which appeared on the scene during my imprisonment, until the lifting of martial law.

Why Did the Movement Start?

The women's liberation movement in Taiwan began in the early 1970s under extremely adverse circumstances—politically, it was a martial law regime of authoritarian autocracy; culturally, it was a patriarchal society full of Confucian and Japanese androcentrism. However, the socioeconomic structure was in the stage of shifting from an agricultural to an industrial economy. Economic prosperity provided the younger generation, both men and women, a good environment for education and for mobilization. The tradition was facing a severe challenge from rapid social development.

The Regime of Martial Law

Taiwan began to be dominated by the Kuomintang in 1945 after Japan surrendered its colony. A brutal massacre was executed to suppress the Taiwanese uprising that took place on February 28, 1947, against the KMT's corruption, pillage, and economic depression. Two years later, Generalissimo Chiang Kai-shek fled to Taiwan where he established the martial law regime. Up until July 15, 1987, when the decree of martial law was lifted, fundamental human rights such as freedom of expression, freedom of assembly, and freedom of the press were infringed upon. Orthodoxy was deeply engraved by the control of thought starting in childhood. Thought control was pervasive in schools as everywhere else in the society.[1]

As a result, various previously taboo topics surfaced. Anyone who dared to express unorthodox ideas or to discuss the sensitive taboo topics was considered a dissident. Dissidents were subjected to political harassment, arrest, torture, incarceration, and even execution. In September 1987 when the Association for Former Prisoners of Conscience was formed, 142 released POCs became its members. Cumulatively, they had spent more than two thousand years in political prisons, including the infamous Green Island. An unverified estimate is that, over the thirty-eight years of martial law, hundreds of persons had been executed and thousands jailed for political reasons, with a total length of six thousand years of imprisonment.[2] In a word, to advocate something different from orthodoxy was to start a journey toward the dark jail.

A Society of Confucianism and Androcentrism

Having historically been ruled by the Spaniards, Dutch, Manchus, Japanese, and Chinese, Taiwan has a complex culture. Chinese Confucianism and Japanese male chauvinism had particularly strong influences on the stereotypes of sexes.

During half a century of colonial rule, the Japanese custom that men are well attended by women while women shall submit to men's domination was transplanted into Taiwanese families. Basically the husbands were masters of the family while wives were nothing but housemaids.

Aside from the tradition that a woman shall be tamed to be a virtuous wife and good mother, many Chinese Confucian disciplines contributed to the androcentric society and were detrimental to women. Among others, the best known "Three Obediences and Four Virtues of Women" had been deeply rooted into the mind of the majority of women.[3] The "Three Obediences" required a woman to obey the father before marriage, obey the husband when married, and answer to the son if widowed. The "Four Virtues" included attention to criteria that women had to meet in order to be "virtuous": morality, skill in handcrafts, appearance, and language for women. These traditional "virtues" plus the custom of foot-binding in effect led to the "Three-Way Bondage of Women," namely, to bind the head by cultivating a belief that to have no talent is a woman's virtue; to bind the waist by condemning severely women's unfaithfulness to their husbands and encouraging men to enjoy extramarital affairs; and to bind the feet by creating a standard of beauty for women with tiny, bound feet. Besides, preference for sons over daughters served as a justification for refusing the implementation of family planning, while the general belief that men are superior to women had prevented women from promoting their talent in many aspects.[4]

The Status of Taiwanese Women in the Early 1970s

Despite the fact that equality of men and women is assured by the Constitution (Art. 7), that both men and women reach their majority on completion of the twentieth year of age (Art. 12 of Civil Code), that both men and women acquire full disposing capacity by either reaching majority or getting married (Art. 13 of Civil Code), and that both men and women are entitled to the same right of inheritance (Art. 1138 of Civil Code), there are many laws that discriminate against women. Among them, the marital property law is the worst.

The framework of the marital property law is based on the following stereotyped assumptions: (1) the husband's obligation to support and the wife's duty to render services; (2) female servitude at home and male employment outside the household; (3) the wife's household service is worth no more than her own support; and (4) every wife needs a guardian, for which purpose the husband is most suited. Being so stipulated, the marital property law infringes on the economic capacity of a woman when she gets married and seriously prevents her from developing economic independence.[5]

Political

Suffrage was granted to Taiwanese men and women simultaneously, when the Constitution of the Republic of China, which provides equality of sexes, was put into effect after the KMT's retreat from the mainland in 1949. Moreover, under Article 134 of the constitution, a quota system is preserved for women in each election in accordance with the ratio of seats elected. Thanks to such affirmative action, women were encouraged to participate in politics, though they still lagged behind their male counterparts.

Up to the year of 1973, altogether 63 of 469 Provincial Assembly members were women (13.43 percent); 14 of 97 Taipei City Council members (28.57 percent) were women, and yet there were no female city or county mayors. As for the congressional level, in the supplementary election held in 1973, 6 of 53 elected National Assembly members were female, and 4 of 56 elected legislators were female. Considering that women comprise 47.55 percent of the population, women's political participation was certainly less than remarkable.

Economic

As traditionally "men go out, women stay in" has been considered the stereotyped role of the two sexes, the labor market used to be a world for men and for poor women only. It is no surprise that in the 1970s the employment level of women was far below that of men. Statistics for 1974 indicate that 30.65 percent of workers were female. The pattern of women's employment bore the following characteristics:

1. The average age of women workers was extremely young: 41.41 percent were age 25 or below. In fact, the older they were, the less the chance that they were employed.
2. The majority of women workers belonged to the blue-collar sector rather than to the white-collar sector.
3. On average, women worked only one day less per month and one hour less per day than men did, but they were paid 62 percent of what men were paid.
4. Women's employment was limited to jobs that had nothing to do with technical knowledge. Women were also excluded from well-respected, well-paid occupations.

Educational

Due to the legacy left by Japanese colonial rule, which did not encourage women to go to school at all, there was a big educational difference between the sexes. The statistics of 1974 indicate that 20 percent of women were illiterate, compared to 7.25 percent of men; that 73.24 percent of women received elementary education or less, compared to 59.74 percent of men; that 3.32 percent of women received college education or above, compared to 6.89 percent of men. The younger generations, however, managed to bridge this gap more and more. For instance, in the 1970s about one-third of the students who passed the Joint Entrance Examination to attend colleges were women. In 1971 the total number of girls entering the three most prestigious universities—Taita, Chengta, and Shihta—was 1,982, only 86 less than boys.

The Feminist Movement Begins (1972–1977)

It was because of the crisis of "waste of education" that a hot debate on how to prevent the surplus of women students in colleges emerged. It was also because of this hot debate that the historic article on "The Traditional Sex Roles" was published in the *United Daily* in October 1971. The author, Lu Hsiu-lien, was a native Taiwanese woman who had just returned from the United States and begun to work for the Executive Yuan. During her two-year study in the United States, she had an opportunity to come into contact with the American women's liberation movement. Earlier she had been struggling in a dilemma between the development of her self-esteem and the social bondage of being a traditional woman.[6] Coming after two girls and a boy in her family, she was expected to be another boy. Her determination and efforts to compete with her only brother made her parents proud of her, on one hand, yet regretful of her gender, on the other. Like her brother, she went to law school. Unlike him, she decided to defend justice outside the courtroom.

Her lengthy article criticizing the stereotyped roles of the sexes attracted wide attention. A young man with his girlfriend came to offer Lu Hsiu-lien their unconditional assistance if ever she would need it. A friend of hers who was a professor of law invited her to his class for a pioneering lecture on feminism. On International Women's Day in 1972, she initiated the movement by giving a formal talk at the Law School of Taita, her alma mater. That summer a Ph.D. candidate murdered his wife, a suspected adulteress. The public gave over-whelming sympathy to the murderer for his misfortune to have married an un-faithful wife. The sickness of the society drove Lu to write another lengthy article, "Which Is More Important, Life or Chastity?" which was published in the *China Times.* Shortly afterward she was invited to become a columnist in the *China Times* and later in many other journals.

Ever since then, her name and women's issues have been popular and contro-versial in Taiwan. From October 1971 to June 1977, her six-year devotion to the movement can be divided into the following categories:[7]

Consciousness-raising

A series of lectures, debates, and writings were undertaken to raise the con-sciousness of women. Speeches were given at university campuses and many nongovernmental organizations. Debates were held on television, and feminist talks were widely reported by newspapers. As a columnist, Lu also wrote com-mentaries to criticize social issues and events.

Business

To provide a space for women as well as to support the activities financially, a coffee shop named *House of Pioneers* opened in October 1972. Three and a half years later, Pioneers Press was started, publishing some fifteen feminist books a year.

Organizations

An attempt was made to organize an Association for the Promotion of Women, but it was denied permission by the Taipei city government. Not until April 1974 was the International Federation of Business and Professional Women, Taipei Chapter, founded. This club sponsored activities such as workshops and a mail box to answer questions raised by career women.

Services

To render free counseling and services for women who were raped or wifebeating victims or who had domestic problems, Protect You Hotlines were set up in the two biggest cities in Taiwan, Taipei and Kaohsiung. Thousands of cases were heard and helped.

Research

In 1976 a Women's Reference Center with a collection of hundreds of feminist books was founded. A survey on the contemporary problems of housewives in Taipei was undertaken. Attention was also paid to women workers, rural women, and prostitutes, and a book entitled *Their Tears, Their Sweat* was published.

Activities

To reverse the stereotyped roles of the sexes, a Men's Cooking Contest and a Workshop on Women Outside of the Kitchen were held to mark International Women's Day in 1976. Based on the results of the survey on housewives, a series of panels on "Love, Sex and Marriage" were held in many cities, which attracted over ten thousand participants.

Obstacles and Supports: What and Why?

The fact that all these activities had been carried out did not mean that there were no obstacles to the advancement of the movement. On the contrary, obstacles existed everywhere. Of course, financial and staff shortages were problems that were to be expected. Attacks from the male chauvinists were predictable yet unbearable. But continual harassment by the KMT was something beyond expectation and tolerance.

Criticism that feminism was a heresy that would destroy traditional female virtues, that women's liberation merely borrowed from Western ideas, and even that the founder was abnormal because she was unmarried were made publicly and privately. Lu Hsiu-lien received almost every type of criticism possible. Quite often there came letters from unidentified persons to curse or to humiliate her in filthy language or pictures. Experience taught her to pray before opening mail.[8] When she could no longer stand such irrational humiliation, she decided to counterattack. She photographed the letters and had them printed in the front pages of one of her books, *The Pioneering Footsteps,* so that the handwriting of the nasty writers was preserved and recognized by readers. Even since then, no one has dared to write to insult her any more.[9]

Obstacles that were more difficult to overcome were those from the KMT. From the very beginning, Lu had had difficulty earning support from the government. Refusal to give permission to form the Association for the Promotion of Women was the first example. A year after the Taipei chapter of the International Federation of Business and Professional Women (IFBPW) was established, Lu was forced out because it was totally under the control of wives of high-ranking KMT officials.[10] The popular Protect You Hotline in Taipei was closed down in two years because the director, a loyal member of the KMT, sabotaged its activities and seduced some of young, attractive female volunteers.[11] On some occasions, invitations to make public speeches were canceled because of political pressure. Without such destructive influence of the KMT, an institutionalized movement would have been formed, which would have been able to better develop financial and human resources for mobilization.

Unfortunately, the KMT's intelligence agents had put their invisible, dirty hands on Lu's shoulders. As early as 1972 when the House of Pioneers coffee house was operated as a woman's activity center, the Investigation Bureau sent one of its investigators to rent a room next to hers.[12] He made friends with her and later invested money in the coffee house and finally became its manager. An editor of the Pioneer Press was subject to report on her daily life. The photographer of the Pioneer Press turned out to be an informant for the Taiwan Garrison Command.[13] There were other enthusiastic supporters who were later proven to have special missions. The most depraved trick was played by the Taiwan Garrison Command on Lu's guiding book of the movement, *New Feminism.* According to martial law, censorship of publications was under the control of the military commander. In addition to having banned two of the feminist books published by the Pioneer Press,[14] the Taiwan Garrison Command used the accusation that Lu's feminism "encouraged promiscuity" to refuse her copyright. The fact was that the term "promiscuity" was mentioned only once, to trace the social development of humankind, and had nothing to with "encouragement" at all. Shamefully enough, none of the officials in the Ministry of the Interior, the Executive Yuan, and the Administrative Court, which were in charge of the litigation brought by Lu, had ever dared to unveil such an open lie.[15]

But why did the KMT so resent the women's movement? There were political and apolitical reasons. Politically, the KMT, as an authoritarian autocracy, disliked any kind of agitation, and as an alien regime on Taiwan, it distrusted any native Taiwanese who did not enter the party.[16] Apolitically, the idea of feminism was contrary to the KMT's women's policy and therefore conflicted with the women's associations that maintained close ties with the KMT.

The KMT's women's policy, which is decided by the Office of Women's Activities of the central party under the leadership of Madame Chiang Kai-shek, has been to preserve the patriarchal and Confucian tradition. Women are encouraged to play supportive and subservient roles at home and in society as well. For instance, every year on Mother's Day, model mothers are selected on the basis of how many children they have raised and what socially recognized achievements their children have made so that a maternal image of women is glorified. The Chinese Women's Anti-Aggression League considers all female civil officials to be its members and requires them to take half a day off once a month to go to the league office to sew a pair of pants for military servicemen. To them, that is the best contribution a woman can make to her nation, no matter how important her official duty is.[17] Under such a political culture, women who are wives of celebrities or were established themselves join a women's club with the intention of promoting their social status rather than of carrying out social reforms. When Lu protested strongly against the patriarchal androcentric tradition, she agitated those women. In fact, the KMT's first refusal of permission for her to form a women's association was made by the Women's Activities Office based on the claim that there were too many women's organizations. Later, members of the Federation of Business and Professional Women's Club refused to cooperate with Lu because her idea to render services for other women was not in their interests.

The fact that Lu had been attacked so frequently and that she had caused so much trouble that the majority of women refused to identify themselves as feminists and that no other woman would commit as much as she had to the cause explained why this stage of the movement was viewed as "a one-woman crusade." However, it by no means implies that there were no other supporters.[18] In fact, for almost every project she could easily recruit a group of volunteers to help, though it was difficult for them to maintain long-term enthusiasm. Interestingly, just as the harshest attacks came from men, the most generous support also came from men. They supported her both spiritually and financially. For instance, half of the capital for the coffee shop was contributed by Lu's male friends. Most of her activities were under the auspices of men's organizations rather than women's. Of course, the most substantial support was from the Asia Foundation. In 1975, the International Women's Year,[19] the Asia Foundation granted Lu an internship to study women's issues in the United States and in Korea. Another grant was given the following year to help set up the publishing house, telephone hotlines, and reference center.

What Is the New Feminism?

To start introducing her ideas of feminism, Lu applied the popular formula of Dr. Sun Yat-sen's Three Principles of the People—that a doctrine is a kind of thought, of belief, and of power. In *New Feminism* she defined feminism as a thought that emerged from the demand of the society along with the tide of history; a belief that the prosperity and harmony of androgynous society shall be founded on the basis of substantial equality between men and women; and a power that will abolish the traditional prejudice against women, reconstruct a new and sensible value system, create independence and dignity for women, and foster the realization of the true equality of sexes.[20]

For further elaboration, Lu reiterates the following three fundamental principles of feminism:

1. Be a person, then a man or a woman. Considering the fact that too often women are limited to being women only, while men are bloated to represent the entire human being, emphasis on the independent personality and dignity of every individual, as a person rather than as a man or a woman, is essential. Let everyone be prepared to be an independent person before he or she identifies his or her gender. Let everyone be treated equally, regardless of sex.

2. Be what you are. Due to biological differences, a certain division of functions between the sexes is undeniable. Such divisions, however, should be limited to reproductive functions, such as pregnancy and childbirth. Beyond that, everyone shall behave according to his or her role in society. Gender is no excuse for privileges. Nor is it justification for discrimination.

3. Let your potential be developed. The stereotyped roles being anachronistic, a readaptation of roles in accordance with one's capability and interest regardless of sex is reinforced. In adapting such a new role, everyone shall develop his or her potential as much as possible. However, to readapt does not mean to reverse. To reverse a stereotype results in creating another stereotype. Not until options are truly open to men and women alike has true emancipation been achieved.

To summarize her ideas, Lu Hsiu-lien described the ideal feminist:[21]

The Portrait of a Feminist

A feminist is a woman proud of being herself.
She is ambitious, responsible, and committed.
She is independent, confident, and sincere to others.

She enriches her intellectual gifts as much as her feminine elegance.
She enjoys the satisfaction of her achievement as much as the sweetness of romance.
She is more attractive than a traditional wife, because she is bright in vision and rich in heart.

She is more maternal than a traditional mother, because she is aware and
informed.
She is more glamorous than a traditional woman, because she is not only a
follower, but also a leader; not only a beneficiary of the invention, but
also an inventor.

In a word,
she is happier than a traditional woman, because she is her own person.
She is no longer living under the shadow of his-story,
but is one of those who create history, our-story!

Is Taiwanese feminism a "Western import"? The answer is yes and no. It is
hardly deniable that Taiwanese feminists have been influenced by Western
thought, not only because Lu Hsiu-lien, Lee Yuan-chen, Ku Yen-lin, and a
number of other leaders went to graduate schools of American universities, but
also because in the early 1970s feminist literature such as Simon de Beauvoir's
The Second Sex and Betty Freidan's *Feminine Mystique* were translated into
Chinese and published in the *China Times* by an overseas Taiwanese feminist,
Yang Mei-huei. Her effort to introduce Western ideas was almost simultaneous
with Lu's movement.

However, with her comparative legal training, Lu Hsiu-lien developed her
feminism on the basis of comparative comprehension of Western and Chinese
culture. To the extent that it does not conflict with the ethics and the foundation
of society, she adopts and advocates. Intentionally she set aside some issues
that were not urgently essential and were too sensitive to advocate openly, such
as sexual freedom and homosexuality. From the strategic point of view, she also
appeared to be moderate with regard to the validity of marriage[22] and the
feminine nature of women,[23] so that objections could be decreased. In a word,
she is critical yet compromising; she is Western-educated, yet still maintains
her originality.[24] By and large, Lu's feminism is a philosophy that appeals to
the universality of human nature and therefore can be shared by women from
all over the world.

The Second Wave of the Movement

After six years of struggle with harassment and frustration, Lu Hsiu-lien decided
to change her arena. She went to Harvard Law School to study, specializing in
women and the law. Two papers on the "Feminist Proposal for the Legalization
of Abortion" and the "Revision of Marital Property Law" were finished. In 1978
she returned to Taiwan to run for Congress, with the intention of promoting the
women's movement as well as advancing democratization. Unfortunately, although her campaign was a miraculous success, the election was aborted on
account of the U.S. advance announcement of normalization with the People's
Republic. She then became an active oppositionist. On December 10, 1979, she

made a twenty-minute speech to mark the International Human Rights Day in Kaohsiung. Later she and virtually all other opposition leaders were arrested and court-martialed. Finally she was sentenced to twelve years imprisonment.[25]

Two years after the political nightmare created by the mass arrest was almost over, the group of feminists, most of whom had worked with Lu, led by Lee Yuan-chen, a professor of Chinese literature, decided to take up the feminist cause once again. They put out a monthly magazine, *Awakening*, for the purpose of "raising female consciousness, encouraging self-development, and voicing feminist opinion." In the absence of a full-time leader, *Awakening* made decisions on a collective basis and projected its image as a group instead of as individuals. In spite of the practical problems of its management and business, *Awakening* served as the mainstay of the feminist movement in Taiwan. It took a firm feminist stand and orchestrated the joint activities of other women's groups.

Awakening put in its agenda an annual theme to focus on. Since 1983 the themes have included "Developing Women's Potential," "Protection of Women," "Rights of Housewives," "Dialogue between the Sexes," and "Women's Right to Work." Almost all of the group's activities have been extensively covered in the media. In addition to publication and annual projects, *Awakening* now also functions as a pressure group. For instance, when the Legislative Yuan was debating the Eugenic Protection Law concerning abortion, *Awakening* called on six other women's groups to petition for better legislation. When the revision of the Family Law was being discussed by legislators in 1985, *Awakening* intended to cooperate with the YWCA to take feminist actions, but the Legislative Yuan passed the law at a surprising speed to avoid being interfered with.[26] As a result, the revised family law is far from satisfactory from the feminist point of view.[27]

Academically, Women's Research Studies, affiliated with the Population Research Center of the National Taiwan University under a grant from the Asia Foundation, was the first women's study group established in 1985. It sponsored in August 1985 a conference on "The Role of Women in the Developing Countries." In September another conference, on "The Future of the Asian Women," was sponsored by Su-Chou University, and in November the Prebysterian Church called an Asian Christian Women's Convention on "The Problem of Asia—Tourism and Prostitution." In February 1987 a symposium on "Women Intellectuals and Development in Taiwan" was held under the auspices of *China Forum* magazine and *Ming-Sheng Daily*.[28]

Although the active feminists currently come from the upper middle class and most are well educated, their concerns are not limited to their own interests. The Protect You Hotline services and the book *Their Tears and Their Sweat* during Lu's period all dealt with problems of their lower-class sisters who suffered worse lives than their own. In the 1980s, efforts were made to cover many aspects of women's issues. In 1984 the Women's Development Center was set up under the sponsorship of the Prebysterian Church to offer job training and employment for housewives whose households are in trouble. In 1985, following the Asian Christian Women's Conference on Tourism and Prostitution, a Rainbow Project was set up to house and rehabilitate escaped child prostitutes.

The year 1987 was a year of blossoming, for democracy as well as for other social reform movements. The world's longest regime of martial law was finally lifted by Chiang Ching-kuo on July 15, 1987. Even before its lifting, so-called self-rescue activities became common occurrences on the whole island. Inspired by such an open and lively air, the women's movement began an epoch of dynamism and multiplicity. Early in 1987, Rainbow and *Awakening* joined hands with thirty other human rights, religious, and women's groups to demonstrate against the abuse of child prostitutes on Hwa-hsi Street, the most notorious red-light district in Taipei. It was the first time that women's issues were brought out on the streets. This action caught the public's attention and was soon expanded to an islandwide movement. In July an antipornography demonstration was launched before the world convention of the Lion's Club when ten thousand male delegates from all over the world arrived in Taipei. And in October, with a view to protesting against the Miss Universe Pageant that would be held in Taipei, a panel on "The Myth of Beauty" following a Mr. Taipei Beauty Pageant was sponsored.[29]

In addition, women's organizations with various functions were formed one by one in the same year. On Mother's Day the League of Progressive Women was formed to recruit women into the opposition movement. On August 2, 1987, the Taiwanese Women's Rescue Association which is made up of lawyers, scholars, and other people concerned with the issue, was formed to render legal services for child prostitutes. There was also a club organized by and for divorced women and widows, named the Warm Life Association, and a group of housewives that advocates consumer rights and environmental protection rights, called the New Environment Housewives Association. In January 1988, the *Awakening* raised one million NT dollars and was legally registered as the Awakening Women's Foundation, a nonprofit organization. The goal of institutionalizing the movement that Lu had dreamed of was finally achieved. The awakening of feminism, coupled with the awakening of consciousness of many other social issues, indicates clearly that people in Taiwan are saying goodbye to the society of authoritarianism and androcentrism and are ready for the horizon of liberalism and egalitarianism.

Conclusion

For better or for worse,[30] the Taiwanese women have been struggling for their independence and equality for over fifteen years. A comparison of statistics over these past years indicates, by and large, that women's status has improved impressively. In education, the increase of the percentage of college women is higher than that of men (7 percent versus 5 percent). In the economic sphere, more and more women maintain their jobs after they are married. The ratio of white-collar women to blue-collar women is about fifty-fifty. The growth in the number of women civilian officials is extremely remarkable. Socially, the average marital age has been deferred and the divorce rate has increased.[31] In politics, although little progress was made for women in the KMT, wives of the oppositionists who were jailed by the KMT ran for election on behalf of their husbands and were elected. Ever since then, women have played a special role in the opposition movement.[32]

In reflecting on the past and present of the Taiwanese feminist movement as well as speculating on its future, a number of questions should be raised. First of all, was it premature to have started women's liberation some sixteen years ago? Compared to many other developing countries, new feminism in Taiwan did start considerably early, only a couple of years after it began in the United States but two years before the United Nations launched the universal women's movement. Candidly admitted, Lu Hsiu-lien was not prepared to sound the trumpet for such a controversial and tough battle when her first feminist article was written. Considering the repressive political environment in Taiwan, it was a little premature for a twenty-seven-year-old woman. But considering the incentive that led Lu to proceed, all that can be explained was the social demand plus her strong driving sense of justice and mission.[33] Had it not met the social demand, how could it have kept going, regardless of the risk? In this context, it was by no means too early to start, although the movement encountered much difficulty.

If Lu Hsiu-lien had not started the movement sixteen years ago, the *Awakening* would not be able to carry on the cause today, since most of its members have been strongly influenced by Lu.[34] Perhaps it would have taken another decade or so for someone else to start the movement. Of course, without the successive efforts of the *Awakening* and other feminist groups, what Lu started would be nothing but a historical dot. After all, thousands of years of tradition cannot be changed in a thousand days.

Certainly the movement is far from successful. Lu Hsiu-lien herself has never been satisfied with what she fought for. If she has made any contribution, she would admit only to having sewn the seeds of feminism on the soil of Taiwan. But for those who overlook the significance of the women's movement, she would remind them that the hardships that she has gone through, especially the political harassment behind the scenes as a feminist fighter, has been twice that which a freedom fighter would encounter. Unlike the opposition leaders who could exaggerate the persecution by their opponents in order to earn sympathy and support from the people, Lu had to hide all the political harassment that she received so that her followers, who were basically apolitical or even very much pro-KMT, were not scared away.

In contrast to the history of the American women's movement in which both the first wave in the nineteenth century and the second wave in the twentieth century emerged from civil rights movements, Taiwanese new feminism was initiated a couple of years before the democratic movement became visibly public. But did the former relate to the latter? Regrettably, in spite of Lu Hsiu-lien's personal experiences, the connection between these two movements is weak.[35] To the conservatives, Lu's involvement in opposition politics was viewed as detrimental to feminism.[36] Nonetheless, those who are far-sighted would agree that not until the ideas of feminism have been enacted into laws and policies will women's rights be truly assured. Therefore the women's movement shall in no way turn aside from politics. On the contrary, the earlier is women's involvement and the more their contribution, the stronger justification they can make for their equality and dignity. In this context, more efforts shall be made to encourage women to be politically active. It is only when women are politically active and powerful enough that they will be able to play the role of policy maker instead of policy follower. It is also only when policy makers are conscious of feminism that the spirit of true equality between the sexes will be respected.

Notes

1. For martial law rule in Taiwan, see *Martial Law in Taiwan,* a Human Rights Report from the Asia Resource Center and Formosan Association for Human Rights (Washington, D.C., 1985).

2. S.C. Lin, *The Wronged Political Cases in Taiwan: 1947–1985* (Washington, D.C.: The Taiwan Foundation, pp. 178–212.

3. Ms. Ban Chow of the Eastern Han dynasty was the first to engrave the Three Obediences and Four Virtues for Women in her book *Commandments for Women (Nu chieh).*

4. For the social background of Taiwan under which the feminist movement was launched, see H.L. Lu, *New Feminism* (Taipei: Tuen-Li Press, 1986).

5. H.L. Lu, "The Marital Property Law in Taiwan—A Feminist Proposal for Reform," LL.M. paper, Harvard Law School, 1978.

6. For her personal struggle, see Lu, *The Pioneering Footsteps* (Taipei: Pioneer Press, 1976).

7. For her experiences of leading the movement, see Lu, *New Feminism.*

8. For the obstacles and support that she had experienced, see Lu, *The Pioneering Footsteps.* Due to the cloudy political climate at that time, however, the book mentioned nothing regarding harassment by KMT intelligence authorities.

9. Ibid.

10. The KMT's women's policy was to reiterate the tradition of "virtuous wife and good mother." Wives of celebrities have little room for their activities except joining a women's association to promote their social status. Lu cooperated with KMT women in order to earn permission to form the IFBPW. Although she succeeded in founding it, she failed in dealing with the KMT women, who have little consciousness of feminism.

11. Mr. Tang, a professor of sociology teaching at Chung-sheng University and Chinese Cultural College, was invited to join Lu to be director of the hotline. Later Lu learned about his demerits.

12. The secret was revealed to Lu by the landlord, a KMT member, who said that he was required by the authorities to lease a room for Mr. Lai, an investigator, and his wife.

13. Mr. Ma, a photographer and mountain climber who used to escort foreign visitors to Taiwan so that information could be collected and surveillance kept.

14. The two books banned were *Sex + Violence = Rape* and *Their Tears, Their Sweat.*

15. For the litigation of this case, see Lu, "My Testimony—Political Persecution behind the Feminism Movement," *The Eighties* II–1, 7 (1979): 44. Not until Lu joined the opposition group were stories of her suffering from political harassment told.

16. "Your motivation to launch such a movement is to destabilize the society, especially to encourage disputes between the husbands and wives of our high-ranking officials so that their marriages are broken." Lu was so accused by the interrogators when she was arrested after the Kaohsiung Incident.

17. For instance, despite the fact that Lu was the section chief of the Commission of Law and Regulation in the Executive Yuan, she had to recess from her heavy duties to sew pants for soldiers during her four years of civil service.

18. For instance, some well-known writers and professors, both men and women, were enthusiastic supporters, though they preferred not to be on the frontline.

19. The United Nations held a World Women's Conference in Mexico City, which Lu was invited to attend. Unfortunately, the Mexican government refused to issue her a visa because of pressure from the PRC delegation led by Deng Ying-chao, wife of Premier Chou En-lai.

20. Lu, *New Feminism.*

21. Ibid., p. 157. She even wrote a "Song of Feminists":

> We are the feminists, of every age and occupation.
> We love our nation, our family, and ourselves.
> Ask not for privileges,
> but stand up against repression.
> We beautify ourselves with knowledge,
> glorify our life with service.
> Science, Arts, and Politics, we participate in everything.
> Our point is clear—
> Let us be our own being!

22. In an interview, Lu contended that since men enjoy life both professionally and domestically, women should also own the office and the kitchen, implying her recognition of the value of marriage and family. See S.W. Chiu, "Balancing Development between Household and Career," *Youth Monthly,* Taipei, April 1972. In a novel she interprets marriage in a more critical way.

23. She does not advocate unisex. Rather, she appreciates the beauty of femininity as much as of masculinity, so long as the standard of beauty is not stereotyped. She therefore contends that the talent of a woman does not damage her feminine beauty. Lu, *New Feminism,* p. 155.

24. Y.L. Ku, "Feminism and the Women's Movement in Taiwan, 1972–87," paper presented at the Symposium on Women Intellectuals and the Development in Taiwan. See *China Forum,* special issue (March 1987).

25. For the Kaohsiung Incident, see Lu, "The Court Martial of the Formosa Case: Sedition or Repression?" a paper written for the Harvard Human Rights Program. See also *Special Issue on the Kaohsiung Incident,* compiled by the Taiwanese Association for Human Rights, California, 1980.

26. Ku, "Feminism and the Women's Movement."

27. When these two laws were debated in the Legislative Yuan, Lu was imprisoned and was helpless, though she had finished proposals for the enactment of abortion law and revisions to the marital property law. For the defects of the revised marital property law, see Lu, *New Feminism,* chap. 9.

28. B.E. Chou and L.H. Chiang, "The Experiences of the Contemporary Women's Movement," paper written at the Women's Studies Center, 1987.

29. All these activities were reported in the *Awakening* monthly (January–November 1987).

30. In the two-day symposium on "Women Intellectuals and Development in Taiwan" sponsored by the *China Forum,* nearly every participant recognized the efforts and contributions that Lu had made.

31. Lu, *New Feminism,* chap. 9.

32. However, the motivation for these women to participate in politics is by no means recommendable, in terms of the feminist spirit. See ibid.

33. Ku, "Feminism and the Women's Movement."

34. Ibid.

35. For instance, very few members of the *Awakening* join the Democratic Progressive party, and very few party members, men and women, are conscious of feminism.

36. After the KMT arrested the Formosa (Mei-Li-Tao) people who were involved in the Kaohsiung Incident, the government-controlled mass media released a series of distorted and defamatory stories about them. Viciously, they accused Lu's feminism as being one of sexual liberation. Those who were close to her had one way or another also been harassed by the security officers stationed at their work places.

Chapter 11

The Social Discourse on Women's Roles in Taiwan: A Textual Analysis

Catherine S. Farris

The textual representation of women's changing roles and statuses in Taiwanese society should be seen as part of that process of change. I suggest here that scholarly and popular discourse on women's roles in Taiwan today also participates in the creation of "women's status" as a social reality and as lived experience, and that this discourse itself is an object worthy of study. This is to be seen as an analysis of native discourses that places in the foreground the discursive properties of texts to reproduce and to transform cultural forms such as "women's status." According to Bakhtin (1981 [1934–35]), every utterance is polyphonic and is part of a dialogue of discourses. Public explanations of women's changing roles and statuses in Taiwan can be read as a text whose many voices call into being Chinese concepts of women's place in the social order. These texts help discursively to construct the social roles and identities that "real" women occupy. Individuals then draw on these discourses to create and transform their own notions of identity and role.

This chapter examines three major voices in the discourse on women's changing roles and statuses in contemporary Taiwanese society: (1) the central authority, (2) the academic establishment, and (3) the increasingly articulate and literate urban middle class. These voices address multiple audiences: each other, their followers, and the "China watchers" in other nations, Communist and non-Communist, the world over. Obviously in one chapter I can neither examine these texts comprehensively nor include other voices in Taiwanese society that

An earlier version of this essay appeared in *Michigan Discussions in Anthropology,* special issue on gender transformations (Spring 1990): 89–105. Ann Arbor: University of Michigan.

animate the discussions on women's roles and statuses. Rather, this chapter is meant to be a first attempt to address the issue of the textual representation of women in Taiwan and to suggest directions in which future investigations might go.

Because language is "ideologically saturated" with socially and historically constructed world views, the idioms of discourse on women's status locate speakers within specific "verbal-ideological" worlds (Bakhtin 1981 [1934–35]: 271). Thus, the unifying language of authority in contemporary Chinese society on Taiwan, embodied in the state and posited as the upholder of the best of traditional Chinese values, contends with the unifying language of the West, especially of the United States, which Chinese scholars returned from study abroad seek to invoke and appropriate as a legitimizing discourse in their native society. At the popular "street" level, voices of the "common folk" (*laobaixing*) appropriate the authoritarian discourse of the ruling class, as well as the Western-derived discourse of the intellectuals, and distill these voices through their own experiences to create and re-create an admixture of voices that is distinctively Taiwanese.

The Republic of China (ROC) exists in counterpoint to the People's Republic of China (PRC), whose official discourse on women is a far more radical one. What impact does the PRC's radical discourse on women have on the ROC's official government discourse and on the discourse of various women's groups in Taiwan? Ku Yenlin (1988) notes that when the Nationalist government moved to Taiwan, "In order to counter the drastic social and political changes on the mainland, it took upon itself the role of maintaining tradition and tightening social control" (1988: 8). When martial law was proclaimed in 1948 (not to be lifted until 1987), restrictions were placed on nongovernmental organizations (NGOs) such that the vast majority of women's groups either were government-controlled ones, such as the Chinese Women's Anti-[Communist] Aggression League, founded in 1950 by Madame Chiang Kai-shek, or were local branches of conservative international organizations, such as the YWCA, the Zonta Club, and the Taipei Jaycettes (Chiang and Ku, 1985). In a continuation of ROC policy on the mainland, women's status was declared to be equal to that of men, based on the 1947 constitution, while their roles were seen to be complementary to those of men; they were expected to contribute to the stability and prosperity of Taiwanese society in their capacities as wives, mothers, and volunteer workers. In the 1960s young women and girl graduates of elementary and junior high school were encouraged by government rhetoric to enter the work force, helping to fuel economic expansion (Gallin 1984a). This economic prosperity in turn contributed to the growth of a new urban middle class in the 1970s, and government rhetoric once again valorized the wife and mother roles as the proper sphere of women (Diamond 1973, 1975). In government and academic discourses, women's enhanced status is measured by rising educational levels, increased labor force participation, legal rights, and control over life decisions such as use of own wages, marriage partner, place of residence, and number of children. The official stance is that this rise in the status of women is a result of government-led modernization policies that are much more beneficial to Chinese citizens than are the policies of the PRC. Therefore, scholarly and popular discourses on women in Taiwan must contend with this official government position.

Much of the discourse on women's statuses and roles in Taiwan, be they governmental, academic, or popular, only implicitly addresses the contrast with Chinese women's lives in the PRC. However, comparisons to other newly developed Asian countries, such as South Korea and Japan, or to Western countries, particularly the United States, are often explicit. I focus here on Western-derived influences on native[1] texts, whether it is an appropriation of Western texts or a contesting of those texts. While native scholars do not always apply Western gender theory uncritically to Taiwanese society, many scholars do assume a universal validity for the theories of gender that they have been exposed to in U.S. universities and scholarly journals. Government and popular discourses are more cautious about embracing Western notions of gender equality (e.g., the fear that "women's lib" will lead to the destruction of the family) and call for a more culturally sensitive model. Between the self-conscious elitism of the intellectuals and the legitimizing discourse of the regime, a growing urban middle class is discursively creating a place for itself through the production of popular texts and is claiming a voice in the construction of its own reality.

The reader will find little discussion here of the textual representation of rural or of working-class women's lives. Government statistics on labor-force participation and educational levels by economic sector exist, along with islandwide household and fertility surveys, as well as some sociological accounts in the academic literature of rural, or, less often, of working-class women (e.g., Chiang 1984; Hu 1985; Xiong 1988). There is a rather large literature on the government's successful family planning program that transcends, of course, rural-urban and class differences (see Chiang and Hsu 1985 for citations). But scholars writing in academic journals, especially women scholars, generally address issues of concern in the lives of the middle class, urban, white-collar, or professional woman. Popular women's magazines are almost totally given over to women's issues in the lives of the urban bourgeoisie. These popular writings emphasize the changing relations between the sexes, primarily within the family, but also in work and in public life, as a concomitant of sociological and economic changes accompanying modernization. Thus, I believe that it is worthwhile to begin with these texts, as they can be seen both as a dominant model of social relations and as a reaffirmation by the bourgeoisie of its own lifestyle.

The voice of the central authority animates the academic and the popular voices and serves as a *subrosa* text in relation to them. Thus, for example, government statistics on women in the work force are appropriated for use in scholarly texts or in the popular press. More often, the popular press stands in a similar relation to academic texts as academic texts do to government ones; for example, government statistics that have been given a certain interpretation in academic discourse are then appropriated by popular discourses from the academic ones. As the unifying language of authority, the government discourse on women's status is the background of the present discussion, while academic and popular voices are highlighted. Regarding the selection of texts, I refer to native sources, both English- and Chinese-language texts, as follows: monographs published by the Women's Research Program at National Taiwan University (NTU), the first of its kind in Taiwan; the English-language journal *Free China Review*, published by the ROC Information Office; the founding text of the modern women's movement in Taiwan, Lu Xiulian's (1986 [1974]) *Xin Nuxingzhuyi* (New feminism); selected articles on gender issues in academic journals; and selections from recent issues of two of the most popular mainstream women's magazines, *Funu zazhi* (Woman) and *Nuxing* (Mademoiselle). Translations from the Chinese are mine; Western sources are cited when relevant. I believe that it is fair to say that these sources represent an accurate, if incomplete, description of the urban middle-class, popular, and academic discourse on women in Taiwan today.

The Scholarly Discourse

In the scholarly discourse, early twentieth-century reform movements and the postwar rise in women's status, as measured by social and economic variables, are cited as evidence of progress toward gender equality. But further improvement is seen as impossible as long as traditional patriarchal values and social structures linger and women remain ignorant of and unconcerned about their legal rights and political participation. In a more open climate for public expression than a decade ago, Lu Xiulian's critique of Chinese gender ideology is being reconsidered. One lone feminist voice, the group of professional women at New Awakening Foundation (Funu Xinzhi Jijinhui), continue Lu's critique of Chinese patriarchy while quietly lending support and guidance to mainstream women's organizations and magazines. The rise of social activism among women's groups is seen as a sign of growing self-consciousness of women's places in a patriarchal society. An increasingly vocal and active women's movement in Taiwan, led by (primarily) Western-educated intellectuals, popular leaders, and a variety of women's organizations, has followed in the wake of increasing pluralism in public and private discourses. Relaxed political controls, the rise of an educated middle class, and the awareness by women of their subordinate status in society have come together to add new voices to the forces legitimizing a rise in women's status on Taiwan.

While it is outside the scope of this essay to address the textual representation of women in Chinese history, I will note here that some native scholars are concerned to invoke an indigenous feminist consciousness in historical perspectives on Chinese women. In these texts, challenges to the traditional roles and status of women in Chinese society are traced to nineteenth century reform movements in the Qing dynasty, which themselves were partially precipitated by the intrusion of Western colonialist powers. In the early years of Nationalist rule on Taiwan, no history of the Chinese women's rights movement was taught in the schools; most publications that appeared in China between 1910 and 1930 were banned, so that "the tradition of Chinese women's suffrage movement and the women's rights movement was completely eliminated" (Ku 1989: 181). Thus, modern scholars feel an obligation—as they do in the West—to write women back into history, and a number of articles and books have appeared in the last ten years that begin with a synopsis of early reform movements for women's rights (e.g., Ku 1987; Bao 1979; Yao 1983).

Socioeconomic and Cultural Perspectives on Chinese Women

Most of the scholarly literature on women focuses on changing gender relations in Nationalist-led, post–World War II Taiwan. In this writing the changing roles and statuses of women are placed in the context of modernization processes. These changes are seen to accompany modernization, while new tensions at the social structural level are seen as firmly rooted remnants of traditional patriarchal thinking, rather than as partially a result of the processes of modernization or congruent with other modernization goals, such as the appropriation of the cheap labor of young women and girls to fuel economic growth. Some of these writings also contain critiques of gender ideology and seek to connect ideology to social structure.

Women's work in the economy, politics, and society in general is frequently discussed in the literature on gender roles in Taiwan (e.g., Chou 1987; Chiang and Ku 1985; Hu 1985). Women's changing educational levels, labor force participation, and legal rights as status markers are herein compared favorably with men's, and recognition of women's crucial role in transforming Taiwan's economy into a newly developed one is, I believe, rightfully demanded.

After touting Taiwan's development, and what this has done *for* women's status, cautious criticism of continuing sexual inequities in education, employment, legal rights, and cultural evaluation is then preferred. This occurs even in the *Free China Review* (*FCR*), in which academic voices present government-sanctioned discourses. As Bakhtin notes, within any utterance a struggle between one's own words and another's words is waged, a process in which they oppose or dialogically interanimate each other: "Language is not a neutral medium that passes freely and easily into the private property of the speaker's intentions; it is populated—overpopulated—with the intentions of others. Expropriating it, forcing it to submit to one's own intentions and accounts, is a difficult and complicated process" (Bakhtin 1981 [1934–35]: 294).

In an *FCR* article on women in small-town politics, Liang Shuang-lian (1987) first speaks in the voice of the central authority, discussing the gains that women have made in politics and how even though "many goals remain unfulfilled," they "seem to have a bright future in this regard." But Liang would force the language of authority to submit to her[2] intentions. All women officials elected in 1986 were from outside the ruling party (the *Guomindang,* or GMD), Liang notes, indicating that the GMD "has not had much interest so far in supporting women for heads of local government." But the intentions of others continue to animate the author's voice. Liang praises the economic achievements of the regime, then tries once again to expropriate that hegemonic language, noting that continued modernization must draw on the skills of men *and* women. "In light of this, women may well expect the ruling party to take the lead in increasing female nominees for elective office" (1987: 15).

In another English-language publication, this one from the Women's Research Program at NTU, Chiang and Ku (1985) are more successful in submitting language to their intentions. They repeatedly stress the restraining effect of the socialization for traditional sex roles and identities on further improvement in women's status. In turn, the Nationalist (i.e., GMD) government is described as conservative and authoritarian, placing "social and political stability, economic growth, and anti-Communist ideology" as top priorities. To ensure stability, the government maintains "a restrictive and traditionalistic social climate" (1985: 27). This authoritarian structure is slowly changing, however; the lifting of martial law in 1987 and the legalization of political parties other than the GMD have contributed to and been shaped by the increasing heteroglossia[3] in public discourse.

The Evolution of "Women's Consciousness"

While the processes of modernization are described as the dynamic behind much of the rise in women's status based on the measures cited above, Taiwanese scholars see traditional social norms and cultural values as a ceiling on further improvement. Ku Yenlin (1987, 1988, 1989) argues that socioeconomic changes are a necessary but insufficient condition for improvement in the status of women. Changes toward gender equality have been and will be brought about by "the burgeoning of female consciousness and collective action" (Ku: personal communication).

A critique of the continuing influence of traditional patriarchal values is called for in much of the scholarly literature. The writings of Lu Xiulian, the pioneer of the modern women's movement on Taiwan, are invariably cited. Lu's (1986 [1974]) book, *New Feminism,* burst on the scene of Taiwan's social consciousness at a time of rising prosperity and the growth of middle-class norms and values. This was a time of sexual politics on Taiwan that Norma Diamond (1975) has characterized as a "variation on the 'feminine mystique,'" in which the traditional cult of domesticity, embodied in the ideal of "a good wife and virtuous mother" (*xian qi liang mu*), valorized housewifery as women's proper contribution to national development. The effect of Betty Friedan's (1963) critique of the sociocultural construction of womanhood in the United States at the time is, I believe, aptly invoked to describe the place of Lu Xiulian and her writings on women's status in modern Taiwanese society.

Historical sketches of the women's movement in Taiwan since 1949 contain obligatory biographical notes on Lu's background, including her training at Harvard Law School, her social activism on Taiwan to promote the cause of gender equality, and her downfall and imprisonment as a result of involvement in opposition party (*dangwai*, literally, "outside the party") activities during the Gaoxiong Incident of 1979[4] (see Chiang and Ku 1985: 38–40; Ku 1987: 46–48). Publication of her book was halted after an overseas female Chinese writer accused the book of promoting "sexual emancipation" (*xing jiefang*) (Ku 1988: ff. 5). Norma Diamond (personal communication) questions the extent to which Lu's imprisonment was due to her opposition activities and the extent to which it was "a case of her being singled out for punishment because of her outspoken and influential feminist views." Indeed, Lu herself suggests this interpretation in her discussion of the harassment she suffered by government security agents during her leadership of the women's movement in the early 1970s—harassment that she dared not let her fellow activists know about lest it alienate them from the movement. During the interrogation following her arrest in wake of the Gaoxiong events, Lu reports that she was reproached for her feminist activities: "Your motivation to launch such a movement is to destabilize the society, especially to arose [*sic*] dispute between the husbands and wives of our high ranking officials so that their marriages may be broken" (Lu 1988: 12, ff. 2). Changing social attitudes and a loosening of government controls over freedom of expression since Lu's book first came out have contributed to a climate in which her critique of Chinese patriarchy is being reconsidered; in 1986 a new edition of *New Feminism* was published in Taipei. The book is not readily available in bookstores, however, and many people are still unfamiliar with it.

In this book Lu describes women's movements in other countries, particularly in the United States, Japan, and Korea; provides a synopsis of Chinese women's history; and details continuing gender inequalities in the legal, political, economic, and educational domains, asking rhetorically if Taiwan needs a women's movement or not. But the heart of Lu's critique is contained, I believe, in the chapter of *New Feminism* entitled "Still a Patriarchal Society." Lu argues that as opposed to visible inequalities, such as economic indicators, invisible concepts of patriarchal values continue to control Chinese women's fates. That is, gender ideology is viewed both as a symbolic system that helps to construct and maintain social structure and as a constraint on further structural changes in women's status. These patriarchal values are four: first, the concept of "continuing the family line" (*zhuanzong jiedai*) generates the phenomenon of "emphasizing the man and deemphasizing the woman" (*zhong nan qing nu*). Second, the concept of "the three obediences and four virtues" (*san cong si de*)[5] generates the phenomenon of "man is respected, woman, debased" (*nan zun nu bei*). Third, the concept of "one-sided chastity" (*pianmian zhencao*) generates the phenomenon of a "double moral standard" (*shuangzhong daode biaozhun*). Last, the concept of "men go out, women stay in" (*nan wai nu nei*) generates the phenomenon of "sex-role differences" (*xingbie jiaose chabie*) (Lu 1986: 87–88).

Scholars generally agree that rising educational levels and labor force participation of women, smaller families, and more neolocal residence signal a rise in women's status by contributing to their increased independence from natal family control before marriage and parity with the spouse over family decision making after marriage. There is disagreement between native and Western scholars, however, as to the nature and extent of an enhancement of women's status due to the above factors. Several Western scholars argue that a patrilineal social structure continues to organize the relations between the sexes. These Western scholars see women's increased value to their natal families or to their husband's family, due to increased earning power of the woman, as largely beneficial to women's parents, parents-in-law, or husband, by placing more resources in control of the family head (e.g., to finance a brother's higher education), while control over women is shifted from primarily parents or husband to society at large (Diamond 1973; Gallin 1984a, 1984b). Native scholars have taken issue with this assessment and argue for real social structural shifts, brought about by modernization processes and an accompanying shift in cultural values (Hu 1985; Tsui 1987).

For many people in Taiwan, however, women are still considered by their natal families as "spilled water" (*pochuqu de shui*) and "goods upon which one loses money" (*peiqianhuo*), as they will transfer their allegiance, earnings, and reproductive powers to their husband's family after marriage. Although women in Taiwanese society are participating in extra-domestic life in increasing numbers and over a longer period of their life cycles, for many men and women, the rationale for that participation remains (both overtly and covertly) different from men's participation in public life. That is, women are seen by many scholars and by the general public as earning supplemental wages that help to raise their family's standard of living and at the same time contribute to national development. By denigrating women's contribution to the family purse as merely "supplemental," women are tacitly discouraged from demanding higher wages and equal opportunities for promotion. Norma Diamond (personal communication) points out that the notion that women's wages are only supplemental also encodes classist assumptions, as the wages of women from working-class and poor families are often crucial to the family's economic survival. Women scholars in Taiwan write optimistically that women's increased participation in extra-domestic life, together with a generational shift in power from the older to the younger, and women's closer ties with their natal families, will result in a lessening of "emphasize the man; deemphasize the woman" attitudes, and that families will come to value girls and boys, and women and men, equally (e.g., Hu 1985; Chiang 1988).

In some of the academic literature, there is an attempt to integrate models of cultural ideology with discussions of social structural change. Tsui's (1987) monograph, "Are Married Daughters 'Spilled Water'?" is based on her dissertation at the University of Hawaii. Tsui applies Barth's (1966) generative model of social organization and Caldwell's (1977) wealth flow model of intergenerational resource allocation to look at the relation between middle- and upper-class urban parents' investment in the education of sons and daughters and the flow of wealth from daughters to parents before and after marriage. She argues that the Chinese cultural construct of "filial piety" (*xiao*) continues to mediate relations between generations within the family, but that the meaning of this construct has been adapted to fit modern realities. Married daughters use their greater financial independence to maintain ties with their natal families—something that previous generations of women would perhaps have liked to do, but were restrained from doing by their structural position in their husband's family. The highly educated, white-collar working women whom Tsui interviewed showed a decreasing preference for sons, as their own value and strengthened ties to their natal families became apparent to them. On the other hand, their husbands still showed a strong son preference (to carry on the family line) and believed that it was primarily or exclusively the son's responsibility to support his parents in old age. Tsui argues that her research demonstrates a shift, for women, from a dominant cultural value to an alternate one, in which increased financial and decision-making abilities translate into an enhanced ability for women to be filial to their natal families.[6] Tsui has published (1987) a popular version of this article, in Chinese, in the widely read women's magazine *Women ABC*, indicating an interest in this topic by the magazine's urban middle-class readership. This research is intriguing and points to the need for further studies incorporating a more diverse population sample.

The one activity that cultural values and social mores still forbid to women and permit to men in the public domain is the pursuit of romantic dalliances. If a sexual double standard is one measure of continuing gender inequality in a society (see Hendrix and Hossain 1988: 446), then Taiwanese society's norm of "one-sided chastity" is a telling indictment of its legal and social ideals of "gender equality" (*xingbie pingdeng*).

The presence in the national language (i.e., Mandarin) of multiple words for men's women friends, with no equivalent for women's men friends, attests to the continuing sexual double standard (see Farris 1988a). Besides women-for-hire, such as prostitutes (*jinu*), call-girls (*yingzhao nulang*), and barbershop misses (*lifating xiaojie*), married men may also have such friends as a "little wife" (*xiao laopo*), a "midday wife" (*wuqi*, a lunch-time affair), or simply "an outside interest" (*waiyu*). It is not unheard of for married women to have an "outside interest" (the only gender-neutral term here), and there is evidence that sex before marriage is becoming more popular and accepted among young people of both sexes. This premarital sex is usually followed quickly by pregnancy and marriage (see Zhang Mingzheng 1982; Chen 1984).

Echoing the fears of many people in Taiwan today, Chen Jiaomei (1984) asserts that the popularization of individualism and the liberalization of sexual attitudes is having a detrimental effect on family life. Changing sexual mores in particular are cited as the reason that marriages today are more fragile, as the lure of outside involvement increases, resulting in unhappy marriages. As I note elsewhere (Farris 1988b: 190–91), "what Chen does not mention is that, for men in Taiwanese society, there has always been a 'lure' of outside involvements. . . . The greater fragility in modern marriages that Chen laments may be due [there-fore], not to an increase in adulterous spouses, but to women's increasing reluc-tance to acquiesce in such an arrangement." The continuing sexual double standard in contemporary Taiwanese society, the stresses of modern marriage, and the discourse on the "problem" of controlling women's sexuality are schol-arly themes that are echoed in popular writings on changing gender roles in Taiwan, to be addressed below.

The Women's Movement and Social Activism

Several themes in the scholarly discourse address and attempt to account for the rise of social activism among women. First, consonant with the cultural value of education as a route to social mobility and increased status in Chinese society, scholars place great faith in the benefits to women of increased education. Sec-ond, there is attention to and invocation of legally recognized "rights" of women. The two themes are intertwined, as the education of women about their "rights" is seen as a consciousness-raising activity for the promotion of gender equality. While the education issue is most likely a product of indigenous discourse, the emphasis on legal rights is probably appropriated from Western discourse.

Economic growth is closely related to rising educational levels and a better-trained work force (Liu 1983). In turn, an increase in education and employment outside the home is seen as increasing women's self-esteem and control over their lives (Chiang 1988: 2). "Education is thus an important social force in altering the lives of women, providing a means for women to realize their poten-tial and advance their status in the family and society" (Chiang 1988: 4). Among the so-called new generation woman (*xinshidai nuren*) in Taiwan, Yin Ping notes, "Advanced education has prompted more independent reasoning and judg-ment while possession of high-paying jobs has led to greater economic indepen-dence" (1987: 27). Although the causal relationship between increased education and high-paying jobs for women is problematic (see Chou 1987; Chiang 1988), it is perhaps true that a better-educated populace contributes to a broader social consciousness and to the heteroglossia of public discourse.

A more highly educated generation of women in Taiwan will also be more aware of its legal rights in society. More education in and of itself, however, is not seen as sufficient to increase women's awareness of subordinate status. Scholars argue that an independent spirit, nurtured by increased participation in the public sphere and decision making in the domestic sphere, is necessary for women to demand and achieve gender equality. Chiang and Ku note that even among college-educated women in Taiwan, there is little awareness of their legal rights (perhaps because it is a foreign concept?), and this fact, coupled with underrepresentation of women in politics, has left the codification of equal rights for women in the hands of men. "Only after the majority of women have been awakened to their human and legal rights and more women leaders have been trained and encouraged to play more active roles in legislation, can true equality be achieved" (Chiang and Ku 1985: 25).

As an outlet for potential discontent, the Nationalist government has allowed the proliferation of magazines and, to a lesser extent, newspapers touting a variety of views and opinions. There is no prior censorship in Taiwan, although the authorities can and have confiscated published editions of newspapers and magazines under the sedition laws. One important way of promoting activism legally in Taiwan is by publishing magazines, which then form foundations to sponsor public activities. Many scholars publish in both academic and popular journals and newspapers, thus playing a part in popular social activism in Taiwan. The increase in the number of women's magazines in the last decade is seen as promoting and reflecting more social awareness of women's changing roles in society (see Yun 1987). With the lifting of martial law and restrictions on NGOs in 1987, a variety of so-called grass-roots women's organizations with membership drawn from both academic circles and the general community have appeared on the scene and strive for the attention of an articulate and active "new generation woman."

Social Activism and Women's Organizations

There has been a growth in the number and kind of women's organizations in Taiwan in the last decade, and an increasing willingness to focus on shared substantive issues (e.g., prostitution and pornography, discrimination in the workplace), despite differences in organizational goals and rationales. Emily Wang notes that such organizations "have moved away from limiting their social concerns to traditional areas such as child care and hospital service ... [and] now address broader social goals" (1987: 30). However, Ku Yenlin (cited in Wang 1987: 30) points out that many of these women's organizations will not openly admit women's rights as their goal because it is not considered womanly to strive for "rights" in their society. Thus, leaders of new women's organizations often couch their goals in less confrontational terms. For example, one of the most successful of these organizations, the New Environment Association, targets the "neutral" issue of environmental protection in order to draw the most isolated of women—housewives—into public life and, in the process, to elevate their status through that participation.

Only one association of women in Taiwan openly promotes feminism and women's rights. Led by women intellectuals and volunteers, Women's New

Awakening Foundation began as a magazine that also sponsors annual theme activities, cooperates with other women's organizations to promote discussion of important social issues, and acts as advisers and resources for other women's magazines and organizations. The magazine is considered "radical" by many people on Taiwan, has a small circulation, and is not readily available on the newsstand.

The stated purpose of *New Awakening* is "to awaken women, to aid women, and to build an equal and harmonious society of the sexes" (from *Funu Xinzhi* insert, October 1986). The magazine aims to arouse women to self-realization, not through trivial and empty articles, but by addressing basic issues about women and the sexes. *New Awakening* calls itself an innovator and trendsetter in initiating questions about women and gender relations, through such activities as symposia, held annually since 1983 on such topics as "the potential and development of women," "the year of the further development of the homemaker," and "conversations between the sexes." By unearthing and discussing controversial questions, *New Awakening* will "promote society, in the domain of knowledge about the sexes, to march toward a new age." Men also need to read *New Awakening,* because society and family structures are undergoing change. While women are searching for themselves, if men hesitate to engage in these questions, it will be more and more difficult for the sexes to communicate. Therefore, in order to build this new and harmonious relationship between the sexes, men must also draw on *New Awakening* (*Funu Xinzhi* 1986).

A coalition of women's, human rights, and religious groups took to the streets of Taibei in early 1987 to protest the trading in underage aboriginal prostitutes. The demonstrations were led by the Presbyterian Church's Rainbow project, which was set up to help rehabilitate child prostitutes, and a group from New Awakening (Ku 1987). Before the demonstration dispersed, Li Yuanzhen, leading the New Awakening group, presented the police precinct head with a proclamation protesting the trade in humans. Ku (1987: 50) notes that, although this was the first time in Taiwan that such public demonstrations about an issue concerning women had occurred and the first time that different groups had joined together in such an activity, the three major television stations did not report the event. This omission by the mass media in Taiwan, Ku argues, reflects the means the media draws on to repress women's opinions (1987: 51).

In the summer of 1987 an even larger coalition of women's groups demonstrated against gender discriminatory employment practices. Ku points out that "insofar as the movement generated enough publicity and social attitudes became less authoritarian and more tolerant, women's rights gradually gained legitimacy as a relevant public concern" (1989: 183). As a native commentator on the discourse about women's roles in contemporary Taiwan, Ku is sensitive to the hegemonic force of the unifying language of political and social legitimacy, and to the potential force that other voices have to contest that hegemony.

Popular Voices

Women's changing role and statuses as a topic of discourse is not limited to the scholarly community or to the central government on Taiwan, as the rise of social activism indicates. The topic is also debated by an increasingly literate, prosperous, and socially active public. Although the texts that help shape this public discourse are many, I will concentrate here on the print media, primarily on women's magazines, as a window onto the popular discourse on women and gender in contemporary Taiwan. In this discourse, changing economic and social factors held responsible for the rise in women's status in the scholarly literature are given "human faces" in popular magazines, and the discussions are given over to the implications of these changes for relations between women and men, and for role adjustments within the family and within society at large.

In the past twenty years, some ninety-six magazines in Taiwan that target women readers have risen to contend for the attention of a print-hungry public. Eugenia Yun notes that many of the successful magazines copy Japanese formats, focus on new trends rather than new ideas, and are sometimes criticized for being intellectually lightweight. Many of these magazines, such as the oldest women's journal, *Mademoiselle* (*Nuxing*), begun in 1966, target the well-educated career woman between twenty and thirty years old. Regular sections include articles on homemaking and childcare, relations between the sexes, "intellectual living," fashion, art, and romance stories. The typical contents of this magazine, as well as other popular ones such as *New Female, Woman,* and *Woman ABC,* reflect mainstream concerns of the urban educated middle-class woman in Taiwan. The editors of these magazines assert that the magazines accurately reflect the "new generation woman" in Taiwan, who successfully combines work and family obligations while contributing to social and economic development. As the editor of *Mademoiselle* notes: "Our women's magazines provide the evidence that we have high education and great capabilities. We can do both family and office work—and do them well. We no longer fit the stereotypes of traditional Chinese women. We are now like women in any advanced country" (cited in Yun 1987: 40). Thus, women in Taiwan are sensitive to images of Chinese women that non-Chinese might possess and are also eager to take their places as educated, competent working wives and mothers just as are women "in any advanced country."

Gender Roles and Relations in Popular Discourse

In this brief survey of various popular women's magazines, I concentrate mainly on articles that address the changing relations between the sexes. In these articles, there is much talk of women entering the public domain and taking up new rights and responsibilities as a consequence of their increased participation in public life. But there is no corresponding emphasis on men's increased participation in domestic life, and working wives and mothers in Taiwan are facing the familiar burden of a double workload: one at the office and one at home. In these texts, there are indications that, as in the West, these new roles for women, their increased consciousness of their continuing subordinate status in society, and the intransigence of men to adjust to women's changing roles or to redefine their own generate strains in family life and interpersonal relations between the sexes. I have selected a few articles from popular magazines published in the last four years to exemplify some of this discourse.

There is a grudging recognition among middle-class men in Taiwan that women's increased responsibilities outside the home necessitate a new division of labor in the home. While housework and childcare are still viewed as women's "natural" responsibility, men are admitting that they are willing to share, or at least take over in a pinch, the least onerous of these activities, such as cooking and playing with the children. An article in *Woman Magazine* (*Funu*) published in 1984 is entitled "Male Students Also Attend Home Economics Class." In a certain senior high school in Taipei, the article explains, boys are taught cooking lessons while girls study shop. These skills are thought necessary for both sexes in modern society, so that together in married life they can take responsibility for daily affairs of the household.

Women's magazines contain a number of articles that seek to discover what men think of the "new generation woman," and how men are adjusting to changing roles in the family and in society. For example, a series of articles in the June 1987 issue of *Woman Magazine* is based on interviews with thirty-five professional and business men in their thirties. Articles address such topics as harmony between the sexes, the "new man" and the "new woman," the roles of husband and father, women coworkers and women supervisors, popular male consumerism, and women's special characteristics (Jin et al. 1987). In another issue of *Woman Magazine* (August 1987) one finds several articles analyzing the father role. The titles—"Must Papa Definitely Wear a Stiff Face?" and "Stranger-Papa"—reflect popular concerns about the stereotypically stern father figure and about the frequently absent father who spends many evenings out at "working" dinners with supervisors, coworkers, and clients (Zhou 1987; Wang Zhihuan 1987). It is clear from this sampling of women's magazines that, among middle-class women, there is a demand from women for a male redefinition of masculinity in Taiwanese society to complement the transformation in women's ideas of femininity.

As mentioned in the section on scholarly discourse above, there is public concern over the problem of controlling women's sexuality, particularly young, unmarried women who are no longer cloistered behind the walls of the family compound as their grandmothers and perhaps mothers were. The hidden text here, I would argue, is that it is important that girls be socialized to be modest and chaste, and to subscribe to the ideal of "a virtuous wife and good mother," regardless of the length and the nature of their participation in the labor market.

It is important that women remain emotionally as well as financially dependent on men, for in this way, they can be more easily controlled. Thus, higher education and work force participation are seen by many parents and by young single women as the route to a high-status marriage. While one might think that the most highly educated women in Taiwan—those who have received a college education—would be most "enlightened" about their subordinate position in society and most unwilling to accept a traditional definition of femininity, this is so only to a certain degree.

According to an article on women in *Free China Review* (*FCR*), women college students these days have "thoughts beyond books, boys, and clubs" (Leu 1987). New attitudes about the education of females, the author asserts, are in part responsible for the equal number of men and women now attending college in Taiwan,[7] while statistics suggest that "women now have plans for a future that includes more options than motherhood and homemaker" (43).

The author asserts that interviews with several female students attending colleges and universities in Taipei support the notion that the "new generation woman" will not be content with only the housewife and mother roles, but hopes and expects to have a meaningful occupation and interests outside the family. As the roles of women in modern society change, personal independence, career orientation, and advanced education are no longer unusual for Chinese women. Leu ends the article on an upbeat note: "Whether they pursue careers instead of—or linked with—marriage and family, the current generation is blazing new trails leading toward exciting opportunities and responsibilities in contemporary society" (47).

The *FCR* is a government-sanctioned organ directed toward the West and the portrait of women that this article paints, as with most of the other articles in this periodical, some of which I have cited above (i.e., Chou 1987; Yin 1987; Wang, and Yun 1987), does not distort the facts of women's changing roles in Taiwan so much as it selectively interprets them to put the best face on things.

An article published in *Mademoiselle* magazine in 1984, entitled "University Coeds Talk About 'Love,'" also containing interviews with several women students, is perhaps a more accurate reflection of the average woman's thoughts concerning the purpose of her education. Although the *FCR* article asserts that women students have more on their minds than boys, that is not evident from the *Mademoiselle* article. Finding a steady boyfriend whom one will keep all through school appears to be a priority. "Love—the college student's most important class" reads the caption under a picture of one couple. Even so, the chances of marrying that college beau are statistically slim, as the obligatory military service for men of two to three years separates the couple (which is considered a "test of love") and usually results in the dissolution of the romance (Zhang Dianwan 1984). While both the *FCR* and the *Mademoiselle* articles probably mirror an aspect of the highly educated woman's lived experiences, women's reality in Taiwanese society remains constructed by their first priority: marriage.

The conundrum for parents in Taiwan today is how to control the behavior of their offspring, in a world in which those children have much more freedom in the extra-domestic realm than their parents did and are developing dangerous independent tendencies. This is a problem with both male and female offspring, as the male's increasing independence from parental control threatens the parents' security in old age (Gallin 1984a, 1984b). The discourse on controlling female children emphasizes control of their sexuality, whereas this is not an issue in the control of male children. In an 1984 article in *Mademoiselle* magazine entitled "Sex, Virginity and Family Planning," it is reported that the Taiwan Family Planning Institute recently released figures indicating that 34.4 percent of newlyweds had had sex before marriage, and of these, 77 percent of the women were pregnant at the time of marriage. This shows, the author asserts, that today's young women are in a transition period emotionally and rationally. The author is perplexed as to why these couples would engage in premarital sex, as most of the couples in the sample had a high school education (Yang 1984).

In interpreting this article, two themes emerge: (1) As mentioned above, unmarried women's sexuality, but not unmarried men's, is to be controlled; that is, virginity is an issue only for women. (2) A sufficient amount of the proper education should inhibit the tendency for immoral behavior such as premarital sex. This faith in the conservative force of education is interesting in light of a 1980 fertility survey of Taiwan, reported by Zhang Mingzheng (1982). Zhang found that from the oldest to the youngest age cohort (women born between 1940 and 1959), their educational level, work outside the home, self-arranged marriage, and premarital sex had all risen steadily. Zhang reports that the single most important factor in encouraging independent behavior appears to be place of residence. Women who lived away from home before marriage were found to be most likely to control their own money, choose their own spouses, and engage in premarital sex. Thus, we see that parents' fears about how to control the sexuality of their unmarried daughters are rational.

The final article from popular women's magazines that I will consider here brings us back to the stresses of modern marriages. This article appeared in the January 1988 issue of *Woman Magazine* and is entitled "Existing in Name but Not in Heart, 'Chinese-Style Divorce'." It aptly points out many of the issues surrounding changing gender roles in Taiwanese society and women's reactions to these concerns. The article begins by noting that in contrast to the high divorce rate in the United States and in European countries, where one out of three marriages ends in divorce, the divorce rate in Taiwan is extremely low. But, the article continues, if we could hide behind the doors of homes, we would see that many couples who share a residence in fact are "united on the outside but divided in spirit" (*maohe shenli*); they "share a bed but have different dreams" (*tongchang yimeng*); and they "quarrel noisily their whole life"(*chaochaodoudou yibeizi*). This sort of married couple hardly speaks to each other, and many people would consider them the same as divorced. This common phenomenon in

Taiwanese society has been called "divorce within the household" (*jiatingli lihun*) or "Chinese-style divorce" (*zhongguoshi lihun*) (Hong 1988: 67).

Why do Chinese people stay in an unhappy marriage whereas a Western couple would divorce? In sections of the article entitled "Because of the Children, Sacrifice a Lifetime of Happiness" and "Women after Divorce Have No Legal Protection," these reasons unfold. First, in this patrilineal society, children "belong" to the husband's family line, so that women who divorce are rarely awarded custody, while some of these women never get to see their children again. At the same time, it is difficult for women to be awarded alimony if they initiate a divorce. The personal experiences of several women are then cited. One college-educated professional woman thought of leaving home to escape constant fighting and no joy, but she realized that she had only two bitter choices if she left—to be a housemaid or a factory worker. Therefore, she stayed in the loveless marriage. Another woman, a high school graduate and a housewife, thought to end her marriage, but when the lawyer whom she and her husband consulted inquired whether she would be a dancehall girl (*wunu*), usually meaning a prostitute, or a factory worker to support herself, she realized the futility of striking out on her own (68). How much less inclined a woman with children would be to do so.

In traditional Chinese society, Hong notes, the only divorce possible was one initiated by the man; the Qing code provided seven causes.[8] The most important social tie was father-son, not husband-wife. The couple knew each other little or not at all before marriage and were expected to maintain a polite distance from each other, to "treat each other as guests" (*xiang jing ru bin*). In this way the matrimonial relationship would become diluted and habitual. In modern marriages, problems can arise because women tend to place much emphasis on emotional expression while men are socialized to show no emotion (69).

Because women are emotionally and economically dependent on men in a marriage, and because men are more likely to have an "outside interest" than are women, Hong asserts that women are more easily harmed. This can give them a sense of meaninglessness and despair that influences the upbringing of their children. Yet a woman will stay in such a marriage, rationalizing that she does so only for the children. Such a home life will have a negative effect on the children as they grow up hearing their parents constantly fighting and realizing that they are the ostensible reason why their parents stay together (70).

Despite this grim depiction of marriage in modern urban Taiwanese society, marriage remains an important and valued part of every individual's life. Hong cites a survey showing that among the most important factors in a happy life, respondents ranked a "perfect marriage" (*wanmei hunyin*) as first and a "happy family" (*hele jiating*) as third. According to Hong, a perfect marriage encompasses understanding and sharing, common activities, sympathy, mutual affection, open communication, and a maintenance of harmony. At the same time, to stay in an affectionless marriage is stupid and unnecessary. However, even if one spouse[9] (i.e., the husband) has had an affair but sincerely wants to reconcile, and the woman still has deep feelings for him, she should accept him back. This generation knows that the contents and the intensity of love will change over the life cycle, and that one's attitude must be rational and positive. Knowing these things, Hong concludes, if people seek out a long and meaningful happiness in marriage, then a "Chinese-style divorce" will have no reason for existence (71).

I have cited this final article at some length because I believe that it exemplifies many of the issues concerning changing gender roles in Taiwanese society that have been discussed in the scholarly literature as well as elsewhere in the popular discourse. Although this article ended on an upbeat note, the tone of the piece indicated a hidden well of dissatisfaction and misery—suffered mainly by women—in modern married life on Taiwan. Sex discrimination in the legal code limits women's options for terminating unhappy marriages. Higher education is no economic safeguard for women as employment opportunities remain limited. The continuing problem of adulterous husbands is mentioned, yet, in the end, they should be accepted back and forgiven (if the woman still cares). Missing from this description of "Chinese-style divorce" is any serious critique of men's roles in constructing a happy marriage, and more tolerance and understanding is called for to maintain this most enduring of Chinese institutions.

Social perception and evaluation of the rising divorce rate as a matter of public concern is not limited to discussion in women's magazines. For instance, in a summer 1988 edition of *Womende zazhi* (Ours), the series of lead articles dealt with the question "Divorce, Is It a Trendy 'Game'?" At the 1988 Hong Kong symposium on Taiwan studies, in which an earlier version of this paper was presented, the sociologist Wen-hui Tsai argued that the rising divorce rate in Taiwan is one of the "costs" of modernization, along with air and traffic pollution and an increase in crime rates and public demonstrations (Tsai 1988: 7). In discussion, I pointed out that the rising divorce rate could be seen as a benefit of modernization, because women who had previously suffered in unhappy marriages now felt sufficiently independent—both economically and emotionally—to end such marriages. Tsai countered that the divorce rate was not beneficial to society as a whole. Thus, in his discursive reification of "society," the benefit of society is to be equated with the benefit of men and not of women.

Conclusion

In interpreting the discourse on women's roles in Taiwan, I have been concerned with three voices: the central authority, the academic establishment, and the new urban middle class. In Taiwanese society of the 1980s, the hegemonic discourse of the ruling class is being challenged by alternative or perhaps oppositional hegemonies (Williams 1977) of the primarily Western-trained intellectuals and the increasingly articulate and vocal urban middle class. These texts, then, are about shifting power relations, that is, contested power structures between men and women, between the older and the younger generations, between the capitalist and the proletariat, and between an authoritarian regime and its opposition. Obviously the vectors of these power relations intersect and overlap such that an examination of one leads into another. The woman born after 1949 has been described by the media as the "new generation woman" and has so come to describe herself. She eagerly seeks the "new generation man" but is often disappointed to find that he has not experienced quite the same evolution of consciousness that she has. Many men are very unhappy about having to renegotiate power in the family, based on women's increased self-confidence due to higher education and work outside the home. Men are also threatened by the challenge to their traditional prerogative to multiple sex partners. The continued diligence in control over women's sexuality implicates both changing gender relations and changing relations of power between the older and the younger generations. Women's participation in wage labor has made them more valuable to both their natal families and their husband's families. As unmarried workers their parents still seek to control their wages and their behavior, while as married workers their husbands seek that same control. Taiwan's economic transformation into a newly developed nation was in large part built on the backs of poorly paid and poorly educated young women, fresh from the farms and the small towns (Galenson 1979), who went to work in the many export-oriented factories. Their labor went to fuel the economy while their wages went to the family purse, which, among other things, provided funds for the advanced education of their brothers and helped underwrite their brothers' marriages. There is very little critique by native scholars of gender-linked class exploitation. The official rhetoric and much of the academic rhetoric assumes that women have shared equally with men in the rising standard of living that modernization has brought to Taiwan. This discourse on gender in Taiwan is also caught up in the changing relations between government and opposition voices. The GMD has variously promoted the "virtuous wife and good mother" motif or the working woman contributing to national development, depending on its economic and political goals. While some of the recently formed women's groups are more or less sympathetic to the opposition party, it remains to be seen whether the leaders of the *Minjindang* (DPP, or Democratic Progressive party)—almost entirely male—have any real interest in promoting gender equality on Taiwan.

Popular literature in Taiwan often uses the rhetorical device of describing a social problem ("the divorce rate is rising") then citing a (usually academic) authority who says something insightful about the matter. This is one way in which popular and scholarly voices interanimate each other. Because the academic establishment is considered to have more legitimacy than the popular press, invoking that legitimacy should enhance its own. While this appropriation may seem one-sided, the scholarly community also appropriates the voices of the masses and interprets those voices in terms of their prefabricated scientific models. At the same time that they contribute their voices to popular journals, the academic community wishes to maintain its distance from popular voices and texts. An anonymous reviewer of an earlier version of this essay noted that it sends several messages to the "intellectual community" (as distinguished from the nonintellectual masses?). Researchers must "answer challenges from the mass media and analyze many taken-for-granted views and popular opinions about women's roles in Taiwan by doing serious, rigid, and systematic research. Furthermore, researchers themselves must clearly and jealously maintain the line between research and journalism to insure Women's Studies a place as a flourishing discipline in the intellectual community." It seems well enough to assert that popular stereotypes should be subjected to scientific inquiry, but a hidden assumption—that the "intellectual community" does not also participate in the discursive construction of "popular opinions about women's roles"—allows the reviewer to privilege academic texts over other discourses, such as popular journalism, and to construct discursively a line between these texts which must then be "clearly and jealously " maintained.

Both popular and scholarly texts contest the most formally legitimate and powerful voice in Taiwanese society, the central authority, by incorporating that voice within their own. Citing government statistics to show the nature and the intensity of the gains that women have made in education, employment, standard of living, and so forth is an obligatory preamble to a critique of continuing gender inequality. In this discourse on sexual politics in Taiwan, at the intersection of language, gender, and power, one finds diverse voices interanimating each other as they come to contest the public and shared symbols that construct "men" and "women" in Taiwanese society today. The growing internal pressure on the government from voices of discontent in Taiwanese society has combined with external pressure (e.g., from their patron, the United States government) to modernize the political process as the economy has been modernized. These pressures convinced the Nationalist government that their grip on legitimate discourse was being loosened and that they should relax that grip voluntarily. We await the discursive processes by which hegemonic forces reappropriate these counterhegemonies.

Suggestions for Future Research

This modest attempt to analyze the textual representation of women's changing roles and statuses in Taiwan suggests a variety of avenues for further research. I will only mention a few here. First, an examination of the historical reconstruction of women's status would give valuable contextualization to the discourses on contemporary gender issues. My reading of native scholars suggests that a discussion of changes in women's status in the late Qing and early Republican period serve to link discursively Chinese women's experiences and government policies under Nationalist-led mainland Chinese society before World War II with the experience of Chinese women on Taiwan after the war and under

Nationalist rule. In the official history of China promulgated by Nationalist historians and taught in the schools of Taiwan, the history of Taiwan is just a footnote. There is little mention of Taiwan as a frontier area in the seventeenth to nineteenth centuries and under Japanese colonialism in the first half of the twentieth century. Historians of Chinese women on Taiwan follow suit in this omission. The government's ban on research concerning Taiwan's history has been relaxed,[10] and simultaneously, nativist sentiments are now more openly expressed. It will be interesting to see to what extent, if any, scholars call for an examination of women's lives in historical Taiwan.

Another interesting topic is the question of the power structures that control discourse directly, that is, through control of the media. How and to what extent does the government, in the past and today, control and censor the media, particularly television and textbooks, and how does this shape conceptions of women's proper roles? Who are the publishers of popular women's magazines, and what is their agenda?

The power of academic scholarship as a legitimizing voice in Chinese society must not be overlooked. To what extent are Western-trained scholars attempting to impose Western values of gender equality on their data? How successful are these scholars in convincing the Taiwanese middle class to adopt these Western values? Finally, are there native critiques of Western feminist theory and, if so, are these models rejected in toto or is there an attempt to incorporate them into a Chinese-derived model?

A follow-up to this chapter should seek to connect the discursive construction of women's roles in Taiwan to women's lived experiences. I agree with Ruth Behar (personal communication) that we need information about how these texts, especially popular women's magazines, are being read—by whom and to what effect. How do women draw on these discourses to "textualize" their own life stories?

I have not begun to address the representation of women and gender roles in modern Taiwanese fiction. Yet contemporary women novelists in Taiwan, in some estimations, are producing some of the best of Taiwanese fiction. This literature also calls for a textual analysis.

Finally, another major voice from outside the country not addressed here is that of Japan. Conversations with people from Taiwan indicate that there is much concern over popular influence from Japan, in addition to concern over Japanese hegemony in the economic realm. The love–hate relationship between Japan and Taiwan is another important factor to be accounted for in deconstructing the native exegesis on women and gender in Taiwan. This chapter is a small contribution to that process.

Notes

I am grateful to Sally Li Xiali and Alice Liou Hsiaohsun for their help in reading and discussing many of the Chinese texts with me. This chapter has undergone a number of revisions since it was first presented at the International Conference on Taiwan's Economy, History, Literature, and Culture, University of Hong Kong Centre of Asian Studies, July 1988. That version will appear in *Conference Proceedings*. A version of the paper was also critiqued by the editor and anonymous reviewers at the *Journal of Population Studies* (National Taiwan University) and was rejected for inclusion in a special issue on women's studies. A later version was presented at the China Humanities Seminar, University of Michigan, April 1989. I have greatly benefited from comments of the conference and seminar participants, the previous journal review, and, finally, the comments of the editors and an anonymous reviewer for Michigan Discussions in Anthropology. Thanks are also due to the following people for a critical reading of earlier drafts: Carol Eastman, Stevan Harrell, Ku Yenlin, Norma Diamond, Nora Lan-hong Chiang, and Ruth Behar.

1. When I refer to "native" scholars, texts, or discourses, I mean the Chinese on Taiwan. I do not distinguish here between Taiwanese and mainland Chinese (both groups are found in government and in academic positions), nor do I mean the aboriginal population, which is extremely small in number and lacking in influence (Gates 1987). "Scholars," "texts," and "discourses" therefore refer to the Chinese, and "Western texts," etc., is the marked term here.

2. This article was written in English, with the author's name in a romanization style. Because there are no Chinese characters (which often are marked for male/female), I am uncertain as to whether the author is a woman or a man.

3. Hetero-, "other" or "different," and -glossia, "tongue" or "language"; thus, in Bakhtin's terms, social discourse is composed of many different "socio-ideological" languages—what we would now call dialects, registers, genres, and, in multilingual settings, different languages—that constitute counter-hegemonic forces (Williams 1977) of decentralization and disunification (Bahktin 1981 [1934–35]:272).

4. In 1979 an opposition magazine, *Meilidao* (Beautiful island, i.e., Formosa) organized a series of protests on International Human Rights Day in the southern city of Gaoxiong, over the Nationalist government's cancellation of elections in the wake of "de-recognition" of the Republic of China by the United States in favor of recognition of the government of the People's Republic of China in 1978. The protests resulted in a violent confrontation with the authorities, and a number of people were killed. Lu Xiulian was one of the editors of the magazine and leaders of the (illegal) opposition party, all of whom were arrested and tried for sedition. Lu received a twelve-year prison term but was released in 1985 because of health reasons, and allowed to travel to the United States for medical treatment. Following a loosening of government restrictions over opposition voices, Lu, among other dissidents, returned to Taiwan in the summer of 1988, where she toured the island to lecture and meet with her fellow activists in the women's movement and in the opposition movement.

5. During the Han dynasty (206 B.C.–A.D. 200) the *Nujie* ("Admonishments to Women") advocated *san cong si de*, "the three obediences and four virtues" for women. The three obediences are: in the natal home, follow the father; after marriage, follow the husband; in widowhood, follow the son. The four virtues are: womanly fidelity, physical charm, propriety in speech, and efficiency in work (cited in Shih 1984).

6. The expression of *xiao* to the woman's natal family is a legitimate value as long as the woman does not neglect her husband's family or fail to give them their due. This alternate expression of *xiao* by women has the potential to subvert the patrilineal principle.

7. In the early 1970s on Taiwan, women's scores on the joint college entrance examination were improving each year, and people feared that they would eventually outnumber men in college. Some suggested that a quota on women students be set (Ku

1989: ff. 5). This brouhaha over competition from women was one of the controversies in which Lu Xiulian involved herself at the time.

8. Women could be divorced for any of the following reasons: disobedience to parents-in-law, barrenness, adultery, jealousy, disease, gossiping, and stealing (Yao 1983:27).

9. Hong uses the word "spouse" (i.e., gender-neutral); the "husband" is my editorial comment on Hong's text.

10. In the last few years, scholarly work has turned to research on the history of Taiwan, including the period of the Japanese occupation. For instance, the Taiwan History Field Research Project, administered through Academia Sinica and supported in part by a grant from the Luce Foundation in the United States, is a three-year (1986–89), multidisciplinary series of projects investigating historical aspects of Taiwan from 1500 to 1945 (*Taiwan Studies Newsletter* 7:2, 1988). The history of Taiwan is therefore becoming legitimate as an object of scholarly research in Taiwan, although Taiwan's history, geography and peoples are still not legitimate objects of instruction in the public schools, except as footnotes to the history of China as a whole.

References

Bakhtin, Michail. 1981 [1934–35]. "Discourse in the Novel." In The *Dialogic Imagination, Four Essays by M.M. Bakhtin*, ed. Michael Holquist, trans. C. Emerson and M. Holquist. Austin: University of Texas Press.

Bao Jialin, ed. 1979. *Zhongguo Funu Shi Lunji*. Taibei: Mutong Chubanshe.

Barth, Fredrik. 1966. "Models of Social Organization." *Royal Anthropological Institute Occasional Papers* no. 23. Glasgow: The University Press.

Caldwell, John. 1977. "Measuring Wealth Flows and the Rationality of Fertility Thoughts and Plans Based on the First Place in African Fieldwork." In *The Economic and Social Supports for High Fertility*, ed. L.T. Ruzicka. Canberra: The Australian National University Printing.

Chen Jiaomei. 1984. "Yi xinlixue de jiaodu tantao fuqi guanxi zhi diaoshi." *Shehui yanjiu*, January 23: 9–14.

Chiang, Lan-hung Nora. 1988. "The New Social and Economic Roles of Chinese Women in Taiwan and Its Implication for Policy and Development." Paper presented at the 30th Annual Conference, Western Social Science Association, April 27–30, 1988, Denver, CO.

———. 1984. "The Migration of Rural Women to Taipei." In *Women in the Cities of Asia*, ed. James Fawcett, Siew-Ean Khoo, and Peter Smith. Boulder: Westview Press.

Chiang, Lan-hung Nora, and Yenlin Ku. 1985. "Past and Current Status of Women in Taiwan." Women Research Program, Population Studies Center, National Taiwan University.

Chiang, Lan-hung Nora, and Meichih Hsu, comps. 1985. *Bibliography of Literature on Women in Taiwan, 1945–1985*. National Taiwan University: Population Studies Center [in Chinese except for citations originally in English].

Chou Bih-er. 1987. "Industrial Reshaping of the Labor Market." *Free China Review* 38, 11 (November): 7–13.

Diamond, Norma. 1975. "Women under Kuomintang Rule: Variations on the Feminine Mystique." *Modern China* 1, 1: 3–45.

———. 1973. "The Status of Women in Taiwan: One Step Forward, Two Steps Back." In *Women in China*, ed. Marilyn Young. Ann Arbor: University of Michigan.

Farris, Catherine S. 1988a. "Gender and Grammar in Chinese, with Implications for Language Universals." *Modern China* (July 1988): 35–67.

————. 1988b. "Language and Sex Role Acquisition in a Taiwanese Kindergarten: A Semeiotic Analysis." Ph.D. dissertation, University of Washington.

Friedan, Betty. 1963. *The Feminine Mystique*. New York: Norton.

Funu Xinzhi (Women's new awakening). 1986. May 10. Taibei.

Galenson, Walter, ed. 1979. *Economic Growth and Structural Change in Taiwan*. Ithaca: Cornell University Press.

Gallin, Rita S. 1984a. "The Entry of Chinese Women into the Rural Labor Market: A Case Study from Taiwan." *Signs* 9, 3: 383–98.

————. 1984b. "Women, the Family, and the Political Economy of Taiwan." *Journal of Peasant Studies* 12, 1: 76–92.

Gates, Hill. 1987. *Chinese Working Class Lives: Getting By in Taiwan*. New York: Cornell University Press.

Hendrix, Lewellyn, and Zakir Hossain. 1988. "Women's Status and Mode of Production: A Cross Cultural Test." *Signs* 13, 3: 437–53.

Hong Xuezhen. 1988. "Ming cun xin bu zai 'Zhongguoshi lihun.'" Nuxing zazhi. Taibei (January): 67–71.

Hu Taili. 1985. "Taiwan nongcun gonyehua dui funu diwei de yingxiang." In *Funu zai guojia fazhan guocheng zhong de jiaose yantanhui*, ed. Nora Chiang. Taiwan: Guoli Taiwan Daxue Renkou Yanjiu Zhongxin Pianyin.

Jin Naixian et al. 1987. "Bian yu bu bian zhi jian: nanren, ni liaojie duoshao?" *Funu zazhi* (June): 49–61.

Ku Yenlin. 1989. "The Women's Movement in Taiwan, 1972–1987." *Bulletin of Concerned Asian Scholars* (1989).

————. 1988. "The Changing Status of Women in Taiwan—A Conscious and Collective Struggle for Equality." *Women's Studies International Forum* 11, 3: 179–86.

————. 1987. "Nuxing yishi yu funu yundong de fazhan." *Zhongguo luntan, Funujie zhuanji* 275: 41–54.

Leu Chien-ai. 1987. "Thoughts Beyond Books, Boys and Clubs." *Free China Review* 38, 11: 42–47.

Liang Shuang-lian. 1987. "Female Dimensions of Small-City Politics." *Free China Review* 38, 11: 17–19.

Lin Xiuying. 1983. "Nansheng ye shang jiazheng ke." *Funu zazhi* (December): 30–32.

Liu, Paul K.C. 1983. "Trends in Female Labor Force Participation in Taiwan: The Transition towards Higher Technological Activities." Nankang, Taiwan: Institute of Economics, *Academia Economic Papers* 11, 1: 293–323.

Lu Xiulian. 1988. "The Women's Movement: Taiwan Experiences." Paper presented at the International Conference on Taiwan's Economy, History, Literature, and Culture. University of Hong Kong Centre of Asian Studies (July 1988). In *Conference Proceedings*.

————. 1986 [1974]. *Xin nuxingzhuyi*. Taibei: Dunli Chubanshe.

Shih Yu-hwei. 1984. "Cong Shehuiyuyanxue guandian tantao Zhongwen nannu liangxing yuyan de chayi. Taiwan, National Taiwan Normal University, *Jiaoxue yu yanjiu* 6: 207–29.

Tsai Wen-hui. 1988. "Social Changes under the Impact of Economic Transformation in Taiwan: From Industrialization to Modernization during the Post–World War II Era." Paper presented at the International Conference on Taiwan's Economy, History, Literature, and Culture. University of Hong Kong Center of Asian Studies (July 1988). In *Conference Proceedings*.

Tsui, Elaine Yi-lan. 1987. "Are Married Daughters 'Spilled Water'?—A Study of Working Women in Urban Taiwan." Monograph 4, Women's Research Program, Population Studies Center, National Taiwan University.

Wang, Emily. 1987. "Women's Organizations Unite." *Free China Review* 38, 11: 30–35.

Wang Zhihuan. 1987. "Mosheng baba." *Funu zazhi* (June): 53–55.

Williams, Raymond. 1977. *Marxism and Literature.* Oxford: Oxford University Press.

Xiong Ruimei. 1988. "Taiwan diqu gongchang nuzuoyeyuan liangxing guanxi yu renkou jiaoyu zhi yanjiu." Taibei: Xingbie jiaose yu shehui fazhan xuexi yantanhui. Taiwan Daxue Renkou Yanjiu Zhongxin Funu Yanjiushi, Qinghua Daxue Shehui-renleixue Yanjiusuo zhuban.

Yao, Esther S. Lee. 1983. *Chinese Women Past and Present.* Mesquite, TX: Ide House.

Yang Dongqing. 1984. "Xing, zhencao yu jiating jihua." *Nuxing zazhi*: 36–38.

Yin Ping. 1987. "No Fear of Flying." *Free China Review* 38, 11: 20–23.

Yun Eugenia. 1987. "Newsstand Power." *Free China Review* 38, 11: 36–41.

Zhang Dianwan. 1984. "Daxue nusheng 'tan lianai.'" *Nuxing zazhi*: 26–29.

Zhang Mingzheng. 1982. "Taiwan xiandaihua yu funu zai qingnian qi zhi xingwei quxiang. *Jingji lunwen: Zhongyang Jingji Suo* 11, 1: 209–26.

Zhou Xiaoqun. 1987. "Baba yiding yao ban liankong ma?" *Funu zazhi* (August): 41–52.

Chapter 12

Changing Patters of Women's Employment in Taiwan, 1966–1986

Bi-ehr Chou

Since World War II, industrialization and increasing participation of women in the labor force have become global phenomena. As a result, the changing role and status of women in the economy has become an important research problem in recent years. These scholastic efforts have led to a rethinking and reinterpretation of the relationships observed. While it is important to explain the universal existence of women's secondary status despite differences in economic development, there are also needs to investigate the diversity and the process through which women experienced industrialization. Moreover, not only is it meaningful to ascertain the role of women in the process of national development, it is also necessary to examine the implications of the process for the well-being of women.

As many studies have pointed out, in the past three decades the economic and social structures of Taiwan society have undergone a rapid and drastic transformation. According to Liu and Hwang (1987), from 1955 to 1985 not only has the socioeconomic structure of Taiwan been transformed from a traditional, agricultural society to an urban, newly industrializing economy, it also has completed the demographic transition from high to low death and birth rates. Its employment structure has also changed from a low skill level to a higher technological level. By the end of this century, Taiwan will be considered an industrialized society.

This article is reprinted with the permission of the Centre of Asian Studies, The University of Hong Kong. It first appeared as "Industrialization and Change in Women's Employment Status in Taiwan: 1966–1968," in *Taiwan: Economy, Society, and History*, edited by Edward K.Y. Chen, Jack F. Williams, and Joseph Wong, pp. 307–26. Hong Kong: Centre of Asian Studies, The University of Hong Kong, 1991.

In contrast to the extensive documentation of Taiwan's economic development, studies of change in gender-role relationships during this process have been few. Recently, however, an increasing number of empirical investigations of the changing role of women in Taiwan have appeared (Chiang and Ku 1985; Chou and Clark 1986; Gallin 1984; Greenhalgh 1985; Kung 1981; Tsai 1986; Tsay 1987; Tsui 1987). In general, these studies document the improving yet still inferior position of women in most spheres of society (Chiang and Ku 1985; Chou and Clark 1986; Greenhalgh 1985). Moreover, there are varieties in the ways through which women experienced this industrialization. Although the educational attainment of women has reached almost the same level as that of men, and the level of labor force participation has increased significantly over the period of intensive industrialization (Tsai 1986), women's participation in political office (Chou and Clark 1986) and sex segregation in occupational distribution (Tsai 1986) remain relatively unchanged over time. Finally, there are also indications of the existence of rural-urban or class differences in Taiwan women's experience with status change in the process of economic development (Farris 1986; Gallin 1984; Kung 1981; Tsui 1987). For example, while rural, uneducated, and older women seem to have suffered status loss from economic development (Gallin 1984), urban, better educated, and younger women appear to have benefited from the opportunities generated by such development (Tsui 1987).

In short, these studies have provided important foundations for assessing the implications of industrialization for women's roles and status in various spheres of Taiwan society. Nevertheless, the question of the relationship between industrialization and women's roles remains. Since employment has been viewed as an important indicator of women's changing roles and status, and since participation in the production system is seen as a mechanism through which the individual is linked with industrialization, this essay focuses on change in this dimension of women's status. Specifically, it examines the nature and pattern of the changes in women's status as reflected in the various aspects of their participation in the employment settings in the recent past in Taiwan. Furthermore, to delineate the change in the relative status of gender, changes in women's employment are compared with men's and analyzed within the context of a changing hierarchy of production systems.

Taiwan society represents an interesting case for studying changes in women's roles and status in the process of economic development because of the existence of countervailing forces. On the one hand, traditional Chinese society was a patriarchal system wherein women assumed a subordinate status. On the other hand, since the Revolution of 1911, the constitution and various laws have granted equal rights to women to participate in politics, education, and employment. Furthermore, with rapid modernization, women have played an increasing role in Taiwan's economy. Interaction of all of these forces should produce contrasting implications for the status of women.

Theoretical Background

Traditionally, economic development was viewed as leading to the expansion of women's participation in the productive sphere of society. This expansion of women's productive role into a nontraditional sphere was expected in turn to elevate their status. This belief was generally unquestioned until Boserup (1970) documented that the relationship between development and women's status may be an inverse one. Since then, many other empirical investigations have demonstrated the continuous existence of a gender gap in status in the industrialization process of many developing societies, despite differences in their paths of development (Elliott 1977; Safa 1977). Similarly, in the developmental history of contemporary Western industrialized societies, such as the United States and Great Britain, the existence of sex segregation in the workplace despite rapid increases in labor force participation among women has been regarded as one of the most persistent social phenomena during the past few decades (Gross 1968; Williams 1979; Beller 1984; Roos 1985).

Theoretical perspectives relevant to the discussion of the persistence of a gender gap in the productive systems of contemporary societies come from three different traditions: the female marginalization thesis, the changing mode of production perspective, and sex segregation theories. The female marginalization thesis emerged from Latin American scholarship and has special relevance to dependency theories, while the mode of production perspective contains elements of both Marxism and feminism. On the other hand, sex segregation theories, being derived mainly from the experience of capitalist industrialized societies, although incorporating a feminist perspective, are more closely related to orthodox economic and sociological traditions.

The Female Marginalization Thesis

Stated briefly, the central idea of the female marginalization (FM) thesis holds that women's marginalization in the productive system resulting from the process of societal economic development is a product of the capitalist organization of production and use of labor. Because capitalist development inherently separates production and reproduction, structures capitalist enterprises hierarchically, requires surplus labor and an industrial reserve army, and engenders mutual accommodation between capitalism and patriarchy, it will result in women's confinement to the home, to inferior jobs, and to the reserve army of labor. Interaction of these processes can have three effects on women. The first produces a withdrawal of women from the labor force, particularly in the early stages of industrialization. The second reconstitutes the female labor force as a secondary market and concentrates women in inferior positions in occupational hierarchies. The third establishes and casualizes women's employment because of their deployment as part of the reserve army of labor. To be marginalized, in dependency theory, means to be excluded from the core sector of the capitalist productive system—export manufacturing or multinational corporations—and absorbed into the peripheral fringe of the economy—the informal or subsistence sectors. In this context, female labor is subject to informalization and tertiarization. Indicators of female marginalization have included (1) a general fall in the global female participation rate at the beginning of industrialization; (2) a decline in women's share of capitalist employment (wage labor and manufacturing); (3) the concentration of women into "informal" and tertiary sectors; (4) the segregation or feminization of marginal sectors or occupations; and (5) inequality between men and women.

Empirical tests of the female marginalization thesis have produced inconsistent results concerning the validity of the hypothesized expectations and thus the generalizability of the thesis. For example, Cho and Koo's (1983) analysis of labor statistics and survey data from South Korea found some support for the marginalization of female employment in the intensification of agricultural work for rural women. On the other hand, there was also an increasing number of urban women moving into factory and clerical work, along with the informalization of married women's work. Similarly, Scott's (1986) analysis of data from Peru's capital city, Lima, between 1940 and 1981 also produced partial support for the thesis. She concluded that "women clearly were marginal to the economy as reflected in a high degree of sex segregation and economic inequality between men and women" (p. 656). However, women do not show a falling labor force participation or an exclusion from the wage sector or an informalization of employment as predicted by the FM thesis. Using the Brazilian manufacturing industry in the 1970s as the basis of analysis, Humphrey (1984) observed that "contrary to the predictions of [the FM thesis], women have not been marginalized from the industrial labor force; [rather] there was a substantial rise in female manufacturing employment and significant change in the sex composition of industry." Although this claim was disputed (Scott 1986), the disagreement is over the interpretation rather than over the analysis.

From the above discussion, it is clear that the female marginalization thesis offers a broad analytical framework capable of explaining the mechanism through which economic development can produce different effects in a population. However, as it is currently being used, marginalization has many meanings and referents. Imprecise definitions and inconsistent measurements may have caused some inconsistency in the empirical findings obtained. Therefore, a discussion of the other two theories may be helpful in providing a basis for evaluating marginalization.

Women and Changing Mode of Production

Since the 1970s, studies have appeared that do not directly examine the applicability of FM but deal with the changing status of women under changing modes of production. These studies generally support the hypothesis that women's status declines with their diminished productive role in the transition from an agricultural, subsistence economy to an urban, industrial economy based on new production factors. But they also point out the complexity of this process and suggest that the process needs to be examined within a particular cultural, historical, and class context. Thus, for rural Java, Stoler (1977) found that while women of the landed class were able to obtain benefits from industrialization, landless women have suffered from income loss caused by mechanization. Similarly, Chinchilla's (1977) analysis of changes in female occupational patterns in Guatemala also showed that poor, uneducated women were increasingly confined to the tertiary sector (e.g., domestic servants), while women from middle and upper classes, often young and unmarried, entered expanding low-level white-collar jobs. In Mexico, Arizpe (1977) also called attention to the uneven effect of reductions of job options for poor women who did not have the choice not to work. In short, these papers demonstrate that the growth of wage labor under capitalism not only widens the gender division of labor but, more importantly, places the primary burden on women at the lower end of the class hierarchy.

Sex Segregation Theories

While FM theories view marginalization as the dynamic by which women are excluded from the core of the production process into secondary status during the course of industrialization in many developing societies, sex segregation theories see sex segregation in the labor market as a persistent social force underlying the perpetuation of status inequality in developed societies beyond industrialization (Gross 1968; Williams 1979; Beller 1984). Occupational sex segregation refers to those situations in which the work force in an occupation does not contain a representative distribution of men and women according to their proportion in the adult population (or appropriate category of adult population) (Tangri 1976). Investigation of the causes of sex segregation and estimation of its contribution to earning differentials have been the focus of many economic and sociological endeavors (Blau and Jusenius 1976; Blau 1984; Strober 1984). While classical economic and sociological theories emphasize individual women's characteristics or employers' taste, institutional approaches stress the structure of the labor market (internal market, dual market, and statistical discrimination) or social institutions (patriarchy, capitalism, unionism) as the factors leading to the allocation of women and men to different positions. According to the latter approach, sex segregation in the workplace is a product of a patriarchal social value system in combination with a capitalist economic value system. Because the labor market under capitalism tends to be divided and segmented into primary and secondary sectors, and since patriarchy emphasizes the economic role of men, men and women are socialized for, hired for, and assigned to different types of work. Then, either through the operation of an internal market and or through statistical discrimination, men are more likely to be in the primary labor market or the internal job market while women are shunted into the secondary market. Jobs in different sectors of the labor market have different characteristics. Primary-sector or internal-market jobs are usually characterized by higher monetary rewards, high skill require-ments, extensive on-the-job training, open promotion schedules, and auton-omy and decision- making power. On the contrary, jobs in the secondary labor market usually pay less and require high initial training, but offer no on-the-job training or firm-specific skills. They are likely to be nonpromotio-nal, dead-end jobs. The effect of these characteristics is unequal achievement by men and women in the economic and occupational status hierarchy. In short, sex segregation is not only prevalent and persistent in the recent his-tory of Western industrialized societies but also closely related to the eco-nomic inequality between genders in contemporary society (Treiman and Hartmann 1981; Blaxall and Reagan 1976; Roos 1985).

The importance of sex segregation theories for our purpose is its explication of dimensions and measurement of occupation segregation. Occupational sex segregation has several interrelated dimensions (Lapidus 1976), but two will be emphasized here. Horizontal segregation refers to a distribution of women to certain sectors or occupations, and of men to others, out of all proportion to their overall participation in the labor force. Horizontal segregation may be measured by the percentage of women and men across types of work, or across different occupational groups or industries.

The second dimension of occupational sex segregation is the vertical stratifi-cation of men and women in an occupational hierarchy. That is the declining proportion of women at successively higher levels of skill, authority, status, and income of job hierarchy. This is also termed by some scholars rank segregation (Miller and Garrison 1982). In addition to rank segregation, there are other forms by which women workers can be vertically stratified. They include the so-called industrial or firm segregations. That is, within occupations, men are more likely to be employed in larger, more capitalized, less marginal, more prestigious firms or industries (i.e., transportation, construction, and durables manufacture) with higher pay and more benefits, while women, on the contrary, are more likely to be employed in smaller, more marginal, less prestigious firms or industries (i.e., retail, nondurable manufacture) that offer lower salary and lower benefits (Bridge 1980; Bielby and Baron 1984). The combination of these forms of vertical segregation has been found to be the dominant factor accounting for the difference in earnings between sexes.[1]

In short, the literature reviewed suggests that segregation may manifest itself in many levels and in different dimensions. Frequently, segregation has been measured at the levels of types of work or major occupation groups. Alterna-tively, segregation can be measured by industries, firms, and jobs within firms. It may also be measured at different strata or positions of occupational prestige or authority scale. Moreover, sex segregation tends to increase as the level of aggregation decreases, or as the unit of analysis becomes more specific. Thus, in the work setting within an organization, women's jobs tend to be completely separated from men's. (For a detailed discussion of this point, see Bielby and Baron 1984.)

From the above discussion, it is clear that although the argument of segregation theories may differ from that of female marginalization, they are complementary. The above review of literature has several implications for the present analysis. First, since the exclusion of females from the core or primary sector of production and the feminization of marginal or declining sectors of production were suggested as factors underlying the gender gap, to adequately analyze the effect of economic development on women's status, research designs must incorporate the historical and structural contexts as criteria for defining the core and periphery of an economy. One such important context for Taiwan society is industrialization. Industrialization has the effect of shifting the hierarchical organization of industries leading to the increasing dominance of manufacturing and decreasing importance of agriculture in the economy. Second, to ascertain changes in status relations, it is necessary to analyze not only changes in the distribution of female employment generated by industrialization but also changes in the sex composition of industries or occupations. Finally, as with segregation when marginalization is analyzed, a research strategy needs to specify the level or the unit of analysis and to consider simultaneously the vertical and horizontal aspects of the phenomenon. In the remaining sections of this chapter, various trend data will be used to take into consideration these points in the analysis below.

Data and Methods

Data for the present analysis came from the *Labor Surveys of Taiwan Area* published annually by the Directorate-General of Budget, Accounting, and Statistics (DGBAS) of the Executive Yuan, which contain information on the various socioeconomic and demographic characteristics of Taiwan's labor force since 1963. Samples for the labor surveys were obtained by a stratified random sampling using neighborhoods as units of sampling. Interviews were conducted periodically several times each year. For the present analysis, data on the distribution of men and women across industries, occupations, and employment strata from 1966 to 1986 were used as the basis for ascertaining the change and persistence of women's status in the process of industrialization in Taiwan. Selection of 1966 as the starting point is both rational and practical. The year 1966 marked the beginning of the period of labor-intensive, export-oriented industrialization of Taiwan (1965–73). It was also the year when annual labor survey statistics became available. Availability of the trend data should facilitate analysis of changes.

To ascertain the extent to which female employment experienced marginalization or segregation in the process of industrialization, both industries and major occupations will be used as the unit of analysis. In addition, gender differences across strata of employment status will be examined to reflect the vertical aspect of status. These three levels of analysis, when interpreted within the context of the changing economic structure of Taiwan in the past two decades, captures the essence of both horizontal and vertical dimensions of the gender gap in status.

Two indicators of changes in women's status will be utilized. The first is the change in the distribution of women's employment across industries, major occupations, and employment strata from 1966 to 1986. These changes will then be compared with those experienced by the male counterparts at the same period of time to assess the change in the relative status of women against that of men. The second indicator is the change in sex composition of occupations, industries, or employment status. Here, females as a percentage of total employed in an occupation, industry, or employment stratum will be used. Change is measured by taking the difference in each of these variables every five years. Since the labor surveys involved a large sample and the purpose of the study is to identify patterns and the nature of changes, rather than analysis of causal relationships, a statistical test of significance of the differences is neither meaningful nor necessary.

Change in Industrial Distribution of Female Employment, 1966–86

To ascertain the change in the degree to which women have been integrated into the core of Taiwan's production system, the distribution of women workers across various industries may be used. Tables 12.1 and 12.2 present the percentage distribution of women workers among industries and the ratios of women workers to the total employed in different industries. The latter statistics are calculated to measure the extent to which industries were feminized. The former is used to indicate the concentration or dispersion of female employment among industries. For comparison purposes, distributions of percentage and ratio of male workers are also included in tables 12.1 and 12.2.

For the discussion of tables 12.1 and 12.2, a brief description of the changing hierarchy of industries in the Taiwan economy over the past thirty years is necessary. In the process of industrialization, the importance of various sectors of an economy shifts. Thus, for the traditional society, agriculture is the most important production system; for the industrialized, manufacturing industry assumes a leading role. For the postindustrial society, service industry contributes a higher share of economic output. In the past three decades of Taiwan's economic development, the importance of agricultural production has decreased substantially. Its share of GNP declined from 33 percent in the 1950s to 20 percent in the 1970s and less than 10 percent in the early 1980s. The share of industry as percent of GNP, in contrast, has increased from 20 percent to 45 percent during the same period. The share of the tertiary sector as a whole remains relatively unchanged. But within it, the shares of finance and transportation have increased twofold (10 percent in 1981–84), while that of commerce has decreased slowly but consistently, from 19 percent in 1951 to 14 percent in 1984 (DGBAS 1986, 26, fig. 24; Liu and Hwang 1987, 115, table 4.16). In short, using the changing share of GNP as a criterion, in the past thirty years agriculture is the declining industry and manufacture represents the core in Taiwan's economy. The tertiary industry as a whole remains an important part of the economy, but within it finance and transportation are gaining weight while commerce appears to be losing and service remains unchanged. Consequently, agriculture, manufacturing, commerce, and service may be viewed as referent industries of criteria for examining the changes in the two aspects of women's status in the production system along the core-peripheral continuum. Agriculture and manufacturing represent the two ends of the periphery and core, and commerce and service are the two medium points along the periphery and core continuum.

Table 12.1 shows the concentration of women's employment in the four critical industries. The percentage of female workers employed in agriculture has decreased consistently from 1966 (47 percent) to 1986 (14 percent), while the percentage of working women engaged in manufacturing more than doubled, from 18 percent in 1966 to 40 percent in 1986. For the tertiary industries as a whole, there was also an overall increase in the percentage of females employed. Among them, the increase is mainly in commerce (from 13 percent to 20 percent) and less in transportation, communication, and finance (2 percent to 5 percent). The percentage of females in service remains essentially unchanged. As a result of these changes, the distribution of female employment has shifted from a predominant concentration in agriculture to manufacturing. At present, manufacturing employs the largest proportion of working women (40 percent). The second largest area of female employment is commerce (20 percent), followed closely by service (19 percent). Agriculture becomes the fourth largest women's employer, currently engaging only 14 percent of total employed women.

When one compares the distribution of men with that of women, a few points stand out. First, although men also experienced a dramatic reduction in agricultural employment, the rapidity of that sector's decline has been slower, and a greater proportion of male workers are still engaged in it (from 43 percent to 19 percent). Second, while there was a significant increase in the percentage of male workers employed in manufacturing (from 18 percent to 30 percent), the magnitude of this increase is far less than that of women, from 18 percent to 40 percent. Third, among other major industries over the studied period, significantly more men are unemployed in the commerce sector, while the proportion engaged in service remains unchanged. Another major increase experienced by men was in the construction industry, where the percentage doubled in twenty years. The consequence of these shifts is a dispersed distribution of men's employment wherein manufacturing workers comprise the largest proportion (30

Table 12.1

Percentage Distribution of Female and Male Workers by Industry in Taiwan, 1966, 1971, 1976, 1981, 1986 (in percent)

Men Workers Employed

Year	Agriculture, Forestry, Fisheries	Mining and Quarrying	Manufacturing	Construction	Public Utilities	Commerce	Transport, Storage, Communication	Services	Others	Total
1966	43.04	1.90	17.70	4.66	0.98	11.24	5.70	13.47	1.31	100.00
1971	34.22	2.65	19.69	8.16	1.03	13.95	6.88	13.34	0.09	100.01
1976	28.93	1.74	25.12	8.54	0.62	13.01	7.68	12.56	1.79	99.99
1981	19.99	0.83	28.62	12.16	0.54	15.47	7.51	12.77	2.11	100.00
1986	18.69	0.58	30.30	9.94	0.62	16.39	7.20	13.88	2.41	100.01

Women Workers Employed

Year	Agriculture, Forestry, Fisheries	Mining and Quarrying	Manufacturing	Construction	Public Utilities	Commerce	Transport, Storage, Communication	Services	Others	Total
1966	46.64	0.38	18.45	0.53	0.17	12.93	1.51	18.74	0.65	100.00
1971	37.22	0.54	25.92	0.87	0.15	15.55	1.67	18.02	0.07	100.00
1976	29.49	0.48	35.32	1.30	0.14	14.02	2.09	15.17	1.99	100.00
1981	16.54	0.22	39.78	2.11	0.13	18.83	2.38	17.35	2.65	99.99
1986	14.28	0.17	39.58	1.58	0.14	20.36	2.09	18.50	3.30	100.01

Source: Annual Report of Labor Statistics, 1966, 1971, 1976, 1981, 1986, Directorate-General of Budget, Accounting, and Statistics, Executive Yuan, R.O.C.

percent), followed closely by agriculture (20 percent), commerce (16 percent), service (14 percent), and construction (10 percent).

Turning to the feminization of declining industries, which is another way of excluding women from core production systems, table 12.2 shows the percentage of women workers to total employed, across all industries from 1966 to 1986. From the table it is clear that with the increase in the female share of the labor force (from 27 percent to 38 percent), the share of women in all industries has increased, including the traditionally male industries. At present there is an almost equal share of men and women working in commerce, manufacturing, and service. The percentages of women in these industries are 44, 42, and 45, which represent 17, 13, and 11 percentage point increases for manufacturing, commerce, and service industries, respectively. In other words, there is almost no segregation in the sex composition of these industries. Compared with the statistics for twenty years earlier, the gains in the ratios of women workers to total employed represent an impressive improvement in women's integration into Taiwan's economy. There is one exception to the general positive direction of change: that is, the increasing feminization of women in agriculture over the past two decades. Table 12.2 shows that, although the concentration of women's employment in agriculture has decreased more than that of men's, in terms of the percentage of women in this industry there is a tendency toward increasing visibility of women in the fields (from 29 percent in 1966 to 32 percent in 1986). In other words, there is some indication of the feminization of agriculture. However, the increase is much less than the total increase in the percentage of females to total employment for all industries.

To summarize, evaluated by the changes in the distribution of women's employment compared with that of men's, data obtained from the past two decades generally do not support the notion of marginalization of women's employment to the extreme of peripheral sectors in Taiwan. From the distribution across the selected industries of the core-periphery continuum, at present, women's employment is concentrated not in agriculture but in manufacture. Moreover, women also made the most gain in their employment entries into manufacturing industry and the least in the agriculture. Today, there is a higher percentage of men than women engaging in agriculture, even though women are increasingly visible in this declining industry. On the other hand, for the other two industries along the medium position of the continuum, women appeared more likely to gain employment opportunities in the declining industries, such as commerce, rather than in the gaining industries, such as services or transportation and finance.

Changes in the Occupational Attainment of Women, 1966–86

In addition to industrial distribution, changes in the occupational distribution between sexes are another aspect commonly examined in the discussion of the changing status of female employment. Over the past two decades, among the

Table 12.2

Distribution of Ratios of Female and Male Workers to Total Employed, by Industry in Taiwan, 1966, 1971, 1976, 1981, 1986

Year	Agriculture, Forestry, Fisheries	Mining and Quarrying	Manufacturing	Construction	Public Utilities	Commerce	Transport, Storage, Communication	Services	Others	Total
				Ratio of Men Workers to Total Employed						
1966	71.34	93.01	72.12	95.96	94.02	70.11	91.04	65.97	84.48	72.95
1971	66.64	91.49	62.27	95.32	93.71	66.09	89.93	61.66	75.00	68.48
1976	67.68	88.49	60.30	93.34	90.57	66.46	88.70	63.88	65.71	68.10
1981	70.72	88.10	58.99	92.01	88.89	62.15	86.30	59.54	61.44	66.66
1986	68.41	84.85	55.89	91.24	88.24	57.12	85.05	55.38	54.72	62.34
				Ratio of Women Workers to Total Employed						
1966	28.66	6.99	27.88	4.04	5.98	29.89	8.96	34.03	15.52	27.05
1971	33.36	8.51	37.73	4.68	6.29	33.91	10.07	38.34	25.00	31.52
1976	32.32	11.51	39.70	6.66	9.43	33.54	11.30	36.12	34.29	31.90
1981	29.28	11.90	41.01	7.99	11.11	37.85	13.70	40.46	38.56	33.34
1986	31.59	15.15	44.11	8.76	11.76	42.88	14.95	44.62	45.28	37.66

Source: Annual Report of Labor Statistics, 1966, 1971, 1976, 1981, 1986, Directorate-General of Budget, Accounting, and Statistics, Executive Yuan, R.O.C.

seven major occupations, administrators and managers and professionals were the top two income-earning jobs in Taiwan. Clerical and sales personnel were the third and fourth on the hierarchy of high income-generating occupations in 1986. But prior to 1982, sales were the third and clerical work was fourth in the order of mean income. At the other end of the scale, agricultural work led the list of occupations with a mean income less than the total average. It was followed by production and service jobs.

Tables 12.3 and 12.4 present data on the occupational distribution of men and women and the sex composition of occupations over time. There were obvious differences as well as similarities between men and women in their concentration across major occupations in the past decades (table 12.3). Between 1966 and 1986 the percentage distribution of men's and women's employment across various occupations appeared to be similar. Not only was the relative concentration of their employment across occupations the same, but the magnitude of the percentage distribution did not differ too much in many occupational categories in the earlier period. Thus, for both men and women, the most dominant occupation in the first decade (1966–76) was agricultural work, followed by production work and labor. About half of the total employed males (44 percent) and females (47 percent) in the early stage of industrialization worked in agriculture-related jobs. However, this proportion has declined consistently since then. It reached a level of less than one-fifth in 1986. On the other hand, the proportions of men and women in production work increased in the same period of time. They increased from 29 percent of the total employed males in 1971 to 43 percent in 1986. Similarly, for women, the increase was from 17 percent to 36 percent between 1971 and 1986.

As a consequence of these changes, the differences in the occupational distribution of men and women became more marked in 1986. Two types of differences are noticeable. The first is the different concentration of male and female employment across occupations. Although production work and labor have replaced agricultural work as the dominant occupation for both sexes in 1986, clerical work was the second largest employer of women (18 percent), followed by agriculture (14 percent) and sales (14 percent). For men, the second largest employment was agricultural work (19 percent), followed by sales (13 percent) and clerical (11 percent). In other words, in the process of industrialization, while manufacturing production appeared to have absorbed the majority of the agricultural surplus labor of both sexes, agricultural jobs were still an important source of men's employment. But agriculture did not appear to retain its capacity to absorb the surplus female agricultural labor. On the contrary, the urban economy, with its expanding clerical work, provided the major source of employment for younger female cohorts. This type of employment, of course, is beyond the access of the agricultural surplus labor of the older generation. Taken together, these results suggest that older female surplus agricultural labor may either become unpaid family labor or go into the informal sector, which is part of the

Table 12.3

Distribution of Female and Male Workers by Occupation in Taiwan Area, 1966, 1971, 1976, 1981, 1986 (in percent)

Men Workers Employed

Year	Professional, Technical	Administrative, Managerial	Clerical	Sales	Services	Agriculture	Mining	Transport, Communication	Production	Total
1966	4.55	4.40	7.30	10.42	5.08	42.37	1.59	4.06	20.22	99.99
1971	3.93	4.10	6.46	11.89	4.33	33.53	2.13	4.70	28.94	100.01
1976	4.99	3.11	7.86	11.87	5.17	28.75	—	—	38.26	100.01
1981	5.24	1.24	11.22	12.90	6.56	19.69	—	—	43.14	99.99
1986	5.97	1.24	11.20	13.32	7.11	18.52	—	—	42.63	99.99
						Women Workers Employed				
1966	5.75	1.42	6.08	12.38	9.76	46.60	0.29	1.15	16.57	100.00
1971	4.55	0.87	7.10	13.31	7.85	37.21	0.40	0.97	27.73	99.99
1976	5.67	0.55	11.92	11.65	6.53	29.36	—	—	34.31	99.99
1981	6.29	0.18	17.53	12.81	9.30	16.40	—	—	37.48	99.99
1986	6.73	0.21	18.00	13.67	10.99	14.22	—	—	36.17	99.99

Source: Annual Report of Labor Statistics, 1966, 1971, 1976, 1981, 1986, Directorate-General of Budget, Accounting, Statistics, Executive Yuan, R.O.C.

344

Table 12.4

Distribution of Ratio of Female and Male Workers to Total Employed, by Occupations in Taiwan Area, 1966, 1971, 1976, 1981, 1986

Year	Professional, Technical	Administrative, Managerial	Clerical	Sales	Services	Agriculture	Mining	Transport, Communication	Production	Total
					Ratio of Men Workers to Total Employed					
1966	68.13	89.33	76.42	69.44	58.40	71.05	93.68	90.48	76.72	72.97
1971	65.22	91.10	66.43	66.01	54.55	66.22	92.03	91.33	69.42	68.51
1976	65.22	92.31	58.49	68.50	62.81	—	—	67.64	70.42	68.10
1981	62.47	93.22	56.13	66.82	58.52	—	—	70.59	69.71	66.66
1986	59.50	90.91	50.75	61.73	51.73	—	—	68.32	66.12	62.35
					Ratio of Women Workers to Total Employed					
1966	31.87	10.67	23.58	30.56	41.60	28.95	6.32	9.52	23.28	27.03
1971	34.78	8.90	33.57	33.99	45.45	33.78	7.97	8.67	30.58	31.49
1976	34.78	7.69	41.51	31.50	37.19	32.36	—	—	29.58	31.90
1981	37.53	6.78	43.87	33.18	41.48	29.41	—	—	30.29	33.34
1986	40.50	9.09	49.25	38.27	48.27	31.68	—	—	33.88	37.65

Source: Annual Report of Labor Statistics, 1966, 1971, 1976, 1981, 1986, Directorate-General of Budget, Accounting, Statistics, Executive Yuan, R.O.C.

reserve army of industrial workers. This suggestion complements the findings of some anthropological studies (e.g., Gallin 1984).

The second difference is with regard to gender differences at the other end of the occupational hierarchy, that is, the professional and administrative. It is interesting to observe that for both sexes, the percentage of administrators has been consistently declining while that of professionals has been slowly increasing. However, it needs to be pointed out that the rate of increase among female professionals (17 percent) was much smaller than that among males (31 percent). But for the administrative jobs, the rate of decrease for females (85 percent) was much greater than that for the males (72 percent). In other words, for the upper end of hierarchy, as industrialization proceeded, the gender gap in status appeared to have broadened.

Table 12.4 presents data on the other indicator of a gender gap in occupational attainment, the sex composition of occupations. This variable can be used to ascertain the validity of the anticipation of the FM theories about the feminization of marginal occupations. A few points about the table deserve attention. Overall, in the past two decades, there was a significant increase (11 percent) in the visibility level of females in the production system as a whole. From 1966 to 1986 the percentage of females to total employed increased from 27 percent to 38 percent. Among all occupations, the increase was most observable among clerical workers, wherein the ratio of females to total employed increased from 24 percent in 1966 to 50 percent in 1986. The magnitude of this increase was more than twice that of the increase of women in the workplace as a whole. Another occupation in which women increasingly found employment was production. This field experienced an increase of more than 10 percent in the period under study. The only occupation in which women experienced decreased representation was administrators and managers. The percentage of women to total administrators and managers decreased from 11 percent in 1966 to 9 percent in 1986. This made administrators and managers the only occupation that is still highly sex segregated and increasingly masculinized. Agriculture is the other occupation in which women did not experience a significant increase in their presence. But from the income-earning ability point of view, increasing female representation may not be a positive sign for women.

In short, the results show that, using occupational distribution and sex composition as criteria, industrialization does not seem to have brought about severe marginalization of female employment in Taiwan in the past two decades. Men and women have an overall similar pattern of change in their occupational distributions across major occupations; moreover, females also experienced the most substantial growth in clerical and production jobs, rather than in agricultural and services, which are declining occupations. However, these positive findings should not obscure evidence on the other side, that is, that women are still much underrepresented in an important part of the occupational system—administrators and managers.

Changes in Class Distribution of Female Employment within Industries

Comparing employment distribution horizontally across industries and occupations along the core-periphery dimension is informative. To capture the vertical dimension of the changing status of women in productive systems, one may incorporate gender differences in employment status within industries. Dividing people according to their relations to the production process—into employers, self-employed, unpaid family workers, and paid employees—one may illuminate the class or stratificational dimension of workers within industries. Tables 12.5–12.8 show the percentage distribution of men and women in different employment classes within agriculture, manufacturing, commerce, and service industries.[2] First, let us examine the class distribution of men and women workers within agriculture from 1966 to 1986 (table 12.5).

It is clear from the table that there are few employers among agricultural workers, men or women, but men have persistently outnumbered women by eight to one for the last two decades. About 90 percent of all employers were men in 1966 and 1986. The majority of male agricultural workers have been self-employed (52 and 68 percent), while most women are classed as unpaid family members (75 and 67 percent).[3] For the class of paid employee, although there is not much overall difference between genders in the percentage distribution, the majority of workers are men, especially in the government sector. At least 80 percent of government employees in agriculture are male.

With regard to change, two contrasting trends are noticeable. First, for both men and women, an increasing proportion of workers falls into the self-employed category, and a decreasing number of workers are counted as unpaid family laborers and wage earners in agriculture. Second, there is an increasing trend of women working as either unpaid labor or private-sector wage earners in agriculture. These statistics demonstrate an increasing shortage of male labor in agriculture and an increasing burden of agricultural production on rural women, even though male dominance in the employer class is not seriously challenged.

Looking at the manufacturing industry (table 12.6, page 348), some interesting points emerge. First, the majority of workers (over 80 percent), both male and female, are wage earners, but the proportion of female industrial workers hired as wage earners is even higher. Second, for the remaining minority of manufacturing workers, men are more likely to be employers (8 and 5 percent) or self-employed (13 and 6 percent). Only a small number of men have ever worked unpaid in family business. For women, the picture is an obvious contrast. Among the remaining one-tenth of female manufacturing workers, most are classed as unpaid family workers. Only a minimal proportion of women have been classified as employers or self-employed since 1966.

As to the trend of change, one point deserves special mention: the polarization of genders into two ends of a stratificational scale. Although for both sexes the overall patterns of distribution across different strata of workers have not

Table 12.5

Percentage and Ratio Distributions of Men and Women Across Employment Status, within Industry, Agriculture, Hunting, Forestry, and Fishing, 1966–1986

	Employer	Self-employed	Unpaid	Private	Govern-ment	Subtotal	Total
					Paid Employees		
Male							
1966	0.87	51.80	28.70	16.51	2.11	18.63	99.99
1971	0.90	56.96	73.02	17.41	1.71	19.12	100.00
1976	0.63	62.98	20.91	14.38	1.10	15.48	100.00
1981	1.58	66.22	16.10	14.08	2.03	16.10	100.00
1986	1.789	67.59	16.54	12.76	1.33	14.10	100.00
Female							
1966	0.26	9.4211	74.87	14.37	1.08	15.45	100.00
1971	0.05	12.38	73.85	13.41	0.32	13.73	100.01
1976	0.14	17.07	71.39	10.98	0.42	11.40	100.00
1981	0.62	22.55	65.76	9.78	1.09	10.89	100.00
1986	0.48	20.43	67.31	11.06	0.72	11.78	100.00
Male/Total employed							
1966	89.36	93.19	48.82	74.09	82.93	75.00	71.33
1971	97.56	90.22	38.45	72.23	91.57	73.62	66.71
1976	90.32	88.54	38.00	73.29	84.48	73.98	67.67
1981	82.35	87.63	37.14	77.64	81.82	78.14	70.70
1986	88.89	87.75	34.73	71.43	80.00	72.16	68.41
Female/Total employed							
1966	10.64	6.81	51.18	25.91	17.07	25.00	28.67
1971	2.44	9.78	61.55	27.77	8.43	26.38	33.29
1976	9.68	11.46	62.00	26.71	15.52	26.02	32.33
1981	17.65	12.37	72.86	22.36	18.18	21.86	29.30
1986	11.11	12.35	65.27	28.57	20.00	27.84	31.59

Source: Annual Report of Labor Statistics, 1966, 1971, 1976, 1981, 1986. Directorate-General of Budget, Accounting and Statistics, Executive Yuan, R.O.C.

changed much, the proportion of male unpaid workers has been steadily declining, while unpaid women workers decreased significantly in an earlier period but have been rising again in recent years. On the other hand, for employers, while there was an overall increase of males (5 and 8 percent), the proportion among female workers decreased consistently from 1966 to 1986. This tendency also shows up in the declining share of women in the employer class. For the self-employed category, it is very revealing that while both males and females have been experiencing a declining trend of decrease of percentage distribution (per-

Table 12.6

Percentage and Ratio Distributions of Men and Women Across Employment Status, within Industry, Manufacturing, 1966–1986

| | Employer | Self-employed | Unpaid | Paid Employees | | | Total |
				Private	Government	Subtotal	
Male							
1966	5.44	13.74	4.43	58.48	17.92	76.40	100.01
1971	6.73	8.53	2.82	71.75	10.17	81.92	100.00
1976	5.88	6.79	2.48	75.82	9.03	84.85	100.00
1981	8.48	5.58	2.44	76.98	6.52	83.50	100.00
1986	8.21	5.54	1.85	79.47	4.93	84.39	100.00
Female							
1966	1.69	12.78	12.13	67.14	6.26	73.40	100.00
1971	0.90	2.58	9.74	83.55	3.23	86.77	100.00
1976	0.71	1.25	4.66	91.11	2.27	93.38	100.00
1981	0.68	1.02	4.63	92.21	1.47	93.68	100.01
1986	0.61	0.87	5.29	92.20	1.04	93.24	100.01
Male/Total employed							
1966	89.26	73.58	43.62	69.29	88.12	72.95	72.15
1971	92.47	84.50	32.29	58.61	83.87	60.89	62.25
1976	92.68	89.15	44.65	55.81	85.78	57.97	60.28
1981	94.74	88.75	43.06	54.54	66.46	56.15	58.96
1986	94.49	89.01	30.68	52.18	85.71	53.40	55.87
Female/Total employed							
1966	10.74	26.42	51.38	30.71	11.88	27.05	27.85
1971	7.53	15.50	67.71	41.39	16.13	39.11	37.75
1976	7.32	10.85	55.35	44.19	14.22	42.03	39.72
1981	5.26	11.25	56.94	45.46	13.54	43.85	41.04
1986	5.51	10.99	69.32	47.82	14.29	46.60	44.13

Source: Annual Report of Labor Statistics, 1966, 1971, 1976, 1981, 1986. Directorate-General of Budget, Accounting, and Statistics, Executive Yuan, R.O.C.

haps resulting from capital intensification) the differences in the magnitude and rapidity of such declines are striking. In short, operation of these two forces in combination has resulted in a "masculinization" of the "have" end (employer and self-employed) of the class hierarchy and the "feminization" of the "have not" end (unpaid) in manufacturing. Ratios of males to totals in employer and self-employed strata have been on an upward swing, averaging 92 percent and 81 percent, respectively. The percentage of females to the total employed for the unpaid stratum also show a rising trend, from 51 percent in 1966 to 69 percent in 1986.

Table 12.7

Percentage and Ratio Distributions of Men and Women Across Employment Status, within Industry, Commerce, 1966–1986

| | Employer | Self-employed | Unpaid | Paid Employees | | | Total |
				Private	Government	Subtotal	
Male							
1966	5.63	57.69	8.32	23.77	4.60	28.37	100.01
1971	7.34	51.38	8.22	26.55	6.51	33.06	100.00
1976	6.38	55.31	6.63	30.34	1.35	31.69	100.01
1981	11.47	48.77	6.24	31.93	1.60	33.53	100.01
1986	10.63	46.58	6.58	34.68	1.52	36.20	99.99
Female							
1966	1.49	34.57	41.64	19.89	2.42	22.30	100.01
1971	1.83	31.47	43.18	19.98	3.54	23.52	100.00
1976	2.17	33.27	36.33	27.54	0.69	28.23	100.00
1981	2.86	24.11	36.28	36.04	0.72	36.75	100.01
1986	2.36	23.10	36.26	37.61	0.67	38.28	100.00
Male/Total employed							
1966	89.87	79.65	31.91	73.71	81.69	74.90	70.11
1971	88.67	76.06	27.04	72.11	78.15	73.23	66.06
1976	85.33	76.71	26.55	68.58	79.41	68.98	66.46
1981	86.81	76.89	22.05	59.30	78.57	60.00	62.18
1986	85.71	72.87	19.48	55.13	75.00	55.75	57.12
Female/Total employed							
1966	10.13	20.35	68.09	26.29	18.31	25.10	29.89
1971	11.33	23.94	72.96	27.89	21.85	26.77	33.94
1976	14.67	23.29	73.45	31.42	20.59	31.02	33.54
1981	13.19	23.11	77.95	40.70	21.43	40.00	37.82
1986	14.29	27.13	80.52	44.87	25.00	44.25	42.88

Source: Annual Report of Labor Statistics, 1966, 1971, 1976, 1981, 1986. Directorate-General of Budget, Accounting, and Statistics, Executive Yuan, R.O.C.

With regard to commerce (table 12.7), a few points of particular relevance can be observed. One is the concentration of women workers into a "working" class, either paid or unpaid. Together they account for 70 percent of all female workers in commerce. The majority of the rest of female commercial workers were self-employed (23 and 35 percent). By contrast, the majority of males in commerce worked either for themselves (57 and 47 percent) or as wage earners (24 and 35 percent). As expected, the least likely position for a man in commerce is as an unpaid family worker. Over the years, no more than 8 percent of men have been thus classified. At present, this figure is smaller than the percentage of male employers.

In terms of changes, some trends are observable. First, there are trends of declining proportions of males and females working as self-employed (58 to 47 percent for men and 35 to 23 percent for women) and unpaid family members (8 to 7 percent and 42 to 36 percent). Second, there is a rising trend of workers of both sexes in the paid employee category. But the pace and magnitude of change is greater for women (a 16 percent change) than for men (an 8 percent change). Third, there is also a tendency for men, as well as for women, to become employers in commerce, but the magnitude is greater for men than for women, even though the rate of increase is slightly greater for females than males. At present, the proportion of male employers accounts for nearly 10 percent of all males in commerce. The same class accounts for only 2 percent of women in commerce.

Finally, examination of the ratio of female workers to the total employed among the strata in commerce delineates another aspect of women's status. Overall, women workers constitute an increasing part of the commercial work force. Not only are women increasing their influence in the wage-earner class, they are also running more commercial establishments, either as employers, self-employed persons, or unpaid family members. Among these three categories, the increase in the unpaid class is the largest, however.

Table 12.8 describes data for the service industry. The most outstanding feature of this industry is the overwhelming concentration of workers of both sexes in the wage-earner class (80 percent for males and 83 percent for females). The next largest class of service workers of both sexes is self-employed (14 percent for males and 9 percent for females). The main difference between genders is in their distribution across strata. It is unlikely for men to be unpaid workers or for women to be listed as employers.

Persistence seems to be more apparent than chance in the service industry. Nevertheless, there are a few noticeable changes. Specifically, they are the increase in proportions of males in the self-employed and employer strata and the decrease of females in the unpaid labor and employer classes. There is also a slight increase in the proportion of self-employed women. When the statistics of women workers as a percentage of total employed are examined, changes become even more noticeable. Overall, as in commerce, the service industry appears to be "feminizing." Female workers comprise an increasing part of all categories except for the employer class. In the last category, the fluctuations over the period do not permit a conclusive statement.

Summary and Conclusions

This chapter has attempted to delineate the dynamic of the changing status of women in employment in the process of industrialization in Taiwan by examining multiple indicators and interpreting them within the context of a changing hierarchy of production systems. The results show that during the industrialization process, Taiwan women have played an active role in re-

Table 12.8

Percentage and Ratio Distributions of Men and Women Across Employment Status, within Industry, Services Industry, 1966–1986

| | Employed | Self-employed | Unpaid | Paid Employees | | | Total |
				Private	Government	Subtotal	
Male							
1966	3.70	9.85	1.98	24.27	60.19	84.46	99.99
1971	4.34	12.33	2.03	32.75	48.55	81.31	100.00
1976	3.01	12.71	1.34	31.66	51.19	82.85	100.00
1981	4.59	13.05	1.41	27.69	53.26	80.95	100.00
1986	4.78	13.75	1.35	30.19	49.93	80.12	100.00
Female							
1966	2.96	6.30	7.20	45.37	38.17	83.55	100.00
1971	2.41	11.51	5.66	41.08	33.33	80.41	99.99
1976	2.01	9.95	4.57	41.00	42.83	83.84	100.00
1981	2.58	8.79	5.17	38.76	44.70	83.46	100.00
1986	2.04	8.91	5.75	42.12	41.19	83.30	100.01
Male/Total employed							
1966	70.89	75.25	34.88	50.97	75.39	66.27	66.03
1971	74.26	63.20	36.46	52.75	70.03	61.87	61.60
1976	73.17	70.09	34.21	57.72	67.88	63.60	63.87
1981	72.22	68.52	28.57	51.14	63.58	58.70	59.43
1986	74.42	65.71	22.50	47.09	60.07	54.42	55.38
Female/Total employed							
1966	29.11	24.75	65.12	49.03	24.61	33.73	33.97
1971	25.74	36.80	63.54	47.25	29.97	38.13	38.40
1976	26.83	29.91	65.79	42.28	32.12	36.40	36.13
1981	27.78	31.48	71.43	48.86	36.42	41.30	40.57
1986	25.58	34.29	77.50	52.91	39.93	45.58	44.62

Source: Annual Report of Labor Statistics, 1966, 1971, 1976, 1981, 1986. Directorate-General of Budget, Accounting, and Statistics, Executive Yuan, R.O.C.

sponding to labor market opportunities generated by economic transformation. This is clearly illustrated by the increasing share of women workers in all industries and occupations. As for equal opportunity in various sectors, Taiwan data do not support the hypothesis that women workers are always excluded from the manufacturing industry or other expanding urban occupations, nor is female employment marginalized to the agricultural sector or service jobs. Although there is some increase in women's share in agriculture, the attainment

of mixed-sex labor composition in manufacturing, commerce, and service industries in the last two decades of industrialization represents an impressive record of
women's access to industrial employment, at least in the horizontal dimension.

However, when one measures in terms of women's vertical integration into
the core of the production systems, the picture does not look as bright. Although women workers have made significant gains in commerce and service
industries at all levels, including the employer class in commerce, the majority
of women are still located in the lower end of the production relationship.
Moreover, the phenomenon of the dominance of men in the employer class and
women in the unpaid category persists over time. Similarly in occupational
attainment, women's representation in the highest income-generating occupations (i.e., administrators and managers) is still very low and has remained so in
the past two decades. In short, it may be said that while women may not have
been excluded horizontally from the process of the emerging urban productive
system, they have not been integrated vertically into the core of the production
process either. Sex segregation at the level of ownership of the means of production remains the biggest obstacle in the way of gender equality.

Finally, due to the limitations of the data, the present study was not able to
delineate fully the variety in which women might have experienced industrialization. Nevertheless, there were indications that as industrialization proceeded and
the urban economy expanded, women with different skills (e.g., educational
attainment) would experience different employment opportunities. To understand fully the effect of this industrialization on women's status and well-being,
further research needs to focus on the variety of women's experiences.

Notes

1. There is a third dimension of occupational sex segregation, that is, the income inequality
or differential between the average male and female wage. Income inequality is not inherently
a structural aspect of sex segregation, although it is in part the effectual reflection of the
horizontal and vertical segregation. Due to limitations of space, it will not be discussed here.

2. Data on other industries are available on request.

3. This is in part explained by the cultural convention that generally describes family
enterprises (farms, shops, small factories) as belonging to husbands, even where wives
contribute equal or greater quantities of capital and labor to them, a circumstance that
occurs more frequently in commerce than in agriculture.

References

Arizpe, L. 1977. "Women in Informal Labor Sector: The Case of Mexico City." In
   Women and National Development, ed. Wellesley Editorial Committee. Chicago: Uni-
   versity of Chicago Press.
Beller, A. 1984. "Trends in Occupational Segregation by Sex and Race, 1960–1981." In
   Sex Segregation in the Workplace, ed. B.F. Reskin. Washington, DC: National Acad-
   emy Press.

Bielby, W.T., and J.N. Baron. 1984. "A Women's Place Is with Other Women, Sex Segregation within Organizations." In *Sex Segregation in the Workplace,* ed. B.F. Raskin. Washington, DC: National Academy Press.

Blaxall, M., and B. Reagan. 1976. *Women and the Workplace.* Chicago: University of Chicago Press.

Blau, F. 1984. "Occupational Segregation and Labor Market Discrimination." In *Sex Segregation in the Workplace,* ed. B.F. Reskin. Washington, DC: National Academy Press.

Blau, F., and C. Jusenius. 1976. "Economists' Approaches to Sex Segregation in Labor Market: An Appraisal." *Women and the Workplace,* ed. M. Blaxall and B. Reagan. Chicago: University of Chicago Press.

Boserup, E. 1970. *Women's Role in Economic Development.* New York: St. Martin's Press.

Bridge, W.A. 1980. "Industry Marginality and Female Employment: A New Appraisal." ASR 45 (February): 58–75.

Chiang, L.N., and Y. Ku. 1985. *Past and Current Status of Women in Taiwan.* Monograph 1, Women's Research Program, Population Studies Center, National Taiwan University. Taipei, Taiwan. October.

Chinchilla, N.S. 1977. "Industrialization, Monopoly Capitalism and Women's Work in Guatemala." In *Women and National Development,* ed. Wellesley Editorial Committee. Chicago: University of Chicago Press.

Cho, U., and H. Koo. 1983. "Capital Accumulation, Women's Work, and Informal Economies in Korea." Working paper 21, *Women in International Development.* Michigan State University.

Chou, B.E., and J. Clark. 1986. "The Political Representation of Women in a 'Reserved Seats' System." Monograph 2, Women's Research Program, Population Studies Center, National Taiwan University. Taipei, Taiwan. May.

Directorate-General of Budget, Accounting, and Statistics, Executive Yuan, R.O.C. 1986. *Annual Report of National Income—Taiwan Area* (in Chinese). Taipei, Taiwan. December.

Elliott, C.M. 1977. "Theories of Development: An Assessment." In *Women and National Development,* ed. Wellesley Editorial Committee. Chicago: University of Chicago Press.

Farris, C.S. 1986. "The Sociocultural Construction of Femininity in Contemporary Urban Taiwan." Working paper 131, *Women in International Development.* Michigan State University. November.

Gallin, R. 1984. "Women, Family and the Political Economy of Taiwan." *Journal of Peasant Studies* 12, 1: 76–92.

Greenhalgh, S. 1985. "Sexual Stratification: The Other Side of 'Growth with Equity' in East Asia." *Population and Development Review* 11, 2: 265–314.

Gross, W. 1968. "Plus ca change . . . ? The Sexual Structure of Occupations Over Time." *Social Problems* 16: 198–208.

Hartmann, H. 1976. "Capitalism, Patriarchy, and Job Segregation by Sex." In *Women and the Workplace,* ed. M. Blaxall and B. Reagan. Chicago: University of Chicago Press.

Humphrey, J. 1984. "The Growth of Female Employment in Brazilian Manufacturing Industry in 1970s." *Journal of Development Studies* 20, 4: 224–47.

Kung, L. 1981. "Perceptions of Workers among Factory Women." In *The Anthropology of Taiwanese Society,* ed. E. Ahern and H. Gates. Stanford: Stanford University Press.

Lapidus, G.W. 1976. "Occupational Segregation and Public Policy: A Comparative Analysis of American and Soviet Patterns." In *Women and the Workplace,* ed. M. Blaxall and B. Reagan. Chicago: University of Chicago Press.

Liu, P.K., and K.S. Hwang. 1987. *Relationships between Changes in Population, Employment and Economic Structure in Taiwan* (in Chinese). Studies of Modern Economy Series 8. Institute of Economics Academia Sinica. Taipei, Taiwan. June.

Miller, J., and H.H. Garrison. 1982. "Sex Roles: The Division of Labor at Home and in the Workplace." *Annual Review of Sociology* 8: 237–62.

Roos, P.A. 1985. *Genders and Work: A Comparative Analysis of Industrial Societies.* Albany, NY: SUNY Press.

Safa, H.I. 1977. "Introduction [to Changing Modes of Production]." In *Women and National Development,* ed. Wellesley Editorial Committee. Chicago: University of Chicago Press.

Saffioti, H.I.B. 1983. "The Impact of Industrialization on the Structure of Female Employment." Working paper 15. *Women in International Development.* Michigan State University.

Scott, A.M. 1986. "Women and Industrialization: Examining the 'Female Marginalisation' Thesis." *Journal of Development Studies* 22, 4: 649–80.

Stoler, A. 1977. "Class Structure and Social Change: A Comparative Appraisal of Turkey's Women." In *Women and National Development,* ed. Wellesley Editorial Committee. Chicago: University of Chicago.

Strober, M. 1984. "Toward a General Theory of Sex Segregation." In *Sex Segregation in the Workplace,* ed. B. Reskin. Washington, DC: National Academy Press.

Tangri, S.S. 1976. "Comment IV." In *Women and the Workplace,* ed. M. Blaxall and B. Reagan. Chicago: University of Chicago Press.

Treiman, D.J., and H. Hartmann, eds. 1981. *Women, Work, and Wages: Equal Pay for Jobs of Equal Value.* Washington, DC: National Academy Press.

Tsai, S-L. 1986. "Gender and Social Stratification in a Changing Society: The Case of Taiwan." Paper presented at the 27th Annual Meeting of the American Association for Chinese Studies, November 22–24, 1985, University of California, Berkeley.

Tsay, C.L. 1987. "Status of Women in Taiwan: Educational Attainment and Labor Force Development, 1951–83." *Academia Economic Papers* 15, 1: 153–82.

Tsui, E.Y. 1987. *Are Married Daughters "Spilled Water"?—A Study of Working Women in Urban Taiwan.* Monograph 4, Women's Research Program, Population Studies Center, National Taiwan University. Taipei, Taiwan. January.

Williams, G. 1979. "The Changing U.S. Labor Force: Occupational Differentiation by Sex." *Demography* 16: 73–78.

Part VI

QUESTIONS OF ETHNIC IDENTITY

Ethnicity has become a dominant and many-sided issue in modern Taiwanese life. The KMT-managed land reform and the economic transformation that followed were made possible in part because the ruling Mainlander-dominated regime was able to take land away from the elite landholders of an occupied and pacified population. Even though the Taiwanese- and Hakka-speaking Han Chinese who came to the island prior to 1945 have gained much from the reforms and from the rapid economic development, they continue to voice the feeling that they are oppressed by the Mandarin-speaking *waishengren* (outside the province) regime. Nor is this oppression simply imagined, for it was manifested in a number of direct ways, including suppression of the Taiwanese spoken language and bias in both university admission and hiring for governmental positions.

The often antagonistic relationship between Taiwanese and Mainlander is but one facet of the ethnic conflict found on the island. There is also a centuries-old problem between the Han Chinese who came from the Minnan (Hokklo)-speaking regions of Fujian and the Hakka-speaking regions of northern Guangdong and the island's Malayo-Polynesian aborigines. The tribes of the island's mountains and western plains—the Yuanzhumin (aborigines)—had long been involved in cultural, economic, and military conflict with the immigrants from China well before the arrival of the Mainlander armies in 1945. The KMT regime played Yanzhumin against Taiwanese and Hakka, using preexisting ethnic tensions as a tactic of divide and conquer. The four chapters in this section explore different dimensions of the ethnic situation.

Robert L. Cheng sets the stage with his chapter, "Language Unification on Taiwan: Past and Present." Cheng's chapter was first published in 1973 and is a pioneering essay that captures the flavor of the times. It provides an overview of the Mandarinization policies of the KMT-dominated regime and is also an argument against that approach.

Joseph Bosco demonstrates that the KMT's conscious efforts to stifle the use of the Taiwanese language did little to prevent the development of a conscious Taiwan-centered popular culture. The chapter focuses on the evolution of a Taiwanese cultural identity, but there is a larger and more challenging theme that serves as a major subtext: the idea that Taiwan has moved from being on the periphery of Chinese civilization to becoming a new center. Bosco asserts that what one witnesses on Taiwan is the erosion of the gap of perception that exists between the "orthodoxy" of "Chinese identity" and the "hetereodoxy" of "Taiwanese identity." The idea that Taiwan is not only the Republic of China but a new and more vital, more viable China is steadily gaining credibility.

One set of actors, the Yuanzhumin, continues to remain outside the mainstream. Shih-Chung Hsieh's chapter offers insights into the changing perceptions of the aborigines as well as their changing self-perceptions. Hsieh asks two basic questions: "What was or is the nature of ethnic identity among aborigines, and how do they create ways for preserving their culture, ethnic group, and identity?"

Taiwan is alive with different ethnicities, with each group redefining who and what they are, and each battling for a slice of the economic pie. The chapters in this section will give the reader some insight into the difficult questions posed by the clash of Taiwan's ethnic communities as well as the larger questions of what it means to be Taiwanese and what it means to be Chinese.

Chapter 13

Language Unification in Taiwan: Present and Future

Robert L. Cheng

For the past twenty-eight years the Nationalist government has promoted Mandarin in Taiwan under two assumptions: (1) Taiwan is a province of China, and (2) Mandarin is the national language of China. This chapter examines the Nationalist language policy in Taiwan to show that the policy neglects proper planning on other vernaculars[1] and, in practice, seeks language unification through monolingualism rather than through bilingualism. This chapter presents the view that unification through bilingualism will achieve the government's proclaimed goals of national harmony, political unity, democracy, and social progress much better than through monolingualism, both in Taiwan and in the whole of China.[2]

The policy of language unification in China through bilingualism I refer to takes the following positions.

In the non-Mandarin areas both Mandarin and the mother tongue will be recognized as official languages of the respective areas. This means that Mandarin is to be learned as a second language by people of non-Mandarin areas and is to be used for communication among people who do not speak the same tongue. The non-Mandarin mother tongues remain the major communication tool in the schools, homes, communities, courts, and local governments. These languages (or dialects) may eventually die a natural death, but this will not be the result of any man-made policy. In the Mandarin areas, Mandarin will be the only official language. Mandarin speakers need not learn a second language unless they want to reside in a non-Mandarin area.

Quite in contrast with the above policy is one that attempts to unify the language of China through suppression of all non-Mandarin tongues. This has as its eventual goal the learning and use of Mandarin as the *first* language by all

This chapter originally appeared in William C. McCormack and Stephen A. Wurm, eds., *Language and Society* (The Haugue: Mouton, 1979), pp. 541–78. Used with permission of Mouton de Gruyter, a Division of Walter de Gruyter & Co.

people in even the non-Mandarin areas. Non-Mandarin tongues would be officially illegal anywhere in public: in schools, in the courts, and at all levels of government. Non-Mandarin tongues would be allowed in communities with the understanding that they be used temporarily only so long as non-Mandarin monolinguals are living. To see to it that non-Mandarin tongues be extinguished as soon as possible, Mandarin will be used between all bilinguals who can speak Mandarin. The well-being of any older members of the community who can speak only a non-Mandarin tongue is to be sacrificed for the sake of national linguistic unity.

Language planning for a population that speaks different languages but has to live under one government is a worldwide problem. Even though my discussion focuses mainly on Taiwan, this essay is intended as part of the joint efforts of scholars in various disciplines to deal with this common human problem.

My arguments for promotion of bilingualism are based on the following assumptions about language and its role in society; I claim these to be universally applicable.

1. An individual's native language is his best communication tool. It becomes an inseparable part of his ego, once his nerve system has internalized it.

2. Old people rarely can acquire a second language, and only a small portion of younger adults are especially talented in learning a second language.

3. A normal individual has a sense of linguistic loyalty to his speech community; if this loyalty is destroyed, his love for and confidence in both his local and national cultures are also lost.

4. Linguistic differences have come into existence as a natural result of man's efforts to adjust to different environments. Differences are not in themselves evil or causes of problems.

5. Language is not only a very important means of communication; it is also a primary feature of group identification. Many other features (geographical, cultural, institutional, etc.) that are also important to group identification can be responsible for linguistic changes. It is useless to destroy linguistic differences in order to obtain a monolithic group identity unless differences in these other features are also eliminated.

6. That linguistic unity through monolingualism is a prerequisite of political unity is a political conviction, not a proven fact. Far more essential for political unity are attitudes of tolerance, understanding, harmony, and lawfulness, together with common interests. To attempt to eliminate language differences because of such a mistaken conviction is no more proper than to attempt to eliminate other facets of social life for purely religious beliefs of what is "best." Not only is the attempt expensive, it also runs the risk of losing the essential features of political unity.

7. When any two speech groups are in contact, there is a tendency for the dominant group to feel superior and the dominated group to feel inferior because of their language differences. Education should not further intensify these superior-

inferior feelings, which result in social disharmony. People should be educated to tolerate and respect linguistic differences and at the same time to increase their ability to communicate with other people.

8. Man instinctively fears people of another linguistic community. He fears contamination of his own linguistic system by alien linguistic elements, and views such innovations as evil. But man is capable of being bilingual and bilingual individuals are more ready to tolerate differences and benefit from cultural interchange than are monolinguals.

While the population of Taiwan shares many features with others with similar conditions and hence is subject to the application of above assumptions, it has certain peculiar features that will be of special interest to language planning specialists: It has a recent history of the consecutive imposition of two languages on the local populace—the implementation of the Japanese language policy to "assimilate the Taiwan population in order to expand the Japanese population" and of the Nationalist policy to assimilate the population of Taiwan into the Chinese population lest it should be "alienated from her mother country again." Both of these language policies aimed at assimilative monolingualism and are in sharp contrast with the British colonial policy, which aimed at segregated monolingualism. The latter is euphemistically "separate but equal," but may only be a strategy to divide and rule.[3] Both also differ from the integrated bilingual policy in Singapore today.

Taiwan's literate population now use Chinese characters, which, though taking much longer to master than a second spoken language would, has the magical power of making their users believe that they belong to people of the characters—the Chinese. As soon as such literate speakers of different "dialects" attempt oral communication, they may discover their speech to be so different that they feel they belong to different peoples.

To my knowledge, no case study of language planning in Taiwan has been done from the viewpoint of modern sociolinguistics.

The Nationalist government has urged solidarity and harmony among the different speech groups in Taiwan in order to cope with its present internal and external political crises. It particularly advocates national unity, love for and confidence in Chinese culture, democracy, social progress, and science as the major goals of government and education. It is timely that specialists in the behavioral sciences discuss the relevance of language planning with regard to these proclaimed goals. No attempt will be made in this particular study to go beyond these proclaimed goals and the Nationalists' claim that the language policy being practiced in Taiwan is identical with its policy for the whole of China.[4]

Sociolinguistic Situations of Taiwan

After the end of the Second World War, the population of Taiwan was about 6 million. Except for the 5 percent Japanese who did not return to Japan immediately and the 2.5 percent Austronesians who were the earliest settlers, the majority of the population spoke either Taiwanese (a Chinese dialect developed through the mixture of South Min or South Hokkien dialects such as Amoy, Chuanzhou, and Zhangzhou)[5] or Hakka as their first language. The ratio between Taiwanese and Hakka is estimated to be seven to one. A great portion of the population were bilinguals, with their first tongue either Taiwanese or Hakka and Japanese their second because under the Japanese, Japanese was the only language allowed at all school levels.

The proportion of such bilinguals compared with monolinguals, and also the degree of Japanese proficiency of these bilinguals, varies greatly according to age groups. Resistance to formal education was stronger in the earlier part of the fifty years of Japanese rule; Japanese was rarely used in the local community until much later when compulsory six-year Japanese education was put in effect in the late 1930s.

Under the policy of Japanization of the Taiwanese (or the so-called policy to assimilate the Taiwanese population into the Japanese emperor's subjects), toward the end of World War II, there were a few families in which Japanese was used. Such families were called National Language (of Japan) families and enjoyed some privileges that other Taiwanese families did not have. The children in these families tended to speak Japanese better than they did either Hakka or Taiwanese. Rarely were these children unable to speak Taiwanese or Hakka if they lived in ordinary communities. In the northern urban areas where Taiwanese and Hakka speakers were mixed or in government housing areas where the Japanese population was proportionally higher, Japanese was used more frequently and monolingual Japanese children existed even in Taiwanese families.

When the Japanese later evacuated, immigrants from China came to Taiwan. It was mainly into these two types of areas that they moved. Therefore, the newcomers unfortunately miscalculated the success of the language policy of the Japanese rulers. Japanese was frequently heard in the urban areas because many people in either group were able to communicate with people in the other group only in Japanese. In the government housing areas, Japanese was often heard more frequently because Japanese monolinguals existed. The habit of using Japanese was impossible to erase overnight, even when the bilingual adults tried to avoid using it.

Another reason for the newcomers' underestimation of the Taiwanese people's desire to maintain their own mother tongue against the Japanese language policy came from the fact that Japanese loan words were used frequently in both Taiwanese and Hakka speech by a majority of the people. Such speech was often thought to be Japanese by the newcomers who did not understand Hakka or Taiwanese.

In spite of the Japanese official discouragement of learning and use of Taiwanese by Hakka speakers and vice versa, Hakka-Taiwanese bilinguals and trilinguals (those who could also speak Japanese) did exist as a natural result of social contacts. Although there are no reliable statistics, there seem to be more bilinguals and trilinguals among the Hakka speakers than among the Taiwanese speakers.

Among the Austronesian people in the mountains, Japanese was used very much as a lingua-franca because there were several small speech communities that could not, and still cannot, communicate with each other except in Japanese.

As for writing, Japanese was used by almost all literates in all speech communities toward the end of World War II. Romanization of Taiwanese was used by churchgoers. Taiwanese texts in Chinese characters were available only in the Bible and hymn books. If one could read romanization, one generally could also write romanized Taiwanese, a sharp contrast with writing in Chinese characters. Romanized Taiwanese was most frequently used for communication among those church members who did not know Japanese.

Outside of the churches there were only two uses of writing of Taiwanese or Hakka: the use of Chinese characters to write folk songs, and the reading of Chinese classics. In neither case was the writing of the vernacular language in romanization or Chinese characters a means of mass communication. It takes several years to learn enough Chinese characters to read and write in the vernacular language, and no school was allowed to give any classes for such training. Only in high schools did students have a course in Chinese classics; even then they had the option of reading it in Japanese or Taiwanese. Although Chinese classics reflect the earlier stages of both Taiwanese and Hakka, they differ from these just as Latin does from French. A few hours of study in high school might be sufficient for reading certain selected texts but not enough to learn to write in classical Chinese.

Romanization would have been easier for people to learn and use. But it was never allowed in any publication outside of churches. The ability to use romanization was taken as a symbol of being a Christian.

There were quite a few studies done on the vernacular languages with a view to popularizing them so as to achieve a higher rate of literacy. No such effort succeeded, because the Japanese authorities discouraged their use.

Since the end of the Second World War, the Nationalist Chinese government of Taiwan enforced its policy of spreading Mandarin under two assumptions: (1) Taiwan is a province of China, and (2) Mandarin is the national language of China. The policy has been carried out without much open opposition in Taiwan.

In 1950 the Nationalist government moved to Taiwan. This has the following implications on language planning.

1. To survive as the legitimate government of the whole of China, the Nationalists have to maintain Mandarin as the national language in Taiwan.

2. Since Mandarin speakers are in the minority, the government has to take extraordinary steps to maintain the status of Mandarin against the natural tendency of Mandarin speakers to be assimilated into the Taiwanese majority.

Besides this language policy and the evacuation of the central government of the Nationalists to Taiwan, new emigration from various parts of the Chinese mainland has been an important factor in the sociolinguistic changes in Taiwan during the past twenty-eight years. The new emigration started even before the departure of the Japanese. It reached its peak around the takeover by the Communists of the Chinese mainland in 1950. The new emigrants are estimated to be 15 percent of the total population, including 600,000 Nationalists troops.

The increase of the population of Taiwan from 6 million to 15 million, however, has been chiefly due to natural increase rather than to new immigration.[6] Furthermore, natural increase is greater among the old settlers than among the new immigrants. One of the reasons for the lower rate of population increase in the latter group is that quite a few were male adults who are unmarried or are separated from their wives. It was not until recent years that marriage began to take place frequently between the old and new settlers.

The sociolinguistic implication of the general natural increase of population is that there are more younger people than older people. Since younger people learn a second language more easily than older people, the above-mentioned distribution of population also means that there are more bilinguals than monolinguals in any language. A sociolinguistic implication of a lower rate of natural increase among the new settlers is that the proportion of Taiwanese or Hakka speakers among the younger generation is even higher than that among the older generation. This means the social pressure on the new settlers' children to learn and use Taiwanese or Hakka in addition to Mandarin is pretty high because they are so greatly outnumbered by their Taiwanese- and Hakka-speaking peers.

Due to the language policy of the Nationalist government and new emigration of Chinese Mainlanders, the sociolinguistic situation of Taiwan has undergone a drastic change in the past twenty-eight years. About 75 percent of the population still speak Taiwanese as the mother tongue and 10 percent speak Hakka. Native speakers of Mandarin are hard to estimate. Chinese Mainlanders who went to Taiwan after the Communist takeover were not necessarily Mandarin speakers at the time of their immigration. Even among Mandarin speakers, dialectal differences are often so great that communication is very difficult, if not entirely impossible.

Since each group among the Mainlanders is relatively very small and since this category of people has generally engaged in occupations that require much contact with other groups (government employees, teachers, and soldiers) there is a tendency for this group to use Mandarin (very frequently with a heavy accent) more frequently than other groups do in their daily life. There is also a tendency for their children to speak Mandarin as their first language, since marriage has tended to take place within this group even though husband and wife may speak entirely different mother tongues. Twelve percent seems to be a reasonable estimate of the group of people who speak Mandarin as their first language, granting that the Mandarin referred to here is not standard Mandarin in the strict sense.

Even if the parents are both from a Mandarin area, there is a strong tendency for the Mainlanders' children to speak a Mandarin that is different from that of their parents. Unlike the Mandarin of their parents, which differs from person to person (i.e., a speaker from Shandong may have some difficulty in understanding one from Sichuan), the Mandarin in their children's speech is more uniform. This is a Mandarin that maintains most of the Peking dialect phenomic distinctions but is different from it in many phonetic and grammatic features. Even children of Pekingese parents speak Taiwan Mandarin except when they are asked to speak "authentic Pekingese."

The borderlines separating the three speech groups are somewhat blurred because marriages take place between speech groups and because individuals may not live in separate speech communities. In rural areas the population of a village is generally either Taiwanese or Hakka speakers, while residential areas for military and government employees are occupied mainly by Mainlanders. Except for these two cases it is very rare for a child to speak a first language that is different from that of his parents. Even in these two cases, the child tends to pick up the mother's language as the first language and the father's language or the language of the neighborhood as the second language. No statistics are available for making generalizations about the pressure of the family, relatives, neighborhood, speech community, or government on the choice of first language for children in the above-mentioned situations.

The bilingual situations of each speech group will be described from four different aspects—the ability to understand, the ability to speak, the frequency of use, and literacy.

Figure 13.1 shows my estimate of the distribution of trilinguals and bilinguals (passive knowledge only is considered here) among Taiwanese speakers according to year of birth. It is equated with ages at 1945, when the war ended, and the present year, 1973. Among those who were born in 1965, more than 90 percent are capable of understanding Mandarin and hence are included in the bilingual group of TM (Taiwanese-Mandarin). Less than 10 percent of those born in that year are monolinguals in Taiwanese (T).

Those who were born between 1933 and 1938 experienced a sudden language shift while they were in primary school (age 7–12). They were exposed to both Japanese and Mandarin at different times in primary school. Some retained Japanese but failed to pick up Mandarin because they graduated too soon to learn Mandarin in school or failed to pick it up elsewhere. These are usually the people whose occupations do not require much contact with a wide variety of people. Some forgot Japanese because they had not used Japanese in school long enough before the time of the shift, or else they have had little opportunity to use their Japanese since then. There is a high proportion of monolinguals in this age group because compulsory education was not enforced after the war, and also because, especially in the countryside, their teachers' Mandarin was in general not sufficient.

Those who were born between 1926 and 1932 were 13–19 years of age at the time of the shift. If these attended high school, they usually picked up both Japanese and Mandarin, though a few older ones may have failed to learn

Age in 1973	Age in 1945	Year of birth
88	60	1885
78	50	1895
68	40	1905
58	30	1915
48	20	1925
38	10	1935
28	0	1945
18		1955
8		1965
0		1973

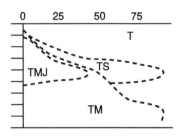

T   = Taiwanese monolinguals
TJ = Taiwanese − Japanese bilinguals
TM = Taiwanese − Mandarin bilinguals
TMJ = Taiwanese − Mandarin − Japanese trilinguals

Figure 13.1 **Percentage of Taiwanese Speakers with Listening Ability in Mandarin and Japanese**

Mandarin (only if they never served in government) and a few younger ones may have forgotten their Japanese. If they attended a middle school, they tend to be trilingual in Japanese, Mandarin, and Taiwanese. If they did not, they tend to be bilingual in Taiwanese and Japanese. Monolinguals in Taiwanese are few among this age group because compulsory education was enforced on them.

Quite a large proportion of the older people have picked up Mandarin mainly through social contacts. These are usually trilinguals. Those who did not learn Japanese at school but succeeded in picking up Mandarin are more numerous than those who did the reverse, because Mandarin is easier to pick up than Japanese for Taiwanese speakers. Among the young people, those who understand Japanese without even a listening ability in Mandarin are relatively few among this age group, because they are exposed to both Japanese and Mandarin through similar channels: mass communication, business contacts, and in government institutions in the urban areas.

Some Taiwanese speakers also speak Hakka. The proportion is smaller than that of Hakka speakers who are able to speak Taiwanese, because Taiwanese speakers do not need to know the language unless they live in Hakka areas. In mixed areas, Hakka speakers usually can speak Mandarin or Japanese rather than Taiwanese. Hakka speakers with wider areas of activities, on the other hand, find some need for learning Taiwanese. Because their group is smaller and in the mixed areas, Taiwanese rather than Mandarin is more frequently spoken by them.

In the above description, my criterion for a bilingual is listening ability in two languages. If we use the criterion of fluent speaking ability, the percentage of bilinguals in Mandarin or Japanese would be reduced by half. Many people's speaking ability is limited to simple conversation. The proportion of those who can speak up in Mandarin even in small meetings is quite low. Four reasons can be given for this: (1) There is a great educational emphasis on writing and an undue neglect of speaking ability. (2) The whole education system trains students to listen and repeat rather than speak and discuss (due to large class size, lecture-type teaching methods, and *improper* way of evaluating student achievement). (3) Most children's ability to express themselves is underdeveloped because the use of their native language is prohibited at school, the time when they are developing their ability to speak in public. (4) Except in some special areas and on some particular occasions, their mother tongue is used in their daily life.

The use of Mandarin between Taiwanese speakers generally happens in two situations: (1) in school or the armed forces, where the ban on any non-Mandarin tongue is strictly enforced, and (2) among children when they play games that they have learned at school.

The use of Mandarin among children varies according to where they live. It is used more frequently in urban than in rural areas, and in mixed areas than in the monolanguage areas where Taiwanese is exclusively used.

There are parents who encourage their children to use Mandarin so that they can achieve a higher academic standing at school. Competition to get into good schools at the higher levels is extremely fierce. Children are compelled to prepare for entrance examinations at the expense even of physical growth. It is common for students to study twelve hours a day, seven days a week, for more than a year preceding an entrance exam. Parents have to bear the idea of having their children sacrifice their health for better schooling; some parents do not mind taking the risk of sacrificing even their children's relationships with their families and relatives. Though small in number, some Taiwanese-speaking parents are beginning to speak to their children in Mandarin with the hope of helping their children to get better grades in school.

In regard to reading ability the population is divided much less clearly horizontally. If one can speak Taiwanese and read Japanese, one has a very good chance of developing a sufficient reading knowledge of Mandarin Chinese. This is because the syntax of Mandarin is quite similar to that of Taiwanese. The lexicons of the two dialects may be very different but they do overlap sufficiently so that at least 70 percent of their monosyllabic etymons are the same. Terms for modern concepts are generally shared by Japanese, Mandarin, and Taiwanese. Many of the same combinations of etymons represented by the same Chinese characters are used in the three languages. Differences are only matters of pronunciation. There is even a high degree of regularity in the similarities and differences among the pronunciations of the same etymons in the three languages.

Compared to people in Japan or English-speaking countries, people of Taiwan are not so dependent on writing for their daily life.

A relatively small portion of the literate depend on reading to acquire knowledge in the arts and crafts, sports, farming, and the like. Books written for the general public are generally in Chinese. Quite a few Taiwanese read Japanese and English for practical knowledge.

Writing ability is much less common than reading ability. Unlike reading Chinese, writing Chinese is not a skill one can pick up by himself through self-study. My estimate is that less than 5 percent of those who have developed a reading knowledge by themselves ever write in Chinese for purposes other than personal communication. Many primary school graduates cannot write even family letters. I have often heard of younger men attending cram sessions for letter writing before they are drafted so that they can write letters home when they are away. Even among college graduates, those who can write articles suitable for newspaper publication are the exception rather than the rule.

Some reasons for this unbalanced ability in Chinese writing and reading are:

1. It is difficult for the average person to write correctly because of the huge number and complexity of the Chinese characters.
2. There is a custom of evaluating one's scholarship by one's own calligraphy. One feels discouraged to write if he feels his calligraphy is not presentable.
3. The norm of modern Chinese is still in flux. Idioms, grammar, and vocabulary from different stages of the development of Mandarin and different dialects are all combined in varying proportions and differing styles in modern Mandarin. Grammar is rarely taught as a guide for writing clear, precise, and easy Chinese. Only the talented who have long years of practice have some confidence in their own writing.
4. The idea that writing is an ornament and a display of learning still haunts people in general. When people read official documents that are full of classical diction strange to modern grammar, it is hard to convince them that simpler and easier writing is good writing because it communicates better. Government business letters have usually been in classical Chinese; not until recently has there been a movement to use modern Chinese for these.

The proportion of those who use romanization of the Taiwanese vernacular has not increased, because the government has banned the teaching of Taiwanese romanization and the printing of new romanized texts. No systematic investigation has been done on the actual use of romanized Taiwanese, so as to compare the efficiency of a phonetic writing such as romanization and logographic writing such as Chinese characters. Such an investigation is very desirable in view of the fact that romanization is rarely used in any other Chinese community.

The bilingual situations of the Hakka in Taiwan are quite similar to those of Taiwanese speakers, especially in the distribution of those who can speak and write Japanese or Mandarin according to age group. As was said earlier, there is a higher proportion of Hakka people capable of using Taiwanese than vice versa. Since the Hakka population is smaller than the Taiwanese and since they therefore need to contact outsiders more frequently than the Taiwanese, and because neither Taiwanese nor Hakka is taught at any school in Taiwan, Hakka people have to use Japanese or Mandarin to communicate with Taiwanese speakers. Some Hakka tend to use Japanese or Mandarin among themselves when non-Hakka speakers are present. This has caused the mistaken belief that the Hakka want to identify themselves with the Japanese or Mainlanders.

The number of those who speak the various Austronesian languages as native tongues is very hard to estimate. The Austronesian peoples have suffered more than the Han (i.e., Chinese) people from the drastic shift of the national language from Japanese to Mandarin. First, Mandarin is a Chinese dialect and is easier for Taiwanese or Hakka speakers to learn and use than for the Austronesian population. Second, the Austronesian population has relied on Japanese much more than the Han dwellers, because each of their speech communities is very small and Japanese is the only language they can use to communicate with outsiders (either other Austronesian tribes or their Han neighbors).

Evaluation of Nationalist Language Planning in Taiwan

My examination of the Nationalist language policy and its practice will center on the question of whether it plans toward language unification through bilingualism or language unification by suppression of linguistic differences.

According to both the description of language policy given by the Ministry of Education on the central level and also its practice on mainland China before the Communist takeover, one would say that it was a policy for bilingualism. Judging from what is being practiced in Taiwan especially in the entire education system, one must conclude that the official language policy in Taiwan is of the second type. However, the official standing of the provincial government on this is not clear.

My claim that the practice of the Nationalists in Taiwan is that of language unification through suppression of linguistic differences is based on the following observations:

1. Taiwanese or Hakka is not allowed as a medium of instruction at any level of school, except in the beginning months of instruction of first graders.

2. No instruction on Taiwanese or Hakka is given at school to help Mainlanders' children communicate with Taiwanese or Hakka monolinguals. Even though bilinguals and trilinguals are more effective and desired in Taiwan than monolinguals from political, economical, and social points of view, the present educational system discourages Mandarin monolinguals from becoming

bilinguals by offering them no facilities to learn Taiwanese or Hakka and by prohibiting the use of Taiwanese and Hakka in school so that Mandarin-speaking children do not feel the necessity of learning Taiwanese and Hakka.

Surrounded by Taiwanese speakers, a Mandarin speaker should be able to use Taiwanese or Hakka if either is taught at school for three months, five hours a week. Not a single class is available at school, however, for those who want to learn Taiwanese for immediate daily use. Quite in contract with this neglect of teaching a language of daily use is the teaching of English, which is rarely used in ordinary life. English is required for every student in middle school (i.e., intermediate and high school) five hours a week every year. More than 80 percent of those who spend three years or more on English never use English in their entire life.

3. No instruction on Hakka and Taiwanese is given to help community members communicate, trust, cooperate, and appreciate each other better in and through their mother languages. Taiwanese and Hakka differ from Mandarin as English does from German or French.

4. No effort is made to teach the linguistic structure of Taiwanese and Hakka so that one can teach or learn Mandarin, Taiwanese, and Hakka more efficiently. The atmosphere is such that any study of Taiwanese or Hakka by native speakers might be viewed as motivated against national policies.

5. No attempt to popularize the vernacular writing in Taiwanese or Hakka is allowed. The government has banned the printing of romanized texts. Romanization is easier for Taiwanese and Hakka illiterates to learn than are Chinese characters. Many Taiwanese and Hakka words either have no characters to represent them or are represented by characters that the average people do not know. Attempts to write down Taiwanese or Hakka are allowed only in folk poetry and proverbs but not in prose. On scholarly subjects, written Chinese in characters may not vary much for Taiwanese or Hakka or Mandarin. Writing in Taiwanese or Hakka, which is intended to faithfully reflect speech, differs drastically from that in Mandarin.

6. The public use of Taiwanese or Hakka is disallowed officially in the troops, schools, and government except in legislative organizations. Their use on private occasions is prohibited in many schools in order to promote Mandarin. Taiwanese and Hakka are prohibited at some schools mainly on the grounds that, in doing so, students will have enough practice in Mandarin. The unfortunate result is that students speak inaccurate Mandarin and non-fluent Taiwanese, Hakka, and Mandarin. Because prohibition of expression in a mother tongue is too much for the average child to adjust to, except for a few talented ones, students cannot speak any language fluently. When students are forced to use Mandarin without sufficient, correct awareness of structural differences, they form the habit of speaking Mandarin with many Taiwanese or Hakka syntactic and phonological features. Undesired habits of speaking inaccurate Mandarin are reinforced by conversation between students with similar habits.

Since there are regular relationships among Taiwanese, Hakka, and Mandarin, the major learning problem is in accuracy rather than fluency. After fluency in the mother tongue is firmly acquired, fluent and accurate Mandarin can be acquired with the help of modern techniques in teaching a second language, especially in making students aware of structural differences among Hakka, Taiwanese, and Mandarin.

Among teachers of Mandarin and written Chinese, there is a general lack of knowledge about the structural relations between Mandarin and Taiwanese or Hakka and their pedagogical implications. There is even fear that study of the Taiwanese dialect will result in its promotion, which will affect the promotion of Mandarin.

7. No efforts are made so that the basic scientific knowledge about the structure and history of Taiwanese and Hakka can be available to students and the general public. People in general still superstitiously believe that Taiwanese and Hakka have no grammar, can never be put into writing, or are inadequate and unsuitable for cultivated discussions. They are miserably ignorant of the truth that Mandarin, Taiwanese, and Hakka were once one and the same language, and that languages change as environments change—not because of community members' evilness, or disloyalty, or incompetence, or inferiority, but because of their ability to innovate as language is passed down from one generation to another. Without such ability to innovate, human beings would make no progress and have no culture. Few efforts have been made to reinforce the facts that Mandarin is no more authentic, correct, or efficient than Taiwanese or Hakka is, that Mandarin has been chosen as the national language of China merely because there are more people who speak Mandarin (or its varieties) than those who speak other tongues, and that Taiwanese and Hakka are not devious forms of Mandarin.

The concept of the standard authentic language and culture results in the following unfortunate value judgment: Differences from the "authentic" culture and language of the Mainlanders are undesirable. If there are differences due to innovation in the "authentic" culture of the Mainlanders, then the conservative feature in the Taiwanese language or culture is viewed to be "backward." If it has been due to innovations in the Taiwanese culture or language, then the innovative features are to be viewed as the results of the Foreign Devil's evil influence.

Many school hours have been spent to emphasize the common history of the Chinese population in Taiwan, and much has been said about the importance of solidarity between different groups. Nothing serves to prove the common history of the Chinese more effectively than the systematic relation that exists between Mandarin, Hakka, and Taiwanese and the common body of vocabulary represented by the same Chinese characters. If history is to be studied to help people understand the present and solve immediate problems, rather than to make them forget the present, the history of the three languages should be included in the curriculum.

8. No legal status is given for either Taiwanese, spoken as their native language by more than 75 percent of the population of Taiwan, or Hakka, spoken by 10 percent. Government subsidies are given to the production of Mandarin television and radio programs and films. Taiwanese TV programs, which are the major source of information and entertainment for the great majority, have been limited to only one hour an evening.

Mandarin is an important qualification for getting any governmental position, or for getting into any high level of school. Taiwanese or Hakka is not required of even those governmental employees who have to serve Taiwanese or Hakka monolinguals in person (clerks, policemen, receptionists in information booths, etc.).

The discrepancies described above between the proclaimed policies of the central government and those of the provincial government, and between the plan and its practice, are symptoms of inadequate planning. It is my conviction that the position of the central government on language unification is the better policy from the modern sociolinguistic point of view. It is also my belief that the discrepancies from the original policy and inadequacy in planning have been chiefly due to misconceptions on the nature of language and language planning on the part of people themselves as well as the policy makers. Through the rest of this section I shall discuss various types of work needed in language planning.[7] Alternatives of major issues will be discussed and the source of these discrepancies identified.

Selection of Planning and Implementation Agencies

The main government agency that has a role similar to that of language planning in Taiwan is the Commission on the Promotion of Mandarin (CPM). It is affiliated with the Education Department of the Taiwan Provincial Government.[8] The CPM was formed in 1946 by the decree of the CPM in the Ministry of Education of the central government of the Nationalists. The CPM in either level of government was an executive body in charge of designing, investigating, and coordinating the teaching of the national language, Mandarin, in the areas with its respective jurisdiction. The policy to adopt Mandarin as the national language and to seek linguistic unification by spreading Mandarin over all of China was decided on long ago by the Planning Committee for Linguistic Unification through a National Language, first organized in 1929. Even so, the Taiwan Provincial CPM has had much independent power since it was not bound to observe any particular method or schedule of implementing the prescribed policy. In fact the policy was carried out in varying degrees and using various methods in different provinces. In Canton and many other provinces the language of school instruction was the native languages up to the twelfth grade. This continued under the Nationalist government until it evacuated to Taiwan. Taiwan is the only place among the non-Mandarin areas that ever taught all subjects in Mandarin at all school levels including even the first grade. What has been practiced in Taiwan regarding the status of non-Mandarin dialects in fact contradicts previous policies and practices of the central (Nationalist) government.

In 1951, soon after the evacuation of the Nationalist government from the Chinese mainland to Taiwan, the CPM was dissolved on the national level. There were some reasons for the Nationalists to dissolve the CPM on the central level, instead of abolishing it on the provincial level or maintaining it on both levels. First, Mandarin was far better promoted in Taiwan than in any other place. Second, the attitude of the central CPM toward non-Mandarin dialects had been too lenient for the nation to achieve the goal of language unity in the mind of those in power. It had recognized that each Chinese dialect is one of the national languages in the broad sense. It had decided on Pekingese as the present-day standard language, or the national language in the narrower sense. It viewed Pekingese merely as one of the Chinese dialects. It even encouraged the study of various dialects so as to enrich and improve the national language and to have more lively national literature. It also stressed that the study of dialects could help improve the teaching of Mandarin.[9] All these views except the last one might have sounded too conservative or out-of-date in the mind of those authorities who were anxious to see that no language but Mandarin be recognized as the official language of Taiwan. They might have feared that Taiwanese and Hakka could be in the way of promoting the teaching and use of Mandarin further in Taiwan.

Two questions can be asked concerning the selection of these committee members who are to be in charge of language planning and its implementation.

1. In selecting the committee members was consideration given so that the interests of each speech group can be best protected?

The conflict of interest between speech communities was not taken into consideration. Qualifications and interest in administering the teaching of Mandarin are the major considerations. Efforts have been made to appoint Taiwanese and Hakka speakers. But these were appointed because of their qualifications to spread Mandarin and not to study the interests of their respective speech communities regarding language policy and its implementation.

2. Do various speech communities have control over the appointment of the committee members?

The committee members of the provincial CPM were appointed by the governor of Taiwan. The provincial government ruled that there be an Institute for the promotion of Mandarin in each district and city. Even the promoters of each such institute are to be appointed by the head of the educational department of the provincial government. Since both the governor of Taiwan and the head of the educational department under him were not elected by the people but appointed by the central government, the people of Taiwan have no control over these organizations.[10]

Theoretically, the people may have their voices heard through representatives in the city, district, or provincial councils.[11] Any bill, however, that such councils might pass would be nullified if it should be in conflict with the decrees of the central or provincial government. Even if the legislators pass bills that do not conflict with decrees on a higher level, they may not be seriously carried out, because neither promoters nor their superiors are responsible to the council representatives in the administrative hierarchy.

There is no special organization at any legislative level that systematically studies the problems of language planning or examines the social, political, cultural, and educational implications of the government's policy of spreading Mandarin.

The fact that neither the population nor its representatives had direct control over the planning and implementing of the spread of Mandarin explains why the original policy of unification through bilingualism in school and community was changed without any serious public deliberation.

Fact Finding

Any planning requires a thorough knowledge of facts. With the present knowledge of various fields of linguistics and applied linguistics, one must seek findings about the following types of facts in order to propose or carry out any language planning.

1. The sociolinguistic situation of each speech community to be affected by language planning.
   a. Analysis of various types of bilingualism of Taiwanese, Hakka, and Mandarin speakers.
   b. Analysis of the general ability to speak, understand, write, read, and translate in each language, and the actual amount of use of the various languages in each of the language skills.
   c. Analysis of the use of writing by various groups of speakers for different types of subject matter.
2. Linguistic study of languages involved.
   a. Description of Mandarin, Taiwanese, and Hakka.
   b. Historical study of the language changes that have occurred in the past due to mutual influence.
   c. Analysis of words borrowed from Mandarin and Japanese into Hakka and Taiwanese, including the two major types of borrowings: (1) compounds pronounced according to Hakka or Taiwanese pronunciation of etymons used in the compounds, and (2) compound etymons pronounced according to Japanese or Mandarin.
   d. Identification of most frequently used lexical items and sentence patterns in each language.
3. Contrastive analysis between languages.
   a. Collection and analysis of errors frequently made by students.
   b. Differences and similarities of each pair of languages.
   c. Degree of difficulty of various learning items.

4. Psychological analysis of various types of language users.
   a. Attitude toward own language, and other languages, toward monolinguals and bilinguals in and out of one's own speech group. Use of native, national language, other languages, and various types of speaking on different types of occasions.
   b. The intelligence and personal traits of bilinguals and monolinguals, especially those who have not had formal education in their native language.
5. The experiences of other countries in language planning.
   a. The soical, cultural, political, economic, and psychological implications of various approaches to language planning.
   b. The achievements, problems, methodology, and theories of language planning in other countries.
   c. Limitation of language planning. (1) Limitations of man's knowledge about the economic, cultural, political, and social goals in the future. (2) Limitation of man's prediction about sociolinguistic changes aimed at in each alternative plan. (3) Limitation in man's ability and facilities to carry out a proposed plan.

With such a highly developed system of government and education in Taiwan, one would expect that a lot must have been done on the above points. From what I have seen so far, I may say that (1) works on points 4 and 5 are rather scarce, (2) works on points 2 and 3 are rather inadequate from modern linguistic or pedagogical points of view, and (3) much has been done on point 1 but quite a few of such works were done rather unscientifically. There is a lack both of overall coordination of efforts and of objective study through fieldwork and using methods and theories of modern behavioral sciences. I have not found good documentation of the works on facts relevant to language planning.

There are two statements in an official report on the language situation of Taiwan,[12] which I would like to comment on because they have some bearing on the main issue of this essay—language unification through bilingualism versus through suppression of linguistic differences.

This report describes the vernaculars of Taiwan as inadequate for academic and cultured communication because these stopped developing and absorbing new elements during the fifty years of Japanese rule. The writer(s) did not seem to be aware that no language can ever stop growing, especially when there is intensive contact with other cultures. There had been intensive mutual borrowing of vocabulary between Japanese and Mandarin. Most Chinese compounds that are used for modern concepts were first coined in Japan by putting Chinese etymons together and then borrowed into Chinese (e.g., *jingi* economics," *lóji* "logic"). What was borrowed by Taiwanese might not be entirely identical with what was borrowed by the Mainlanders, since each group might have coined its own compounds for new concepts instead of borrowing from Japanese or other sources. When new words were created for new concepts existing only in China (e.g., *Zong hua Min guo* "Republic of China," *Guofu* "national father"), borrowing was a matter of a very short time since all Mandarin words are represented in Chinese characters and all Chinese characters have at least their dictionary pronunciations in Taiwanese or Hakka. As for the grammar of Taiwanese or Hakka, either one is even more precise than Mandarin because Mandarin has many patterns taken in from other dialects which have not been normalized into the structures of Mandarin.

These same reports also say that people in Taiwan were generally more competent in Japanese than in Taiwanese or Hakka. If there were a scientific investigation, the report would have said that people of a certain age group in certain types of areas tend to speak more fluent Japanese than Taiwanese or Hakka. Usage of words, even function words, borrowed from Japanese into Taiwanese or Hakka speech of certain age groups is very common all over Taiwan. As I described earlier, incorrect interpretations of data by the Nationalists have resulted in an overestimation of the power of language planning and an underestimation of the universal love and respect for one's own native language. The Taiwanese did not abandon their languages easily; it can be proven that Taiwanese and Hakka are still the main means of communication in their communities, in spite of the fact that their use is banned from grade school onward. The government has tried with all its power to spread Mandarin at the expense of Taiwanese and Hakka.

Purposes of Language Planning

Granted that changes in people's ability in and use of languages can be planned in spite of many unknowns, one asks whether a plan is needed or not to change the people's ability in and use of various languages and, if a plan is needed, for what purpose we do language planning.

Much has been said to justify the policy of language unification through Mandarin in order to convince people in general to support government policy. This has been necessary since language unification itself should not be the eventual goal of language planning. If language unity is a sociolinguistic goal, there should be some nonsociolinguistic goals of language unity. To my knowledge there has been no systematized proposal for the purposes of language unification with clear concepts about their cause–effect relations, and with the priority of each purpose well defined. These clearly stated purposes should be the guiding principles in selecting among alternative plans and evaluating the implementation of the plan adopted.

There has been a lack of a balanced analysis of the costs of unifying the language of China against the benefits of having a Chinese linguistic unity. While many people see the benefits of language unification, only a few have seen that changing people's language costs a lot in many respects because it brings many undesired effects and that linguistic unity should not be the end in itself.

Among the purposes given for the language unification of China are typically the following. These are arranged under the Nationalist Three People's Principles: nationalism, democracy, and livelihood. (1) National harmony and integration of various speech communities and patriotism so as to have a stronger nation. (2) Political unity and equal opportunity to make democracy work better. (3) Social progress to attain a better livelihood for all members of the nation.

The relationship between language unity and some of these goals (or goals of a goal) are not frequently mentioned. For example, the existence of minority speech groups alongside a dominant group often results in discrimination in job opportunities. Differences in language require a high cost in communication and stand in the way of communication and cooperation between speech groups. Hence, it slows down the rate of social progress. These goals are, in my opinion, legitimate ones since they are all desired goals of government and education in general. Linguistic unity does result in these goals, other things being equal.

In addition to the above goals it should be clearly understood that language planning and its results should not contradict any of the general goals of education and government. The Goals of Education state among other things that government and education should aim at the cultivation of self-respect and self-confidence for the nation as well as for the individual. They also state that education should aim at healthy development of the individual's body and mind. The Constitution of the Republic of China recognizes equality among various ethnic or linguistic groups within China. Since language planning and its implementation are merely a part of government and education, they should not contradict any of these goals. Even with such an understanding, the interests and well-being of such a huge number of people are so much at stake when language changes are planned that I think it proper to identify such goals as negatively stated goals of language planning lest any language policy should result in abuses.

Long-Range Sociolinguistic Goals

The main body of language planning should include the sociolinguistic goals, the strategy to achieve such goals, and nonsociolinguistic goals of language planning. While the identification of nonsociolinguistic goals (such as national harmony and political unity) is not the sole responsibility of a language planner, the identification of sociolinguistic goals should be his sole responsibility. Since the goals of government and education, especially the priority of each of these goals, are not clearly given, a language planner usually needs to present alternative plans, with his prediction of how each educational and government goal can be achieved by each alternative. As a strategy one may set up several phases of planned sociolinguistic changes and specify the (short-range) sociolinguistic goals of each phase.

What is the eventual goal of the Nationalists with regard to the question of who learns and uses what language(s) in Taiwan?

1. Eventual goal for Mandarin. What is clearly agreed on is the goal that eventually everybody should be able to use Mandarin.

2. Eventual goal for Taiwanese and Hakka. With regard to the eventual goal for Taiwanese and Hakka, there is no agreement. Three alternatives can be considered. (1) Each of the major languages is to be used by its respective community without interference. (2) Each of the major languages shall eventually become extinct. (3) Uncommitted.

On paper the central government took the first position for the whole country.[13] In Taiwan, there is no legal status for Taiwanese and Hakka, and there is no clear written indication as to whether Taiwanese or Hakka should be eventually wiped out or not.

I shall now evaluate the merits of each of the above alternatives in terms of how it helps to achieve the claimed purposes of language planning.

Two reasons have been given for the second alternative that the final goal be the extinction of non-Mandarin tongues. Each can be counterargued.

1. To assimilate the people of Taiwan into the Chinese people without any discriminatory features, the mere ability to use Mandarin by everyone is not enough, since language functions not only as a means of communication but also as a symbol of group identification. As long as there is language difference there is difference in group identity. This argument can be countered as follows: Although a single language group identity is very desirable, the cost of achieving it is much higher than its benefits.

Taiwanese, Hakka, and Mandarin were once one and the same language. They are different today because each speech group has had geographical, cultural, and institutional differences over the past several thousand years. One might attain the goal of a single speech group without internal linguistic difference over all of China by extraordinary means, such as killing off all the adults, or by mixing up the members of each group. An extraordinary means, such as killing off all the adults, or by mixing up the members of each group. An extraordinary means is needed to attain such a goal because normal people usually learn a second language with features carried over from their native tongue. It is conceivable even then that each speech group might speak Mandarin with features peculiar to that group. New dialectal differences would be bound to develop even if the goal were be reached temporarily unless all extralinguistic differences were also wiped away.

Language, moreover, is not the only means of group identification. Even if human technology should so develop that linguistic differences did not develop, geographical, cultural, and institutional differences are themselves also features of group identity.

Monolingualism in the same language, to be sure, is not a necessary condition for political unity or national identity. Peoples of Switzerland and Singapore[14] have national harmony and political unity without language unity. Nor is language unity through monolingualism itself a sufficient condition for true unity:

Nationalist and Communist Chinese both speak the same language, but they are deadly enemies of each other. The Irish speak English, but they adamantly refuse to belong to the British. Suppression of their own language is one of the unpleasant experiences with the British that the Irish will not forget.

It is not so much for a monolithic group identity as for communication that Mandarin is to be learned by the people of Taiwan or elsewhere. To advocate elimination of linguistic differences for the purpose of eliminating all non-Mandarin group identity in a country bigger than the whole of Europe shows great naïvité about the nature of language learning, of language change, and of group identity. Among the older generations in Taiwan different group identifications are made whenever these people speak Mandarin. Young people in Taiwan, moreover, are already using a Mandarin that is different from that of Peking. By their language alone they have an identity that is different from that of the young people in China.

Given that linguistic differences cannot be eliminated entirely and that there are linguistic as well as extra-linguistic features that are pertinent in group identity, it is more realistic for education to play the role of enhancing people's ability to tolerate and respect human differences than to make people look down on them as some evil to be eliminated. Unless people are educated to accept that Taiwanese, Hakka, Cantonese, etc. are all languages of China, China will soon become many countries like Europe.

2. If Mandarin is to be learned by future generations of those now non-Mandarin speakers, it is more economical in the long run to have Mandarin learned as a native language by everyone as soon as possible. The costs for learning Mandarin as a second language can be saved once and for all.

Treated as an economical issue the above argument is valid. But elimination of the use of a language is not purely an economic issue, either for an individual or for a government. In an extraordinary situation an individual may decide to teach Mandarin to his children as the first language purely on the basis of long-run economy. A normal adult will, however, also consider the change of language within his family as a moral and social issue as well. He will ask: Do I have an obligation to maintain my father's language? If I should give up my father's language for the language of others, what else can I give up also? What principle do I have for giving up what my family has cherished, for something strange to our family tradition? Will differences in language, or differences in degree of competence in Mandarin cause wider generation gaps and isolation of the old from the young and, consequently, from the new developments of our community and the world? By alienating my children from my parents do I violate my filial piety, the highest virtue of the Chinese people? Will my children be socially acceptable to their community, which still speaks Taiwanese or Hakka? Even if I do shift my identification from the Taiwanese or Hakka community to the Mandarin one, can I be accepted by the latter without discrimination? Which is more desirable, to belong to both or to either of the communities?

A responsible government should, by its knowledge and ability, provide unbiased guidance so that each individual can do a balanced deliberation and make the best decision from the economic, moral, and social points of view.

If it is not a purely economic issue for an individual to give up his own language, it is even less a government right to make its goal the elimination of the major native language of 13 million people.

Several noneconomic problems must be considered by a government thinking of eliminating Taiwanese and Hakka.

1. The cultivation of confidence in and respect for one's own community, culture, and people is an important task of a changing community that aims at modernization. This confidence and respect include a desire that one's community undergo only healthy cultural changes, that it not give up its own system blindly, nor slavishly accept any other system from the outside. To achieve such a confidence, a community should develop the ability to compare the new thing with the old intelligently before it abandons the latter for the former. An old system should be abandoned when and only when it is certain that the latter is better than the former. Unless a community is able to exercise such a judgment, its individuals may tend to value any cultural feature of a dominating group from inside or outside the country as superior to that of their own group. Many Nationalist leaders themselves have been able to see the importance of self-respect and self-confidence during their process of modernization. While they see standardization or unification of language as a feature for modernization, they have generally failed to see that in their efforts to persuade people to learn and use the national language, they often commit the following errors.

a. Individuals of local communities are not given enough chance to compare carefully whatever they are considering adopting with what they traditionally have. Localisms are generally suppressed as being backward and reactionary. The Nationalists have not emphasized the point that a local language can be abandoned only when it is no longer used by the majority—not because it is inferior to Mandarin as a symbolic system. As a result, individuals may lose confidence in and respect for the culture, tradition, and people of their own community. Some national leaders may not be worried about such cultural suicide on the local level; but lack of confidence in one's own community may extend to each of confidence in one's own nation. People who are once indoctrinated to abandon their own system for that of others, because of the prestige of its users rather than because their own is truly inferior, may tend to admire all things that are used by any other nations that have higher prestige. Nationalists of course do not want cultural suicide on the national level.[15] They should know that language loyalty is the most basic of cultural confidence for individuals. Once it is destroyed, cultural confidence is apt to be destroyed on the national level as well as the local level. If Taiwanese can be given up for Mandarin, why not Mandarin for English? English is used more widely internationally.

It is noteworthy that those who spoke Japanese most of the time under the Japanese rule tend to speak Mandarin in Taiwan and English when they come to the United States more than Taiwanese or Hakka today.

This shows that people tend to seek after the language and culture of a more prestigious group once their primary language loyalty is destroyed.

Japanese tend to borrow words from prestigious cultures too fast. This seems to be a symptom of a similar trait—eagerness to adopt prestigious features. Japan has been able to borrow very fast from other cultures without causing too much internal disruption because her people has a strong sense of social responsibility. Those who adopt a new feature from a foreign culture make efforts to spread it to their fellow countrymen. Their fellow countrymen also make efforts to follow the change lest they should be lagging behind in the cultural changes.

In a country like China, which is so big in territory and population and so burdened with the cultures of the past, to start a cultural change is always hard. But when a cultural change is promoted without cultivating cultural confidence, group loyalty, and a strong sense of social responsibility, there is a danger of national disruption and social confusion.

b. If people are taught to subjugate their own sentiments and interests to those of the nation, they do not learn to understand and work for the interests of their local community, nor do they get much experience in negotiation with other groups for the best interests of various groups. If one is not trained to understand and work for the interests of one's own community in the midst of other communities, he tends to be incapable of doing so for his own country. The whole nation becomes separate crowds who are easily controlled by any powerful interest group who monopolizes the interpretation of national interests.

c. Loyalty and confidence in the local community are an important safeguard against the tendency for the strong to suppress the weak domestically and internationally. In order to spread Mandarin, the Nationalists seem to have overemphasized the following theme adopted from a Chinese proverb: since the rule is that the bigger fish swallows up the smaller fish, individuals should join the bigger group and the people should become a big fish that swallows, rather than remain many small fish and be swallowed.

Japan's success in the standardization of its language may be the envy of developing countries. However, her harsh measures in suppressing the dialectal differences in Japan or in her colonies are not worth copying. Some people in Japan even committed suicide because they were put to shame when they violated the rule of not using their local speech. Such measures have resulted from, and have reinforced the jungle law of, suppression of the "weak" by the "strong" rather than the civilized tradition of tolerance of differences and respect for the interests of one's own group and other groups. Japan's past aggression in Asia might not be purely accidental.

2. Men are blessed with the capacity to change their language according to their environment. Such an ability to change makes human progress possible.

Each language is undergoing constant changes, and linguistic differences are a fact of men's evolution. It is totally wrong to regard Taiwanese or Hakka as a deviation from an authentic language and therefore an evil to be eliminated.

3. If the members of a country are equal before the law, it is hard to justify the view that the languages of that country are not equal before the same law. It is also hard to justify the fact that some parents are forbidden to teach their own language to their own children while others may, and that some cannot receive education in their own language while others can.

4. Since the Taiwanese people are regarded as Chinese, their language should be regarded as a Chinese language. The Nationalists took over Taiwan on the very ground that the languages spoken by the Taiwan dwellers are Chinese. It would be an irony to eliminate their languages in order to make them have "complete" identification with China. If bilingualism in Mandarin and Taiwanese or Hakka is not enough to identify the Taiwanese as Chinese citizens, that is, if Mandarin monoligualism is the essential requirement for being a Chinese citizen, then the Taiwanese people should not be considered Chinese citizens at all.

5. There is a natural tendency for the members of a minority group to develop an inferiority complex about their own language in the midst of the majority group. If mass education is used to promote Mandarin with the final goal of eliminating Taiwanese and Hakka, it is playing the role of reinforcing such an inferiority complex among the underprivileged people. When there are human differences and group conflicts, the education of a democratic society should play the role of emancipating people from fear, ignorance, suspicion, and misunderstanding.

Short-Range Sociolinguistic Goals as a Strategy to Minimize Undesirable Results

Since the eventual status of Taiwanese and Hakka is not clearly recognized or denied by the provincial government, there are three alternatives: (1) official recognition of their legal status for a clearly defined period of time; (2) immediate official denial of their legal status; (3) no official position. The second alternative would be justifiable if Taiwanese and Hakka speakers were too small in number to be granted any lawful status or if these languages were spoken primarily by newly arrived immigrants who expected to adopt the customs of the host community. Since Taiwanese and Hakka are in neither of these categories, this alternative should not be adopted.

The first alternative might be refuted on two grounds. (1) If the Taiwanese and Hakka are legally allowed, Mandarin will never be learned. (2) The length of transitional period during which Taiwanese and Hakka should have a legal status is hard to determine.

The first ground might stand if Taiwan were a closed community that had resisted learning any language having a wider communication value. On the contrary, Taiwanese has modern facilities for the spread of Mandarin. Its population, though not willing to give up its own language, has been quite ready psychologically to learn Mandarin for its wider communication possibilities. This readiness is a result of their experience with Japanese, which they at first refused to learn but later found to be of benefit after they did learn it. The Taiwanese are, if anything, too eager to learn new things. Some measures are needed to slow down their changing if they are to avoid the evils of too rapid sociolinguistic changes.

If a period of transition from Taiwanese and Hakka cannot be defined absolutely, it might be stated on the basis of various conditions. For example, the legal status of Taiwanese and Hakka could be recognized for seventy-five years (this is not arbitrary, because it takes seventy-five years for a generation to die out) with possible consecutive seventy-five-year extensions until certain sociolinguistic conditions are met and the peoples approve the denial of legal status to Taiwanese and Hakka.

There are several reasons for setting up a plan that will state unequivocally sociolinguistic goals for Mandarin, Taiwanese, and Hakka at each stage.

1. Confusion and disputes can be avoided. There has been a general lack of agreement on what to do with Taiwanese, Hakka, and Mandarin; such uncertainty results in suspicion and fear. The majority of Taiwanese suspect that the Mainlanders are attempting to maintain their superior position by banning Taiwanese and Hakka. The Mainlanders fear that the continued prevalence of Taiwanese is a symptom of Taiwanese nationalism that may result in persecution of the mainlander minority.

2. It enables efficient implementation and fair evaluation of its results.

3. It safeguards against undesirable side effects of too rapid sociolinguistic changes, and abuses of language planning for self-interests.

The following are some possible undesirable side effects of language planning in which bilingualism is not legally recognized at least for a considerable period of time.

1. *Conflicts of Interest between Mandarin and Taiwanese and Hakka Speakers.* The policy of spreading Mandarin at the expense of Taiwanese and Hakka brought incalculable advantages to both Mandarin speakers and those who learned it before others did; it also brought disadvantages to the Taiwanese and Hakka speakers that were felt in almost all aspects of their life— economic, political, social, and educational. Many teachers and government officials lost their jobs or could not get promoted merely because of their language backgrounds. Taiwanese and Hakka children have less chance of succeeding in college and high school entrance examinations than do Mandarin children, mainly because Mandarin is the language of both instruction and such examinations. One such exam had a Mandarin composition topic written

with three Chinese characters: "Huochetou." These characters mean "Loco-motive" in Mandarin but "Railway Station" in Taiwanese. Taiwanese parents naturally felt very bitter since this examination discriminated against their children's educational opportunities. Such inequalities in opportunities for jobs, in government, and in schooling naturally have resulted in group conflicts.

2. *Enormous Generation Gaps in Taiwanese and Hakka.* Big generation gaps are a problem common to changing societies. The problem is much worse in Taiwanese and Hakka families and communities since the parents were given their schooling in Japanese but their children are given theirs in Mandarin. Thus the children sometimes use language that older generations cannot understand. These generation gaps would be much smaller if Taiwanese and Hakka were used in schools at least for the beginning four years, since they are languages that would be common to both the parents and the children. Parents could thus be of some help in both their children's homework and their application of school learning to their life at home. Since communication on school-related topics between generations is poor at home and in the community, the parents' care for their own children tends to be limited to provisions of food, clothing, and shelter. This is a great loss to a community, since it is the parents and not the teachers who should best be able to guide their children in their present problems. What has made things worse is the tendency for schools in Taiwan to teach too many things about the "then and there" rather than the "here and now" and its application to daily life. Taiwan is having new generations who are isolated from their own community, who know very little about the history, the function, the problems and the hopes, the sorrows and joys of their own people, but who, instead, memorize the names of territories of different dynasties, and get excited over Western, Russian, and Japanese aggressions of China.

The new generation has been indoctrinated that localism and provincialism are bad, narrow-minded, and backward, and are barriers to national unity and national modernization and progress. Even the recognition of differences is regarded as evil and intolerable. In creating high student motivation to learn Mandarin (which has no use in society or at home), some teachers tend to discourage a real understanding and tolerance of cultural and linguistic differences among different localities; they think tolerance may encourage indifference toward or even opposition to the promotion of Mandarin and thus decrease students' drive to learn Mandarin.

3. *Psychological Depression.*
   a. The following psycholgical problems may exist among Taiwanese and Hakka children who begin to attend a school where they have to use a strange tongue. (1) Their ability to express themselves orally in public may never be developed, as has been pointed out in a UNESCO report. "Ideas which have ben formulated in one language are so difficult to express

through the modes of another, that a person habiltually faced with this task can readily lose his facility to express himself. A child faced with this task at an age when his powers of self-expression even in his native tongue are but incompletely developed, may possibly never achieve adequate self-expression." (1953, p. 47) (2) A guilt complex may be developed and their self-confidence and self-respect affected when the use of their own mother tongue is either not allowed or discouraged at school; one's mother tongue is a very important part of one's ego. (3) Frustration may result due to wide generation gaps. This is especially felt when parents want to check their children's progress at school and when children want help from their parents.

b. Mainlanders' children are psychologically no better off, even though they are privileged in many senses. Their language privilege becomes the target of envy and resentment by the Taiwanese majority. Not until recently when Mainlanders and Taiwanese speakers began to speak the same type of Mandarin—i.e., a Taiwanese variety of Mandarin—were they often accepted by their Taiwanese peers at school. An ability to use Taiwanese or Hakka is still needed for social acceptance in many Taiwanese and Hakka areas.

c. The older generations in Taiwanese and Hakka communities are unhappiest of all, because of generation gaps and the lack of status of their own language. They feel left behind by the changing society and alienated from their own children. Nothing is unhappier than an elderly person in a Chinese community whose prestige is not dearly respected by the younger ones.

d. The older Mainlanders have had similar psychological experiences with their children. They are actually in a worse position, because without proper facilities they cannot pick up Taiwanese or Hakka as easily as their children do. They are very slow in regarding Taiwan as their home. It is rather embarrassing for them to claim that they want to serve the community without knowing its language.

4. *Deterred Social Progress.* Taiwan has witnessed rapid economic growth in the past two decades. This does not mean that what has been done is the best among all alternatives with regard to language planning and other aspects of government. I believe that if the alternative of language unification through bilingualism is adopted, there will be more rapid growth and a healthier outlook in other aspects of social progress. A population that left their isolated village life on the Chinese mainland and sought adventure in the new land, a population that has been stimulated by the mixture of new and old settlers and has had the impact of modern ideas through intensive contacts with American and Japanese peoples, such a population should have made more social progress than they have. Social progress may be deterred by language planning that neglects a proper coordination of the language of the school with the

language of the community and between the languages between speech groups for the following reasons: (1) General psychological depression as discussed above. (2) Inefficient learning of all subjects at school. Too big a portion of school time is spent on learning Mandarin. For children, especially, language is best learned through life rather than only in class. Less time could be spent on Mandarin if the language of school were coordinated with the language of the community. Instruction in a student's second language is not so effective as instruction in his first language.[16] Lack of direct application of school-learning to the students' community and home environment usually leads to lack of interest, motivation, and effectiveness in learning. (3) Lack of understanding of one's own community. Students in Taiwan spend too much time on books, partly because of the ineffective learning mentioned above. The exclusive use of Mandarin at school separates school from local community. By not teaching students to express themselves in Taiwanese or Hakka, teachers are discouraging them from contacting their own community leaders and receiving benefits from their community experiences. Any education that aims at suppression of linguistic differences tends to teach more about national events than about local matters. Students are thus ill-trained to locate and solve the problems of their own communities or to understand and serve their own people. Love, respect, and concern for their immediate environment are not cultivated along with nationally oriented interest. (4) Lack of coordination and cooperation between generations. This tendency is a result of the wide generation gaps described above. The young think that the old are unqualified and uninformed because they cannot even understand the official language. The old think the young know too little because they seldom take advice from their elders. (5) Lack of coordination and cooperation between speech groups due to economic and social isolation of the Taiwanese and Hakka monolinguals. Since the medium of mass communication is mostly Mandarin, Taiwanese and Hakka monolinguals are ill-informed of the happenings of the changing society. Their business tends to be limited in scale, and their ways of production slow in improvement. Farmers in isolated villages who have heavily depended on television for entertainment and information found themselves suddenly left behind when Taiwanese programs were cut down drastically. Their inability to understand Mandarin weather forecasts has resulted in failures to take precautionary measures for their crops against bad weather.

5. *Failure of Democracy at the Local as Well as the National Level.*
   (1) The newer generations are less outspoken in public in either their native tongue or Mandarin. (2) Through too much emphasis on learning Mandarin in addition to the memory work on Chinese characters, students have lost much of the time that could have been used to learn other subjects that would improve their creativity and critical thinking abilities. Thus the people tend to become a mass that blindly follows and worships its leaders. (3) People know

too little of their own community as mentioned above to serve as public servants or to exercise their right to control their local government. Democracy works when people know their own interests and their own desires as well as those of other groups, when they are prepared to compromise and tolerate differences, and when they are bound by laws in their struggle for their own interests. (4) On the national level democracy is also likely to fail. If people of various local communities have insufficient training and experience in the practice of democracy on the local level, they are even less prepared for democracy on national level. There, people cannot see what is going on easily, because national matters are more heterogeneous and complex than are local matters. Even if they do know interests of their own communities and those of others, they may not be able to act for the best of all communities because they lack experience in doing similar things on a smaller scale. If people are taught to suppress their most natural group instinct—their language loyalty—they are at the same time being trained to suppress their own interest and dignity as an individual, as members of their local community, and as citizens of their country. Such suppression is euphemized by the motto that says "Sacrifice the small ego to accomplish the big ego." The people are being prepared to follow anyone who can dictate the big ego for the small ego.

Feedback

All good planning should leave some room for constant revision by checking output against both the input and the expected output. If there is good work on feedback, the practice of aiming toward monolingualism might be rectified. How public opinion is treated and how information on the results of language planning is provided to improve language planning will be discussed.

Since the policy on spreading Mandarin brings so many advantages to Mainlanders and so many disadvantages to the Taiwanese people, it is expected that arguments such as I have presented would be raised and demands based on these arguments for a more enlightened policy would be voiced.

Voices for a more rational and humane policy are heard only in private conversations. In public one finds the following themes reiterated in newspapers and radio broadcasts:

a. The "language unification" of Taiwan has been too slow. Taiwan should learn from Italy, where language unification was accomplished in ten years.

b. It is progressive and patriotic to use Mandarin. Many Taiwanese feel ashamed and inferior for being unable to use Mandarin. They are very enthusiastic in participating in speech contests in Mandarin as a gesture for supporting the policy of promoting Mandarin.

c. The government has been considerate toward Taiwanese, often to the extent that it is too lenient toward the use of dialects. Taiwanese people have been very thankful for the government's moderate approach on the matter of language unification.

The only voice urging for the protection of the interests of Taiwanese speakers I have heard appeared in the *Central Daily News,* a Nationalist newspaper (January 19, 1973). It was a letter to the editor by J. Bruce Jacobs, an American graduate student doing research work in rural Taiwan. He points out that half of the population of Taiwan are farmers, most of whom do not understand Mandarin. Although one out of every three families has a television set, farmers cannot get enough information and entertainment through television after Taiwanese programs were drastically limited. Many farmers once suffered a great loss of crops, which could have been saved if news and weather forecasts were reported in Taiwanese *also*.[17]

The lack of open opposition to the government's policy for promoting Mandarin at the expense of Taiwanese and Hakka can be explained as follows:

a. There is a general lack of scientific knowledge about language and language change.

b. There is a general incompetence in identifying and working for local and national interests with respect to language planning. The political, economic, social, and cultural implications of language planning are only vaguely understood. Practical aspects of language education are not fully understood.

c. The traditional emphasis on the written language and classical Chinese tends to make people think that as long as their children have competence in writing, they have an equal opportunity in education.

d. The internal and external political situations have given rise to a phobia against any open disruption or disharmony between the Taiwanese and the Mainlanders. Language policy is one of the most touchy issues. People were afraid of raising this issue lest they be accused of causing group conflicts, a serious crime under the martial law, when it was in effect.

e. Mass communication media are almost exclusively in the hands of Mainlanders.

f. Censorship has been very strict.

A lack of reliable estimates of sociolinguistic changes in the past is another cause of failure in feedback. Reliance on impressions rather than on an objective investigation has characterized sources of information on sociolinguistic situations of the past and present.

Those in charge of language planning tend to exaggerate the success of the promotion of Mandarin in order to claim more credit for their own service, and to encourage people to use more Mandarin. Those in power are happy with exaggerated reports because they serve to confirm their own impressions. They tend to have contact with only Mandarin speakers. Monolinguals in Taiwanese or Hakka either live in different areas or keep quiet in the presence of Mandarin speakers. Their judgments tend to be misled by their own wishful thinking that soon Taiwan will be peopled by only Mandarin monolinguals. Businessmen are more realistic, since they support Taiwanese programs on television or radio rather than Mandarin ones for their commercial advertisements.

There are certain facts that the Nationalist government prefers not to reveal in public even though it does know that these have close relationships with language planning. Unequal job and education opportunities and conflicts between groups, for example, have never been admitted to be the results of language policy.

Evaluation

I shall discuss the Nationalist government's evaluation work of its own language planning mainly on the basis of its own criteria for evaluation, and the relative weight it puts on each criterion.

To my knowledge there is no set of criteria as to how nonsociolinguistic goals of language planning are being realized. This is unfortunate because language unity itself is merely a means to some goals. Regular evaluation on the achievement of such goals as national harmony, political unity through democracy, and social progress are needed for improving language planning and its implementation. Criteria such as the following might be considered for measuring the achievements of these goals.

a. The attitude toward the individuals, speech, and ways of life of different speech groups.
b. The frequency of contacts between individuals of different speech groups.
c. The range of subject matters in the verbal communication between generations of the same speech groups and different speech groups.
d. Equity in job and educational opportunities.
e. The proportion of individuals of different speech groups who have access to encoding and decoding in various modes of exchange of ideas, including mass communication.
f. The proportion of individuals of different speech groups who participate in various types of political and social activities.

The whole official concern of evaluation of the language planning and its practice in Taiwan has been skewed toward the spread of Mandarin. The number of people who can speak Mandarin, their proficiency and frequency in the use of Mandarin, maximum use of Mandarin, and minimum use of Taiwanese or Hakka are almost the sole criteria for evaluating the achievement of language planning. A situation with 100 percent Mandarin monolinguals and 0 percent Taiwanese or Hakka monolinguals would be most highly valued. One gets the impression that the spread of Mandarin has been taken as the eventual goal of language planning in itself.

No criterion was given for people to tell whether knowledge in Taiwanese or Hakka is a desirable thing to have or not.

If it is recognized that old Taiwanese or Hakka speakers cannot learn Mandarin easily while young Mainlanders can easily learn Taiwanese or Hakka, a bilingual ability by the latter should be highly valued to promote interspeech group harmony, integration, and cooperation.

The Nationalists' failure to evaluate the overall effect of language planning results from the fact that there is no government organization that has anything to do with language planning except the Action Committee on the Spread of Mandarin. Assigned with the task of spreading Mandarin, the committee has no concern or jurisdiction beyond their assigned task.

Conclusion

I have defended the earlier official Nationalist position of language unification through bilingualism rather than the present practice of working toward linguistic unity through monolingualism. I discussed possible language planning alternatives. The main source of problems in Taiwan's language planning has been the misconception that the promotion of Mandarin is the sole task of language planning. My suggestions for improvement for the future of language planning in Taiwan have been implicit in my discussion. The following points summarize my main suggestions.

1. In place of, or in addition to the present CPM, a commission on language planning should be established on both the central and the provincial level and should be charged with the task of comprehensive language planning in Taiwan.

2. The legal status of the Austronesian, Taiwanese, and Hakka languages should be clarified; the interests of their speakers should be protected by law for at least a clearly defined period.

3. Taiwan should carry out the 1953 UNESCO recommendation for the use of vernacular languages in education. To this end, instruction in Mandarin should be delayed until students in primary school have firmly acquired the skills to express themselves in their mother tongue. Instruction in Mandarin can be introduced pretty early, however. Instruction in Taiwanese and Hakka should be continued in some way so that students can use both their native tongue and Mandarin for the discussion of all subject matter.

4. The reality that a bilingual or trilingual is a more effective and desirable member of the community than a monolingual in Taiwanese, Hakka, or Mandarin should be officially recognized, and education should take up the responsibility of the production of competent bilinguals and translators from one language to another.

5. Basic scientific knowledge on the history and structure of Mandarin, Taiwanese, and Hakka should be made available to students so that all language teachers and high school and college students may have an unbiased view toward the various vernaculars, use their own mother tongue more effectively, and learn a second language more efficiently.

6. The plan of the central CPM to promote vernacular literature should be carried out. This includes (a) instruction on folk literature at school and through mass media to help the population appreciate and create folk literature with a proper attitude, (b) instruction on a phonetic writing system of Taiwanese or Hakka (in romanization or in Chinese phonetic symbols) as is being done for Mandarin, and (c) study of Chinese characters that have been newly created or that have special usage in Taiwanese or Hakka folk literature.

The principle of one and the same writing need not be destroyed except in literature intended for faithful representation of the spoken language[18]— which in fact is merely a new style of written Chinese already emerging in Taiwan. The present colloquial style of writing is closer to various Chinese dialects than to any classical style, especially in vocabulary. A decrease of instruction in classical Chinese for more instruction in Taiwanese and Hakka is justifiable because the language of the living is more important than the language of the dead, and it helps for better understanding of the latter. This innovation should make language education much more interesting and meaningful.

To sum up, I propose a comprehensive language planning that aims at integration and bilingualism in society and at school. It will bring some changes in the school system for which the population of Taiwan has sufficient financial, technological, and manpower resources. More than 85 percent of the present elementary school teachers are competent bilinguals, for example. Outside of schools it will significantly increase understanding and cooperation between different speech groups without much cost to the government. The present colloquial style of written language will not be affected except for an increase of literary works, which appeal more to the general population, and use of phonetic writing to represent Taiwanese and Hakka in the elementary schools.

Notes

1. Whether Taiwanese, Hakka, Cantonese, and Mandarin, etc., are different languages or different dialects of the same language is a problem. Western linguists have regarded them as different languages on the ground that they are not mutually intelligible. Some Chinese patriots view this to be an attempt by imperialists to divide China. I use the two terms "language" and "dialect" interchangeably. For language planning in general, see Fishman, Ferguson, and Das Grupta (1968), Rubin (1971).

2. For the general background of the language policy in China, see DeFrancis (1950).

3. I am referring to the British policy of allowing different schools for different vernaculars. Under the Japanese and Nationalists only the national language was used at all school levels. The main difference between the two is that the Japanese set up separate schools for Japanese children and Taiwanese children, whereas the Nationalists mix children of different language backgrounds in the same *classes*.

4. There are views that the Nationalists have the intention to divide various groups to prevent united opposition, that the Nationalists at this time want to alienate the population of Taiwan from China so as to cope with Peking's efforts to take over

Taiwan, and that Taiwan has been a separate political entity and its dwellers desire independence. Discussion of such political goals will go beyond the scope of this study. I do believe, however, that bilingualism should be the choice for any population that is similar to that of Taiwan under any government that is responsible to the people.

Whether the Taipei or Peking government or people active in the Taiwanese Independence Movement like it or not, bilingualism of the Taiwan variety of Mandarin, Hakka, and Min is a reality that serves as a feature of group identity in addition to other features of group identity: geographical, institutional, educational, etc.

5. The terms Taiwanese and South Min (or South Hokkien) are both problematic. In the South of the Min (or Hokkien) provinces, Hakka is also spoken, and the South Min dialects are also spoken in the province of Canton. I follow the general use of the term, namely, the Taiwanese people include Taiwanese and Hakka speakers who immigrated to Taiwan before World War II. When referring to language, the term includes only the Min variety of Chinese spoken in Taiwan.

6. Hsieh, pp. 205–28.

7. The headings throughout this discussion are adopted from Rubin (1971), who has attempted to identify a language planner's work and its evaluator's work.

8. Ministry of Education, (1948), pp. 1162–77.

9. Ibid., pp. 1162–63.

10. It also ruled that each mayor automatically be the director of the city's Institute for the Spread of Mandarin. Although the mayors are elected by the people, the mayors have no control over personnel action, policy making, or administration of the institute; they must follow the plan for promoting Mandarin prescribed by the provincial government. Each mayor's record in carrying out the orders of the provincial government is part of the provincial government's grading of his service.

Very frequently the mayor himself does not speak Mandarin at all or can speak it only very poorly.

Incidentally, election campaign speeches are almost invariably in the vernacular, as candidates try to woo votes from the 85 percent Taiwanese population.

11. Meetings of such councils are usually conducted in Taiwanese rather than Mandarin.

12. Ministry of Education (1948), p. 1178.

13. Ibid., pp. 1162–63.

14. Race riots that took place in Singapore were symptoms of racial conflicts. It was due to the multilingual and multiracial policy, not a policy to suppress human differences, that racial conflicts have been eased off.

15. Symptoms of cultural suicide, which can be caused by many other factors, include opportunism among talented individuals, neurotic condemnation or glorification of one's own culture, and extreme attitudes toward other cultures.

16. The principle of using vernacular language in education was stressed in UNESCO (1953) p. 11. The difficulties in carrying out the principle of teaching in the students' vernacular language are discussed by the same writer and by Le Page (1964) also. Few of the difficulties are applicable to Taiwan which has highly developed educational facilities and large, uniform speech communities that can financially afford bilingual education.

17. I have discussed elsewhere the relevance of degree of remoteness between the lexicons of related languages and the degree of difficulty for speakers of one language to learn that lexicon of another (1972, 1973).

18. A writing that represents Taiwanese or Hakka faithfully needs to be discussed separately. I am for a writing combining the use of Chinese characters and a phonetic script.

References

Cheng, Robert L. "Second-Language Learner's Classification of Chinese Dialects and Related Languages." *Gengo Kenkyu,* Tokyo Linguistic Society of Japan (1973).

————. "Memorizing the Pronunciation of Cognates in a Target Language." In *Papers in Linguistics in Honor of A.A. Hill,* ed. E.T.C. Tang, Jeffrey C.H. Tung, and A.Y.T. Wu (1972, pp. 33–62).

DeFrancis, John. *Nationalism and Language Reform in China.* Princeton, 1950.

Fishman, Joshua A., Charles A. Ferguson, and Jyotirndra Das Gupta, eds., *Language Problems of Developing Nations.* New York: John Wiley and Sons, 1968.

Hsieh, Chiao-min. *Taiwan-Ilha Formosa, A Geographic in Perspective.* Taipei, 1964.

LePage, R.B. *The National Language Question, Linguistic Problems of Newly Independent States.* London. 1964.

Ministry of Education, Republic of China. *Second Year Book of the Chinese Education.* Shanghai (1948).

Rubin, Joan. "Evaluation and Language Planning." In *Can Language Be Planned,* ed. J. Rubin and B.H. Jernudd, Honolulu, Hawaii (1971, pp. 217–52).

UNESCO. *The Use of Vernacular Languages in Education.* Monographs on Fundamental Education, 8. Paris: UNESCO, 1953.

Chapter 14

The Emergence of a Taiwanese Popular Culture

Joseph Bosco

The sense of Taiwanese identity has grown twice this century, both times, ironically, not because of isolation from mainland China but because of contact with it. First, after retrocession of Taiwan to China, early euphoria that Taiwan was returning to the motherland dissipated as Taiwan natives recognized the differences between themselves and those who, even before 1949, were already formally called *waishengren* or mainlanders. In one village in Pingdong County where I did field work, informants remember that there were puppet shows and festivities at retrocession, but that attitudes changed. As one informant from Kaohsiung put it, the defeated Japanese lined up and marched to ships that would take them back to Japan. Out of the ships of victorious China ambled mainlander soldiers in straw sandals, dressed in partial uniforms, carrying pots and food on their shoulders. The sense of difference from those encounters and from the rebellion and terror of 1947 lingers to this day. Many rural Taiwanese, when speaking Hokkien,[1] refer to mainlanders as *Tiong-kok-lâng* or "Chinese," implying that Taiwanese are not Chinese. I even recorded this usage from a sixty-two-year-old woman whose husband was a KMT village faction leader and whose son was a party cadre. From 1945 to the 1980s, the relevant division was between all native Taiwanese (a category that reduces the difference between speakers of Hokkien and Hakka) and all "mainlanders" (a category that lumps together persons from all the provinces in China despite the many differences of dialect, class, and custom among them).

The second period of contact began in the mid-1980s when surreptitious exchanges with the PRC began. In November 1987, the ban on travel to the mainland was lifted. By mid-1990, one in fifteen adults on Taiwan had traveled to China (*Far Eastern Economic Review*, October 18, 1990). Trips to the mainland became popular for business, tourism, and religious pilgrimage. But the "mainland fever" that broke out in Taiwan has had the ironic effect of turning all

---

This chapter originally appeared in *American Journal of Chinese Studies*, vol. 1, no. 1 (April 1992).

residents of Taiwan, both mainlanders and native Taiwanese, into "Taiwanese."

For mainlanders, trips home are often intensely disappointing. Economic backwardness and the discovery that the land of their memories is lost forever is often depressing, forcing the realization that, especially if they have married, Taiwan is now their home. They no longer see themselves as exiles on the periphery. Other mainlanders find their trips home satisfying: they can eat the food they grew up with, people speak their language, and relatives and old friends, though changed, provide a sense of connectedness that mainlanders lack in Taiwan. But even for these mainlanders, the benefits they and their relatives enjoy stem from their status in the PRC as *"Taiwan tongbao"* or "Taiwanese compatriots." They cannot relocate permanently to the PRC or they would lose their privileges there, which are based on being Taiwanese. The PRC's very use of the term *"tongbao,"* "compatriot" (literally "from the same womb"), indicates an attempt to hide differences. In Taiwan, the obvious differences between Han Chinese and Malayo-Polynesian aborigines are also obfuscated by referring to the aborigines as *"shandi tongbao,"* or "mountain people compatriots." Thus the PRC's official terminology of inclusion admits that Taiwanese are somehow different.

For native Taiwanese, trips to the mainland also strengthen their Taiwanese identity. They find the PRC sufficiently different from their society so that as one informant put it, "I felt like I was a tourist in a foreign land." They find the PRC dirty and unhygienic (ironically, the same charge that many mainlanders made against Taiwan in the early 1950s), and are shocked by the rude public behavior on buses and in shops and restaurants. One informant was on a train when a fellow passenger commented that it was good for him to visit Xi'an to "seek his roots" (*xungen*). My informant corrected him, saying that his ancestors may have been from China but that his roots were in Taiwan. The feeling of differentness may seem surprising in that Taiwan and PRC residents can converse in Mandarin, and Taiwanese are indeed credited with savvy and successful investment in Xiamen precisely because of common Hokkien language and culture. But it is only surprising if we assume that identity must be based on previous cultural differences; instead, culture and identity are created.

Residents of Taiwan often resent what they feel are the patronizing attitudes of PRC citizens. Taiwanese say they are often viewed as rich cousins who came upon their fortune fortuitously or illegitimately. On Taiwan, many argue whether the economic miracle is the result of hard work or government planning, but PRC residents often feel that the KMT's plundering of the central bank's gold reserves, and foreign aid and preferential treatment from the United States were the main factors in Taiwan's development. Taiwan residents come to feel that the PRC views Taiwan as a plum to be picked to benefit the PRC. At the same time, Taiwan residents feel more sophisticated and modern than PRC residents.

Being Taiwanese thus has two meanings. First, in contrast to mainlander, it means Hokkien (or Hakka) speakers whose ancestors came to Taiwan before 1895. Second, in contrast to the PRC, being Taiwanese means everyone on

Taiwan. This second meaning is growing in importance because of current political, strategic, and economic forces. The emerging new Taiwanese culture reflects this second meaning of Taiwanese, but is heavily influenced by native Taiwanese culture.

Until 1949, Taiwan was in the periphery. Then the central government moved to the island and Taiwan suddenly became a peripheral center, or a self-defined center temporarily in the periphery. The Nationalist government first defined itself as the bearer of cultural orthodoxy; Taiwan, as periphery, was heterodox (on center and periphery, see Tu 1991). This paper argues that the struggle between orthodoxy of the center and heterodoxy of the periphery has given way to the unorthodox cosmopolitanism of Taiwanese popular culture (see Lee 1991:224). At a time when many question whether one can be both modern and Chinese, and when scholars note a loss of center in Chinese culture (Tu 1991; Lee 1991:224–25), a new Taiwanese popular culture is emerging that destroys the distinction between orthodox and heterodox and between center and periphery.

Cultural Form of the Emerging Taiwanese Identity

Identity must take a cultural form; persons adopt behavior, symbols, and rituals that allow identity to be recognized. The emerging Taiwanese popular culture is noticeable in three areas: language, religion, and the arts and entertainment.

Language

Language is one of the most common markers of identity. Before about 1987, Hokkien was a primary marker of being native Taiwanese. Indeed, it is called "*Taiwanhua*" or "Taiwanese language" in Mandarin (*Tâioâne* in Hokkien). The prohibition against speaking Hokkien in school and strict time limits on Hokkien programming on radio and television reflect government attempts to promote Mandarin as a common island-wide language and to prevent language from becoming a focus for opposition.

Since about 1987, however, Taiwan has become increasingly bilingual. Of course, native Hokkien speakers have had to be bilingual all this century, first with Japanese and then with Mandarin. But the new Taiwanese culture requires competence in both Hokkien and Mandarin for everyone. Young mainlanders find they need Hokkien to work effectively. One young mainlander told me in 1986 that in his work for a U.S. bank, he would meet with clients who would switch into Hokkien and discuss strategy among themselves without even leaving the room since he could not understand them. He added that often the family patriarch only spoke Hokkien, so the meeting had to be translated. At that time, it was illegal for my informant to register for Hokkien language training, but since liberalization, mainlanders have been flocking to Hokkien classes (FEER August 30, 1990). Second generation mainlander politicians like Jaw Shau-kong (Zhao

Shaokang) publicize their ability to speak Hokkien, and it is even reported that General Chiang Wei-kuo began studying Hokkien in 1990 (ibid.). In fact, the attitude is that everyone on Taiwan should know some Hokkien; not knowing Hokkien is a disadvantage. A discussion on the radio in February 1990 caught my attention when during an interview, a guest chided the interviewer for having lived so long in Taiwan and still not being able to speak Hokkien. The interviewer playfully came back with a heavily accented "I can speak Taiwanese" (*goāe-hiáu kóng Tâoânōe*), indicating that she accepted the premise that Taiwan residents should know some Hokkien.

Taiwan's Mandarin is different from PRC Mandarin in lexicon and pronunciation.[2] Words common in the PRC like *shuiping* (level; instead of *shuizhun*) sound comical in Taiwan. Taiwan's *zhanshi* (temporarily) is pronounced *zanshi* according to PRC dictionaries. Tones are sometimes different: *yanjiū* (research) in the PRC is pronounced *yanjiù* in Taiwan.[3] Most noticeable, however, is Taiwan Mandarin's loss of palatalization in retroflex initials; *zhi* becomes *zi*, *chi* (eat) approaches *ci*, *shi* (is) merges with *si*, a pronunciation that had been typical of Chinese with a southern accent. This process began with Hokkien speakers trying to pronounce the Mandarin imposed on them after 1945 (DeFrancis 1984:59). Many of these differences merely reflect a southern accent and the inability of Hokkien speakers to reach standard Mandarin; they do not necessarily reflect the creation of a Taiwanese identity. But in the last five years the standard for Mandarin itself has shifted to accept this Taiwanese pronunciation. Media personalities speak with a noticeably stronger "Taiwanese" accent, and reporters whose pronunciation would at one time have been insufficiently "standard" (*bubiaozhun*, with Peking as the standard) are now heard on the air. As late as the mid-1980s it was still common to hear jokes about native Taiwanese mispronouncing Mandarin (*Guoyu* laughingly referred to as *Go-yi*). Now it is common to hear mainlanders sprinkling their Mandarin with phrases of Hokkien. And in Taiwan, there is less embarrassment about, if not an actual pride in, a southern accent. Mainlanders (and schoolchildren) who speak with perfect northern pronunciation (not to mention the *er-hua* of Peking) are ridiculed for putting on airs and acting superior. Standard spoken Mandarin in Taiwan now incorporates a Hokkien accent.

Language use often reflects patterns of social dominance. Sociolinguists often find that a subordinate group learns the language of the dominant group but that the dominant group does not deign to learn the language of the subordinate group. In Taiwan's Pingdong County, the mainlanders generally do not learn Hokkien or Hakka, native Hokkien speakers learn Mandarin, but not Hakka, and Hakka businesspersons often learn both Hokkien and Mandarin. Mainlanders consider local languages subordinate, and native Hokkien speakers consider Hakka subordinate.

Given this pattern of language dominance, the recent shift to bilingualism in Taiwan shows the emergence of the new Taiwan culture. Announcements in

Hokkien are now a feature of Taiwan's trains and Taiwan's flagship air carrier, China Airlines. News broadcasts and talk shows include Hokkien phrases and sayings and interviews with persons on the street speaking in Hokkien. The television subtitles, once presumably aimed at Hokkien speakers who did not understand Mandarin, now also serve for Mandarin speakers who do not understand Hokkien. Although the increase in bilingualism has been most dramatic since about 1987, the process began earlier. As early as 1980, the *chuxi* (the eve of lunar new year) presidential address was broadcast live in Mandarin and then rebroadcast with a voice-over in Hokkien and Hakka.

Religion

Taiwanese identity first formed around religion when the Japanese, late in their colonial rule, began to try to assimilate the Taiwanese by, among other things, promoting Shinto religion and suppressing Taiwan's popular religion.[4] In Pingdong, the Japanese banned religious festivals and prevented residents from repairing local temples, many of which collapsed. After the war, "there was a strong revival of popular religious practices" that, "together with many other traditional elements, were increasingly redefined as identifiers of 'being Taiwanese' in the context of the growing hostility between the local population and the mainlander-dominant Nationalist government" (Cohen 1991:131–32). The KMT, following the anti-traditionalism of post–May 4th intellectuals, has long been an opponent of popular folk religion, viewing popular religion as superstition and a waste of money that could be invested to build the nation. This stance led the party to promote campaigns to limit the size and expense of festivities (see, e.g., Jacobs 1980:31–39).

As a result of KMT opposition to popular religion, popular religion's *baibais* (festivals) and their feasting and display of the pig became symbols of Taiwanese-ness. In Pingdong, the mainlanders I knew refused to eat at popular festivals: one considered the display of the pig carcass and uncovered food unhygienic, and others either had no relatives who would invite them or were Christian and refused to participate. To the Hokkien, however, religious festivals were celebrations of family and community (which excluded mainlanders). Mazu in particular, whose temples at Beigang, Dajia, and Lugang attract tens of thousands of pilgrims, became the patron deity of Taiwan. With traditional popular religion redefined as being Taiwanese, the KMT was unable to pursue its attacks against tradition and superstition in the name of progress with the same vigor as it had in the mainland.

The KMT's own local politicians are among those who undermined the mainlander anti-traditionalist policies. Politicians are expected to curb their religious expenditures; offerings to the gods are limited to fruits and incense, and their weddings and religious banquets are not to exceed three tables of guests. These rules are not always enforced, however, as expensive feasts make valuable ritual displays of generosity and power. Indeed, most successful politicians use religious organizations and ceremonies to build electoral support for their campaigns. In Pingdong, nearly all Hakka politicians for county-wide office begin their campaign by offering incense at the Zhongyici, the Six Camps (*liudui*) temple that during the Qing period was the ceremonial political–religious center of southern Taiwan's Hakka. In Wandan Township, the 1986 and 1990 township executive campaigns began with a rally at the candidate's campaign headquarters and a procession to the Mazu, Jade Emperor, and other local temples throughout the town. At each temple, the candidates offered incense to the gods. In addition to the candidates' use of religious rituals, the temple organization and body of followers can be used as support for politicians or political factions (see Seaman 1978). Thus, despite KMT official hostility toward popular religion, its local politicians have used religion to build up their support.

Whereas the post-war Japanese government has promoted Japanese village festivals as tourist attractions that celebrate Japanese tradition, the KMT government attitude toward festivals in Taiwan has been one of embarrassment at the traditionalism and superstition of the natives. In the 1980s, however, the KMT in many ways shifted to accommodate popular religion, muting the May 4th anti-traditionalism of mainland intellectuals. Recent government publications have shifted to a more sympathetic tone, listing religious festivals in tourist magazines, and lauding temple art and some aspects of popular religion in glossy magazines. The government's embrace of popular religion is in part an attempt to claim it as Chinese and deny its Taiwanese-ness, but by validating it and including it among government-approved cultural elements, the government is also reducing the opposition between Chinese-ness and Taiwanese-ness. Myron Cohen (1991:132) has noted that this transformation "was dramatized in 1980 when President Chiang Ching-kuo . . . presented an image of Mazu to her major temple on the island" in Beigang. This came just eight years after he promulgated his Ten Rules of Reform, which sought to fight "waste" and "superstition." It seems likely that in the more competitive electoral environment of the 1990s, the KMT will completely abandon its historical hostility to popular religion as its candidates use religion to mobilize voters.

Arts and Entertainment

Movies, music, and clothing styles from Taiwan have helped to define modernity for the PRC, in the process changing the island's image in the mainland (*New York Times* May 4, 1989:1). "Tapes of Taiwan singers like Su Rui, Wan Shalang and Pan Anbang are extremely popular on the mainland, and so are books by Taiwan authors" including Bo Yang (ibid.). Music, movies, and clothing styles from the island are cosmopolitan and tied to international trends and fashions. Discos and beauty pageants, though only legal in Taiwan since the late 1980s, are signs of Taiwan's participation in a modern, cosmopolitan, popular culture.

Although Taiwan does not influence U.S. fashion like Japan does, Taiwan has great influence in China and Southeast Asia, contributing to the setting of a sort of "four dragons" style. From a peripheral backwater, Taiwan has become the trendsetter for the PRC.

Thus, an element of the emerging sense of Taiwanese identity is the feeling among Taiwan residents that their movies, songs, clothing, and other elements of popular culture are far superior to the backward cultural products of the PRC. Taiwan residents pride themselves on the popularity of Taiwanese popular music in the PRC, and feel their clothing styles are more sophisticated. They ridicule the platform heels and knee-high nylon stockings of mainland residents, as well as other PRC styles that mark the country as not fully cosmopolitan in fashion.

Government policies in the past sought to prevent any sense of even regional identity for Taiwan. As recently as the summer of 1989, a debate raged on a bitnet electronic mail bulletin board in the United States (mostly among immigrants and students from Taiwan) over whether there is such a thing as a Taiwanese cuisine, or whether it is merely Chinese food cooked by chefs from Taiwan. Within Taiwan, however, interest in local history is booming (see cover story, *China Times Weekly*, March 16, 1991). Some of the books were written out of sympathy for the independence movement, but public interest and the market are much wider, ranging from Yuanliu Publishers's children's series on Taiwan history and traditional culture to the founding of the Taiwan History Field Research Office at Academia Sinica. Since Hou Hsiao-hsien's (Hou Xiaoxian) movie *A City of Sadness* broke the taboo on discussion of the February 28 Incident (1947), many books and articles have appeared and KMT leaders have memorialized the victims, in the process defusing much of the tension surrounding the various interpretations of the event.

Whereas earlier Chinese nationalism (both KMT and CCP versions) included an iconoclastic anti-traditionalism (Cohen 1991), Taiwan residents now seek traditional roots in Taiwan. The government began in the 1980s to take an interest in historic preservation. The homes and temples preserved are at the same time examples of pan-Chinese high culture and creations of Taiwanese leaders in a Taiwanese style. The ambiguity allows everyone to agree that significant architectural monuments must be preserved. The market for Taiwan's antiques has grown phenomenally since the 1980s. Wooden puppets that appealed only to foreigners a decade ago (most residents in Taiwan considered them "used," "dirty," and "old" because they were wooden and not plastic, which was "modern" and "new") are now expensive and accepted as antiques. Artists painting Taiwanese themes and vistas a decade ago were mostly ignored, but they prospered even more than other artists in the art boom of the late 1980s.

Many books and movies in Taiwan explore specifically Taiwanese themes, including the experiences of mainlanders in Taiwan (e.g., *Jin dabande zuihou yiye* [Hostess Jin's Last Night], *Laomo de dierge chuntian* [Old Soldier Mo's Late Marriage]), and the nostalgia of Taiwanese who have left parents, the *renqingwei* (human feelings) of relatives and friends, and the beautiful and serene countryside for the prestige, money, and temptations of urban life. When the *xiangtu wenxue* (native or local literature) of authors like Huang Chunming, whose *Sayonara zaijian* describes lives of ordinary and poor Taiwanese, was published in the mid- to late-1970s, it was attacked by mainlanders such as Yu Guangzhong and Peng Ge for promoting communist "worker–peasant–soldier art" (Li and Xue 1991:329). This hypersensitivity to social realism and localist topics has been transcended, and the *xiangtu wenxue* is now credited with promoting the preservation of folk culture. Taiwanese glorify rural life and folk culture much like German romanticists because many Taiwanese grew up in the countryside and see rural society and values as the source of Taiwan's tradition.[5]

The fate of Taiwanese opera (*gezaixi*) and puppet shows (*budaixi*) perhaps best illustrates the emergence of a Taiwanese popular culture. For decades, the only government-supported opera group was a Peking opera school, not the Hokkien-language opera most native Taiwanese watched at temple festivals and later on television. Peking opera was presented as the orthodox high culture; *gezaixi* was officially merely an inferior local variant of Peking opera, part of "folk culture." Peking opera was promoted as part of the government policy of presenting itself as the true heir and preserver of traditional Chinese culture. The Peking opera school was named Fuxing juxiao (*fuxing* meaning "revive, rejuvenate" and referring to the slogan *fuxing zhonghua wenhua*, "revive Chinese culture"); it received government subsidies and was the opera performed in a theater to which foreigners were brought to see Chinese culture. Taiwanese opera is, however, tremendously popular. Performances at village festivals are still crowded (even though they compete with television for younger spectators), and most rural families watch the Taiwanese opera that is part of the 6:00 to 7:30 P.M. Hokkien programming.

Government hostility toward Taiwanese local culture has dissipated, however. The *Free China Review*—published by the Government Information Office—focused squarely on the mainland until the 1980s, but it now offers glossy reports on Taiwan's cultural and economic trends. In 1969, the magazine featured articles on Dunhuang, Chinese religions, and Nanking in 1937. As recently as 1979 the magazine focused primarily on anti-communist news and propaganda (including its monthly column, Mainland Periscope) and economic development projects (the completion of the North–South Highway, the new airport, and the modernization of Kaohsiung and Taipei), though it did have one photo story on woodcarvers of Sanyi. But in 1990, the *Free China Review* focused exclusively on Taiwan affairs. It featured special issues on folk arts (April 1990) and on cultural preservation (November 1990) that stressed the value of Taiwan's traditional arts as examples of Chinese tradition.

In 1989, the Ministry of Education named seven leading masters, including *budaixi* puppeteer Li Tianlu, as "living national treasures," albeit under the guise of "folk culture." The Art Heritage Awards, established in 1985 to increase the prestige of traditional folk arts, have been shown live on television since 1990. And the Ming Hua Yuan *gezaixi* Taiwanese opera has become recognized as an artistic troupe. This opera company was even invited to Beijing by the PRC to accompany the "Chinese-Taipei" athletic team to the Asian Games as representatives of Taiwanese art.

Conclusion

It is popularly assumed that nations exist first and that out of a nationalist struggle the nation wins a state. Nationalists argue that their nation has always existed, and that "the political and national unit should be congruent" (Gellner 1983:1). Recent scholarship on nationalism, however, argues that struggle comes first and that out of the struggle a nation may be created (Waldron 1985:433; Gellner 1983:48–49; Hobsbawm 1990:10). This chapter has taken the perspective that identity and culture are created, not fixed, and applied it to the Taiwan case.[6]

Ernest Gellner (1983) argues that the industrial state requires interchangeable workers and thus seeks to homogenize the population.[7] When the KMT arrived in Taiwan in 1945, it found a population that had not gone through the nationalist experiences of the 1911 Revolution, the May 4th Movement, and the Anti-Japanese War. KMT policies sought to homogenize this population and make it nationalistic. Even disregarding charges of looting and other abuses by the 1945–47 Chen Yi regime, native Taiwanese and mainland Chinese were on a cultural collision course. KMT military and police power assured that the homogenization would take place on the mainlanders' terms.

Scholars of nationalism also note that identity is rooted in politics (Waldron 1985:433). Certainly the debate surrounding unification and independence is intimately connected with political control within Taiwan. But the Taiwanese popular culture discussed in this chapter unites what appear to be irreconcilable nationalisms. The election process with which the KMT institutionalized its rule has led since the late 1980s to greater pluralism and the emergence of localist, Taiwan-centered interests. The forced retirement of mainland representatives completes the Taiwanization process. The KMT will soon no longer be able to rely on mainlander-dominated national bodies for control. Democratization of Taiwan politics is easing the resentment against mainlanders and the KMT; it will no longer be necessary to argue that independence is necessary to remove the dominant mainlanders and achieve democracy. At the same time, however, democratization is localizing politics: KMT candidates now pledge to protect the interests of all Taiwan residents rather than focusing primarily on the mainland. Now, especially after the June 4 incident, even the KMT argues that Taiwan is different economically, socially, and politically from the PRC and cannot be reunited with the mainland in the near future. Uncertainty and instability in the PRC and over forty years of anti-communist propaganda leave few Taiwan residents eager for immediate reunification. A poll of delegates to the KMT National Congress found that 84.8 percent wanted to preserve the status quo and only 14.04 percent thought Taiwan and China should reunite now (*Hong Kong Standard* June 11, 1991). The new sense of Taiwanese identity is emerging not from Qing-period nationalist longings, as argued by Taiwan independence activists, but from the current relations between the island and the mainland. As a result, this new sense of Taiwanese identity finds mainlanders and native Taiwanese both becoming "Taiwanese" in contrast to the PRC.

This political force forging a Taiwanese identity is clearest in the drive to reapply for membership in the United Nations. Many Taiwan residents are galled by the lack of U.N. representation for the island's 20 million people; the reapplication bid was supported not only by independence activists but also by many second generation mainlanders (*South China Morning Post* June 15, 1991) and liberal KMT politicians.

This chapter has not discussed the continuing independence/unification debate so as to focus on a common Taiwanese identity at a higher level. The Taiwanese identity I have described does not imply Taiwan independence. Taiwan nationalists use cultural evidence to bolster claims of nationhood, but this "tendency to fetishize cultural 'authenticity' is a peculiarly modern phenomenon" (Evans in FEER July 18, 1991:53). Just as Hong Kong will continue to have a Hong Kong identity after it is politically reunited with the PRC in 1997, Taiwan's growing sense of identity does not imply independence. KMT nationalism grew out of China's struggle against Western and Japanese imperialism. Native Taiwanese nationalism first developed in the conflicts with Japanese colonial rulers and later with mainlander domination. The new Taiwanese identity, however, rises out of the interaction with—and the threat of forcible incorporation into—the PRC.

Chiang Ching-kuo has dramatized many of the shifts that have brought on this newly emerging Taiwanese identity (for example, his presidential addresses with simultaneous Hokkien and his offering of an image of Mazu to the Beigang temple). This shift was most dramatic in his announcement on July 27, 1987, when, because he had lived in Taiwan nearly forty years, he said, "I am Taiwanese." This statement offended some conservative mainlanders but endeared him to most of the population. Like the political reform process that his seal of approval made possible, this statement legitimized the emergence of the new Taiwanese identity. Chiang Ching-kuo's statement also marked the end of KMT hostility toward tradition. Much of the questioning of Chinese tradition by intellectuals was the by-product of Chinese economic and political weakness. Taiwan's economic success is now leading its intellectuals to reclaim tradition. Whether Taiwanese or Chinese, tradition is no longer to be swept away to reach modernity, but is a source of strength and identity in an increasingly industrialized and individualistic world.

Notes

This paper benefited from many suggestions and ideas from Chen-chia Cheng and Mingtong Chen. It was presented November 9, 1991, at the Thirty-third Meeting of the American Association for Chinese Studies in Charlottesville, Virginia. Helpful comments were received from Richard Lufrano and June Teufel Dreyer. Remaining errors are my own.

1. Hokkien is also often referred to as Minnan, or Southern Fukienese.

2. Taiwan's Mandarin is also sociolinguistically different. The hyper-feminine and baby talk of *sajiao* is more common and pronounced in Taiwan, as is the use of the final particle -*a* which softens the intonation of the sentence. PRC speakers often sound more gruff and abrupt to Taiwan listeners than the speaker intended.

3. Differences of this kind are natural for any language; similar differences can be noted in the United States. For example, Easterners distinguish between "marry," "merry," and "Mary" while Midwesterners merge the three, and different parts of the country say "soda," "pop," and "softdrinks." In Mandarin, it is the standardization of official Mandarin in the 1950s as Putonghua in the PRC and Guoyu that has led to differences in the official pronounciation on the two sides of the straight (Li and Thompson 1981:2).

4. The core of my argument on religion follows Cohen 1991.

5. The parallel in the PRC is the *xungen* literary movement that began in the 1980s (see Lee 1991).

6. Nothing in this article should be construed to support the claims of either Taiwan independence or Chinese nationalism. The author agrees with Hobsbawm (1990:12) that "no serious historian of nations and nationalism can be a committed political nationalist. Nationalism requires too much belief in what is patently not so."

7. This process is perhaps best described in Eugene Weber's classic *Peasants into Frenchmen* (1976).

References

Cohen, Myron L. (1991). "Being Chinese: The Peripheralization of Traditional Identity." *Daedalus* 120 (2): 113–34.

DeFrancis, John. (1984). *The Chinese Language: Fact and Fantasy*. Honolulu: University of Hawaii Press.

Gellner, Ernest. (1983). *Nations and Nationalism*. Oxford: Oxford University Press.

Hobsbawm, E.J. (1990). *Nations and Nationalism Since 1780*. Cambridge: Cambridge University Press.

Jacobs, J. Bruce. (1980). *Local Politics in a Rural Chinese Cultural Setting: A Field Study of Mazu Township, Taiwan*. Canberra: Contemporary China Centre, Research School of Pacific Studies, Australian National University.

Lee, Leo Ou-fan. (1991). "On the Margins of the Chinese Discourse: Some Personal Thoughts on the Cultural Meaning of the Periphery." *Daedalus* 120 (2): 207–26.

Li, Charles N., and Sandra A. Thompson. (1981). *Mandarin Chinese: A Functional Reference Grammar*. Berkeley: University of California Press.

Li Yonshi and Xue Huayuan, eds. (1991). *Taiwan lishi nianbiao*, Volume 2. Taipei: Institute for National Policy Research.

Seaman, Gary. (1978). *Temple Organization in a Chinese Village*. Taipei: The Orient Cultural Service.

Tu Wei-ming. (1991). "Cultural China: The Periphery as the Center." *Daedalus* 120 (2): 1–32.

Waldron, Arthur N. (1985). "Theories of Nationalism and Historical Explanation." *World Politics* 37 (3): 416–33.

Weber, Eugen. (1976). *Peasants into Frenchmen: The Modernization of Rural France, 1870–1914*. Stanford: Stanford University Press.

Chapter 15

From *Shanbao* to *Yuanzhumin:* Taiwan Aborigines in Transition

Shih-Chung Hsieh

In spite of the fact that there are four main social groups that more or less possess relationships of mutual antagonism in Taiwan—*Minnan*-Taiwanese, Hakka people, Mainlanders, and Austronesian-speaking aborigines, in some particular situations, the first three belong to the same ethnic group—they all recognize that they are Han people and their first ancestor was Huangdi. In essence, in their attitude toward aborigines, these three groups also form a single interest group in pursuing ethnic benefits (cf. Keyes 1981). In other words, from a broader viewpoint, there are just two ethnic groups in Taiwan—Han and aborigines.

Traditionally, both Japanese and Chinese scholars divide the Taiwanese aborigines into nine or ten groups.[1] Their whole population in 1985 numbered 317,936—1.64 percent of the total population of Taiwan (19,358,000) (Guo 1985, 3; Hsieh 1987a, 10). Originally, each of these nine or ten groups had its own distinct identity. After lengthy contact with immigrants (Han Chinese), the nature of ethnic identity among Taiwan aborigines has been changing.

In this chapter I use historical and anthropological approaches to discuss how the ethnic positions and ethnic identity of the aborigines changes against the background of ethnic contacts and situational adaptation. What was or is the nature of ethnic identity among aborigines, and how do they create ways for preserving their culture, ethnic group, and identity?

Taiwan Aborigines in a Passive Position, Before 1983

I have divided the history of ethnic contacts of Taiwan aborigines into four stages: (1) being the only master, (2) being one of the masters, (3) being conquered, and (4) ready-to-disappear (Hsieh 1987a, 14–25). The term "master" under my definition indicates that the group identifies itself positively, and that its sociocultural institutions are still effective. It does not refer to relationships between the majority and minority groups in the sense of population. In other words, the master may be a superior one (e.g., the aborigines before the coming of invaders) or an inferior one (e.g., the aborigines after immigration of a great number of Han Chinese in the eighteenth and nineteenth centuries). But if one takes the position of aborigines and observes that although objectively the Han Chinese had already become the superior group, some aboriginal groups, having almost no contacts with the outerworld, still interpreted the whole world in their own terms. Their ethnic position was not different from the time when alien powers had not yet arrived. They were still masters, so to speak.

In table 15.1, one can clearly see the changing positions of aborigines from the first stage to the third stage. As for the fourth stage, if the aborigines are ready to disappear, I would explain it by three approaches. The first is the policy of assimilation. In Taiwan, the policy of the government toward the mountain area is to "plainize the mountains"[2] or to "amalgamate mountain people and plains people" (i.e., Han people) (Institute of Ethnology 1983, 7; Provincial Government of Taiwan 1953). Although the government did not use the term "assimilation," it is in fact trying to assimilate aborigines. The second approach is a "mythical belief" among Chinese, especially intellectuals. That is, "whatever the people or culture is, whenever it encounters Chinese culture, it must be sinicized." Based on the "mythical belief," Han Chinese feel that it is a matter of course that non-Han people are sinicized, and that it is a glorious event for those being assimilated. Therefore, in the eyes of Han Taiwanese, the Taiwan aborigines are going to be assimilated sooner or later because Chinese culture possesses a great charming power, and the aborigines must be naturalized.[3]

Government policy and the "mythical belief" of the Han people combine with the third element—the problems of adaptation, ethnic antagonism, discrimination, and ethnic identity, including new tensions over government plans to open the mountain reservations. These policies cause the aborigines (including aboriginal urbanites and people in mountain areas) to encounter serious hardships in their living,[4] and some people pessimistically predict the worst future for the aborigines. Some aboriginal intellectuals have hearts loaded with worry about the possibility that the aborigines will be destroyed.

Stigmatized Identity

Originally, the term "stigma" referred to "bodily signs designed to expose something unusual and bad about the moral status of the signifier" (Goffman 1963, 1). Goffman has divided stigma into three aspects, one of which is the "tribal stigma." Harald Eidheim (1969) adopted the concept of stigma to study ethnic relationship between Lapps and Norwegians. But neither precisely defined ethnic stigma (or tribal stigma, in Goffman's term). I suggest the following definition:

Table 15.1

Historical Change of Aboriginal Status in Taiwan

Position of Aborigines	Period	Alien Powers	Key Phenomena
Only master	ca. 1620 B.C.	None	There were just Austronesian groups living in Taiwan.
Mostly masters	1624 —→ 1661	Holland and Spain	Parts of plains aborigines under rule of Spain (northern Taiwan) and Holland (southwestern Taiwan) lost their dominant position. But most aborigines were still not affected.
Half masters	1661 —→ 1875	Zhen Chenggong and Qing Empire	Aborigines who lived in plains and mounds and some aborigines in mountain areas lost their superior position. Most aborigines who lived in high mountain areas still kept position of master.
Masters in fewer areas	1875 —→ 1930	Qing Empire and Japan	In 1875 the Qing government began to develop power to mountain areas. In 1885 Taiwan became province of China. In 1895 Japanese occupied Taiwan. During the period, aborigines always fought against alien powers. In 1930 after the Wushe rebellion was quelled, the aborigines were completely conquered.
Lost position of master completely	1930 —→ present	Japan and China	The bloody ending of the Wushe rebellion stood for complete victory of alien powers. China regained Taiwan in 1945. The KMT government escaped to Taiwan in 1949, and many Han people followed. Meanwhile, almost all plains aborigines had been assimilated.

An ethnic group, especially a minority, has a real, fictive, or imagined "feature" that not only makes people who contact this group keep them at arm's length, but is disgusting to the group itself. This feature usually is exactly the group itself. In addition, this feature also always had intimate relations with poverty, dependence, rejection, and inferiority. In the expressed attitude or behavior, members of this group may defend themselves because of their uncertainty or insecurity. Furthermore, they may "cringe," "make a deceptive show of power," evince "strong self-slight," and show "exaggerated self-esteem" in their social lives.

In the case of Taiwan aborigines, besides several studies that indicate that they possess a serious feeling of stigma toward their ethnic background, my investigation and analysis also reveal deeper phenomena.

I interviewed fifty-nine aboriginal students in Yushan Seminary. Most of them feel that they are treated in negative ways by Han people. They told me that Han people always think "We are stupid," "We are savage people," "Our brain is very simple, and the four limbs are strong," "We are barbarians," "We do not have knowledge, intelligence," or "We are just like animals."

Although the aboriginal informants felt that these features are simply the opinions of Han people, many cases reported in other studies indicate that aborigines do not hold their ethnic background in esteem and possess serious feelings of self-slighting. One may thus assume that those negative features are also recognized by the aborigines themselves.

In addition, in the public sphere, aborigines try to show off their "Hanness"; they try not to let people recognize their ethnic background. But in their own ethnic community, they often express indignant emotions about Han people. For instance, some told me, "We are not afraid of Han people, because this is our land," "What is there to be afraid of, our population is bigger," or "O.K., let's compete fiercely, I am not scared." These reactions reflect the complicated psychology of the people who feel unafraid of Han people. On the one hand, they try to protect their self-esteem; on the other hand, they cannot conceal their feelings of shame. What they respond with is a kind of "exaggerated self-esteem."

Figure 15.1 illustrates the process of formation of the stigmatized identity among Taiwan aborigines.

I divide the factors that help form stigmatized identity into two spheres: external and internal (Hsieh 1987a). The external factors include (1) the traditional Chinese world view of *Hua-Yi* (or Han versus non-Han barbarians), (2) the worst symbol of stigma—Wu Feng, a mythical man who sacrificed himself to stop the "bad" aboriginal head-hunting custom, and (3) stereotyping, prejudice, and discrimination by Han people (i.e., the aborigines are stupid, strong, brainless, ugly, dirty, lazy, and drunken). Internal factors include (1) shared historical experiences (all are called "Mountain People" and conquered), (2) loss of function of the sociocultural tradition (i.e., traditional norms are becoming inferior), and (3) the situational reactions of aborigines (feel small while in contact).

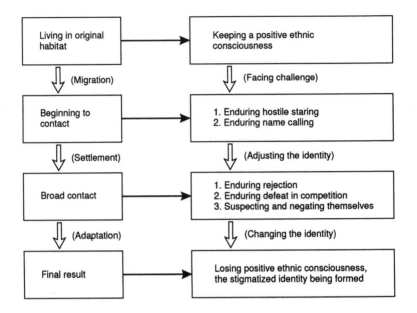

Figure 15.1

Under these circumstances, a number of aboriginal college students began to worry about the future of their people. The young aboriginal intellectuals of different groups therefore united to search for a new identity to enhance their power to save "the original master of this island" (Hsieh 1987a, 59–100).

New Voices from the Aborigines, 1983–1987

The so-called pan-movement is "dedicated to the unification of a geographic area, linguistic group, nation, race, or religion" (Kazemzadeh 1968, 365). At present some Taiwan aborigines are actively forming a sociopolitical movement that possesses the nature of a pan-movement (because there are ten Taiwan aboriginal groups participating) but is also a mininationalism (in Shaukat Ali's term [1976]). I call it pan-Taiwan aboriginalism or a pan-ethnic identity movement among Taiwan aborigines.

There were at least three groups participating in the movement at the end of 1984: *Mountain Blue* magazine (published in 1983 by aboriginal students at National Taiwan University), the Committee of Minority of the Conference of Editing among Non-KMT Writers (founded in 1984), and the Alliance of Taiwan Aborigines (also founded in 1984). Figure 15.2 shows the process of development of these units.

Since 1985 the Alliance of Taiwan Aborigines (ATA) has been the most important organization in initiating the ethnic-political movement. I will describe its formation and main ideology and claims below.

409

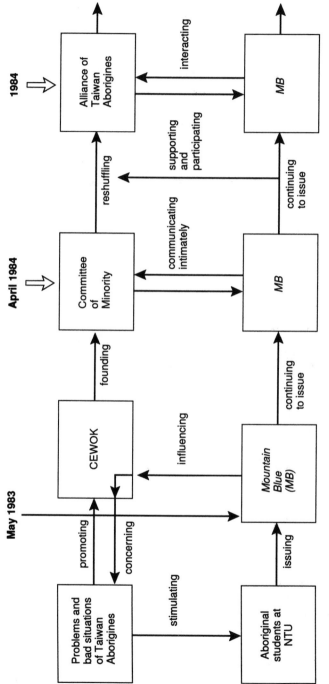

Figure 15.2

Table 15.2

ATA Members and Their Backgrounds

December 29, 1984	August 1985		October 1987	
Total = 24	Total = 53		Total = 94	
No data	Han:	14 (26.4%)	Han:	22 (23.4%)
	Aborigines:	39 (73.6%)	Aborigines:	72 (76.6%)
	College and up: 23 (43.3%)		College and up: 27 (34.1%)	
	Seminary:	17 (32.1%)	Seminary:	25 (31.6%)

On December 29, 1984, twenty-four young people formed the Alliance of Taiwan Aborigines in Taipei. It was the first nontraditional social organization of aborigines. There have been three kinds of activities undertaken by the ATA: formulating theories, positive action, and establishing principles (Hsieh 1987b). In the first period, the movement members theorized that the ATA had to be organized. They wanted the organization to be accepted. Therefore, they tried to describe the tragic condition of the aboriginal community. In the active period of the movement, from the first general assembly on March 15, 1987, the ATA members began to go into the streets to disseminate their ideas, to oppose the minority policy of assimilation, and to complain against the invasion of Han people since ancient times.

In other words, instead of taking just a passive role, the ATA played an active role. This lasted until October 26, 1987, when the ATA convened its second general assembly and proposed a "Manifesto of the Taiwan Aborigines" (ATA 1987c). This was the beginning of the period of establishing principles (table 15.2).

The ATA's ideas about territory and territorial rights have changed or modified according to the different approaches being undertaken at various times.

The First Period (December 29, 1984 to March 15, 1987)

Because the ATA had just been founded, it paid attention to services for urban aborigines, making the unit stable, and receiving financial aid. The claim on territory was not evident. The five major articles[5] about this topic in the newsletters of the ATA by its members were concerned with accusing Han people of invading aboriginal lands, criticizing the activities of the Department of Forestry of the provincial government of Taiwan, and asking for land in the cities for urban aborigines.

Obviously, in this period, members of the movement knew that their inherited lands had been taken by the state or the Han people, but they responded simply by complaining rather than proposing a more integrated concept of the relationships between Han Chinese and aborigines on lands and territories.

The Second Period (March 15, 1987 to October 26, 1987)

After the new president of the ATA was been elected on March 15, 1987, he designed a series of activities that were very different from those of the previous period. On the questions of lands and territories, there were seven articles published in the newsletters of the ATA in just half a year.[6] The question of lands was emphasized much more than before, and although the nature of the movement members' ideology pertaining to lands was not really different from that in the first period, their method of disseminating their ideas changed to include talking on the streets or speaking through microphones in front of central administration halls.

On the one hand, this phenomenon illustrates that the ATA felt that the problem of lands was probably the most important element in the survival of the aborigines. On the other hand, they understood that the Taiwan aborigines were a people with no territory. No territory means no security, identity, or freedom (Bakker and Bakker-Rabdau 1973, 33–47). The ATA found that they had to go beyond complaining about the Han invasion and find a way to establish their territory for the future.

The Third Period (October 26, 1987 to Present)

Although the Taiwan government has set aside some mountain reservations for aborigines, those reserves belong to the state instead of to aboriginal tribes. The reservation for aborigines means that aborigines rent land from the government, which may levy and reclaim those lands for public use. The ATA interpreted that the reservation policy was a main element in the strategy of destroying aborigines through lack of territorial protection (Duo Ao 1985). It is no wonder that Bawan's article (1987) is entitled "Land Is Life, and the Reserve Is Exactly the Identity," and Ifan stated that "our ancestors' lands are synonymous with our lives" (1987).

On October 26, 1987, when the ATA held its second general assembly, it announced a "Manifesto of Taiwan Aborigines." Six of the seventeen articles relate to territory and lands:

1. The aborigines have rights of basic protection for their lives (including . . . rights of lands) (Article 2).
2. The traditional aboriginal areas should practice local autonomy (Article 3).

3. The state must recognize population, regions, and social organizations of aborigines (Article 7).
4. The aborigines have their ownership of lands and resources. All lands that were gotten by illegal means should be returned to the aborigines (Article 8).
5. The rights of lands include surface, subsoil, and marine rights (Article 9).
6. The aborigines have the right to take advantage of their resources for satisfying needs (Article 10).

The key essence of these claims is a request for territorial rights. "Territory," to the ATA, refers to political, economic, social, cultural, ethnic, and psychological dimensions. Their basic belief is the "truism of aborigines" (Hsieh 1987b). In other words, the consciousness on territorial rights is based on the ATA's interpretation of what rights the aborigines should naturally have.

The Alliance of Taiwan Aborigines (ATA) is the first social group whose members are mostly aborigines. It is also the first pan-ethnic organization that systematically develops an ethnic movement. Most of the members came from general intellectuals and graduates of Christian schools (especially the Yushan Seminary).

One of the most obvious marks of pan-ethnic identity in the systematic pan-aboriginalism initiated by the ATA is that all members have given up their Chinese names and taken advantage of Chinese characters to spell their original (aboriginal) names. Identifying with their original names directly stands for identification with aboriginal culture.

In addition, they use a new term, *Yuanzhumin* (aborigines), to replace the traditional *Gaoshanzu* (high mountain people) or *Shanbao* (mountain siblings). According to the ATA, the term *Yuanzhumin* is a "pure and clean" name, because it had never been used formally before. They oppose the use of *Gaoshanzu* because 45.4 percent of aborigines live in valleys or plains. Furthermore, the term *Shanbao* is just a demonstration of the fact that Han people regard minorities as secondary people. In sum, they are trying to ask all aboriginal people to identify with the aspect of "aborigines," to make people more confident of themselves.

Although members of the ATA, or resistant elites, indicate that they are optimistic about their movement, and most elementary intellectuals (i.e., educated at the high school level) express their support, the "political elite" and some "intellectual elite," or party elites, who support the traditional ideology of unification of China and the politically rational concept of the KMT, oppose the ATA movement. The ATA emphasizes identification as "aborigines" and tries to integrate all aboriginal groups of Taiwan, whereas the political elite emphasize identification with the "Chinese nation" or *Zhonghuaminzu* and endeavor to maintain the present conditions of cooperation with the government.

Development and Dilemma, 1984 to 1990

The indigenous resistance movement has gained efficiency and made achievements in the last six years. The number of new resistance organizations has grown to more than fifteen. The power of the resistance ideology seems to be much greater than before. In addition, the story of Wu Feng, which was regarded as the main reason for stigmatized identity among indigenous people, is being deleted from textbooks in primary schools. Wu Feng *hsiang* has been changed to Alishan *hsiang,* a name preferred by resistance groups. Moreover, the Interior Department of the provincial government of Taiwan has set up a Section on the Affairs of Indigenous People to replace the lower-level Mountainous Administrative Section, which had been the highest-ranked office to administer indigenous affairs.

However, such concessions by the government, the enlargement of the ATA organization, or an increase in support by voluntary societies are totally meaningless in terms of power relations. That is to say, the state's compromises on ATA's struggle have not affected its absolute control in indigenous communities. All reforms so far have merely been superficial. The heads of Alishan *hsiang* and the Section of Affairs of Indigenous People are still appointed or recommended by the KMT. Most of the members of the new resistance organizations are also members of the ATA, and some organizations contain only a few members. For example, most articles published in the *Aboriginal Post (Yuanbao)* and Hunter's Culture (*Lieren wenhua*) are written by four people: Luoladeng Wumasi, Kaliduai Kabi, Taibang Shashale, and Walishi Yougan. The number of indigenous supporters of the resistance movement has in fact not increased at all.

From 1984 to 1990, resistant elites participated twice in general elections for provincial counselor and legislator. Ale Lusuolaman, one of two indigenous candidates from the anti-KMT group, was proud of participating in a campaign that symbolized the end of the KMT's monopolization, in spite of the fact that both candidates lost (Ale 1986). A belief of that all indigenous peoples will be awakened through the work of resistant intellectuals has been cultivated into the minds of these young elites.

The election in 1989 was very significant to the young radicals, especially members of the ATA, because they universally felt that, based on their implementation of the indigenous movement, a great number of supporters would appear. The *Aboriginal Post* estimated that the ATA candidate in the plains indigenous region might win or at least come very close to winning the election. For the mountainous region, the *Post (Yuanbao* 1989a) said, "ATA's Chen Zhengshu . . . , under the assistance of the ATA, will get support from a new generation of indigens." Another candidate, Duo Ao, even publicly said that he would not be defeated, because he believed that the missionary organizations absolutely supported him (*Yuanbao* 1989b). In other words, this election was the apex of collective dreams among resistant intellectuals. However, the second crushing defeat was undeniable. All resistant elites were hurt, for they now proved to be a group of "elites without people."

The president of the *Aboriginal Post,* Kaliduoai Kabi, said, "The participants in the indigenous movement do not know where the people are" (*Yuanbao,* 1990a). His observation reflects not merely a general depression of resistant elites about the overall unsuccessfulness of ethnic movement, but points out the most critical element in formulating relationships between ATA leaders and indigenous communities—never touching people's hearts. The ATA and other resistance leaders seemed to live in an illusory world, constructing a blueprint of an indigenous feature. They have exhausted themselves in their effort to distribute their *Yuanzhumin* ideology and claimed lost or exploited rights in metropolitan areas, but no base has been established in their homeland. I thereby call them "elites without people." This phenomenon is also the most serious dilemma in the indigenous movement.

Although it is true that the establishment of the ATA and the initiation of an ethnic movement are unprecedented events in the history of Taiwan's indigenous people, I somewhat agree with Huang Ying-kuei's criticism that my discussion (Hsieh 1987a) about the founding of the ATA being a distinguishing symbol in ethnic change of indigenous people was exaggerated (Huang 1989: 236). After all, the "flourishing" development of the ATA in the past six years has only shown its characteristics of elites without people.

The crushing defeat in the 1989 election (some candidates gained even fewer votes than in 1985) caused the resistant intellectuals' strong feelings of crisis about the indigenous movement. Many leaders attempted to return to their home communities to serve local people in accordance with their recognition of the fact that two unconnected worlds existed—traditional indigenous areas and the metropolis (*Yuanbao* 1990a). Others called for retrospection about the entire ideology and strategy of the indigenous movement (Walisi 1990). Although these young leaders have expressed such a mood, I find no concrete projects on implementing the resistance ideology in local communities. A tendency exists, instead, of accommodation between long-lasting, mutually antagonistic parties: resistant elites and KMT-oriented elites.

Integration

There are at least three elements restricting the ATA's attempt to expand its influence to tribal locations. In the first place, the KMT and the state still firmly control ethnic administration in every indigenous community. Second, the indigenous peoples are sparsely and widely distributed in nearly all of Taiwan, and the limited number of ATA members is not able to reach everywhere. Third, the Taiwan indigens consist of many mutually unintelligible ethnic groups, and even though most younger people are able to use Mandarin to communicate, the concept of an ethnic-political movement is still very unfamiliar and not under-standable for those peoples with various cultural traditions or in different living spaces. Moreover, even if the ATA sends all of its 100 or so members to tradi-tional indigenous communities, the organization may not be able to put its proj-ects into practice because of the isolation of its widespread members.

Since new people's representatives have been elected, all publications issued by resistance organizations have paid much attention to their activities in the Legislative Yuan and in the provincial and local councils. Many resistance elites at this very moment feel that the KMT-oriented indigenous representatives are still speaking for the *Yuanzhumin*. They look forward to "good" and "just" expression from these representatives.

Radical sociopolitical change in recent years in Taiwan has made the resis-tance ideology much more positive. Indigenous representatives are not as quiet as before. They have begun to criticize some unreasonable policies of the gov-ernment, as well as the distorted history of and discrimination toward the indige-nous people. Opinions and questions mentioned by those representatives in some aspects are identical to the ATA's original appeal. Most instances are praised by resistance elites. Gao Tianlai, a newly elected legislator, for example, advocates abolishing the Council of Mongol and Tibetan Affairs and setting up a Depart-ment of Indigenous Affairs in the central government (*Yuanbao* 1990b). Hua Jiazhi, another legislator who had once been seriously attacked by resistance elites, is also proposing a draft plan of indigenous autonomy that has been supported by resistance groups for several years (Zhang 1990).

It is obvious that traditional features of KMT-oriented indigenous elites are changing. They seem to realize that resistant elites are a new power, and they take the ATA's contentions into careful account. Based on this recognition, these representatives and even some indigenous officials have sought the support of radical young elites. This is a tendency of integration between the two parties. Although there are some objective elements, such as radical social change in Taiwan, that facilitate the appearance of integration, I would suggest another interpretation, from the viewpoint of ethnicity or, more accurately, the operation of *Yuanzhumin*.

Conclusion

In this chapter, I have discussed how Taiwan aborigines, a completely passive people, have been manipulating their ethnic identity to originate a powerful ethnic-political movement within the past ten years. I have basically told a gen-eral story about ethnic relationships between the aborigines and Han Taiwanese, and among aboriginal groups with different ideologies.

Although we may not be able to comment optimistically that the ethnic move-ment among Taiwan aborigines is already successful, it actually has brought an originally weak and passive people to a much more positive position. Especially when the integrative phenomenon among aboriginal elites with different ideologies appears, people believe that the aborigines will have more and more influence in ethnic politics in Taiwan. Certainly the global phenomenon of ethnic revival since the 1990s will directly stimulate the aboriginal movement in the future in Taiwan. We have already begun to observe its interactive process, and the reaction of the Taiwan government and residents toward it.

Notes

1. They are Atayal, Saisiat, Tsou, Bunun, Paiwan, Rukai, Puyuma, Ami, and Yami (see Ruey 1972), as well as Thao (Chen 1968, 8–14). Most are scattered in the mountain areas or valleys of northern, central, eastern, and southern Taiwan.

2. Traditionally, Han Chinese have called Taiwan aborigines "Mountain People" or "Mountain Siblings." They feel that these aborigines should live in higher mountain areas. However, in reality, only 54.6 percent of the aborigines now live in mountain areas (Guo 1985, 4; Hsieh 1987a, 13). The Taiwan government basically does not recognize that Taiwan aborigines are an independent minority people. It feels that the aborigines are "mountain people" and Han Chinese are "plains people."

3. Because the previous regime in China (the Qing dynasty) was established by non-Han people (Manchus), both the Republic of China (ruled by the Kuomintang or Nationalist party) and the People's Republic of China (ruled by the Communist party) have deliberately formulated theories of the relationships among all peoples of China in order to maintain unification of the multi-ethnic state. Dr. Sun Yat-sen, the founder of China's Republic, defined five nations in China: Han, Manchu, Mongolian, Hui, and Tibetan. He said: "Chinese nationalism, we claim, is not a five nations' nationalism. We should . . . assimilate the five nations to be a Chinese nation or *Zhonghuaminzu*" (Sun 1921). Chiang Kai-shek expanded Sun's theory with some modifications. He said, "Our Republic of China is founded by the whole Chinese nation. The 'Chinese Nation' is an integral term which refers to the idea that the nation is composed of five lineages or *zongzu*—Han, Manchu, Mongolian, Hui, and Tibetan. The reason why I use the term 'lineage' instead of 'nation' is because all of us belong to the Chinese nation. It is just like several brothers in a family" (Chiang 1952). The proposal of Dr. Sun was to make China become a nation-state even though he realized that it would include some non-Han peoples. His main concept was the assumption that one nation, one state would be able to keep a state peaceful and united. As for Chiang, he even denied the independence of each "nation." According to him, all Chinese people came from the same origin. Therefore, there was just one nation in China; Han Chinese and non-Han Chinese were brothers. It is evident that Dr. Sun only suggested a course of development of Chinese ethnic-politics. However, Chiang, based on the philosophy of Han-ethnocentrism, believed that all of the Chinese people must identify themselves as descendants of Huangdi or the Yellow Emperor, a mythical figure who is traditionally interpreted by Han Chinese to be a common ancestor. As we know, in Republican China, the words of Dr. Sun and Chiang are regarded as "truth." Not only does the design of the constitution reflect the sayings of the two "saints" of the KMT, but all of the citizens are asked to obey and believe them. Under the circumstances, in the KMT's system of education, students are seriously taught to identify with the Chinese nation. In Taiwan, because of this phenomenon, even the aborigines who are Austronesian speakers feel that they belong to the Chinese nation rather than to the nondescendants of the Yellow Emperor. To summarize, in the mind of Han Chinese in the KMT's China (including the previous KMT on the mainland and the contemporary KMT in Taiwan), the Han Chinese is the big brother, and other non-Han peoples are younger brothers in the same family (Zhou 1984, 3). These younger brothers supposedly should be

glad to be assimilated by the big family—*Zhonghuaminzu*—because this family is an origin of "light," and all of the non-Han members living in "darkness" must be very eager to find the warm and light "big brother" (cf. Ruey 1977, 482–506; Hsieh 1987a, 24). Therefore, Chinese, without the experience of recognition of multi-ethnic context in a state, always accuse people who show any ethnic consciousness, other than that of the Chinese nation, of betraying ancestors or being traitors. The territory of China cannot be divided (see the Constitution of the Republic of China, Article 4).

4. Owing to the decline of the economic system in aboriginal regions in prolonged contact with the capitalist economy, the young aborigines could not make a living in their homeland. They could not help moving to urban areas to find jobs. However, because of the discrimination and prejudice of Han Chinese toward aborigines, and the difficulty of cultural adaptation among the aboriginal immigrants, the "mountain people" in the cities have been pushed to the lowest level of the social hierarchy. The only jobs they can find are low paid and low status: truck drivers, packing laborers, sailors on deep-sea fishing boats, or prostitutes (see Fu 1985, 70–71; Lin 1987, 26–27; Huang 1985, 91; Hsieh 1987a: 50).

5. The five articles are Duo Ao (1985), Lusuolaman (1985), Lawa (1985), and ATA (1987a; 1987b).

6. They are ATA (1987a; 1987b), Ifan (1987), Bawan (1987), Lin (1987), and Shashaler (1987).

References

Ale, Lusuolaman. 1986. "Tu Po Si Shi Lian Lai de Tong Er Jin Xuan: Yi Jou Ba Wu Nian Sheng Yi Yuan Xuan Ju de Hui Gu." *Yuanzhumin* 3, July 15.

Ali, Shaukat. 1976. *Pan-Movements in the Third World.* Lahore: Publishers United.

Alliance of Taiwan Aborigines (ATA). 1987a. "Shan Di Guan Zhi Qu Yu Yuan Zhu Min Zi Zhi Qu" ('The Enclaves of Mountains' and 'the Aboriginal Autonomy'). *Aborigines* 5, June 30.

———. 1987b. "Qiang Lie Kang Yi Guo Min Dang Zheng Fu Lan Wa Yuan Zhu Min Fen Gong Tong Sheng Ming" (A common announcement to resist the KMT government to dig the ancestor's bones out). *Aborigines* 4, May 20.

———. 1987c. "Tai Wan Yuan Zhu Min Zu Xuan Yan" (A manifesto of the Taiwan aborigines). Taipei: ATA.

Bakker, Cornelis B., and Marianne K. Bakker-Rabdau. 1973. *No Trespassing!* San Francisco: Chandler & Sharp Publishers.

Bawan, Yumin. 1987. "Tu Di Jiu Shi Sheng Min Bao Liu De Jiu Shi Ren Tong" (Land is exactly life, and the reserve is the identity). *Aborigines* 5, June 30.

Chen, Chi-lu. 1968. *Material Culture of the Formosan Aborigines.* Taipei: The Taiwan Museum.

Chiang, Kai-shek. 1952. "Zhong Hua Min Zu Zheng Ge Gong Tong Ze Ren" (The common responsibility of China nation). In *The Frontier's Policy of the Three Principles of the People,* ed. Zhou Kuntian. 1984: 24. Taipei: KMT.

Duo Ao. 1985. "Qing Kan Kan Wen Ming Guo Jia Ru He Dui Dai Yuan Zhu Min Zu" (Please take a look on the aboriginal policies of the civilized states). *Aborigines* 1, February 15.

Eidheim, Harald. 1969. "When Ethnic Identity Is a Social Stigma." In *Ethnic Groups and Boundaries,* ed. Fredrik Barth. Boston: Little, Brown.

Fu, Yang-chi. 1985. "Du Shi Shan Bao Yan Jiu De Hui Gu Yu Qian Zhan" (An overview of studies on aboriginal urbanites). *Word and Thought* 23, 2: 65–81.

Goffman, Erving. 1963. *Stigma: Notes on the Management of Spoiled Identity.* Englewood Cliffs, NJ: Prentice-Hall.

Guo, Xiu-yan. 1985. "Dang Qian Shan Di Xing Zheng Zhong Yao Cuo Shi Yu Zhan Wang" (Contemporary policy and development for administration of mountain areas). Document of Provincial Government of Taiwan (unpublished).

Hsieh, Shih-chung. 1987a. *Ren Tong De Wu Ming: Tai Wan Yuan Zhu Min De Zu Quin Bian Qian* (Stigmatized identity: A study on ethnic change of Taiwan aborigines). Taipei: Zi Li Wan Bao.

———. 1987b. "Yuan Zhu Min Yun Dong Sheng Cheng Yu Fa Zhan Li Lun De Jian Li: Yi Bei Mei Yu Tai Wan Wei Li De Cu Be Tan Tao" (Toward dynamic theories of initiation and development of aboriginal movement: The cases of North America and Taiwan). *Bulletin of the Institute of Ethnology, Academia Sinica* 64: 139–77.

Huang, Mei-ying. 1985. "Du Shi Shan Bao Yu Du Shi Ren Lei Xue" (Aboriginal urbanites and urban anthropology). *Word and Thought* 23, 2: 82–107.

Huang, Ying-kuei. 1989. "Jin Liu Nian Lai Tai Wan Di Qu Chu Ban Ren Lei Xue Lun Zhu Xuan Jie." *Newsletter for Research in Chinese Studies* 8, 4: 227–38.

Ifan, Yugan. 1987. "Li Shan Da Xian 1989" (The death of Mt. Li in 1989). *Aborigines* 5, June 30.

Institute of Ethnology. 1983. Shan Di Xing Zheng Zheng Ce Zhi Yan Jiu Yu Ping Gu Bao Gao Shu (A report on the study of the policy of the mountain's administration). Taipei: Academia Sinica.

Kazemzadeh, F. 1968. "Pan Movements." In *International Encyclopedia of Social Sciences*, ed. David Sills, vol. 11, pp. 365–70. Macmillan and The Free Press.

Keyes, Charles F. 1981. "The Dialectics of Ethnic Change." In *Ethnic Change*, ed. Charles F. Keynes. Seattle: University of Washington.

Lawa, Kafei. 1985. "Han Ren Qing Zhan Yuan Zhu Min Tu Di De Bai Zhong Shou Duian" (A hundred ways of the Han people to invade our lands). *Mountain's Mountain* 1, July 15.

Lin, Jin-pao. 1981. "Tai Wan Bei Bu Di Qu de Du Shi Shan Bao" (Aboriginal urbanites in northern Taiwan). *The China Overview* 12, 7: 24–28.

Lin, Mei-rong. 1987. "Jia Shan Di Kai Fa Zhi Min Wa Jue Zu Fen Yuan Zhu Min Bei Puo Zhou Shang Jie Tou" (Under the name of development to dig their ancestor's bones out, the aborigines walked down to the streets). *Aborigines* 4, May 20.

Lusuolaman, Aler. 1985. "Huan Wo Zu Fen Huan Wo Jia Yuan" (Return the ancestor's graves to me! Return the homeland to me!) *Mountain's Mountain* 1, July 15.

The Provincial Government of Taiwan. 1953. "Cu Jing Shan Di Xing Zheng Jian She Ji Hua Da Gang" (The outline for promoting the establishment of the mountain's administration). In *A Report on the Study of the Policy of the Mountain's Administration*. Taipei: Academia Sinica.

Ruey, Yih-fu. 1972 [1952]. "Tai Wan Tu Zhu Ge Zu Hua Yi Ming Ming Ni Yi" (A suggestion for the unification of the tribal names of the Taiwan aborigines). In *China: The Nation and Some Aspects of its Culture*, ed. Yih-fu Ruey. Taipei: Yiwen.

———. 1977. "Zhong Guo Min Zu Go Cheng de Chu Bu Yan Jiu" (A primary study of the formation of Chinese peoples). *An Essays Collection of Sociology*. Taipei: Hua Gang.

Shashaler. 1987. "Ji Jiang Xiao Shi De Mei Shan Cun" (The disappearing village Mai Shan). *Aborigines* 6, June 30.

Sun, Yat-sen. 1921. "Shan Min Zhu Yi Zhi Ju Ti Ban Fa" (The practice of the three principles of the people) (oral lecture). In *The Introduction to Frontier Policy*, ed. Zhou Kuntien. 1984: Taipei: KMT.

Weaver, Sally M. 1984. "Struggles of the Nation-State to Define Aboriginal Ethnicity: Canada and Australia." In *Minority and Mother Country Imagery*, ed. Gerald L. Gold. Newfoundland: Memorial University of Newfoundland.

Walisi, Yougan. 1990. "Zhai Li Shi Zhong Yan Mo?—Cong Xuan Ju Tan Yuan Zhu Min de Fang Xiang." *Yuanbao* 2, January.

Yuanbao (Aboriginal post). 1989a. "Yi Jou Ba Jou San Xiang Gong Zhi Ren Yuan Xuan Ju Yuan Zhu Min Xuan Qing Zhuan Ji." *Yuanbao* 1, November 18.

———. 1989b. "Tai Ya Zu Xuan Jiang Xiang Wai Shen Chu Jiao." *Yuanbao* 1, November 18.

———. 1990a. "Ba Kang Zhen Liu Gei Du Shi, Ba Jia Xiang Liu Gei Zi Ji." *Yuanbao* 2, January 1.

———. 1990b. "San Shi Si Wan Ren Dui Qi Bai Er Shi Ba Ren." *Yuanbao* 4, May 10.

Zhang, Renjie. 1990. "Yuan Zhu Min Li Wei Cai Zhong Han Huan Jia Zhi Qiang Lie Yao Qiu Yuan Zhu Min Zi Zhi." *Yuanbao* 5, July 10, 1990.

Zhou, Kuntian. 1984. *Shan Min Zhu Yi de Bian Jiang Zheng Ce* (The frontier's policy of the three principles of the people). Taipei: KMT.

Part VII

RELIGION IN TRANSITION

The socioeconomic transformation examined in this book has had its effects on Taiwan's religious life, as the two chapters in this section demonstrate. Each piece explores two religious bodies whose belief systems and organizational structures evolved in response to the attitudes and actions of a hostile government, one a syncretistic Folk–Buddhist-related sect and the other a radical Charismatic/Pentecostal church. Both also developed as a response to the island's changing social and cultural conditions and may be seen as indigenous Chinese responses to modernization and Westernization.

In his chapter "Yiguan Dao: 'Heterodoxy' and Popular Religion on Taiwan," Joseph Bosco explores a modern-day variant of a major Folk–Buddhist sect. His study is both a useful new look at the Yiguan Dao as it functions in one specific part of Taiwan, and a well-reasoned argument against the way scholars have made use of the orthodoxy/heterodoxy diad in their analysis of the Chinese religious tradition. What he shows us is that the Yiguan Dao can be seen as a sect that shares many beliefs and practices with mainstream folk religion.

Bosco begins by examining the structure of the Yiguan Dao and shows how its leaders have created a hierarchy and their own network of private temples. He also shows what role the masters—those individuals who have special religious power and have authority inherited from the pioneer who brought Yiguan Dao belief and practice from the Chinese mainland—play in administering and helping to expand the sect.

Next Bosco examines the belief system of the Yiguan Dao. He introduces the major gods of the canon and then provides an overview of certain basic ideas, most notably the concept of salvation developed by the group's theologians. Millenarianism is another important idea in the Yiguan Dao system and here again Bosco shows how this concept is linked to more mainstream ideas of the End of Days. This picture of ritual suggests the links that exist between this ostensibly heterodox sect and the rituals practiced in more orthodox and mainstream systems. Bosco does not argue exact replication, but he does make a case for congruence.*

Congruence is a term I have used in my attempt to understand the appeal of certain Christian groups in Taiwan. For a detailed introduction to the idea, see Murray A. Rubinstein, *The Protestant Community on Modern Taiwan: Mission, Seminary, and Church* (Armonk, NY: M.E. Sharpe, 1991), chapter four.

Murray A. Rubinstein's chapter explores the history, theology, and political activities of a unique Taiwanese church, the New Testament Church, which had its origins in Hong Kong and since its formation in the early 1960s has won converts in Southeast Asia, Taiwan, and the United States.

Rubinstein begins by focusing on the life and the thought of the founder of the church, Gong Duanyi. This mainland-born singer and actress was raised in a mainstream Anglican church but underwent a religious conversion during a period of physical and perhaps mental illness in the late 1950s. As a result of this conversion, she founded her own highly charismatic (i.e., Gift of the Holy Spirit–centered) church based on her highly eclectic reading of the Bible. The scene then shifts to Taiwan and to the planting of the church on the island in the 1960s. The rise of Elijah Hong, a new leader, is traced as is his fight for control of the church with Sister Gong's daughter. His theology and his conflicts with the KMT-dominated state—in the aftermath of his attempts to settle the church's holy mountain—are then traced.

Chapter 16

Yiguan Dao: "Heterodoxy" and Popular Religion in Taiwan

Joseph Bosco

Chinese religion has generally been divided into "orthodox popular religion" and "heterodox sects."[1] Popular religion has referred to the mixture of Buddhism, Taoism, spiritism, and ancestor worship that centers on family altars and village temples. Heterodox sects, on the other hand, have been groups of believers claiming to have found the way to individual salvation, implicitly rejecting the worldly hierarchy (emperor to local official) reflected in popular religion's pantheon (Jade Emperor to Earth God).

Heterodox sects, though usually meditative and quiescent, have been responsible for several of China's largest millenarian rebellions (see Naquin 1976; Overmyer 1976). A tradition commonly called "White Lotus" has persisted in a recognizable form since the sixteenth century (Naquin 1985:255), and even as early as "1305 most of the fundamental elements of later White Lotus belief and practice were already present" (Overmyer 1981:182). Despite ruthless state suppression, sectarian religious groups of the White Lotus tradition surfaced in nearly all parts of China over the past four centuries and still exist in Southeast Asia and Taiwan.

In part because of its association with rebellion, sectarian religion has been viewed as separate from popular religion. Traditional village-level popular religion has been seen as influenced by—and in turn influencing—the state religion (see Watson 1985; Taylor 1990; Smith 1990). In imperial times, this has been seen as maintaining ideological support for the emperor and the bureaucratic

This paper is based on field work in Taiwan carried out from June 1984 to August 1986 and supported by a Columbia University Traveling Fellowship, an American Council of Learned Societies Pre-doctoral Dissertation Research Fellowship, and a Fulbright–Hays Doctoral Dissertation Research Abroad Fellowship. Additional research in Taiwan in January–February 1990 was supported by the Taiwan Area Studies Program of the East Asian Institute, Columbia University, a program supported by a grant from the Institute of International Relations of National Chengchi University. An earlier version of this paper was presented November 17, 1988, at the American Anthropological Association meetings in Phoenix, Arizona.

elite. Even with the demise of the imperial system, popular religion has been seen as supporting the social hierarchy and state power. Sectarian religion has been viewed as a totally different tradition that offers a radical critique of society and a rejection of the worldly order.

This chapter focuses on a contemporary sect in Taiwan, the Yiguan Dao, to challenge this orthodox view. It examines several elements of Yiguan Dao belief and practice and shows how they are rooted in popular religion. By rooted I mean that the practices may be slightly different from practices in a village temple but that believers and nonbelievers make sense of these beliefs or practices in terms of popular religious "orthodoxy" and not as a separate tradition. Certainly no one considers these beliefs and practices bizarre.

The Yiguan Dao

While doing field work in Wandan Township in southern Taiwan, I was initiated and able to study a modern-day White Lotus–type sect known as Yiguan Dao. This sect was organized in China in the 1920s and spread widely throughout Japanese-occupied areas during World War II. After the war, missionaries brought Yiguan Dao to Taiwan. Today it has spread widely; press reports in 1984 suggested that as many as 20 percent of all Taiwan residents had had contact with the sect and been initiated, despite its illegal status. The religion was legalized in 1987 as part of Taiwan's democratization, and government figures show almost a million members in 1991 ([Government Information Office] 1991).

Roughly translated, *yiguan dao* means "unity way" or "the way of pervading unity." As the name implies, Yiguan Dao claims it unites "the world's five great religions": Buddhism, Taoism, Confucianism, Islam, and Christianity. Scriptures from all these religions are believed to be sacred texts, but the current followers of the five religions are believed to be misguided. Initiates are told they are fortunate for they have just received the *dao* or "way," which supersedes all previous religions. Religions merely urge humans to be good; the *dao*, on the other hand, allows believers to escape from the cycle of death and rebirth (reincarnation) and reach nirvana.

Yiguan Dao operates secretly, in keeping with White Lotus tradition. Its temples are in ordinary homes and members seek converts discreetly. Its ceremonies are only open to initiated members. Initiation involves receiving the secret three treasures: a mantra, a hand position, and the symbolic opening of a door in the body so the soul may depart from the proper exit and not from one of the body's other orifices.[2] After initiation, new members are taught the three treasures meaning, which is the core secret of the sect.

Popular Religion

Popular religion is a mixture of many elements. In Taiwan, Buddhist nuns typically recite sutras the evening before a burial to help the soul pass the rigors of Hell. The actual burial is often organized by a Taoist geomancer. A Taoist priest leads the rituals on the evening before a groom's wedding, but the matchmaker herself is usually in charge of the wedding-day rituals. Many temples have shamans or spirit mediums who hold seances to help residents consult the gods on important decisions or problems. Village temples hold a variety of gods from the folk pantheon; most people are not exactly sure who all the gods in their village temple are, and the statues and rituals frequently allow multiple interpretations (see Weller 1987). Taiwanese generally depend on specialists for most religious activities and know only the general scheme of the religious system.

Because of the variety of traditions and the lack of any central authority ruling on religious matters, local temples and their committees can innovate and reinterpret rituals and beliefs. As a result, a variety of beliefs and rituals coexist in one area. Ritual specialists of different traditions offer different perspectives and advice, and most residents simply follow the advice of whomever they hired for the moment (Weller 1987).

Out of this varied and constantly changing local popular religion come the seeds of sectarian beliefs. Yiguan Dao is representative of sectarian religion because it is the best organized sect on Taiwan (Jordan and Overmyer 1986) and because it preserves the practices and beliefs of White Lotus groups described by historians (see below). In many cases, Yiguan Dao rituals and beliefs that at first appear heterodox in fact have clear roots in popular religion. Rather than view the Yiguan Dao and its Chinese predecessors as heterodox sects, it is more useful to see them as simple transformations of Chinese popular religion. With those same processes used to create popular religion's local temple cults, believers have created alternative sectarian religions.

A great deal of attention has been paid to the origin and transmission of White Lotus documents and beliefs (see Naquin 1985; Overmyer 1976 and 1981; Berling 1980). As Esherick (1987:326) has argued, however, finding the origin of beliefs and practices does not explain their rise, persistence, and meaning to members. Space considerations do not allow a discussion of the reasons for the current popularity of the Yiguan Dao. This article shows that the basic elements of the Yiguan Dao exist in the beliefs and practices of temples and cults that are accepted as part of orthodox popular religion in Taiwan. This argument not only helps us to understand the Yiguan Dao today but shows that because the seeds of the sect were rooted in popular religion, they sprouted repeatedly throughout China despite severe state pressure.

Organization

The Yiguan Dao is organized as a secret sect, with temples located on the top floors of private homes. Believers are organized in temple cells of eight to ten core followers per temple. Religious activities include morning and evening prayer sessions but only the most devout attend them daily. Believers are expected to attend at least on the full and new moon. The ceremonies themselves involve group kowtowing to a long list of gods.

Temples are organized in districts under the loose leadership of a master. The master presides over initiation ceremonies and guides the activities of the district faithful. He is treated with great respect. He links the district with the island-wide hierarchy. At the top of the hierarchy is the man who brought Yiguan Dao to Taiwan from China in 1945. The people he and his followers have converted form what is known as a line (much like a lineage of teacher–pupil links). Each missionary who came from China has a line of followers behind him, forming in essence separate—though loosely federated—sects.

At first glance, Yiguan Dao temple organization seems very different from popular religion. On closer examination, however, Yiguan Dao can be placed within the range of temples that are found in popular religion on Taiwan.

Public and Private Temples

Natural villages[3] in southern Taiwan have a public temple where community festivals are held. Village temples are community centers; indeed, many of these temples have the village office in one of the temple wings. The temples typically are named after the primary god whose large statue sits behind the central altar; this is the god whose birth date the village celebrates. Other smaller gods sit on the altar or behind secondary altars on the sides. The public temple symbolizes the unity of the village and is the focus of village solidarity. Many villages have a smaller separate public temple for the Earth God (or tutelary deity) which also belongs to the village as a whole. All the gods are part of the Chinese pantheon which in imperial times both mirrored and was integrated with the state bureaucracy. The Earth God was the lowest local official in the religious hierarchy.

The public temple represents the village, and the temple's leadership often coincides with village leadership (see Seaman 1978). All villagers are expected to participate in public offerings to the gods in front of the temple and to make financial contributions to the renovation of the temple and to public festivals. The only villagers who do not contribute to the temple are the few Christians. One major complaint that many Wandan residents express against Christians is that they cut themselves off from the village.[4]

Village temples are socially and economically independent of one another. The only higher level of organization is the public temple in the market town whose procession includes all the district's temples. In Wandan Township, the Mazu temple known as the Wanhui Gong is the focus of a procession that passes in front of all the township's temples. Each village sends a troupe of entertainers followed by its gods in a carriage. Though once a three-day annual parade, the event is now held once every three years and only for two days. The Mazu temple is also the focus for an annual lantern festival procession of the town's temples (excluding the temples of the outlying villages). This is still held annually, but whereas the procession once passed by each temple three nights in a row, now the town—which has grown much larger—is divided into two districts which are covered in two nights. A village temple may participate in one or two such processions, thus symbolizing the village's participation in one or two larger communities. The village is thus subordinate to the Mazu temple; informants from Xinghuabu, whose temple is also dedicated to Mazu, explain that they participate in the procession because the Wandan Mazu is "bigger" (*bijiao da*), that is, ritually higher. But the Mazu temple does not have a say in a village temple's affairs; temples are autonomous, though they observe each other's rituals and compare and judge styles and innovative elements.

There are three other public temples in Wandan Township. Chishayan is located on the only hill in the Wandan area. The hill is slightly volcanically active, giving off steam and burning gas for a day or so in December of each year. It, no doubt, has had a temple for centuries. Several decades ago the temple had resident monks and was run by a committee of prominent area worshipers, but a local entrepreneur, who for physical reasons was not able to marry, took over the management, upkeep, and expansion of the temple, and thus singlehandedly controls it today. He has been making the temple increasingly Buddhist, and no longer allows the temple gods to leave the temple for the township-wide processions. Although the manager controls the temple today, it is not his or his family's property. His investment of time and money in the temple gives him greater say in the temple's functioning, but it will revert to the control of other interested persons after his death.

Two higher-level temples in the town of Wandan have also come to be controlled by a single individual, but since in this case the manager is poor, the temples have lost their splendor. They are the Chenfu Chenghuang Miao (the temple to the local ruler of the spirits of the dead who would otherwise become hungry ghosts),[5] and the Wanquansi, a temple to the Jade Emperor. These temples were both founded during the Qing dynasty. The lantern festival procession originally began and ended at the Wanquansi, but because of that temple's lack of resources, the Mazu temple has held the procession for over twenty years.

In Wandan Township in southern Taiwan, public temples (*gongde*) like the village or the Mazu temple are distinguished from temples that are privately owned (*sirende*).[6] Private temples usually belong to an individual, sometimes to an association. Devotees of a god may establish an altar in their house, or more elaborately, build a small temple to the god next to their house. Sometimes these private temples belong to more than one person (a committee), or they may belong to a larger organization such as a Buddhist association.

Private temples are the focus of religious activity for a community of believers instead of for a whole village. Believers are a subset of villagers, and may include nonvillagers. Followers of a certain god may come to the private temple to consult the god, especially if the particular god gains a reputation for being efficacious (*ling*).

Private temples come in a wide range of complexities. The simplest are the cults that develop around figures of gods on private altars. These cults do not have a separate temple building, but can be viewed sociologically as a temple community. One Kheliau[7] family has several figures of gods that they say are particularly *ling*. Friends and neighbors, the young family head says, sometimes come to worship or consult his gods. Another family, the Zhengs, have devoted the center of their family altar to the cult of the family head's grandfather, Zheng Wenyi. A nephew of the altar owner (i.e., a grandson of Zheng Wenyi) is one of the village's shamans, and he regularly serves at his uncle's house. Clients consult Zheng in return for small monetary gifts. This cult to Zheng Wenyi not only serves a group related by kin, but anyone who believes in the power of the god. The cult is modest, owning only the god's joss (statue) and incense burner.

The next step up in degree of complexity is the cult that actually has its own structure. In the town of Wandan most private temples are housed in store fronts; only during processions, when banners are hung outside and shamans parade in front of the site, can temples be easily identified. In more rural parts of the township, separate structures may be built to house the cult. In the village of Lamsekak, for example, a temple called Nanhaisi, dedicated to Guanyin, the goddess of mercy, belongs to one family and is next to their house. These more elaborate temples often accept contributions from worshipers to help defray the cost of daily worship or to support the temple's construction. Conceivably, if the owner so desires, he can dismantle the temple and make it his residence (as many skeptics often suspect will happen). The Guo family, fairly wealthy with over two hectares of land and a dowel factory, built a sizable temple that looks like a two-story house except for its swallow-tail roof. The temple was built on farmland and is surrounded by rice fields, one hundred meters from the edge of Lamsekak. One of the Guo sons is a shaman, and the temple has a cult that includes consultations with shamans on specific days of the lunar month.

A higher order of private temple belongs to an association. Two such temples have recently been built in Wandan. The first is a large temple with guest rooms, belonging to a Buddhist association. The nuns who manage the temple lived in a more modest temple (until about 1987) and provided Buddhist services, such as sutra readings for the dead. The new temple has been built on a gigantic scale in a new location, surrounded by rice paddies to serve as a retreat for urban believers. The second private temple also belongs to a Buddhist association. Its resident nuns had a falling out with the neighboring Chishanyan and so built their own temple and pagoda for the ashes of donor–believers.

Neither size, style, nor name is a reliable guide to whether a temple is public or private, though a rule of thumb is that temples called *gong* are public and those called *si* are private. In terms of size, many villages have built enormous new public temples that look like private temples. Some private temples are large and stand out from their surroundings, looking very much like public temples, while others are mere storefronts or rooms in a house and are clearly private.

In general, however, private temples are more likely to have a resident spirit medium and/or to be the site of an active cult to a god. Private temples must be perceived as *ling* (powerful and efficacious) to survive and prosper. They are often built to offer the services of a particular spirit medium (or shaman; *tâng-ki* in Hokkien). Temples often have regularly scheduled sessions when the spirit medium can be consulted. One private temple, for example, has the resident spirit medium present on days of the lunar calender that are divisible by three (3, 6, 9, 12, etc.). Private temples that begin to operate like businesses, however, destroy the social illusion and lose their following (see Sangren 1987).

Public temples also often have spirit mediums associated with them (see Jordan 1972; Seaman 1978). But in Wandan, the more exciting and popular shamans work in private temples, where they can better control the workenvironment—and perhaps the funds. Public temple festivities, however, are an important occasion for shamans to perform in front of the public temple, where they build up their prestige by demonstrating sufficient ritual mutilation to convince observers of their sincerity and power. Some of the more exuberant performances at public temple festivals are thus from shamans who regularly consult at private temples.

The organization of temples is ritually expressed in the order of palanquins at religious processions. In the Mazu procession, for example, the palanquin bearing Mazu herself will come at the end of the procession, in the most honored position. Just before Mazu's palanquin are her two giant guardians, Thousand League Eyes and Favoring Wind Ears, and other attendants carrying signs telling the public to look away and be quiet, the same signs that once preceded the palanquin of the imperial county magistrate. The other high-level public temples have palanquins at the end of the procession but before Mazu. Thus, the Wanquansi palanquin goes next to last[8] and the Chenfu Chenghuang Miao palanquin is third from the end.

The rest of the procession is organized by village in a random order to indicate the equality of the village temples that participate. A month before the procession, village leaders meet at the Mazu temple and draw lots to determine the order. At one time, placement toward the back of the procession was desirable because it was ritually higher, but now placement toward the front is felt to be better since the end of the procession often does not return to the Mazu temple until five or six in the morning. Whereas the agricultural society had many youth able and eager to participate, allowing heavy work to be rotated, an industrial society prevents many villagers from participating, making the burden greater on the few who do. But each village temple has an equal chance of being first or fourth from the end, just before the higher-level public temples.[9]

Within each village contingent, the honorific rear position is reserved for the public temple's palanquin. Before it comes the troupe of entertainers (drum and cymbal dancers, stilt-walkers, martial arts braves, etc.) that represents the village. In front of them come private temple groups, if any have the resources and desire to participate. Only the more elaborate private temples have the necessary palanquin, and ideally a troupe of entertainers should precede it. But the key structural point is that though many private temples have devotees in other villages, they are ritually considered part of the village in which they are located and are lower than the village temple in the ritual hierarchy. Temples that reject the folk temple hierarchy, like the Buddhist temples mentioned above, allow the procession to visit their temples, but do not join the procession to visit other temples. They interpret this as allowing the visiting gods to pay respect to their temple's bodhisattvas, which they feel are superior to the folk gods.

Sectarian Temples

Sects that have temples in more than one village do not participate in the folk religious hierarchy; their temples form a hierarchy of their own. Yiguan Dao temples are very much like private temples. The primary difference lies in their affiliation with other temples of the same cult in an organization independent of the folk religious hierarchy. There are numerous such sects in Taiwan today; Yiguan Dao is simply the largest and the most organized.

The basic Yiguan Dao unit is the private temple in which a community of faithful perform the regular rituals. To the uninitiated, this temple is much like any private temple, albeit more elaborate. Typically a scroll to Guanyin, the goddess of mercy, or to Guangong, the god of war and commerce, forms the central panel. Scrolls of calligraphy with Buddhist themes hang on each side. Statuettes of Jigong, the drunken monk, and Milefo, the Maitreya Buddha (the fat and smiling seated or reclining buddha), lie on the altar, as is common in other family altars. A large censor (a bowl in which sticks of incense are set for offerings) and elaborate brass oil lamps are on the altar table, but nothing appears odd. There is even an ancestor tablet on the stage right side of the altar, in the same place as on all Hokkien family altars. Kneelers like those at Buddhist temples suggest the home of a devout Buddhist. Only an initiate knows that together these elements are characteristic of Yiguan Dao.

Taiwan's private temples can be placed along a scale of organizational complexity. Jordan and Overmyer (1986), in their study of spirit writing in sectarian religion on Taiwan, studied three sects, which they chose in terms of such a scale. First was the individual temple with a group of believers and associated shaman(s) or spirit medium(s). Second and more elaborate was the "Compassion Society," a temple that had given rise to branch temples in other parts of Taiwan. The branch congregations "develop spontaneously out of local initiative" (Jordan and Overmyer 1986:137) but follow the same organization and rules as members of the founding temple. Finally, the Yiguan Dao was presented as the most highly organized of the sects.

The Yiguan Dao has several branches, each centered on a founder who brought the *dao* from China in 1945. Since a dozen or so people brought the *dao* from China, there are about a dozen different branches or "lines," each of which is largely independent. In Wandan Township, there is at least one other active branch, but the branch I researched was the largest and most active locally, and members of different branches did not mingle. Each branch is organized by geographic units all under a central authority. Wandan Township, for example, is one unit under one master. The master reports to a "venerable master" (*qianren*) in Taibei who first spread the *dao* in Pingdong County. This degree of centralization helps keep the Yiguan Dao united, and helps to counteract the centrifugal forces that are generated by localism, secrecy, and personal ambitions.

Township organization is also hierarchical. Wandan Township, for example, is divided into an eastern and a western district. Each district has a leadership structure that manages the affairs of the district's temples. Followers are affiliated with the temple nearest to their home or sometimes with the temple in which friends or persons with similar lifestyles (e.g., shopkeepers or farmers) are active. But the township-wide organization of the sect is important because initiates are usually first brought to one of the township's larger, newer, and more luxurious temples for the initiation ceremony. Excursions to other areas' temples to welcome the new year (*bainian*) and field trips for youth are organized by the district or township to include a larger group of followers of similar background. Otherwise, a follower's contact with the sect is through his local temple.

At the local temple, the leader is the temple owner. He leads believers in worship and is the ritual expert. To be qualified to have a temple his family must eat only vegetarian foods. Any willing individual can, with the sect's approval and about eight followers, construct a temple (known as *fotan*, literally a Buddha altar or hall). Masters are the only persons who can consecrate new temples and initiate new members; temple owners must hold ceremonies twice a day and purchase fruit offerings for the full and new moon ceremonies, as well as snacks for believers and guests (believers make voluntary monetary contributions, however).

Masters are chosen by the gods in planchette séances and are the key leaders. Wandan's master currently serves nearly one hundred temples. Most are in the Wandan and Pingdong City areas, but several are in Gaoxiong and other parts of the island, and four are in Japan, one is in Toronto, and one is in Flushing, New York. The Pingdong unit (*Pingdong danwei*), of which Wandan believers are a part, is also contributing labor and money to the construction of an enormous temple complex in Jiayi County in central Taiwan. The temple will seat two thousand and is already a major focus of pride and effort for believers. The planning and construction of this complex has been the master's major task since 1988. Up to now, except for a central headquarters and a home for the branch founder in Taibei, all temples were built by private individuals; this will be the first major sect-owned property that Wandan faithful can visit and use.

Spirit Writing

Yiguan Dao uses spirit writing to receive encouragement and direction from deities. Spirit writing has a long tradition in China. In its simplest form a spirit medium in trance writes in the air or on paper, but the writing is scribbled and open to interpretation. The Yiguan Dao uses a more elaborate and impressive form known as a planchette (writing on a board covered with sand), and spirit writing is held in the district's larger and more luxurious temples. Three specially selected and trained youngsters represent heaven (*tian*), humankind (*ren*), and earth (*di*). "Heaven" writes, "humankind" reads, and "earth" writes. Writing involves moving a wooden stylus attached to a hoop over a tray covered with a thin layer of sand. The child holds the hoop and writes from a side of the table so that the characters face "humankind." The hoop is moved rapidly (and seems to move on its own, with the child barely holding on), but produces easily legible characters said to have the calligraphy not of the child but of the god who descends on the child and makes him or her write. "Humankind" reads the characters out loud and glides a flat rake over the sand to erase the three or four characters and prepare the sand for the next characters. "Earth" writes the message on paper. The message typically is in doggerel rhyme and encourages followers to work for the *dao*. Names of persons present are often sprinkled in the text, sometimes with puns on their names, identifying them as persons especially counted on to do the *dao*'s work. Since the youngsters are not from the area and do not know the people they name, and since the message appears too long to be memorized, participants are impressed by the power of the *dao*.

Several features distinguish spirit writing in Yiguan Dao from the more common forms of spirit writing in private temples. First, these séances are very rare in Yiguan Dao, occurring perhaps once or twice a year in one township, while they are typically the regular feature of small cults. Second, only one spirit medium goes into trance in Yiguan Dao séances, not the followers as occurs in some cults (see Jordan and Overmyer 1986:184–85). This medium is not a *tâng-ki*, the shaman of folk religion. Third, the Yiguan Dao séance involves receiving messages (typically exhortations to work harder for the *dao*) from Heaven for all the congregation, while small cults typically answer personal questions.

Esherick (1987:325–25) notes that the transformation of religious exuberance into the Taiping movement required controlling the outbreak of spirit possessions that occurred in Guangxi while Hong Xiuquan was away. Similarly, the Yiguan Dao has carefully controlled spirit writing to gain the immediacy and power from interacting with gods without losing control over theology.

The greater control over organization and over spirit possessions sought by Yiguan Dao is necessary for any local cult to develop into a broadly based religion. The strong organization of the Yiguan Dao, which holds together many followers, is satisfying to believers and proves to them that their enterprise of spreading the *dao* and saving souls is valid and important. Yet because of its secret nature and its reliance on temple cells tied to a hierarchy of masters, the sect cannot fully control its members and sometimes even local leaders go astray. In Wandan Township, one temple owner began to make claims of personal religious power and was thus expelled from the organization, but he took all his temple's congregation with him. There are thus limits to the strength of the Yiguan Dao organization, but it is its organization that makes it distinct from small private sects.

Beliefs

A number of Yiguan Dao beliefs appear to be heterodox but are in fact part of the variegated—and sometimes contradictory—beliefs of popular religion. Many religious symbols and rituals allow alternative interpretations; sectarian beliefs combine with alternate beliefs to create a "heterodox" theology.

Gods

Yiguan Dao members worship all gods; this synchretism is typical of Chinese religion. Yiguan Dao differs from popular religion primarily in its focus on the Maitreya Buddha and in its belief in the Venerable Heavenly Mother. Yiguan Dao followers believe the Maitreya Buddha, the Buddhist Messiah known as Milefo, has already arrived and given humankind the *dao*. Buddhists also worship the Maitreya Buddha but do not believe he has or is about to return (Weller 1987). Neither the deity nor the idea of his return were invented by Yiguan Dao.

Yiguan Dao believers worship an all-encompassing spirit known as Laomuniang, the Venerable Heavenly Mother, who has existed since before the universe. The Heavenly Mother is a sectarian invention; as a female figure outside of but giving order to the cycle of growth and the destruction of *kalpas* (eras), she challenges the orthodox concepts of patriarchy, linear time, and worldliness. Many believers, however, interpret her as merely another among the many gods and goddesses of the religious pantheon. In fact, she is often confused with Guanyin, the goddess of mercy, in part because representations of the Venerable Heavenly Mother are not allowed and statues and pictures of Guanyin are frequently used as substitute symbols. Only after periods of study do the more intellectual and theology-minded followers learn of her special role. One informant, a grandmother who had been attending the full and new moon services regularly for several years and had even made a vow to be a vegetarian, answered my question of why she believed in the *dao* by saying, "They are all gods, they all require incense, they are all the same."

Salvation

The Yiguan Dao belief in individual salvation also appears heterodox at first glance. According to Yiguan Dao beliefs, those who have not been initiated have no way of delivering themselves from the cycle of death and rebirth; they are doomed to being reborn in this bitter world rather than attaining bodhisattva status and going to Western Heaven. Believers try to earn "merit" (*gongde*) to

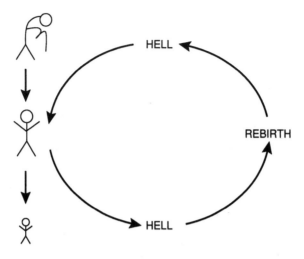

Figure 16.1. **Sources of Karma**

improve their karma so as to be worthy of bodhisattva status. Their karma, they believe, is primarily determined by what they did in past lives (see Figure 16.1). Believers are urged to earn as much merit as possible while they are healthy and able, so that in case a spirit they killed in a past incarnation returns to cause them trouble and demand repayment, they will have a storehouse of merit to overcome this challenge.

In contrast to this individualistic view of karma accumulation, ancestor worship emphasizes the dependence of the entire family on the karma and behavior of its ancestors. In ancestor worship, a person's karma comes from his or her ancestors. Taiwanese commonly suggest that a string of bad luck may be due to the past evil behavior of one's ancestors (see Figure 16.1).

While it may appear that individual karma and ancestral karma are conflicting ideas, and that Yiguan Dao is therefore heterodox because it contradicts ancestor worship, popular religion accepts both sources of karma. The concept of individual karma, borrowed from Buddhist tradition, is also popularly used to explain individual misfortune. While the emphasis in sectarian groups is on individual karma, they do not deny ancestral karma. In fact, believers often mystify the social selection of believers by saying that the inheritance of good karma from both ancestors and past lives is responsible for an initiate's being among the few chosen to receive the *dao*.

Popular religion allows the two sources of karma to coexist. The karma from ancestor worship focuses on lineage and emphasizes the mutual responsibility of ancestors and descendants. Individual karma, from the Buddhist tradition, stresses reincarnation, individual salvation, and cyclical time. Yiguan Dao does not contradict popular religion or introduce any new elements. It simply shifts the emphasis from ancestors to the individual. This same shift occurs in Buddhist temples and in other small temple cults that dot the Taiwanese landscape, and is an integral part of traditional popular religion.

The most unconventional belief of Yiguan Dao is that the end of the world is imminent and that only believers will be saved. Expressed in its most direct form, this millenarian view certainly seems rather "heterodox," or outside Chinese popular religion. Several factors mitigate the heresy of this belief. First, the end of the world is couched in the Buddhist terminology of *kalpas* (eras) and the savior Buddha. Although these beliefs are partly the messianic message of the White Lotus tradition, they are based on traditional Buddhism (Weller 1987:166). Second, these beliefs are widely current in present day Taiwan: not only do fundamentalist Christian missionaries talk of the coming end of the world (to scare Taiwanese into converting), but the Taiwanese are very aware that invasion from the PRC or nuclear annihilation are real possibilities. Furthermore, most believers are not consumed with the idea of the end of the world. In fact, initiates are only told of this idea months after they have learned the basics of the rituals and beliefs. Millenarianism is consciously played down to avoid frightening converts and the government. One leader said this element had to be spoken of carefully because Taiwanese could not simply stop working to build the economy and defend against the communists. Yiguan Dao millenarianism is not unrelated to traditional popular religion and is not dominant in its belief system, as it is in doomsday cults (see Lofland 1966; Festinger, Riecken, and Schachter 1964).

Ritual

Much of Yiguan Dao belief and ritual is borrowed from popular religion. Sect members are able to discuss the texts of planchette séances in the open with non-members present, because the contents of the texts resemble those produced by shamans in local temples. The discreet propagation of the faith depends on the fact that little of Yiguan Dao belief strikes most prospective and new initiates as strange or heterodox (*xie*), though the fervor of believers often repels new members. Many loosely associated members, especially older persons, are often naive as to the meaning of the rituals. The grandmother mentioned above, for example, on one occasion about a year after her initiation, invited all her neighbors to join her at the supposedly secret temple for what she simply called *bai-bai*, or "prayers," a term from popular religion. She understood that the praying gave her karmic merit, and was able to participate with just a background in popular religion. For her, this was simply a way to pray.

Yiguan Dao praying involves very rapid kowtowing in a kneeled position while a cantor on the right announces the names of gods and a cantor on the left counts out the kowtows. This bowing is similar to that performed by the family of the groom on the evening before a wedding, though some of the details such as hand position and the speed of portions of the kowtowing are different. The chanting is typically Confucian, much like the state-sponsored ceremonies on Confucius's birthday, which are broadcast on television each year. Furthermore, the chanting and bowing resemble in a general way the ceremonies held at a local Buddhist temple.

Although there are similarities with other religious bowing, Yiguan Dao bowing is obviously different. Nevertheless, Taiwanese families accept the idea that there are different ways of bowing for different gods and different occasions. Buddhist, Taoist, and Confucian rituals are each different, and an individual will perform different rituals on different occasions. Not only are there variations between occasions, but there are personal variations as well (if one observes closely at temples). Some of the faithful bow deeply from the waist, others rock three times, or hold the incense in special ways. This is all within the acceptable range of variation.

Heterodoxy and the Bizarre

Because until 1987 the Yiguan Dao was defined as "heterodox" by the state, the state-controlled press, and other religious groups (especially the Buddhist organizations; see Shi 1985), its rituals are assumed to be bizarre. My assistants, who knew I was researching the Yiguan Dao but had not been initiated into the sect, on several occasions pointed out persons bowing unconventionally and suggested perhaps these persons were "heterodox." In one case the person held the incense slightly above her head; in another case, the person was bowing on her knees. Although these forms were acceptable variations within popular religion and would not normally have provoked comment, my assistants revealed their assumption that Yiguan Dao members practice a strange new religion. The rumor that Yiguan Dao rituals are performed in the nude is also widely repeated. Stories of heterodox rituals in the nude date at least as far back as the eighteenth century (see De Groot 1903), and are no doubt made believable by the secrecy of such groups and their reputation as "heterodox." "In China as elsewhere, underground sects are subject to extravagant suspicions, and hence to unrealistic legal charges, which are easily believed by a populace that lacks firsthand knowledge of them" (Jordan and Overmyer 1986:246).[10] The Yiguan Dao has in fact survived the state proscription because police arrive on a scene expecting bizarre rituals but find instead teachers and well-educated believers studying Buddhist or Taoist classics in an ordinary-looking if elaborate temple. During the martial law period (1949–1987), the police could only reproach a temple owner for conducting a meeting without a permit. Significantly, the term *xie* (heretical, evil, unhealthy) is used by those with little or no contact with Yiguan Dao. Persons who have been initiated may consider believers to be fanatics, but I never heard them refer to Yiguan Dao as "heterodox."

My point is not, however, to argue that "heterodox" sects are the same as popular religion. The salvationist, otherworldly content and congregationalist organization clearly make the sects different from village- and family-based popular religion. Most importantly, they define membership in terms of belief and not in terms of natural categories such as residence or descent. The state correctly perceived the sectarian message of individual salvation as a threat to its control, and preferred to stress the interconnection of humans with gods and ancestors as opposed to the escape from Earth to Western Heaven (Cohen 1988).

Nevertheless, the use of the notion of "heterodox" has led scholars to over-emphasize the split between sects and popular religion. It has been common to suggest that sects like the Yiguan Dao reject the secular order and reject popular religion that is a projection of the worldly order and state bureaucracy. It has even been argued that heterodox sects glorify chaos and disorder (Sangren 1987:177–82).

These views rest on the conventional assumption that groups like the Yiguan Dao are "heterodox" and therefore perversely contrarian. Although a number of Yiguan Dao beliefs do contradict the traditional order, many ordinary believers are able to understand the initiation and participate in rituals with just their background knowledge in popular religion. Indeed, even the most articulate and intellectual believers must at first understand the message of the Yiguan Dao in terms of the popular religion with which they are already familiar. Where Yiguan Dao does challenge tradition, it is not necessarily subversive. Shek (1990) argues that sectarian millenarianism leads to a propensity toward revolt and violence, but Christian millenarianism has justified a variety of responses, from crusades and colonial conquest to pacifism and passive otherworldliness.

Many of the characterizations of heterodoxy are thus simplistic in drawing too sharp a line between it and popular religion. Because believers speak of cyclical time and *kalpas* (eras), it is assumed that this represents disorder. Instead, Yiguan Dao also presents order, albeit a different order. Believers are as fasci-nated by order as are other Taiwanese. For example, one evening session with a group of believers that I attended seemed to digress from theological discussion into a long series of examples of the orderly mutation of Chinese writing from pictographs to modern characters. I remarked in my notes at the time that I had no idea why my informants spent so much time on this topic. They repeated again and again, after each example, "This is not just random change; there are laws governing it." In retrospect, I believe this is an example of the equally strong attachment of Yiguan Dao believers to the sense of order. Coming after a discussion of the value of the *dao* and of the coming end of the world and the rise of a new *kalpa*, the imagery of evolving characters as a symbol for orderly mutation is clear.

New religions often claim to have found the "correct" interpretation of tradi-tional religions or claim to possess revealed truths that supersede earlier religions. Scholars generally treat these claims as part of the new religion's ideology, and do not accept them uncritically. Claims by the state and by traditional religious authorities that the new religions are perversions of tradition (i.e., heterodox) have, however, been accepted by sinologists and anthropologists.

The division of Chinese religion into orthodox and heterodox has created an artificial division within popular religion that makes the persistent emergence of millenarian movements difficult to understand. The focus on the survival and transmission of heterodox or White Lotus ideas and texts in the face of government oppression overemphasizes the difference between heterodox and popular religion. Documents such as *baojuan* and the ritual knowledge passed from teacher to pupil are at most only the seeds of White Lotus. Though important for the continuity of any one group or tradition, they had to find fertile ground to grow. Fertile ground includes the socioeconomic conditions that may strengthen religious fervor. Local private temples also offer pieces of practice and belief that can be used to form a sect. Sectarian groups only had to systematize into a semi-coherent doctrine the beliefs and practices of local cults. These popular cult elements are already widely known so that converts interpret and make sense of sectarian beliefs in terms of the cult elements.

The state's branding of the Yiguan Dao as heretical frightens many potential believers and prevents them from participating. Similarly, emphasis on the different or odd nature of Taiwanese sects leads us to emphasize the "conversion" of believers because of role stress and economic and social dislocation. The implied question is: "Why else would a Taiwanese join such a different group?"

This line of questioning is mistaken because it assumes a great gulf between heterodox sects and popular religion. Between Yiguan Dao and popular religion are many small temple cults, some less salvationistic than others, many simply emphasizing solutions to everyday health and economic problems. Yiguan Dao must compete with these temples and healers in this folk religious environment. Although Yiguan Dao offers a more fully spelled-out salvationistic view of the world, it articulates many of its beliefs and rituals in terms of popular religion. Yiguan Dao ideology in fact urges believers to continue participating in popular religion while following the precepts of the *dao*.

Yiguan Dao leaders know they compete with other forms of popular religion. Members are warned not to attend other sects' rituals, and competition from other sects and local cults is recognized as preventing the expansion of the Yiguan Dao. One village in Wandan Township, Xinghuabu, has a very active cult temple life. These small temples have shamans who, in a state of trance, offer advice to worshipers. Illness, investment questions, or personal problems can all be resolved through consultation with the god who is believed to enter the body of the shaman. Yiguan Dao leaders blame their lack of inroads in Xinghuabu on the power of the "demons" that they claim are controlling the shamans. They mystify the social nature of the competition by giving it a religious interpretation, but they recognize the source of their competition.

To understand Yiguan Dao, we must view it as part of the growing revitalist religious activity of modern Taiwan. This resurgent interest in religion includes many competing sects and religions, now also including evangelical Christians (chapter 17 in this volume). College students searching for answers find them in new churches. In working-class neighborhoods and the countryside, spirit mediums in new temple cults offer consultation on life's problems. Yiguan Dao is merely the most organized and widespread of these private cults.

The underlying difficulty we have in understanding sects like the Yiguan Dao stems from the use of the terms "orthodox" and "heterodox." These terms are often used uncritically without recognizing who has the power to determine what is "heterodox." "Heterodox" means "beyond the pale" according to a standard of ideological purity. In Europe, powerful churches (especially the Roman Catholic and Eastern Orthodox) determined what was heterodox; China since at least the Yuan dynasty (1280–1364) has not had such powerful theocratic authorities. Since ideological correctness or purity was defined by the state, "orthodox" and "heterodox" largely overlapped with "legal" and "illegal."

The state cult and popular religion were orthodox and legal. State rituals—those held by the emperor and locally by county magistrates—set the model for popular religion (Taylor 1990). Although the state cult has disappeared, popular religion still supports social hierarchy and state power: in present-day Wandan, the Mazu temple committee is made up of the township's wealthy businessmen and is chaired by a wealthy contractor and industrialist who founded the local Rotary Club. In an interview, he volunteered that religion, though perhaps not true in a scientific sense, is good for social order. He said that large temples give families a wholesome destination for family outings.

The Qing state branded Buddhism and Taoism as "heterodox," but because it controlled their organization, it made them legal. The state controlled the Buddhist and Taoist establishments through licensing and registration requirements, and by keeping their monasteries far from major urban centers and thus far from centers of influence (Yang 1961). These religious groups survived, in other words, by accepting the state's supremacy.

Sects and local cults, however, did not seek state recognition. When they remained local and innocuous they normally did not come to the state's attention, or if they did, no action was necessary. When they became more powerful they were branded "heterodox" and thus illegal. The label, it must be emphasized, was fixed by the state. The fact that organized religions such as the Buddhist *sangha* (or "church") have also been vehement in their opposition to sects like Yiguan Dao is of no consequence except as it reinforces the position of the state. Other "heterodox" groups (notably Christians and Muslims) were tolerated, so long as the state could control them.

A number of scholars have written about sects as though their odd beliefs make them obviously "heterodox" and evil (*xie*). Anecdotes of the fear and horror of informants with regard to these sects are recounted to show that this is a popular attitude, not merely the opinion of the scholar. Popular attitudes are not formed merely on the basis of doctrine, however. The fact that well-organized sects such as the Yiguan Dao face orchestrated assaults from the state and from other religious groups, and that the group was illegal until 1987, are important factors in evaluating people's response. If a standard of reasonableness of belief is to be used, what standard is to be used? The faithful of some of the world's dominant religions believe that a stick was turned into a serpent and believe in a resurrection, beliefs that cannot appear reasonable by any scientific standard and that are bizarre and "heterodox" to others. Since there is no central religious body in China that decides on matters of faith, it is tempting to apply some other intellectual standard of authenticity, be it modern historical scholarship or Buddhist doctrine. This stance, however, assumes that there is only one correct interpretation, and that this interpretation is timeless. Both these assumptions can be shown to be empirically false: texts have a number of possible interpretations and the dominant interpretations change over time. When scholars make these assumptions, they are unconsciously denying the power of the state and the bureaucratic elite to determine what is orthodox and legal.

Sects like Yiguan Dao are often referred to as "White Lotus," but Overmyer (1981:169) argues that "the term 'White Lotus' should be understood to represent a characteristic type of association, not a firm historical tradition." The lack of a firm tradition is a consequence of state suppression. The fundamental elements of White Lotus belief and practice (which Overmyer [1981:182] notes were present by 1305) persisted in the face of state suppression because they were part of popular religion. It is likely that pious persons repeatedly rediscovered the sectarian possibilities of popular religion.

In sum, the Yiguan Dao is not as divided from popular religion as the distinction between "heterodox" and "orthodox" suggests. The Yiguan Dao takes many traditions, beliefs, and practices and integrates them in a new way. It has a stronger hierarchy and organizational structure than popular religion, and its beliefs do not buttress the worldly order and the state, as does popular religion. Some of its beliefs offend state and religious authorities, but these same authorities have had to tolerate similar beliefs when they existed in isolated temple cults. It is the Yiguan Dao's organization into a larger secret organization that has caused it to become the target of state scorn.[11] In studying sects like the Yiguan Dao (especially those known only through court documents written on the suppression of the sects) it is important to see the sects not as bizarre groups with esoteric rituals kept alive by a rebellious tradition but as arising from the local cults typical of popular religion. Sectarian groups are not separated from or rejections of popular religion but are enmeshed with popular religion. This is what explains their resilience over centuries, despite brutal state suppression.

It might be argued that these small private temples have been freer to develop in modern Taiwan than in Qing China and that the connection between popular religion and the sects is only true in Taiwan. Although popular religion has grown in postwar Taiwan, resulting in an expansion in the number and size of temples (see, for example, Overmyer 1986), there is ample evidence that such temples were also common in Qing China. Naquin (1985) describes prayer groups that were either cells or independent sects. The missionary Arthur Smith (1970:105) noted them at the turn of the century:

> The countless secret sects of China, are all of them examples of the Chinese talent for coöperation in the alleged "practice of virtue." The general plan of procedure does not differ externally from that of a religious denomination in any Western land, except that there is an element of cloudiness about the basis upon which the whole superstructure rests, and great secrecy in the actual assembling at night. Masters and pupils, each in a graduated series, manuscript books containing doctrines, hymns which are recited or even composed to order, prayers, offerings, and ascetic observances are traits which many of these sects share in common with other forms of religion elsewhere.[12]

Smith noted this religious activity in the years leading up to the Boxer uprising and considered this religious activity to be unremarkable. Just a few years later, however, the area described by Smith was found to be teeming with "heterodox" sects.

Conclusion

The distinction between orthodoxy and heterodoxy in Europe was determined and enforced by religious authorities. Roman Catholic bishops and popes decided whether apparitions were genuine and whether scriptural interpretations were acceptable (see Ladurie 1979; Badone 1990). No such religious authorities existed (or were allowed to exist) in China. It is often assumed that independent intellectual standards can be used to recognize heterodoxy, or that popular opinion or community sentiment can provide a standard. This overlooks the power of elites and the state to establish, define, and protect an orthodoxy. In the Chinese case, the state and the bureaucratic elite depended on the maintenance of Confucian orthodoxy to buttress the leadership of the imperial dynasty and the scholarly elite.

In modern Taiwan, however, Confucian orthodoxy is less of an underpinning to the state and its mainlander bureaucratic and Taiwanese business elite. Certainly many elements survive, but the Confucian cult and its texts are not important pillars legitimizing the modern state. Alternative sources of legitimacy are at work: elections legitimize political elites; capital gives businessmen power; and now, increasingly, farmers, workers, women, and other interest groups struggle for power in the emerging pluralistic government.

In the 1980s, more and more persons questioned the wisdom of making the Yiguan Dao illegal. Chu Hai-yuan (1982) wrote a magazine article describing the Yiguan Dao as a harmless religion and advocating its legalization. Song Guangyu (1983) wrote a well-illustrated book that described the sect's rituals and made the same argument. Many Yiguan Dao members had a copy of the book on their shelf in the mid-1980s and interpreted its publication as an official endorsement of the religion. Only its secret meetings—a violation of martial law—made the sect illegal. Ultimately, in February 1987, the sect was allowed—and agreed to—register as a religion, ending its status as illegal and heterodox.

Notes

I wish to thank Murray Rubinstein, Sara Bosco, and Richard Lufrano for comments on an earlier draft of this paper. Remaining errors are of course my own.

1. I follow Jordan and Overmyer (1986:7) in defining a sect as "the group of believers and its organization" and a cult as "its system of ideology and religious practice." I use the terms "folk religion" and "popular religion" interchangeably for the religion as it is practiced at the local level, with no derogatory meaning implied.

2. The term "three treasures" or "three jewels" (*sanbao* in Mandarin) is also used in Buddhism, but in Buddhism it refers to the Buddha, the dharma, and the sangha.

3. Natural villages are the social units that recognize themselves as a village, in contrast to administrative villages, which are artificial government units that combine or divide natural villages to make administrative units of roughly equal size.

4. The other complaint is that Christians are unfilial for abandoning ancestor worship. Many asked, "Why can they not pray to Jesus and venerate their ancestors too?" The Yiguan Dao, in contrast to Christianity, encourages its members to maintain participation in their previous religion.

5. Although this temple is named like a city god temple, according to the inscription on the wall and to the caretaker it is a *yimin* shrine.

6. Feuchtwang (1974:268, 272–73) has called these local and nonlocal temples.

7. Lamsekak and Kheliau are pseudonyms for two villages in Wandan Township, Pingdong County.

8. If the Wanquansi were to organize the lantern festival procession, as is the custom, then its palanquin would be last and the Mazu palanquin would be next to last. In other words, these two temples are traditionally at an equal level in the hierarchy, each becoming highest only for the procession that it organizes.

9. The only exception, which is instructive, is that the six Hokkien villages in the predominantly Hakka Zhutian Township are allowed to be at the front of the Mazu procession in the third lunar month. This is done in recognition of the greater distance these villagers must travel to participate in the procession. In essence, Wandan villages sacrifice by going later in the procession in order to maintain the participation of these outlying villages, which are threatened by—and the first line of defense against—the Hakka majority. Although ethnic tension has declined considerably over the past hundred years, it is still expressed in such rituals.

10. A number of scholars accept unsubstantiated charges against the Yiguan Dao; see especially Deliusin (1972), who repeats Communist charges of collaboration with the Japanese.

11. When the government legalized the Yiguan Dao in February 1987, it merely required Yiguan Dao chapters to register with the proper authorities as a religious organization. In requiring registration, the state shows it is more concerned with knowing the association's organization (names of leaders and number of followers) than with knowing

the association's beliefs. In a parallel fashion, when legalizing opposition political parties, the state has required that they register by providing not their party platform but their organizational chart.

12. Smith goes on to say, "The[y] have also definite assessments upon the members at fixed times without which, for lack of a motive power, no such society would long hold together" (ibid.). This comment is aimed at the prevailing elite attitude that sects cheated simple people. Like De Groot (1903), Smith is identifying with the religious sects, finding them misguided perhaps, but kindred spirits in the struggle against state "orthodoxy."

References

Badone, Ellen, ed. (1990). *Religious Orthodoxy and Popular Faith in European Society.* Princeton: Princeton University Press.

Berling, Judith A. (1980). *The Synchretic Religion of Lin Chao-en.* New York: Columbia University Press.

Chu, Hai-yuan. (1982). "Thoughts on the Relationship between Politics and Religion, Part 2: Yiguan Dao" (in Chinese). *Lianhe yuekan* 7 (February): 38–41.

Cohen, Myron L. (1988). "Souls and Salvation: Conflicting Themes in Chinese Popular Religion." In *Death and Ritual in Late Imperial and Modern China*, ed. James L. Watson and Evelyn S. Rawski, 180–202. Berkeley: University of California Press.

De Groot, J.J.M. (1903). *Sectarianism and Religious Persecution in China: A Page in the History of Religions.* Amsterdam: Johannes Muller.

Deliusin, Lev. (1972). "The I-kuan Tao Society." *Popular Movements and Secret Societies in China 1840–1950*, ed. Jean Chesneaux, 225–33, 277–78. Stanford: Stanford University Press.

Esherick, Joseph W. (1987). *The Origins of the Boxer Uprising.* Berkeley: University of California Press.

Festinger, Leon, Henry W. Riecken, and Stanley Schachter. (1964) [1956]. *When Prophecy Fails: A Social and Psychological Study of a Modern Group that Predicted the Destruction of the World.* New York: Harper Torchbooks.

Feuchtwang, Stephan. (1974). "City Temples in Taipei under Three Regimes." *The Chinese City between Two Worlds*, ed. Mark Elvin and G. William Skinner, 263–301. Stanford: Stanford University Press.

[Government Information Office]. (1991). *Religions in the Republic of China.* Taipei: Kwang Hwa Publishing Company [Government Information Office].

Jordan, David K. (1972). *Gods, Ghosts, and Ancestors: The Folk Religion of a Taiwanese Village.* Berkeley: University of California Press.

Jordan, David K., and Daniel L. Overmyer. (1986). *The Flying Phoenix: Aspects of Chinese Sectarianism in Taiwan.* Princeton: Princeton University Press.

Ladurie, Emmanuel Le Roy. (1979). *Montaillou: The Promised Land of Error.* Trans. Barbara Bray. New York: Random House, Vintage.

Lofland, John. (1966). *Doomsday Cult: A Study of Conversion, Proselytization, and Maintenance of Faith.* Englewood Cliffs, NJ: Prentice-Hall.

Naquin, Susan. (1976). "Millenarian Rebellion in China: The Eight Trigrams Uprising of 1813." New Haven: Yale University Press.

———. (1985). "The Transmission of White Lotus Sectarianism in Late Imperial China." In *Popular Culture in Late Imperial China*, ed. David Johnson et al., 255–91. Berkeley: University of California Press.

Overmyer, Daniel L. (1976). *Folk Buddhist Religion: Dissenting Sects in Late Traditional China.* Cambridge: Harvard University Press.

————. (1981). "Alternatives: Popular Religious Sects in Chinese Society." *Modern China* 7:153–90.

————. (1986). *Religions of China*. Religious Traditions of the World. New York: Harper & Row.

Sangren, Stevan. (1987). *History and Magical Power in a Chinese Community*. Stanford: Stanford University Press.

Seaman, Gary. (1978). "Temple Organization in a Chinese Village." Taipei: The Orient Cultural Service.

Shek, Richard. (1990). "Sectarian Eschatology and Violence." In *Violence in China: Essays in Culture and Counterculture,* ed. Jonathan N. Lipman and Stevan Harrell, 87–114. Albany: SUNY Press.

Shi, Wentu. (1985). *Wo zemma twoli Yiguan Dao* [How I Broke Away From Yiguan Dao]. Taibei: Fuojiao Chubanshe.

Smith, Arthur H. (1970) [1899]. *Village Life in China*. Boston: Little, Brown and Co.

Smith, Richard J. (1990). "Ritual in Ch'ing Culture." In *Orthodoxy in Late Imperial China*, ed. Kwang-Ching Liu, 281–310.Berkeley: University of California Press.

Song, Guangyu. (1983). *Tiandao Gouchen: Yiguan Dao Diaocha Baogao*. Taibei: Yuanyu Chubanshe.

Taylor, Romeyn. (1990). "Official and Popular Religion and the Political Organization of Chinese Society in the Ming." In *Orthodoxy in Late Imperial China*, ed. Kwang-Ching Liu, 126-57. Berkeley: University of California Press.

Watson, James L. (1985). "Standardizing the Gods: The Promotion of T'ien Hou ('Emperess of Heaven') along the South China Coast, 1960–1960." *Popular Culture in Late Imperial China*, ed. David Johnson et al., 292–324.Berkeley: University of California Press.

Weller, Robert P. (1987). *Unities and Diversities in Chinese Religion*. Seattle: University of Washington Press.

Yang, C.K. (1961). *Religion in Chinese Society*. Berkeley: University of California Press.

Chapter 17

The New Testament Church and the Taiwanese Protestant Community

Murray A. Rubinstein

A specter is haunting Taiwan—the specter of a radical, millenarian, charismatic Christianity. This is the self-proclaimed one true church, an apostolic sect that calls itself the New Testament Church (*Hsin-yueh Chiao-hui*). Since the time of its founding in Hong Kong, over a quarter century ago, the church's prophets and apostles have proclaimed loudly to all nations and peoples their message of a purified Christianity, and their God-ordained mission to announce the long-awaited "end of days." Planted on Taiwan in the mid-1960s, the New Testament Church (NTC) has become an all too visible entity in Taiwan's spirit-filled (Pentecostal/charismatic) church community. And, as Protestant church leaders will sadly admit, it has also become a factor in national Taiwanese life—one that casts all Christian organizations in a bad light.

The Place of the New Testament Church within the Taiwan Protestant Community

The New Testament Church is part of the Taiwanese Protestant community and within that the Pentecostal/charismatic sub-community.

The Protestant community in Taiwan is organized, as are similar communities within the United States, along denominational lines. Thus, there are conciliar churches, such as the Taiwanese Presbyterian Church. There are also evangelical churches, such as the Taiwan Baptist Convention and the various Taipei-based "Mandarin Churches." Finally, there are the churches belonging to the Pentecostal/charismatic communities.[1]

The churches within the Pentecostal community make up yet another spectrum (or continuum). At one end of this spectrum are churches that are very

---

This chapter was prepared for delivery at a conference entitled "Christianity in China: Indigenization," held at Taiwan National University in December, 1988.

close to their Western roots and that remain linked to the mission bodies that helped to establish them. The Taiwan Assemblies of God is one such church. It is a Chinese Pentecostal church that is close to its Western origins and to the missionaries who helped found it. This church was founded by and continues to have strong ties to the Springfield, Missouri–based Assemblies of God, the largest of the American Pentecostal denominations. A second mission-centered church is that founded by the Ramapo, New York–based Christian and Mission Alliance.

In the middle of this spectrum are churches that owe their origins to Western theologians and that maintain a careful relationship with these spiritual father churches but which, at the same time, exist as aggressively independent entities. These may be called "bridge" structures. The Assembly Hall (or Little Flock) represents a church that occupies the middle ground and is just such a bridge. It remains close to a small Western church, the Exclusive Brethren, in its theology and its ecclesiology, but is, at the same time, an independent religious body that has developed its own doctrines and patterns of evangelism.

At the other end of the spectrum are those churches that are both independent and indigenous. Such churches were founded by Chinese and have developed theologies that demonstrate both the church's doctrinal independence and their leaders' ability to create a Chinese context for the Christian message. The True Jesus Church represents a truly indigenous form of Chinese Pentecostalism in its history, its organizational structure, its doctrines, and its pattern of worship. It began on the Chinese mainland and was planted on the island of Taiwan in the 1920s. The New Testament Church fits into the indigenous wing of the spectrum as a church founded and run by Chinese.

Questions of History

"God works in many ways, his wonders to perform." The sympathetic observer might cite this passage of scripture to explain the origins and the evolution of the Kaohsiung-based New Testament Church. However, one who has been attacked by the church would tend to see its development in a less sympathetic light. As a longtime student of the Chinese religious scene, I have the obligation to seek a middle ground. Using the church's own published materials, as well as information derived from interviews, I will present a close-to-the-source, but objective, portrait of the church's development over the course of the past thirty years.

The New Testament Church was founded 1963 in Hong Kong by a movie star and popular singer, Mui Yi. Using her own name, K'ang Tuan-yi, rather than her now famous stage name, she renounced her life as a celebrity, gathered around her a body of followers, and began to preach a new set of charismatic Christian doctrines.

K'ang Tuan-yi was a complex, and often tormented, woman whose life of forty-four years, with its many transitions, crises, and conflicts, may be seen as a microcosm of the modern Chinese historical experience. She came from a gentry family in South China who had seen better days. Her grandfather was a well-known Ch'ing official historian who had served at the court in Peking. However, by the time Tuan-yi was born in 1923, he had become an opium addict (K'ang 1966: 201–2). Her father was also a government official who, like many of the elite of his generation, had received an education outside China and then served in Peking. Like his father he wasted his talents, leaving his wife and family to suffer before finally abandoning them (ibid., 203–4). The family then moved to Shanghai to search for the man who had abandoned them. Things became so desperate that K'ang Tuan-yi herself was sold to another family to pay off a debt. However, she stole a piece of jewelry from that family, sold it at a pawn shop, and then gave the money to her mother, who paid the debt and bought her back. The family then returned to Canton, where times continued to be difficult. It was during these years that Tuan-yi became aware of the glamorous world of the movies. She saw the movies as a way out of poverty, and when she was fifteen she was mature, attractive, and ambitious enough to journey to Hong Kong to try to break into film. She was discovered at a screen test and cast in a major production. She soon became a star and remained so until she abandoned her career in 1959. Tuan-yi was clearly a woman who learned to use her beauty and her talent, but at an emotional cost. She admits that because of her success she grew up too fast (ibid., 203–4).

Tuan-yi's life from her teen years to her late thirties sounds more, in her telling, like soap opera than reality. She became a movie actress and then clawed her way to stardom. She married twice, once for passion and once for wealth. She drank, she partied, and she gambled. This last was an addiction she often indulged in. But, as she asserts in the autobiographical sections of her first and most important book, *A Life to Testify to the Full Gospel of Jesus Christ*, she was not happy; life's pleasures could not make up for the generalized sense of dissatisfaction she felt nor for the pain she suffered from a number of ailments and chronic conditions (ibid., 204–7).

Her mother had become a Protestant and had had Tuan-yi baptized. However, neither the experience of baptism nor the participation in Christian rites and ceremonies meant much to the actress during most of her life. Satan's temptations, as she terms the many attractions of the secular world she lived in, were too strong. She remained a nominal Christian until the late 1950s (ibid., 205, 213–15). However, in the year 1957 her life reached a turning point. During this year, one in which she experienced outward success but also inner torment (she underwent episodes of both physical and mental illness), she began to study Christianity and underwent a deep conversion experience (ibid., 208–9).

Something happened to this woman who was rich and pampered yet deeply troubled. She became more and more committed to her old-yet-newfound faith. The conversion to an evangelical form of Protestantism allowed her to see the

world in a new way (ibid., 209). From 1957 until she announced her retirement from the screen in 1959, she began to do Christian service. She
began to give of herself to good works and, though she had not yet defined
her own form of Christianity, she tried to evangelize and bear witness (ibid.,
219–20, 222–24).

Even after she retired from the stage she was not yet ready to devote herself
completely to Christian work. It was at this time that she underwent an even
deeper form of Christian experience. She wrote in her memoirs that God talked
to her through "an old servant." In these visions she was told to become an
evangelist and to forsake any normal means of employment (ibid., 229–31). She
had her doubts but the Holy Spirit continued to speak this message to her. She
then gave away all her worldly possessions, convinced that God would provide
for her needs. She also assumed a more ordinary appearance, giving up the
makeup and the fine clothing she had worn during her days as a celebrity (ibid.,
231–33).

In March of 1959 she began her new life as a full-time evangelist. She
purchased a flat which she made both home and chapel and began to hold
weekly Gospel-reading sessions at the site. At these services, she taught herself
how to present God's word and how to preach. She found it difficult to write
these early sermons but one may assume that her long experience as an actress
served her well; she did have a stage presence and the ability to read convincingly from a prepared text, and such skills are of great value on the church pulpit
or on the "bully pulpit" that the president possesses (ibid., 235–36). In the
months that followed, she gained attention and the number of people attending
the services increased.

Work in the chapel was but one part of her effort during these years. She also
visited hospitals and visited the sick. She found she was able to counsel people
and to hold them, and she also discovered that she was able to heal through the
laying on of hands (ibid., 236–37).

In the months that followed this initial period she went on a preaching
tour. As her fame as an evangelist grew she found that she was given ever
greater opportunities to spread the word of God. Her message at this time was
a simple one: she gave testimony to her own spiritual and moral transformation, talked about redemption through the Blood of Christ and the nature of
the end of days, and, finally, testified to the power of the Holy Spirit (ibid.,
237–38).

She continued to preach, to distribute tracts, and to communicate in person
and through letters to more and more people. These activities forced her to begin
the process of clarifying her own thoughts on doctrinal and theological matters.
As day followed day and month followed month, it became clear to her that she
was moving toward accepting the Pentecostal vision of Christianity. Her acts and
her preaching of the word reflected the concepts of this spirit-filled form of
Protestantism (ibid., 239, 241–43).

But she had not yet been baptized in the Holy Spirit. Thus she lacked the one spiritual experience necessary for her to be able to truly give form and structure to her ideas on matters of doctrine and practice; she was not yet able to articulate what would be her unique contributions to Christian doctrine. This much-needed event took place in 1961, when she writes she experienced a series of charismatic visions and was, only then, fully and completely baptized in the Holy Spirit (ibid., 244–45). The precipitating event may well have been the discovery that she, the former singer and actress, was suffering from throat cancer. It was at this moment in her life that she gave herself to God as a living sacrifice. She knew now that her time on earth was limited and she prayed to be able to continue to preach and do good work. It was during these months that she had her ecstatic visions.

She described the scene at length in *A Life to Testify,* telling that she felt the Holy Spirit pour out on her and that He spoke in tongues she had not heard before (ibid., 305–6). For her, the experience was an affirmation of her growing faith.

The months that followed demonstrated to her the power of the Holy Spirit: her illness did not feel as painful as before and she found the inner strength to deal with her own flaws as a person. She was also able to focus on expanding the work of her ministry.

These first visions and those that followed changed her in other ways. God now gave her a vision in which she saw herself taking up the cross and following him. But, she wrote, God also asked more of her. It was at this time that He commanded her to denounce all heresies and to build a new church that would restore Christianity to its pristine Apostolic state. It was now her new God-given task to restore the foundation of the early church. As she did so she was commanded to strike out against all other churches that had perverted the message of Christ. Thus she was both a reformer and a crusader against heretics (ibid., 318–21). With these powerful visions before her she was almost ready to title herself a prophetess and an apostle. One step remained. God prepared her for this step in February of 1962. That month she had yet another vision. In that vision God told her that, as his handmaiden, she had to go on a personal retreat. He warned her of the tribulations to come and told her that in two months hence she would have to withdraw from the world. The tribulation he warned her of came in March in the form of an earthquake. Tuan-yi saw this as God's warning to all people. Thus she continued to preach, building her church and preparing its members for the days and months she would be away from them learning of God's plan (ibid., 321–24).

This period of seclusion began on May 1, 1962, and lasted for a hundred days. She was not allowed to have contact with anyone but her children and those living in her house. Over the course of these days and weeks she "had intimate fellowship with the Lord and was taught by many things. Morning after morning, He opened my ears to hear, that I might know what is the good, acceptable, and perfect will of God and walk according to it" (ibid., 326).

During these days she fasted, she prayed, and she wrote, defining as she did her vision of Christianity, her view of the denominations and their doctrines, her analysis of the workings and the power of the Holy Spirit, her concept of Baptism of the Holy Spirit and of glossolalia, and finally, her concrete and practical proposals for the way the true Christian believer had to conduct himself. With God as her source and her guide she wrote *A Life to Testify to the Full Gospel of Jesus Christ* and in doing so laid out a concrete set of doctrines for her small band to study and follow.

So convinced was she of the validity of her experiences and of the truth of her new vision of Christianity that she returned to the everyday world and formally founded the New Testament Church. The next three years were ones of preaching, in Singapore and Malaysia, of planting churches, of writing tracts and epistles to her growing number of new followers, and of helping her followers plant churches in Taiwan (K'ang 1978b; 1978a). She was also able to devote time to writing books that described her evangelical work. The two volumes of *The Acts of the Holy Spirit* give detailed accounts of the major evangelical campaigns and of the internal problems the new church faced (K'ang 1979). These accounts also show that the church suffered because it stood in opposition to major denominations and challenged the leaders of the various Chinese religious communities in Southeast Asia. The narratives show just how much the church was able to progress, in spite of its militancy, from 1962 when it formally came into being until 1965. K'ang Tuan-yi's church was a militant body from its very beginning. As a result of this militancy, it often came to the attention of local authorities who had little, if any, regard for Christianity in the first place. The problems of the church on Taiwan can be traced to the militancy of its founder, the prophetess and apostle, Sister K'ang.

In 1965 evangelists planted the church on Taiwan. The prophetess saw Taiwan as the center for a vast evangelizing enterprise. She visited Taiwan in late 1965 and remained until early 1966. Here she met Elijah Hong, the man who would, in time, assume the leadership of the New Testament Church. She was already suffering from the throat and tongue cancer that would kill her, but she was able to get her message across. In a dramatic farewell, photographed by Hong and his associates, she gave the mantle of leadership of the church on Taiwan to Hong. The passing of power was subtle and not recognized for what it was at the time. However, it was a moment Hong and his followers would recall as evidence of Hong's legitimate claim to power in those months in 1976 when they fought K'ang's daughter Ruth for control of the church (Hong, undated: 5–6,.15–24, Appendix I).

Sister K'ang died of cancer in April 1966. Her death was painful, but she persevered to the end and continued to evangelize, write, and counsel her followers. Leadership of the church then passed to Ruth Cheung.

By 1969 it was clear to the more traditional and doctrinally conservative elements of the church that Ruth Cheung had "strayed from the truth." Elijah

Hong and his followers on Taiwan blamed Ruth Cheung's new husband for this change. However, a close reading of K'ang Tuan-yi's writings show that Ruth had had a troubled childhood and had revolted against her mother's authority. Furthermore, after 1959, she had resented her descent into semi-poverty and had run away from her new and less affluent lifestyle. Thus she was, from the first, more worldly than many of her followers believed a leader of a radical and puritanical sect had to be. As Sister K'ang's chosen successor, she was able to hold on to power until the early winter of 1976, when she was challenged by the key figure in the Taiwan branch of the church, the dynamic and visionary Elijah Hong.

Elijah Hong had been a local leader of the Assembly Hall Church (Ti-fang Hui). He had broken away with a number of followers and joined the charismatic New Testament Church in 1965. However, he, like Sister K'ang, believed he possessed a special vision of the church and thus disagreed with the path Sister Cheung had charted. He challenged Sister Cheung at the church's winter conference in 1976. Armed with his own special visions of the church and his own sense of the working of the Holy Spirit within him, he preached against the apostasy of Sister Cheung and began a bitter battle to assume the leadership of the New Testament Church (ibid., 25–44). Ironically, it was Ruth Cheung who conferred upon Hong his new name, Elijah. She was also the one who approved of the project that Hong was developing on a mountain in Kaohsiung County, a mountain that has become the New Testament Church's own holy mountain, Mount Zion (ibid., 4–5).

The dramatic struggle for control of the New Testament Church was waged between 1976 and 1979. During this time, according to Hong, it was the power of the Holy Spirit that led him to a deeper sense that he, like Sister K'ang, was chosen by God to lead his church in a holy war against the other Protestant denominations and against the Catholic Church.

Even as Hong fought his battles with Sister Cheung he was busy defining his vision of the church and his plan for its center and refuge. He would later spell out this vision in more precise terms in a number of short books and in his magnum opus, *This Man and this Mountain* (ibid.). It seems clear from the tone and the mode of argument in these works—*Apostleship* (Hong 1984a) is one example—that they were worked on during the period when Hong was trying to wrest control from Sister Cheung and was attempting to gain the favor of church members in Taiwan and throughout East and Southeast Asia.

The dream of establishing the sanctuary and home for the New Testament Church on Mount Zion created the most serious problems for the young and small church. It was, as Hong saw it, his mission to lead the New Testament Church and also to establish as its home and center of evangelism, the holy mountain of Zion. He and his followers continued to develop the property in the mountain reservation, which they had obtained in 1964 after considerable difficulty and struggle with local people and governmental officials (Hong, undated).

Sister K'ang had called for a new holy mountain, one to be found on Taiwan. Her daughter had shown just where on the island that mountain was. Now it was the task of Hong and his followers to convince the members of the many denominations the New Testament Church was at war with, that the new center of Christianity, the new Mount Zion, now existed in a mountain reservation deep in the far reaches of southern Taiwan's Kaohsiung County (*KMT Persecuted NTC for 20 Years* 1986: 4).

Over the course of the 1970s this vision of a holy mountain grew stronger, and in the years from 1976 to 1979, when Hong assumed leadership as the newly anointed latter-day prophet Elijah, that dream took a concrete form. The key event occurred when Hong led his followers to the new Mount Zion and was revealed on that very site as the prophet for the new age (Hong, undated: 123–46; *KMT Persecuted* 1986: 4–5).

The church leaders had worked to establish themselves on the mountain by building fish ponds, planting crops, engaging in reforestation, building a prayer hall, constructing guard towers, and even building a cable car to improve access to the site. Hong, having declared the beginning of a new age, now expected many of his followers to move to the site and to make it a paradise on earth (*KMT Persecuted* 1986: 5).

Elijah Hong's timing was unfortunate, however; he undertook much of this development in the months in which the Taiwanese Independence Movement of the late 1970s was reaching its height, cresting in the Kaohsiung incident of November 1979. The local authorities, acting, one may assume, on the orders of higher authorities, challenged the church's lease to the mountain land, destroyed the settlement, and drove the small band from the property that was now not officially theirs to occupy (Hong, undated: 146–55; *KMT Persecuted* 1986: 6).

When church members were driven from the mountain they attempted to settle in the village near the reservation checkpoint. They lived for a while in a pigsty, and when they attempted to return to Mount Zion for the census that took place in late 1980, they lost even that modest dwelling. They then moved to a dry riverbed at the base of the mountain. Here they set up tents and tried to make a life for themselves. However floods came—eight of them—and local authorities began to challenge the church members' right to occupy this land. This struggle began in late 1981 and continued for the next two years. During this time the tents and property of the church members were destroyed, the police kept close watch on all activities, and finally church members were arrested. The church fought back with lawsuits and with incredible patience. The various projects they had built on the mountain were destroyed during this time by persons unknown—the church suggests the government was involved. Even in the face of what they saw as an increasing level of persecution, the church members continued their efforts to return to the mountain and, as a result, confrontations with the authorities and subsequent arrests became more frequent (see Lau, undated; Liu 1984; *KMT Persecuted* 1986: 6–29).

Matters continued to escalate when church members brought their plight to public attention and tried to get the Taiwanese and Western media to cover the rising tide of confrontations. New Testament Church leaders went so far as to challenge the government in the Western media. A full-page advertisement attacking the Nationalist government was taken out in the *New York Times*.[2] During this time, church members in the United States tried win over human rights advocates by presenting them with materials that told their side of the story.[3] Further confrontations occurred in airports and in other public locations between 1985 and 1986.[4] In the summer of 1987 the storm let up. A key figure in the academic world stepped in to negotiate between the church and the government.[5] Hong and his followers were allowed to return to the mountain and have been there ever since. They have worked to rebuild the site. They also hold services, training sessions for church workers, and religious retreats on their newly reclaimed mountain home.

This, then, is the history of the New Testament Church. It is a church with a complex past, a stormy present, and an uncertain future. What the history of the church—a history I have written using the words of the church's own leaders—demonstrates is this: This is a radical and Pentecostal sect that has evolved and grown because it reflects the will and the personality of its two powerful, dynamic, and "charismatic" leaders. One cannot ascertain the validity of the claims of either K'ang Tuan-yi or Elijah Hong that they were driven by the need to fulfill the explicit commands of the Holy Spirit. Deep religious experiences of this sort cannot be verified by formalized, rigorous scientific testing, although psychologists have attempted to understand both trance states and glossolalia and have attempted to define each as a natural phenomenon.[6] One can say that both individuals were disaffected and were outside of mainstream society, and each seems to have been suffering from various types of identity crises. Their way of dealing with these crises was, first, to find some measure of security in an alien (i.e., non-Chinese) and non-traditional religious system and then, because they were as dynamic and visionary as they were, to redefine that tradition in ways that fit their own particular vision of the world and of God. Because each individual tried to change the religious and political institutions of their local environments and each met with resistance and overt opposition from religious and secular establishments, each individual came to see the world around him or her as hostile and antagonistic. This led to a certain pronounced militancy in their words and deeds which, in turn, provoked further confrontation and conflict with religious authorities and local government powers. The result was what seemed to them to be overt harassment and persecution. But these crises served their purpose: suffering and the demands for martyrdom were incorporated as permanent elements in the theology of the New Testament Church.

Just what is the nature of the faith system these leaders defined for their church? This question will now be examined.

The Doctrines of the New Testament Church

The New Testament Church is a Pentecostal church that accepts the basic tenets of other Pentecostal/charismatic churches. Given the personality and the visions of both its founder and its present leader, however, its theology is not simply Pentecostal. While Pentecostals and charismatics may agree on certain basic doctrines—the inerrancy of the Bible, the need for "rebirth" as exemplified by full-immersion baptism, and the need for Baptism of the Holy Spirit[7]—there can be, and on Taiwan there are, important differences that separate the various mission-centered, bridge, and indigenous churches that, together, make up the island's Pentecostal/charismatic community. This will be demonstrated in this discussion of New Testament theology and doctrine.

The basic doctrines of the New Testament Church were first spelled out by K'ang Tuan-yi in her book *A Life to Testify to the Full Gospel of Jesus Christ* (1966). This book still serves as the basis for all New Testament exposition of doctrine and theology, although much has also been written on these subjects by those church leaders who succeeded her. *A Life to Testify* is an interesting, if crudely written, volume that combines somewhat abstract theology with pragmatic advice for the new believer and powerful and revealing passages of confession and witness.

Sister K'ang continued to write even after she had concluded this powerful work. Her next book, *Acts of the Holy Spirit* (1979), is a narrative of the NTC's development from late 1962 until 1965. It was modeled after the Acts, I and II, which traced the triumphs and travails of the early church. If *A Life to Testify* is Sister K'ang's own Synoptic Gospels, then *Acts of the Holy Spirit* is her own modern-day Book of Acts. But what of the Epistles? Here, too Sister K'ang followed the New Testament precedent with *The Golden Candlestick* (1978b). This two-volume work consists of letters to church members throughout Southeast Asia. It deals with questions of faith, problems of doctrine, and suggestions on how to deal with those Christians and non-Christians who threaten the NTC and its followers. K'ang Tuan-yi saw herself as both prophetess and apostle, and her written works, modeled so closely on the work she revered above all others, the New Testament, were her instrument for making her claim as the true Christian leader of the only orthodox church that could exist in a period so close to the long-awaited "end of days."

The second major figure who defined the theology of the church was Victor Pi Sing. An apostle of the church and co-worker of Elijah Hong, Pi felt the need to spell out in clear and concise form the ideas that Sister K'ang had scattered like diamonds throughout the many hundreds of pages of her books and tracts. In two small, but most useful, tracts he does this. These works are *The Gospel of the Heavenly Kingdom* (1979a) and *The Truth on Spirit Baptism* (1979b). These brief works are important for two reasons. First, they reinforce the power of Sister K'ang's message, showing how unique such ideas are. Second, at the same time they demonstrate that the new leaders of the NTC, Victor Pi Sing among them, are true to the founder's vision of the church and that her daughter and would-be successor is the apostate who led the church in the wrong direction.

Elijah Hong, who now leads the church and who describes himself as "the prophet for this age," has written a number of books that may be seen as new contributions to church doctrine. Hong's task was to build on the original theological concepts that Sister K'ang had developed in her own writings. His major book, *This Man and This Mountain* (undated), describes the struggles of the church in the years from 1964 to 1984. This narrative was meant to parallel Sister K'ang's sections of narrative and witness. Three of his other books demonstrate the other major patterns to be found in Sister K'ang's work and were written to teach his followers and to prove that he was the first apostle's true and legitimate successor.

In *The Book of Nehemiah* (1981) he uses the Book of Chronicles to argue that his church has much in common with the Second Temple, the restored sanctuary built by the priest Nehemiah. He sees his church as the restored true church and sees his role as the leader of this restored church. He interprets the message of the Old Testament to suggest that it speaks not only of the past but of what is now and what is to be. True to the spirit of Sister K'ang, he links his church to Old Testament practices and ceremonies. We see this pattern in the writings of Sister K'ang and Victor Pi Sing and we see it again here.

Another Hong book, *Apostleship* (1984a), makes the case for Hong as the successor of Sister K'ang and lays out the theory of church leadership. It serves two purposes. First, it argues that he and the other new apostles are the legitimate leaders of the church and rightful successors to the mantle of Sister K'ang. Second, it makes the case for a charismatic means of defining church leadership. In this book Hong also uses Old Testament examples to make his points.

A third book by Hong deals with day-to-day conduct and with the way an individual can purify himself once he has been baptized with the Holy Spirit. This book is *Spirit Exercise and Self-Riddance* (1984b). It, too, follows the precedent established by Sister K'ang. While she developed doctrine and theology in her writings, she also wrote in very practical terms of the way the individual could transform himself or herself. Hong makes use of this tactic in this particular book.

New Testament Church theology today is based on a close reading of the Bible and is spelled out in the books and tracts I have mentioned. But there is more to it than that. While the Bible is the central book of the church, and is the book that is used to justify all of Sister K'ang and Elijah Hong's doctrines and concepts, it is not a book that all can understand. Church leaders assert that for one to be able to understand the true message of the Bible (the New Testament Church makes use of the Old and the New Testament) one has to be baptized with the Holy Spirit. One first becomes a born-again Christian, one is then baptized in the water, and one finally is baptized with the Holy Spirit. Once that

process has taken place, then, and only then, can an individual truly understand
the true and authentic message of the Bible. What this means is that, as church
leaders see it, there will always be a barrier between the true believer and the
outsider, though he or she might be a good Christian in his or her own right. It
also means that no one but an NTC member can truly understand the doctrines
and the theology of the church.[8] Although I am not an NTC member, and am
thus handicapped and limited by this reality, I will proceed with my own external—and in church eyes, false—analysis of NTC doctrine.

Sister K'ang's (i.e., the New Testament Church's) theology begins with a
vision of God. In the eyes of the NTC apostles, God is the Triune God—Father,
Son, and Holy Spirit. Thus she rejects the modalist position that some Pentecostal churches have espoused (one such is the True Jesus Church) that God is truly
one but manifests himself in three different forms at given stages of human
history (see Hollenweger 1972: 311–12).

Sister K'ang also sees man as having a three-part nature—spirit, soul, and
body. Man, in NTC theology, as in mainstream Christian theology, is seen as
evil. The only way man can change his nature is to undergo conversion: "But
whosoever will repent and confess his sins humbly before and receive Jesus
as his Saviour shall be forgiven and shall be given the blessings of grace"
(K'ang 1966: 15). Here we see the apostle again accepting mainstream evangelical beliefs.

The Devil is another major concern of theologians, and in recent decades
evangelicals and Pentecostals have focused on the work of the Devil as an
explanation for the prevalence of evil in the modern world. Like many of her
evangelical and charismatic peers, Sister K'ang accepts the Devil as real. It is
the Devil, the angel who became God's enemy, who leads men from God and
who "deceives, lures, oppresses, bruises, destroys and afflicts men." Furthermore, it is because of the Devil "that men become independent, doubtful, and
even hostile to Him. Because of the Devil's work men reject the Bible, refuse
salvation, and worship idols" (ibid., 16). In Sister K'ang's eyes, this doctrine
of the Devil as the agent and the source and the embodiment of evil in the
world has broad implications. She uses the Devil and his influence as an
explanation for much that has taken place in man's history and in the history
of her New Testament Church.

Man cannot help but be touched by the presence of this omnipresent force
who is the very source of Sin, and thus it is Satan who, with God, helps define
man's very nature. There are, as Sister K'ang sees it, but two types of men: those
who belong to God and those who belong to Satan. The most basic of sins is the
disobedience of God's word. At the very heart of this act, of Adam and Eve's
failure to heed God's command in the Garden of Eden, is their willingness to
listen to Satan's lies. In Sister K'ang's words, "Sin did not come because of the
eating of the fruit but because man obeyed Satan and violated the commandment
of God" (K'ang 1966).

I see this stress on obedience, one which is manifested in the way the NTC leaders run their church as well the way they define and teach their doctrines and theology, as a clear example of the NTC's indigenization of Protestantism. The principle of absolute obedience, so basic to Sister K'ang's theology, reflects her upbringing as a member of a gentry family. It was obedience and acceptance of hierarchy and one's role in a strict hierarchical family system that was the social cement of traditional China. When this society broke down under the strain of Western pressure and the internal need to modernize, the family system and the power of obedience within the hierarchical construct also broke down. Sister K'ang's family history and her life until the moment she became a born-again Christian reflect this process of breakdown. In her stress on obedience she reconstructs both the hierarchy and the source of authority, but it is now the Father, not the father, who is the ultimate source of that authority. Whether consciously or not, she has appropriated the Confucian ideal of filiality in her charismatic Christian doctrine. This same integration of Confucianism can also be seen in the way the church deals with the world, as I will argue at a later point.

We now move from sin to the types of sinful and unbelieving people. First among these are those she defines as ungodly. These are people who simply do not believe in God and will thus suffer His wrath (K'ang 1966: 18).

A second category is made up of those who mock God. They know Him but refuse to return to Him. These down-sliders smoke, gamble, drink, eat to excess, and seek pleasure, all those things the movie actress Mui Yi engaged in when she lived in the limelight. Here we see that Sister K'ang is in agreement with viewpoints held by those Protestants to be found in the more moralistic and fundamentalist wings of the neo-evangelical and Pentecostal movements. But Chinese who are not Christian would also accept much of this: it reflects a type of puritanism often expressed by the more radical Maoists who feel, even more strongly today, that their revolution was corrupted by cultural pollution.[9] Thus, romanticism and the desire to return to a simpler past unite very different types of people.

The third category of the ungodly consists of those who worship idols. Here Sister K'ang attacks those Chinese who continue to believe in the traditional deities and who continue to both maintain the folk practices and celebrate the holidays of the Chinese festival year. Her basic argument is simple: "Idol and ancestor worshipers receive no blessing but provoke the wrath of God."[10]

A fourth category of sinners Sister K'ang describes as "the unrighteous." She cites a number of acts and activities as unrighteous. There is no logic to her list. The only link between the categories is that they are each mentioned in the Bible. The comprehensiveness of the list is useful to Sister K'ang and to the apostles and prophets who now lead the church for it allows them to attack many facets of traditional Chinese life as well as both East Asian and Western forms of modern existence as ungodly. Among those she sees as ungodly are liars, prostitutes, and sorcerers (K'ang 1966: 19).

The consequence of such ungodly and unrighteous behavior is death, and after death, the many tortures of Hell. Eternal damnation is the price the sinner must pay. But there is an escape from this fate: salvation through the grace of the Word-made-flesh, Jesus Christ. Sister K'ang sees the suffering messiah as the core of her teaching. She writes, "To redeem mankind from Sin, the Lord came into the world to experience poverty, contempt, shame, suffering, sorrow, grief, whipping, mockery, bloodshed, and, finally, death" (ibid., 22). Before her own conversion in 1957 Sister K'ang had lived a life that was, on the surface, very successful. However, it was also a life filled with deep pain and much mental suffering. Thus it is natural for her to identify with the suffering savior and to make his death a center of her theology. She talked of the born-again experience as "baptism in the Blood." She told her readers, "dirt on our bodies can be washed away but the sin in our hearts can only be cleansed by the Blood of Christ. The cleansing process is the confession of all sins to Christ" (ibid., 23). This is a mainstream evangelical/Pentecostal theme, one that is discussed in many Sunday sermons. However, Sister K'ang and her successors discuss it at such length that it assumes a greater significance in NTC theology than it does in the theologies of churches that are otherwise quite close to the theology of the New Testament Church. Elijah Hong continues to stress blood and the sacrificial nature of the Christ and he develops this theme even more fully in his own books and tracts. Suffering and purification through suffering and martyrdom came to play a central role in the doctrinal system of the church, in its ritual practices, and in its relationship with the outside world.

After Christ's death came His resurrection: "God's judgement upon our sins was met by the Blood of the Lord Jesus. His resurrection has answered God's demand for righteousness. . . . All who believe in His Beloved Son become righteous. . . . Christians today can live a Christ-like life because they have the life of the risen Christ" (ibid., 24–25).

The Triune God does return to earth again, some fifty days after the resurrection in the form of the Holy Spirit. The Holy Spirit as he manifested himself on the day of the Pentecost is the central event in the history of the early church. The baptism of the spirit that the apostles and those early Christians experienced in the upper room is central to any Pentecostal theology and is another key element in NTC doctrine. Sister K'ang argued that Christ commanded his disciples to receive the Baptism of the Holy Spirit. "After a Christian receives the Holy Spirit he will have a host of spiritual blessings and these include the power to love, to witness and to serve him." The Holy Spirit will also "guide all into truth." Finally, "the power of the Holy Spirit will keep us till God's return" (K'ang 1966).

The Holy Spirit is also essential to the true revival of the church in the period we now live in, which is but the prelude to the "end of days," which will mark the first phase of the millennial age. Sister K'ang sees such a revival of the church as essential, and her task as prophet and apostle of the New Testament

Church is to bring about such a revival. However, it will be a true revival only if a core of Christians become true Christians—Christians who are baptized in the Holy Spirit. If Christians are baptized in the Holy Spirit they will demonstrate it by speaking in tongues. This small band of Holy Spirit–baptized Christians will then be the vanguard of the church and prepare the way for the end of days.[11]

Sister K'ang, like many of her Pentecostal contemporaries, accepted the eschatology of the Book of Revelations. She also seems to have been a Dispensationalist, accepting the Dispensationalist schema worked out by Darby and then concretized in the famous Schofield Prophecy edition of the Bible. This widely used Bible with its voluminous marginal notes remains the text used by many American Pentecostal denominations.[12] She sees signs of the End of Days, the prelude to the millennium, in all the disasters that the people of the world have suffered through in the twentieth century. But if the end of history as we know it is coming, is it not also the end for the true believer? The answer is no, for a New Testament Church member will be raptured up with fellow church members on the day the Lord descends to begin the period of tribulation that precedes the establishment of the millennial kingdom. Here again we see that Sister K'ang is a good evangelical/Pentecostal. However, as shall be demonstrated later, she did add her own unique interpretation to this basic fundamentalist eschatology.

K'ang Tuan-yi was not a well-educated or a very subtle theologian. Her strength as a writer and a crafter of church doctrine lay in her ability to make her ideas clear to the lower- and lower-middle-class Chinese audience. She demonstrated the ability to simplify and to personalize theology—to bring it home to her reader. She was able to link the individual to an abstract belief system. This is demonstrated in her discussion, "How to be a genuine Christian" (K'ang 1966). In this chapter, she shows just how key topics such as Christology, Salvation, Holy Spirit Baptism, and Eschatology are related to the daily life of each reader. The first step is to accept Christ as one's personal Savior. The next is to receive baptism according to the NTC rite. In this discussion she lays out the NTC format and also criticizes other churches, such as the Catholic Church, for its way of performing the sacrament. She then introduces her idea of the "Full Testimony of God." She writes: "When we accept Jesus as our personal saviour we receive not only Blood (regeneration) and water baptism (baptism and obedience to the word of God) but also the Baptism with the Holy Spirit" (K'ang 1966: 43). These three forms of ritual are essential for they are the core evolutionary moments in a Christian life. Later, in *A Life to Testify*, and also in those books written after she had formally founded the NTC, she expands on this notion of the triad of blood, water, and spirit and links it to a complex system of belief and behavior. Here she was content to introduce it to her readers in its most basic form.

But passage through a given set of rites is not enough; it is only the beginning of the life of a true Christian. A true Christian must love man, as well as God, and must be willing to bring others into the fold. Thus, each believer is also a missionary. Love for man is expressed in love for other church members and thus, she urges, all must work to create a strong and tight-knit church community. Loving also means giving up all worldly goods and renouncing the material gifts of the world. One must contribute all one has to the church and then one must work to spread church doctrines. Here we see the justification for the Christian commune on Mount Zion that Elijah Hong established in the mid-1960s. In her books, Sister K'ang demonstrates that she gave up material things when she gave up her career as a movie star. She had acted and she felt that she could urge others to follow her in abandoning the sinful secular world.

But one must be willing to redefine one's inner life as well as one's outer life. One must watch and pray. One must constantly read the Bible and draw strength from it. One must be aware that Satan and his unholy minions are ever ready to tempt one. Only by reading the Bible, by praying, and by keeping God in one's heart and mind can one conquer Satan. Prayer is personal but it does have a defined form. To pray one must be free of sin. One must then be filled with a deep and abiding faith. If one is in this frame of mind then one can proceed by making the specific request in the name of Jesus Christ. At that point one must simply put oneself in God's hand and let Him do His will. Sister K'ang urges that one should put God, not man, at the center of one's life.

The call to Christian service is a familiar one and the basic message Sister K'ang preached was common enough in evangelical and charismatic ranks. What is different is the power of the call to commitment and the accompanying demand for sacrifice. There is an air of fanaticism in these words and in various comments in Sister K'ang's later tomes and commentaries. Here a question must be raised: Can an individual who works only for the church and for the salvation of mankind—and who gives all he has in the world to support this evangelization effort—exist as a citizen in a state that lays strong claim to his loyalty and that often demands self-sacrifice? Implicit in Sister K'ang's words are a challenge to secular authority, a challenge that Sister K'ang's followers have made explicit over the course of the twenty-five years following the birth of the New Testament Church.

That the church can challenge the state may be explained by its eschatology. If one is sure that the world as we know it is soon to end then one may be willing to risk all in an effort to evangelize mankind. Sister K'ang (1966: 55) concludes her pragmatic linking of theology to individual behavior when she urges her followers to "wait for the Lord's return." She warns that all will be judged and urges that each person labor for the Lord in order to obtain "the heavenly inheritance." She warns that the final period will be most difficult, that the devil will be doubly active, and that he will not leave Christians undisturbed unless they love the Lord Jesus.

In these words she again demonstrates her talent for linking theology to practice, here the theology of the end of days with pragmatic suggestions for personal action and behavior.

Sister K'ang Tuan-yi was able to read the Bible through the lens of her own personal experience and then forge new sets of insights on the very nature of Christianity. She possessed a unique personal vision of the meaning of the Bible and the nature of the true church, which she was able to articulate during months of retreat and contemplation. Inspired by, or as she put it, directed by God, she established a new set of doctrines which she used as the basis for what she saw as the one true church, the New Testament Church. Underlying these doctrines is what I see as a decidedly Chinese gestalt. She was a charismatic Christian but she is also a *Chinese* charismatic Christian, and this subtle Chinese sensibility is demonstrated by her argument for establishment of formal and hierarchical authority structures and her pointed reliance on text as the ultimate source of behavior. She also demonstrated her Chinese background in the way she dealt with competing theologies, as will be shown in a later part of this chapter.

But a church is more than one person. Sister K'ang developed the form of the church and laid out its basic theology, but it was her successors who carried on her work and further developed her ideas. Victor Pi Sing and Elijah Hong, both leaders and apostles of the NTC that now exists on Taiwan, involved themselves in the process of doctrinal development. Their contributions were developed, as suggested earlier, in a number of tracts and books.

One can quickly sum up Victor Pi Sing's contribution: He took Sister K'ang's ideas, extracted their essence, and then presented them in a crisp and easily understood form. He was thus important as a transmitter of doctrine but not as a real innovator (see Pi 1979b; 1981). What he did was of great value for he was able to show that Sister K'ang had created a doctrinal system that linked the Old Testament to the New. In doing so he laid out the NTC's major theological innovation. In *The Full Gospel of Jesus Christ* (1981), he discusses the significance of the "Seven Feasts of the Lord." In doing so he demonstrates that the church leaders had been able to show how the doctrines and the theological concepts of the Old Testament led directly to the revelations of the New Testament, thus clarifying the link between both books. To be sure, both Catholic and Protestant theologians, following the lead of Christ and the apostles, had made such links. What K'ang and her successors did was to show how the Hebrew ritual year may be interpreted as a Dispensationalist-like schema that charts the path to the day of Christ's return. The prophetess had suggested this but had not spelled it out all that clearly.

This same schema also serves to demonstrate where the NTC core concepts of blood, water, and Holy Spirit sacrifice fit into the larger Judeo-Christian holy history. The Passover is the first of the seven feasts. It is seen as symbolizing Christ as the Lamb of God sacrificed by the Hebrews before their deliverance. Because of this the festival is also seen, within the context of the Full Gospel system, as representing the Witness of Blood. Finally, on the level of personal belief, it is seen as reminding NTC members that they must trust in "the efficacy of the Precious Blood." The second of the festivals is the Feast of the Unleavened Bread. In Pi Sing's eyes this is a distinct festival, but it is one that is celebrated by Jews as the Passover. In the NTC schema, it is the moment in the New Testament when Christ is buried. In Full Gospel terms, it represents the Witness of Water. For the believer, it is the symbolic act of leaving behind one's old life—of dying and being buried with Christ. The third of the festivals is the Feast of the First Fruits— the Jewish Shevuoth. The NTC sees this as the celebration of the day Christ rose from the dead. It is thus seen, within the Full Gospel system, as the reality of the Witness of Water. For the believer this festival signifies resurrection with the Lord. In doing so one abides by the Word of God and lives for him. The fourth of the NTC festivals is Pentecost, the day that the "Lord sent down the Holy Spirit to build the New Testament Church." Within the Full Gospel system it is the Witness of Holy Spirit. The believer must receive the Holy Spirit, must abide by the apostles' doctrines, and must strive to maintain the unity of the NTC. These four festivals are part of the church's present. The final three represent moments in the NTC's version of the Dispensationalist theology.

The first of this second set is the Feast of Trumpets. It is the equivalent of Rosh Hoshanah, the Jewish new year festival. In Jewish eyes, this is the beginning of the Ten Days of Awe, days that are seen as making up the holiest period in the Jewish festival year. NTC theologians such as Victor Pi Sing see this as the time when the Lord shall descend. In the Full Gospel schema, this is a time when all must hold fast to the Full Gospel and wait for the Lord's advent. It is also the moment when the dead shall rise and the believers shall be raptured up. Thus, it is the first moments in the period of the Final Days. The Yom Kippur, the Day of Atonement, is the festival that marks the second phase of this final period in man's history. This day, celebrated as one in which the Book of Life is closed for the year, is, in NTC eyes, when the whole house of Israel will be saved during that time of tribulation. Furthermore, all sinners shall repent. It is, in Full Gospel terms, the time of holding fast to God's word and of witnessing. It may also be a time of martyrdom. Finally, those who are overcomers—those who have been saved before the end of days but have died—will be resurrected and raptured up. The Feast of Tabernacles, the Succoth, is the last of the NTC festivals. It marks the final stage of the drama of the end of days and the millennium. It is during this time that the Lord will descend with the tens of thousands of saints to establish the millennial kingdom. This millennial age is then followed by a final period in which a new heaven and a new earth are established. This is the New Jerusalem and it is here that God and men will live together. This is also the time when the Full Gospel is fulfilled, for those who are believers—the overcomers—will descend with Christ to become the priests of God. Finally, for the individual, this is period in which he will serve as a king, working with Christ for the thousand years of the millennium and for the eternity that follows this first thousand years (Pi Sing 1981: 1–28).

This creation of a fully developed schema linking personal act to divine history may be seen as an important innovation in Pentecostal thinking. It is, at the same time, a clear example of the NTC's sinification of Protestantism. One of the most striking characteristics of those who developed Chinese religious and metaphysical thought was their ability to construct systems that linked together seemingly disparate elements into a concrete and organic whole. Certainly this is what the Han Confucian T'ung Chung-shu did in his works and it is what the major Neo-Confucian thinkers did in Sung and Ming times. It is also what the modern leaders of the I Kuan Tao do in their own pamphlets and books. I would argue that K'ang Tuan-yi did much the same thing when she introduced her own version of Dispensationalism. As I have also demonstrated, Victor Pi Sing did this when he pulled Sister K'ang's ideas together in a clear and comprehensible form that allowed church members and outsiders to see just what the prophetess had contributed. In doing this he also set the stage for his fellow apostle, Elijah Hong.

Hong is the more ambitious and the more original of the two. Furthermore, he has the need to justify his claim to be the "prophet of the new age." He, too, uses Sister K'ang's work as the basis for his own thought. His stress is not on pure doctrine but on the linkages between doctrine and church structure and between doctrine and personal discipline. These are themes in Sister K'ang's own work, but she was more interested in larger theological issues, as is demonstrated in her own writings and in Pi Sing's synopses. Hong seems content to use Sister K'ang's ideas as his framework. However, he is more political than she was, and he is more involved in establishing a church in a hostile political climate. Thus he stresses both those doctrines that will enable his church to survive and those doctrines that will secure his own power base as a charismatic leader. He is the leader of the church militant—and the church besieged—and his own writings reflect this aggressive sensibility.

Why is the New Testament Church so militant? The answer lies in both Sister K'ang's and Elijah Hong's need to see the church as the one true church. Theirs is, by definition, a radical and sectarian form of Christianity that needs to see the world as threatening to create a stronger in-group identity. How does the NTC see its enemies, both religious and secular? The NTC vision of the outer world must now be examined.

The Church Militant: the New Testament Church
Attack on the Chinese Christianity Community

The New Testament Church sees all other churches as corrupt and heretical. The wide-ranging attack on all other facets of Christianity was defined by Sister K'ang and has been refined and carried forward by Elijah Hong.

Sister K'ang's experiences as a nominal and then a born-again Christian and her own special reading of the Bible, as filtered through the process of Holy Spirit baptism, had convinced her of the heretical nature of many of the churches she had observed and studied. In *A Life to Testify* and in later works she attacks these churches and openly condemns what she saw as their heresies. Her attack is all-inclusive: church bodies as different as the Roman Catholic Church, the Presbyterian Church, and the True Jesus Church are examined and found wanting in the eyes of the prophetess. She sees these churches either as false bodies that represent the will of Satan or as institutions that are in error, having misread or misinterpreted the instructions and injunctions found in the books of the Old and New Testaments.

The Roman Catholic Church is taken to task on a number of grounds. She argues that first and foremost among the many sins of this "universal" church is the fact that it dares to claim descent from the apostle Peter. Because Catholics do this they distort the fabric of Christian history. Furthermore, the Catholic Church has had the arrogance to create a Christianity that is more than simply biblical, as is the NTC and many of the neo-evangelical and charismatic churches. The very depth and richness of the Catholic tradition and its ability to integrate patterns of existing pre-Christian and localized religion into its system are seen as the work of the Devil (K'ang 1966: 65).

The Pope and his role as head of the universal church are also attacked. The institution of the Papacy demonstrates the satanic pride of Catholicism. In Sister K'ang's eyes Catholics equate the Pope with Christ: "He is Christ in the Flesh and believes he can never be wrong" (K'ang 1966). At the core of her attack is her belief that Peter himself was insincere and that he was succeeded by others who were even more corrupt.

Aspects of the Catholic sacramental system are also seen as false. The way Catholics perform baptism is seen as incorrect. The doctrine of transubstantiation and the very way the eucharistic rite is performed are scoffed at as ridiculous. The sacraments of Confession and Holy Orders are seen as incorrect and the very idea that the church stands as intermediary between man and God is rejected.

Catholic glorification of Mary, the worship of saints, and the veneration given to certain holy objects are also seen as heretical and as contradictions of biblical injunctions. Here the Catholic Church is condemned for allowing its members to practice a lightly concealed form of paganism (ibid., 66–72).

Such attacks are not unique in Pentecostal or neo-evangelical circles. Books attacking Catholicism could be found in the Taiwan Baptist convention's own reading room in Taipei in 1983, for example. Furthermore, the now discredited (but still televised) Pentecostal evangelist Jimmy Swaggert was often criticized for his own bitter and inflammatory attacks on Roman Catholicism, attacks that were witnessed by millions of television viewers in the United States and around the world. What is notable is the savagery of the NTC's attack, and the ignorance of the Catholic tradition that Sister K'ang too often displays.

A second favorite target of Sister K'ang is Mormonism. Mormons are attacked for distorting the basic nature of God. Their concept of Adam as God is seen as blasphemy, as is their perception of Jesus. According to Sister K'ang,

Mormons believe that Jesus was the son of Adam and Mary. This, she says, provides them with a rationale for their belief in polygamy. She attacks such an idea as false and totally unbiblical. She also suggests that Mormons disregard the Holy Spirit, and this opens them to condemnation. She concludes her critique by stating that those who join the Mormons are becoming members of a religious system that will only lead them to Hell (ibid., 73–74).

Yet another body that is characterized as semi-Christian, and is thus open to condemnation, is the Jehovah's Witnesses. Sister K'ang sees them as a group that rejects the Triune God and the idea of the eternal condemnation of the sinner. She also condemns as false their idea that the millennium has already arrived and that Christ lives among us (ibid., 83–87). While similar views might be held by other churches, it is the stridency of her attack that sets her apart from the more moderate and consciously denominational mainstream.

The Seventh-Day Adventist Church, a somewhat more mainstream millennial Christian body, is also condemned by Sister K'ang. It is attacked for its concept of the soul and for its acceptance of Saturday as the Sabbath. She is willing to concede that Adventists do good works, but in her eyes this only means they are successful heretics, but heretics nonetheless (ibid., 74–83).

The True Jesus Church, the largest of the indigenous charismatic churches found on Taiwan and a church with considerable strength in Southeast Asia, is also attacked by Sister K'ang. She discusses the True Jesus Church in some detail in one of her epistles in *The Golden Candlestick, Vol. I* (1978b). In this piece she comments on what she believed were the major errors of the church. What is clear in her discussion is that the points that divide her own new church from this older and more established church are, to an outsider at least, seemingly minor, and they revolve around questions of practice as much as theology. That she devotes such attention to these questions of True Jesus faith and practice demonstrates that she sees the church as a major competitor whose doctrines must be confronted directly. If there is a subtext in her comments it is that she saw the True Jesus believer as a potential NTC follower, and thus tried to show that while the churches are close in their theologies the differences that exist demonstrate the superiority of her system of theology and her interpretation of scripture.

In addition to these semi-Christian bodies, millenarian sects, and other indigenous charismatic churches, Sister K'ang lashes out at what she called "the social gospel." Using this rubric she is able to broaden her attack to include all Protestant Conciliar churches, most especially the powerful Anglican Church, which is found in Hong Kong, and the Presbyterian Church, which is so well established on Taiwan. She sees in the social gospel the hand of Satan and condemns the "modernist" church leaders for mistaking black for white. In good fundamentalist fashion she condemns these churches for their use of "Higher Criticism." She suggests that this opened the way for a variety of heresies such as the devaluation of the divinity of Christ, the denial of the validity of miracles described in the Bible, and the denial of virgin birth and the Resurrection. She also condemns these churches for what she sees as their worldly organizations, their illegal activities, and, finally, their willingness to have ongoing dialogue with the Roman Catholic Church. She sees such activities as misguided and sees these churches as preaching falsehoods. Thus she calls upon all true Christians to condemn them (ibid., 88–106).

The church leaders who succeeded her continue to press forward this many-sided attack on the Christian world. In a recent tract, *Depart from Idols and False Gods* (undated), while condemning the governments of the world, they also lash out against all religions that are man-made. All varieties of Chinese religion are thus attacked as are all churches not willing to accept NTC doctrine. The tract is a document written by angry men that demonstrates, in a clear and direct fashion, the militancy of the New Testament Church's leaders. Sister K'ang would be proud of these new leaders for they hold high the sectarian torch and use the published word as a weapon to do battle with all whom they see as heretics.

Christian churches and traditional Chinese religions are seen as spiritual ene-mies that must be defeated. But there is another enemy to be overcome—the state—and the leaders of the NTC have demonstrated their willingness to do battle with the political authorities who dare to oppose them and who act to prevent them from carrying on their God-inspired labors.

The New Testament Church and the State, 1960–1988

The New Testament Church sees government as a problem wherever it may be. In their writings, church leaders from Sister K'ang to Elijah Hong condemn at length the power the state possesses. The arguments church leaders make are theological in nature, but what is clear from NTC documents and the various historical narratives church leaders have written is that such arguments are in-variably made after some incident has taken place or some resistance to its work on the part of a local, provincial, or national government has been encountered. This can be seen as we explore the way the NTC sees the state.

It was Sister K'ang who encountered the first resistance and who began the process of defining a theology of church–state interaction. In the two volumes of *Acts of the Holy Spirit* (1979) she describes her first evangelistic campaigns, when she attempted to win converts to the NTC in Southeast Asia. What emerges from these tales of trauma and occasional triumph are her methods and her heavy-handed iconoclasm, which served to stir up considerable opposition wherever she preached. She did draw crowds but many among those assembled were hostile toward her and her methods. Public authorities began to see her as a threat and, because many of these areas were Moslem in faith, began to use statutes that prohibited evangelism. With other, less militant and less strident Christian groups they often looked the other way, but with K'ang Tuan-yi they invoked the letter of the law. As a result, police were usually on the scene when she spoke, ready to move in if a breach of public security seemed about to take place. On a number of occasions she was taken to police headquarters and told to shorten her stay. She would obey and move on, only to find that authorities in the next city were ready for her. In *Acts of the Holy Spirit* she describes the events simply, but her tone is one of condemnation as she describes the actions of the authorities. They are, she implies, agents of Satan in their efforts to prevent her from preaching her unique and "true" version of God's word. Running through her writing is the idea that true Christians—meaning NTC members—must be willing to martyr themselves if necessary and must oppose the godless leaders of the states of Southeast and East Asia.

The New Testament Church leaders on Taiwan found that they too were confronted by a godless state, whatever professions to Christianity its leaders might make. They found that their attempts to colonize Mount Zion were opposed from the very start. Elijah Hong documents this opposition in his own long book, *This Man and this Mountain* (undated). After presenting a detailed account of the building of the site that was to become the center of the New Jerusalem, he gives an even more detailed and equally emotional account of the way the local and county governments destroyed this church center and condemned those who lived there to years of desperate wandering. There is no formal theology of state–church interaction presented in these pages. Rather, Hong is content to let the actions of the state and the responses of his followers speak for themselves. The idea of NTC member as martyr which Sister K'ang introduced is spelled out in great detail in these chapters and in the documents the church published in the eight years that followed.

Subtlety of argument and the will to write calm, soft-spoken prose are not gifts NTC leaders possess. Instead, following the lead of Sister K'ang, they press forward and loudly condemn all who are in their way. The KMT was seen as the enemy and essays, tracts, and pamphlets were written to make this clear to the public on Taiwan and to the Christian public worldwide. Through its overseas evangelistic organ, the Grace of Jesus Crusade, the church leaders tried to reach all who would listen.

The message of all these materials—and they served as the source of numerous news stories about the NTC–KMT confrontation—is that the KMT has persecuted the church for three generations. NTC writers see this persecution as similar to that the line of Herod visited on Jesus and the early Christians. The author of the pamphlet *KMT Persecuted NTC for 20 Years* (1986) traces this conflict from its origins in 1963 until 1986. He discusses the early problems of the church, the destruction of Mount Zion, and the attacks on Elijah Hong. It is his basic contention that the KMT "turns out to be an anti–Christ regime which trusts in deceit rather than in Truth, takes preference in unrighteousness, wants face and never admits its wrongs" (ibid., 2). He then argues that this can be demonstrated in the way the regime treats the prophet Elijah Hong. He contends that Hong is a man the rulers of Taiwan hate and fear. One reason is that Hong is willing to confront the KMT directly, as he did in 1985 when he stated, "the enemy, the adversary who intends in his heart to liquidate NTC is this evil man, Chiang Ching-kuo (today's Haman)" (ibid., 30–32). With these words the leaders of the church made it clear to all that they had declared war on the state. The way the NTC fought that war was to use the press and to use its weapon of personal prayer. Thus it launched a full-scale press offensive and its leaders and followers denounced the KMT in public forums and at demonstrations. Whenever they could, the leaders of the church prophesied the end of the KMT and used quotations from the Bible to demonstrate that God's wrath would be visited on the KMT authorities.

But why engage in this conflict? One answer is spelled out by the author of *KMT Persecuted NTC for 20 Years*. He states that while the autocratic KMT might rule the political system, the economy, the culture, and the educational system of Taiwan, it does not and cannot control the New Testament Church. He argues, "the NTC submits herself only to God and refuses to come under man's control." He adds, "Since the KMT fails to take control over the NTC or disunite the NTC, it exerts all its strength to persecute the NTC with the intent of liquidating the NTC" (ibid., 33). Thus the church is fighting an oppressive state that is attempting to wipe it out. It has no choice but to declare war.

The war that began in 1985 continued to be waged in the three years that followed and the rhetoric the church used became even more fierce. Tracts and sheets that brought the message home with great force were prepared and distributed. One example is a large handout that condemned the KMT. Titled *NTC's Divine Obligations—Vanquish Tyrannies and Rescue Mankind* (1987), this tract was an attempt to answer criticisms other churches had leveled at the NTC for its ongoing propaganda offensive against the KMT. The author of the tract argues that the NTC was acting for God in an attempt to exercise divine justice. Even as the church defended its actions it continued its attack on the KMT. Thus its author argues, "Heaven will not tolerate Chiang Ching-kuo" and goes on to say to the president of Taiwan, "Don't you know that before Heaven, Truth, law, and justice, you are only a criminal? . . . Heaven will not tolerate your obstinacy and impenitence! You will speedily step down, fall to the pit and perish."

A second handout contains a similar message. Titled *Give the Government Back to God* (undated), it condemns all secular governments and argues that "the kingdom and the power are God's." It states further that "the kingdom of men is an Anti-God rebellious bloc," and warns, "Christ shall destroy all rulers and hand over the kingdom to God." This tract demonstrates that the church leaders were willing to used their Dispensationalist and Millennarian theology as a weapon in the war against the state. Prophecy and prayer and the words of the Bible were all used in the war against the oppressive KMT regime.

The New Testament Church was willing to wage a full-scale battle: its leaders' theology of martyrdom allowed it to take no other course. But how has this affected the course of Christian development on Taiwan? In the conclusion to this chapter I explore this question.

Conclusion: The New Testament Church and the Development of Taiwanese Protestantism

The New Testament Church presents a many-faceted threat to the Protestant community on Taiwan. That this is so is a reality Christian leaders must face. To say that the church as it now exists poses a threat to the development of Christianity in the Republic of China is not to make a biased statement: rather it is to read the record of NTC history and to accept the NTC leaders' words—their statements on theology and doctrine and on church–state relations—at face value.

The NTC is a threat because of its theology, a theology that openly and loudly condemns the belief systems of all other churches and all other religious institutions on the island of Taiwan. It is, its leaders proclaim, the one true church and all Christians must come to it or they will burn in Hell. This, in essence, is the message of the leaders of the church.

The NTC is a threat because it sees itself as at war with all other churches. All other churches are heretical, and willingly and loudly promote false doctrines. Thus the NTC sees attacking these churches as basic and fundamental duty—as God's own work. Working for Christian unity and for inter-church cooperation in a nation that is 96 percent non-Christian is an unacceptable strategy for Elijah Hong and the other apostles.

The NTC is also a threat because it is willing to attack the KMT and its government, a government that has, by and large, been tolerant of many diverse religious bodies and a government that has opened its doors to Christian missionaries. The leaders of the NTC have not read the history of the KMT nor of other, more ancient, Chinese regimes. If they had they would have learned the most basic of all postulates: the Chinese state, whether imperial or republican or Marxist, will tolerate a religious body as long as that body is willing to accept the basic political, moral, and social norms of the larger society and to not confront the state, the agency that defines and defends those fundamental norms and principles.

Finally, the NTC is a threat because it has such a visible and public presence. It demonstrates. It propagandizes. It stages confrontations designed to embarrass the powers that be. As a result the NTC is seen to represent Christianity in the eyes of many of the people of the island. This was demonstrated by an incident I witnessed in 1986. It took place at the annual meeting of the Taiwan Mission Fellowship, held at the Morrison Academy in T'aichung. Local authorities met with the leaders of the fellowship and asked if they were connected to the New Testament Church. They proceeded to keep watch, from a distance, as the meeting continued. In the eyes of those police, all Christians were somehow connected to the NTC.

But how will this church affect the development of Taiwanese Christianity and, more to the point, how will it affect the evolution of an indigenous Christianity on Taiwan? I see the church as having the potential to do much harm in the ongoing effort to create a Protestant Taiwan. The church has upset the careful balance between church and state. It is not content to bear witness nor to work within the system, as did the Presbyterian Church. Nor is it content to "render unto Caesar" as does that other charismatic body, the True Jesus Church. It must stridently move forward and make itself an all too visible force on the Taiwan scene. When people outside the church risk their "personal capital" and influence to work on behalf of the church in settling its disputes with the KMT, church leaders accept the help but see it not as an act of reconciliation but as a demonstration that God has forced His will on the evil ones.

The government is now wary and will be less tolerant. One of the regime's spokesmen gave voice to its bemused frustration in dealing with a church that wishes to confront the regime on one issue after another. When frustration turns to real anger, all the island's churches, not the NTC alone, will be at risk.

This creation of a confrontational public persona is but the more obvious way the church has hurt the course of Protestant development. It has affected the course of Christian progress in a more subtle way as well. With its radical indigenized theology and its attitude toward other churches, as well as its communitarian style of organization that centers around obedience to an exalted, powerful, and divinely inspired leader, the church can be seen as a Christian version of a radical Chinese popular sect. Such sects were an important element in various sections of China throughout the long centuries of imperial rule. In times of economic dislocation and governmental decline, such heterodox groups were seen as threatening to regional and sometimes national social stability. The KMT viewed the I Kuan Tao in much the same way until the millenarian and ecstatic sect was legalized a few years ago. The New Testament Church can be seen as a Christian version of just such a heterodox sect and those who join it are viewed with suspicion. But, as I suggested earlier, most Chinese are not apt to discern the differences between a mainstream—and law-abiding—Christian church and a heterodox and politically radical Christian church. Thus, those Chinese who might otherwise be attracted to Protestant Christianity might fear association with any form of this now seemingly dangerous alien religion.

The merits of New Testament Church theology and of the church's unique vision of the Christian message must be weighed against its militant and somewhat paranoid vision of the outside world. Its defensiveness, its antagonism toward other churches, and its hostility toward the state make it a threat to the Taiwanese Christian community at large. It is my considered opinion that the New Testament Church is an interesting, and even important, attempt to create an indigenous Pentecostalism, but it is also a danger to that community, even to the Republic of China, a country that already lives each day on the brink of national extinction.

Notes

1. Whatever its protestations, the New Testament Church is not unique; it can be defined as a form of spirit-filled Pentecostal/charismatic Christianity. What is charismatic Christianity? Just how can this belief system that mainland Chinese, Taiwanese, and mountain people in the Republic of China have come to believe in be defined?

Following the lead of Paul Pomerville, an Assemblies of God missiologist, I begin with a definition of evangelicalism, one that demonstrates the Pentecostal/charismatic tradition's closeness·to the basic orientation of the older, and numerically stronger, evangelical tradition. Pomerville (1985) discusses this in his important book *The Third Force in Missions: A Pentecostal Contribution to Contemporary Mission Theology*. Evangelicalism was one of main strains within American religion that produced the Pentecostal revival of the early twentieth century. The other was the Methodist-derived Holiness tradition. I then define spirit-filled Christianity itself.

According to Pomerville (ibid.), the basic elements of evangelicalism are: the absolute authority of the Word of God (inerrancy); orthodoxy (correct belief); personal salvation by Grace; dedication and commitment; and a heavy stress on evangelism and missions.

Pentecostal/charismatic Christianity shares each of these orientations. How, then, does it differ from evangelicalism? Pomerville (ibid.) argues that spirit-filled Christianity possesses a number of distinct characteristics. One of these is a deep and abiding sense of ecumenism. There exists a sense of a fellowship in the abiding belief that the Holy Spirit works in the world, and this common faith blurs denominational distinctions. It is this characteristic that allows Pentecostals and Charismatics to be true to their own churches yet have close contact with those Roman Catholics who share in the gifts of the spirit. It is this same characteristic that has allowed Charismatics to remain members of their mainline conciliar or evangelical denominations even while speaking in tongues and healing with the laying on of hands, practices often scoffed at by the mainstream denominational churches.

A second, and more important, element separating Pentecostal/charismatic churches from evangelical churches is the abiding faith in the direct and active work of the Holy Spirit. Pomerville (ibid.) spells out this difference in detail. He argues that because of the active role the Holy Spirit plays in the lives of the Pentecostal/charismatic church members, these churches represent a return to the first-century Christian experience and to the Apostolic church itself. Pentecostalism (and the more recent Charismatic movement), "brings a dimension of the Christian faith to light which has all but been eclipsed in Western Christianity—the experiential dimension."

Pomerville takes this further. He argues that this principle of experiential Christianity, what he terms the dynamic nature of the Christian faith, is one of eight basic principles. This power, the power of the Holy Spirit, infuses the other principles (other characteristics of the evangelical/charismatic faith system) with a new tension and a dynamic dimension.

This principle, the belief in the indwelling of the Holy Spirit, can be defined in experiential terms as follows: a believer can experience, in an immediate and direct way, the power of the Holy Spirit and can be "baptized in the Spirit"; because of such a "baptism" one can "speak in tongues" (glossolalia) and can heal by the "laying on of hands." What binds the charismatic/Pentecostal movement together is this belief that the Holy Spirit is at work transforming the lives of all those who accept it in their lives.

Those doctrines I have defined as Pentecostal/charismatic are shared by the spirit-filled churches that now exist on Taiwan. At their core is the idea of the ongoing and ever present work of the Holy Spirit. This is accepted as a fundamental reality in each of these Taiwanese religious entities—the churches and the interdenominational parachurch, the

Prayer Mountain Movement—that are part of the island's charismatic/Pentecostal community.

2. These articles cover 1985 and 1986. They are part of the NTC press packet sent to those Westerners interested in the struggle of the church. (See also *KMT Persecuted NTC for 20 Years* 1986: 30–42).

3. For example, James Seymour, a political scientist and head of the Society for the Protection of East Asian Human Rights, was contacted in 1986, as was Linda Gail Arrigo, wife of Shih Ming-te, the imprisoned advocate of Taiwanese independence and herself a sociologist and most articulate and able observer of the Chinese scene. I interviewed a member of the church in 1986 and was also sent a variety of materials, materials which I have used in writing this part of the chapter. I also obtained information on the way the government sees the NTC.

4. See *KMT Persecuted NTC for 20 Years* (1986: 34–35). These confrontations are covered in the materials in the NTC press packet.

5. This comment is based upon interviews with Chu Hai-yuan of the Institute of Ethnography, Academia Sinica, a specialist on religion on Taiwan who has studied the problem of the confrontation and served as the intermediary between the government and the NTC leadership.

6. See the important and provocative essays in Bourguignon 1973.

7. The best comprehensive study of pentecostalism we have, one that explores history and doctrine in detail is Hollenweger 1972. His discussion of pentecostal theology is found in part 2, chapters 21–29.

8. Based on an interview with Fidelia Ng, pastor of the Church of New York, Queens, New York, August 16, 1988.

9. It is ironic that a number of Western commentators who write about the PRC also reflect this mood of puritanism and talk about the good old days of the Cultural Revolution. On this see Schell 1988.

10. An excellent introduction to the festival year is in Thompson 1988.

11. Sister K'ang has much to say about the true revival of the church and the nature of Holy Spirit Baptism. I will discuss these ideas at some length in a full-length study of the NTC. This paragraph serves as a brief introduction to her concept of the Holy Spirit and its work. (See K'ang 1966: part 2, chapters 1–5.)

12. The Springfield, Missouri–based Assemblies of God is perhaps the largest denomination that makes use of the Schofield Bible.

References

Bourguignon, Erika, ed. (1973) *Religion, Altered States of Consciousness, and Social Change.* Colombus, OH: Ohio State University Press.
Depart from Idols and False Gods (undated) Kaohsiung, Taiwan (pamphlet).
Give the Government Back to God (undated) Kaohsiung, Taiwan (pamphlet).
Hollenweger, W.J. (1972) *The Pentecostals.* Minneapolis, MN: Augsburg Publishing House.
Hong, Elijah. (1981) *The Book of Nehemiah.* Kaohsiung, Taiwan (pamphlet).
———. (1984a) *Apostleship.* Kaohsiung, Taiwan (pamphlet).
———. (1984b) *Spirit Exercise and Self-Riddance.* Kaohsiung, Taiwan (pamphlet).
———. (undated) *This Man and this Mountain.* Kaohsiung, Taiwan (pamphlet).
K'ang, Tuan-yi. (1979) *Acts of the Holy Spirit,* 2 vols. Kaohsiung, Taiwan (pamphlet).
———. (1966) *A Life to Testify to the Full Gospel of Jesus Christ.* Hong Kong, (pamphlet).
———. (1978a) *Entering God's Kingdom.* Kaohsiung, Taiwan (pamphlet).

————. (1978b) *The Golden Candlesticks,* 2 vols. Kaohsiung, Taiwan (pamphlet).

KMT Persecuted NTC for 20 Years. (1986) New York (pamphlet).

Lau, Fidelia, et al. (undated) *A Living Political Persecution: The Tormented New Testament Church and Holy Mount Zion* (pamphlet).

Liu, Chai-tse. (1984) *The Most Outrageous Injustice of the 20th Century.* Hsiaolin, Chiahsien, Kaohsuing, Taiwan (pamphlet).

NTC's Divine Obligations—Vanquish Tyrannies and Rescue Mankind. (1987) Kaohsiung, Taiwan (pamphlet).

Pi Sing, Victor. (1979a) *The Gospel of the Heavenly Kingdom.* Kaohsiung, Taiwan (pamphlet).

————. (1979b) *The Truth on Spirit Baptism* (pamphlet).

————. (1981) *The Full Gospel of Jesus Christ.* Taipei, Taiwan (pamphlet).

Pomerville, Paul. (1985) *The Third Force in Missions: A Pentecostal Contribution to Contemporary Mission Theology.* Peabody, MA: Hendrickson Publisher.

Schell, Orville (1988) *Discos and Democracy.* New York: Pantheon.

Thompson, Laurence. (1988) *Chinese Religion: An Introduction.* Revised ed. Belmont, CA: Wadsworth Publishers.

Index